The Ordeal

Michael Jay Harris

Cadmus Publishing
www.cadmuspublishing.com

Cover art by Michael Jay Harris

Published by Cadmus Publishing
www.cadmuspublishing.com
Port Angeles, WA

ISBN: 978-1-63751-126-8

Table of Contents

ONE

I met her online at Match.com and she was beautiful. A real blue-eyed beauty with blonde hair. Her name was Kerri Guthrie and we hit it off right away. She had twin daughters, named Martha and Chelsea, who were ten years old. It was the end of 2001.

They lived in Nevada City, California, about twenty miles from Lake Tahoe. Kerri skied, rode horses, and loved the outdoors. And so did I. My name is Mike Harris and I lived in Bishop, California, about two-hundred miles south of Kerri's four-acre spread. I lived on the eastern slopes of the High Sierra Mountains. I was a computer whiz and had created the website www.395.com, which showcased the Eastern Sierra corridor of Highway 395, a route that travels from Southern California to Canada.

I skied a lot and did a weekly video ski report featuring Mammoth Mountain, CA. The video report was seen by thousands on the internet. Kerri was impressed. I rode horses at a walk, up trails. Kerri was vastly more experienced. She rode dressage, did equestrian jumping, had packing experience, raised her own horses; she was awesome. I wanted to learn how to ride like she did.

Kerri did all of this with a vision disability that hindered her eyesight as a result of Albinism. Basically, she had to move her eyes slightly from side to side in order to see. If she just stared at something, it would blur out. She had a companion dog named Farley, who was a Black Labrador

Retriever and he went everywhere with her. I had three Dalmatians and our dogs got along great. I skied with Kerri and she followed right behind me so she could see better and we had a ton of fun. She had the horses and I had the skiing. It was a match made in heaven.

Kerri owned her home and I rented a single wide trailer with a small yard. Kerri had four acres of forested land at 4,200-foot elevation. This was good for horses in the summer but the winters were tough. As time went by, Kerri decided to move to Bishop. She had roommates in Nevada City and so, as her visits to Bishop lengthened, she still had her home cared for.

My trailer was not very large but the equestrian facilities near my home were world-class, and most importantly, below the snowline. Kerri moved her horses over and we groomed, fed, rode, and took pictures. Kerri had been having trouble with Chelsea and so, in early 2002, Chelsea went to live with her dad in Coloma, California. Martha and Kerri, with Farley, moved into my mobile home in Bishop. Kerri went back to Nevada City every week or two and Martha stayed with me since she was in school. Every few weeks we would all go over to Nevada City together for the weekend. Martha was in the Bishop school and had made several new friends, including Michelle Jackson and Shaylynn Ellis.

Kerri had her home up for sale and we worked on it to get it ready to sell. During the summer, we spent a lot of time at the stables and I did my internet work gathering video and pictures of the area for use on the website. Late in the summer, Chelsea moved over, having heard from Martha how great it was to live in the Eastern Sierra. Martha and Chelsea entered fifth grade and were in class together, which they really liked, although their teacher, Ms. Ginter, thought they were troublesome together.

We kept the same schedule traveling between Bishop and Nevada City. We all enjoyed the road trips, because we could go shopping and eating at places not available in our small towns. We especially liked the all-you-can-eat buffets in Reno and Carson City, Nevada.

2002 merged into 2003, with our routine staying the same; skiing, horseback riding and watching movies. I cooked and Kerri and the girls cleaned up. I was really happy with domesticated life. I had been a bachelor for decades and I wanted to settle down. I was 42 years old, had never been married, never had kids; my dogs were my family at that point.

In the spring of 2003, Kerri sold her house. There weren't many homes for sale in Bishop to Kerri's liking and budget. She wound up buying a place thirteen miles north of Bishop in the Chalfant Valley. She got a double-wide on half-an-acre, zoned for horses. It wasn't perfect, but it was a great starter home. In July 2003, Kerri moved from Nevada City to Chalfant and she asked me to move in with her. So I did.

We worked on the new property cleaning it up, fixing it up, and setting up the horse corrals.

There was an apple tree and a pear tree. We had satellite TV with hundreds of channels. Life was good. We got an exemption so the girls could still go to the Bishop schools even though we lived in the Chalfant district.

The girls made friends in the neighborhood as several of the kids were also in the Bishop school. One of their friends was Raeanna Davenport. The girls played with Raeanna and sometimes she came over. In October 2003, Raeanna came over to the house with her grandma, who wanted me to watch Raeanna while the grandma went to town. I was hesitant, but Raeanna pleaded that she didn't want to go all the way to her uncles in Benton. She wanted to stay and play with Martha and Chelsea. Kerri was at work.

As afternoon stretched into evening, I put on a movie and started dinner. I told Raeanna she could stay for dinner. It was all good. We had baked halibut nuggets, noodles romanov, and spinach. Just about dark, Raeanna's grandma called her to come home from out on the street and Raeanna went home. The next afternoon, while Kerri was at work, I heard a knock on the door and I answered it. It was a Mono County Sheriff's Deputy who asked me to step outside. I was placed under arrest. I asked what was going on and he said he would tell me later. A CHP lady officer came to the house and took control of Martha and Chelsea, because Kerri wasn't at home. I was transported to the Mono County Jail in Bridgeport, CA., some ninety miles to the north. In the car, the deputy explained that Raeanna's grandmother had reported that Raeanna had been touched inappropriately the day before. I immediately became hostile and professed my innocence.

Once I had been booked into jail, I made a phone call to Kerri and explained how I was in jail because of Raeanna and told her to ask the twins what happened in order to get me freed. She said she would get to the bottom of it and our call ended. I was in jail for almost two days before I was interviewed by Frank Smith, a police officer from Mammoth Lakes who specialized in sexual abuse cases. I told him it was all a crock and that I should be let go at once. I told him the girls knew nothing happened and he should go talk to them right away. I wanted him to test for touch DNA in order to clear myself and he said that was beyond their capabilities.

When it came to be forty-eight hours after my arrest, I was not charged and I was set free. It was October 22nd, 2003, at 5:00pm, and it was cold outside. I had no jacket. I eventually got a ride home and I went straight to bed. It was late. The next day, we all went about our routines, which included me driving the twins to school.

Within days, the twins were interviewed by CPS at school without their mother's knowledge or permission. They denied that anything happened with Raeanna and they denied they had ever been sexually abused. The CPS found Raeanna's claim to be unfounded. I was never charged and the Child Protective Services made no report to Kerri.

Fall turned to winter and another Christmas came and went. December 25th was Kerri's birthday, so we celebrated both. In early January 2004, I went down to my dad's house in Southern California. My dad lived near Kerri's dad, so we decided that I would take the girls down to their grandfather's house and Kerri would stay at home. Kerri didn't like LA or "smell-ay" as it were. The girls and I went to my dad's place for a night and then the girls went to their grandfather's house for a couple of nights while I went to the Palm Springs Kennel Club dog show. I won Best of Breed and it was awesome. The next day I picked up the twins and we went home.

As winter turned to spring, we took Kerri's mare, Sue (a Thoroughbred), down to Lancaster, CA., to breed with a real nice Appaloosa. The breeding wound up not taking, so after a couple months, we brought her back home. About this time, I sold my internet business in order to go into construction full-time. In mid-2004, the internet business was slowing and home building and repair were booming. One reason I sold my business was Kerri's insistence that I couldn't pay my bills based on web income. I had a lot of ads on my website with a ton of traffic, but I struggled to monetize it.

Kerri also had a problem with my dogs. They were indoor dogs and she didn't like that. I had had to put down one dog and he had made some big messes in the house on his way out. I decided to buy a brand-new 24-foot travel-trailer to put in Kerri's yard, so my dogs would have a home to live in. It was either this or move out completely. I was in love with Kerri, but I was living in her house and that was new territory for me. I was used to being in control of my home.

Come June, the girls and I went down to my dad's house again. He was remodeling his house and we helped by painting and cleaning up. He offered to pay for us to go to Disneyland, so the girls and I went. It was a lot of fun. We especially liked the FastPass feature where you could reserve your time on a ride and avoid the line.

We came back to Chalfant and it was hot. I wanted to use the air-conditioner on my trailer, which was plugged into Kerri's house. She didn't like that. She didn't like my dogs. She thought me and my dogs were soft. She thought that if I wanted to be in control of my house, I should buy one. We decided maybe it would be best if I put my trailer in a trailer park and keep my dogs there. Basically, I moved out, but I still spent time at Kerri's cooking and working with the horses.

I still had my computer and photo-grade printer. I still had my video equipment and my digital camera. I loved taking pictures and shooting video. I wanted the best of both worlds: the domesticated life and the life of adventure. I still had my office in town with high-speed internet, so I kept on working on web projects even though I had sold my business.

I was waiting for the right opportunity to come along, and in October of 2004, I got a great offer. I was hired as a lead framer at the Lodges project in Mammoth. As fall turned to winter, I moved my trailer up to Mammoth and saw less and less of Kerri and the girls. Just me and my dogs. I missed my domesticated life.

As winter roared in, it got brutal. Eight to ten feet of snow and cold. I was still framing and it was crazy. During one of the storms the girls ran away to the neighbor's house, saying Kerri had hit them with the broom. Kerri called me to come help, saying she knocked the broom out of one of the girl's hands and they were overreacting. The neighbor called CPS. I scrambled down the mountain and on to Chalfant hoping to save the day. The neighbors, the Worley's, were definitely anti-Kerri. Eventually, the Sheriff's Deputy showed up. The CPS worker was patched in by phone and, after several hours, the girls came home. This was an example of the battle between the twins and their mother. This was beginning to dominate their relationship. I was in the middle and sometimes I took the girls side, and sometimes I took Kerri's side.

By late January 2005, a big storm was coming in with another six to eight feet of snow predicted. I didn't want to get buried in, so I decided to quit my job and move back down to Bishop. The storm dumped two feet of snow in Bishop, but at least I wasn't buried. After all that was over it and said "that's enough snow for me" and moved my trailer down to Orange County near my dad's house.

All it did in Orange County was rain, but I was out of the snow. I worked indoors at my dad's house remodeling. My dad suggested I do repair and remodeling work for others in the neighborhood. I placed an ad in the Penny Saver and I was overwhelmed by calls for estimates. I did a lot of rain damage repairs. It was the second wettest winter on record that year, to my detriment or advantage depending on how you looked at it. I also specialized in gate repair, there was a ton of that work as well. In April, I bought a new truck and started commuting to Kerri's every weekend. I was in love with her, but had ambitions beyond living on her half-acre. We had a fundamental difference between us: She made little money and was frugal; I made lots of money and spent it at will. Kerri would chop her own firewood and try to heat the house with one wood-burner. I would light the furnace, and pay for propane. The trouble was, Kerri would not let me pay for her heat. She was too independent and that in essence was why I loved her so much. I, too, was independent, it was the living together that took some work. I learned to sit by the wood-burner.

In the spring, we took Sue down to Lancaster to try breeding her again. This time it took, so we left her down there to board. It became our routine that I visited Chalfant on the weekends and worked in Orange County during the week. In July, I took the girls down to my dad's house for a week. We went to Magic Mountain, Knott's Berry Farm, and Hollywood. I discussed with Kerri at length about us moving to Orange County together. I would buy or rent a nice house, and she could rent out her half-acre for income. She said maybe, but wanted to have her horses.

Well, horse property in Orange County is expensive, if it is available at all. I took Martha down to my dad's house for a week and we went and checked out houses and stables. There were stables in Huntington Beach and Long Beach. Homes were renting for $2,500 a month, and at that price, purchasing was the better option. Kerri, Martha, and Chelsea were onboard with moving. They had a rough go of it on the "Ranch" with no heat, no a/c, and lots of chores. I spoke with my dad about getting a home to "flip" and he was interested in helping me get one.

I thought long and hard, but eventually decided to move back to the Eastern Sierra and try to buy land to build on there. I talked with Kerri and she agreed with me moving my trailer back onto her property. She even said I could hook up my electrical, if I made sure to pay for it. I bought the food and cooked, she liked that. The girls liked that I ran cover for them and kept their mom off their back by helping out with chores. I even got Kerri to let me use my portable electric heater if I paid the electricity. My trailer had propane heat. I was now down to one dog and he was special. A liver spotted Dalmatian who loved running. I took him everywhere in my truck. His name was Rusty.

I took out an ad in the local paper for my business, Can-do services, and I got a bunch of work. Drywall, painting, tile, wood flooring, electrical... you name it and I was doing it. I also bought a season pass at Mammoth Mountain ski area. Work, ski, drive back and forth. I was busy. Kerri was busy. The girls were busy. The girls were busy with school, sports, hanging out with their friends. The girls were in the Benton school by then instead of the Bishop school. Kerri had a couple of horses and we still had Sue down in Lancaster pregnant as could be. We all went down to Lancaster a few times and we especially loved the Hometown Buffet. There was also this little Chinese buffet in Ridgecrest that we adored. We would drive for two hours one-way just to eat there.

I kept on working and skiing, and suddenly it was 2006. That year came in with a bang. A huge blizzard dumped two feet of snow in Chalfant, then a couple inches of rain on top of it. Tree branches were breaking and then the power went out for four days. It was a good thing Kerri had a wood-burner. My trailer was toasty for Rusty. Kerri still wouldn't let him in the house.

The skiing was great and I was plenty busy at work after the blizzard. I also still had my website www.GoMammoth.com where I published my weekly ski report. As winter turned to spring, Sue gave birth to a beautiful little Appaloosa colt. We went down to Lancaster after he was born and brought mama and baby home. We cut them in Kerri's backyard and it was great. His name was XY, but I called him "Baby". His registered name was Majestic Hi Sierra and he was. By July, Baby was ready to be weaned and that meant separating mom and son. Kerri and I had a difference of opinion and we argued about what should happen next. We decided that I would take the colt up to stable in Mammoth and I would move my trailer there as well. It was hot in Chalfant that July. Mammoth was perfect. I kept working and commuted down to Kerri's house every couple of days. The girls and Kerri were having arguments about chores and freedom to come and go as they pleased. Soon thereafter, with a bit of coaching, their behavior improved. I had to go down to Anaheim to buy some specialty lumber and hardware for a project I was working on, so down we went. Kerri did not want to go, so I took Martha and Chelsea for a lap in Disneyland since the lumberyard was right next door. We got down there expecting to stay at my dad's house, and he said "no way!" He was having a bridge party. We decided to look for a motel that would take a dog near Disneyland. I had Rusty along and Baby was still in Mammoth. Kerri wanted nothing to do with Disneyland and the crowds, smog, heat, etc.

Finding a motel was not easy. The prices midsummer in Anaheim were outrageous. We finally found a room for $400 for two nights. It was a double bed setup, two separate beds, one room. I wasn't going to pop for two rooms and Disneyland. I thought nothing of sharing a room with the girls since we had stayed together with Kerri in motels before. I was like a dad to the twins.

Well, we went to Disneyland and it was the 50th anniversary, with lots of special features, like an upgraded Space Mountain and Jack Sparrow in the Pirates of the Caribbean ride. The next day we bought supplies and went home.

By late September, it was getting cold in Mammoth, so I moved my trailer and Baby down to Bishop. The stable in Bishop was really nice. I built my own tack shed, so I was able to store supplies and tack and begin training my colt. I started spending more time at Kerri's and things were good between us. Things were strained between the girls and their mom however. The girls were freshmen in High School.

TWO

Bishop Union High School opened up a whole new world for the girls. A world of freedom. They were sneaking off campus for lunch. They were riding around in cars. They were enamored with boys. It was all perfectly normal, but Kerri had some concerns. She set down some rules and insisted that the girls follow them. The girls were in band, so they stayed late at school for practice and got to hang out with their friends. The twins were also helping me at work, so they could buy their dresses for the Homecoming Dance. Kerri did not want them to go, seeing as they were only freshmen and they were not behaving all that well. I talked Kerri into letting them go since they were buying the dresses and I would drive them and pick them up. They went and had a great time, according to their stories of dancing and taking pictures with their friends.

Soon, it was November, and one morning I drove out to Chalfant to give the girls some lunch money and I saw them getting into a van, not the school bus. I confronted them about the rule their mom had about riding around in boy's cars. They were 14 at the time. Martha said she was sorry, but Chelsea got belligerent. I told Chelsea to say she was sorry or I would take her off the ski team, which I was paying for and driving them to. Chelsea called me an asshole and said "you aren't my dad" and then stormed off. I went to work and thought nothing of it. Later, Kerri called me and asked what was up. The CPS had called her and brought the girls home. They said they were scared of me, because I had yelled at them in the street. I went over to Kerri's to work things out, and in the end, it was all good, almost. Kerri told Chelsea she was off the ski team, but Martha could still do it.

A couple weeks later, it was time for the Christmas band concert and Kerri and the girls did not invite me to go and I was upset. I was so upset, I ignored them at Christmas and Kerri's birthday. I bought them nothing and went to Utah by myself for a ski vacation. I had a great time, though it was a very dry winter throughout the west. I kept working into January 2007 and Kerri and I worked out our differences. We all did the ski team activities together. I skied with Chelsea and all seemed okay. In March, Martha made the state final in giant slalom, so I went to Mount Shasta to watch and videotape Martha's runs. Kerri and Chelsea stayed at home. Martha stayed with the ski team and I stayed with Rusty at a motel.

By the time we came back from the state finals, Kerri was in full-blown school mode. Martha and Chelsea both had final reports to write and that was a big project. It was creating conflict, so I only went to Kerri's a couple times between March and the end of the school year. I had a lot going on with my computer projects as well. Kerri was working with a new colt she had bought and she had her hands full with Martha and Chelsea. The girls wanted more freedom, but their behavior was costing them. They fought with their mother and each other. I was told by Kerri to stay away until school was out, because she was setting some ground rules and didn't want any interference from me.

Well, school was finally out, and within a week, Chelsea ran away from home. I was at work in Mammoth when I heard a call on my radio scanner that Kerri had called the Sheriff's Department reporting that her daughter had run away the night before. I immediately called Kerri and she told me Chelsea had run away from home, but Kerri couldn't talk to me right then, because she didn't have call waiting and she was expecting a call. Kerri really was frugal. I called later and spoke with Martha who told me she didn't know where Chelsea was and they were going into town to put up missing person flyers. I wanted to help, but there wasn't much I could do.

A couple of days later, the girls' best friend forever, Shaylynn Ellis, called Kerri and told her that Chelsea was at her boyfriend's house. Kerri was mad that the boyfriend's parents hadn't called her. Kerri called the sheriff who called CPS. The sheriff's deputies and Alex Ellis, the CPS case worker (no relation), went and got Chelsea. They brought Chelsea home and there was a big confrontation in the front of Kerri's house. Chelsea said, if she had to go home, she would just run away again. Kerri said fine, take her, and so Alex Ellis took Chelsea to a foster home. A couple of days after that, on June 30th, 2007, Kerri had a court date with CPS in Mammoth, but Kerri refused to go. She was saying to hell with Chelsea, if that's how she felt.

Kerri got some papers from CPS delivered to her home that day and she called me right away. It seemed that Chelsea was alleging verbal and physical abuse by me and Kerri. It was craziness. Chelsea had never been abused. If anything, she had been abusive towards Kerri and Martha. I couldn't figure out how I fit in, since I had helped Chelsea for years including helping her go to the Homecoming Dance. It was Kerri who ultimately said Chelsea couldn't be on the ski team. Nevertheless, Kerri wanted nothing to do with Chelsea or the CPS.

In early July, Kerri told Martha to box up Chelsea's stuff and load it in my truck to take to the dump. I wasn't going to do that but I didn't tell Kerri. I took the stuff to Alex Ellis of the CPS so she could give it to Chelsea. There was important stuff in there, including irreplaceable gifts from her now deceased father. I eventually told Kerri where I took the stuff, and she really didn't care at that point. On July 6th I took Martha over to Michelle Jackson's house while I went golfing. Martha stayed there about six hours. If she contacted CPS or Chelsea while she was there, I never heard about it from her.

On July 8th, late at night, Martha snuck out of the house. Kerri discovered her missing and called me. I drove out to Chalfant and Kerri told me someone had been circling the house as though they were looking for Martha. We spotted the car and I went and followed it. I eventually boxed in that car and asked the driver who he was and why was he circling the Guthrie's house. He said he was Dylan Clarke, which I knew was BS, because that was Chelsea's boyfriend's last name. Tyler was her boyfriend's name and I knew there was no Dylan in that family. I let the guy go and followed him to his house, which was the Medrud residence. I figured he was Leif Medrud. I should mention that calling the cops in Chalfant is not really an option, because it takes hours to get a response. Bishop is close by, but it is in a different county. In an emergency, the CHP will respond if they have an officer in position.

Early the next morning, with Martha still missing, Kerri asked me to go over to the Medrud's house and get Martha. I went over and there was a confrontation about the fact they said Martha had come over the night before, but she left around 11:00pm. I asked why they would let her walk home alone at such a late hour. They had no response but anger. I went back to Kerri's and not a half hour later Martha showed up. Kerri was mad, but she told Martha if she wanted to go like Chelsea had after all Kerri had done for her, then so be it. I told Martha we could go talk to CPS and see if she could talk to Chelsea. Martha said she wanted to go.

We drove to Mammoth and met with Rose Douglas, because Alex Ellis was not in. Martha asked about Chelsea and was told it was confidential and that Martha could not know how Chelsea was, or even where she was. Martha then asked about foster care in general and Ms. Douglas explained the ins and outs of foster care: the rules, the limitations, etc. Martha decided she liked it at her mom's better than foster care, so we went back to Chalfant.

A week went by and it was July 16th, the next court date, for Kerri. Kerri did not go. She wanted nothing to do with Chelsea. Kerri felt that Chelsea was out to ruin her life and cost her thousands of dollars in restitution to the State for Chelsea's care. Martha told me that her mom was going mental and explained what led up to Chelsea's running away episode. Martha told me that Kerri had received an SSDI settlement and got a lump sum payment. Kerri had then bought the girls bikes and clothes and such. Chelsea was mad that Kerri was now getting SSDI money every month as well as Chelsea's SSI death benefit money from her deceased father Dale Guthrie. An argument ensued and Kerri wound up telling Chelsea that she was going to box up her stuff and sell it on eBay. Chelsea sassed back "dot com" like in the commercials. Kerri then told her that Martha was going to switch bedrooms with her and Chelsea said "whatever." Chelsea had a much larger room with a queen-sized bed. Martha had the small bedroom with the bunkbed. Martha continued to tell me that Chelsea had left behind stuff that was very important to her and she didn't feel like Chelsea had planned on running away that night. It just happened. In any event, I talked Martha into writing her mom a note of apology if she really was sorry. Martha said she really was sorry, so she wrote her mom a beautiful apology.

Within the hour, the police and Ms. Ellis were at the door with a court order to take Martha into state custody for placement in foster care. Kerri was really mad. I was confused. Martha was crying. Talk about some homewrecking. Later that night, Kerri became very despondent and got really drunk, which is something she never did. Losing Chelsea was one thing, but to lose Martha was extremely upsetting to her. Kerri was seriously worried that she couldn't pay the state for foster care and that the state would seize her property to cover the costs. Kerri was worried she would never see Martha again. She thought that the CPS would turn Martha against her. I stayed with Kerri and pleaded with her that she could fight the CPS in court and get Martha back. I told her the state would even give her an attorney to help litigate the case.

Kerri got an attorney and she gave him a detailed explanation of what had happened, including events going back to the late 1990s. It seemed this wasn't Kerri's first run in with CPS. The girls had called CPS about their mom neglecting to feed them, leaving them alone, even physical abuse. These claims all proved to be unfounded. Nonetheless, CPS was raising all the past issues and they were blaming Kerri for the alleged verbal and physical abuse by me. I wanted to defend myself, but I had no standing in Kerri's Juvenile Dependency Hearing.

Kerri kept on working with her attorney, David Hammon, to at least get Martha back. Kerri actually attended the WIC §300 hearing on July 30th. Nothing came out of the hearing other than keeping the girls in foster care pending a final placement decision on August 13th, 2007. In early August, Mr. Hammon asked Kerri for a statement which she provided:

My Statement for the Record

Kerri Guthrie

The girls have been sneaking out at night and has been a recent problem that only came to light after Chelsea ran away to be with her boyfriend. Notes that I have in may possession and which have been turned over to Deputy Bowman with the Mono County Sheriff's Department outline her secret life of violence, deviant sex, and deceptive relationship with a boy I know nothing about. The girls secretly hid everything from me, and when Mike tried to help, they became belligerent, rebellious, and they threatened to run away, believing that they can't be put in juvenile hall for running away, even though they could have been placed in custody with a WIC §601 petition instead of the WIC §300 petition they can get lying as a duo. I attempted to enlist the support of the Sheriff's Office in gaining control of the girls, but they helped perpetuate the problem by saying it's not illegal to run away, and it's bad. parenting that causes them to be physically and verbally abusive towards one another. Secret MySpace and text messaging is precipitating all problems with the kids that are in trouble in the Bishop School District. Furthermore, the schools open campus policy, which allows 14-year olds to mingle with, and ride in cars with, 18-year olds is patent child endangerment.

Mono County Mental health is encouraging the girls with the sharing of confidential and personal information with numerous people leading to the appearance of nepotism in this case. I feel external and private evaluations are in order due to the bias of the entire Mono County Mental Health and Human Services Department and their acceptance of Chelsea's story in light of the deviant lesbian nature contained within the notes. The liberal activist mindset of the CPS/Mental Health Dept. does not coalesce well with the mandated disclosure of all the facts regarding this case and their bias towards a predetermined outcome is obvious when you consider all the statements I have made that are not in the report. I do not trust Alex Ellis and want her replaced immediately.

Riding in cars with restricted drivers is illegal. Martha and Chelsea have both been sneaking out at night and riding in cars with 16-year-old restricted drivers after curfew in violation of California law. Notes regarding violent attitude, Chelsea's notes, scare me tremendously. The deviant content of the notes is being ignored. I am shocked at the content of Chelsea's notes and she needs a secure and restricted environment until she acknowledges the notes and her actions are wrong.

Chelsea wanted to be with her boyfriend, so she left home without permission and went to Don Clarke's house, and hid there until she was ratted out by one of her friends. I called the Sheriff and told him where she was. They then picked her up. I have since tried to ascertain why she was there for four days without anyone knowing, and why Don Clarke and Kathleen Trainor-Reeder have not been criminally charged with aiding and abetting a runaway. They should be held responsible for what they put me through and they should be held financially responsible as well.

Martha complained of Leif as mean and as a stalker and had Mike call the sheriff and report the Leif information while I talked with her privately about not riding in cars with boys until she was older. I also told her she wasn't mature enough to date and this made her mad.

Chelsea does not follow the house rules. Chelsea is a threat to anything or anyone who gets in her way. Chelsea is very vindictive and has been making false claims to anyone who would listen since she was five years old. The children have never witnessed domestic violence. The federal court has ruled this is not applicable in removing a child anyway. (Nicholson v Williams 181 F.Supp.2d.182 (2001).) My children have been talked to without my parental consent and absent any emergency in clear violation of my constitutional rights. (Doe et al. v Heck 327 F.3d 492 (9th Cir. 2003).)

Martha had every opportunity to seek help and guidance and instead ran away to be with her boyfriend. She also got caught just like Chelsea, but she wanted to return home. I called Mike to see if he knew where Martha was, and he didn't, but said he could try to get her via text message since she wasn't responding to phone calls. She failed to respond to text messages and so I asked Mike to come over and look for her. He finally was able to contact her via text after some contact with Leif Medrud. Martha was with Leif all night and returned at 7:30 in the morning after I sent Mike over to 221 Hunter in one last effort to remove her from the Medrud's house. Both girls are scared of the consequences of the lies and deceitful actions in regards to their boyfriends.

Sending confidential emails violates some kind of confidentiality procedure within state and county governments.

Chelsea has grown increasingly abusive towards me, both physically and verbally since entering Bishop Union High School. She recently began telling me "I don't have to listen to you, crazy bitch." She even spray painted it.

I want to instill a sense of family tradition. I want the girls' school and roots to be in conservative, normally upstanding homes out of the Bishop area, Northern California or Reno/Carson City preferred. The Jackson family is not a part of the Guthrie extended family in any way, shape, or form. We used to babysit their daughter while they went out to parties and they now leave their daughter at home alone, and if Martha is there, this is a recipe for more problems

Kerri Guthrie

On August 3rd, 2007, Kerri and I ran into Chelsea, Tyler, and Leif in Bishop near the theater. It was heated as I gave the boys shit and Kerri gave Chelsea a hard time. Eventually, the police were called, and when they showed, up so did Alex Ellis, Chelsea's caseworker. It just so happened that Ms. Ellis had a restraining order for me that ordered I have no contact with the girls. Kerri was already under a no-contact order as part of the WIC §300 proceedings. A couple of days later, Ms. Ellis came over to Kerri's and got Martha's stuff, even though Kerri was hopeful that Martha would be returning home. Kerri's next court date was August 13th. My next court date was August 16th for the restraining order hearing. Kerri's hearing was brief. The court ordered continued placement with review in six months. Kerri was disappointed, but she had mentally prepared for the court to rule against her. Kerri thought that the county and state were not listening to her. I agreed with Kerri's assessment on many levels. I felt that Ms. Ellis in particular did not like me or Kerri. We thought she was a bleeding-heart liberal.

My court date was rather eventful. First, I met with the county attorney, Mark Magit, and I agreed that I did not need to have contact with the girls. I did, however, oppose the order barring me from contacting a list of people the girls knew. I convinced the court to only order no contact with Chelsea and Martha. In a way, I won my case. On the way out, Detective Rutkowski asked me and Kerri to stop by the sheriff's substation in Crowley Lake to meet with him. When we got there, we sat in an interview room with cameras and microphones and it was intimidating. He got right to the point. He said that the girls had reported being forced to watch Kerri and I having sex. This was unbelievable. Then Det. Rutkowski said one of the girls was claiming rape. This was overwhelming. I immediately told the detective that it was total bullshit. He said he wanted me to take a lie detector test and I said okay. Then after a few minutes of further allegations, I said fuck that, have the girls take a polygraph. Kerri was then asked some questions and she was shocked as well. There was no way the girls watched us have sex, and Kerri said so.

It came time to leave and Det. Rutkowski asked me if he could take a picture of my penis for a lineup and I told him that was ridiculous. Finally, I asked if we were under arrest and he said no, but he was still looking into the matter. On the way out, Kerri told him the sheriffs should do a better job in Chalfant, because the underage kids were drinking and smoking and shooting things late at night. It was unsafe. Kerri added that there was a party spot where they all went and she drew him a map and he said he would look into it. Well, Kerri and I drove back to Chalfant and we were dismayed. I reminded her that her attorney, Mr. Hammon, had advised us not to fuck with Alex Ellis. Of course, Ms. Ellis was the impetus to the restraining order, which made no mention of sexual abuse. Ms. Ellis was also responsible for the Welfare and Institutions Code §300 action for both girls and Martha's forced removal from Kerri's home. Ms. Ellis was a real homewrecker, IMHO.

After dinner, I went home to Bishop and began looking for legal help, because Kerri's attorney was really limited in his area of expertise. He knew Mono County, but there were never any rape or molestation cases there. Besides, he couldn't represent me and Kerri both, if things got dicey.

On Monday morning, August 20th, 2007, I drove to Mammoth for work, and right after I got there, Det. Rutkowski showed up and placed me under arrest for child molestation. I told him I had nothing more to say than already had been said, other than to say take me to court so I could get a release on my own recognizance (OR). I got to jail and my bail was $100,000, or ten-thousand cash and $100,000 collateral through a bondsman. I owned my truck and trailer but they weren't worth 100K, and I sure didn't have 10K laying around. I needed a bail reduction or an OR release.

THREE

The jail was very small, with a 42-person capacity in the small town of Bridgeport, population 500. They put me in my own cell with a TV, phone, shower, and no cellmates. I was in protective custody. This was the same cell that Sean Penn had stayed in when he came to Mono County to serve a sentence in his assault case. The next day, August 21st, I went to court and Randy Gephart was appointed, and he told the court I wanted an OR release. The initial charges were §288.5 continual sexual abuse of a minor. The District Attorney was Todd Graham.

Mr. Graham: We expect the charges to multiply greatly based upon my conversation with Detective Rutkowski, and I would like to talk about that when we get into his custody status.

I entered not guilty pleas to the two counts and asked to be heard on the bail or own recognizance issue.

The Defendant: Your Honor, I was before you for a $250,000 bail on a terrorism charge, I forget the exact number, that was about five years ago in the Kathy Shultz case. You were forced to put me on bail, and then I bailed out and I went and appeared before you and you exonerated my bail. I basically appeared and I obeyed all of your orders in that case, every last one of them. I completed my probation. I didn't do anything wrong for years. And so, I would ask you, on your faith of knowing me, for an OR release because I have lived here for thirty years. I vigorously defend these charges. I am not running away. I am pissed at

Mr. Graham. I am pissed at the sheriff. And I am pissed at the system which has brought us here today.

Following this, Mr. Graham took to the lectern and went into a lengthy diatribe related to the girls' allegations:

Mr. Graham: ...they both recount years of molestation by this man, including one of them alleging forcible rape...in speaking with Detective Rutkowski, just a few minutes ago, the abuse, the molestation going on at least in Mono County, was continuous, repeated, one of the girls used the word every day. The girls were threatened to be killed if they reported the abuse. Although they are not charged, yet, I expect this case to be one of, if not the most, serious molestation case that I have seen in my years in Mono County, going on eight... So, we object to any kind of OR release of this man.

Mr. Graham then went on to state that no bail should be granted, since I faced decades in prison:

The Court: Okay. Under Penal Code Section 1270.1, because of the nature of the charges, before the court either increases or reduces bail or OR's a defendant, it must conduct a hearing, a noticed hearing.

The Judge, Hon. Stan Eller, continued on to set a bail review hearing for one week hence on August 28th, 2007. Mr. Gephart then spoke to the court:

Mr. Gephart: I understand. I can only say, look, these are allegations. Mr. Harris has denied those. I know from Mr. Graham there has been a pretext call with negative results or showing any culpability, and he has denied the allegations, and that's all they are, is allegations, so I will get a motion on file, and we can hear it next week.

Following this, a date of September 4th, 2007, was set for a preliminary hearing. I was then hauled back across the street to the county jail. The jail was modern and it sat in juxtaposition to the original jail from the 1800's, which was built out of rock. The courthouse was also built in the 1800's and was white with red trim, and had vaulted ceiling and a truly pioneer style of architecture.

My happy little abode was cold and dreary, even though it was a beautiful late summer day. I was agitated and upset. I called Kerri and talked about things and she was very supportive. Kerri had numerous CPS records from the prior years, which showed the girls making false claims of abuse against her many times in the past. I was adamant that nothing ever transpired between me and the girls. Kerri said they were liars and I should be extra worried about Chelsea. I spent the next few days getting ready for my bail review hearing. That is when I thought I would be set free on my own recognizance.

Tuesday came, the 28th, and I found out I would have to wait until the afternoon for court. I waited until just before 2:00pm. I was stressed out. My boss, Alex Reichl, was there and so was Kerri. Mr. Gephart called Kerri to the stand and she was sworn in. Immediately, Mr. Graham got involved talking about §1270.1(c) and the fact he did not think Kerri's testimony was pertinent to the bail review hearing.

Mr. Graham: …the court under (c) "shall consider evidence of past court appearances of the detained person, the maximum potential sentence that could be imposed, and the danger that may be imposed to other persons if the detained person is released."

Mr. Graham, continued by asking the court if this was going to be a full-blown evidentiary hearing involving Kerri, regarding her beliefs about the truthfulness of the allegations and is this appropriate under (c). The court said it assumed it was, that it's quite relevant stating:

The Court: …because of the fact that one of, and I think the primary, consideration in this case is not whether Mr. Harris is going to show up in court or not; frankly Mr. Harris shows up in court. I don't have an issue with that. It's the danger to other persons, the other persons I believe, I can't speak for the DA; are the children…

Mr. Graham: I would agree, as well as the maximum potential sentence and how that would have an effect on Mr. Harris' willingness to appear. Obviously, if you are facing, which would be indicated in the first amended felony complaint, at least on 15 years-to-life, which is what the allegations are going to be added here, that would have at least a potential effect on your willingness to come to court.

The Court: I stand corrected. I haven't seen that amended complaint, but sure, that is going to be a consideration.

It was time for Kerri to testify and she looked a bit nervous, but pretty all the same. It was great to see her, because I had been in jail a week and I missed her. Kerri was asked some preliminary questions. Mr. Gephart had met with her over lunch and discussed the areas he would be covering.

Mr. Gephart: And I made you aware of allegations that your twin daughters have made in this case, specifically, one of the serious allegations as I understand it, is that you and Mr. Harris have, on many occasions, had sex in front of your daughters.

The Court: I am going to stop you right there, Mr. Gephart. I am concerned about this witness' possible incrimination under the Fifth Amendment. I didn't realize we were going to talk about that sort of thing.

Mr. Gephart: Well, that line of questioning, Judge, addresses the concerns that Mr. Graham raised, which does she have personal knowledge and can she testify to personal knowledge regarding the allegations, and so it's important she be in a position to address through personal knowledge, specifics of the allegations.

The Court: I agree.

Mr. Gephart: I can represent to this court that Ms. Guthrie's counsel was present during my interview with her. I don't know where he is now. I think it would be appropriate, given the court's concern, that he be present.

The Court: I am not saying there may be Fifth Amendment information. I am saying only if there was a possibility, I would be derelict in my duties to not at least raise that.

Mr. Gephart: I understand the court's concern. Can I just note for the record that there is another person sitting at counsel table? Can we identify who is sitting at counsel table?

The Court: Alex Ellis, from Child Protective Services.

Mr. Gephart: Thank you.

After a short break to get Kerri's attorney, Mr. Hammon, who is assigned to her in the CPS proceedings, the court assigned Mr. Hammon for Fifth Amendment purposes as well. The Fifth Amendment to the United States Constitution addresses, among other issues, the right not to be compelled to testify against oneself. No self-incriminating testimony can be forced.

Q. by Mr. Gephart: Let me ask it this way, Ms. Guthrie, are you aware of any instances in your relationship with Mr. Harris where you and he had sex in front of your twin daughters?

A. No, I am not, not at all.

Q. If your twin daughters told someone that that had happened, would they be lying?

Mr. Graham: Objection…

The Witness: They lie a lot.

Mr. Graham: Objection, speculation and…

Mr. Gephart: That's not speculation.

The Court: Overruled. She has personal knowledge. That's not speculation.

Mr. Graham: He asked are you aware.

The Court: Overruled. You can answer and you did. What did you say?

The Witness: They lie a lot.

Q. by Mr. Gephart: And in the specific response to my question whether they would be lying if they told someone that you and Mike Harris had sex in front of them, they would be lying in that instance, as well?

A. Yes, they would, because they lie all the time. They are kids.

Q. Are you aware of other instances where they have told lies to people, in essence, which got you or Mr. Harris in trouble?

A. Yes. They lie about things with me.

Q. On how many occasions?

A. Too many to count.

Q. Over what period of time?

A. Pretty much most of their life. Since I divorced their father.

Mr. Gephart: Thank you. I have nothing further.

The Court: Thank you. Mr. Graham, any questions?

Mr. Graham: Yes.

Q. by Mr. Graham: How long have you known Michael Harris?

A. About six years.

Q. How did you first meet Michael Harris?

A. We met online.

Q. And when did you first begin seeing each other? Can you give me a month and a year?

A. About December 2001.

Q. Can you explain how you met and got together and started your relationship? You met online, I understand that, keep going.

A. We found we had lots of things in common, and we met and we liked each other and we dated.

Q. And eventually you ended up in Bishop, living in Bishop; is that correct?

A. Yes.

Q. And when you started living in Bishop did you live with Mr. Harris at that time?

A. Yes.

Q. When did you start living with Mr. Harris in Bishop?

A. In 2002. I also have a mutual friend in Bishop.

Q. And where did you live with Mr. Harris in Bishop?

A. On See Vee.

Q. Is that a trailer?

A. Yes, it is. It's a street in Bishop.

Q. While you lived with Mr. Harris in Bishop, did you live there with one of your daughters?

A. Yes, I did.

Q. And what daughter was that?
A. I lived there with Martha.
Q. She has a twin sister named Chelsea; is that correct?
A. Yes, that's correct.

Kerri went on to describe the fact she owned a home in Nevada City and that she was back and forth all the time. She was asked if Martha was back and forth with her and Kerri said she was, whereupon she was asked:

Q. by Mr. Graham: You lived with Martha here at this trailer in Bishop and you spent time also in Nevada City; is that right?
A. Yes.
Q. And during that time that you lived with Mr. Harris in Bishop, in the trailer, at any time during that time, did Martha complain to you about any abuse from Mr. Harris?

The court overruled an objection by Mr. Gephart and so Mr. Graham asked his question again:

Q. by Mr. Graham: Did she ever, did Martha, while Mr. Harris lived in this trailer and you frequented that trailer, did Martha ever complain to you about any kind of abuse from Mr. Harris?
A. Never. Not at all. She was really happy.
Q. So, if she is coming forward today and making allegations along these lines of continued sexual abuse beginning with the time where Mr. Harris was living in the trailer, are you saying she is an outright liar?
A. Yes.
Q. Did Chelsea ever come over and live with you at all at the trailer on See Vee?
A. Yes. Chelsea came over.
Q. Did she stay there and actually have residence there at the trailer?
A. Yes, for a short time.
Q. And did Chelsea, at any time during that period of time in the trailer in Bishop, complain to you about any kind of abuse, sexual or otherwise, from Mr. Harris?
A. No. They were very happy.
Q. So again, if she is making similar allegations, are you saying she is an outright liar?
A. Yes, I am.

During the summer of 2003, I had moved into a double-wide trailer Kerri had bought in Chalfant. Mr. Graham next went into why I moved out to LA and he discussed the period of time I lived in the Guthrie home.

Q. by Mr. Graham: Was there any tension between the girls at the time he moved out?
A. No, the girls liked him.
Q. So, again, all of these statements you probably heard about the abuse, the physical abuse, the sexual abuse, is all made up according to you; is that correct?
A. Yes.
Q. During your period of time in Chalfant where Mr. Harris would come and go at that residence where the girls were living, at any time during that period of time, did either of the girls complain to you about any sexual abuse by Mr. Harris?
A. No, not at all.

Mr. Graham went on to discuss the trips I took with the girls down to LA, but he made no mention of the trips Kerri, the girls, and I took to Nevada City, Reno, and Lancaster to name a few. Mr. Graham focused in on a trip Martha and I took to LA.

Q. by Mr. Graham: Did she say anything to you about any kind of sexual abuse by Mr. Harris when she got back?
A. Neither kid has ever mentioned that at all. She did not mention that.

Then Mr. Graham honed in on another trip to LA with both girls and tried to ask the same question as before but referring to both girls. Judge Eller sustained Mr. Gephart's objection and that was that. Mr. Graham then delved into Kerri's relationship with me, asking if I was more than a friend, and Kerri answered "he's my boyfriend." Mr. Graham pressed the issue and the court intervened asking "Do you have a romantic relationship with Mr. Harris?" Kerri replied, "No, he's in jail." The court burst out in laughter. The court then asked if, prior to his incarceration, did you have a sexual relationship with Mr. Harris. Kerri answered, "Yes, I did."

The Court: There you go. Is that what you wanted to ask Mr. Graham? And that shows bias. I agree with that. 352 may play into this eventually.

Evidence Code §352 is the code relied on during most every objection made in the course of a trial in California. The trial court, in its discretion, may exclude evidence if its probative value is substantially outweighed by the probability that its admission will (a) necessitate undue consumption of time or (b) create substantial danger of undue prejudice, of confusing the issues, or (c) of misleading the jury. Relevance is also measured under this standard. Basically, to be admissible under Ev. Code §352, the evidence must be relevant, that is, it must tend logically, and by reasonable inference to establish a material fact.

Next up was some questioning about when I moved out of the Chalfant residence and where I moved to.

Q. by Mr. Graham: When Mr. Harris moved out of the Chalfant residence, you were still living with the two girls; is that correct?

A. Yes.

Q. He moved out to Los Angeles; is that correct?

A. Yes.

Q. And I want to know about your relationship after he moved to Los Angeles.

A. We have seen each other off and on the whole time.

The Court: Did you have any financial dependence on Mr. Harris after he moved out?

The Witness: No, I have my own house.

Q. by Mr. Graham: Do you receive any monetary support from Mr. Harris today?

A. No.

Q. Before he was arrested, did you receive any monetary support from Mr. Harris?

A. No.

Mr. Graham then had a discussion with Judge Eller about whether Kerri could testify about different ways the girls had lied in the past that qualified her statement that "they lie a lot."

The Witness: They have taken money and I have found it in their room. They have taken things forbidden from the kitchen and I found it in their bedroom. They have hung out with people that they are not allowed to hang out with and I have caught them.

Mr. Graham then wanted to understand why the girls would lie about physical and sexual abuse.

Q. by Mr. Graham: I am focusing on what do they have to gain to come forward and say this about this man, who is not even living there anymore?

A. They are very revengeful with me and anyone else in my life, they are jealous and revengeful, and they have been that way since I divorced their father.

Q. Let me make sure I understand this. Is it your opinion that they are making up all these allegations up against Michael Harris and also including you in some of the allegations for revenge?

A. Yes. And to be with their boyfriends and to date. I told them they weren't allowed to date until they got out of high school.

Q. Have they done anything else that you can think of that you would consider revenge towards you, because of your strictness with them over boyfriends?

A. Yes. After we had an argument about not dating, the next day and the subsequent weeks I kept finding hair in my food when it was their turn to cook.

Q. So hair in your food. What else?

A. They stole a $200 X-Box game station and I don't know where it went. And they spray painted "Bitch" on my garage wall.

Kerri went on to describe her love/hate relationship with the girls. Kerri loved them because she was their mother, but she set the rules and the girls hated her for that. The court then asked Kerri if she knew who Raeanna Davenport was and Kerri replied:

A. Yes. She is one of the Mono County kids.

Mr. Graham: I have a police report here involving an allegation by a young girl involving molestation.

Q. by Mr. Graham: Are you aware of that allegation by her?

A. Yes, I am.

Q. And has Mr. Harris ever spoken to you about Raeanna Davenport and that allegation?

A. Yes.

Q. What did he say?

A. He said he didn't do anything. And the kids said that to me.

Q. What kids?

A. My children.

Q. Did he tell you that he never touched her?

A. Correct. He never touched her. That's what the kids said.

So that was finished and Kerri was excused. Next it was my turn to read my statement. I had spent the week thinking about it and I had a lot to say but I whittled it down to a few paragraphs. I begged the court to release me OR in order to use my resources for defending myself and not to be subject to solitary confinement for weeks on end.

I felt the DA was using the shotgun approach by charging me with anything he could in order to keep me in jail and limit my ability to defend myself. I told the court that I didn't have unlimited resources and I needed an OR release in order to move forward to the case-in-chief instead of having several bail review hearings so the DA could put me in jail under some absurdly high amount of bail.

Next, I argued that the complexities of the case were going to warrant me to waive my right to a speedy trial in order to adequately prepare. I asked the court to consider all this in my request for an OR release. I noted to the court that the State may have valid beliefs, but their beliefs were based on tales I could disprove. I begged upon the discretion of the court to allow me an opportunity to prove my innocence unburdened by the financial ruin that high bail would impose on me.

The Defendant: I am able and willing to check-in with the court daily if released on my own recognizance. In the past, the prosecutor has been overzealous towards me and this may also be the fact now. I am not a threat to flee, I am not a threat to the complainants. I am an innocent person who wishes to help my attorney in my defense. And I feel the DA, in concert with the sheriff, hopes to keep my defense in check with a bail that renders me unable to defend myself. Thank you for your consideration Your Honor.

The Court: Mr. Graham. I had a question for you. Mr. Harris indicated he was interviewed on August the 16th by the Sheriff's Department and apprised of the charges against him and yet he stayed and did not flee and was arrested on August 20th, some four or five days later; is that correct?

Mr. Graham: That's my recollection, Judge.

The Court: Okay. All right. Mr. Gephart, anything further?

Mr. Gephart then addressed the court regarding the impact incarceration has on a defendant's ability to assist in the preparation of a defense. Mr. Gephart added that I wasn't a flight risk or a risk to the accusers, reiterating that to be precluded from being released by high bail in a real sense precludes his ability to assist and effectively prepare his defense in this case. Of course, Mr. Graham had his own idea on bail and it was $500K up from the S100K, which was the bail at that time.

Mr. Graham: The People are going to be asking to file a first amended felony complaint that alleges that Mr. Harris falls within the provisions of the one-strike law, which requires a 15 year to life sentence based on molestation, continuous molestation of more than one victim under §667.61(B)... These are extremely serious allegations. I understand Mr. Harris has a very serious desire to conduct his own defense investigation. We welcome that. The People in no way seek to prohibit Mr. Harris from doing that. If, at any point during this process, the People have a reasonable doubt as to the allegations being made by these two girls, we would stop the whole process from going forward.

The court then inquired whether there was already a restraining order in place and Ms. Ellis said there was, whereupon the court ordered a reduction in bail down to $50,000 from the current $100,000. Following this ruling, the prelim was set for September 4th, unless I bailed out and then I would waive time and postpone the preliminary examination in order to better prepare for it. Mr. Graham was to bring a motion to amend the complaint and the Judge was going to allow it to be heard and considered on the same day as the prelim, and if the motion is granted the evidence will be heard as to all the charges that are before the court at that time. There was to be no continuance based on lack of notice or surprise.

I think this was where Mr. Gephart started to show signs of weakness. For example, he just failed to seek a continuance he desperately wanted even when the court was inviting him to plead his case. I went back to my cell and started plotting how I could get $5,000 for the bondsman and $50,000 in collateral.

Immediately, I zeroed in on my friend Greg Johnson. I had just purchased a snowmobile from him for $5,000 and I still hadn't picked it up from, his house. Surely he could help me out and refund my money in order for me to bail out. I tried and tried to call Greg, but he wasn't taking my calls.

I tried calling Dee Berner, who was a dear friend, and she said she would do what she could. I called my dad and he was willing to put up his car as collateral, so that was a plus. I waited until the next day to talk with Kerri. She was petrified the DA was going to have her arrested and put in jail, so she didn't want to extend herself right then. I understood her belief that this was a witch hunt.

I then called Steve Cupp, a family friend of Kerri's who lived in Bishop and who I knew on a friendly basis. He was receptive to helping me out, offering to get the money from Greg, handle the car title from my dad, and deal with the bondsman, Buckaroo Bonds out of Bishop.

Finally, after several days, on Friday, August the 31st, Greg decided he wasn't going to refund me the $5,000 I needed and so it was back to square one. Steve hatched a plan where my boss, Alex Reichl, and Steve would both cover the now $5,500 fee and Steve would let the bondsman lien against his home in Bishop for the $50,000 collateral. At 6:00pm, I bailed out and the bondsman, Bob Kimball, drove me back to Mammoth in his new Audi TT. I was on cloud nine as Bob dropped me off at my truck, which was still in Mr. Reichl's driveway. The battery was dead. My phone was on life support. Somehow, I managed to call AAA and they came right out, which made me feel better. I headed for Kerri's house, stopping on the way for some Chinese takeout. A little sesame beef and sweet and sour pork never hurt anybody. Kerri gave me a big hug and Rusty went crazy. Kerri had bailed Rusty out of the dog pound and she had been taking care of him. Kerri quickly noticed that I had lost weight. Stress and skimpy portions of food sure takes its toll.

We spent a relaxing weekend watching tennis, hanging out with the horses, including mine at the stables and hers at her house. We also went shopping for court clothes since I had a court date set for Tuesday the

4th. I called Mr. Gephart and told him I had bailed out. He was glad and told me to be sure and show up in court on the 4th. He opined that we didn't need to meet before then, because he would get a continuance, because the 10-day requirement only applies to defendants in custody. So, Tuesday came and Kerri and I made the lengthy drive to Bridgeport for my preliminary hearing.

FOUR

We got to court with minutes to spare. Mr. Gephart was in a tizzy. It seemed that the DA was going to amend the complaint and he wanted my bail increased. Mr. Graham was none too pleased that I had bailed out. I appeared before Judge Eller again and it turned out that Mr. Graham had not formally filed his amended complaint nor had he provided discovery. Mr. Gephart felt confident he would get a continuance. Mr. Graham objected to Mr. Gephart's request for a continuance, and asserted that he had a right to the preliminary hearing as scheduled, pursuant to §1048. (All references are to the California Penal Code unless otherwise indicated.) Mr. Graham also introduced evidence purporting to show that I was a threat to Martha and Chelsea in what was tantamount to an unnoticed bail review hearing

The People were seeking to remand me immediately. Martha's boyfriend, Leif Medrud, spoke to CPS over the Labor Day weekend and said I was stalking the girls. This was all a bunch of malarkey since I was with Kerri the entire time. Martha's psychiatric specialist also wrote a letter detailing the fact that Martha had tried to kill herself and was emotionally unstable. Kerri was flabbergasted that the state would take Martha out of her true home and place her in a foster home where she could attempt suicide or go out late at night and get in fights. Mr. Graham believed the girls were emotionally distraught and any delay in the prelim would be harmful to them.

The Court: Mr. Graham, have you provided, I know you are not required to do it prior to prelim as opposed to prior to trial, but your office has always been good about doing this, have you provided all of the discovery of the anticipated testimony and evidence you are going to present at the preliminary hearing to the best of your knowledge?

Mr. Graham: Yes, I have provided defense counsel everything that I have.

At this point, Mr. Gephart failed to argue §§1048(a)(3) or (b)(3), even though the required threat of force of violence was not present. There is a difference between §288(a) and §288(b) and Mr. Gephart missed this fact and failed to argue for a continuance based on that difference. Judge Eller ordered a one-day continuance to allow Mr. Gephart time to prepare and told him to make good use of his time.

The next day, I appeared in Mammoth before a different judge, the Honorable Richard Specchio, who had been brought in from the neighboring Alpine County, population 1,200. He was there just to hear my case. This was not going to end well, was my first thought. Immediately, Mr. Gephart tried to get a continuance as he was still not ready for the prelim.

The previous afternoon and evening Kerri and I had met with Mr. Gephart and Kerri had provided him with hundreds of documents from her daughters' false reports to CPS. The reports ran the gamut from "Mom doesn't feed me" to "she beats me," for example. Now Martha was ready to take the stand and Mr. Gephart was still digesting the information he had received thus far. After some perfunctory niceties, the prelim began with Martha:

Mr. Graham: For the record on this document that's going to be entitled Touching Locations MG under 14, I have written in "Defendant's trailer in Bishop, couch"; "Chalfant trailer, Mom's bedroom"; "Chalfant trailer, living room floor".

Q. by Mr. Graham: Were there any other places in the Chalfant trailer where any touchings occurred?

A. No.

Q. Other than the Bishop trailer and the Chalfant trailer, were there any other locations at all that Mike touched you that you didn't like?

A. It was at his dad's house in LA.

Q. And was there a room that occurred in?

A. It was in the living room on the couch.

Q. Were there any other places that Mike touched you in a bad way while you were under 14, or do we have all of them?

A. No, you have all of them.

Martha went on to describe my hand supposedly touching her boobs or vagina between 2 and 100 times at the Bishop trailer. Martha was then asked about any other touching.

Q. by Mr. Graham: Did Mr. Harris' mouth ever touch you in the trailer?

A. No.

Q. On any part of your body?

A. No.

Q. Did he ever do anything with his fingers when he would rub you?

A. No, not when I was at that house.

Q. Did he ever put his fingers inside you?

A. No.

Now, at first glance, this is horrific testimony, but on further review, the question looms, how is it possible that I could rub her vagina up to 100 times without using my fingers? The perplexities of this case were starting to appear, but for Mr. Gephart, he just wasn't getting it. Or he was preoccupied.

Q. by Mr. Graham: Did you ever see his penis during this time when he was touching you like this?

A. No.

Q. And at any time while you were — during this period of time when you were being touched on the couch in Bishop — we're talking about these two different kinds of touchings — did you ever tell anyone, including your sister about what was happening to you?

A. I told my sister but nobody else.

Q. Why didn't you tell your mom about what was going on with you?

A. Because Mike would have gotten mad and then I know my mom probably wouldn't have listened to me.

The Court: You were afraid that your mother would…

The Witness: Get mad? Yes, at me.

Q. by Mr. Graham: Did Mike, during this time when you were — would come into — where you were, on the couch in Bishop, did he ever tell you anything about what he would do if you were to tell anybody?

A. If I told anybody, he said he was just going to lie about it.

Q. Did he ever tell you he would do any harm if you told anybody at this time?

A. Not at that time.

Mr. Graham next moved on to the Chalfant trailer residence. Martha described the same kind of touching in her mom's bedroom, but instead of using Mr. Graham's estimate numbers, like 2 to 100 or 2 to 50, she was now using "more than one time". There was a distinct difference in her answers when Mr. Graham was leading her along. When pressed, Martha said the inappropriate touchings occurred almost every day.

Q. by Mr. Graham: Now, was there another kind of touching that you wanted to talk about?

A. Yeah.

Q. And did this happen one time or more than one time while you were under 14 at the Chalfant trailer in your mom's bedroom?

A. I can't give you days, but I can give you how many times, because I remember.

Q. How many times?

A. He only did it, like, five times. He didn't do it very much.

Martha then described me supposedly putting my penis on her vagina a lot and kissing her all over including her lips. At this point, I was exceedingly frustrated that Martha could get away with lying so flagrantly and I couldn't even whisper a response. I just sat there and stoically took it. Further questions involving the Chalfant residence led Mr. Graham to ask:

Q. by Mr. Graham: Did he ever put his penis even any way partly inside your vagina?

A. Yes.

Q. How many times did he try to put his penis inside your vagina in your mom's bedroom while you were under 14?

A. Like, a lot.

Q. What did he do?

A. And he tried to put it in.

Q. And when you say "tried to put it in," was he able to get his boner any way inside of you?

A. A little bit inside.

Q. And how did that feel?

A. It hurt.

Martha then described another instance of penile penetration and, upon questioning, estimated that three to four days a week I raped her. Yet, didn't she just say I rubbed my penis on her vagina "like five times"? This was supposedly when she was 11 or 12 years old.

Q. by Mr. Graham: How long after you moved into the trailer did any of the touchings here start?

A. One or two weeks.

Q. How many days or weeks or months passed before he started putting his penis or trying to put his penis inside your vagina?

A. I think I was 13 at the time.

Q. So you think you turned 13. Is that when he started trying to put his penis inside your vagina?

A. Yes.

Martha then described the "bucket incident" where she peed in my dog's water dish and then lied about it. I got mad and Martha says I threw the bucket at her when we got home, but in reality, I threw the water dish/bucket at the trash can and it bounced out and hit her. This was never an issue until years later when she was in CPS custody fighting to stay out of her mom's home. Martha was then asked what I said would happen if she told anyone about my rapes and molestations, to which Martha replied "If you tell anybody what I did to you, I'll lie and I 'll kill you."

Martha next said this happened when she was 13. So, are we supposed to believe this little 10, 11, 12-year-old girl was being repeatedly molested and raped, some three to four days a week, and yet never told anyone and was under no threat if she told until she was 13? I was upset Martha was saying she told her sister when her sister was actually living in Coloma with their father, Dale. Martha said she wouldn't tell her mom, because her mom wouldn't believe her and now after a year of purported abuse, she goes through two more years of purported abuse with nary a mention of a threat should she tell. Martha was then asked about the incidents in the living room of the Chalfant trailer where Martha claimed that, on two occasions, I rubbed her vagina with my penis. Mr. Graham asked:

Q. by Mr. Graham: Was there a reason why — did he tell you a reason why he didn't do it more on the living room floor with you?

A. No.

Q. Can you tell us, do you know why?

A. Because my mom was in her room and then if my mom was not in her room, then that's where it would happen.

It was obvious that twice in the living room spanning years and 3 to 4 times a week in mom's bedroom didn't add up.

Q. by Mr. Graham: During any of these times that Mike touched you, as we've described so far in the Chalfant trailer on the living room floor or in your mom's bedroom, was your sister present in either of those rooms to where she could see you?

A. Yes.

Q. How many times?

A. I don't know how many times.

Q. Was it more than one time?

A. Yes, it was more than one time.

Q. Was it more than ten times?

A. Yes.

Q. Was it more than 20 times?

A. I don't think it was more than 20 times.

Just more leading the witness to a number after she said initially "I don't know how many times."

Q. by Mr. Graham: But is it fair to say she saw some of the touchings going on?

A. Yes.

Q. And when she was in either of the rooms when some or all of the touchings were going on, did Mike ever say anything to her about what was going on with Mike and you?

A. No.

Q. So, he never told her anything?

A. No.

Q. Now this is the last place and time where touchings occurred, is that correct, when you were under 14?

A. Yes.

Q. And we've talked about a lot of different — we talked about three different locations where touchings occurred, lots of touchings, and now you're going down to Mike's dad's house with Mike, with your sister. Did you ever tell your mom you did not want to go to LA with Mike because of all this other stuff that happened?

A. Well, we got in a big argument.

Q. Who did you get in an argument with?

A. My mom and me and my sister got in an argument with my mom.

Q. About what?

A. That we didn't want to go to LA.

Q. But did you tell your mom you wanted to go or didn't want to go?

A. Like the first time, me and Chelsea wanted to go to the beach and the amusement parks.

Q. But even — and this is with Mike, correct?
A. Yes.
Q. And did it — a lot of sexual touchings had occurred prior to that; is that correct?
A. Before that?
Q. Prior to going to LA the first time?
A. Yes.
Q. And yet, you still wanted to go down there with Mike; is that right?
A. Yes.
Q. Tell the court why you would go down to Los Angeles with Mike even though a lot of bad things had happened prior to that.
A. Well, the first time, because I knew that he wasn't — we were going — we were going to spend the night but I knew he wasn't going to do anything.
Q. Why did you think he wasn't going to do anything the first time?
A. Well, because we were in a whole different room than him. Plus, his dad was at the house.
Q. Did you tell your mother before you left to go down to LA to Mike dad's house, this first time, did you tell your mom during the argument or any time leading up to when you left about what Mike had been doing to you before then?
A. No.
Q. And again, I want to ask you why didn't you tell your mom about what was happening?
A. Because I knew she wasn't going to believe me, because one time I tried telling her but — because Mike had another incident with another girl that he touched and he went to jail, and then my mom asked if he ever touched us and I said "yes, he has," and she didn't believe me.
Q. While you were under 14, from the very first touching Mike ever did to you up to your 14th birthday, how many times did you tell your mom about what Mike was doing to you?
A. Just once.

Martha then related being raped at my dad's house with full penetration and ejaculation inside of her. She noted a bloody discharge afterwards. It was some pretty tall tales going on from one thing to the next.

Q. by Mr. Graham: Did you tell anybody about this incident down at Mike's dad's house?
A. I told my sister.

A lunch break was taken after this graphic fibbery. After lunch, Mr. Graham revisited the living room floor location and Martha's description of "spooning." Mr. Graham. finally asked:

Q. by Mr. Graham: Now, how many times did he do this spooning thing? One time or more than one time on the living room floor when you were under 14?
A. Just the one time.
Now remember that, just before lunch, Martha was asked:
Q. by Mr. Graham: And did he touch his penis to your vagina one time or more than one time?
A. On the living room floor it was only, like, a couple times he did.
Q. Could he have done it more than twice?
A. Yeah, just a couple times, like twice.

Martha's demeanor was unflinching and unemotional. I was chomping at the bit to point out some things. Mr. Gephart couldn't care less what I thought. I wanted to scream out my objections but court rules don't give me standing to object. It is up to Mr. Gephart to object or argue, and so I continued to sit in silence, my freedom hanging in the balance. Mr. Graham then continued:

Q. by Mr. Graham: Were you ever in the room when Mike and your mother did anything together?
A. Yes.
Q. What did you watch them do together?
A. They had sex.
Q. How old were you when you — the first time that you watched where you were in the room when Mike and your mom were having sex?
A. Ten.
Q. And which room was that?
A. The house in Nevada City.
Q. Is that in California?
A. Yes.
Q. And when you say you saw them having sex, are you talking about intercourse? Do you know what that means?
A. Yeah.
Q. Were they having intercourse?
A. I don't think it was fully sex. She was giving him a blow job.
Q. Did Mike ever talk to you at any point in time prior to your 14th birthday about blow jobs?
A. No.
Q. At any point in time before you were 14 did you ever put your mouth on his penis?
A. No.
Q. When was the first time that you told anyone else, other than your sister?

A. Just my mom.

Q. Other than your mother, when was the first time that you told anybody?

A. I didn't tell anybody else — well, I told Alex.

Q. Before Alex got involved, and her department got involved, had you told anybody else?

A. No.

Q. So, you never told any of your friends -

A. No.

Q. -What Mike was doing to you?

A. No.

Q. Why didn't you tell any of your friends what was going on?

A. It was hard to talk about.

Martha then alleged that I had hit Kerri between 10 and 30 times, but then retreated by saying, "He mainly just pushed her around and threw stuff at her." And I admit, there have been a few scuffles and broken doors, but I never hit Kerri and Kerri never hit me.

Q. by Mr. Graham: And you were describing an earlier event back at the beginning this morning [the bucket incident]. Has he done anything more than that?

A. Yes, he has — one time I got caught. I took my report card from the mailbox and so he got real angry and he took me and threw me up against the wall.

Q. Where?

A. In the Chalfant house in my room.

Q. What part of your body hit the wall?

A. My back.

Q. And was your mom present during that incident?

A. Yes, she was.

Q. Any other times when he's committed any violence on you? Hitting, pushing, that type of thing?

A. No.

Q. Did you ever try to leave the house yourself at any time to get away from Mike? Ever try to run away or anything like that?

A. Oh no.

Mr. Graham was finished. Finally. It was now time for Mr. Gephart to show his stuff cross-examining the little liar Martha with the pants on fire. He started out by asking Martha if she had run away, knowing full well that Kerri and I had told him about the running away incident July 8th, where Martha left for the night to be with her boyfriend. Martha flatly denied running away however, but at least Mr. Gephart was paying attention. Martha was then asked about who she had told in order to prepare for the prelim.

Q. by Mr. Gephart: In preparation for today's testimony, can you tell me the people that you've spoken with in getting ready to testify here today?
A. Todd.
Q. That's Mr. Graham, the DA, that's asked you all the questions?
A. Yes. Alex.
Q. Alex Ellis?
A. Yes.
Q. From CPS?
A. Yes.
Q. The woman sitting to your right?
A. Yes… and Rat.
Q. And who, Rat?
A. Yes.
Q. Detective Rutkowski?
A. Yes… Trish.
Q. Who is Trish?
A. My foster parent.
Q. Person you're living with currently?
A. Yes.
Q. Anyone else that you can think of that you've spoken with in preparation for today's testimony?
A. And my friend Jessikah.
Q. Jessikah?
A. Yes.
Q. How old is Jessikah?
A. 15.
Q. Anyone else?
A. No.
Q. Have you spoken about this matter with anyone else you can think of, other than the five people you have listed for me?
A. I forgot one person, my counselor, Mike.
Q. Mike?
A. Yes.
Q. Apart from the people you've spoken with in preparation for today, have you spoken with anyone else about the events you've testified to here today?
A. No.

Q. Well, you've spoken with your sister, correct?
A. Sorry. My sister.
Q. Your twin sister Chelsea?
A. We didn't really talk about it though.
Q. You and she haven't spoken at all?
A. But we don't talk. We haven't been talking about testifying here.
Q. I understand, but without limitation as to time or place, I'm asking if you've spoken with anyone else about the events you've testified to here today, and I was asking haven't you spoken with Chelsea about these events?
A. Yes, I have.
Q. And there was testimony from you today that you've spoken to, at least in some regard, to your mother about the events or some of the events, correct?
A. Yes.
Q. Anyone else you can think of?
A. No.
Q. But, prior to initiation of actions which resulted in you living someplace else away from your home and Chelsea living someplace else. Prior to that happening, would you and Chelsea talk about Mike Harris and these events on a regular basis?
A. No.

Martha next described the fact that she and Chelsea spoke approximately once every other week about these matters since she was ten. Mr. Gephart deftly moved into detailed questions about the various locations and touchings. The first location was the couch at the Bishop trailer. Martha alleged that she was repeatedly touched between 2 and 100 times, some of which reportedly occurred while Chelsea was asleep at the other end of the couch.

Q. by Mr. Gephart: Do you. recall any instance where Chelsea woke up while this was going on?
A. No.
Q. Not a single time?
A. No.
Q. Was there ever a situation where, the next morning, where one of these 2 to 100 episodes occurred where Chelsea woke you up and you said "Hey, didn't you see what was going on" or "Didn't you hear what Mike was doing in the middle of the night?" Ever have any discussion like that with Chelsea after one of these episodes?
A. No.

Q. Same question with regard to your mom. Did you ever after one of these episodes say to her, "Hey, you know what Mike did to me last night?"

A. No.

Q. During the time you were sleeping in the bunk beds at the Bishop trailer, did any of these touchings, whether it be your boobs or your vagina, occur?

A. No.

Q. Only while you were on the couch?

A. Yes.

Q. And then, I take it, at some point you moved off the couch on to the bunk beds?

A. Yes.

Q. And the touchings had stopped by then, at least with regard to the Bishop trailer, correct?

A. Yes.

Mr. Gephart then proceeded to go through the touchings and locations at the Chalfant trailer with Martha, getting a bit confused regarding daytime/nighttime — mom was at home/mom was not at home. Martha did, however, stick to the "it happened almost every day" theme. Always in Kerri's bedroom. With more detailed questioning, Martha tended to not remember exactly. For example:

Q. by Mr. Gephart: But, in any event, it would happen in the bedroom. Would it be on your mother's bed?

A. Yes.

Q. And you would be on the bed watching TV —

A. Yes.

Q. — whether it was at night or whether it was day, and he would enter the room and put his penis on your vagina? That's what you remember?

A. Yes.

Q. Is it your memory that sperm would come out of his penis on your vagina when this occurred?

A. No... What?

Q. Did he ejaculate during any of the times when he would put his penis on your vagina?

A. Yes.

Q. In your mother's bedroom?

A. Yes, but he would pull it out before it came out except for that one time.

Q. So anytime he ejaculated — and you said he ejaculated almost every time?

A. Yes.

Q. But it was always —

A. But he pulled it out.

Q. But he would always pull away, correct?

A. Yes.

So, what gives? It was on the vagina and now it's in the vagina, just another inconsistency. Mr. Gephart then covered the trip to LA:

Q. by Mr. Gephart: ...You described a situation where you and Chelsea were leaving for Los Angeles with Mike, and there was a fight that occurred involving Mike and your mother. Do you recall?

A. No, it was just my mom and me and my sister.

Q. But I understood your testimony to be that the fight was in the context of something involving the arrest of Mike Harris at about that time?

A. That wasn't before LA.

Q. What were you remembering and testifying to with regard to an arrest of Mike Harris?

A. Well, he asked if I've ever told anybody about what happened, and so I told him I told my mom, and then he asked when and so I said when Mike got arrested for molesting the other kid.

Q. So the arrest didn't have anything to do timing wise with your trip to Los Angeles?

A. No.

Q. Am I correct in that?

A. It was before.

Q. What do you understand Mike to have been arrested for?

A. He touched, molested another girl.

Q. And you saw him do it?

A. Yeah.

Q. And what did you see him do?

A. He put his hand down her pants.

Q. And you understood Mike to be arrested for that?

A. Yes.

Q. And did you have an opportunity to discuss that event at about the time it happened with any law enforcement or any other officials that you understood to be investigating that episode?

A. Nobody came and asked me anything.

Q. And you were never interviewed by any policeman or social worker or anybody regarding this incident?

A. No. Nobody asked me any questions.

How can this be? I told the investigator, Frank Smith, to go and ask the girls what happened and he went and talked to somebody and then closed his investigation and released me from jail with no charges ever being filed. Mr. Gephart went back to the living room incident that Martha said occurred a couple of times and then changed it to once and then described four incidents under specific questioning. When lying, it appears to be best to not remember like Martha was doing pretty steadily but Martha was not that shrewd. She was caught and Mr. Gephart knew it. He asked her about the alleged rape in LA one more time and then he rested.

Mr. Gephart told the court he was unavailable the next day and a chambers conference was held outside of my presence. When it was over, Mr. Graham put his objection on the record that I be remanded into custody with a new bail amount of $500,000. The Honorable Judge Specchio noted his request but declined to raise the bail, stating to me, "But I trust that you will be here tomorrow. And secondarily, I had represented to your counsel that I would hear all evidence before I would even consider raising bail". I told the judge, "thank you," and then day one of the prelim was over.

Kerri and I drove back to her house while I described the day's events. Kerri had waited all day outside the courtroom, since the hearing was closed to the public. While she was waiting, Det. Rutkowski pressured her to stop helping me out and Kerri told him to bug off. Clearly, Kerri was in my corner. Once at the house, we BBQ'd some hamburgers out in the yard then spent a quiet evening watching TV. In the back of my mind, I kept thinking about going back to jail and Kerri worried that she was next.

The next morning, we were off early because court was supposed to start at 8:00am sharp. I entered the courtroom only to be told that Judge Specchio's father had passed away the night before and there would have to be a continuance. I thought, all right, a continuance was a good thing, but there was a catch. The judge was going to remand me to jail and set my bail at $500,000. Mr. Graham and. Mr. Gephart argued back and forth, but in the end the court said:

The Court: Okay. You know we are consuming a lot of time and I know where I am going on this... And Mr. Harris, you have been an absolute gentleman through the course of this, but I feel, I feel compelled to remand you.

After this, I made a brief statement pleading to remain free in order to fight my case, but it really didn't matter, my fate was set. I did, however, waive the single session rule, which provides that a preliminary hearing be handled in one continuous series of hearings. I did this because I didn't want to rock the boat with Judge Specchio.

So, off I went to jail. It was a beautiful day and I still had my street clothes and my sunglasses, so it wasn't like I was bound and gagged or anything. When I arrived at the jail, I was ushered into my private cell and my books and the TV were still there. I had been free for five days and it had cost me $5,500. Wow.

I waited for day two of the prelim on September 13th, 2007, by watching TV and sleeping.

FIVE

On Thursday the 13th, I walked across the street doing the perp walk to the stately old courthouse; its white paint and red trim stark against the deep azure backdrop. I was going to court for day two of the bifurcated preliminary hearing. It turned out that Mr. Graham wanted to put Raeanna Davenport on the stand. She was the girl who claimed I touched her back in 2003. I wasn't being charged with molesting her; she was there as a California Evidence Code §1108 witness.

Section 1108 states:

In a criminal action in which the defendant is accused of a sexual offense, evidence of the defendant's commission of another sexual offense or offenses is not made inadmissible by section 1101, if the evidence is admissible pursuant to section 352.

Section 1101 states:

(a) Except as provided in this section and in sections 1102, 1103, 1108, and 1109, evidence of a person's character or trait of his or her character (whether in the form of an opinion, evidence of reputation, or evidence of specific instances of his or her conduct) is inadmissible when offered to prove his or her conduct on a specified occasion.

(b) Nothing in this section prohibits the admission of evidence that a person committed a crime, civil wrong, or other act when relevant to prove some fact (such as motive, opportunity, intent, preparation, plan, knowledge, identity, absence of mistake or accident or whether a defendant in a prosecution for an unlawful sexual act or

attempted unlawful sexual act did not reasonably and in good faith believe that the victim consented) other than his or her disposition to commit such an act.

(c) Nothing in this section affects the admissibility of evidence offered to support or attack the credibility of a witness.

As for Evid. Code §352, I described that previously that it has to do with the admissibility of evidence and that the judge has the discretion to allow any relevant evidence unless it is unduly prejudicial, would confuse a jury, or would take up too much time. I was confused about §1108, because the Raeanna allegation was an uncharged event and proper notice and discovery had not been provided. But, into the fire we went. Mr. Gephart started off by telling Judge Specchio that he had represented Greg Davenport, who was Raeanna's uncle and who I had told investigators back in 2003 that he probably molested her based on my conversations with Raeanna and her unwillingness to go to his house.

A chambers conference was held and it was decided that, for the day at least, Mr. Gephart had no conflict of interest. During the in camera hearing:

The Court: Do you have any other objections to Raeanna Davenport?

Mr. Gephart: I don't feel I have a basis to object under §1108, because that is where she is being offered.

That wrapped up the conference and Mr. Gephart, Mr. Graham, and the Judge all came into the courtroom and Raeanna began to testify.

Q. by Mr. Graham: And at some time before today were you someplace in Chalfant where something happened to you with Mr. Harris?

A. Yes.

Q. And where did this thing happen?

A. In his house.

Q. And do you know which room in the house?

A. His bedroom.

Q. And how old were you when this thing happened?

A. About 10.

Q. And when this thing happened, was there anybody else in the room with you?

A. Yes.

Q. Can you tell us all the people who were in the room when this happened?

A. Martha and Chelsea.

Q. And when Martha and Chelsea were in this bedroom you spoke about, was Michael Harris also in the bedroom?

A. Yes.

Q. Describe what happened. Just tell us what happened.
A. We were watching TV and then he came in and —
The Court: Meaning Mr. Harris?
The Witness: Yes, and he started rubbing my legs and then I was wearing shorts and he went a little too far up and, yeah.
Q. by Mr. Graham: Okay. You said he was rubbing your legs. Were you in the room when he was doing that?
A. On the bed.
Q. And was there anybody else on the bed with you when he started rubbing your legs?
A. One of the girls. I don't know which one.
Q. Did he rub up and down more than once?
A. Yes.
Q. More than five times?
A. Yes.
Q. And after he was done rubbing your legs, what did he do with his hand?
A. He put it up my shorts.

So, there it was, the story had unfolded and I immediately found fault with the testimony, mainly, Martha had said I reached down Raeanna's pants while Raeanna said I reached up her shorts, an obvious discrepancy.

Q. by Mr. Graham: You just told him to stop it and he pulled his hand out. Did anything happen after that?
A. No.
Q. What did you guys do? Did you guys continue to watch TV or did you play or where did you go?
A. We watched TV and then ate dinner.
Q. After that happened, did you eventually tell somebody about what had just occurred?
A. Yes.
Q. Who was the first person you told?
A. My grandma.
Q. Now there were the girls there. Martha and Chelsea were there when this happened; is that correct?
A. Yeah.
Q. And did you tell them what had just happened?
A. The next day I did.

Why did Raeanna have to tell them something they saw? Just wondering.

Q. And did either of the girls, either Martha or Chelsea, tell you about anything in their lives that had happened to them?

A. No.

Q. After this incident, let's say we go on for months and months and months go by, and you would see Mr. Harris or Mr. Harris' truck for that matter, how would you feel?

A. Scared.

She says she was scared, but she never mentioned any threats, never got a restraining order and stayed in the same house across the street for months and months and months. Hardly a scared little girl.

Now it was Mr. Gephart's turn. He started off asking Raeanna if she remembered the event and she said she did. Then Mr. Gephart asked her a series of specific questions to which Raeanna replied "I don't remember."

Q. by Mr. Gephart: Was Mr. Harris in the room with you and the girls for the entire time or did he enter the room sometime after you and the girls were already in the room?

A. I don't remember.

Q. But at some point in time he was in the room with you?

A. Yes.

Q. And he was on the bed with you?

A. Yes.

Q. Was he sitting on the bed watching TV?

A. I don't remember.

Q. You don't remember his position on the bed?

A. No.

Q. Okay. Okay. Let me go back to the way you reported this to your grandmother then. You went home. Do you recall how you got home that night? Did you walk?

A. I walked.

Q. And you went in the house and your grandmother was there?

A. Yes.

Q. And did you say to her, Mr. Harris touched me?

A. I don't remember how I told her.

Q. Do you recall talking to any police officer or sheriff's officer about this incident?

A. Yes.

Q. Do you remember your grandmother asking you that night whether something was wrong with you?

A. Yes.

Q. What do you remember?
A. She asked me what had happened and I told her.
Q. What did you tell her? Do you remember?
A. That Mike touched me.
Q. Do you remember your grandmother asking you about blood on your underpants?
A. No.
Q. Do you recall when you first talked to a policemen or a sheriff's officer?
A. I think it was that same night.
Q. Was your grandmother there while you were talking with the police officer?
A. Yes.
Q. The next day then, Raeanna, did you tell what had happened to anyone else? And by that, I mean any other person who came to talk to you about this?
A. I don't think anybody else came to see me the next day.
Q. And you've already told Mr. Graham that you told the girls about it the next day?
A. Yes.
Q. Did you tell Martha and Chelsea about this event the next day?
A. I only told one of the girls.
Q. Do you remember which one?
A. No.

Now it was just one girl who she told and she doesn't remember which one. What exactly does she remember? Anyway, she finished up and it was Chelsea's turn to make believe. That was going to be interesting.

SIX

Chelsea, was asked some preliminary questions by Mr. Graham, such as how old she was, how old she was when she met me and the like.

Q. by Mr. Graham: Since you were approximately 10½ - 11 has Mike ever done anything to you?

A. Yes.

Q. And can you tell us, generally, what he did to you?

A. He's touched me, he's hit me, he's molested me.

Chelsea then described all the inappropriate touchings that occurred in the Bishop trailer bedroom or her bedroom in the Chalfant trailer.

(A discussion was held off the record, between defense counsel and the defendant.)

The Court: I don't know what's going on over there but I would suggest, Mr. Harris, that you don't point towards the witness.

Mr. Gephart: Judge, what Mr. Harris was concerned about was that Ms. Ellis appeared to be talking to the witness and we'd object to that going on Judge. We understand she's here for support. But we're not going to agree to having communications passing between them or coaching or anything else going on while the witness is testifying or thereafter for that purpose.

The Court: Well, a support person is there for a lot of reasons; however, up to this juncture, I haven't seen any communications during the course of examination.

But I will admonish you not to speak with Chelsea during the course of her examination.

Ms. Ellis: I apologize Your Honor.

The Court: Have any questions been asked that you, in any way, assisted or suggested answers?

Ms. Ellis: Not at all. I apologize. I did say something, and I'll tell you what I said.

The Court: Okay.

Ms. Ellis: I said, 'breathe.'

The Court: 'Breathe?'

Ms. Ellis: Yes.

The Court: And that's a good suggestion.

Alex Ellis is no joke. She knows the rules, and yet crushes right through them as though she has a vendetta.

Q. by Mr. Graham: Did you over take any trips at all with Mr. Harris?

A. Yes.

Q. Where it's just you and Mr. Harris alone or you and Mr. Harris and your sister?

A. It was me and my sister and Mike. We went lots of places; Disneyland, Knott's Berry Farm, Magic Mountain.

Q. And were there any… anytime, whether you were under 14 or over 14, were there any bad touchings on any of these trips?

A. Yes.

Q. And how old were you when the first bad touching occurred on one of these trips?

A. I was 13 or 14.

Q. And we'll get back to that. Let's just go back to the locations where these touchings occurred when you were under 14, all right?

A. All right.

Q. And let's start out with the first one that you mentioned, the defendant's trailer in Bishop on See Vee. You said it was in the bedroom on the bed?

A. Yes.

Q. Tell us about any kind of touching that he did to you in there.

A. His hand touched my — my belly, and my chest, and my legs, and that's when he started taking off my clothes.

Q. And did he do this in the bedroom in the Bishop trailer one time or more than one time?

A. More than one time.

Q. Tell us how many times his hand or hands touched your breast in that bedroom in Bishop?

A. Ten.

Q. When you say "ten" were these on ten different days or just ten different touchings on possibly the same day?
A. Ten different days.
Q. Did he touch you with his hand on your - on your thigh part of your leg one time or more than one time?
A. More than one time.
Q. Can you give us how many different days this kind of touching occurred? How many occasions?
A. Twice a week.
Q. Any other kind of touching?
A. With his mouth.
Q. Okay. Tell us the different parts of your body or part of your body he touched with his mouth to your body?
A. My neck, my face, chest and belly.
Q. And did he engage in this kissing activity one time or more than one time in his bedroom in the trailer in Bishop?
A. More than one time.
Q. And can you give us how many times he engaged in this kind of activity, this kissing activity on your body?
A. The same, ten.
Q. Ten?
A. Occasions. It's the whole time when he did everything it was - he did the same thing.

And then Chelsea got mad and frustrated and asked for a break. Her demeanor was much the same as Martha's: stoic and unemotional, hardly a victim of years of abuse. After a short break, the Judge admonished me for pointing out that Alex Ellis was coaching Chelsea. I had no response. Chelsea was then asked by Mr. Graham to return to the discussion of the bedroom incidents in the Bishop trailer.

Q. by Mr. Graham: Did he kiss you on any other places on your body other than the places you spoke about?
A. No.
Q. Did any other part of his body other than his mouth or hand ever touch any other part of your body? In other words, any other kind of touching in his bedroom in Bishop?
A. No.
Q. Did he ever make you go into his room?
A. No, not that I remember.
Q. Did he ever use any threats at all to get you into his room?

A. No.

Q. And do you recall Mike ever saying anything to you during those times, any kind of words, or things that he would say to you while you were in the room with you and he was touching you like this?

A. "If you" - he just threatens that "If you ever told anybody, I would kill you."

Q. How did that make you feel?

A. Scared.

Q. And how many times during the nighttime episodes did he make a statement like that?

A. It was only twice and then he stopped.

Q. Let's ask this question: How many times when you were living in the trailer in Bishop did Mr. Harris threaten to kill you if you told anybody?

A. It would be every day, so about — I don't remember how long we lived in the trailer, probably about a year or six months. I don't remember.

Q. But if you were to give us - when, you say "every day," if you were to think about a number of times, can you give us an estimate as far as a number of times he actually said to you "I'm going to kill you if you tell anybody about what I'm doing to you?"

A. I don t know, like 30.

Q. But it was more than twice?

A. Yes, more than twice.

The Court: Then I'm confused. When you said this happened twice, what were you referring to?

The Witness: During the time he was touching me.

The Court: You mean on each of these occasions he would — he threatened you about 30 times and usually once before and after the incident?

The Witness: Yes.

So even the Judge is getting it and we had just started. Let's review. First, there was no threat, then there were two threats, then there was every day, then there were thirty threats, then there were thirty threats before and after thirty and the same exact touching occurred ten times. I sure hoped the Judge would see through this farce. Chelsea went on to describe the same touchings during the weekend days that had happened during the nighttime incidents. Finally, Mr. Graham moved on.

Q. by Mr. Graham: And when this was happening in the trailer in Bishop, did you and your sister ever discuss what was going on?

A. Yes, we did.

Q. And this is in the trailer, or while you were living in the trailer; is that correct?

A. Yes.

Q. All right, what did you tell your sister about what was happening?

A. I just told her what happened and I asked if he touched her and she said "yes."

Q. I want you to go back in your mind if you can to the very first time that this kind of touching occurred in his bedroom on the bed. Can you remember the first time?

A. I can try. I remember some of it.

Q. Do you remember how long it was after the first time he touched you that you told your sister about what was going on?

A. It was about a week after.

Q. During that week, were there any more touchings as you've spoken about?

A. Yes.

Q. So how many occasions of touchings — episodes of touchings occurred before you told your sister?

A. About two or three.

Q. Did you tell your sister what you told us today was going on?

A. Yes, I did.

Q. And how did she respond?

A. She was scared and shocked, because then she told me the same thing happened to her.

Now wait a minute. Isn't Martha already scared by having been abused for months before Chelsea arrived? And, if Martha had been abused, what did she think was going on with me and Chelsea in the bedroom in the Bishop trailer? How could Martha be shocked if it's been happening to her for months? The lies the girls were telling were outrageous and nobody was seeming to get that but me. Mr. Graham continually led the girls to an answer and deftly ignored the contradictions.

Q. by Mr. Graham: Did she ever give you any details of what was happening to her?

A. No.

Q. Did she ever tell you anything about what was happening to her?

A. Yeah. She didn't tell me all of it though.

Q. At any point while you were staying in that Bishop trailer did you tell your mother about what was going on with Mike?

A. No.

Q. Can you tell us why you didn't tell your mother?

A. Because I was scared she wasn't going to believe me.

Q. While you were living in the trailer and these kinds of touchings were going on by Mr. Harris, did you tell anybody else other than your sister?

A. No.

Q. Did you tell any friends?
A. No.
Q. Did you write it down anywhere?
A. Yes.
Q. While you were living in the trailer in Bishop, you wrote down something about this; is that correct?
A. Correct.
Q. Do you have that?
A. No I don't.
Q. Where did you write something down about this?
A. Just in a journal. A notebook.
Q. And what did you write in the journal?
A. What he did to me.
Q. And do you know what happened to that journal?
A. No, I don't. All I know is it's in Chalfant, but I don't know what happened to it.
Q. Is it fair to say you just lost it since then?
A. No. After I left the house, I don't know, my mom packed up all my stuff, and I don't know where anything is.
Q. Is there — is it possible that we could find that journal if we were to go look for it today?
A. Maybe. Maybe if my mom and Mike didn't do anything with it.
Q. Do you have an idea or any kind of idea about where it is right now?
A. My stuff is packed up.
Q. In what?
A. Boxes, I think. I don't know, my sister packed it up.

If Chelsea knew that Martha had packed up her stuff, then why didn't she ask Martha about the journal? Why doesn't Chelsea know that I gave all of her stuff to Alex Ellis and, more importantly, why didn't Chelsea tell Ms. Ellis about the journal? Food for thought.

Q. by Mr. Graham: Just to be clear, there were no other kinds of touchings other than what we talked about inside the Bishop trailer?
A. Yes.
Q. Let' s go to the second location that you spoke about, which was your bedroom in Chalfant. And in your bedroom, tell us any of the kinds of touchings that Mr. Harris did to you in that bedroom.
A. His hand doing the same thing I told you he did in the other house on See Vee, touching up and down my body.
Q. So hands all over your body?

A. Yes, and kissing.

Q. Did he touch his hbecauseands on your body one time or more than one time?

Q. Can you give us a number of occasions, meaning episodes that occurred on separate days, where he would touch his hands on your body in [your] bedroom?

A. It would be once every day.

Q. You said he kissed you while you were in the — in your bedroom in Chalfant. Describe the kind of kissing.

A. It was up and down my neck and then when he was getting my shirt off it would be on my chest, on my breasts, and on my belly.

Q. Any other place on your body that he put his mouth on?

A. No.

Q. Did this happen one time or more than one time, this kissing type of activity?

A. More than one time.

Q. Can you give us how many episodes this kissing activity occurred?

A. Every day. Once every day, or the days if my mom didn't go horseback riding that day nothing would happen.

Chelsea next described me supposedly touching my penis to her leg and her vagina more than one time. In fact, she related that I "always tried to put it in."

Q. by Mr. Graham: Can you give us an estimate of how many episodes he tried to put his penis in your vagina?

A. Mostly every day, except the days my mom didn't go riding.

Chelsea then said she didn't try to get away, because she knew she would get in trouble "because he knew I was going to tell someone."

Q. by Mr. Graham: What made you think he knew that?

A. Because he always said: "If you tell anyone, I'm going to kill you" and he knew if he did then I was going to tell.

Say what? On what planet does this make sense? But wait, it got better.

Q. by Mr. Graham: How many times did Mr. Harris threaten to kill you if you told anyone while you were living in Chalfant?

A. About, at least twice a week.

Q. And would he say this kind of threat during the touchings or would he say it before or after?

A. Afterwards, after him and my mom would get in an argument he left and he moved out, he would say "If you tell anyone, I'll kill you." So mainly afterwards.

Q. Would it be immediately after he stopped? In other words, you were in the bedroom and it's all done, and then he's leaving, would he said it then, or when? I don't quite understand.

A. It would be a little bit afterwards, not right after.

You know it is a lie when the DA doesn't understand the testimony and drops the subject like Mr. Graham did. He moved on to the first incident in Chelsea's bedroom in the Chalfant trailer.

Q. by Mr. Graham: You're saying during that first episode, he tried to put his penis inside of you?

A. Yes.

Q. And during that first episode where he tries to put his penis inside you, before that, had he ever done that before?

A. No.

Q. He gets on top of you and could you feel his penis?

A. Yes.

Q. Was it hard or soft?

A. I don't remember.

Q. Do you know what a boner is?

A. Yes.

Q. Could you tell if he had a boner or not?

A. Not that I remember.

Q. Was there any part of his penis that actually made it, however slight a distance, inside of you?

A. Just a little bit.

Q. Can you show us?

A. About that much.

Chelsea then held up her hand and showed about an inch between her thumb and forefinger.

Q. by Mr. Graham: Now, when Mr. Harris did this, at any point in time during this first episode in the bedroom, did anything come out of his penis that you saw?

A. No.

Lunch recess was taken and then we started right back up.

Q. by Mr. Graham: All right. Now when you stated that he tried to put his penis inside you mostly every day, okay, you testified to that. Do you recall?

A. Yes.

Q. Would it be the same kind of behavior by Mr. Harris, essentially the same kind of thing?

A. I don't get what you mean.

Q. Well, what I mean is, he would take your clothes off, get on top of you, as you've described, and tried to put his penis inside of you?

A. Yes.

Q. And during these times when he would do this, would he just push once with his penis inside of you or would he do it — try to push more than one time?
A. More than one time.
Q. And how many times would he try to push his penis inside you on just the average time?
A. Three or four.
Q. And do you know what would make him stop?
A. Hearing my mom come in or me squirming enough or Martha walking in.
The Court: Who was walking in?
The Witness: Martha, my sister.
The Court: Okay.
Q. by Mr. Graham: We'll get to that. Was he ever able to get his penis all the way inside of you?
A. No.
Q. Did your sister ever enter the room to a place where she could see him doing this to you?
A. Yes.
Q. And how many times did your sister come into the room when Mr. Harris was trying to put his penis inside you?
A. Once.
Mr. Graham then asked a few more questions, then digressed to the Bishop trailer issue.
Q. by Mr. Graham: Did he ever ask you to do anything to him, perform any kind of sexual acts on him at the Bishop residence?
A. Not that I remember.
Q. Okay. After you moved in to the Chalfant residence, did he ever ask you to perform any kind of sexual activity on him on any part of his body?
A. No.
Q. At any time when he was trying to put his penis inside you, did you ever see anything come out of the tip of his penis?
A. No.
Mr. Graham then shifted gears to the Nevada City home Kerri had owned.
Q. by Mr. Graham: When you were living in Bishop with Mr. Harris, did you occasionally go up to Nevada City?
A. Yes.
Q. Did anything of a sexual nature occur up in the Nevada City location at all with Mr. Harris?
A. Yes.

Q. Did it happen one time or more than one time?
A. Just once.
Q. And who was in the residence just before this happened?
A. Mike, my mom, and my sister.
Q. Tell the court what happened in that incident.
A. We were up in my mom's room.
Q. Who was? Who?
A. Me, my sister and my mom and Mike. It was at night and we were watching a movie. And we were just sitting there watching it and Mike and my mom started having sex and —
Q. What do you mean, they were having sex. Describe what they were doing.
A. I don't know what they were doing.
Q. What did you see them do?
A. There were blankets over them. I don't know what they did.
Q. And what made you think they were having sex?
A. Because my mom moaned.
Q. And how was Mike situated to your mom? Was he next to her? Was he under her?
A. My mom was laying on her side and he was laying on his side too with his, like, front part of his body against my mom's butt, and me and my sister saw mike moving back and forth, so we knew what was happening.
Q. What happened next?
A. Mike called me over and the blankets were off them at that point and Mike's penis was inside my mom's vagina and Mike made me put my hand on his penis while it was going in and out of my mom.
Q. How did you know to put your hand on his penis?
A. Because he grabbed my hand.
Q. And where was your sister?
A. In the room.

Wow. What an incredible story. Strange how Martha described a blow-job being performed, when Chelsea says it was during intercourse. The DA's attitude is the girls can't be making this stuff up. They would, if that's the case, just say they got molested once and be done with it, was the DA's thinking. Mr. Graham's opinion was that they had every chance in the world to exaggerate the molestations, and instead they are limiting the exaggerations from what they could be saying. Of course, I disagreed. All the stories were exaggeration based on continual leading questions from the police, the CPS, the DA's office, etc.

Next, Mr. Graham waded into the 14 and older accusations which involved trips to LA to go to Disneyland and other attractions.

Q. by Mr. Graham: How many total trips did you make down from Chalfant down to that area?

A. Three.

Q. So you made one trip to this motel and two trips where you stayed at his dad's house?

A. Yes.

Q. Now at this motel in Disneyland, you say you spent two nights. Did any kinds of touchings occur during those two nights by Mr. Harris on you?

A. Yes. The first night.

Q. And where was your sister when these touchings happened during the first night?

A. In the motel room.

Q. Was she awake or asleep?

A. I don't know. She was laying down, but I couldn't tell if she was awake or asleep.

Chelsea goes on to describe me getting into the bed she is asleep in and tells how I did the same things as at the Chalfant residence.

Q. by Mr. Graham: Was there any reason why he stopped?

A. Maybe Martha woke up. I'm not sure.

Q. Before you went on this first trip, did you ever tell your mother that you didn't want to go?

A. No.

Q. Before you left, was there any discussion with anybody about how you didn't want to go?

A. Just my sister.

Q. What did you tell your sister?

A. I really didn't want to go, because I knew what was going to happen and she told me she didn't want to go either.

Q. Is it fair to say you did not want to go to Disneyland?

A. Yes.

Q. But you did anyway, with your sister?

A. Yes.

Q. Without mom?

A. Yes.

Q. Why didn't you just say, I don't want to go to Disneyland alone with Mike?

A. Because I know she would ask why.

Q. You knew that she would ask you why you wouldn't want to go down to Disneyland?

A. Yes.

Q. And so why did that thought in your mind make you still go?

A. Because I didn't want to have to tell her what Mike has been doing to me.

Q. Why didn't you want to tell her about what Mike was doing to you?

A. Because, I would have been scared and also because she wouldn't have believed me.

Q. You go on a trip with your sister to Disneyland, on a trip where, in your mind, you believe you are going to be touched some more and yet you still go; is that correct?

A. Correct.

Q. After you turned 14, how many times did you try to tell your mother about what was going on?

A. None.

Q. After you turned 14, who, other than the people recently, like the CPS and the Sheriffs, who else did you tell about what was going on?

A. Just my sister.

Q. Did you tell any friends?

A. No.

Q. How many times, if any, did you — were you present in the room when your mother and Mike were having sex?

A. I don't know how many times, but it happened a lot.

Q. And were there any other times where Mr. Harris asked you to touch him during [his] having sex with your mother, other than what you've already described?

A. No.

Q. That only happened one time?

A. Yes.

Chelsea them continued to describe me grabbing and pushing her against the wall, leaving a mark around her neck, and also me having hit Kerri a lot and then with that said Mr. Graham's direct examination was in the books. Next up was Mr. Gephart's cross-examination and I couldn't wait.

Q. by Mr. Gephart: The journal that you described earlier this morning, do you recall that?

A. Yes.

Q. When did you start keeping a journal?

A. About the first time he started touching me.

Q. So, the reason you started keeping it was because he was touching you?

A. Yes.

Q. How often would you write down in the journal what he did to you?

A. After everything happened, whatever he did to me, I'd. write it down afterwards. Not every day.
Q. So, sometimes an entry would say, okay, for the last three days, Mike has been touching me again, something like that?
A. Something like that.
Q. Did you ever tell anyone else that you were keeping a journal?
A. No. Just my sister.
Q. Did you and she discuss this?
A. No.
Q. So you told her one time you were keeping a journal?
A. Yes.
Q. And did she ever ask to see it?
A. No.
Q. Can you describe your journal?
A. I don t really remember what it looks like.
Q. Did you ever get to the end of the journal so that it was totally filled up and then you had to go out and get another one?
A. Yes.
Q. And you discussed this journal with —
A. My sister.
Q. Martha?
A. Yes.
Q. On one occasion?
A. Yes.
Q. Where was the first journal the last time you saw it?
A. It was in my bedroom, between my desk and my bed.
Q. You haven't seen it since then?
A. No.
Q. When was that?
A. It was after — the last time I saw it was before I ran away.
Q. So, when was the last time you actually looked at it?
A. It was maybe a month before June.
Q. Where was the new journal that you started after you filled up the first journal? Where was the new journal the last time you saw it?
A. I gave it to my sister.
Q. When was that?
A. It was the night I ran away, before I left, I said "can you hold onto this for me?"

Q. And, at that time, did you also tell her, and the other journal is between the desk and the bed?

A. No, I didn't tell her.

Q. You gave the second journal to Martha for safekeeping at the time you ran away?

A. Yes.

Q. You did not give to her the first one?

A. No.

Q. Why not?

A. Because I didn't want to, it was mine.

At this point, I was getting confused by the testimony. Compounding this was the fact Kerri had found a collection of notes that showed the deviant behavior the girls engaged in with their friends. Suddenly, out of nowhere, Chelsea has this story about journals that doesn't even make sense. I felt a glimmer of hope. Chelsea gave the second journal to Martha, but wouldn't give her the first one? What about the math? She is claiming to have been molested every day for five years and yet she only filled up one and a half journals? That is one magic journal. None of this is based on any reality, so I digress.

Q. by Mr. Gephart: Have you ever discussed the object of your testimony here today in any detail whatsoever with Ms. Ellis at any time?

A. I just — well, she was there during the meeting with Todd.

Q. So, she was with you during the meeting with Todd? [Mr. Graham]

A. Yes.

Q. So, she heard what you discussed with Todd?

A. Our discussion, yes.

Mr. Gephart then elicits testimony that Ms. Ellis was present at all of Chelsea's interviews and, in fact, was the only social worker to interview her. Chelsea went on to state that she had discussed these allegations of molestation with Martha on an ongoing basis since she was 11 years old.

Q. by Mr. Gephart: Have you discussed any of the details of the allegations of molestation with any of your friends?

A. No.

Q. At any time?

A. No.

Q. Have you ever told any of your friends, at any time, that Mike Harris was molesting you?

A. No. I just said he was a weirdo.

Mr. Graham then took to the lectern and asked a couple of redirect questions and then Mr. Gephart asked the proverbial one last question.

Q. by Mr. Gephart: Chelsea, did you receive any personal possessions or your property at the time after you ran away and after you were placed in foster care?

A. Yes, I did get some of my stuff.

Q. And that was given to you by the people at CPS, Ms. Ellis specifically?

A. Yes.

Q. And when you say, "some of my stuff," what did you get?

A. The stuff I wanted. There's still some stuff I want, but I haven't got it back yet.

Q. Did you specifically ask Alex, or anyone from CPS, to go find your journal?

A. No.

Q. Why not?

A. Why would I?

Q. Why not?

A. Because it's mine. I don't want someone else getting my stuff.

Q. Didn't you say to Alex Ellis, look, go find that journal.

A. I want to go get it myself.

Q. Didn't you say to Alex Ellis, you better go find that journal, because I have recorded in that journal on a daily basis Mike molesting me?

A. No, I didn't.

Q. Why not?

A. Because, I wanted to get it myself. I told my sister about it, but I didn't want to tell — before because, we didn't — I didn't tell her about the molestations until like a month ago. I didn't want to tell her what was in there.

Q. After you told Ms. Ellis about the molestations, did you say to her at that time, a month ago, go find my journal?

A. No.

Q. Why not?

A. Is that a problem?

The Court: Just answer the question.

The Witness: I said I wanted my stuff back and I said "there's private stuff in there that I need," but I wasn't going to explain what it was. I told my sister what I was looking for.

Thus, ended Chelsea's testimony. It struck me as odd that Chelsea said she told Martha what she was looking for and yet Martha is unaware of any journals. And the whole gave her the second journal but wouldn't give her the first one is obvious prevarication.

The Court: I want to let you know, Mr. Harris, that I appreciate your absolute cooperation in not having any contact or allowing any inferences to be drawn from your presence with these girls. I appreciate that. You have been a gentleman throughout these proceedings.

Yeah, whatever, just let me bail out, I thought.

SEVEN

The rest of day two of the prelim was pretty mundane, although I was hoping for a bail review hearing since Judge Specchio had told me he would consider resetting my bail after all the evidence was in.

Next up was a discussion about jurisdiction. Then, to my surprise, Mr. Gephart submitted it to the court on the record. No argument. No evidence. I was pissed. I wanted to go piece by piece, tearing down the wall of fabrication right then and there. Mr. Gephart wanted to wait for trial. I wanted to bail out, so our priorities were crossed.

Mr. Graham then went through all the counts, dismissing the Chalfant living room floor count alleged by Martha since Martha was all over the place on that count. Mr. Gephart had gotten Martha to say the living room event happened four times, but she told Mr. Graham it only happened once. I was seething. Mr. Gephart was not arguing my innocence, he was not objecting or anything. I guess you really could indict a ham sandwich, and that was me.

In all, Mr. Graham charged me with ten counts of §288(a), lewd and lascivious acts on a child under 14, and asked the court to find that §667.61, the One-Strike law, applied since there were multiple victims. The judge did so. Section 667.61 provides for a 15-year-to-life sentence as to each count, and they could be applied consecutively. I was now seething and worried too. Ten 15-year-to-life sentences was 150 years-to-life of exposure. I was way up the mountain with no rope. My life was already in ruin, but this added a depth of despair unknown to me. This was serious shit and my chances for bail were shrinking by the minute. Then, Mr. Graham asked for a holding order for §288(a) for Raeanna and Mr. Gephart finally spoke up:

Mr. Gephart: He hasn't been charged with that. How can he be ordered —

The Court: Your asking for — well, but if the evidence produced supports that finding —

Mr. Gephart: To a new victim?

Mr. Graham: Yeah.

The Court: Why not? Do you have — would you check some authority for that?

Mr. Gephart: Thank you, Judge.

Then a short break was taken, but Mr. Gephart didn't look up, any authority regarding the Raeanna count, nor did he raise the specter that he should have received notice and discovery regarding the Evid. Code §1108 witness Raeanna prior to her testimony.

The Judge then went on to issue holding orders for all counts that §667.61(b)(8) applied. It should have been §667.61(c)(7), but Mr. Gephart said nothing. Finally, the Judge agreed to keep bail as set, but he would come back to Bridgeport to hear argument about bail at the arraignment. That was set for October 2nd, 2007. I couldn't wait.

As for me, I went back to me cell and called Kerri. She didn't travel to Bridgeport since it's 120 miles one way from her house and it's tough with her vision issues and she couldn't have come in the courtroom anyway. Kerri answered the phone right away, but she couldn't talk, because the sheriffs were searching her house for the journals. She gave them the notebooks with all the notes, but they wanted to search anyway, so I said "I love you" and "goodbye." Kerri told me she loved me too and would come visit soon. That made me feel better. I was trying not to seethe and so I turned on the TV.

It was telling that they were searching now even while Chelsea was testifying. Obviously, she had never mentioned a journal before that day at all. Martha never mentioned a journal either. I wanted Mr. Gephart to recall Martha and show the contradictions that were plain as day.

I settled into a routine that was simple; food, TV, sleep, repeat. Every Tuesday was court day in my small little town, with the old-fashioned courthouse and the population of 500. I was looking forward to my arraignment and the chance at getting my bail lowered so I could keep my life from completely imploding.

But alas, the 2nd came and there was no Judge Specchio. He was never to be seen again. The Judge was the Honorable Stan Eller who had cut my bail the last time we met. I felt a glimmer of hope, but Mr. Gephart quickly dashed my hopes telling me that Mr. Graham was now charging me with 24 counts of §288(a), the lewd and lascivious charge, and two counts of §269(a)(1), aggravated rape of a child under 14. These all fell under the One-Strike law and so I was now facing 390 years-to-life. I was mad, scared, tired, and still slightly hopeful.

Judge Eller let me speak first and I pleaded for an OR release and then said:

The Defendant: A case of this magnitude requires me to have a local, well respected attorney, but also to have an expert specialized attorney from out of the area or out of state in order to avoid the trappings and politics our quaint little community affords.

Judge Eller denied my request for an expert to assist Mr. Gephart, but left it open for Mr. Gephart to file a motion later. I felt tremendous pressure facing life in prison to be decided by a jury pool of exclusively registered voters. Nobody I knew was a registered voter. Who would these people be, I wondered?

A week went by and it was court day so I made another perp walk across the street where I was formally arraigned on 26 felony counts mandating 15 year to life sentences for each count. I asked for a speedy trial and a date of December 10th was set for a jury trial. In the meantime, Mr. Gephart sought the same CPS records Kerri had from the CPS. Apparently, these records are not allowed to be used in court without the court's approval. The documents Kerri had showed the lies the girls had told about Kerri and also showed the time leading up to and including their removal from Kerri's home.

On the jail front I was moved from my luxurious cell to a small cell in A-Pod. There were eight two-man cells adjacent to a large dayroom. The cells had a bunkbed and a desk as well as a toilet and sink. No TV. The dayroom had a TV, a shower and a couple of tables. There was also a phone. I was locked in my cell all day long since I was in protective custody, segregated from the other inmates. This was because I was a suspected sex offender. This protective custody was not very protective since the jail staff kept accidentally opening my door when all the other inmates were in the dayroom. The same inmates would always yell threats and such at me through my window all day, so being out in the dayroom with them was pure crazy. Fortunately, after a couple of weeks of complaining by both sides, I got my luxury suite back all alone.

While all that was going on, Mr. Gephart managed to hire a specialized forensic psychologist supremely experienced in §288(a) cases. Her name was Dr. Linda Meza. I met with her and she was sharp. She was hired by my trial litigator, Michael Berger, who was Mr. Gephart's partner. It turned out that Mr. Gephart was just the front man, not the main attraction.

Mr. Berger came and met with me and explained his need for more time to prepare for trial. I was adamant that I wanted to go to trial right away. I spoke with him, Mr. Gephart, and Dr. Meza about reopening the preliminary hearing with a California Code of Civil Procedure §995 hearing in order to put on evidence of the lies that were told. They all said that was not a good idea. Basically, Mr. Graham could just pile more charges on me and I would be facing 100 counts. My attitude at that point was "whatever" bring it, in for a penny, in for a pound. In the end, they called the shots and I was displeased with their choices.

Mr. Gephart hired an investigator, Brian Grice, who did some preliminary investigating. When he came to visit me in jail and conduct an interview, he concluded that I was lying and left the team. Obviously, we didn't hit it off, but the facts spoke for themselves. I wanted my team to go after the truth aggressively, but they wanted to play it slow and careful.

November 13th, 2007, came and it was Tuesday, court day in Bridgeport. I went to court and waived my right to a speedy trial. I may have had the right to a speedy trial, but the reality of the justice system forecloses meaningful justice in a scant 60 days. The wheels of justice and lawyers grind very slowly. I basically caved in to pressure from my attorneys. Very concisely, Mr. Berger told me to waive my right to a speedy trial or I would get some other attorney to wave goodbye to me as I headed off to prison. Harsh words indeed. Okay, I said, and a tentative trial date was set for some time in the spring of 2008.

While this was going on, I was fighting with Mr. Gephart to locate the couch Martha said she was raped on at my dad's house in Seal Beach, CA. I insisted that DNA testing be done on the couch to show there was no blood or semen on the couch matching Martha or myself. I was adamant that a rape had not occurred on my dad's couch and I meant to prove it.

Mr. Gephart finally got around to it and an expert was called in. The expert did luminol like testing and said he discovered microscopic material that may or may not be semen or blood. In order to do the DNA testing, I was told me or my dad would have to pony up $25,000. I said that ain't gonna happen and Mr. Berger said he wasn't going to ask the judge for that kind of money, because the DA would find out. Mr. Berger's opinion was that my defense position was that there was no physical evidence. My personal position was that there never is physical evidence in a molestation case. Regrettably, I had to go along with the attorneys because I had no say in strategy or tactics.

Thanksgiving 2007 came and went and on November 27th I went to court and a trial date was set for March 3rd, 2008. I settled into a stable routine until February 14th, 2008, when my attorneys decided they needed even more time and so a new trial date was set for June 9th, 2008. My team was doing nothing as best I could tell. No motions, no discovery.

Meanwhile, the computer hard drive that had been seized from my trailer when I was arrested, and which was physically inoperable, was miraculously working and showing evidence of child porn. This was concerning. I had told Mr. Gephart that there was some questionable material related to searching I had done on the internet, but I was certain there was no porn of any type on my hard drives. I was certain that if there was, it had been planted there by the cops. They would have had to rebuild that drive to get it working, I said.

But now I truly felt terrible. Child porn in a child sexual abuse case is a death knell. I told my team that I had looked at some child glamour sites that were in the news, but I hadn't viewed the pictures. I had just looked at the code. There was a big fight going on with Yahoo! messenger user created chat rooms and I was fascinated with the Dateline Predator series, having been falsely accused of child molestation before. I figured Raeanna and her grandma set me up like the Michael Jackson case circa 2003. I never viewed or saved any type of porn, let alone child porn.

Mr. Gephart and Mr. Berger still hadn't received a ruling on the CPS records and they still needed to file motions for California Evidence Code §1101 for the computer evidence and a motion regarding the admission of Child Sexual Abuse Accommodation Syndrome, or CSAAS for short. They were trying to exclude the evidence as nothing more than psychobabble.

April 22nd rolled around and the computer evidence still hadn't been provided to my defense team. I was getting anxious as my court date grew nearer. Mr. Gephart was making me nervous by constantly talking to me about taking a plea. No way was I going to plead guilty to a crime that never even occurred. Besides, the offer was ridiculous. 32 years in prison and register as a sex offender. Like I said, ridiculous. I wanted less plea bargaining and more investigation based on the CPS files Kerri had shown them.

On May 6th, I appeared before Judge Eller who was opting out of being my Judge, and the Honorable Patrick Canfield was assigned for all purposes. He was retired out of Bishop, CA. That was in nearby Inyo County. We appeared before Judge Canfield on May 21st for the hearing on the motions in limine where we were trying to exclude the computer and CSAAS evidence. Mr. Berger filed the first motion, so he led off.

Mr. Berger: With respect to many of the "discoveries" found on the hard drive seized by the government, although there are some jpeg photographs that are part of the hard drive, there are references to other sites called newsgroups or other sites that are suggestive of either child pornography or incest that do not have depictions saved. So, we want to object at the very least to any present depictions.

In a nutshell, Mr. Berger was saying the computer hard drive visited nefarious websites but the sites weren't cached on the drive and so the prosecution expert, Lydell Wall, had visited the sites on his own and printed his own depiction of a URL which was how the site looked now instead of in the past, like three years prior. Mr. Berger seemed to have a handle on the issues somewhat, but he insisted I take a plea, because with the three girls and child porn supposedly on the hard drive, I was going to be found guilty on all counts and would be sentenced to 390-years-to-life in prison.

After Mr. Graham spoke about his need to have the jury understand that I was a pervert with a sexual interest in young girls, the judge made his rulings.

The Court: Well, it would be my intention to allow those images that were actually on the hard drive which illustrate an interest and/or sexual interest in underage girls. I am disinclined to allow present depictions on those sites that were accessed on the dates indicated where no images were actually discovered. But I am inclined to allow testimony as to what those sites contain by way of verbal testimony.

Now as for the CSAAS evidence to be presented by Cathy McLennan, Judge Canfield chose to put off any decision until an Evid. Code §402 hearing prior to her testimony related to further limitations on the scope of her direct testimony. The CPS files issue was addressed next.

The Court: We did not address the petition filed by the District Attorney for CPS records and I am not sure what resolution was reached.

Mr. Graham: I think the issue is not ripe yet, Judge, given that I have not selected out the documents that I will seek to have admitted.

Mr. Gephart: Well the motion was filed by the DA. We, on the other hand, have orally joined the motion to make these records available. And we have discussed in chambers our intent with regard to those records.

It had become apparent to me that my team was not ready. The CPS files were explosive and important to show the inclination of the girls to lie in order to get things to go their way. And we had the files already. Kerri had provided all the reports and statements. So, to let the DA decide what to release is pure treachery. Those files should be admissible through Kerri's testimony at the very least. I also felt that the computer evidence was suspect and I wanted more investigation, especially on the integrity of hard drive number one. As the trial date neared, I felt further delay was absolutely necessary, but Mr. Berger said, no way. He said "if there is a delay, I won't be available" for any further hearings or trial. If he left, then Dr. Meza was going to leave with him. I then met with Dr. Meza in late May and she explained that she would be unavailable to me at a later date as well. She went on to tell me about a procedure, a Marsden hearing (People v Marsden, 2 Cal.3d 118 (1970)) which would let me substitute counsel. I thought this was a great idea since I was getting nothing but take a plea from my defense team.

So, on June 4th, 2008, I made a Marsden motion and entered the courtroom with only Mr. Gephart present. No gallery. No Mr. Graham. Once again, Judge Canfield presided and he was very receptive to my concerns, such as the collegial nature of the Mono County Justice System, the lack of privacy between me and my defense team in the county jail, and the pressure to take a deal. I told Judge Canfield that I didn't think Mr. Berger wanted to be on my case anymore. The computer evidence was overwhelming to my defense, he had argued. I wanted more time to investigate the computer evidence, the CPS and school records, and the whole series of events which preceded the girls' placement in foster homes. I raised a litany of complaints, but in the end, Judge Canfield ruled that I was to keep my attorney, Mr. Gephart, and he ruled that there would, in fact, be a delay in the trial.

This concluded the Marsden hearing and Mr. Graham was called back into the courtroom to argue the state's position on the continuance motion. Mr. Gephart argued that the computer evidence had just been provided in the last few weeks and more time was needed to effectively prepare for trial. Mr. Graham argued that the girls were "very nervous about coming in to testify" and he was objecting to a delay on that basis. The judge then discussed a need to balance the needs of the girls and the potential lifetime in prison I faced. He felt that a short delay would not be that damaging to the girls relative to the year they had already waited. Judge Canfield granted the motion for a continuance. Mr. Gephart, at my behest, offered to go to trial right away without delay if Mr. Graham would not produce the computer evidence at trial. Mr. Graham declined the offer.

The trial setting hearing was scheduled for June 17th before Judge Eller who had opted out of sitting for my trial, but who would handle scheduling matters at the Bridgeport court. Continuing on, Judge Canfield, after setting the trial date, went on to discuss the in camera hearing the previous October 22nd, 2007, where Judge Eller ruled that five jurisdictional reports from the CPS be released to my defense team. Mr. Gephart then spoke:

Mr. Gephart: The documents that were produced pursuant to that order after an in camera inspection by Judge Eller, what was given to him and represented to him to be the entire juvenile file, were limited to five specific documents that can be generally described as the documents reflecting the communication and reporting of the incident or incidents giving rise to the filing of criminal charges here. So, in other words, what Judge Eller ordered to be turned over back in October of 2007, were juvenile court, more, correctly stated, CPS documents reflecting the reporting of molestation in late summer, early fall 2007.

As reflected in my letter to you, Judge, of May 29th, we had been provided a stack of documents [Kerri's file], an entire stack of documents. We don't know if it was the entire file. We were trying to figure out what to do in order to, on the one hand, keep the confidentiality of those records in place, but on the other hand, prepare the defense for Mr. Harris, because as we reviewed these documents, it was clear to us that there was a history of CPS involvement dating back, as I say in my letter, to 2001 that could and probably would be relevant in this case. It is the documents that go to the history of CPS involvement dating back to 2001 which we consider important and essential to the defense of this case. And the documents that were provided under court order of October of last year are not those documents. They are a more recent set of reports which specifically allege child molestation.

The Court: And Mr. Graham, have you provided to Mr. Gephart with the totality of the juvenile records?

Mr. Graham: I don't believe I can until the court allows me to.

I analogized to Mr. Gephart that to put the DA in charge of deciding which reports to release was the same as letting a card dealer decide which cards to deal in a game of poker. The court then asked Mr. Graham:

The Court: But you did provide certain records?

Mr. Graham: We had original CPS documents that were provided to us and certain cover letters. I would prefer to have the court and all parties be privy and to have a common set of documents that we can go over and discuss which are going to be released for public viewing at trial and which ones would not be. So it puts us in a bit of a quandary as the prosecution because we have a legal and ethical obligation to disclose this information and I am sitting on it and I believe it would be helpful to the defense, essentially helpful to us, but most likely to the defense, and I want to find the most expeditious way to get these documents to the defense in a legal fashion.

The Court: But you didn't receive the totality of the files?

Mr. Graham: I don't have the files. I have documents that were selected by our investigator. We don't have the CPS files.

The Court: And neither does the court. And so, you, Mr. Gephart, wish the court to go through all of these files and to make those all available?

Mr. Gephart: I think the stated intention of our motion back in October was for the court to review the juvenile court records without limitation and to make available to us all Brady [Brady v Maryland 373 US 83 (1963)] material, all documents that might be discoverable under §1054. We were aware of a history of reports that we felt were essential to this case. We didn't get those out of that motion. We have been sitting on those documents as we prepare for trial, not quite knowing how those documents were going to get introduced.

Talk about crazy. Mr. Gephart and Mr. Berger are asking me to take a plea, when in fact, they haven't even investigated any of the CPS reports and notes Dr. Meza had recently interviewed Kerri about the reports and there was plenty of investigation left to do on that front, as well. I didn't understand why Mr. Berger was already saying there was no defense to my case and he couldn't get his arms around it. I thought he had given up.

The court, Mr. Graham, and Mr. Gephart continued to argue through the next few days about how to get a handle on the large volume of documents, the need for confidentiality, and the right to defend against false allegations. The girls had made numerous documented false allegations against Kerri, and these were at the center of the debate.

Suddenly, it was June 17th, and I was once again doing the perp walk across the street to court. Once inside, Judge Eller set my jury trial for August 6th, 2008, nearly a year after my arrest. I was wondering what had been decided about the CPS files, so I spoke up:

The Defendant: With regards to my previous Marsden hearing held on June 4th that was just held, there are some issues that came up with that. There was also supposed to be a CPS records setting date today.

The Court: Oh, that wasn't done? I thought that was done on the last —

The Defendant: He says there is going to be a meeting and I opposed the last time when all this went down in camera without my knowledge and Randy [Mr. Gephart] has told me one thing, and it's now come to light that another result, you released five records. Randy told me one of the records released actually wasn't.

I then told the court that I wanted to be in attendance at any further meetings regarding the CPS records. I then decided I wanted another Marsden hearing in regards to the handling of the CPS issues. I went on to state that I wanted to be in attendance for any further argument related to the records and Judge Eller said the visiting Judge would decide that, as there may have been some confidentiality issues.

EIGHT

June 26th rolled around and I was back in the historic Bridgeport courthouse before a new judge, the Honorable David DeVore, visiting from nearby Alpine County. It was time for my second Marsden hearing. Judge Canfield had recused himself from further proceedings, so I had my fourth different judge. And this time, I really wanted a new attorney. Mr. Gephart had become problematic for me. He was basically telling the DA's computer expert details of my assertions, violating attorney/client privilege. This was unacceptable.

The Court: And your complaint in this hearing is that your attorney has in some way impaired the integrity of the attorney/client privilege?

The Defendant: And possibly disclosed evidence that isn't in the possession of the District Attorney. It may or may not be exculpatory.

This was my concern. In order to plead out my case, they had to talk about relative strength and weaknesses of my case with the District Attorney. This all revolved around Mr. Gephart's passing of papers to me in the jail through the jailor that were not sealed in an envelope and could be read by anybody. The papers were from a printout of a file called key.dat.

Mr. Gephart: But there clearly has been discussion between Mr. Harris and me regarding this issue and the computer printout. And I can tell you what the docu-

ment is. It is a printout of computer records from Mr. Harris' computer that are in the possession of the DA.

Here, Mr. Gephart was using semantics to lure the judge into a false belief. The printout was not in the possession of the DA. the corrupted hard drive was. The key.dat file printout was from Evan Asher, our own computer expert.

The Defendant: That document isn't in the possession of the DA. He [Mr. Gephart] is trying to do what he does. Cover his ass.

Mr. Gephart: The information and the line by line printout that you see before you comes from Mr. Harris' computer, first analyzed and confirmed and printed out by Detective Wall, who was working for the District Attorney, and then confirmed by our computer expert, Evan Asher.

The Court: Who printed out these four pages of printouts? Evan Asher or someone from the prosecution's office?

Mr. Gephart: It could be Asher; I can't say for sure.

The Court: Are you telling me that these [printouts] in your possession that you received through the discovery process?

Mr. Gephart: Yes.

That was utter bullshit. He could say, but he didn't want to. Discovery has a number written on it identifying it in a sequence and this printout did not have any number on it. The printouts were not in discovery. Period.

The Court: What else did you want to say about this, sir?

The Defendant: These were not generated through the discovery process. This is not information the DA has yet. Our expert has discovered this information on the computer. It was not discovered by Mr. Wall. It was not discovered by the DA. It is not listed in any reports. It is information they are using to extort me into taking a plea, that they will disclose this to the District Attorney if I don't go along with their deal.

Mr. Gephart: I disagree.

Now, at first glance, it would appear that I am paranoid. I mean, why would my lawyer lie? But, alas, there exists a report from Det. Wall, dated April 25th, 2008, where he lists all the nefarious items he found on hard drive no. 1, and he in no way lists or mentions a key.dat file. The printouts are not in his work product. Mr. Wall produced a detailed report and listed numerous items except the key.dat file.

I really needed to get rid of Mr. Gephart, and as the Marsden hearing progressed, I attacked. I alleged hypocrisy and bias for a start.

The Court: Tell me what they have done that constitutes hypocrisy and bias.

The Defendant: What I would say, in general, would be that there is a difference. And they provide me lip service vs meaningful conversations or discussions. Because my discussions with my attorney are very often ignored or forgotten. He has a very large workload. I discuss things with him that completely don't even show up in any further communications.

So, whether I'm able to communicate with him effectively or whether he's able to absorb what I am communicating effectively, there is a problem, we are unable to mesh.

And then, when you throw into the mix Dr. Meza the jury strategist and consultant from LA and his senior partner, Michael Berger, who is the trial litigator, based in Santa Barbara, there is a three-way lack of communication and error of communication down the line.

The Court: Do you want to respond to that Mr. Gephart?

Mr. Gephart: …I can assure, and have assured Mr. Harris, that we don't tell him one thing and do another. We've been candid and brutally honest with him.

The Defendant: Their position is that, based on the information they have found on my computer, their position is that if they put me on the stand, the only thing I can do is lie through false, perjured testimony and so, therefore, they probably don't make me do it. I can go up there and tell my story which would be narrative testimony. They are not preparing for my testimony in any way, shape, or form, which is detrimental to my case.

I believe that my attorney's decisions have been based on assumptive conjecture or inferences which are reserved for the trier of fact. My attorneys have ignored my statements and direction in an arrogant and prejudicial way, without any basis for their bias other than opinion and speculative supposition and innuendo.

So, on June 18th, Mr. Gephart says that they are against me testifying, even though they have done no investigation. Then, three weeks later, he wrote to me and said that, while they recommend I don't testify, they will continue to prepare. What preparation? He is just covering his ass.

Mr. Gephart told the court at the second Marsden hearing that he would test the DNA to see if it excludes Martha. Then, in a July 7th letter to me, he wrote that they are going to refuse to do it. He wrote "to continue to pursue court-ordered testing would be legal malpractice" He told the judge he would do it and then took it back. I may have jumped ahead a bit, but isn't it legal malpractice to divulge attorney/client work product to the prosecution without authorization?

The Court: Well, I'll tell you as a matter of law, attorneys have an obligation not to participate in the presentation of false evidence. And there's a line to walk, a spe-

cific way of allowing a person to present his or her testimony without an attorney running afoul of the attorney's ethical obligation.

The Defendant: Or bias. They have no factual basis for that position.

I continued back and forth with Mr. Gephart, and Judge DeVore started getting frustrated. I told the court:

The Defendant: If I have to go to trial and be convicted based on their lack of effort and then come back on appeal, that they should have followed these items up to fruition, then where am I?

The Court: We don't want that to happen. And I respect your concerns here bringing the motion. But many of the things you are telling me, seems to me, are part of a work in progress and can't be adequately assessed unless and until the trial proceeds.

The Defendant: This isn't a work in progress. That mischaracterizes the office's effort at this point.

Mr. Gephart: Our communication, Judge, has disintegrated where Mr. Harris has not done that or refused to do that or wants to yell at me and has yelled at me. So, I have been attempting to supplement what we have with Mr. Asher with communications we have with Mr. Harris, but have been unsuccessful in doing that.

Which is really the gist — goes to the gist of this motion, Judge, which is not incompetence of counsel, but failure to communicate an unreconcilable conflict between Mr. Harris and his view of what we're doing and our credibility and his total loss of and lack of confidence in our office.

The Defendant: Just as a point of the contradiction, it is very glaring right there in the fact that I have given them a ton of stuff they can use, and then he wants me to give him and then he says I won't give it to him. There is a contradiction there.

The Court: I appreciate and have the greatest respect for the concerns that you have. You are facing very serious charges, very serious consequences should you be convicted of those charges. However, I don't see any objective evidence of ineffective assistance of counsel at this point. Again, I respect your concerns, your issues. Some, many of them, are anticipatory and can't really be addressed at this point. I do appreciate your comments about going through a trial and then having to appeal on ineffective assistance of counsel grounds. Again, you can't gainsay what may happen in the future.

On each of the assignments raised today on this issue to have Mr. Gephart, his office relieved and new counsel appointed, I do not find sufficient evidence to warrant that occurring, and therefore the motion is denied.

Mr. Gephart: Judge, can I be heard? Because I don't believe the rift can be repaired, and I would join in the motion. I would also initiate my own motion to be relieved from this initially under the cannon of ethics and professional rules of conduct, which makes it permissive to withdraw if the relationship is such that counsel cannot effectively represent the client.

The Court: Respectfully sir, I am going to deny your motion to be relieved, and again, caution you both that you are six weeks away from trial. It is important that you work together as harmoniously as possible. That is the order of the court.

NINE

So, I was stuck with Mr. Gephart. Mr. Berger and Dr. Meza were gone and no longer available. I sat in my cell and stressed out. I had a trial date in just a few weeks. No investigation had been done, the CPS files hadn't been reviewed or released, I had no judge, and I had lost my defense team. No big deal, right? A couple of weeks later, a bright ray of hope appeared. Mr. Gephart filed some motions to be relieved as counsel, and by the looks of them, he was serious. On July 17th, I was back in court for a civil relievement hearing California Code of Civil Procedure §§284 and 285. Mr. Gephart made his pitch. He claimed I had threatened him and that I was going to lie at trial. During this in camera hearing before visiting Judge DeVore, Mr. Gephart offered up some pretty strong stuff. I retaliated by pointing out what a two-faced liar he was, but in the end, Judge DeVore bought none of it and said to Mr. Gephart:

The Court: I don't believe that your strongly held belief that there has been such a breakdown is the end of the story here. I accept what you say, but I believe, having heard at length the Marsden motion last week, that Mr. Harris does not understand the nature of the relationship that the law establishes between counsel and defendant and that he is, in effect, attempting to manufacture an issue by failing to effectively communicate with you, including expressing threats.

So, I don't question your integrity or the sincerity of the statements you are making in your heartfelt belief that there has been such a breakdown. Nonetheless, I don't think that dictates an order of withdrawal under these circumstances.

Mr. Gephart: I expect then, based on your comments, that you are about to deny the motion, my motion to withdraw.

The Court: Respectfully so.

Mr. Gephart then fought long and hard to get a stay in the proceedings and I was against a delay. I wanted the lawyers to do their job and they wanted me to take a plea deal. Plain and simple. I wasn't anything but a witness to Mr. Gephart's motion. The judge was sure I was manipulating the system, but in my mind, I was pursuing the truth. The nature of the law regarding attorney/client roles is one that is totally unfair IMHO. The law is the "Captain of the Ship" doctrine, (See In re Horton 54 Cal.3d 82) whereby the attorney makes all strategic and tactical decisions and the defendant is left with only the most fundamental decisions, such as the right to a speedy trial, the right to testify or not, the right to a jury trial, and the right to act as one's own attorney. The appointed attorney cannot waive these fundamental rights, but the attorney can offer no defense at all if he or she chooses. The system is skewed toward those with money, because they can fire attorneys who don't go along with their wishes. Appointed attorneys have enormous power over a defendant and so did Mr. Gephart.

Soon after this, Mr. Gephart filed a petition for a writ of mandate put together by his partner, Robert Hanna. In this petition, Mr. Gephart renewed his claim that he was threatened, his legal assistant Alicia Beale was threatened, and that he had an ethical obligation to withdraw based on my expected perjurious statements during testimony. He said he couldn't present a defense based on lies. So, there I sat in jail, hopes buoyed by the allure of new counsel. At least I had decent accommodations. As I said before: I had a TV, a shower, a phone and a window to look out. Not only that, I could see the clock in dispatch, so I always knew what time it was. Believe it or not, but a window and a clock are basics that, once taken away, put you in a bad place.

That being said, I bid my time until my next court date, of which I had no idea when it would be. Turns out, it was July 28th, 2008. I was before the Honorable Ed Forstenzer, the presiding judge for Mono County. Mr. Gephart was there with me and it was awkward since he had filed the writ of mandate petition. I was confused because I wanted to appeal, too. I did not know how to file a petition, but I knew I could figure it out.

Judge Forstenzer kept mentioning a new judge, the Honorable John Darlington out of Nevada County. What was that all about? He was like my fifth or sixth judge. Mr. Graham and Mr. Gephart argued like cats about a trial date, because August 6th wasn't going to happen. They finally agreed on September 16th and Judge Forstenzer asked if I had anything to say, so I said:

The Defendant: I am opposed to any delay.

The Court: I understand that, but given the circumstances, I think the continuance is inevitable, and I think this is the most workable thing that I can see in this case. There is a judge assigned to hear this case.

The Defendant: What happened to Judge Canfield?

The Court: He has refused to continue to hear the case.

The Defendant: Your Honor, are you continuing to deny my request for a Marsden hearing?

The Court: I believe that's already been ruled on, Mr. Harris. I am not going to rehear that matter. I believe that's the subject matter of the writ that's been talked about.

The Defendant: I have no way of knowing if that writ is being filed on my behalf in regards to my Marsden hearing or not.

The Court: It may not be filed on your behalf. You may need to file your own.

The Defendant: Then, therefore, could you instruct — the Sheriff's Department denies me access to the law library, and I am not able to do research in addressing or forming what I may need in order to submit my writ.

The Court: Defendant is being denied access to the law library?

The Defendant: Yes, Your Honor, since August of 2007, they absolutely deny me access to the law library within the Mono County jail. And that's a standing policy until or unless I am pro. per.

The Court: Since he is not pro. per. but yet at odds somewhat with his counsel, I think he should be given the right to file a writ with the Court of Appeal on the denial of his motion to have new counsel appointed for him. And so, for that reason, I am going to order that he have access to the law library.

I thanked the judge and began my odyssey into the realm of legal literature. Meanwhile, all eyes were on the Court of Appeal (3rd DCA) awaiting their decision on Mr. Gephart's petition. I filed a request for the appointment of counsel to help me appeal and I waited in my cell. Finally, on August 15th, the 3rd DCA made its ruling. Judge DeVore could either vacate his July 17th order denying Mr. Gephart's motion to withdraw or submit argument as to why he shouldn't. Six days later, Judge DeVore vacated his order and removed Mr. Gephart as my attorney of record.

A few days later, the court appointed Ms. Therese Hankel as my attorney. I kind of knew her, since it's a small town and we had friends in common. I was satisfied that Mr. Gephart was gone and I had a fresh start to prove my innocence. Ms. Hankel came and saw me right away and things went pretty well until I brought up the DNA issue. She insisted she wasn't going to touch that issue and I should drop it. She added that she was Captain of the Ship and she would be deciding tactics and strategies, but she welcomed my input. I sent a request to Mr. Gephart to return all my stuff, including documents I gave him for safekeeping, as well as my trial clothes. Ms. Hankel met with Mr. Gephart and got all my things and he told her his thoughts on the case. Ms. Hankel thereafter met with me once a week more or less for a couple months and gave me her rapt attention as I pointed out why I was innocent.

On November 10th, 2008, I went to court with Ms. Hankel before the new Judge, the Honorable John Darlington. A trial setting hearing was held. The date of March 16th, 2009, was set as the jury trial date. The Judge then invited discussion on the trial location; Mammoth Lakes or Bridgeport. Ms. Hankel voiced her concerns about a south county jury and Mr. Graham said it could be a blend of north and south county jurors. The Clerk spoke up, saying, "Though usually in the wintertime we don't do that."

Ms. Hankel: My only problem with that is I don't want to antagonize a juror coming from a long distance during that period of the year.

Mr. Graham then noted that everybody but me was from the south county. Nobody lives in the north county, was my take on things. It seemed as though it was going to be me traveling from Bridgeport to Mammoth for trial each day, though Judge Darlington put off a final decision until later.

Next, the issue of motions came up and Ms. Hankel wisely brought up the CPS records issue and that piqued my interest. I knew then and there that she had been listening to me. More discussion ensued and it was decided that March 16th would be the motions date and the jury trial would commence on May 12th, 2009.

As my meetings with Ms. Hankel became more detailed, I mentioned the document I had created for Dr. Meza, which outlined all the contradictions and inconsistencies of the girls between their initial interviews and their prelim testimony. Ms. Hankel said she didn't have that document but that she would give me copies of the transcripts. I got those and went to work straight away, writing out my observations.

TEN

Martha was initially interviewed on August 3rd, 2007, at the Crowley Lake substation by Detective Rutkowski of the Mono County Sheriff's Department. Martha started out with quite a tale:

Det. Rutkowski: Okay. How many times has he sexually assaulted you?

Martha: A lot.

Q. Okay. Can you give me an estimate? Is it once a month? Once a year?

A. He used to do it every day.

Martha then described living in the Bishop trailer in 4th grade, about ten or eleven years old, then she spoke about the Chalfant trailer.

Q. by Det. Rutkowski: How about your sister? I remember she — twin sisters as - have you two talked about this, you and your sister?

A. by Martha: Uh-huh.

Q. And so she knows this?

A. Yes. He's done it to her, too.

Q. Okay. So, when you guys talk, did you ever go to your mom and talk to her about it?

A. (inaudible)

Q. Okay.

A. She won't listen to us.

Notice Martha said "us".

Q. by Det. Rutkowski: Okay. She won't listen to you. Why do you think that is?

A. by Martha: Because (inaudible)
Q. Okay. And how long ago was that?
A. That was like 6th or 7th grade when Mike got in trouble for molesting another girl.
Q. Okay. And who was the other girl?
A. (inaudible) her pants and she called the cops on him.
Q. Okay. Did you think of calling the cops on him yourself when your mother wouldn't listen?
A. No. I was scared to.
Q. That's common. Who got molested first, do you think, you or your sister?
A. Me.
Q. You?
A. My sister came here in fifth grade.
Q. Okay. She lived with your dad or something?
A. He died.
Q. So she didn't move in until he passed away?
A. Well, she lived in foster care. Then she came here in the fifth grade — when he died maybe - we were in the sixth or seventh grade.
Q. Can you remember the very first time it [the molest] happened?
A. (inaudible) on the couch and watching a (inaudible)
Q. Okay. And he put his hand down your pants and how did you respond to that?
A. I got up.
Q. And did you say anything?
A. No.
Q. And then that was all that happened, is he put his hand down your pants?
A. Yes.

Martha then described a second and third time of touching her vagina and boobs, then added that on the third time I tried to kiss her. This is odd since at the later prelim she said flatly that she was never kissed in the Bishop trailer. From the prelim:

Q. by Mr. Graham: Did Mr. Harris' mouth ever touch you in the Bishop trailer?
A. by Martha: No.

In reviewing the interview and prelim transcripts, it was obvious kissing was an afterthought or embellishment. After the initial mention of kissing in the interview, Martha only mentioned kissing in response to direct questions about kissing. During the prelim, Mr. Graham repeatedly asked about other kinds of touchings and Martha failed to disclose kissing unless provoked, and then when specifically asked:

Q. by Mr. Graham: Would he ever kiss you?

A. by Martha: Oh yes.

So, Mr. Graham was leading her along. All through the interview and prelim the detective and the DA led Martha along with prompting and cueing. The investigation was basically one-sided. Another document Ms. Hankel provided me for my report was an email from Martha dated August 29th, 2007. This email was sent after the interview but before the prelim. There is no mention of kissing in the entire email. Detective Rutkowski jumped around a bit in his questioning with Martha after she had described the first three episodes.

Q. by Det. Rutkowski: Okay. So, what's the next time this happened?

A. by Martha: I don't remember.

How is this possible? Only if she is making believe was that possible she said that.

Q. by Det. Rutkowski: Okay. So pretty much, you're 15 now. How long has it been since he's done something to you?

A. by Martha: It's been a year.

Q. Okay. So, it's been at least a year? So, he pretty much quit when you were 14? Can you remember the last time it happened, which would have been the most recent, where you were, what kind of sex it was?

A. The last time was when we were in Los Angeles.

In the email, Martha stated that nothing happened when she was 14, because I wasn't there, but when she was 15, she was molested and raped two times in her mother's bedroom. During the prelim Martha said:

Q. by Mr. Graham: Where were any of the locations where Mike touched you sexually, if he did when you were 14 years of age or older?

A. by Martha: The Chalfant house.

Q. In any particular room?

A. In my bedroom.

Q. Any other places after you turned 14?

A. No.

Martha further contradicted herself when, during the prelim, she was asked:

Q. by Mr. Graham: What was the very last touching of you that Mr. Harris did to you, the very last one?

A. by Martha: The very last one was when he touched my boobs, and that's the very last one.

Q. And which room was that?

A. The living room.

So, now it's in her bedroom and in the living room? I wondered if anybody was keeping track of this.

Q. by Mr. Graham: Did any touchings go on after you turned 14 in any other rooms other than your room and the living room?

A. by Martha: No.

Despite this, here is what Martha said in the email:

Q. by Mr. Graham: Please tell me about all the things Mr. Harris has done to you since you turned 15.

A. by Martha: Same as before I was 14. Mike also raped me two times in Chalfant, in my mother's bed.

Returning to the interview with Det. Rutkowski, Martha was asked when the last time was, and she said LA.

Q. by Det. Rutkoski: LA? Okay, and why were you in LA?

A. by Martha: He had to go down there for work.

Q. He had to go?

A. Yeah. And my mom made me go with him because he got mad that he was going to go alone.

So, Kerri was forcing Martha to go to LA with me, even though Martha had told her mom after the Raeanna allegation that I had been molesting both of the twins. This was proof positive of fabrication. Martha wanted to go to LA. according to Kerri and as shown in Martha's note to her friend in 9th grade, in which Martha talks about going to LA shopping and to Disneyland. Next, Det. Rutkowski went into the specifics of the LA rape:

Q. by Det. Rutkowski: Okay. And what did that sex act entail?

A. by Martha: He raped me.

Q. Okay. And I need to know specifics about how it started and how long it lasted and what you mean by — rape?

A. He put it in me.

Q. Okay. And had he put it in you any time before that?

A. No.

Q. That was the first time you actually had intercourse with him?

A. Uh-huh.

So, let's look at the specifics. In the interview transcripts I located this colloquy:

Q. by Det. Rutkowski: Okay. So, tell me what happened. How did it happen?

A. by Martha: I was sleeping on the couch and he came in. He started undressing me and then he started rubbing me like he did when I was little.

While in the email to Mr. Graham, Martha stated:

A. by Martha: When I was laying on the couch watching TV, he came over and he started to take off my pants and he took off his, he took out his wee-wee and he started to put it inside of me.

Then, in the prelim, Martha testified:

Q. by Mr. Graham: Tell us what time of day or night this started?

A. by Martha: It was at night.

Q. And you were sleeping on the couch in the living room?

A. I think we were watching a movie.

So, which was it? Watching a movie or sleeping on the couch? The only way you get confused on this detail is if you are lying. So, after this trip to LA. Martha and I drove back:

Q. by Det. Rutkowski: Now, when you are driving all the way back from L.A., you're alone with him in the truck. Did you guys talk about this at all or did he say anything to you about it?

A. by Martha: He asked if we were going to do it again, and I said (inaudible) "I'm telling my mom," and then I tried to tell her and she wouldn't listen to me.

So, there is Martha, in the middle of nowhere, driving home across the desert and she threatens to tell on me even though I had supposedly threatened to kill her if she told. This was pure craziness; it doesn't make sense even in make-believeland.

Q. by Det. Rutkowski: Now, this last time when there was intercourse, what did you tell her?

A. by Martha: I just told her that Mike raped me.

Q. And what did she say?

A. She said Mike wouldn't do anything like that.

Q. Yeah. And did you say – did you try to convince her at all?

A. Yeah, I did. And she wouldn't listen to me.

Moving on, Det. Rutkowski asked specifically about Chalfant:

Q. by Det. Rutkowski: Okay, so how many times do you think in Chalfant you had sexual contact with him?

A. by Martha: Not very much (inaudible). I'd say once a month he'd try and do it.

Q. Okay. So maybe a dozen acts total.

A. Uh-huh.

Q. And this is – what room is this in (inaudible).

A. This is my room, because our mom would go to work, because she had a job then.

Q. Okay. And so, he'd come in your room at night or daytime or whatever?
A. My mom had the night shift.

During the prelim, Martha said it was always in her mom's bedroom and it happened almost every day with penile penetration, like maybe three or four days a week. Regarding Chalfant, again Martha said "more than ten times," "almost every day" and "more than 20, Less than a hundred". Clearly, she was inconsistent.

Then, Mr. Graham asked after she had turned 14 then nothing happened in her mother's bedroom and Martha replied "No." But then, a bit later during cross-examination, she was asked by Mr. Gephart: "only in your mother's bedroom or in the living room?" referring to the Chalfant home and Martha said "Yes." So, Mr. Gephart then asked her, "so you don't recall him ever coming in to your bedroom at night after you were asleep and doing any of these things to you?" and Martha said "no." Just as a thought, Martha seemed to not describe having sexual contact in her bedroom because she always slept with the door shut. Clearly, Martha described being sexually assaulted in her bedroom even though in her testimony at the prelim she said nothing happened in her bedroom, then changed her story to say it happened in her bedroom after she turned 14. However, in the email, she had said it happened in her mom's bedroom same as always and she was raped two more times. During the interview, Det. Rutkowski asked her directly:

Q. by Det. Rutkowski: Okay. Did you ever have intercourse in Chalfant?
A. by Martha: No.
Q. Did he just rub you sometimes?
A. Uh-huh.
Q. How many times do you think he actually what you called "fingered" you?
A. I'd say once or twice.
Q. Okay. How did your sister find out this was happening to you?
A. Because I told her.
Q. And then did – did she say – what?
A. She said he was doing the same thing to her.
Q. Meaning fingering and intercourse? Do you think your sister had intercourse with him too?
A. I don't know — I don't know about that. She hasn't told me anything.
Q. About intercourse. What did she tell you about?
A. She said he was rubbing her too.

Now if you recall during the prelim, Chelsea said that Martha had seen me trying to put my penis in her vagina at least twice and said that her and Martha always talked about stuff. It's strange that neither girl mentioned talking about the threats they allegedly received. Another interesting point is that during the interview, Martha described having seen my penis one time, because she watched me and Kerri having sex, not because of the many sexual assaults she claimed I did to her. The episode of sex between Kerri and me supposedly happened at the Nevada house. Martha described her and Chelsea having to watch me and Kerri having sex. There seemed to be a major discrepancy in their stories.

Q. by Det. Rutkowski: And your sister was there too?

A. by Martha: Yeah, she was there — like it was during the day and we were watching a movie in my mom's room.

Q. Okay, and he just decided to have sex with your mom while you guys are still sitting there watching a movie?

A. Yeah.

Q. And you don't say, you know, "mom" or "gross" or —

A. I told her that when he's not around.

Q. Yeah. And what's her response?

A. She said, "I'm a grown adult. I can do what I want."

Q. Okay. Now as far as abuse, you talked about being thrown against the wall and a bucket thrown at you. How about your sister?

A. Yeah, he's –

Q. Does he spank you guys? Does he –

A. No. He's hurt my sister, too. He's grabbed her and left marks.

Q. Okay. And for what kind of behavior has he -

Kerri had warned me that Chelsea was a liar, and when she stole something and lied about it, I got really mad at her.

Q. by Det. Rutkowski: Okay. How many — well I'm talking to your sister. You know we're looking at maybe 10 - 12 times with you actually in Chalfant. And — and everything from touching you. Did he kiss you in Chalfant too or —

A. Uh-huh.

Q. Okay. And describe the kind of kissing.

A. My lips.

Q. Okay. And did he kiss you anywhere else on your body?

A. He would try to kiss my boobs.

Q. Okay.

A. He never tried to kiss me down there.

Q. Okay. And then the fingering part, how many times do you think you were actually fingered?
A. Like — like one to three times. He didn't do it very much.
Q. The full length of the finger?
A. Yeah.
Q. Can you — Okay. And would he say anything?
A. (inaudible)
Q. "Does that feel good"?
A. And "Do you want more"?
Q. Now your sister recently — and you know we've been out there and stuff — ran away. What was that? Was that because of Mike or because of your mother?
A. My mom.
Q. Because of you mother?
A. And some Mike, but mostly it was my mother.
Q. Okay, and was it anything to do with Mike and your mom or was it just between your mom and your sister?
A. Just between my mom and my sister.
Q. Oh, okay. And do you think your sister has told your mom about Mike making sexual advances to her?
A. She's never told me anything about that.

A couple points to ponder. The reason Chelsea left was because of the argument between her and her mom where Kerri threatened to sell her stuff on eBay and Kerri gave Chelsea's larger bedroom to Martha. In addition, Chelsea left without taking any of her important stuff, so the fact that she ran away had more to do with activities which occurred after she left that night rather than some premeditated act. There is also the note Martha left in Chelsea's stuff wondering why Chelsea never came back and never told Martha she was leaving. Also, Martha says Chelsea never told her anything about whether Chelsea had told their mom about sexual contacts, even though Martha talked about telling their mom. Martha stated in the early part of the interview:

Q. by Det. Rutkowski: So, when you guys talk, did you ever go to your mom and talk to her about it?
A. by Martha: She won't listen to us.

Note the "us" in that response.

Q. by Det. Rutkowski: What do you think would happen to you if you were lying right now?
A. by Martha: I'd probably get in a lot of trouble.

Q. What benefits are there to telling the truth?
A. Knowing that Mike's not going to do this to another kid.

So, this is Martha's motivation? Helping other kids, not getting help from being either killed or not being raped or beaten anymore? Finally, Martha was asked:

Q. by Det. Rutkowski: Is there anything you haven't told me?
A. by Martha: I told you everything.
Q. So, if there's something else, now is the time to talk to me about it.

Martha said she had nothing to add even though she failed to disclose the two rapes noted in her email to Todd, the third trip to LA in Disneyland, seeing me trying to rape Chelsea, the whole Chelsea's hand incident, as well as many others.

ELEVEN

With that done, I started in on Chelsea's interview/prelim comparison for Ms. Hankel. I was literally overwhelmed by all the contradictions. I was also astounded that, with all the allegations, there was only one corroboration; the bucket incident. Chelsea was interviewed five days after Martha, on August 8th, 2007, also at the Crowley Lake substation. The interview was conducted by Sergeant Smart of the Mammoth Lakes police department.

Q. by Sgt. Smart: I'm going to let you kind of give me the overview of what's happening right now that caused you to come forward to law enforcement to Officer Snell.

A. by Chelsea: Well, we used to live with Mike in his trailer on See Vee.

Q. Tell me what that was like.

A. When my mom and he would get in arguments, she drove back to her old house in Nevada City. And so, when she did that, that's when he would start doing this touching, trying to have. sex. The first time it happened, I think it was two weeks after I came back from my dad's trailer. That was when he told me to go in his room. He closed his door. I knew something was up, but I didn't realize it was — he was going to try to have sex with me.

Q. And what happened after that?

A. I sat in this chair and then he told me to lay on the bed, and then he — I didn't want to. I wanted to stay in the chair. He forced me on the bed and then be tried to have sex with me.

Q. Do you remember what he said to you about anything? Did he ask you to do anything to him that you didn't understand or you didn't know what was going on?
A. Well, first he (inaudible) blow job, but I didn't know what that was, because I was young, but I knew it was something I wouldn't like.
Q. You said he tried to kiss you?
A. Yeah.
Q. Where did you get kissed?
A. All over.
Q. Okay. Did he touch you anywhere in addition to kissing you?
A. After he took my pants off, he stuck his hand down my panties.
Q. Okay. What happened after that?
A. He told me he would kill me if I told anybody.
Q. Was it just the two of you or did anybody overhear that conversation?
A. It was just the two of us.
Q. Okay. And where was your sister at the time?
A. She was in the living room. We were in his room — But I don't know what — I think she was with my mom when he did it to me, but I don't remember where she was.

Chelsea goes through all this and doesn't tell her sister, her mom or her dad? How is this possible in today's stranger danger Amber Alert world? Next, Sgt. Smart asked a series of questions about my temper.

Q. by Sgt. Smart: So, his thing was always if he was angry, he would just try to take it out on everybody?
A. by Chelsea: Right.
Q. And then threaten to kill anybody who was going to say something about him?
A. Uh-huh.
Q. Can you remember the next time after the first time that something happened sexual?

Chelsea then proceeded to describe a trip to Disneyland where she claimed to have been raped right in front of Martha. There is a several year gap in this statement. We lived in the Bishop trailer in 2003 and went to Disneyland and stayed at a motel in 2006.

Q. by Sgt. Smart: And how long were you down there?
A. by Chelsea: I think a week.
Q. And then what happened?
A. He got a room with two beds and me and Martha were going to sleep in one bed together. He was going to sleep in the other bed, but he wanted one of us to sleep with him and we didn't want to but he (inaudible) first and then he — when I

was sleeping, he woke me up and he was pulling down my pants, taking off my shirt and that's when he tried to put it in.

Q. And he put his penis where?

A. Into my vagina.

Q. What happened?

A. Then he tried to stick it in — Martha woke up and then she was getting upset. He said, "Martha, go back to bed," and she laid back down, and then I tried to get him to stop, and he wouldn't.

Chelsea then described an encounter with Martha the next night that Martha never mentioned. Martha had never described anything sexual at all during the trips to Disneyland. Chelsea did describe many threats.

Q. by Sgt. Smart: Okay. Okay. And so, it was always "If you say anything to anybody, I'll kill you," sort of thing?

A. by Chelsea: Uh-huh. Or, "If I go to jail, when I get out, I will hunt you down and kill you."

Q. Okay. And what did you take that to mean? What did you think was going to happen?

A. That he was actually going to do it.

Q. Okay. Okay. So that happened at Disneyland?

A. Uh-huh.

Q. Then what's the next time in your life that you remember happening that was sexual in nature?

A. It was the rest of 6th grade, 7th grade, and 8th grade.

Q. So, various places in Bishop and then out in Chalfant?

A. Yeah, we were in Chalfant in the sixth grade.

Q. And how would that usually happen? Would you guys be in the house by yourself, or were there other people there?

A. My mom would go out riding, and I didn't want her to leave, my mom, because then he would ask — he would try and do something, but she wouldn't listen. The first time I told her that he tried to have sex with me, she didn't believe me.

Q. How old were you when you tried to tell her the first time?

A. 11.

Q. Okay. And her reaction was she didn't believe you?

A. Uh-huh.

Whoa now. Wait a minute. Chelsea told her mom when she was 11, but she said she was molested the first time when she was 10 and the second time when she was 14. She was making this up as she went along.

Q. by Sgt. Smart: Okay. And how did it usually go. Do you remember any specific incidents?

A. by Chelsea: He would push me down on the bed, take off my clothes, and push his penis in.

Q. Okay. And how — was he ever successful?

A. No.

Q. Even partially?

A. A little bit, yeah.

Q. Okay. Okay. And did you get hurt when this happened?

A. Uh-huh. Because he would hit if I was squirming.

Chelsea missed the whole point of the question. Her vagina should have been sore if she was partially raped, but her first thought is hitting.

Q. by Sgt. Smart: Where would he usually hit you?

A. by Chelsea: My arms, my stomach, my face.

Q. Okay. Slap you? Punch you? What would he do?

A. Punch, slap, scratch, anything.

Q. Did you end up with bruises a lot?

A. Yes.

Q. Okay. So, you always made excuses for having bruises on your arms or your neck?

A. Right.

Q. But you would also try to cover them up and hide them from people?

A. Yeah.

Q. Did you approach your mom again anytime in those probably two and a half, three years?

A. No.

Q. Did you talk to her again about what was going on?

A. No. Because she would never believe me, anything I told her about Mike.

Q. Do you remember her in that time in the sixth, seventh, eighth grade, her ever asking you about bruises, seeing bruises on you?

A. No.

Q. So, we're basically up through the eighth grade and many attempts on his part to try and have sex with you, and you felt like sometimes he got his penis in partway?

A. Yes.

Q. Can you tell me how often this happened? Was it a couple times a week or a couple times a month or what?

A. Couple of times a week because my mom would go riding.

Q. Okay. Would you try and get out of the house, or anything like that?

A. I snuck out.

This was a non-sequitur. Chelsea was asked how she would get away from me and answers about sneaking out of the house in the middle of the night, which Martha and her did in the ninth grade when I wasn't even living or staying there.

Q. by Sgt. Smart: Okay. You told me that you never said anything to your mom because you didn't believe she would believe you?

A. by Chelsea: Uh-huh.

Q. Did you ever try and tell anyone else?

A. No.

Q. But anyway, so you made it through the ninth grade with him sort of coming in and out of —

A. Right.

Q. — your life and at some point in time, you decided to run away and I guess that's why Alex is in your life now?

A. Uh-huh.

Q. So, you've done some foster home stuff. Okay. What was your last sexual contact with Mike?

A. It was after the eighth grade in the summer.

Q. Okay. Still no real complete penetration of his —

A. No.

Q. — penis in your vagina? Okay. Those times that you were struggling and he was trying to do that, was he doing the kissing thing again?

A. No.

Q. Okay. Did he ever touch you in the genital area?

A. Yes.

Q. How would he do that?

A. He would (inaudible) start with hugging me and then I would kick his hand away and that's when he hit me because I hurt him.

Q. Okay. Did he ever stick a finger or fingers in your vagina?

A. No.

Q. Did he ever take anything else; a bottle, a vibrator, anything, and try to stick it in you?

A. No.

Q. Did he ever kiss you down there?

A. No.

The skeptics in the crowd would probably like to point out that if Chelsea was lying then she would have said yes to these questions. She was given the chance to easily expand her allegations and declined to agree with the answer Sgt. Smart was looking for. I would counter that the contradictions, the discrepancies, the illogicality of her statements proved she was lying. Take for example, the fact she said she told her mom when she was 11, then says she never told her mom because her mom wouldn't believe her. Another example — the hugging and kissing then the kicking the hand away statement. Can anybody please ask her to demonstrate this activity? Anyway, back to the analysis.

Q. by Sgt. Smart: Okay. And you said that, way back, when this started, he'd ask you if you'd give him a blow job, and you didn't know what that meant. Did he continue to keep doing that?

A. Yes

Q. Did that ever happen?

A. No. Because I wouldn't do it.

Q. Did he ever try to force you to do it?

A. Yes.

Q. How would he do that?

A. He would shove my head down.

Q. And you said he would actually force your mouth open?

A. Yeah.

Q. How would he do that?

A. He would grab my jaw and my chin and try to open it.

Can we please get a demonstration of the gymnastics involved in this allegation, which curiously contains no mention of threats, hitting, slapping, scratching, or punching? I can't believe the cops were taken in by the debauchery, blinded to reality.

Q. by Sgt. Smart: Okay. Did you ever try to ask him why he was doing that, or what — what it was he wanted from you? You know, or to have a conversation with him about it?

A. by Chelsea: No.

Q. Okay. So, you felt like you couldn't go to your mom. You couldn't confide in anyone else. You and Martha are twins. How much information did you exchange, the two of you?

A. Well, she told me about the incident when she (inaudible) down in Long Beach and she was alone with him.

Q. Okay. Did the two of you talk about being afraid of him or anything about the threats?

A. Yeah.

Yeah, but didn't they consider that talking to each other would get them killed?

Q. by Sgt. Smart: Okay. Did the two of you ever talk about trying to talk to your mother again together? Do you remember that?
A. by Chelsea: Well, we knew that she wouldn't believe us. We — we could never talk to her about anything. She just wouldn't listen or sit down and talk with us.
Q. So, anyway, there's this rumor that Mike liked to have sex with his girlfriends and make the kids watch.
A. That's true.
Q. Was that you then? Were you the kids —
A. Yes.
Q. — that people were always kind of —
A. I didn't know anybody knew that unless he goes and tells people.
Q. Yeah, he's kind of weird — so tell me about that. What was — how many times did that happen?
A. A lot. When him and my mom — we'd be watching a movie, and he would try to — he would start having sex, and me and Martha would look at each other and we'd try to walk out of the room and Mike would say "no," watch the movie. Sit there and watch. And then he'd make us sit there and watch because we tried leaving once but it didn't work.
Q. What happened that time?
A. He told us to stay in the room, and my mom was like, my mom didn't say anything (inaudible). I don't know why she didn't say anything, but he made us stay in the room.
Q. Did he physically make you stay in the room?
A. No.
Q. So, how old were you guys when this first happened?
A. 11.
Q. So, it wasn't too long after your mom and Mike hooked up?
A. I think it was only — maybe it was a year after.
Q. And then how many times afterwards has that happened?
A. It was every time we were ever watching a movie.
Q. Okay.
A. The last one was Easter.
Q. Okay. Maybe how long — how long ago? Can you remember?
A. I think it was like March or February.
Q. Okay. And did your mom say anything?
A. No, she didn't say anything.
Q. Okay. Later, did she ever try to explain to you or offer some excuse for why that was happening?

A. No. She didn't — she didn't talk about it at all.
Q. Okay. Did you ever ask? Do you remember asking her?
A. Well, the first time I asked why wouldn't she say something she said "Well, I don't care."
Q. So, this is what you remember her saying?
A. Uh-huh. The first time.
Q. And you said that your mom and Mike had sex — what happened basically?
A. He would just do normal sex stuff with her.
Q. Okay.
A. Oral sex.
Q. Okay. When that was happening, did he ever say anything to you and Martha?
A. No, he just looked at us.
Q. He never asked you to do anything as well?
A. No.

Okay. Okay, Okay. I get it. These cops were force feeding a bunch of foolish ideas down these girls' throats and they were spitting it back out ad hoc. Let's see, Martha said in the interview that me and Kerri were having sex in front of her at Nevada City and Chelsea was there, yet Chelsea made no mention of Nevada City, going so far as to deny ever being asked to do anything as well. During the prelim, Martha says that me and Kerri are engaged in oral sex, not "fully sex," and now Chelsea's story during the prelim is that me and Kerri were having intercourse and during this time I forced Chelsea's hand onto my penis while I was moving in and out of her mom, all the while in plain view of Martha. I'm thinking to myself, how is it I am still in jail after this complete and obvious fabrication and uncorroborated hooey. Sgt. Smart then moved on to the theater incident, August 3rd, 2007.

A. by Chelsea: On Friday, I called out that he was a child molester.
Q. by Sgt. Smart: So, you actually accused him to his face?
A. Yeah, in front of everybody.
Q. Who's everybody?
A. Well, people I don't even know.
Q. So, this was in public somewhere?
A. Yeah, at the movie theater in Bishop.
Q. Good place. So, you called him out on it?
A. He stopped for a minute then he started yelling and my mom started yelling.
Q. When you made that accusation to him, you said it kind of shut him up for a minute, and then he went off again. Did he respond to it at all or —

A. (inaudible) lying piece of shit.

Q. So he didn't - he didn't acknowledge it. He just accused you of lying about it?

A. (inaudible) there were people there.

Q. Yeah. I guess there were a bunch of people there. Did he threaten you at all at that time?

A. He said he was going to kill me.

Let's review:

• In the interview, Chelsea described being forced to give me a blow job causing bruises, then in the prelim she said she was never asked to perform a sex act;

• Chelsea never mentions sleeping on the couch while Martha said molestations occurred on the couch with Chelsea there;

• Martha said the molestations stopped when she started sleeping on the bunkbeds. This was before Chelsea moved in;

• Martha described a blow job in Nevada City and Chelsea says nothing in the interview and Chelsea said she was never asked to perform a sex act, then in the prelim the whole hand on penis story came out;

• Tried to tell mom, told mom, once, twice, three times?

• Martha denies knowing if Chelsea had intercourse with me, yet Chelsea described Martha walking into Chelsea's bedroom and seeing me trying to put it in and then there's the whole Disneyland motel story;

• How did Chelsea find out about the things I was doing to Martha — Martha told her — not because of the 20 plus times that Martha said Chelsea saw her being molested and never mentioned it either;

• One journal or two, or what? Why only two? Martha had it? Or not? Who had what when?

• Martha described being kissed in the Bishop trailer during the interview, but in the prelim said it never happened;

• Martha said she had been molested maybe 12 times in the Chalfant residence, then in the prelim stated "almost every day," "more than ten times," "a lot," what gives;

• Martha said it happened in mom's bedroom, then says it happened in her bedroom, then she said she slept with her door closed so she wouldn't be molested. Basically, Martha said one thing then said another;

• LA rape — in the interview, Martha said she told her mom afterwards, but at the prelim said she only told her sister;

• Living room floor — sperm came out or didn't? This happened one time, two times, four times? How many did you count?

• Raeanna said I reached up her shorts and Martha said I reached down her long pants.

TWELVE

Ms. Hankel was receptive to my analysis, even though it totaled 200 pages of notes and over 300 pages of highlighted transcripts. I continued to meet with her about once per week and then one week she brought up the physical findings from the Sexual Assault Response Team (SART) nurse. It seemed that back in February, the girls underwent a sexual assault exam by nurse Cathy Boyle from UC Davis. She looked at their vaginas for evidence of rape. Now, right off the bat, I considered this nonsense. This happened six months after my arrest and the girls had boyfriends (more than one). The exam did not show the absence of hymen. Nurse Boyle stated in her opinion there was a healed cleft, but my expert said that was not true and there was no evidence of repeated and forced intercourse.

The next phase of my case was to be the pretrial motions and, on March 9th, 2008, Ms. Hankel filed several. On March 16th, there was a hearing and Mr. Graham said he wasn't ready to respond, because there were so many motions. There was continued discussion of whether the trial should be in Mammoth Lakes or Bridgeport. No decision was reached that day. The next date for a motions hearing was set for April 28th. By then, I was starting to get frustrated. I had pointed out all the provable lies, the flawed physical exam, and the like, and I was still in jail.

It was going on two years in jail and I was over it. Mr. Graham was being dichotomous. On one hand, he wanted the trial right away for his alleged "victims" well-being, but yet on the other hand, he couldn't put in the work to respond to Ms. Hankel's motions in limine. On March 19th, Judge Forstenzer ruled that the trial would begin in Bridgeport on May 4th, 2009.

On March 27th, Mr. Graham fired back with a motion to admit prior threats and domestic violence. I was worried. I had a past involving domestic violence, but that didn't mean I was a child molester. But having my life dragged through the mud was disheartening. Mr. Graham filed additional motions in limine and so did Ms. Hankel. All this was heading for a showdown on April 28th.

On April 17th, Judge Darlington divulged that his daughter had been a victim of molestation and so Ms. Hankel filed a verified challenge for cause. Judge Darlington declined to accept the challenge for cause and asserted that he could hear the matter impartially. Ms. Hankel decided to file a peremptory challenge, Cal. Code Civ Proc. §170.6, but I was opposed to that, because we still had a hearing coming on the challenge for cause. Ms. Hankel said she was worried about the 5-day/10-day rule so close to the trial date. My argument was that there was no way in hell that the trial was going to start on May 4th. We hadn't even resolved the motions, the computer evidence, and the CPS records issue.

Even though Ms. Hankel's §170.6 challenge was untimely, Judge Darlington accepted it and stepped down. The motions on both sides were voluminous. On April 20th, the Honorable Romero Moench was assigned for all purposes. On April 28th, the judge showed up late to the Bridgeport courthouse for the motions hearing and promptly fined himself $50. He then proceeded to go through the motions one by one. He was an animated fellow; old, experienced. I thought he was a breath of fresh air. He said we were in trial now and would be working straight through. There were a total of 28 motions and responses to go through and only a few days before trial.

My hopes were becoming dashed at that point, since another continuance seemed likely. I was torn. I wanted to go to trial and be free at last, but I didn't want to get screwed because the court and the lawyers weren't ready. Straightaway after lunch, Mr. Graham made a §1050 continuance motion and Judge Moench quickly denied it, stating that we were going to work 24/7. Mr. Graham asked if we were going to start picking a jury on Monday and Judge Moench said "No."

The Court: And I'll want your schedules for the next couple of months when we talk again on Monday. If you have conflicts — you think you have conflicts, no, you don't, not anymore. You're out at trial now.

Whereby the court adjourned until Monday, May 4th, 2009. No sooner had we wrapped that up with my new friend Judge Moench than Mr. Graham filed his own §170.6 peremptory challenge of Judge Moench and he was gone.

Monday, May 4th, came and I was transported to Mammoth Court. I had tried to oppose Mr. Graham's challenge, but I had no standing to challenge anything, appointed counsel has to do it for me. My argument was that Mr. Graham was untimely since he had to make his challenge five days before trial. His challenge was made on April 30th, only four days before the trial date. Ms. Hankel did not want to contest Mr. Graham's challenge, because she thought Judge Moench was a loose cannon which could go off in any direction.

So, next up was Judge Forstenzer again who told us that Judge DeVore of Marsden fame was back in the saddle. He was assigned for all purposes, so I was in it deep. The next hearing scheduled was to be May 14th. I then addressed the court:

The Defendant: Your Honor, in regards to Judge DeVore, previously Judge Darlington — Judge DeVore previously ruled on some matters as to Marsden in my case. Judge Darlington was appointed at that time. Judge Darlington made a disclosure eight months into my case that warranted a cause hearing, but since it was so close to my trial date my counsel, Therese Hankel, felt it necessary to pull the trigger and file a peremptory challenge of Judge Darlington, because we were so close to a trial date and we couldn't risk going to a cause hearing because that would have gone into the timeliness issue of the §170.6 challenge.

The Court: That's not accurate at all. My understanding is that Judge Darlington, that he had given little time to file any disqualification, and so he, therefore, permitted a peremptory challenge to be filed so there was no time issue.

The Defendant: Maybe I misspoke then, owing to my lack of legal background. However, my position is that the peremptory challenge should not have been filed and it should have gone to a cause hearing based on items (ii) and (iii) within the pertinent section of Cal. Civ. Code Proc. §170.1. The fact that it didn't go to a cause hearing, I believe, is unfair and which warranted the use of the 170.6 in order to achieve a result, which should have come from the 170.1 challenge, thereby preserving my 170.6 challenge. So, therefore, I would like to withdraw my 170.6 6 peremptory challenge of Judge Darlington at this time.

The Court: That's not going to be permitted. I am going to deny that, Mr. Harris.

The Defendant: And so, therefore, Judge DeVore, I feel I deserve a cause hearing to disqualify him.

The Court: Very well. Thank you.

The Defendant: Furthermore, I would like it on the record as to why you personally, pursuant to 170.8, aren't qualified to hear this case?

The Court: I am not going to hear the case because I don't feel that I can proceed in an unbiased manner. I proceeded as you well know in the juvenile proceedings for a number of the witnesses that are going to testify in this matter and so I am intimately familiar with the facts of this case and don't feel I can proceed in an unprejudiced manner.

The Defendant: Thank you, Your Honor.

Mr. Graham the proceeded to discuss motions and timing of the trial and the like, and the judge asked him if there had been time waivers in my case and I told the court that I was withdrawing my general time waiver and requested a trial with 60 days. That had been my right all along. I felt it was time to light a fire under some ass or I would never get out of jail.

With that taken care of, I left to go back to Bridgeport and my luxury suite. One item of note. Judge Forstenzer immediately filed his recusal notice and thus prevented himself from hearing any matters in my case. That meant I had lost both of my local judges and four visiting judges. I was stuck with Judge DeVore, because I didn't have any peremptory challenges left as you only get one. To challenge him for cause was not something Ms. Hankel was going to do. She liked Judge DeVore. He had been her judge when she was a victim of arson and he had been very fair, she claimed.

Next up was the May 14th first hearing before Judge DeVore. I hadn't seen him since my Marsden hearing. The day's topic was the CPS records. Alex Ellis was there with county counsel Mark Magit. They were adamant that the records were confidential, but Judge DeVore wasn't buying it. This was good news for me. I knew what was in those records since Kerri had them all boxed up and saved. The issue was that the CPS felt it was a trial right as opposed to a pretrial right. My defense position was that I was entitled to have the court review those records in camera in order to create a fair gatekeeper to the information. To let the CPS and the DA decide what should be released was simply unacceptable. Also, it was imperative that the documents be released pretrial so investigations could commence. Otherwise, if we waited until trial, we would then have to delay the trial anyway to allow for investigations.

Mr. Magit: I would also indicate, Your Honor, Mr. Mohun, who has been appointed to the juvenile case to represent the minors, has asked me to appear on his behalf and would join with the county's positions.

So now Mr. Magit is representing the girls' interests? This would prove pivotal much later. Ms. Hankel was making a broad request for notes, reports, logs, anything which went to the girls' previous discussions and disclosures about their mom and lack of discussion or disclosure about me.

The Court: There is enough confusion in interpreting these documents than was in my mind before and there is more now that it seems to me due process would require, particularly in the circumstances of. new counsel and the passage of a couple of years, that we visit this issue anew and it would be my intention to do that.

Well, alright, maybe this Judge DeVore was OK like Ms. Hankel said. Judge DeVore said he would look at the entire file and cull the relevant documents and then give them to both sides, deferring and ruling on admissibility at trial to an ad hoc basis.

Ms. Hankel: By admission, it is a broad cast, however, it's warranted given the facts of the case and given the huge disparity in one month. Between the interviews given by the girls and the date of the preliminary hearing, there is probably a hundred discrepancies in that testimony I have documented, a hundred of them, which speaks not only to stories being planted, but to downright fabrication. And my client is entitled to know all of the people to whom they have made disclosures about these alleged acts of molestation and what they said, how they said it, ways it happened, who they said was present, when it occurred and how long it happened. And to suggest that my client should find out on the first day of trial the breadth and depth of all these disclosures — And, in fact, as I made mention before, the first disclosures were made to therapists working for the CPS and Mono County Mental Health, and I have never been provided any discovery other than that fact these disclosures were made to them. In terms of them being mandated reporters, yes in fact those two individuals reported it, now I am getting word a month ago that Rose Douglas, a Mono County Child Protective Services worker, a mandated reporter, apparently interviewed one of the girls and said, oh yes, she just disclosed child abuse to me and she didn't report it. And so, the fact that, gee, all these people who got all this information would have reported it has just been shown to be false. This is information given to me by the District

Attorney in this case, I am certain he wouldn't have told that if he hadn't at least received some information from Rose Douglas that it's true.

Unfortunately, Mr. Magit's not aware of that, but it's a fact that she is now claiming that one of the girls did make a disclosure in 2003, which of course turns everything on its ear. To suggest that my client has not shown good cause for those records is just ludicrous.

The Court: Well, with respect Mr. Magit, I think both in the pleadings and in the argument here, Ms. Hankel makes a compelling argument that, over the course of five years, there were numerous reports of physical and emotional abuse against the mother and former boyfriend, I forgot his name, he's mentioned somewhere along the line here, to a variety of people in a variety of settings: law enforcement officers, neighbors, social workers, foster parents, and there was no such allegation even with the opportunity to do so against Mr. Harris during that period of time. That certainly is relevant, it seems to me, to the allegations that then did pop up in 2007, or maybe 2003, I don't know.

So, with all that being said. I felt better than I had in a while. I felt so good, I waived time to July 20th for trial in order to accommodate Judge DeVore's busy schedule. He was a visiting judge who went where he was needed and he had scheduled matters that couldn't be changed. Ms. Hankel was optimistic since we had most of, if not all of, the records and we hoped we might even get more. And we had the girls' notes between them and their friends, including the "red letter" which detailed Chelsea's abhorrent behavior while sneaking out with "those boys."

So now it was sit and wait to get the documents. I wanted Ms. Hankel to investigate Martha and Chelsea's friends but she couldn't get an investigator. I was concerned, but I still felt good that the truth was going to blow the girls out of the water. The next hearing was May 18th and I waived my time further to August 24th, 2009, in order for Ms. Hankel and Judge DeVore to have time to prepare. I wasn't going to force the issue when it was obvious there was a lot of work left to do.

About a month later, Judge DeVore issued his ruling on the CPS records. He stated that he had gone through three boxes of material and was releasing the segregated relevant documents, but he pointed out that discovery does not ensure admissibility at trial.

The CPS records were a treasure trove of information. The contents included:

- All screener narratives;
- All reports;

• All notes of discussions by an employee of CPS or others with the twins;

• Reports of suspected child abuse not previously disclosed;

• Case notes and files related to Chelsea's El Dorado County case in 2002;

• Many other miscellaneous notes and records in the CPS/Social Services/Juvenile Court system.

Of great importance were the screener narratives in which the girls completely contradicted themselves once again. I undertook the arduous task of making a comparative report and immediately noticed a discrepancy between the referrals, as the reports were called. Corresponding dates between the notes, reports, and referrals did not align with each other, and when you factored in the DSL log files, I was bewildered. I took exception with the Suspected Child Abuse Reports (SCARs) which were not produced in a timely or contemporaneous fashion and were not presented to the sheriff of DA as required by state law.

THIRTEEN

On July 8th, 2009, an in camera hearing was held in Mammoth court. The unreported discussion centered on the many motions before the court. Attending the hearing were myself, Judge DeVore, Ms. Hankel, and Mr. Graham. Judge DeVore tentatively ruled on many of the motions in limine, including one involving Kathy Shultz and her ridiculous claim that I threatened to kill her if she caused me to go to jail. Mr. Graham was reaching too far this time. Her claims were utter nonsense but they fit in to Mr. Graham's wheelhouse, so she was going to be allowed despite my protestations. The only limitation on her testimony was that she could only talk about the purported threats.

On July 14th, I went to Mammoth for an Evid. Code §402 hearing related to CSAAS evidence involving defense expert Dr. Lee Coleman, and the prosecution expert Ms. Cathy McLennan. Mr. Graham wanted to exclude Dr. Coleman and my position was to let him testify despite my hate for psychobabble. Dr. Coleman's area of expertise was interviewing techniques, "suggestibility", and CSAAS.

Q. by Ms. Hankel: Do you believe that children want to accommodate an interviewer who is an authority figure?

A. by Dr. Coleman: They certainly may. I mean that certainly can happen.

Q. What would you look for in an interview to see if that is occurring?

A. Well, I would be comparing what a child has said to people before the interview or what they're saying now in the interview and I would be comparing what they're saying as the interview progresses. For example, I've studied so many interviews where a child will say they can't remember something and the interviewer indicates that it's really, really important that they try to remember and they try really hard to remember, and a minute or two later they are describing things which they just got done saying they couldn't remember, which raises the question whether you're actually then witnessing the very process by which a new memory or a new mental picture is being created.

So, if you begin to see that kind of pattern where the child's statements start changing and it seems to be directly in response and followed a certain kind of direction that the interviewer is going then that to me would indicate that the child is trying to satisfy their interviewer for different reasons, sometimes to get done with it, sometimes because they have a need to please and so forth.

Q. Well then Doctor, can you describe the term "suggestibility"?

A. Suggestibility means the vulnerability of human beings to be altered in their feelings and memories by what are called post-event influences, that is, contact with other people, alterations or changes in their life, their attitudes that can interact with an actual event that did occur or can create a whole new picture mentally that didn't occur or some combination. So, suggestibility is the tendency of human beings to be susceptible to those kinds of influences.

Q. Doctor, are you familiar with the Child Sexual Abuse Accommodation Syndrome?

A. Yes, I am.

Q. Can you explain what that is?

A. That first was coined by Dr. Roland Summit, a psychiatrist. I believe he's retired now, but at that time, 1983, when he published the article he was at the UCLA Veterans Hospital Psychiatry Consultation Division, and basically in this article he described what he claimed were the typical behaviors of a sexually abused child, especially with regard to disclosure, and what he - and so the article did not discuss the molested vs. non-molested children. In fact, in the article he said false allegations of sexual abuse simply don't happen. So, he was talking about children who he said were abused and that they can show these five characteristics. One was that they can keep the abuse a secret; that is, they may never tell anybody, but obviously if you come into contact it's because they are now telling somebody, but there is a secret held for a certain…

He then said that they can be — while the abuse is occurring, they can be helpless to do anything about it; that is, they can't figure out a way to stop it by telling somebody or by, you know, refusing or something like that. Then he described next what he called entrapment and accommodation, and what he was saying there is that professionals who are in contact with a sexually abused child shouldn't fall into the trap of believing that because the child is functioning okay, how could they be a sexual-abuse victim, that children who are victimized could be doing okay in school, they could be doing okay in the in the playground, they could be doing okay with their family. So, don't take that to mean that abuse cause the child to fall apart.

Next he said that when the child does say something it's what he called delayed and conflicted disclosure, that the child may — don't expect the child to give you a running account in perfect time sequence and not leaving anything out of everything that happened like you'd expect of John Dean when he went to testify about Richard Nixon. You know, don't have unrealistic expectations of children.

And finally, he said that children may retract an allegation. But don't forget that children can be surrounded by adults who don't want to believe it occurred and be pressuring the child. So, therefore, they can make a false retraction. So that is what was called the Child Sexual Abuse Accommodation Syndrome.

Q. Did Summit ever retract any of his original opinions with regard to the Child Sexual Abuse Accommodation Syndrome?

A. Yes, he did. Basically, he said that, in his opinion, his article was being misused sometimes or often — I can't remember — in the courts, that it wasn't meant as a way to help decide whether children had been molested, it wasn't a diagnostic tool, that maybe he shouldn't have used the word "syndrome," maybe he should have called it a pattern. So in that way he was backing away from a good bit of what he had said in his article.

Q. Do you have an opinion as to the propriety of the interrogation methods used in this case?

A. Yes, I do

Q. What is that opinion?

A. I don't think they were very good. I think they were the kind of methods which could both — that would ignore potentially, factors, which might raise questions about the allegations and also methods which could encourage further elaboration on allegations which were already there. In other words, I don't believe the interviews I studied were creating allegations out of whole cloth. They already existed. But in my opinion, the methods used were ones that, instead of helping to clarify factors which would support accuracy versus inaccuracy, but ones which would further cloud and confuse the process of trying to decide what is the truth. So, I thought they were very poor methods, very - lacking in neutrality. And just basically lacking the objectivity I would look for in a well-done interview.

Q. Were there any specific examples of, shall we say, an evidence of a lack of neutrality on behalf of, for example, the CPS worker in this case?

A. Yes. The nature of the relationship between the social worker Alex Ellis and the girls I found to be highly, highly troublesome. I mean, if you were to set up a scale of lack of neutrality, she would be at the far end. When she was chanting as a cheerleader p-r-i-s-o-n that they were going - the whole idea was "Let's get this guy into prison" with the child present. And all kinds of other communications clearly indicated that the main social worker was basically acting as an advocate to — for conviction, as an agent of the process which would get Mr. Harris in prison and convince people that's where he belonged. I think that the methods used here by all the people talking to the girls, whether it was police, social workers, therapists, with the kind of methods that if what they were saying was not true, it would encourage and nurture a kind of comfort zone for them to say it because every time they say it, they're surrounded by people who are rewarding them for saying it and just kind of indicating that "this is really good and we're going to go forward together as a team and we're going to do something about it." Well, that in turn, by giving some comfort, giving that comfort zone, could influence the way they present their statements to other people. That is why it is so critical for everybody who has to decide, to go back to the very beginning, and not just look at how they say what they say now.

Q. In examination of the materials in this case, did you see any indication at all that any investigator contemplated that there were false allegations being made in this case?

A. No, I didn't.

Q. Same question with respect to the social workers?

A. No.

Q. Is it important in your opinions whether the allegations against mom, the various and numerous allegations against mom were unfounded or unsubstantiated?

A. I think it's terribly important, yes, because if they were founded, it would support the girls' reliability, maybe not prove the reliability on the sexual abuse but it would be a factor. If they were found to be incorrect, then it would raise a serious question about whether or not they had gotten into the habit of telling people things because, after all, these girls were veterans of the system. They had a lot of contact with agencies and social workers. And people learn. So, you know, that would be, I think, very important and that's one of the things from what I can see wasn't done.

Ms. Hankel clearly did her homework for Dr. Coleman, but this hearing still had a way to go. Mr. Graham was next and he was going to cross-examine the hell out of Dr. Coleman. Mr. Graham was going to try and prove that (a) Dr. Coleman is a quack, not a doctor; and, (b) the evidence of interviewing techniques, suggestibility, and Dr. Coleman's take on CSAAS should be excluded at trial. Mr. Graham came out swinging for the fences:

Q. by Mr. Graham: What is your opinion regarding the fact three victims or three girls pointed the finger at Mr. Harris accusing him of molesting them? Does that factor in your mind at all regarding the reliability -

A. by Dr. Coleman: No. No. And I assume you mean, in other words, the number three as opposed to one. The reason I don't think it's —

Q. Well, let me clarify. You made direct points regarding the investigators and their attitude towards the case. Would the fact that three girls had disclosed regarding Mr. Harris affect the overall ability of the investigators' outlook on the case as opposed to one?

A. No. If they were truly independent allegations then I think maybe you could consider it a factor, but the girls were all caught up in a network in which they're interacting with some of the same people, in other words, some — or the interviewers have been influenced by other interviewers. So, a lot of the problems that you see of potential influence doesn't mean that the people have actually had contact, but there is some common source, similar methods being used, let's say. So, the fact that it's three, I think the data is pretty strong that that should not be taken to support or deny anything that's said, just that number itself.

Q. In a general sense — and I'm going to use a generalization to characterize your testimony — you have talked about - you used the word "network" just then, you talked about the way questions were asked and attitudes of interviewers and influences on these girls and how that might potentially impact the way the information came out of their mouths. Is that a fair statement of your overall testimony and your critique of that process?

A. Yes. The only thing that I also added that it's not just that the interviewers could be responsible for any influence, that there were other factors in addition to the interviewers. But what you said, I think, is a reasonable summation, yes.

Q. And though you've testified numerous times that it is not your role here to form what — state an opinion as to the reliability of what the girls said — Is that correct?

A. Yes.

Q. - and you are in essence, doing that by your critique of the overall case. Isn't that the import of your testimony?

A. I don't think so. I think basically what I'm doing is using some experience and information that lay people wouldn't have, because, after all, I've watched hundreds and hundreds of hours of children being interviewed, studied, thousands and thousands of pages. Lay people don't get access to that stuff. So, I'm using that background to say that, in my opinion, certain problems exist that could impact the reliability of what's being said and that, in my opinion, it's important to pay attention to those things.

The Court: Doctor, do I understand that basically, your proposed testimony is two-fold? One is that there are recognized factors in influencing memory reporting and such as a general proposition that are recognized by the relevant scientific field.

The Witness: Yes.

The Court: Secondly, in this case there are present a number of factors among those?

The Witness: Yes. I wouldn't have to change a word of what you said.

The Court: And it doesn't go any further than that?

The Witness: No. I think that is —

The Court: And you identified the ones that are present in this case?

The Witness: Exactly. Yes.

The Court: All right.

Q. by Mr. Graham: Were you ever provided any information regarding the defendant's own sexual interest in young girls?

A. I have not been provided anything, I was told and I think for the first time yesterday — I couldn't be completely sure — that there is some computer issue.

Q. Did you ever inquire as to what that was?

A. I did.

Q. What did you find out?

A. Not very much. That basically there is something that might be considered by some people to be relevant, but on the other hand it might be links, that it wouldn't be relevant. And obviously that's all I know about it.

Q. Would the fact that the defendant, hypothetically, has been shown via the information on his computer to have a sexual interest in young girls of similar age and look to the victims in this case, would that factor into your mind at all?

A. Not as far as what I'm doing. In other words, it doesn't influence what I'm talking about because the factors stand on their own. Now, of course, whether that is a relevant issue for a juror, I have no comment on that. That is for them to decide.
Q. Regarding Child Sexual Abuse Accommodation Syndrome, I'll use the acronym CSAAS — It has been used hundreds of times in California; isn't that correct?
A. Yes, it has.
Q. In fact, there's a jury instruction discussing it, correct?
A. Yes.
Q. Is there a jury instruction regarding suggestibility of children specifically?
A. I'm not sure. I don't know.
Q. And CSAAS was never meant to be used as a diagnostic tool; isn't that fair to say?
A. That's fair to say.
Q. And what are the myths the courts are trying to or allowing the prosecution to dispel by calling the witness?
A. The idea that — of what someone talked about, that children who have been molested would report it right away; that when it was going on, they would have a way to try and stop it, they would have the power and the influence and where-withal psychologically to do something about it; that they would give a clear and convincing and time-sequenced presentation; that, you know — and that they might take it back if they were pressured to do that.
Q. Is there a dramatic social stigma commonly held social stigma of a girl who has been molested as opposed to physically abused?
A. There can be. It can also be the other way. It can be — if you got caught up in the right network, it can be a badge. It can be something that actually gets you out of a lot of trouble, where you go from being the one who's on the hot seat to explain behaviors that are not okay — drug taking, truancy, running away, sex, all, kinds of things — to the person who is given all the TLC that anyone could muster because now they're the victim.
So, I agree with you, but I also think there's another side to it. And that's where studying each case has its own merits is so critical form the beginning to the end.
Q. When an officer is conducting an investigation or an interviewer is conducting an investigation and he is receiving information out of the victim or the alleged victim, ultimately he has to make, whether it's through subsequent investigation or not, a call on the case. Isn't that correct?
A. Up to the point he makes a decision whether there is sufficient material to send to the DA. He doesn't really make any kind of final call. That's your department.

So — but he might make a preliminary decision not to take it that far. Yes. That can happen.

Q. So, at some point the officer, the officer who is conducting the forensic interview has to make a decision to pass the case on down the line, correct?

A. Yes.

Q. And he goes from neutrality in your ideal world to a subjective view that this case is worth sending on to the DA. correct?

A. Yes.

And then Mr. Graham was done. He was really trying to make hay about the "kiddie porn" and was implying that the interviews were based on that information, but the reality was that it was way beyond the time of the prelims and interviews before they ever looked at the computer evidence allegedly seized from my trailer. There was no investigation and the points Dr. Coleman was making were skewed by Mr. Graham's insinuation that there was no investigation because of the kiddie porn.

Mr. Graham next called Ms. Cathy McLennan to talk about why Dr. Coleman and his testimony should be excluded from my trial. Ms. McLennan is an expert child forensic interviewer and she began with an overview of the evolution of the field of child forensic interviewing and then she discussed CSAAS and how she doesn't testify about it anymore because it is somewhat outdated by more recent research.

The Court: Excuse me. I'm having a little trouble following this. "That" being CSAAS?

The Witness: Yes.

The Court: The research that you referred to, post some of the research if you will, and more recently has been more focused on the component parts of what he [Dr. Summit] described as separate entities as opposed to a syndrome as he characterized it?

The Witness: Which he lived to regret.

The Court: But I did understand, you correctly?

The Witness: Correct.

The Court: So, the research is into what I think Dr. Coleman correctly identified as the five or so component parts of what Summit described and that people are taking these as stand-alone concepts and doing research into them?

The Witness: Correct.

Q. by Mr. Graham: You disagree with Dr. Coleman on an issue that you just — relating to the issue you just spoke about. What was that?

A. He made the statement that there were not — that every case was different, that of every 2,000 he had reviewed, they were all different and there were no patterns per se. I agree, on one level, in that the children that I have personally interviewed and evaluated, that there is no two alike in terms of the history they provide, but there are most absolutely, in my experience, supported by the research, there are patterns in the way children disclose about child sexual abuse or don't disclose.

Q. Can you discuss those, patterns now?

A. Typically children do not tell anybody right away when somethings happened to them, when they've experienced child sexual abuse with the exception of a stranger assault or abuse. They — kids — the research indicates that kids tend to disclose very quickly if it has been a stranger. About 90 percent of children who experience abuse, it is by someone they can name, they even know well, they're related to, they live with, but they know that person. Again, it is about two-thirds of kids don't tell anybody on an immediate basis.

Q. Regarding partial disclosure, what is your knowledge of that?

A. We know that some children will later provide more information, that is not unusual then for them to get into treatment and add additional information, and it doesn't necessarily reflect that they made a deliberate omission or lied in the first place. It's not necessarily inconsistent. It's that they sometimes can give disclosures incrementally, and we know that is the case.

Q. And I'll tell you in this case, as Dr. Coleman discussed, there was a previous molest allegation against Mr. Harris by Raeanna Davenport. Do you recall hearing —

A. Yes.

Q. — along those lines?

A. Yes.

Q. And assume, for purposes of this hearing that no prosecution was carried forward in that case and that the two main victims in this case, who disclosed some years later had known about that non-prosecution, would that be consistent with this idea of not disclosing they would be afraid, that they wouldn't be believed?

A. I believe so.

Q. Regarding suggestibility, you heard Dr. Coleman speak about suggestibility in general, as well as how age affects suggestibility?

A. Correct.

Q. What is your view on suggestibility?

A. Well, I don't — I hesitate to say it is my view, because, again, there is a very large body of research now on suggestibility that is largely driving the changes, the positive changes that have happened in the field, of child abuse investigation, not just on one discipline's part, but on everybody's part. And again, that harkens back to the mistakes that were made in these cases in the 80s and that is that there was little regard for the fact that small children are highly suggestible. There is a very large body of research on suggestibility in children. Most of it is directed at children under the age of about 10 because the research that was done indicated that a high degree of suggestibility could only be proven in very young children, preschool children between the age of about 3 and 5, and that as children developed and hit the age of about 9 or 10 they were clearly no more suggestible in these studies than the adults were.

Q. You heard Dr. Coleman dispute that. He didn't essentially agree with the way these studies were performed or the conclusions that were drawn. Is that correct?

A. Yes.

Q. And your comment in relation to what he had said?

A. Well, I disagree.

Ms. McLennan continued to describe some studies stating "one person isn't always more suggestible or gullible than somebody else, that for certain circumstances we could all have our memory or accounting of something changed" and that seemed to be agreeable with Dr. Coleman's opinion. But overall, the issue was really moot in my mind because the girls were obviously making it up as they went along. Mr. Graham thus continued:

Q. by Mr. Graham: Let me ask you a question about that. Do we know under what circumstances that that [suggestibility] would happen? Do you have an idea on that?

A. Well, I have an idea of what the research indicates. I don't work with adults; I work with children. So, I know what the research says about suggestibility in general, and that is that age is number one, the number one predictor of suggestibility.

Whether or not it was an observed or an experienced event tends to be for people of all ages. But again, I think with regards to adults, yeah, all of us have some degree or some potential of suggestibility around certain memories or events. In the studies, kids over ten perform like an adult with regard to suggestibility.

Q. And Dr. Coleman essentially agrees with that, correct?

A. Yes. Yes, he did.

Q. But then he made some qualifiers or stated a qualifier to that, namely that with teens there would be external pressures that would make them more suggestible. Do you feel that is a caveat to the overall statement that equates teens with adults in suggestibility?

A. No. I don't think so with regard to suggestibility. I do think it's important to qualify. There's been discussion around things that are kind of in terms of defining in my mind are getting mixed up about what is suggestibility versus what is a false allegation. They are two very distinctive things, and that really needs to be defined.

Q. Who was mixing that up?

A. Well, I think in the discussion this morning, there was a lot of talk about suggestibility as someone saying something that they knew to be untrue because someone else had talked to them about it. That's not technically suggestibility. That — if you are making a statement, regardless of whether somebody else talked to you about it or not suggested it to you, at 15 if you know that that statement is not true and did not happen, that no longer falls into suggestibility. What we're talking about is a false allegation. The person knows that it's false and still tells the story.

Q. So is it your testimony — and just so we capsulate it here, is it your testimony with regards to suggestibility a 15-year-old teen should be treated and viewed the same as an adult without any huge exception?

A. Correct.

So that was Mr. Graham's presentation. It was becoming clear to me that each side was trying to insinuate that the veracity of the accusers was impacted by the influences of others or by patterns of behavior. Both Dr. Coleman and Ms. McLennan felt their positions were justified by their research and depending on Judge DeVore's ruling then ultimately a jury would have to decide who was right. Next up though was Ms. Hankel and her chance to cross-examine Ms. McLennan:

Q. by Ms. Hankel: In a case of delayed disclosure where a child says "that happened two years ago," that could be because the child is delaying disclosure because she is a victim of child abuse, correct?

A. by Ms. McLennan: Yes.

Q. And you said that that's a typical way that a child may disclose, after a delay.

A. Even in studies in which the abuse has been confirmed, it is — the statistics remain static.

Q. Isn't it true, that a child who's making a false allegation could, say "that happened to me two years ago?"

A. Yes.

Q. And with respect to the second factor of CSAAS - and I may have them out of order but —

The Court: I'll give you the order. The second is helplessness. First is secretive. Second is helplessness. That was the order they came out this morning.

Q. by Ms. Hankel: Where the child doesn't disclose, he can't do anything about it. If there's nothing to disclose, and the child is accommodating i.e.; doing well in school, that can tend to show that nothing was occurring, correct?

A. Sure, it could.

Q. And the third factor —

The Court: Entrapment and accommodation.

Q. by Ms. Hankel: And I may have blended that into the helplessness, secrecy and helplessness, but the accommodation would be, of course, what we just discussed. They're doing well in school. They're not acting as if anything is occurring.

A. The child has chosen to live with the behavior.

Q. But that can also occur if nothing is happening to them, correct?

A. Sure, it's not a diagnostic tool.

Q. And the —

The Court: Inconsistent and conflicted disclosure.

Q. by Ms. Hankel: If a child is making a false allegation, wouldn't it be true that their disclosure may be inconsistent and/ or not convincing?

A. It certainly could be.

Q. And finally the recantation. If the child has actually made a false allegation of sexual abuse and then they recant that, wouldn't that factor also be shown if — be applicable, rather, to a false allegation, the recantation.

A. Yes, we agree that it's not diagnostic.

Q. And you're not testifying here today that children never lie about sexual abuse?

A. That's correct.

Q. And would you agree with me that there are several reasons or motivations that children could lie or make false allegations of sexua1 abuse?

A. I would agree with you that there are false — that false allegations exist.

Q. What are some of those reasons?

A. In the literature it is that false allegations primarily come from an adult and again more commonly the smaller children because they're more suggestible, but coming from an adult. So, it's generally the adult that's been motivated

Q. So in the literature is it your testimony that children never make false allegations?

A. No.

Q. You testified earlier, I think, that you conducted some 2,000 interviews of children.

A. Correct. Or more.

The Court: More than 2,500.

Q. by Ms. Hankel: 2,500 actually. Thank you. In those 2,500 interviews, or more, at any time did you ascertain or determine that a child was making a false allegation of sexual abuse to you?

A. *Not within the context of an interview. That's, again, not my job to determine credibility in the context of an interview. It's my job to develop questions that are developmentally sensible and defensible in order to try and collect information from a child that might allow the investigator to collect further information that may corroborate what the child has to say or not say. So, it is not ever my determination as to whether an allegation is either true or false. So no, I have not had that experience.*

Q. *Is it appropriate in your mind to use leading questions in an interview?*

A. *People will disagree on what the definition of a leading question is. I'll tell you what mine is before I tell you that it is inappropriate. To me, a leading question is one in which the answer is implied within the context of the question. So, I am asking the child to either confirm or deny the information I'm presenting to them, and that is not appropriate and should never be included in an interview.*

Q. *In your experience of interviewing children, do you typically permit social workers, case workers, to sit with the child during the interview?*

A. *No. But that's the protocol of my particular center. I do not.*

Q. *Do you think it's appropriate for a social worker to participate in an interview of a child?*

A. *I think it depends on the practice of the area in which the child is being interviewed.*

Q. *So let me clarify and make sure I am hearing you. The propriety of who participates in an interview depends on the county you're in?*

A. *It can. It can be defined by the county. Again, who has the most experience with children, who's done this before, what their protocol is, you know, what their practice is. There are counties, again, that don't have the luxury of a designated person to do that. In my area, because there are a number of people that have the need to know what the child says and we're attempting to limit the number of child - times the child is exposed to an interview. I'm in an interview room on the other side of a one-way mirror. I very often have the child protective services workers, a law enforcement worker, and a district attorney sitting in the room observing, so they're privy to what's going on.*

Q. *In your mind is it ever appropriate for a child being interviewed for the first time by a law enforcement officer to have a social worker assist the child in responding to questions from the interviewer?*

A. *That would not be ideal.*

Q. *Aside from it not being ideal, is it appropriate?*

A. *I would want to see what the questions were. Were they abuse related questions? Are they questions like what's your name or what's your grade? Or are they abuse related? What kind of impact it might have on the process would definitely depend on what the question was.*

Q. Would you agree with me that the Child Sexual Abuse Accommodation Syndrome, what Mr. Graham has been referring to as CSAAS, is only one explanation for delayed disclosure?

A. You know, again, I mentioned I haven't testified about that in years because it's grown to be – again, it was one man's observations. A lot of people agreed with it. It was proved, but it's not diagnostic.

Q. And the situation of false allegations has nothing to do with Child Sexual Abuse Accommodation Syndrome, correct?

A. Not really. I mean not —you know, not - no I mean I don't - in general, again., it was just a framework. It does not prove or disprove anything.

The Court: It also does not explain anything does it?

The Witness: Not really.

The Court: The question was couched in terms of an explanation. In fact, as far as the state of the law goes, it's whether or not somebody's conduct was not inconsistent for someone who has been molested for purposes of permitting the trier of fact to evaluate the believability of the alleged victim's testimony. That's different than an explanation isn't it?

The Witness: Correct. Correct.

Mr. Graham followed this colloquy with some redirect questions for Ms. McClennan:

Q. by Mr, Graham: Just so we're clear, you're saying a 15-year-old has the same suggestibility as an adult. Start off with that, correct?

A. Correct

Q. And if interviewing techniques were used that were suggestive, pushed a person in a certain -- that — assuming the person is a 15-year-old, that person should give you the same answer as an adult in that situation being interviewed; is that correct?

A. Yes.

The Court: How do we know there is still a myth out there?

The Witness: In my exposure to people when I do public education around child sexual abuse prevention, it's routinely — routine feedback that I get from people that everybody says if that happened to my child I would know because they would tell me immediately.

Following a few more questions involving memories and suggestibility the day was done. I was exhausted and all I did was take notes. I knew I was going to have to get in shape for the fight ahead. Judge DeVore was going to take the matter under submission and the attorneys were going to brief it further with a ruling sometime before trial. That trial was still scheduled for August 24th, 2009, a scant month away. I was whisked off to Bridgeport amidst the beautiful eastern Sierra evening.

FOURTEEN

I awoke to a beautiful midsummer morning locked in a box. I was going to head back down to Mammoth for the computer evidence 402. hearing. My expert, Rick Albee, was having open heart surgery that day so he was not going to be at the hearing. However, the prosecution expert was going to be there. Mr. Lydell Wall was going to get to testify unopposed essentially. Ms. Hankel was going to wait until Mr. Albee was well before cross-examining Mr. Wall at length. I wanted to testify since I felt I was more of an expert than they were. Ms. Hankel put the kibosh on that plan but she did agree to get me a transcript right away so I could point out inconsistencies to her and Mr. Albee. I knew that the computer evidence was problematic. I had told Mr. Gephart and Mr. Berger from the beginning that the hard drive was mechanically inoperative. I mentioned the child model sites and some Google searches. I was ready for Mr. Wall since I was certain there was no kiddie porn on my computers.

Q. by Mr. Graham: Mr. Wall, how did you get involved in this case?

A. by Mr. Wall: I was contacted in, I believe -- I believe it was September of 2007 by DA investigator Wade McCammond, who told me that he had several hard drives that he wished we would analyze.

Q. Was there a name associated with the package that you received, a suspect named?

A. Yes.

Q. What was that?

A. Michael Jay Harris.

Q. And you received this — just tell, me again, when did you receive this package?

A. This was on September 27, 2007.

Q. And tell me, what did you receive?

A. I actually received three pieces of evidence that were documented from Wade McCammond that were identified as item No. 1 which was a Maxtor hard drive with a serial number of A50F8WCC. Item No. 2 was identified as a Maxtor hard drive with a serial number 5LS67MVK. And the third item of evidence which was identified as item No. 3 Was a SONY model PCG-7X2L. There was no serial number on the exterior of the laptop.

Q. And what did you do to prepare for any kind of analysis of the evidence that you received?

A. After we received the evidence it was returned to our office in Turlock. The hard drive was removed from the laptop for the duplication process, and each of the hard drives was duplicated from a virus free Windows environment using EnCase 5 and a write blocking device.

At that point Mr. Graham asked the court to find Mr. Wall a computer expert and Ms. Hankel objected.

The Court: Well, why don't you voir dire on it right now. Let's get that issue out of the way.

Ms. Hankel then proceeded to query Mr. Wall regarding his certifications which included EnCase and certificates from the FBI, Department of Justice, and the Search Institute.

Q. by Ms. Hankel: And can you tell me, do you have any certifications in internet programming?

A. Internet programming? I'm not familiar with anything called internet programing.

Q. Are you familiar with the concept of internet programming?

A. I'm not a programmer.

Q. Okay. Do you have any certificates in internet access or usage and protocols?

A. Internet access? I'm not aware of or familiar with any specified training on internet access.

Mr. Wall then went on to outline his training in Windows and Internet Explorer and that Internet access was in fact part of that training but Mr. Wall conceded he had no specific training in news servers or mail servers. The court then wanted an offer of proof to continue grilling Mr. Wall about internet software and malware. Ms. Hankel then asked the court to reserve ruling on that issue.

Mr. Graham: Can we have this individual he deemed an appropriate computer expert for purposes of today's hearing, judge?

The Court: Yes, subject to Ms. Hankel's later, further developed, objections, if she has any.

Mr. Graham: That's fine.

Mr. Graham then began his presentation of evidence, moving directly to the images portion of the hard drive No. 1 on the overhead ELMO display.

Q. by Mr. Graham: Moving on to the child pornography section on the list.

A. The child pornography link on the left would open this folder here labeled Child Pornography and that was the - then directs you to a set of images that were identified on the computer from a compressed file that was found in the Windows directory of the temp folder.

Q. Can you describe what you see going from the top to the bottom of the photographs?

A. Yes. The first image was located in the C:\windows directory in the Temp folder. It was titled pst1002.tmp. That's where the image resided. The image is of a young girl under the age of 18, completely disrobed with her genitals clearly exposed and where the focus of the image is directing the viewer to the genital region.

Q. What about the next image?

A. The next image is of a younger female lying on a bed, again, completely disrobed with her genital region completely exposed. There appears to be a hand, a left hand from an adult male near her vaginal region, and it appears she is holding a yellow - I don't know. Looks maybe like it's a cup. But she has pigtails, and she's clearly her -- genital area is clearly openly exposed.

Q. What about the third image?

A. The third image is of a young female with her legs spread open exposing the genital region. She is completely disrobed, facing the camera, and the focus of the image is at the it focuses the viewer to the genital region.

Q. What is your opinion regarding how these images were installed on the hard drive?

A. Each of these images required user intervention.

Q. Can you explain that?

A. It takes an individual on the keyboard to access this image for it to be saved on the computer. Now there are many ways images can be saved on the computer. In this particular instance they're in -- these top two photos were in a folder titled pst1002.tmp in the windows directory in the temp folder. This methodology is accomplished by user intervention by accessing the image through the Outlook Express email client and most likely from the evidence that's present on the defendant's computer system, through a newsgroup posting. What happens when a user is on the computer using their software or their email client software it creates a temp folder in the event that something happens that the data can be recalled, and most people are familiar with the Word program, Microsoft Word, and a lot of people here had that program crash. And you think, Oh, I've lost all my work, but as soon as you reopen the program or reboot your computer, the program opens back up and lo and behold, there is your Word program because it's been recovered from a temp file or a temporary file.

This is the same methodology that Widows uses in the Outlook client where Outlook records the data in a portion of the program that they call Explorer; and it creates a temp file with the default location in Windows 98, which is the version that we're using here. 4.1 is the actual designation from Windows.

The temp file gets created when the program crashes, and the user has generally no knowledge of where that temp file goes or that it's even there, nor can they access it through any other normal means because it is a compressed file.

Q. Going back to the primary issue, is it your opinion that Mr. Harris had to click on something to get to these images and these images came up on his computer?

A. Absolutely.

Okay. Wait just a minute. I really wished that Ms. Hankel had been objecting, but she was standing mute. I knew for a fact that Mr. Wall was full of it on so many levels. The hard drive No. 1 was mechanically inoperative, so assuming his hypothesis is true, the drive still couldn't have written a temp file when it crashed. More importantly, the version of Windows I used, Windows 98 release 1, created cache files based on a user login ID or user "default" if no user has logged in bypassing the login screen. This pst1002.tmp file is as suspect a file as I have ever seen. It's kind of like a Photoshop temp file but it's not and it's in a location not configured on my system. Even more to the point, Photoshop temp files are individually created for example court.tmp for the image you are working on called court.jpg or another example would be sky.tmp for the image file sky.jpg. The pst1002.tmp file was one file with hundreds of images in the one file, three of which were kiddie porn. Interestingly enough there were no html, text, audio, video, or script files in pst1002.tmp. Also, no email or newsgroup messages associated with the three nefarious images.

An image doesn't display in Outlook Express, instead Microsoft's Internet Explorer associates jpg files and displays them for Outlook Express. It's built-in functionality. An image goes to the cache when it is viewed but it also goes with the text file or the html file or the email/newsgroup message holder. One caveat is that if you click on a link in

Outlook Express it opens in either the message pane of Outlook Express or in a standalone window of Internet Explorer. Just the image, no holder and only one image at a time.

This then puts the cached image in the users directory under c:\windows and it would never be a temp file; it would be in a folder with the name of the folder in Outlook Express being the file name in Windows, such as inbox.dbx for the inbox folder you are familiar with in Outlook Express.

Mr. Graham then went into emails from the girls and their friends sent to me and then he dove headfirst into the Newsgroups, how they worked and how many I had subscribed to. Supposedly, anyway.

Q. by Mr. Graham: But it's your opinion or based upon what you've found that these tabs below and what you have shown describe separate individual newsgroups that the defendant or that Michael Harris had clicked on to go and view content?

A. And subscribed to, yes. He actually subscribed to them. They were in Outlook Express client ready for him to view at any time he wanted.

The next one is alt.sex.fetish.tinygirls. And in this one, in this particular volume, we know that there was a story that was a newsgroup posting, a story that was actually accessed, and it was — I copied it out. In this particular newsgroup posting it's a story about: "Oh, Daddy, I like it so much when you slide down my pink little panties and rub that big red mushroom redhead that you have down there against tight pink kitty." And it's a whole story about a girl describing her incestuous relationship with her dad.

Q. So were clear on this story, is it your opinion going back to the basic issue, that Mr. Harris had to affirmatively select this story off of the newsgroup and it was brought into his computer voluntarily?

A. That's correct. It was selected from alt.sex.young and it resided in a — in the Outlook Express volume.

By then I had grown extremely frustrated. Mr. Wall was not specific about the path that that file had, he just said it's there, he viewed it, end of story.

Next Mr. Graham focused in on a set of pages called Exhibit 5.

Q. by Mr. Graham. Mr. Wall again, you created this exhibit how?

A. This exhibit was created from the web pages that were contained within pst1002. trap which was located in the c:\windows\temp directory.

Q. And when you say "Web Pages" again, going back to the primary issue, are you saying that these are web pages that Mr. Harris clicked on and went to?

A. Yes. More specifically, what he typed in to request specific content and then had the computer search out that specific content using Google, that was the search engine.
Q. What was requested by Mr. Harris?
A. On item No. 8 [of 56] a Google search was requested and the word "Lolita" was typed in the search bar. You can see the word "Lolita" right there. And then the content would be displayed below.
Q. Now we have the content that we see here below the typed word "Lolita" we have a number of photographs, approximately 21; is that fair to say?
A. Yeah. Yeah, there's 21.
Q. Can we say that these photographs that Mr. Harris -- or that came up onto the computer and reviewed by Mr. Harris when he clicked on a search for "Lolita"?
A. No. I cannot. And the reason why is when I activated this specific link, there had been some time -- you know a year or two of time had elapsed so these images weren't the exact images, the content is going to change but the basic type of content would be very similar based on the current keyword, but I cannot validate that these were the exact same images because when I accessed the URL link that was recorded on his computer, it's going to give me the most recent images because I had an active connection to the internet at that time.
Q. Is it your opinion that a similar set of images would have been viewed by Mr. Harris after his search with the word "Lolita"?
A. Yes, when conducting a keyword search for the word "Lolita" it will deliver content specific to child pornography - related images or child erotica, and typically those images will be specific to young girls.

It is worth mentioning at this point that the images from the searches were not found in the pstl002.tmp file where Mr. Wall said the URLs came from. There were no follow up pages or linked pages either. Mr. Graham moved along to talk about page one and the search for the word "Nymphet" and "3D preteen" among other questionable searches such as incestart and newstar.krissy.net. The inference Mr. Graham was hoping to draw and Mr. Wall was stating was that I went to all these pages.

Q. by Mr. Graham: And again, does each page infer that he clicked on something to get to that new page?
A. Yes.
Q. And again, in his Google search we can't say this is what he viewed, but in your training and experience, in your opinion this would be something similar that would come up?

A. Yes, and quite frequently with web pages of this nature, the content is based on basic theme, but the actual content changes to entice the user to return to check out the new content.

Q. All right. Let's out that exhibit together. I'd ask to move this exhibit into evidence.

The Court: Excuse me.

Mr. Graham: Move this exhibit into evidence?

The Court: Ms. Hankel?

Ms. Hankel: I am maintaining my objection as to foundation because the representations of the websites are not what the computer user would have seen at the time of the search nor is there any -- there hasn't been any foundation laid that the computer user actually viewed any of these websites. It is my understanding that this is the result of a search.

The Court: I am going to admit it for today's proceedings with that objection.

Q. by Mr. Graham: Let's get to the PST file images. Can you, just so we're onboard, explain the PST file images term?

A. Yes. The "pst images file" term was derived from the pst files that were described as the pst1002.tmp and there were multiple files that were created when the Outlook Express client crashed. These files were present in the Windows directory subdirectory called Temp under Windows. What I did was conduct a search of images to recover images from those pst files and that's what we're going to bring up right now.

Q. Let me ask you a question. Unlike the Exhibit No. 5, the products of the search via Google, are these images the ones that you would say Mr. Harris actually viewed?

A. Yes, because they are associated with his Outlook client and during his -- during his activity on the computer, whether Outlook was on or not -- I mean Outlook being on and then closing -- not closing properly created the file that had all these images that had been viewed and then saved in this pst format. Does that make sense?

The Court: No.

The Witness: Okay.

The Court: The question wasn't "why." It was just "if." Does this mean - does what you have on the screen now reflect something that was actually viewed by the user of this computer at some point in time?

The Witness: Yes.

Mr. Graham then proceeded to go through all the images, which included images of tile saws, horse stuff, child erotica, a segment of an incest cartoon, a wide variety of stuff. But where was the html, text, email, newsgroup massages, cookies, scripts, or videos? All he showed were jpg images, even though he had just been saying that the Google web searches were in the pst.1002.tmp file.

Q. by Mr. Graham: Based upon your training and experience and the result of your investigations, did you form an opinion as to whether or not the user had any preference for young girls?

A. Yes.

Q. What was that?

A. It was my opinion that based on the contents of the defendant's computer that he was actively engaged in searching out pictures of young girls under the age of 18 in sexually suggestive poses and the three images of child pornography that were viewed on his computer.

It seems that, according to Mr. Wall, I viewed images that I never saw. There is no way I viewed those images, but I did do some research on "Child Models" and "Entrapment" like the "Predator" series on "Dateline" and "Perverted Justice."

I also did a lot of research on Google and Yahoo! Messenger, including user created chatrooms and "bots" [little embedded scripts]. Mr. Wall's investigation was pretty one sided. And it is interesting to note that Mr. Wall made no mention of the key.dat file I so aggressively argued that Mr. Gephart had disclosed to the prosecution. Mr. Gephart said it was already in the possession of the prosecution because the DA had given it to him in Discovery. I said bullshit then and I say bullshit now. Next Ms. Hankel was going to ask some basic questions on cross-examination and then continue her cross when Mr. Albee was ready as my defense computer expert.

Q. by Ms. Hankel: Detective, I don't recall if you testified with respect to your experience as an investigator working for a specific police department or law enforcement. So can you refresh my recollection?

A. Yes. 34-year law enforcement veteran. Started in 1979 with the Sheriff's Department.

Q. Can you tell me when you began any work involving analysis of computers for sexual-predator type data?

A. Yeah, that was in 1999. We actively, my partner and I, actively developed a proactive program to go after sexual predators on the internet who were preying on young children and as a result of that, those undercover operations, we began conducting computer analysis work to obtain the evidence relating to those investigations.

Q. And going to the analysis of computers, looking for sexual content -- can you estimate for me how many computers you have analyzed?
A. Well, well over a hundred.
Q. In what time frame?
A. From 1999 to 2009.
Q. Of those hundred, do you have in your mind any idea of the average number of child pornography pictures you would have located using the EnCase or any other software forensic analysis program on each of those computers?
A. The average number of child pornography images on a computer involving cases that involved child pornography?
Q. Yes.
A. Some were as low as five and some as high as 30,000.
Q. Is it fair to say that if the user of the computer had clicked on a newsgroup that you would have subsequently found evidence of that somewhere in your analysis?
A. And we did, yes.
Q. And the extent to which you found something, can you look through the evidence that you put up on the screen today and can you look through the hard copies and point to anything that you saw that was actually accessed —
A. Yes.
Q. - from the newsgroups?
A. The incestuous story was one.
Q. When you say the incestuous story was one, I'm handing you a document that's been received into evidence as Exhibit 3 entitled newsgroup postings. Is that what you just referred to as the incestuous story?
A. Yes and it came from the newsgroup alt.sex.young.
Q. And there is - on the top of the exhibit there are the words "last accessed" with a date of May 6th, 2006?
A. Uh-huh.
Q. Is that correct?
A. Yes.
Q. With a time of 3:16:13pm?
A. Yes.
Q. And then file created date with the exact same time and date?
A. Yes.
Q. And then there's a path?
A. That's correct. That's very common.
Q. Other than this particular exhibit, is there anything else that you believed was accessed by a computer user from those lists of newsgroups?

A. Yes.

Q. What else?

A. Those files that were contained in pst1002.tmp and the other subsequent pst files.

Q. So stop there. The first one that you mentioned, the files in the pst1002.tmp?

A. Yes. It's pst1002.tmp.

Q. That's the three images?

A. Most of the content we are dealing with is from that pst file and those are as a result of the content from the Outlook Express email newsgroup client.

Wow. Can you believe this guy? He keeps saying Outlook then he says Outlook Express as though they are the same program. And he is supposed to be a world-renowned expert. I guess it takes a real expert, like my Mr. Albee, to know they are two different programs. We'll see. Moving ahead in the proceedings:

The Court: Hold on. What we've had marked as Exhibit B consists of how many pages, and how is it described?

Ms. Hankel: I have and will show the witness an exhibit that's been marked for identification as Defendant's Exhibit B. It's a two-page document entitled Child Pornography Images. It contains pictures of three images.

Q. by Ms. Hankel: And your testimony is that these three images were also viewed from the newsgroups?

A. That is correct.

Q. Can you identify or have you identified which newsgroups they were viewed from?

A. No.

Q. Do you have any idea what the headers of the newsgroups were?

A. I'm sorry. The what?

Q. The headers or the titles of the newsgroups.

A. The category, no.

Q. Do you have any idea of the date of access?

A. pst1002.tmp was accessed, I believe on June 11, 2006. Or I'm -- that pst file was created on that date.

Q. And do you have any idea of the date of access, or is it the same as the creation date?

A. The access of content can vary that is contained in a pst volume similar to this or a compressed volume. And like I mentioned before, it's a result of Outlook not closing properly. If Outlook Express closes properly then all that data that's contained in that pst temp file gets flushed out to unallocated space.

C'mon, really? Outlook or Outlook Express, chewgotta pick one and stick with it, Mr. Wall. And how can there be an access date of an image inside the pst when it's a compressed volume file inaccessible to the computer user, whoever that is? Just wondering. Ms. Hankel continued her cross of Mr. Wall.

Q. by Ms. Hankel: So my question is: Can you tell the exact date of access from any of these three images that you have there that's in Defense Exhibit B?

A. No. I cannot.

Q. Is it fair to say you're making an assumption that the computer user is always Mr. Harris?

A. I am making an opinion that he is the primary user of that computer and accessed the data contained on it.

Q. But let me make sure than I understand your testimony. Windows 98 did not require a user login?

A. That's correct.

Q. We have Outlook Express as a program on this computer?

A. That's correct.

Q. And Outlook as a program on this computer?

A. That's correct.

Q. When the computer user accesses email on the computer are they using Outlook or Outlook Express?

A. They are both email clients. One, Outlook Express is a slimmed down version that is also used as a newgroup reader, and it creates a specific set of -- volumes, we call them volumes on the computer and it's called the dbx volume. If the person is using Outlook, it creates a pst container or volume to store the data. So they store it in two different methodologies. I mean the methodologies are similar, but they're two different file extensions.

By that point, I was getting flustered because Mr. Wall is wrong. I wanted to cross-examine him myself. For example, the file pst1002.tmp is a temp file, yet Outlook uses a cache file system. So does Outlook Express. The user login determines the placement of the user configuration files and Mr. Wall was avoiding this topic. The pst1002.tmp file is as suspicious as it gets from a forensic point of view. I wanted the judge to understand these nuances.

Q. by Ms. Hankel: So how do you know which of these programs the computer user was using to access email accounts on this computer?

A. The primary one was Outlook Express. There may have been some pst files but I think it was minimal.

Q. So for the most part I can assume that Outlook Express was being used to access the email accounts on that computer?

A. Yes.

Q. And would that be the same for the newsgroup?

A. Yes, that is the newsgroup. That is the methodology that you would obtain newsgroups from in Outlook Express.

What did he just say? I can't make sense of it. Is it just me or is this guy talking out of both sides of his mouth? He had said that the three kiddie porn images were in the pst file and then he said that Outlook created the pst file and then he said that Outlook Express was the newsgroup reader or client and he said the images came from a newsposting, yet does not know which one. Hmmm.

Q. by Ms. Hankel: I was asking you what you could tell that the computer user had actually viewed from the newsgroups and you had identified Exhibit 3, the incestuous story, and you had identified the three what you had termed as child pornographic images. And is there anything else that you can specifically identify as having been viewed from the newsgroups?

A. Yes. The child erotica that was present in the pst containers because when you're using Outlook Express that is the program that creates the pst numerical sequence tmp file, and it's created when the program doesn't close properly.

I was really confused at that point. Did Mr. Wall just say that Outlook Express creates the pst file? I thought he said the pst file was created by Outlook and the dbx volumes were created by Outlook Express?

Q. by Ms. Hankel: You have testified earlier that the child erotica pictures -- that each of those images required user intervention. And my question to you is: Isn't it true that each of these images could have been from a pop-up or spam?

A. No.

Q. Why not?

A. Well spam comes in the form of email, it still requires you to click on the email for that image to be displayed on the screen. A popup is -- has become somewhat of an archaic term, although there are still some technologies out there that push data to a computer. But I don't know of any instances where child erotica and child pornography would be associated with a popup unless that's what you are already looking at.

Q. So if a computer user was looking at erotica, is it fair to say you may get spam of erotica?

A. The possibility exists. Depending on their methodology of capturing your email, you could get spam to your email, but popups, what appears on your screen and what goes to email are two separate things.

Q. Is it fair to say that I could be looking at a web page and have a popup right behind my webpage that I may never even see in my screen?

A. Yes, it's possible.

Q. And is it fair to say that in the child erotica pictures that we looked at just a moment ago, the 6 or 7 images, that none of those images was purposely saved to a folder?

A. That's correct.

Q. Can you say with any certainty today that none of the pst images were spam or popup?

A. No.

Q. With respect to the URL listings, did your analysis identify any cookies on this computer that related to those URLs?

A. No.

Q. Did you bring anything here with you today that will show the court the concurrent use of an email account which you testified to earlier and any viewing of any image and/or message?

A. No, I did not.

Ms. Hankel: At this time Your Honor, I would like to reserve the completion of my cross for a time when I can consult with my expert.

Judge DeVore agreed and so it was Mt. Graham's turn to ask some redirect questions. Before he could even get started though, Judge DeVore got mad and sent Mr. Wall out of the courtroom so he could talk with the attorneys. It seemed he was upset with all the techy-talk and especially the assumption by Mr. Wall and Mr. Graham that it was my computer. The judge had not even addressed the issue of whether he was going to allow the evidence in and then it was the jury that would decide if it was my computer and if I was a pervert and whatnot. The judge opined that he was in the detail business and didn't paint with a broad brush. He wanted specific proof before he was even going to let the jury view the presentation of evidence of kiddie porn and that made me feel a little better that this judge still had an open mind after all the content displayed thus far.

Finally Judge DeVore wrapped up by saying:

The Court: If the scope of this motion is can he then provide some evidence of nexus with the defendant here, somebody better get that answer out and better get it straight and clear and succinct without getting into techy-talk.

So, following this, Mr. Graham rethought his strategy and decided to hold off on his redirect. Ms. Hankel then said she had one last question.

Q. by Ms. Hankel: In your analysis of item No. 1 was there any single image that was purposefully saved by the computer user?
A. No.

That finished up another arduous day. I was spent and actually enjoyed myself on the way back. I thought Ms. Hankel had scored some points. I thought about Mr. Wall's dichotomous testimony, but I tempered that with the knowledge that I had done some questionable Google searches and had looked at some questionable sites. And there was still that pesky key.dat file looming in the distance. But all I ever did was look at code. I never looked at images. This was evidenced by Mr. Wall's statements that there wasn't any user saved images on the computers. There were no email messages or newsgroup messages either, except the one questionable incestuous story, which had the same creation and access date stamp. An anomaly for sure. I was anxious to see what Mr. Albee thought since I had yet to meet him and see what his skill set was.

FIFTEEN

A couple of weeks later, I was back in the Bridgeport Courthouse for a hearing about subpoenaed evidence not being produced. Nothing happened and it just got rescheduled. However, Judge DeVore did issue a favorable ruling allowing Dr. Gabaeff to testify on my behalf. He was going to testify that, based on the girls' SART exams, there was no way they were repeatedly raped as they had claimed. Mr. Graham had fought hard to keep Dr. Gabaeff out, he was really good for me and hopefully the computer evidence was just a sideshow.

My next court date was August 12th, and that gave me less than two weeks to get the computer evidence hearing transcript with Mr. Wall's sworn testimony and then highlight it and make notes for Ms. Hankel and Mr. Albee. Some of my concerns were:

• Were there multiple users or logins on item No. 1?

• Do multiple users require Windows to create multiple cache/temp locations?

• If Mr. Wall is opining that someone owned item No. 1, then why didn't he look at the configuration settings and other system files to more accurately show use and user?

Mr. Wall said that Windows 98 did not require a user login, but that was deceptive because it did permit them in order for a user to customize the configurations and settings. User login profiles are located in Windows starting with Win95 and are located at c\window\users and subsumed by program for example c:\windows\users\ski\programfiles\outlookexpress\cache\mail and then at that path location would be the file inbox.dbx or sent.dbx for example. Simply put, this means that when a user logs in they are using their custom directory structure.

If somebody accesses the computer by clicking on the cancel button on the login screen then they are using the setting for the user named "default". This would be the same path with the user being default instead of ski. In either instance, the user is using cache files, not temp files (.tmp). Mr. Wall said that it was like Word, but he forgot to mention that the version of Word that used tmp files was not in Win98 1st release, which is what my hard drive had on it.

Everything I told Mr. Albee went right over his head, lights out. Ms. Hankel liked him though; he was a medal of honor cop who had shot and killed a suspect who had shot and killed his partner. Heady stuff. He had his own computer forensic company. I felt hopeful that I could coax him to an understanding of the nuances of Mr. Wall's rhetoric. August 12th came along way too quickly and I was confused because I had heard nothing from Mr. Albee regarding the user login and configuration issues we had discussed. Ms. Hankel postponed her cross of Mr. Wall, so Mr. Graham could reopen his direct examination.

Q. by Mr. Graham: Mr. Wall, since our last court appearance, have you done further examination of the ghost image - created image of the hard drive in question, item No. 1?

A. by Mr. Wall: Yes, I. have.

Q. As you sit here today do you recall anything out of the ordinary as far as the physical operation of that drive when you began to operate it?

A. Nothing abnormal. No.

Q. Is it fair to say the only issue that you saw was the failure of the program, the Outlook Express program to close properly?

A. There was evidence that it did not close down properly, that's correct.

Q. Did you see any other – I'm going to use the term "defects" or issues relating to the drive, other than that when you examined the drive?

A. No. I did not.

Q. Okay, now you created a new report, correct, relating to identifiers on the hard drive, correct?

A. Yes, I did.

Q. On this page [Exhibit 7] there is a line entitled "Registered Owner"; is that correct?

A. That's correct.

Q. And what -- after that what is the word there?

A. The word is ski. S-K-I.

Q. This document, People's 7, relates to information that was created at the beginning of the use of this drive, is that correct?

A. That's correct, when the operating system was installed, the user entered in the name for the registered owner as "ski".

Q. And does it show any kind of date associated with when this drive was -- began its use -- user?

A. Yes, it does. January 7th, 1999.

Mr. Graham then produced Exhibit 6, which was a compilation of email, chat, correspondence, business materials, and the like which he proffered definitively linked me to the hard drive No. 1.

Mr. Graham: Your Honor, without having to go through this document paragraph by paragraph, I'd ask that it stand on its own as an exculpation of what Mr. Wall found as to identifiers.

The Court: Well, if it does, it's evidence and its contents are certainly subject to perusal and -- I think it's pretty understandable -- I don t think for my purposes at this juncture unless -- there may well be some cross-examination but, yeah, for my purposes the point is made here.

Q. by Mr. Graham: Based upon the numerous -- I'm going to use the term "identifiers" that you list in Exhibit 6, were there any of those identifiers linked to any of the specific activity relating to child sex or images of child – children in sexual poses, anything like that?

A. Yes.

Q. Can you explain to the judge what specific identifiers would be linked to that activity?

A. During the reanalysis, I identified a file called key.dat. When I viewed the key.dat file the key.dat contained actual keystrokes and programs accessed during a specific period of time.

Q. What are key strokes?

A. Any time a user pushes a key, this program records all the activity and any programs that are opened.

Q. And as far as specific key strokes that are indicative of the user showing by inference and interest in, sexual interest in, children, did you mention that in your report?

A. Yes, I did.

Q. Can you explain it to the Court?

A. Yes. The first indication that I observed was on 3/13/06 at 2:32:52pm where Internet Explorer was activated and the keyword "pre" hyphen "pubescent" was typed and then the key enter was struck and recorded. And then the word "child" with a space and then the word "models" and the keystroke enter was hit again.

Okay. I admit I put a keystroke logger on my computer and did those searches, but I did so trying to catch some malware and scripting which could access my configuration settings in regedit.exe. What is interesting to note is there are no image accesses and no text or email or newsgroup messages related to anything sexual. Also, why is Mr. Wall playing this card now after having the hard drive all that time? I was betting that Mr. Gephart or Mr. Berger tipped them off. The odds that Mr. Wall would find that file after all his scanning and reporting were exponentially against him. Mr. Gephart told Judge DeVore in July 2008 that the People already had the key.dat file, and yet now they had just discovered it. Somebody is lying, and it sure isn't me.

Mr. Graham spent the morning going through documents, business cards, et cetera... hoping to prove that hard drive item No. 1 was mine even thought it had two different serial numbers according to Mr. Wall's testimony.

Q. by Mr. Graham: Mr. Wall, there was mention the last time we had you – I'll loosely call it the pop-up defense, namely, that the content relating to, by inference, an interest sexually in young girls could have been involuntarily created on the drive without some user knowing via a pop-up or some other involuntary action from outside the computer, do you recall that -- that discussion we had previously?

A. Yes, I do.

Q. Did you do any further analysis relating to that?

A. Yes. I did.

Q. Can you provide the court your opinion of — relating to that here today?

Mr. Graham, Mr. Wall, and the Court then went into a lengthy discussion about Mr. Wall searching for popup.htm or window.open as though it was that simple. Scripting language to pop windows is much more sophisticated than html or JavaScript. PHP and CGI offer hidden options that I don't think Mr. Wall ever heard of. Regardless, there were no text or html files in the pst file. What blows my mind is that, as a web developer, I had hundreds, if not thousands, of scripts on my 20-gig drive, and many of them popped windows in one way or another. Mr. Wall came up with nary a one. Besides, if an email is sent as html and the Outlook Express email client is configured to receive it as html, then spam can pop windows all day long. As easy as pie. Mr. Wall was techy talking and I needed Mr. Albee and Ms. Hankel to get it or I was sunk.

Q. by Mr. Graham: Did you see evidence in that document [the key logger printout] that related to photographs that were — that were shown to the court either of child pornography or child erotica?

A. No. There would be no evidence of actual images that were being displayed in that document.

And there you have it: no evidence of actual images proves I wasn't looking at images. I was looking at code, tracking it as it were. Well, Mr. Wall got one thing right: Mr. Wall showed images as URLs in his pst history file, yet now said that a picture URL wouldn't show up in key.dat even if an email or newsgroup message would pop an image into a new window if clicked. Mr. Wall said the keystroke logger showed programs that opened. Oh well. It was time for Ms. Hankel to cross-examine Mr. Wall and then directly examine Mr. Albee. Ms. Hankel wasn't even talking to me at that point: her brain was full.

Q. by Ms. Hankel: Mr. Wall, were you ever provided by the DA with a copy of the return of search warrant which identified the serial numbers of the hard drives that were later forwarded to you for analysis?

A. No.

Q. So am I correct in assuming that you have no way of knowing whether the serial numbers of the hard drive you analyzed was the exact hard drive that was seized by law enforcement from my client's trailer?

A. In way of a search warrant return format, no. But it was the one handed to me and it was recorded at that time when it was entered into our system.

The Court: Do you have that serial number handy?

The Witness: Yes

The Court: Can you read it into the record for us please?

The Witness: Item No. 1 Maxtor hard drive, serial number 91080D5.

The court then took a break for lunch. After lunch, a printout was provided by the DA of the front label of the hard drive No. 1. We had requested to inspect the drive physically, but Mr. Graham was balking at that. It was hinky. For the purpose of that hearing, Ms. Hankel entered into a stipulation that their item No. 1 was in fact the hard drive seized from my trailer. Then Ms. Hankel resumed her cross-examination of Mr. Wall.

Q. by Ms. Hankel: Mr. Wall, are there additional parts of your report that have not been produced to the defense in this case?

A. by Mr. Wall: No.

Q. If we take the CD that was generated ... would that constitute your full EnCase report in this case?

A. My prepared report, yes. But obviously you're referring to something else that was discussed during the lunch break, which is called the EnCase case file.

Q. And is that an additional report that you made of the hard drive in this case?

A. No, it's not an additional report, it's work product.

Q. Okay, what do you define as work product?

A. When we enter in a keyword to conduct searches, to obtain specific results that we were looking for ... it's just a portion of work product that we do and it's part of the EnCase program, can only be opened with EnCase.

Ms. Hankel was done with Mr. Wall and she looked eager to get Mr. Albee on the stand. I was hoping for a home run and freedom at long last.

Q. by Ms. Hankel: Mr. Albee, have you had experience and education working with the EnCase software program?

A. by Mr. Albee: Yes, ma'am. I am a certified EnCase examiner.

Q. Have you received a portion of an EnCase report from Mr. Wall in this case?

A. Yes, ma'am.

Q. Did that EnCase report look complete to you?

A. It is -- it contains extractions from the full EnCase report. What Mr. Wall just identified as the case file.

The question was reread after an admonishment from the judge to stick to yes or no answers.

Q. Did that EnCase report look complete to you?

A. No, ma'am.

Q. by Ms. Hankel: Why not?

A. Because the EnCase report that is generated by the EnCase software has considerable information in it.

Q. Without that information, can you render an opinion in this case?

A. Perhaps.

The Court: But what was there is what's been provided to you and what you do not see in Mr. Wall's report is something that would cause you to question the validity of what he has reported and testified to that he did find?

The Witness: Perhaps, I'm sorry.

Q. by Ms. Hankel: Would the additional information change your opinion with respect to the authenticity of the hard drive?
A. Perhaps.
Q. Would the additional information change your opinion with respect to the connection between my client and any of the child erotica on the hard drive?
A. I don't know ma'am.
Q. Would the additional information change your opinions with respect to any connection between my client and the alleged child pornography images on the hard drive?
A. I don't know ma'am.
Q. Would the additional information change your opinions with respect to the connection between my client and the recovered pst file images on the hard drive?
A. I don't know ma'am.
Q. Would the additional information change your opinions with respect to the connection between my client and the newsgroups that were found on the hard drive?
A. Perhaps ma'am.
Q. Would the additional information change your opinions with respect to the connection between my client and the email information on the hard drive?
A. Possibly, yes.
The Court: What are we doing here … Is this premature? I mean, can you -- it appears you cannot complete your opposition to this proceeding, to this -- to this request for the admissibility of evidence.
Ms. Hankel: That is -- that's my concern Your Honor.
The Court: When are we coming back? We've got -- let's see. We've got 12 days until we start trial. Maybe we ought to sit down and talk about some further scheduling. I don't think we can conclude this hearing.
Ms. Hankel: Can I have -- may I have a -- you know, maybe the court can meet with the state and I, the District Attorney and I in chambers and discuss the issues?
The Court: Let's go.
(Whereupon a discussion was held off the record between the court and counsel)
Ms. Hankel: Your Honor, I wanted a moment with my client before we proceed.
The Court: Sure. If you need to speak in private?
Ms. Hankel: I would like to.
The Court: Can you guys use the hall there?
Ms. Hankel: Sure.

(A discussion was held between defense counsel and the defendant)

Ms. Hankel advised me that they had decided in the chambers conference that there would be a delay in the trial. I objected to any further delays and insisted on my right to a speedy trial. Judge DeVore was told of my objection and a further private conversation was had between me, Ms. Hankel, and Mr. Albee in the hallway. I didn't understand Mr. Albee's need for more time since the information in the missing report was trivial compared to the evidence he was supposed to be ready to testify about that day. Mr. Albee said he couldn't do so without the report that was missing from the discovery provided by Mr. Wall. I disputed Mr. Albee's assertions, pointing out that Mr. Albee had told Judge DeVore that he was unavailable the first week or two of September as he had other commitments and so I pressed Mr. Albee in our private meeting to explain how he planned to testify in my current scheduled trial, just days away if a delay wasn't granted that day due to the developments regarding the case file. Mr. Albee responded that he did not anticipate the evidence being allowed in and that he had made his commitments prior to the new trial dates being set the preceding May.

I told Ms. Hankel and Mr. Albee that they had already had enough time to prepare and had extensive information provided to them by me, and if Mr. Albee had a scheduling conflict since May, he should have notified Ms. Hankel and myself long ago. I concluded my tirade by telling Ms. Hankel that I wasn't going to accept another delay for what appeared to be delay's sake. I told Ms. Hankel I preferred to put Mr. Albee on the stand as is and let the judge rule that day. If Judge DeVore admitted the evidence, then we should seek a writ of prohibition from the 3rd DCA to exclude it as unduly prejudicial and irrelevant.

Ms. Hankel and Mr. Albee were quick to point out that only two percent of appeals are successful and I should let them do their work even if I didn't believe it would help my case. I insisted that I was not going to waive time again. Instead, I told them to put me on the stand as an Evid. Code 702 witness to testify in my own area of expertise, an expert in my computer. Not all computers, mine.

My internet experience, my experience with Windows and my programming experience would be plenty to blow Mr. Wall out of the water. I had the most riding on it, so what the hell, let's do this I said. Ms. Hankel put on the brakes to that idea faster than I could say it. We then reentered the courtroom.

Judge DeVore accepted my decision to preserve the trial date, but asked counsel to brief the issue of granting defense counsel's request for a continuance §1050 request, over the client's objection. He then scheduled a telephonic conference call for Friday August 14, 2009. I was shocked that it was possible that my speedy trial rights could be waived by my new attorney. I had been in jail for 2 years and my life was in ruin. Enough was enough was my mantra.

Ms. Hankel: Your Honor, we had spoken in chambers about a discovery issue. My expert, Mr. Albee, has not had a portion of the materials regarding the analysis of the computer at his disposal, to analyze prior to his forming of his opinions in this case. He deemed it necessary to be able to review the same prior to making his opinions in this case. We met in chambers to discuss the availability of my expert, counsel, and the court, to do that, to keep our trial date in this case. We were not able to arrive at that conclusion. I believe it is critical for the defense that my expert have the necessary materials to be able to arrive at a fully considered opinion, with respect to the computer evidence in this case. I've so advised my client. My client does not wish to waive time any further than the time that's been waived on the record in the case so far. My client does not wish to waive time from August 24th to December 1st unless the Court is inclined to release him on his own recognizance. He has been in jail 720 days. It is his desire to maintain his trial date at this point.

The Court: And I absolutely respect that -- Mr. Graham?

Mr. Graham: I'd like to provide some briefing on this issue if the court would so entertain.

The Court: I will certainly entertain it but as I mentioned at sidebar, I am aware of how long Mr. Harris has been in custody and I absolutely respect his interest in having this matter brought to trial…

I know about the conundrum between the defendant's speedy trial and his right to counsel and counsel's being in the rock and a hard place position of saying "I don't feel I can be effective without having his expert assistance."

With that being said, Judge DeVore scheduled a telephonic conference where he would hopefully make a decision to exclude the computer evidence.

SIXTEEN

Despite having told the court that I didn't want to participate in the telephonic conference call, I woke up that Friday morning on August 14th so stressed out that I told the jailor I wanted to participate after all. Arrangements were made and I was connected in at the appropriate time. Included in the unreported call were Judge DeVore, myself, Mr. Graham, Mr. Albee, and Ms. Hankel.

A discussion broke out related to briefs which had just been filed on the continuance issue. After some debate, Judge DeVore advised Mr. Graham that he best prepare to proceed without the computer evidence in light of the repeated delays in the State's production of the computer evidence. Mr. Graham voiced the opinion that the total exclusion was a rather draconian remedy. Judge DeVore acquiesced and scheduled a hearing for August 19th. The judge asked me to provide him with information regarding the delays which had occurred and led to my withdrawal of my general time waiver. Judge DeVore concluded by asking counsel to further brief the issue of defense seeking a continuance over a defendant's objection.

Five days later, I was back in Mammoth Court hopeful that the judge was going to exclude the computer evidence once and for all. I submitted documents explaining why there had been delays not of my choosing. Judge DeVore lodged my documents but did not file them, nor did he allow me to argue my positions. I had no standing. My attorney, appointed by the State, speaks for me at all times and stages of a criminal proceeding. This is because I asked to have counsel appointed because I was indigent when I was arrested. When this happened, unbeknownst to me, I gave up most of my rights. Appointed counsel gets to choose all tactics and strategies within acceptable professional norms. (See Strickland v Washington 466 US 668 (1984).) After much commentary by Ms. Hankel and Mr. Graham, Judge DeVore granted Ms. Hankel's request over my objection citing Townsend v Superior Court (1975) 15 Cal.3d 774.

I felt that, just as in the Marsden hearings, I was not represented by counsel at that critical stage of the proceedings. I believed that Ms. Hankel was laboring under an actual conflict of interest in that her own interest in having extra time to prepare superseded my wishes to go to trial within the constitutionally proscribed 60 days.

At the close of the hearing Kerri, showed up and attempted to be heard regarding her motion related to Fifth Amendment issues and whether the state was offering her immunity. Judge DeVore declined to hear from her because her attorney was only available by phone. Kerri had made extraordinary arrangements to appear in court that day and the cold rebuke by the Judge was intimidating to her. Kerri, who was to be an important witness if not crucial, was already fearful of the actions that may have been taken against her by the State, the DA, the Sheriff's Department. her daughters, her daughters' friends, and others. Kerri was living alone in the middle of nowhere and she was receiving threats.

Kerri's inability to be heard by the court did little to help her overcome the perception she had that my trial was a witch hunt. Judge DeVore set a new trial date of October 26th and the resumption of the computer evidence §402 hearing for October 23rd. On August 27th, Kerri gave two interviews. The first was with Ms. Hankel and the second was with Wade McCammond, the DA's investigator. Kerri's attorney, David Hammon, was present at both interviews and they were recorded. Both parties got a copy of both recordings after the interviews. During both interviews, Kerri confirmed all her previous statements made to the following:

- Det. Rutkowski re: "the red letter";
- Det. Rutkowski and the suspect interview 8/16/07;
- The bail review hearing;
- The Gephart meeting;
- Emails to the CPS;

- Statements filed in court in her WIC §300 case;
- The DA in response to his subpoena;
- Letters and phone calls to me in jail.

Kerri told both Ms. Hankel and Mr. McCammond that she was never told of the molestations, rapes, or abuse of any type by Martha or Chelsea. Kerri stated that she was never told by Martha that I had molested Raeanna, was never told that the girls did not want to go to Disneyland, go shopping, et cetera. Kerri said she never had sex in front of the girls with me, nor did she make them watch or participate in sex with herself and me. Ms. Hankel did not question Kerri regarding numerous issues including the runaway timeline and the escalation of complaints by Chelsea and then later by Martha. Ms. Hankel also failed to ask about Steve Cupp, Shaylynn Ellis, the Jacksons, the ski team, the van incident, and Martha's claim that she was being stalked by Leif Medrud. Kerri was also not asked about her own issues related to being threatened by her daughters, her daughters' friends, the district attorney's office, the sheriff's office, as well as all the topics I had spoken to Ms. Hankel about prior to the interview. Kerri was the key to my "escalation defense."

Nothing happened in the next couple of months. I met with Ms. Hankel about once a week and we went over Kerri's interviews. Then, all of a sudden, the Mono County Jail in Bridgeport flooded. Over 3 inches of rain fell while the roof was being replaced. There was basically no roof and it was a certifiable disaster.

I was transferred along with all the other prisoners to the Inyo County jail in Independence, CA. This was about 135 miles south of Bridgeport and about 90 miles south of Mammoth. Most importantly though, even though I was transferred in a private car, I had lost my luxury suite with all the amenities. I almost got placed in with the general population, but I screamed bloody murder and got a single cell with no amenities. I did get a book though. The jailers took away all my legal papers and I was steamed. I made them call Ms. Hankel in an effort to resolve the impasse. In the end, they stored my papers for the night then let me have them the next day. I was going to be there indefinitely, so I tried to get along. The food was awesome. I mean restaurant quality.

The flood and resulting move came at a most inopportune moment. Ms. Hankel had finally hired an investigator recently, Nathan Morganstein, and he was developing some leads, but I did not meet with him or Ms. Hankel until just days before my trial was set to begin. I was not able to review any of their materials regarding the Jacksons, Leif Medrud, Tyler Clarke, Jordan Moriarty, Kathleen Traynor and others. The Inyo County jail did not honor the Mono County court order permitting me contact visits with my defense team. The development of information regarding witnesses was a welcome relief at long last, however the limitation of time and space hindered my ability to discuss the veracity of the facts being ascertained. The preparation by Ms. Hankel was decidedly turning toward the plan defense despite substantial evidence that there was no plan by the girls to disclose sexual abuse. Instead, the evidence showed that the girls' accusations against their mother and then me actually escalated over time based on queries, not unsolicited complaints.

Clearly, the discussions about the specific facts leading up to the disclosures, and the involvement of the witnesses being developed were limited and incomplete and this led to a negative impact on strategic decisions being made without my input. I was only able to meet with Ms. Hankel and Mr. Albee one time before October 23rd and the §402 hearing. This was with the same no-contact format, so I had no ability to review evidence on Mr. Albee's computer laptop. In my meeting with Ms. Hankel and Mr. Albee, I reiterated my concerns regarding the pst files, the cache vs. temp issue, as well as the need to identify the user directory which housed the cache file structure and thus disprove the temp file assertion central to Mr. Wall's damaging opinions.

The next day I spoke on the phone with Ms. Hankel and Mr. Albee. Mr. Albee was excited with the news that he had found evidence of other users on item No. 1, the hard drive, and he was going to testify that there were several users of the hard drive besides me. I was confused by this revelation and without being able to see or review his newly found evidence first-hand, I was at a decided disadvantage being housed all the way down in Inyo County.

SEVENTEEN

A few days later and it was October 23rd. It was crunch time. I really wanted to talk with Ms. Hankel and Mr. Albee, but that never happened. I was still concerned with Mr. Albee's contention that he had discovered multiple users on the hard drive. I knew that other people had used my computer over the years, but I had set up only one login, otherwise the hard drive used the default settings. Ms. Hankel got right to it examining Mr. Albee.

Q. by Ms. Hankel: Mr. Albee, since the last time we were in court, did you have an opportunity to complete your analysis of the hard drive in this case?

A. by Mr. Albee: Yes ma'am, pretty much.

Q. Can you tell me, Mr. Albee, whether you agree with Mr. Wall's conclusion that Mr. Harris is responsible for the nefarious images on the hard drive in question?

A. No ma'am, I do not agree.

Q. Why not?

A. For several reasons. I don't believe that the hard drive has enough evidence on it -- well, the hard drive doesn't have any evidence on it that the images have ever been accessed. So to say that Mr. Harris is responsible for possession is an entirely different matter.

Mr. Albee then described 20 purported users of the hard drive, but immediately I knew I was in big trouble. Mr. Albee was relying on spam addresses in my spam folder in my email settings under spam.dbx. These were from my catchall email filter on my dedicated web server. Against my desires, Mr. Albee was not using the user profile in the login structure c:\windows\users. He then discussed profiles for Yahoo! and it was obvious Martha, Chelsea and Kerri had used my computer besides me.

Q. by Ms. Hankel: And do you agree with Mr. Wall's contention that the Windows 98 operating system did not require a user login?

A. Yes, I do.

Q. And so any person could sit down and operate that computer without entering a password to log on?

A. Yes ma'am.

Q. Mr. Wall said he could put my client on the computer through his use of sending and receiving concurrently with viewing images or accessing data on the computer. Do you agree with that assertion?

A. No.

Q. In the transcript of July 15th, 2009, page 112, lines 6-11, Mr. Wall stated "So can I tell when Mr. Harris was on the computer? Yes, I can tell when he sent email and when he received email, when he looked at webpages, on what dates those webpages were viewed, because they correlate with the times he was on his using email." Mr. Albee, do you agree with that assertion?

A. No, I do not.

Q. Why not?

A. Because I took the disc that was provided by Mr. Wall, which had the spreadsheets on it for all the newsgroup subject pages, and I compared the dates and times that we have from the key logger with all the dates and times listed by Mr. Wall as to the newsgroup dates and times listed and they did not correlate, there was no correlation between those, I took the -- well, there is no email.

Q. What would you expect from your training and experience and investigating child molestation cases and in your training and experience in analyzing computers for evidence of pornographic or obscene material, what would you expect to find if you were looking at a group of newsgroup subjects?

A. Well, for one thing, I would expect to see just a plethora of it, a huge amount… The second thing I'd expect is access.

Q. The three pornography, what you called child pornography pictures, were not accessible to any computer user on this computer, correct?

A. That is correct.

Q. And in fact did you find any of what Mr. Wall characterized as child erotica or child porn, pictures that had been purposefully saved by any computer user on this computer?

A. No, I did not.

Q. Did you find any webpages that had been purposefully saved by any computer user that depicted child porn?

A. No, I did not.

Q. Did you find any purposeful saving of any child erotica material on this computer?

A. All the child erotica on this computer was extracted from unallocated space.

The Court: But if you find it there, in the unallocated space, you can't know whether it was viewed, used, printed, or simply deleted without ever having a person access, or look at, or make any use of?

The Witness: That's correct, Your Honor.

The Court: What's the significance?

The Witness: pst1002.tmp is an active file but that file is an active temp file that is used by a couple different programs for when the program either crashes or the program stashes its active stuff for like -- pst stands for Photoshop Temp. But that's not the only program that uses that type of a temp file. Mr. Wall stated that it was when Outlook crashed that it was put -- that whatever was in Outlook - so somebody was looking at Outlook when it was put into that file, that's not correct, that is not an Outlook temp file for several reasons, but it's absolutely not an Outlook temp file.

The Court: Okay -- would you expect to see a larger volume of pornographic material if this were a computer utilized by a person with prurient sexual interests in young girls?

The Witness: Yes.

The Court: Let me ask, is it an affirmative action that somebody has to do, to delete something as opposed to not shutting a computer down properly and having things get dumped into a temp file?

The Witness: Affirmative action to delete something? Yes, Your Honor, I believe so.

The Court: Okay, go ahead.

The Witness: But -- okay.

The Court: Oh, I'm sorry. Go ahead.

The Witness: Well, the problem with this is that I would disagree I with what Mr. Graham said in his objection. I have never agreed and I believe I testified that specifically on the temp file, that pst2001.tmp I believe it is .tmp.

Ms. Hankel 1002.

The Witness: 1002. That temp file there was testimony that the temp file exists because Outlook crashed and that is not correct.

Q. by Ms. Hankel: Mr. Wall said that much of the material on the computer was due to a crash of a program and you disagree with that analysis, correct?

A. Yes, I do disagree with that.

Q. And why?

A. Because Mr. Wall stated that the information and specifically the child pornographic images were put into the pst1002.tmp file as a result of Outlook crashing and that is categorically incorrect for a couple of reasons.

Outlook, number one, does not use a temp file - the only time Outlook can use a temp file is in Outlook 2007 or later. And it can only use a temp file when it is using the NTFS system. New Technology File System. This computer is running FAT 32. This gets a little techie but it's inconsistent. It won't work.

The Court: Let me make sure I understand that. I understand that not until 2007 did Microsoft have a process by which an improper closure, crashing, would result in data going to a temp file?

The Witness: The program Outlook 2007 – the Outlook program on this computer is really old and there's nothing in it. I don't think it's ever been used or - everything is out of it… but more importantly, it had to have a NTFS file system. The file system on this computer is FAT 32 [File Allocation Table 32] and they are not compatible.

Q. by Ms. Hankel: Do you agree with the statement by Mr. Wall that - that the material [pstl002.tmp] would have been created because Outlook Express crashed?

A. No, I do not.

Q. Why not?

A. Because Outlook Express uses cache files.

The Court: In your analysis of this hard drive, do you get any indication, any clue one way or another, whether this computer is being used by one or more sophisticated computer users or unsophisticated?

The Witness: There's not a lot of information on the hard drive so to go one way or another on that, Mr. Wall said that Mr. Harris - I believe he called him a power user. In looking at the hard drive there's not a lot of indication that the user of this hard drive took great pains to erase anything.

The Court: Or users?

The Witness: Or users, yeah -- whoever was on it at the time, although I understand Mr. Harris made a website — the unallocated space was not wiped, the slack space was not wiped. And the programs that are on the computer are kind of what you would expect to see.

The Court: Basic stuff?

The Witness: Basic stuff, yes sir.

Q. by Ms. Hankel: There are some sophisticated programs that people who have an interest in pornography might use, correct?

A. I'm sure.

Q. And there are certain files you would look for?

A. Certain files, definitely yes.

Q. Would you look for something called a Bit Torrent file?

A. Yes, I would.

Q. And when a sophisticated user who was interested in - had a sexual interest in child porn, be using a Bit Torrent file?

A. Very probably.

Q. And what about a ZIP file?

A. A ZIP file has a number of uses, and that would be one of them, because a person who's collecting a lot of photographs or movies will ZIP them to make them smaller on the hard drive and also to be able to send them to someone else without being a large file.

Q. And did you see any use of ZIP files on this computer?

A. No.

Q. Did you see any use of Bit Torrents on this computer?

A. No, I did not.

Q. I'm going to ask you Mr. Albee, would you have expected to have seen purposefully saved images of child porn on this computer if the computer user had a sexual interest in little girls?

A. Yes, I would.

The Court: Was any there?

The Witness: No there was not.

Q. by Ms. Hankel: If a computer user had actually looked at those URLs wouldn't you expect to find the image on the computer itself, in either the cache or in the unallocated space?

A. Yes.

So far, so good. I was hopeful that Judge DeVore would see through this farce. Now it was time for Mr. Graham to cross-examine Mr. Albee.

Q. by Mr. Graham: Regarding all of the -- and I'm going to use the term "bad material," material that shows a sexual interest in young girls, we'll just call, of the bad material.

A. by Mr. Albee: I understand sir.

Q. The dozens of photos of young girls, the Google searches, the website hits, the newsgroups, are you saying that all this material was inputted on the drive through a random process and not by any choice by the user?

A. Well you -- you've -- no. Because you've mixed information that doesn't get on the hard drive the same way.

Q. Okay. And so, when I use the term -- when I say all of the material got there randomly, not by choice of the user of that drive, that's not an accurate statement, correct?

A. That is correct. That is not an accurate statement.

Q. I want you to tell the court what you believe was not inputted randomly or by some kind of spam or outside influence but by choice of the user?

The Court: What, bad material?

Mr. Graham: Bad material, yes.

The Witness: The -- well, let's start with the newsgroups. Because the newsgroups are obviously action accessed and whatever's on that - I'm not agreeing that they were viewed -- but whatever is on the hard drive, if you count that as used, the newsgroups that were -- somebody did that, somebody went and downloaded the title pages or the subject pages.

Q. by Mr. Graham: When you say the word accessed, I hear that but I don't know what you mean by that?

A. Yes. The -- from the CD that Mr. Wall gave us, he's got the -- he did a very good job of categorizing out the separate title pages, and under the title pages are subject lines. He took all of those and put them in an Excel spreadsheet, actually spreadsheets, and with the Excel spreadsheets he put the created date and the last accessed date and the created dates and the last accessed dates are the same. And keep in mind there is no data associated with these. They are only text. So the text messages are — these lists are created within a span of seconds and they all match the created time.

So you get this list and if you go back and you access any of the data or try to see what's in it, you're going to change the last access time and it's going to be different from the created time.

Q. For you the newsgroups were purposefully accessed by the user, correct?

A. No, they were not accessed, they appear on the computer but they were not accessed. The subject line was accessed. There's a big difference.

Q. I asked what does the word access mean? Tell the court.

A. Access means you went back to it and looked at it. After it was created — however you call it, downloaded, whatever you did to get it [the list] out of the server — you went back and looked at the message and opened it or whatever.

Q. What other category of bad material that we've been talking about would you say was affirmatively accessed by the user or users of that drive?

The Court: He's already said nothing was accessed. He found nothing that was accessed. Did I get that wrong?

The Witness: That's correct Your Honor.

In the end, it just didn't matter. Judge DeVore ruled the evidence was admissible, all of it. The computer evidence was going to take up more time than the alleged victims. Mr. Albee had discussed many topics, but most importantly he had erroneously testified about finding a variety of users on the hard drive and Mr. Graham had caught him making a big mistake.

Mr. Wall had testified that individual users did not need to log on to a Win98 system, when in fact they could. Mr. Albee was instructed to research his copy of hard drive No. 1 in order to impugn Mr. Wall and his take on the log in attribute and its relationship to the cache files used by Win98 first edition. Mr. Albee did a fine job in some areas, but in others he fell short. Ms. Hankel was to blame for relying too heavily on him instead of me.

Mr. Albee said it wasn't his job to inspect the whole hard drive but instead to respond to evidence put forth by the prosecution. The problem with that strategy was that the State was constantly producing new evidence, such as the key.dat file and they had Mr. Albee on the ropes. The State's position was that the hard drive had been turned over in discovery and we were responsible for responding to anything they presented from the drive, ad hoc. A daunting task and the authenticity of the drive was still in question. The pst1002.tmp file was an unexplainable anomaly, as though it had been planted on the drive. I guessed privately that it was a dump file for some kind of gallery tool or viewer that put all locatable images in one viewer, like the newer version of windows did with its file manager. But that was a guess on my part. I did not have the hard drive to work with and time was out. Enough of all that, it was time to focus on the trial starting in three days on Monday, October 26th, 2009.

EIGHTEEN

Monday morning couldn't come soon enough, but it did. I was awakened at 5:00am in order to be ready for my 6:00am transport to Mammoth. I was being transported by the Mono County Sheriffs, so they had to drive down from Bridgeport just to pick me up. I ate a quick breakfast of homemade waffles and scrambled eggs. I then got dressed in my nice clothes, put on a tie and donned my blazer. Leaving the jail with Mono County deputy Burbine, I was greeted with a glorious sunrise with golden hues blanketing the eastern slopes of Mt. Williamson and beyond. I really enjoyed the 90-minute drive north on US Highway 395 along the Eastern Sierra.

At the courthouse in Mammoth, which was in a strip-mall type shopping center only three stories high, I was escorted up the back stairs to my new home away from home: my holding cell. A six-foot square room with a window in the door and a wooden bench along one wall. The potential jurors were filling the small lobby, spilling into the halls which ran the length of the building. It was a crazy scene with all types of people and outfits. The one thing I noted was they were all white and they looked conservative. Not a good sign for an accused baby raper. Ms. Hankel was still attempting to resolve issues with Mr. Albee and the computer evidence, while also attempting to corral all the issues surrounding the witnesses and still get ready for 200 veniremen, as the potential jurors are called. As this was going on, I noticed her voice was going out, her health appeared sketchy and things were generally looking scattered. She had no time to discuss all the last-minute witness developments with me, nor was she able to provide me with documents from my attorney-client file which I needed.

I am not going to rehash the minutia of selecting a jury. Suffice to say the 200 veniremen are randomly placed on a list after those with major excuses are released. The leftovers on the list are called and the first six are seated on six chairs setup in front of the jury box. This row of chairs is referred to as the six-pack. Those first six are questioned or Voir Dired and any that are unsuitable are dismissed for cause. If they survive this initial screening, they are placed in the jury box, starting with Juror No. 1. Once they are in the jury box, the process is repeated until the box is filled. Then the jurors in the jury box can be peremptorily challenged and excused with no reason given. Each side gets 20 peremptory challenges, so this went on and on for four days. During the four days of voir dire, I sat next to Ms. Hankel and expressed my concerns mostly with notes passing between us. I had a variety of issues, such as the inconsistent initial questioning of each individual juror, the lack of detailed questionnaire, the failure to conduct voir dire in camera so that other potential jurors didn't bias one another, and also the judge made an error and changed the selection process which let the People leave the last pick each round.

I was told by Ms. Hankel that Juror No. 11 was actually a friend of Mr. Graham's. Another Juror, No. 12, was a clerk in the very court we were in. This was all very disconcerting to me, but I wasn't going to be disruptive before the judge or jury.

After lunch on the fourth day of jury selection with a jury selected, sworn, and seated, the opening statements were given. These cannot be argumentative and are not to be considered as evidence, they are to be outlines of what lies ahead more or less.

Mr. Graham went first and worked his way through the counts and explained the way he was charging me. He was using one count as a first time and another count as the last time for each particular act and location. He was planning on having Martha and Chelsea simply say "more than one time" to satisfy the jury. I didn't like that generic approach one bit. Mr. Graham then went on to discuss details of the alleged abuse and also a bit about Raeanna Davenport. He also prepared the jury for the girls' demeanor, which wasn't what a person might expect. He just didn't know how it was going to go. He next talked about the medical exam and the computer evidence. Mr. Graham spent a fairly long amount of time on the computer evidence, and I didn't like that either. He then spoke about Kerri and her history. Mr. Graham then closed up with argument:

Mr. Graham: But at the end of the day, you are not going to hear enough evidence for you to believe that these girls manufactured this history, this sexual assault history against Mr. Harris.

The Court: This is argument.

Mr. Graham: At the end of the evidence, you are going to find the defendant guilty of all the charges. Thank you.

The Court: Ms. Hankel

So now it was-my turn. Mr. Graham had basically violated my right to the presumption of innocence when he transferred the burden of proof over to me, but that being said, here we were, after all the preliminaries, it was time to present my side of the story. Ms. Hankel prefaced her comments by saying she would be quoting some material that was pretty graphic and she didn't want to offend anyone. She then laid out the twin's history and their parents who divorced and their dad who ultimately died on September 11, 2003. Ms. Hankel outlined the twins calling CPS numerous times on their mom, lodging complaints. She discussed Chelsea being sent to her dad's in 2002. He didn't have adequate housing, so Chelsea wound up in a foster home. Ms. Hankel mentioned some of the facts involving Raeanna Davenport and noted that the CPS interviewed Martha and Chelsea at school, away from home secretly, and both Martha and Chelsea said nothing happened to Raeanna and nothing was happening to them. Ms. Hankel then mentioned that the twins' home life was not to their liking.

Kerri wasn't allowing them to date, so they were sneaking out late at night to be with boys and to pay back Kerri for disciplining them. Then Ms. Hankel introduced the "plan" defense, which I didn't like at all.

Ms. Hankel: The evidence is going to show the girls came up with a plan. The girls came up with a plan to get out of the house.

Ms. Hankel segued into a presentation of the evidence, including statements not made at the time of disclosure and all the discrepancies between the girls' interviews and their preliminary hearing testimony.

Ms. Hankel: I suggest to you to keep the word "manipulation" close in this case, because these girls have not only manipulated their mom, they not only have ma-

nipulated their social worker, they have manipulated law enforcement. And they have manipulated the district attorney. When Martha responds to Mr. Graham when she is 15 years old, "tell me all the things that Mike Harris did to you when you were 10," I suggest to you she's trying to think what does a child say about allegations of child abuse. And Martha responds, "He would put his wiener in between my legs and he would start moving back and forth." When he asks her, "Please tell me all the things Mr. Harris did to you when you were 12," Martha's 15-year-old response is, "Mike would try to put his wee-wee inside of me."

Ms. Hankel then pointed out a contrast saying 15-year-old Martha and Chelsea, who are too afraid to make an allegation against me, could make the following statement to Michelle Jackson a mere 60 days after the wee-wee response to Mr. Graham.

Ms. Hankel: "You know what you fucking little skank, I can fight my own battles. You just haven't seen yet. I can kick your ass. You are just too pussy. You are a slut. All the guys you date, date you for is they want to get some. I am going to laugh one day when you get fucking raped in the alley because of the way you dress."

That is 15-year-old Martha. The same one who's writing to the DA about the wee-wee. Chelsea is the same way. "So if you want to fight me bitch, I am ready. I can kick your ass any day, you fucking pussy. You are so fucking fucked up."

Ms. Hankel closed out with a recap of her assertions with more examples then stated:

Ms. Hankel: Because the state's case is so weak, they are going to try to put on evidence just to make you dislike my client. What can we find to make you dislike my client? You may not like my client or you may like him just fine. You may think there are certain things in his life you don't like, you don't appreciate or agree with. But he did not molest three girls.

With that done the battle lines were clear and I felt a little better. I thought Ms. Hankel did a good job, but the whole "plan" defense was worrisome. Also of concern was Juror No. 12, Larry Petrisky, who was a clerk in the Mammoth Superior Court of Mono County.

The Clerk: Your Honor, is Juror No. 12 available to go back to work if we don't have to be here until 9:30 in the morning?

The Court: Yes.

The Clerk: Can he go to work at 8:30?

The Court: Any problem with you?

Mr. Graham: No.

Ms. Hankel: No.

The Court: If we are back in the area of the library which is serving as my chambers for the time being, make certain there are no conversations occurring in the hallway. Everything occurs behind closed doors. And of course, clerking. Alise and Karen both will be careful as will reporter and Bailiff. Okay?

Ms. Hankel: Okay, thank you.

Is it just me or is this kind of crazy? It's a small town and this case was the subject of much discussion. I didn't understand how a clerk could be in the jury, but Ms. Hankel said "relax" and so I did … for a bit.

NINETEEN

Suddenly, the reality set in and it was Monday morning November 2nd, 2009. The trial was underway and Martha was taking the stand first

Q. by Mr. Graham: Good morning, Martha.

A. by Martha Guthrie: Good morning.

Q. Do you want to be here today?

A. Not really.

Mr. Graham then went through the basics as he saw them, such as Martha having lived in Nevada City, Chalfant, and Bishop. He discussed with her the fact that Martha said she was touched inappropriately by me on her "boobs and vagina" . Martha was then asked about me yelling and hitting her and the ever present "if you tell anybody, I will kill you." These were all the same things she had said before. Then, Mr. Graham led her through the different locations where Martha alleged the touchings occurred, Bishop, Chalfant, LA. This is where it got interesting.

Q. by Mr. Graham: Now at the Bishop location, can you describe that location?

A. It was a trailer in a trailer park.

Q. And was there a particular location, or room, or place inside that trailer or places where that touching occurred?

A. Yes.

Q. Where was that?

A. In his bedroom and in the living room.

Now this is the first time Martha had said my bedroom in the Bishop trailer and Mr. Graham just blew through it. Ms. Hankel and I get it though, Chelsea has said it happened only in my bedroom and Martha said only on the couch, so this was already suspect in my mind. I would have been charged for the bedroom activities had that issue been raised previously.

Q. by Mr. Graham: Going to the Chalfant location. Can you describe what that is?
A. It is a trailer.
Q. And are there any particular places in that trailer where sexual touchings occurred?
A. Yes.
Q. Where was that?
A. In the living room and my mom's bedroom.
Q. And again, can you tell the jury where in the Bishop trailer he did any kind of sexual touching to you?
A. In his bedroom and the living room.

Martha then described me touching her boobs and her vagina more than one time in the living room on the couch in the Bishop trailer.

Q. by Mr. Graham: Do you remember the first time he touched you in the Bishop trailer sexually?
A. Yes.
Q. Could you tell us what you were doing before that started?
A. Me and my mom and Mike were laying down watching a movie. And I was laying, like sideways, next to my mom. And then he reached down and put his hand down my pants.
Q. And which part of your body did he touch?
A. My butt.
Q. And your mom was present, correct?
A. Yes.
Q. Did she see what happened?
A. I don't think she saw that part.

Martha then went on to describe another time I supposedly woke her up on the couch and fondled her and then she was asked:

Q. by Mr. Graham: Can you recall any other incidents that occurred on the couch in the Bishop trailer? Can you think back to any other times when he touched you?
A. No.
Q. You said there were touchings in the bedroom; is that correct?
A. Yes.
Q. How many events or occasions do you believe you were touched in his bedroom?

A. Just a couple, I think, that was actually in his bedroom. I don't remember though.

Q. And can you think back to an occasion when he touched you in his bedroom? Can you think back and can you describe for the jury the event or events?

A. He just did the same thing he did on the couch when he was rubbing my vagina and my body with his hands.

So far, Martha was only able to describe a few occasions and that was without any specific details. I was getting restless for Ms. Hankel's cross-examination, even though we were just getting started. Ms. Hankel and I were passing notes back and forth at our defense table and I was cautiously optimistic.

Q. by Mr. Graham: Regarding the sexual touching of his hands touching your boobs, his hand touching your vagina, how often did those kind of things happen?

A. Every day.

Q. Did he ever make any statements to you about what he would do to you if you were to tell anyone about what he was doing to you? I am going to the Bishop trailer.

A. Not at the Bishop trailer. He didn't say anything that I remember.

Q. Can you remember any other specific events or incidents in the Bishop trailer where he sexually touched you where you can describe for the jury here how this event happened? Do you remember anything else.

A. No.

Q. Do you know whether or not – during your time in the Bishop trailer, do you know whether or not Mr. Harris was touching your sister Chelsea in a sexual way.

A. I don't – I don't know.

Q. And did you, when you were living in the Bishop trailer, did you speak with your sister, Chelsea, about what was happening to you?

A. No, I didn't.

Q. In the Bishop trailer, when you were living there, did you tell any friends about what Mike was doing to you?

A. No.

Q. Now when you were 10 or 11 years old living in this trailer, did you feel that you could trust your mom? Did you trust her?

A. I don't trust my mom.

Q. Back at that time you were living in the trailer with her and Mike, did you feel enough trust with her to go and tell her about what Mike was doing to you sexually?

A. No.

Q. In the Bishop trailer, when you were approximately 10 or 11 years old, did you ever see Mike's penis? Do you recall seeing his penis when you were living there?

A. No, I don't recall.

Q. Do you recall him ever doing anything with his penis to you or your body when you were living in the Bishop trailer?

A. Yes, I remember.

Q. Can you recall an event when you lived in the Bishop trailer as you sit there now?

A. He made me give him a blow job.

Q. Do you recall whether you mentioned what you just mentioned at the preliminary hearing?

A. No, I don't remember.

Q. Do you remember ever telling anybody that at the Bishop trailer you gave Mike a blowjob in the Bishop trailer?

A. I don't recall saying that but afterwards I remember that he did do that.

Q. I am going right to the time when you moved into the Chalfant trailer. At that time, did you want to tell anybody about what Mike was doing to you sexually? Did you want to tell anybody?

A. Yes, I wanted to.

Q. Up to the time when you moved into the Chalfant trailer, do you recall the people you told about what Mike was doing to you sexually?

A. I just told my mom.

Q. When did you tell your mom? Was it in the Bishop trailer or when you were in the Chalfant trailer?

A. It was in the Chalfant trailer when we first told her.

Q. But prior to moving to the Chalfant trailer, tell us the people or person that you told about what Mike was doing to you sexually.

A. Nobody but my sister.

Wasn't it just a bit ago when Martha said no, she hadn't spoken with her sister at the Bishop trailer? I was getting angry.

Q. by Mr. Graham: Tell us about that day you told your mom.

A. Mike got in trouble for touching another girl, one of my friends that came over that lived across the street from us. He was in jail and my mom asked us if he ever touched me and my sister and that is when we told her.

Q. When you say "we", are you saying you were with your sister Chelsea and told her?

A. Yes, I was with my sister.

Q. And what was your mother's response?

A. That he wouldn't do anything like that.

Q. Did she believe you?

A. No.

Martha next told of sexual touchings in her mom's bedroom and the living room; "And a couple of times he tried to stick his penis in my vagina." This one time, more than one time overbroad generalization was going to be hard to fight against. How do you present an alibi to an unknown event? It was impossible to prove a negative. Then came this:

Q. by Mr. Graham: Same location [mom's bedroom], how many times did he touch his hand or hands to your vagina? Did it happen one time or more than one time?

A. More than one time.

Q. Can you tell us how often that would occur?

A. Every day.

Q. Regarding his penis and your vagina, what did he do?

A. He tried to stick it in.

Q. How many different events did Mike try to stick his penis in your vagina in your mom's bedroom in the Chalfant trailer when you were under 14?

A. I don't know.

Q. Was it more than one time?

A. More than one time.

Q. Do you recall if your sister observed this incident where he tried – where he put his penis inside your vagina and it hurt?

A. No.

Q. [on the bed, Chalfant] After he got your pants and underwear off, what is the very next thing he did?

A. He touched my vagina with his hand.

Q. Did he do anything with his fingers to your vagina?

A. He fingered me.

Q. When you say fingered you, what do you mean?

A. He put his fingers inside of my vagina and started going in and out.

So there you have it, penis and fingers in and out, approximately 11 years old, certainly there should be some physical damage that can be shown. We will see.

Q. by Mr. Graham: How many times did he move his finger or fingers in and out of you? Do you remember that?

A. More than one time.

Q. After he finished putting his finger inside of you what did he do next?

A. Tried to put his penis inside of me.

Q. When you say he tried to put his penis inside of you, did you feel his penis actually go inside of you?

A. It didn't go all the way in yet.

Q. Can you tell us how far it went inside as far as – hold up a measurement, use your fingers if you want.
Mr. Graham: May the record reflect the witness is holding up her thumb and forefinger indicating approximately an inch and a half, Judge?
The Court: Yes, that is fine.
Q. by Mr. Graham: How often would he put his penis on your vagina and just rub your vagina with his penis?
A. Like every other day or every three days or something. I don't know. I wasn't keeping count.
Q. Did he ever do anything with his mouth to you in your mom's bedroom at the Chalfant trailer?
A. Yes.
Q. What did he do with his mouth to you sexually?
A. He made out with me, he kissed my boobs, and he licked my vagina with his tongue.
Q. Did he do this one time or more than one time?
A. More than one time.
Q. At any time when you were under 14 at this Chalfant trailer, did Mike ever make any statements to you about what he would do if you were to disclose to anybody or tell anybody about what he was doing to you sexually?
A. He said he would kill us.
Q. He used the word "us" or "you"?
A. Me. Sorry. He would kill me.
Q. Did you go down to Orange County to his dad's house with anybody else besides Mike?
A. No.
Q. And in what room of this, his dad's house, did this incident occur?
A. In the living room.
Q. Could you tell us what you were doing just before this incident occurred?
A. Watching a TV show.
Q. How did this incident start?
A. As soon as his dad went to bed he came over to my side of the couch.
Q. What was the first thing he did?
A. Took off my clothes.
Q. What happened next?
A. He took off his clothes and then he put his penis inside my vagina all the way.
Q. Did you tell anyone after this event in Orange County at his dad's house?
A. No I didn't. I told my sister.

Q. How long after that event did you tell your sister?
A. When I got back from Orange County. I think it was two days later.
Q. Did you try to say anything to your mom about what happened?
A. No, because I knew she wasn't going to listen.
Correct me if I'm wrong, but during the interview with Det. Rutkowski, didn't Martha say she threatened to tell her mom while we were driving back and then said she told her mom too? Anyway…
Q. by Mr. Graham: I want to go back to the point in time when you told the first person that you told about what Mike was doing to you sexually. Do you recall who that is, who that person was?
A. My sister.
Q. Other than your sister who was an outside person you told about what Mike had done to you sexually?
A. Alex.
Q. Did you and your sister at any time prior to telling Alex get together and communicate with each other and come up with a plan to make this whole thing up against Mike?
A. No.
Q. How many times did you try and tell your mom about what Mike had done to you sexually?
A. You know, I tried that once.
Q. Did you ever make any complaints that got CPS, Child Protective Services, involved in your family – that you believed got CPS involved in your family?
A. Yes.
Q. When was that?
A. I was in the sixth grade.
Q. Where were you living?
A. Chalfant.
Q. And what made you want to get CPS involved?
A. Mike was verbally abusing me, he stopped us in the Field road on the way to the bus stop because we were talking to one of our guy friends. And he started yelling at us. So we didn't want to go home, and our friend called the CPS on him.
Q. Do you recall the CPS worker that showed up in response?
A. Alex.
Q. And what did you tell Alex happened?
A. That we were scared to go home because Mike was really angry that day and was verbally abusing us.
Q. Did you tell Alex about the sexual abuse that had been occurring in the house?

A. No.

Q. Why not?

A. Because of what Mike told me if I told anyone.

Q. Now you made your first outside disclosure about sexual abuse to Alex Ellis. Approximately when was that? What month and what year?

A. Two months. As soon as I got into foster care I was 15. So I think that was 2007.

Q. What made you feel that it was okay to tell about the sexual abuse?

A. My sister is the one who told Alex first, and Alex was taking me to a foster home. And she told me in the car that my sister told about what Mike was doing to you guys. Then she asked if it was true and I told her, yes, it was.

Q. Did your sister tell you – prior to telling Alex Ellis about your abuse – did your sister tell you that she had disclosed the sexual abuse by Mike Harris?

A. No, she didn't tell me, I found out by Alex Ellis.

Q. Let me be clear. When you first heard from Alex your sister had disclosed what went through your mind?

A. I just – I can't believe – I didn't know she was going to do that.

Q. Before you heard from Alex Ellis that your sister had disclosed, did you want to tell somebody on the outside what had been occurring as far as sexual abuse from Mike Harris?

A. Yes, I wanted to tell somebody.

Q. Yet why didn't you?

A. Because I was scared.

Q. After you spoke to Alex Ellis in the car briefly, when was the next time you spoke to Alex Ellis about the sexual abuse of Mike Harris?

A. When the courts gave me a counselor.

Q. What was the counselor's name?

A. Mike Hultz.

Q. Do you recall an incident that was investigated in 2003 involving Raeanna?

A. Yes.

Q. And who was in the residence, the Chalfant residence, who was in the residence at the time?

A. Me, my sister, Raeanna, and Mike.

Q. What happened?

A. We were lying down and Mike came and laid down next to Raeanna. And then he started like giving her a back massage, and then he put his hand down her pants.

Q. Do you remember what kind of lower clothing she was wearing?

A. She had jeans.

Mr. Graham them concluded his direct examination of Martha with some questions going one by one through each count asking if it happened one time or more than one time. Martha always responded "more than one time" to each count. Next up, after the lunch break, was Ms. Hankel, and boy was I excited. Ms. Hankel dug right in and asked Martha like 25 rapid fire questions, to which Martha repeatedly replied, "I don't remember." Then Ms. Hankel asked:

Q. by Ms. Hankel: Can you describe how Mike gave Raeanna that back rub?
A. I don't remember how he gave her the back rub.
Q. But you remember that he gave her the back rub?
A. Yeah.
Q. And she was laying on her stomach on the bed?
A. Yeah. She was laying on her stomach.
Q. And you testified that she had jeans on?
A. Yes.
Q. You said that you saw my client put his hand down Raeanna's pants?
A. Yes.
Q. Did he do that while he was rubbing her back?
A. Yes.
Q. Did he out his hand down the back of her pants?
A. Yes.
Q. Do you remember she had long pants on?
A. Yes, she was wearing jeans, long jeans.
Q. Some time after that, did you hear that my client had inappropriately touched Raeanna Davenport?
A. Yes.
Q. Who told you that?
A. My mom did because the cops came.

Martha just got through saying how she saw it happen and now she is saying she found out about it from her mom, "Because the cops came." What about the whole long pants issue, too? Man, I was peeved.

Q. by Ms. Hankel: Do you remember when CPS came and talked to you in school about that?
A. Yes, I remember when they came to my school.
Q. And do you remember you told them that nothing happened?
A. No, I don't remember telling them that.
Q. What do you remember telling them?
A. I don't remember everything we talked about?

Q. Who do you remember coming out to talk to you?
A. Alex Ellis.
Q. Did Rose Douglas come and talk to you?
A. Well, she also did come to talk to us.

Martha was then asked a series of questions related to whether or not she had talked with her friends about her mom being mean and not allowing her to date. She finished this discussion by asking about the twins' boyfriends.

Q. by Ms. Hankel: Do you remember talking to Leif and Tyler at the same time with Chelsea about how mean your mom was?
A. Yes.
Q. And do you remember telling them you wanted to come up with a plan to get out of your mom's house?
A. No.
Q. Do you remember whether you and Chelsea were sneaking out of your mom's house at midnight to go meet with Tyler Clarke and Leif Medrud?
A. Yes
Q. And telling the boys you wanted to get out of your mom's house?
A. Yes.
Q. And do you remember telling the boys way back, six weeks before Chelsea ran away, that Mike Harris was raping you and that's why you needed to get out of the house?
A. I don't remember telling them that.
Q. When you spoke to Det. Rutowski do you remember telling him that you had only told Mike Hultz about Mike Harris molesting you?
A. He already knew. We told Alex because Alex was there.
Q. Did you tell him that you told Leif Medrud.
A. I don't think so.
Q. Do you remember telling the district attorney that you didn't tell any friends?
A. Yes.
Q. Do you remember telling anyone that Steve Cupp was a child molestor?
A. Yes.
Q. Do you think that is a pretty serious thing to call somebody?
A. Yes. Because if you know that they are and you know that they have done it to one of your friends, yes.
Q. When you told Alex Ellis that Steve Cupp was a child molester, what did you base that on?
A. What my friend's mom and my friend told me.

Q. Do you remember testifying at the preliminary hearing in this case?
A. Yes.
Q. Do you remember being asked whether or not you had ever given Mike Harris a blow job when you were under 14?
A. Yes.
Q. And do you remember saying "No, I never did that."
A. Yes. Yes. I remember saying that.
Q. Do you remember that you were asked if he ever tried to get you to perform one on him?
A. Yes. I remember that.
Q. Do you remember your answer was "no"?
A. Yes, I remember.
Q. And do you remember being asked if, at any point in time before you were 14, did you ever put your mouth on his penis?
A. Yes, I remember.
Q. And what was your answer?
A. No, but I remember now.
Q. Did you ever tell Det. Rutowski in August of 2007 that you had given Mike Harris a blowjob?
A. I don't remember.
Q. Do you remember testifying at the preliminary hearing that you never saw Mike Harris' penis while you were in the Bishop trailer?
A. Yes.
Q. Do you remember when Randy Gephart [at the prelim] asked at any time whether you were being touched in the couch in Bishop – we're talking about these two different kinds of touching here – did you ever tell anyone including your sister, about what was happening to you?
A. I told my sister but nobody else.
Q. Do you remember telling Det. Rutowski at the interview that the very first time that Mike put his penis in you and you had intercourse was in Los Angeles at his dad's house?
A. Yes, I remember that.
Q. When Chelsea ran away, you didn't agree with her decision to run away, did you?
A. No. I didn't want her to go.
Q. And did you try to talk her out of it?
A. Yes, I did.
Q. And did you agree with her plan to tell CPS that Mike Harris was molesting her?
A. I didn't know she was going to do that.

Q. Before she ran away, she never gave you a journal and told you to keep it secret, did she?
A. I don't remember that.
Q. Did she ever give you a journal and tell you to make sure nobody else looked at it?
A. Yes, I remember that. She did.
Q. Did you ever read the notebook?
A. I am sure I did read it.
Q. Do you remember anything in the notebook?
A. No.
Q. How many times did you talk to Alex Ellis about the molestation?
A. Whenever she asked about it.
Q. Did you tell her about being molested by Mike Harris before you toke Mike Hultz?
A. Yes.
Q. Do you remember when you were removed from the Jackson home?
A. Yes, I remember.
Q. Do you remember talking to CPS and telling them that Michelle Jackson had choked you after you had been removed from the Jackson home?
A. This was while I was in the home she choked me. I was sitting at the kitchen table.
Q. Do you remember talking to CPS about that after you had been removed from the Jackson home?
A. Yes, I think I talked to Alex about it.

Obviously, Alex Ellis played a major role in CPS with the Guthrie twins. It was the end of the day and I was ready for more. I felt the jury was attentive and getting the inconsistencies, as most were taking notes. Martha conveniently couldn't remember all the major events which happened to her, but could remember that during the Raeanna incident that we were eating mac and cheese and that Raeanna had on long pants. Of course, we know from the prelim that Raeanna said she was wearing shorts. Even more interesting is that Martha said the first time I touched her, I reached down her pants and touched her butt and Martha also said that's what I did to Raeanna in an amazingly similar description.

TWENTY

After a long commute to Independence and back, I was ready for day two of my trial. Things got started with a mini §402 hearing related to Mr. Graham's desire to present evidence of sexual abuse after the age of 14, even though he didn't charge those crimes.

Ms. Hankel objected, but failed to brief the issue or present a motion in limine. Judge DeVore stated that Evid. Code §1103 made propensity evidence legal, which would otherwise be illegal under §1101. Ms. Hankel agreed but said it was still subject to Evid. Code §358. Judge DeVore referenced People v. Yovanov, (1999) 69 Cal.App.4th 392, which also involved twins and §1108 evidence of past uncharged acts against the same victims. In the Yovanov case, the court was concerned that there is a consideration that the jury may be inclined to punish the defendant for acts that were not charged and were not subject to proof beyond a reasonable doubt. Ms. Hankel had no argument, so I was toast. Judge DeVore ruled the evidence admissible with a limiting instruction CALCRIM No. 1191. So off we went to conclude cross-examination.

Q. by Ms. Hankel: Did Alex Ellis give you a copy of your testimony from the preliminary hearing for you to look at?

A. Yes.

Q. Did it help you to remember what you said at the prelim?

A. Yes.

Q. Did you sneak out and drink alcohol when you were at the Lindsay's foster care?
A. I did.
Q. You never saw Mr. Harris sexually touch Chelsea in the Bishop trailer, did you?
A. No.
Q. And you never saw Mr. Harris sexually touch Chelsea in the Chalfant trailer?
A. No.
Q. And you never saw Mr. Harris sexually touch Chelsea in any other location, did you?
A. No, I don't think so.
Q. And you never saw Chelsea give Mr. Harris a blowjob?
A. No.
Q. And you never saw Chelsea touch Mr. Harris' penis?
A. No – yes, I have.
Q. Do you remember talking about – Do you remember talking at the prelim? Do you remember testifying about what you saw in Nevada City?
A. Yes.
Q. You didn't testify at the prelim about seeing Chelsea with her head on Mr. Harris' penis, did you?
A. No, I didn't.
Q. Why not?
A. I don't know. Because I was young then. I was scared to say everything. It is not that easy.
Q. That prelim was in September of 2007, right?
A. Sure.
Q. A little more than two years ago?
A. Yeah.
Q. Do you remember what you said about what you saw in Nevada City?
A. No, I don't.
Q. What is your testimony today about what you saw?
A. That my mom was giving Mike Harris a blowjob and he put my sister's hand on his penis. That is what he did in Nevada City.

Ms. Hankel then got Martha to admit that while she said I touched her in the Bishop trailer, the Chalfant trailer, and at my dad's house; she was never touched any place else, including at the park, in the car, somewhere along the road while we drove somewhere, nor in my travel trailer parked on Karri's property, or in the trailer park in Bishop. Nowhere else.

Q. by Ms. Hankel: Do you remember telling Det. Rutowski that you didn't know Chelsea had ever had sexual intercourse with Mike?

A. Yes, I remember that.

Q. Do you remember telling CPS that you did not want to be placed in the same foster care home with Chelsea?

A. Yes, I remember that. We weren't doing so well at the time.

Q. Do you remember telling Alex Ellis?

A. Yes, I remember. That is CPS.

Now it was time for Mr. Graham to conclude his presentation with a redirect examination. Things started off with the Evid Code §1108 limiting instruction discussing the different burdens of proof that being a lesser burden of proof for the §1108 evidence, simple a preponderance of evidence was required to allow the evidence to be considered.

The Court: Evidence of another sexual offense is not sufficient alone to find the defendant guilty of the charged sexual offenses or any of them. The People must still prove each charge and allegation of the information beyond a reasonable doubt.

Mr. Graham then began his questioning of Martha by going into sexual abuse which occurred after she turned 14.

Q. by Mr. Graham: Okay. After you turned 14 did Mike continue to touch you sexually?

A. Yes.

Martha then said I touched her boobs and vagina more than one time in the Chalfant residence. She did not, however, provide any details of the touchings.

Q. by Mr. Graham: You stated Chelsea ran away on June 26th, 2007; is that correct?

A. Yes.

Q. Did you know what she was going to do at that time just prior to her actually running away?

A. I didn't know exactly everything she was going to do. She just said I am going to – well I knew she was going to run away. So yeah, I did know.

Q. Prior to her running away, did you and Chelsea ever sit down and talk about a plan together to get Mike Harris in some form or fashion?

A. No. Why would we want to put ourselves through all this stuff?

Q. When you spoke to Ms. Ellis, had you planned with Chelsea or planned in your mind to just disclose to Alex Ellis just a bit about what Mike had done?

A. No, we didn't plan any of this.

Q. Have you ever told anyone that this didn't happen, the sexual abuse didn't happen?

A. When I was younger I guess.

Q. Who did you tell?

A. Some of my friends because they said they seen signs and I said "No, he is not doing anything."
Q. Why would you tell them that?
A. Because I was scared. I wasn't – I just didn't think I should tell them. I didn't know what to do.

Martha was then asked a few more questions by Ms. Hankel during re-cross, but she only pointed out that Martha told Det. Rutowski that the last sexual touching was at my dad's house when she wasn't even 14. Ms. Hankel did, however, raise the issue of why the sexual abuse (SART) physical exam didn't occur for more than six months after my arrest if the girls had said they were being raped right up until the time Chelsea ran away.

During Martha's testimony, Ms. Hankel failed to cross-examine her completely in regards to the substantial contradictions and inconsistencies of Martha's prior statements and testimony. In addition, Ms. Hankel failed to confront Martha with the relevant CPS documents and properly introduce them. The CPS documents went to the heart of Martha's prevarications.

Ms. Hankel and I continued to debate the strategy she wanted to employ at trial, name the "plan" defense, which I argued relied on theory instead of fact. She wanted to shoehorn facts into her theory instead of developing theory and strategy from actual facts. Any facts which did not conform to Ms. Hankel's theory, she wanted to ignore. She also insisted on asserting that Chelsea had a plan to get out of her mother's home by reporting sexual abuse by me.

I had given Ms. Hankel evidence that showed that the girls did not have a plan. This was well before trial began, even before the hiring of an investigator. Ms. Hankel did not want to pursue any other defense than the one where the girls had a plan to get out of their mother's home. Ms. Hankel did have a fallback theory of reasonable doubt as a catchall defense. When in doubt, raise reasonable doubt as a defense, right? These two strategies were at odds with one another in actuality. Ms. Hankel wanted to say they had a plan and then she wanted to use suggestibility to show reasonable doubt. It seemed oxymoronic, because on the one hand they had a plan and on the other they were led into the claims.

The deficiency of Ms. Hankel's "plan" defense was showcased almost immediately when Martha testified that she did not plan any of this. Compounding the deficiency of the "plan" defense was the lack of coherent strategy to outline times and dates relative to the sequence of events, which either did or didn't demonstrate the "plan". I posited that a timeline would actually have shown there was no plan and that there wasn't even consistent or credible evidence that the girls had ever disclosed sexual abuse other than in response to queries from authorities. For example, Martha testified that she did not know that Chelsea had been raped or have been having intercourse with me, even though Chelsea said that Martha had seen her 10-20 times being raped when Martha purportedly walked in on me and Chelsea. Ms. Hankel had this direct and credible evidence of a major contradiction, which showed a false statement of allegation, but Ms. Hankel chose to ignore this and persist in accepting the premise that the girls had a plan. This instead of the "escalation" of allegations reality of the girls' statements to authorities escalating in seriousness to suit their needs.

I had suggested to Ms. Hankel that if the girls had a plan, then why all the contradictions and confusion over how it was carried out? Ms. Hankel did not press the issue with Martha that, if she was saying there was no "plan" then Ms. Hankel should have brought to the fore evidence of "suggestibility" that she was planning on using during my case-in-chief. Ms. Hankel did not want to ask Martha about the specific events surrounding Chelsea's running away incident, which preceded any disclosures of any type of abuse by either me or Kerri. I wanted Ms. Hankel to ask Martha about her best friend Shaylynn Ellis' involvement in this period of time, including the locating of Chelsea at her boyfriend's house.

I also wanted Ms. Hankel to ask Martha about the argument between Chelsea and her mom the night before Chelsea ran away, the personal items Chelsea left behind and their intrinsic value and other general questions which would have showed the girls had no "plan", nor that Chelsea even planned to run away on that night. Ms. Hankel had not even investigated these issues despite my repeated requests. I specifically asked Ms. Hankel to talk to Shaylynn Ellis and subpoena the sheriff's log from 6/28/07 related to the events involved in the locating of Chelsea before any claims of abuse were made. Martha was a prime witness, as was Shaylynn Ellis. Ms. Hankel knew that Kerri, with the help of Shaylynn Ellis, located Chelsea and this fact was of paramount importance, because it would show several witnesses were outright lying, since Chelsea never called the CPS or the police while a runaway. Martha knew this and wasn't asked about it.

There simply was no plan. There was only an escalation of accusations based on queries from authorities. The allegations began with verbal abuse, then escalated to physical abuse and finally sexual abuse when all else failed. Ms. Hankel never confronted Martha with her CPS records that said she never called CPS on the day she was removed from Kerri's house on 7/16/07. This line of questioning would have been important in light of the fact there were major discrepancies in the documentation and the veracity of the CPS records themselves, which needed to be tested. Ms. Hankel told me to stop being a conspiratorial theorist. Martha was not asked about the "oh those boys don't know anything" statement made to Det. Rutowski by Chelsea in May of 2008.

In fact, Ms. Hankel did not want to impugn "those boys" (Leif, Tyler, and Jordan) since their combined evidence of a plan was crucial to Ms. Hankel's misguided defense strategy. Why was Ms. Hankel using the enemy to try and help me? It was stupidity in my opinion. I felt it was sabotage. Ms. Hankel told me to get over it. If Ms. Hankel would have questioned Martha on this issue specifically, Martha would have said she never told them anything. The notes and other documentation would have shown she never told "those boys" anything until after her purported disclosure to Alex Ellis. Martha was specifically asked, "Who did you tell?" Her initial response was nobody, then she said her mom, then she added her sister and the dialogue in court seemed leading, yet Martha never mentioned telling "those boys" anything. I desperately wanted Ms. Hankel to ask Martha why she would need to tell her sister if her sister was a witness to the abuse? Moreover, why would Martha tell her sister if I had threatened to kill her if she told anybody? Isn't her sister anybody? And then if she felt okay to tell her sister, why not somebody else, like Shaylynn or Michelle? I wanted Ms. Hankel to ask her why she needed to tell her sister if they were both being forced to watch sex and they both said they told their mom about the abuse together? I wanted Ms. Hankel to focus on the irrationality of Martha's statement that she told her mom and her sister who were allegedly participating in the abuse. Remember Martha's initial response was she told nobody.

Now let's compare all that with the fact of the lack of statements by Martha that she told her friends who were now ready to testify they knew about the abuse for some time because the girls had told them so. Ms. Hankel's opinion was that all the witnesses and CPS workers and documents couldn't conspire to "get me". Yet I countered that they all couldn't have kept a secret either. I said it was as it appeared, nothing happened. Ms. Hankel was not pursuing the truth and was apparently content to bolster her theory regardless of the facts coming out of trial. These already known facts and the facts coming out at trial were casting serious doubt on Ms. Hankel's hypothesis.

Of special import was the fact that Mr. Gephart and then Ms. Hankel knew of the girls' best friend, Shaylynn Ellis, and failed to talk to her, much less ask Martha questions about her involvement in Martha's life since 4th grade. A proper investigation would have revealed I had extensive interaction with Shaylynn and a thorough examination of Martha would have revealed I drove the girls to numerous activities.

Neither Shaylynn nor her mother had any concerns about me or my behavior and that should have come out at trial. Ms. Hankel did not question Martha about Michelle and Trish Jackson regarding the same issues, such as sleepovers and babysitting Michelle when Trish and her husband Rick went out. We knew them since the 4th grade, too. The Jacksons heard no report of any type of abuse at home. These interrogatories would have been pivotal to my defense, especially when combined with a thorough impeachment of the girls' "other friends'" testimony.

Ms. Hankel never asked Martha about the numerous trips to LA and elsewhere, the rape allegation at my dad's house and Martha's statement to Det. Rutowski that she told her mom about the rape in LA when she got home. Ms. Hankel also did not ask Martha about the several rapes that she described in her email to Todd. Martha initially wrote to Mr. Graham in an email that she was raped in her mother's bedroom, but at the prelim she said the rapes occurred in her bedroom. These rape allegations that were never charged as rape were important in testing Martha's veracity. Ms. Hankel never challenged Martha in this area. Remember that Martha could describe a mac and cheese dinner, yet was utterly confused on this major area of interest.

I fully expected Kerri to testify. She was in the courthouse lobby every day waiting to be called. Her testimony, combined with Martha's statements about telling her mom at least two times, seemed to be to be among the most critical disputed facts in this case. Kerri had provided handwritten notes between the girls and their friends, and in one Martha was asked, "What do you want to do over the summer?" and Martha replied, "Go to Disneyland and go shopping." This note was from late in the school year of 2007. The activities in Southern California were something we had been doing since 2004. This note Martha swapped with her friend belied any plan that Martha had to disclose abuse in order to be removed from her home and was contemporaneous to the purported disclosure to "those boys."

Ms. Hankel also failed to press Martha about the choking incident at the Jackson's foster home, the partying at the Lindsay's foster home, Martha's alcohol and pot use, and the inference that Martha's behavior in CPS custody and care was decidedly different than that in her mother's home. Martha had a reason to be out of her mother's home, a reason based on freedom to act irresponsibly, and this reward was integral to my assertion that the accusations were the result of escalating disclosures to authorities based on repeated questioning. Without making the allegations, Martha's new found freedom would have been at risk.

Ms. Hankel also never pressed Martha about calling her dad in Coloma, CA, before and after Chelsea's move to Bishop, including details about the move itself. CPS records show that Martha knew how to call her dad and did in fact call him on several occasions, after the alleged abuse began. Ms. Hankel never asked Martha about the fact that after Chelsea came to live in Bishop and the girls were supposedly talking to each other about sexual abuse they never told their dad anything was wrong when they called him. In the spring of 2003, the girls' dad, Dale Guthrie, and their grandma, Sharon Cole, along with Dale's sister, came to visit Martha and Chelsea privately in Bishop. They came to explain that Dale was dying and he was moving to Michigan to live with Mrs. Cole. Ms. Hankel knew all this with Mrs. Cole in the audience at court no less and yet she didn't ask Martha why she didn't seek help from her dad and family.

I took Martha and Chelsea to LA several times, and on more than one occasion they were dropped off at Kerri's dad's house for several days at a time. Ms. Hankel failed to elicit this testimony or ask Martha why she didn't seek his help. Ms. Hankel never asked Martha to describe anything she may have told her friend, Jessikah Luffman or Jessikah's mom, Gina. This was another important lapse in Ms. Hankel's judgment in my opinion, because there was a major discrepancy between Martha's statement to Det. Rutowski that she told Jessikah about the alleged abuse only after reporting it to Alex contrasted by Jessikah's statement to my defense investigator, Mr. Morganstein, that Martha's disclosure occurred more than a year before Martha told Alex Ellis.

Gina Luffman, Jessikah's mom, told Mr. Morganstein that she knew for a year or two about the sexual abuse but did nothing to report it herself, telling him that she had been a victim of sexual abuse in the past and that is why she kept it a secret. Martha wasn't asked to explain why or how all of her friends had kept her secret that she said she never told them about. It wasn't logical in perspective and Ms. Hankel was missing important points I wanted to raise. Gina Luffman also confided to Mr. Morganstein that Martha and Chelsea were mad at me for moving out and leaving them to fend for themselves and deal with their mom's erratic behavior alone. Ms. Hankel wanted nothing to do with my strategy choices.

Martha claimed her mom had physically and emotionally abused her, but Ms. Hankel left that alone as well. I was pretty frustrated, but I just kept sending her notes in the hopes that some of it might rub off. Ms. Hankel not only didn't ask Martha important questions, but was caught off guard when Martha answered a question by asking rhetorically, "Why would I want to go through all this?" Why indeed. Ms. Hankel and I had discussed this motive issue and she understood the reward as a motive component to all of this, yet she failed to segue into the "why indeed" line of questioning. She should have asked, "How could you not go through all of this?" Perhaps the girls got in too deep and had no way to backtrack. Ms. Hankel should have explored this area in light of Kathleen Traynor's statements. Ms. Hankel should have asked Martha about her email to Todd and why did you send all those emails to Todd in which you complained that "I don't think I can go through with this, I just want it to be over." What rewards were associated with testifying vs. repercussions if she didn't testify.

Ms. Hankel should have asked Martha if I was even living or visiting at the Chalfant trailer in 2007 at any time. Ms. Hankel should have pursued a lack of corroboration line of questioning, even though corroboration is not required in a §2838(a) case. It's a he said/she said situation. Both girls had said that they had been seen by each other, but never once did they validate that claim. What Martha saw was a major issue worthy of inquiry. Ms. Hankel should have set up a veracity test by asking each for verification or corroboration. Ms. Hankel failed to confront and cross-examine Martha effective and by failing to exploit the evidence there was no "plan" she actually fortified the People's case.

TWENTY-ONE

I spent the lunch hour wallowing in my holding cell. I really wanted a radio for some reason. Chelsea was to start her testimony after lunch. I wanted to meet with Ms. Hankel, but she was too busy, which I hoped was a good thing. Chelsea no sooner than took the stand and she was crying but it seemed contrived to me. I mean her being a bald-faced liar and all. But there we were, waiting for her to compose herself. Finally, Mr. Graham was able to ask some perfunctory questions about her age, where she lived, stuff like that.

Mr. Graham then laid out the locations of the alleged molestations in the Bishop trailer, the Chalfant trailer, and the Nevada City house. I was also being charged with the rape of a child under 14. The actual locations alleged were in my bedroom at the Bishop trailer, in Chelsea's bedroom at the Chalfant trailer, and in her mom's bedroom at the Nevada City house. Then Mr. Graham, just as he did with Martha, went through the specifics of the touchings, asking Chelsea:

Q. by Mr. Graham: Was it one time or more than one time?

A. More than one time.

Q. And could you tell us how often these touching type events would happen in the Bishop trailer when you were under 14? Give us an estimate.

A. Maybe twice a week.

Q. What did Mike say to get you to go into his bedroom at the Bishop trailer.

A. "Let's go in my room and watch TV."
Q. And did you immediately go in his room with him or wait for a period of time?
A. I waited a few minutes and then I went in there.
Q. At the time you got up to go into his room, what were you thinking?
A. I was scared.
Q. About what?
A. I didn't know what he was going to do.
Okay, bullshit alert. Why would she be scared to go and watch TV? Mr. Graham saves it a bit:
Q. by Mr. Graham: What happened next?
A. We got in there, and you know there was a bed in there. And then there is only one chair and so, you know, Martha and I would always sit on the bed, and that is when Mike shut the door, and so I was scared.
Q. What happened next?
A. He started touching me.
Q. What happened next?
A. Pretty much he kept doing that for a while, just kissing and touching. Touching was for about five minutes and kissing was for a while. And that is when he started taking off my clothes.
Q. And what did he do to you after he took off your clothes?
A. He tried having sex with me.
Q. What do you mean by that?
A. That is what I meant.
Q. Did you try to do anything to try to resist, either verbally or physically?
A. I said "No I don't want to do this."
Q. And what happened?
A. And so he did what he did. But then my mom came home. He didn't – like I explained last time, he didn't get it in all the way. But he tried.
Q. About how long did you live in the Bishop trailer?
A. Maybe a year.
Q. And during that year, did you tell anyone about the sexual abuse and the touching?
A. No.
Q. Why not?
A. I was scared.
Q. Scared of what?
A. Scared of Mike.
Q. What kind of physical abuse occurred in the Bishop trailer by either your mother or Mr. Harris?

A. Well, hitting definitely. And one thing I will never forget is when he grabbed my by the neck and brought me up to the ceiling and after that threw me on the bed.
Q. What was happening before that?
A. It was Tri-County fair night and my sister had to go to the bathroom. And she peed in a bucket, and Mike got mad because it was in a dog bucket or bowl thing.
Q. Where did he get mad?
A. He got mad at the fairgrounds.
Q. What happened next?
A. He was yelling all the way home.
Q. Were both you and Martha in the car with him?
A. Yes.
Q. What happened next?
A. He started yelling at us, and he got very aggressive and verbally abusive. And then I don't really recall what he said. I don't remember. I just remember him throwing the bucket at my sister and picking me up by the throat.
Q. Based upon what you were seeing at the time, why did he direct his attention and physical abuse towards you instead of your sister?
A. Because I was standing up for my sister.
Q. What did you tell Mike in order to stand up to him?
A. I don't remember. I just remember standing up for my sister, and then that is when Mike grabbed me and said "Do you want to go call CPS?"
Q. What did you say in response to that?
A. I said "No" because I was scared.
Q. Did you know at the time what CPS was?
A. Yes.
Q. Why?
A. Because it had been called before on my mom in different houses.
Q. Do you know whose – had you called CPS – had you called CPS prior to Mike saying that?
A. No.
Q. But you knew what CPS was?
A. Yes.

That's quite a story and it's partially true. I did tell her to call CPS since Kerri had told me about Chelsea's lying and stealing and calling CPS on Kerri when Kerri got mad. I did leave a mark on her neck from her t-shirt, but I never hit her and I never molested her. I did throw the bowl/bucket at the trash can and it bounced off and hit Martha. The girls had lied about peeing in the bucket and then argued with me about it. I got mad. I was wrong. But what is important to note is that this story is the only incident the twins specifically describe in detail and did so in the same way. I put forth that is proof that they are lying about all the other stuff. There is nothing wrong with their memories. Mr. Graham then moved on to the Chalfant trailer and touchings of Chelsea's whole body by my mouth, hands, and penis. He next started asking about me putting my penis inside of Chelsea's vagina and Chelsea asked for a break. She wasn't crying anymore, she was getting impatient, even mad. After the break, Mr. Graham reversed direction and returned to the Bishop trailer incidents and asked:

Q. by Mr. Graham: Did you ever in the Bishop trailer physically resist him?

A. Yes.

Q. Did he ever try to force his penis in your vagina when you were in the Bishop trailer?

A. Yes.

Q. How many times?

A. I don't remember how many times.

Q. Going to the Chalfant trailer, the incident you were describing previously, the specific incident where he was taking off your clothes, you say he tried to put his penis inside you; is that correct?

A. Correct.

Q. How far did he get his penis inside you during this incident you were describing? Can you show us with your fingers the depth, if there was any?

A. I'm not sure how far, but I know it wasn't in all the way, maybe that far (indicating).

Mr. Graham: May the record reflect the witness is holding up her thumb and finger separated with a distance of approximately two and a half inches.

Ms. Hankel: I'd say more like three inches.

The Court: Between two and a half inches and three inches, is that an accurate – what you are trying to indicate with your fingers?

The Witness: Sure.

The Court: Thank you.

Q. by Mr. Graham: Was it one time or more than one time?

A. More than one time.

Q. Can you tell us what happened at the Nevada City residence?

A. We went up there – I don't know if we went up there to see my mom; Mike and my sister, but my mom was there at the house we owned there and we were watching a movie.

Q. Approximately what time was this during the day?
A. It was at night.
Q. Who all was present when this event happened?
A. Mike, my mom, my sister, and me.
Q. Why don't you walk us through this event. What happened?
A. Well, we went in my mom's bedroom and we were going to watch a movie together.
Q. What was the first thing that happened?
A. Me and my sister sat in the two chairs and Mike and my mom laid on the bed.
Q. What happened next?
A. We started watching the movie, and that is when Mike and my mom started having sex.
Q. Describe what they were doing.
A. They were under the covers kissing. That is what I saw: kissing. And that is when he grabbed my hand and made me put it on his penis while it was going in and out of my mom.
Q. When he did that, did you see anything about your mom that told you she knew what was happening at that time?
A. She had to know what was happening because my hand was right there.
Q. Could you tell the jury why you didn't just take your hand away and stop?
A. Because it was holding it on there.
Q. Is there any indication that your sister saw it?
A. I think so, yeah, she was right there.

I think so? I thought they talked about this stuff. Martha said I put Chelsea's hand on my penis while Kerri was giving me a blowjob in the daytime and now Chelsea had said it happened while I was having intercourse with Kerri at night. These girls can remember a bucket incident verbatim, but when it comes to a dramatic sex scene, they fail to corroborate each other. They never mention talking about it so that could have at least got their stories straight. And why would they need to tell their mom about sexual abuse if she was participating in it?

Q. by Mr. Graham: What was the first time Mike made a statement to you if you were to disclose his sexual abuse?
A. What he said?
Q. Yes.
A. He said "If you ever tell anyone, I will hunt you down and kill you."
Q. And do you recall what location you were at when he made that statement?
A. The Bishop trailer.

Q. Tell the jury what you remember him doing to you sexually after you turned 14 when you were living in the Chalfant house?

A. Just like the other times, try to have sex with me. And you know, "It will be okay" you know, even when I said no.

Q. Did Mr. Harris do anything sexually to you at any other location that you can recall after you turned 14?

A. Yes. That was in LA.

Q. And what kind of location was it?

A. In a hotel room.

Q. And who was there at that time?

A. It was me, Mike and my sister.

Q. And what were you doing just before this event happened?

A. I was sleeping.

Q. Describe the room you're in.

A. It was a two-bed bedroom with two beds in it.

Q. And who was sleeping where?

A. My sister was sleeping in one bed and Mike insisted that I sleep in the bed with him.

Q. And what happened?

A. I woke up to him trying to take off my pants.

Q. What happened next?

A. He pulled off my pajamas and underwear, and I tried stopping him, but there was no way, even saying no or doing anything wouldn't stop him.

Q. Your sister was in the room?

A. Correct.

Q. Did you do anything to let her know what was happening?

A. Yeah, I said "Martha." She knew what was happening.

Q. Did you see her or make any observation of her that would make you believe she saw what was happening?

A. Yeah, she turned over and looked at me.

Q. How did she react?

A. She just turned back over because she knew she couldn't do anything.

Q. Before you ran away on June 26th, 2007, as you sit here today, do you remember who you had spoken to about the sexual abuse?

A. Before I ran away?

Q. Yes.

A. Just my sister.

So now, clearly both Martha and Chelsea have said that they told nobody of the alleged abuse except each other. This will become important as Ms. Hankel delves deeper into her "plan" defense abyss.

Q. by Mr. Graham: Had you tried to tell your mom at any point up to June 26 --

A. Yes.

Q. – going back all the years?

A. Yes.

Q. Do you recall approximately when you tried to tell your mom about the sexual abuse?

A. Yes, it was the incident with Raeanna. And he was in jail, and my mom asked, "Did this ever happen to you?" And Martha and I said "yes" and she didn't believe us.

Q. How did that affect your willingness over the course of the next year, up until you ran away, to want to tell her about what happened?

A. I wanted to tell her but I knew she wouldn't believe me.

Q. After you ran away on June 26th, who was the first person that you told there was any kind of sexual abuse going on?

A. My social worker Alex.

Q. And did you tell her about all the abuse that Mike had done to you or something less?

A. Well first I told her about the physical and verbal abuse from him. And then, about – I think it was a few weeks later, she asked me if Mike had ever done anything to me and I said "Yes."

Q. And up to the time you ran away, had you had previous contacts with Alex Ellis?

A. There was one, I think it was when we had that incident with Mike and Raeanna and social services came and talked to us, Rose and Alex.

Q. How many times did you have contact with CPS prior to your disclosure to Alex Ellis?

A. There were a lot of CPS calls.

Q. But you never told CPS or law enforcement for that matter, that Mike had been sexually abusing you; is that correct?

A. Correct.

Q. Chelsea, around the early part of August after you had made some disclosures to Ellen Thompson and John Rutowski, were there any incidents with Mike Harris in Bishop?

A. There was one with him and my mom at the movie theater.

Q. Can you tell us what you were doing just before this incident started?

A. I was waiting at the corner right there at the movie theater.

Q. Who were you with?
A. My boyfriend and my friend.
Q. Who was your boyfriend?
A. Tyler Clarke.
Q. And who was your other friend?
A. Leif.
Q. And what is the first thing that happened that started this incident?
A. I was waiting there at the corner, and Mike yells out the window, "get the fuck out of my town."
Q. How did you respond when Mike said "get the fuck out of my town?"
A. I said leave me alone, go away.
Q. Do you recall what he said in response?
A. He pulled into the parking lot and started yelling at me.
Q. What did he say to you?
A. I don't remember the exact words.
Q. Do you remember the gist of what he was telling you?
A. Pretty much get out of this town. You know, no one wants you here. My mom was yelling stuff, and then Mike was trying to fight my boyfriend and my friend, and then he said I was the one who started the whole thing.
Q. How did that make you feel?
A. About Mike? You know, I was pissed off. And I was scared for my life, because I didn't know what he was going to do.
Q. Did Mike make any physical threats to you during this incident?
A. No, not that I remember.
Q. Did Mike make any physical contact with you during this incident?
A. No.

I did tell her to get the fuck out of town and that she started it because I knew that Martha was just going along with Chelsea's ruse. That wrapped up Mr. Graham's direct examination and it was suddenly time for Ms. Hankel's cross. I prayed it would go better than Martha's did. I had given all my notes related to Chelsea's direct testimony to Ms. Hankel and off she went, raspy voice and all.

Q. by Ms. Hankel: Good afternoon, Ms. Guthrie.
A. by Chelsea: Good afternoon.
Q. Did you talk to Mr. Graham about your testimony today?
A. Yes.
Q. And did you talk to him prior to you testifying at the prelim?
A. Yes.

Q. And did anybody provide you with a copy of the testimony from your preliminary hearing?
A. Yes.
Q. And did you take a look at it before you testified?
A. No, I gave it to my counselor.
Q. Have you reviewed that testimony?
A. Just once.
Q. Do you remember that there were some problems with you and your mom before your mom dropped you off at your dad's to have your dad look after you?
A. Yes.
Q. Do you remember that you and your mom and dad talked to you about stealing?
A. Yes.
Q. Do you remember when, before you went to live with your dad, and you were living in Nevada City, that you had some discussion with CPS?
A. Yes.
Q. And do you remember telling CPS that you liked your home a lot better after your mom's boyfriend, Marty Teichmann, moved out?
A. Yes.
Q. Do you remember telling CPS that your mom's boyfriend was mean and angry?
A. Yes.
Q. Do you remember telling CPS that he hit and yelled?
A. Yes.
Q. Do you remember telling CPS that your mom's boyfriend got mad at Martha and picked her up and threw her in her room?
A. Yes.
Q. And that she bounced off the wall and into her bed?
A. Yes.
Q. Do you remember telling CPS, while you were living in Nevada City in 2001, that you witnessed Marty Teichmann pushing your mom down and breaking her china and knick-knacks?
A. Yes.
Q. Do you remember telling CPS at the same time that you didn't like your mom?
A. Yes.
Q. Do you remember telling CPS that your mom wouldn't buy you any food?
A. Yes.
Q. Do you remember telling CPS that your mom wouldn't buy you any backpacks?
A. Yes.
Q. Do you remember telling CPS that your mom wouldn't buy you any clothes?

A. Yes.

Q. Do you remember telling CPS around the same time that your mom always makes you do all the work?

A. Yes.

Q. And do you remember a time in February 2002 around February 7th or 8th, 2002, when your mom was in Bishop, and do you remember having some discussions with CPS while your mom was away?

A. Yes.

Q. And you and Martha were still in Nevada City; do you remember that?

A. Yes.

Q. And do you remember telling CPS that you were often left alone overnight to fend for yourselves?

A. Yes.

Q. Do you remember telling Nevada County CPS about that same time that your mom said you couldn't eat for a week?

A. Yes.

Q. Do you remember telling CPS that same time that your mom was trying to get away from you?

A. Yes.

Q. Do you remember telling Nevada County CPS at that same time that your mom is always angry with you?

A. What does this have to do with anything?

The Court: We do need to – you have to bear with us and answer the questions.

The Witness: Can I take a break please?

The Court: Let's take a five-minute break. (Whereupon the witness and the jury exits the courtroom)

The Court: Let's go on the record again in the matter of People v. Harris. Counsel and Mr. Harris are present, the jury is out of the room. The witness Chelsea Guthrie and her support person are out of the room. When the witness requested the opportunity to take a break and we allowed her to depart, the jury was still seated in the room. She and her support person went out a back door to a hallway, and counsel asked me to put on the record the outburst that occurred at that time, which was clearly audible to the entire courtroom, certainly to me on the bench.

I am aware that the jurors heard the witness' statement "This is fucking bullshit." And it appears there was a blow struck on the door or a wall or a door was slammed. I am not sure. The bailiff indicated a need to get a band-aid as apparently the witness injured her hand and indeed did strike a wall.

The outburst occurred and the jury was excused subject to a recall. And we propose to recall them now.

(Whereupon the witness and the jury returned to the courtroom)

Q. by Ms. Hankel: We were talking about conversations that you had with CPS in 2002 right around February 7th or 8th. Do you remember telling Nevada County CPS that your mom is often sad?

A. Yes.

Q. Do you remember telling Nevada County CPS, around that same time period that your mom takes pills to make her feel better?

A. Yes.

Q. Do you remember telling CPS, around that same time period, that you would rather stay at the neighbor's house or your dad's house?

A. Yes.

The Court: Keep your voice up, please.

The Witness: I am speaking as loud as I can.

Q. by Ms. Hankel: Do you remember telling El Dorado County CPS on March 12th, 2002, just a little bit later that your mom had hit Martha with a belt?

A. Yes.

Q. All the stuff we just talked about, was it difficult to tell CPS workers about your mom?

A. Sometimes. Sometimes now.

Q. Was it embarrassing?

A. No.

Q. Was it humiliating?

A. No.

Q. Was it easy?

A. It wasn't easy.

Q. How did you feel when you told them about it?

A. Relieved.

Q. After you came to live with your mom and sister in Bishop in July 2002, you were still close to your dad, weren't you?

A. Yes.

Q. And your dad had a close relationship with you; correct?

A. Yes.

Q. Do you remember that you actually had to call the campground and have somebody go get him. Is that how you did it?

A. Yeah.

Q. Do you remember that you were able to talk to him pretty regularly?

A. Not as regularly as I would have liked to.
Q. Did you ever get to live with him again?
A. No.
Q. And isn't it true that he died on 9/11/2003?
A. Yes.
Q. About a year and a half later, after you came to Bishop?
A. Yes.
Q. Did your dad come and visit you before he died?
A. Yes.
Q. Did some other relatives come with him?
A. Yes.
Q. Did they stay for a few days?
A. Yes.
Q. Did you visit with them?
A. Yes.
Q. Do you remember if you went out to dinner with them?
A. Yes.
Q. Do you remember anything else you did with them while they were home?
A. We went back to the hotel room and sat by the pool and talked.
Q. After your dad died, do you remember relatives coming back to Bishop to visit with you?
A. My aunt did, yes.
Q. From July 2002 to September 2003, you never told your dad that Mike Harris was molesting you, did you?
A. No.
Q. You never told your dad that Mike Harris was touching your breasts?
A. No.
Q. Or touching your vagina?
A. No.
Q. Did you ever tell any of his relatives that?
A. No.
Q. So when is the first time, the very first time you ever told anybody that Mike Harris was molesting you?
A. After I ran away from home.

The truth always rears its head on instinct. Martha and Chelsea both said the same thing.

Q. by Ms. Hankel: And who did you tell?
A. Alex.

Q. Are you sure about that?
A. Yes.
Q. You went with my client, Mike Harris, to the Los Angeles area three times, do you remember that?
A. Yes.
Q. And do you remember you went with Martha the first time?
A. Yes.
Q. Just you and Martha and Mike Harris the first time?
A. Yes.
Q. And then it was just Martha and Mike, did they go another time without you?
A. Yes.
Q. And you testified today about the trip that you and Martha and Mike made down to the Disneyland area, correct?
A. Correct.
Q. And that is the testimony where you said Martha was in the bed next to you?
A. Yes.
Q. Do you remember the testimony? Do you remember the interview telling Karen Smart that Martha woke up while my client was forcibly trying to rape you?
A. I never said the word "rape."
Q. So, when you said he tried to stick it in, were you talking about a rape, or were you talking about something else?
A. Could be molesting.
Q. What was it he was trying to stick in?
A. His private part.
Q. Where was he trying to stick it?
A. My private part, where it doesn't belong.
Q. Do you remember saying that Martha woke up, then my client said "Martha go back to sleep." Do you remember that?
A. No, I don't.
Q. Do you remember that you told Karen [Smart[that Martha then laid back down?
A. Yeah.
Q. Do you remember testifying at the preliminary hearing about another time that Martha walked into your bedroom and saw Mike trying to rape you?
A. Yes.
Q. Do you remember saying that night you nor Martha said anything? Mike just looked at Martha, and she walked out and closed the door.
A. Yes.
Q. Is it your testimony today that you have never given my client a blowjob?

A. I never have.

Q. Then why did you say that at the interview to Karen Smart in August 2007?

A. You were talking about today. Not the last testifying.

Q. Do you remember when you told Karen Smart that?

A. Yes.

Q. Miss Guthrie, I am handing you a document … I am going to ask you if you recognize that document. Would you take a minute to look at it?

The Court: Are you done with it?

The Witness: Yes.

Q. by Ms. Hankel: Did you have a chance to look at it? Do you recognize this as a journal entry?

A. Yes.

Q. Is this your handwriting?

A. Yes.

Q. Is this your journal?

A. Yeah.

Q. In this journal entry, are you talking about planning to be emancipated from your mom?

A. Correct.

Q. Miss Guthrie. I am handing you another document … And I'll ask you if you recognize that document … Have you had a chance to look at it?

A. Yeah.

Q. Is this another journal in your handwriting?

A. Yes.

Q. And the date is August 13, 2005?

A. Yes.

Q. And does this journal entry describe a trip that Martha took to LA with Mike Harris for a week?

A. Yes.

Q. Is it the second trip we talked about just a moment ago?

A. Yeah.

Q. And does the entry state "Martha gets to go to LA for a week. It sucks I can't go."

A. Yes.

I am handing you two separate pages of a document – Have you had a chance to look at that?

A. Yes.

Q. Are these entries, separate entries from May 4th, 2007, and May 5th, 2007?

A. Yes.
Q. And is this your journal?
A. Yes.
Q. And you signed the one on the left-hand side Chelsea, correct?
A. Correct.
Q. And on the left-hand side does this journal entry describe how you're feeling, like all your friends hate you?
A. Yes.
Q. And that you'll never date again?
A. Yes.
Q. And on the right-hand side, does it, the journal entry, describe how your mom blames stuff on you every day?
A. Yes.
Q. And do you identify your mom in this as Kerri instead of my mom?
A. Yes.
Q. And do you describe an incident where Martha broke the door and Kerri blamed it on you?
A. Yes.
Q. And you describe an incident where Martha wrote on the garage door "Kerri is a bitch" in spray paint, and you got blamed for that?
A. Yes.
Q. And you were made to scrub it off?
A. Yes.

Ms. Hankel then went on and on with journal entries and notes about sneaking out and boyfriends and how Kerri is a bitch and so on and so forth and so ended day two with another long drive home, er, to jail.

TWENTY-TWO

It was already day three and when you factored in four days of jury selection we had already been at trial for seven days of an estimated ten day trial. One a witness and a half had testified. This was looking to go on a lot longer than the judge had planned, and I was concerned. Chelsea was back on the stand for Wednesday morning of day three and Ms. Hankel started right in.

Q. by Ms. Hankel: The TeaBag email message appears to be stating that they know who Mike is and what he has done and what he has been doing. Yesterday I believe you told me that you hadn't told anybody about Mike Harris except for Alex Ellis. And is it true that at the interview, when you were answering questions by Det. Karen Smart you told her that you hadn't told anybody at all about Mike Harris molesting you. Do you remember that?

A. Yes.

Q. Do you remember at the prelim you were asked whether or not you had discussed any of the allegations with your friends, and you said you never told any of your friends that Mike was molesting you?

A. Yes.

Q. And that you had never told any of your friends that Mike was molesting you?

A. Does this message say that he was doing by molesting? Does this say that we told my friends about him doing this to us?

The Court: Miss Guthrie, we ask that you do not argue with the person questioning you.

Q. by Ms. Hankel: You never told any of your friends that he was a molester, correct? You said that at the prelim?

A. Correct.

Next, Ms. Hankel went through a stack of emails that the girls and their friends sent to me calling me a perv or a sick mother fucker and stuff like that. I told them to call the cops because I had and I did. I showed the emails to the Bishop PD and they told me it was a Mono County case. Bishop is in Inyo County. These emails didn't begin until the girls had made their initial disclosures to Alex Ellis.

Q. by Ms. Hankel: I am handing you what has been admitted as Exhibit 8, which is an email from you to skibumgonegood. It says "Hi Mike, this is Bob from security." Mr. Graham showed this to you yesterday. Which friend helped you draft that email?

A. Bob.

Q. Bob who?

A. I don't know his last name.

Q. How do you know Bob?

A. A friend from school.

Q. What school?

A. Bishop.

Q. What did you tell Bob – was it Bob who drafted the email?

A. Yes.

Q. And were you sitting next to Bob when he drafted the email?

A. Yes.

Q. The date of the email is August 1, 2007, correct?

A. Yeah, I see that.

Q. In the email your friend writes that Mike is a little perv, a sick little perv that needs to be thrown in jail for touching little girls. Did you talk to Bob about Mike Harris touching little girls?

A. I didn't.

Q. How did he know how to write this email?

A. Because of my sister.

Q. Martha talked about it?

A. Yes.

Q. Who is Bob in the email is my question to you?

A. I already told you I don't know his name.

Q. How many times have you met him?
A. I know him from school.
Q. What classes was he in with you?
A. I don't remember.
Q. How did you come to be sitting with him writing this email?
A. Because we hung out.
Q. Where were you hanging out?
A. Michelle's house.
Q. Whose computer were you using?
A. Michelle's.
Q. Whose idea was it to write this email?
A. My friends.
Q. Bob's or Michelle's?
A. Bob's.
Q. Why did Bob want you to write this email? Did he tell you?
A. Because we were wanting him to write back and see what he would say.
Q. Aside from Bob and Michelle and Martha, is there anybody else that you were meeting with and talking about writing to Mike?
A. No.
The Court: Alright, we are going to need to take a break and we may have to do this more frequently today. Ms. Hankel has some medical issues that she is dealing with.

After a short break, Ms. Hankel went through more emails which Chelsea sent and Chelsea said she sent them by herself and her friends did not participate nor send any more emails. The one email, the "Tea-Bag" email which I actually replied to by saying "Call the cops, I know I have" Chelsea forwarded to Alex Ellis on August 1st, 2007. This is an important issue in that Alex Ellis must have known about Martha's and Chelsea's allegations at that point, but Ms. Ellis still hadn't reported any molestation to the Sheriff or DA in a Suspected Child Abuse Report (SCAR). This despite her being mandated to report abuse immediately. Basically, they were trying to set me up.

Q. by Ms. Hankel: All of these emails were written before the preliminary hearing in this case, and they were written before the interview that you had with Karen Smart; correct?
A. Correct.
Q. Isn't it true that he never told you that you couldn't hang out with boys?
A. Yeah. That we weren't allowed to.

Q. Do you remember at the preliminary hearing being asked by Mr. Graham:
Question: Did Mr. Harris ever tell you he did not want you to hang out with boys?
Answer: Not that I remember.
Q. By Ms. Hankel: Do you remember that testimony?
A. Yes.
Q. Did my client bring you to a prom?
A. Prom? No. Prom is in high school.
Q. Did he transport you to a prom?
A. No. It was Homecoming.
Q. Homecoming, is that a dance?
A. Yes.
Q. What year did he transport you to the Homecoming dance?
A. I was in 9th grade, 2006 I think.
Q. When you were dating Tyler Clarke, you couldn't go to a movie with him, could you?
A. No.
Q. Couldn't go out to dinner with him?
A. No.
Q. Couldn't go out for pizza with him?
A. No.
Q. Couldn't go out to his house and hang out with him?
A. No.
Q. You had to sneak out of the house in order to be with him?
A. Yes.
Q. And you were hanging out at the park with Tyler and Leif and Martha?
A. Yes.
Q. And the park I am referring to is the park out at Chalfant, correct?
A. Yes.
Q. You'd been doing that for quite a few weeks by the time you decided to run away; correct?
A. Correct.
Q. And you were planning on running away?
A. No. That was the day that – well, I was planning on it, but I figured out that was the day.

Clearly Ms. Hankel dropped the ball on that last question. Chelsea started to say that was the day of the big fight with her mom and the reason why she ran away. There was no plan and Ms. Hankel was ignoring that at all costs, including my continued incarceration. Ms. Hankel continued with a different track.

Q. by Ms. Hankel: Is it fair to say you had been thinking about it for quite some time?

A. Yes.

Q. Do you remember telling Tyler Clarke, six weeks before you ran away, that my client was molesting you and you needed a place to go and stay?

A. No.

Q. Do you deny ever telling Tyler Clarke that my client was molesting you?

A. No. I don't deny it.

Q. Do you remember telling Tyler Clarke that my client had raped you twice and raped Martha three times?

A. No.

Q. When do you remember telling Tyler Clarke that you told him that Mike Harris was raping you?

A. It took a long time before I told him. I think like after I told the investigators and everything.

Q. Did you tell Michelle Jackson that my client had never raped you.

A. No.

Q. Never had a conversation with her like that?

A. I did, but it was after I told Alex about it.

Q. Describe to me what you – your conversation was with Michelle Jackson.

A. I told her – well, Martha told her first and then she asked me, and I said yes, he did touch me and my sister.

Q. Okay. Do you remember having a discussion with Rose Douglas from CPS after you ran away and before your interview and before the prelim in this case where you told Rose Douglas that Mike had molested Martha and had tried to molest you?

A. I don't remember that conversation with her.

This was where my conflict with Ms. Hankel came to a boil. In the CPS files we had was a Delivered Service Log (DSL) file which said that Chelsea contacted Rose Douglas and made that very claim. However, Ms. Hankel didn't want to impugn the CPS records from 7/9/07 or 7/12/07 which clearly showed somebody entered this report at some point. Chelsea had denied the report being made. Ms. Hankel was adamant that we didn't want to look like conspiratorial theorists, but my attitude was I was getting screwed. I didn't think I was going to lose any more credibility than I had already lost anyway. I told Ms. Hankel facts are facts and to get in there and argue them.

Q. by Ms. Hankel: Do you remember in November of 2006 talking to Rose Douglas when she came out after the "van incident" in Chalfant?

A. The what incident?

Q. The van incident. When I refer to the van incident, that is the incident where you guys were waiting for the bus?

A. I don't know what you are talking about.

Q. Do you remember going in November of 2006 and talking to Aaron Storey?

A. Yes.

Q. What do you remember about it.

A. All I remember was when I was walking to the bus stop – I was telling him about what happened that morning while I was walking to the bus stop that Mike did.

Q. Tell me who Aaron Storey is?

A. He was the old counselor at Bishop High School.

Q. And you went to talk to Aaron Storey about what had happened that morning; correct?

A. Correct.

Q. And CPS was called out; correct?

A. Yeah.

Q. And you had a conversation with CPS about what happened that morning; correct?

A. Yes.

Q. And you made some statements to CPS about my client that morning; correct?

A. I did.

Q. Do you remember telling CPS that my client was physically abusive to you?

A. Yes.

Q. Do you remember telling CPS that you were afraid to call anyone?

A. Yes.

Q. Do you remember telling CPS that Mike had a temper?

A. Yes.

Q. And when you said all those things to CPS, were you nervous about what might happen?

A. I was.

Q. Were you scared about what Mike might do if you made those statements?

A. Yes.

Q. Were you fearful that he might hit you?

A. Yes.

Q. Were you worried he might do something even more drastic?
A. Yes.
Q. Do you remember telling Karen Smart your mom blamed you when Mike Harris left?
A. Yes.
Q. Do you remember your mom telling you that you were a problem in her relationships?
A. Yes.
Q. Did that make you angry?
A. For what my mom said?
Q. Yes.
A. Yeah.
Q. Did accusing Mike of sexually abusing you make your mom angry?
A. I am not sure. She didn't believe us when we told her.
Q. And what about after you ran away, do you know if she was angry when you accused Mike of sexually abusing you?
A. I don't know. I didn't talk to her about it. I didn't talk to her at all after I ran away.

What about the showdown in Kerri's front yard on June 28th, 2007, when Alex Ellis tried to place Chelsea back in Kerri's home and Chelsea said she would just run away again? Wasn't that talking to your mom after you ran away? Wasn't that the perfect time to claim sexual abuse? Martha and Chelsea both made allegations when it became apparent that the court was going to place the twins back in Kerri's home. But back to Chelsea's cross-examination:

Q. by Ms. Hankel: But you saw her outside the movie theater in August; correct?
A. Correct.
Q. And you talked a little bit about that?
A. Yes.
Q. And she seemed pretty angry at the time, didn't she?
A. Yes.
Q. In 2003, you were sitting in a room with Raeanna Davenport and your sister; correct?
A. Correct.
Q. Do you remember that folks from Child Protective Services came out to talk to you at your school after that incident?
A. Yes.
Q. Do you remember telling them that nothing had happened?

A. Yes.

Q. Do you remember telling your mom that you didn't see Mike sexually touch or inappropriately touch Raeanna Davenport?

A. Yes.

Q. Do you remember when you were speaking to CPS after the incident, that they came out and talked to you at your school? Do you remember telling them that you had not been sexually abused by my client?

A. Yes.

Q. We talked for a moment yesterday, and I think I probably confused you somewhat because I am a little confused about whether or not you had testified about giving my client a blowjob.

A. Right.

Q. And you didn't testify yesterday with Mr. Graham that my client had ever had you give him a blowjob; correct?

A. Correct.

Q. Do you remember when you talked to Karen Smart at the interview in 2007 in August and do you remember specifically talking to her about how my client had forced you to give him a blowjob?

A. Yes.

Q. And do you remember telling officer Smart that he would try to force you by shoving your head down and holding your jaw?

A. Yes.

And that concluded Ms. Hankel's vigorous cross. Mr. Graham quickly jumped up to right the ship.

Q. by Mr. Graham: You have given statements both here and to law enforcement, that you hadn't told friends about what Mike had done to you; correct?

A. Correct.

Q. And so is it fair to say that you did not tell the truth about telling your friends about what happened? Is that fair to say?

A. That is.

Q. Why did you not want to tell law enforcement or anybody else that you had disclosed to your friends?

A. Because it was embarrassing, you know, just having my friends know. And I didn't –

Q. When you were asked, did you tell any of your friends, why didn't you want us in law enforcement in other words Karen Smart of John Rutowski, CPS to know that your friends knew.

A. I didn't want to get them involved in this. I didn't want them to have to be involved in all this.

Q. Were you trying to protect your friends?

A. Yes.

So now, Mr. Graham is on the "plan" defense band wagon supporting the earlier disclosure theory that the girls have repeatedly denied during pretrial and trial proceedings. They didn't tell their friends because they didn't tell their friends, period. Next, Mr. Graham went into the journals which were actually more like notebooks.

Q. by Mr. Graham: I am going to hand you this bag that contains three notebooks – do you recognize those notebooks?

A. Yes.

Q. Are those yours?

A. yes.

Q. And had there been examination of you by Ms. Hankel of some of the contents of these notebooks?

A. Yes.

Q. Now when Det. Rutowski came out and showed you these note books did you go over them with him present?

A. Yes.

Q. When you reviewed the notebooks, did you observe any writing of yours reflective of you writing about sexual abuse by Mr. Harris?

A. There was none of that in there.

Q. Were you surprised when you opened any of the notebooks that there was no writing about Mr. Harris?

A. Yes.

How convenient. Chelsea's evidence of abuse which she never cared about until after the fact suddenly disappears. Martha testified that the notebooks contained poems and stuff like that. Martha never mentioned writings about sexual abuse and she testified she thought she had read the notebooks.

Q. by Mr. Graham: When you ran away at the end of June 2007, what did you take with you?

A. My purse, makeup, and that is pretty much it.

Q. Did you take a duffel bag full of clothes?

A. Sort of. I had a pair of underwear and socks, and that was pretty much it.

Q. When you ran away on June 26th did you bring those journals with you?

A. No.

Q. Why not?
A. Because I wasn't thinking at the time, I just up and left.
Q. What was your primary focus when you left on June 26th, 2007?
A. Just to get out of there as soon as possible.

So, what's up Ms. Hankel? Can anybody find out why she left that night, clearly she did not have a "plan". I said that the big fight with Kerri made Chelsea mad and she left to be with Tyler and after that they decided to shack up at Tyler's. There was no call to the cops or to CPS. And most importantly, Chelsea said she wasn't thinking, she just left which speaks volumes for a lack of "plan."

Q. by Mr. Graham: You engaged in some messages to Mike; correct?
A. Correct.
Q. Why did you do that?
A. Because I wanted to get him to write back.
Q. Why?
A. So I could get him in trouble.
Q. Did you plan the gradual release of information?
A. No.
Q. Did you plan to do that?
A. No.
Q. Did you scheme to do that?
A. No.
Q. Did you plan and scheme to give all the inconsistent answers in all the different interviews?
A. No.
Q. Who were you hanging out with just before you ran away?
A. Tyler Clarke and Leif Medrud.
Q. And of those two, who did you tell about any kind of abuse, sexual or otherwise, by Mr. Harris?
A. Neither of them at the time, until after I told Alex Ellis.
Q. I just want to be sure we are clear. Did you tell any of your friends prior to June 26th, 2007, about sexual abuse?
A. No.

And then it was over. Ms. Hankel had a few more recross-examination questions, but it didn't matter. She wasn't touching the no plan position I held regardless of what the girls said. Simply put, no telling friends before the running away incident equals no plan. Period. Why was I still in jail?

Chelsea testified haphazardly and Ms. Hankel failed to confront and cross-examine her completely, including the core issues, in a manner consistent with the available facts, the credible facts being ignored. Ms. Hankel was sticking with the "plan" defense, but failed to press Chelsea about the plan in any meaningful way. Chelsea was never asked about the events which led up to her running away incident. These questions would have included was I living at the Chalfant house in June of 2007 or was I molesting her every day. Stuff like that seemed relevant at the time. I wasn't, by the way. Chelsea also was not asked specifically, although it can be inferred that she didn't, but she was not asked if she told anybody about the alleged abuse while she was at Tyler's house. This was while she was a runaway and before the big scene in Kerri's front yard, with the Sheriffs and Alex Ellis.

Mr. Graham ventured into this territory, asking Chelsea who she had disclosed abuse to, and yet Chelsea clearly said she told Alex Ellis first. Not her mom. Not her sister. She said she told nobody before Alex. Then after prodding from Mr. Graham, Chelsea said she told Detective Rutowski second. Mr. Graham then led her to change her answer to Ellen Thompson second and Det. Rutowski third. Ms. Hankel never objected to this or any other leading questions posed by Mr. Graham. Chelsea did not mention her mom, her sister, Jessikah or Gina Luffman, Tyler Clarke, Jordan Moriarty, Kathleen Traynor, or any other person like Rose Douglas. CPS records that Ms. Hankel did not want to use to show faulty and suspicious activities by the CPS in this case and they show clearly that on either 7/9/07 or 7/12/07 Chelsea supposedly called the CPS (Rose Douglas or Alex Ellis depending on which record you review) and stated that I had been molesting Martha and tried to molest both of them.

My discussions with Ms. Hankel related to this topic involved my assertion that the documents in CPS referral No. 10 plainly showed that the reported contact with Chelsea was not a contemporaneous entry, nor was it even entered consistently. Ms. Hankel did not ask Chelsea at any length about this important event, especially in light of the fact that Chelsea testified that Martha disclosed first. Martha was still in Kerri's home until 7/16/07. This is where a timeline would have been helpful and would have shown that the incredulous perception I had towards the CPS documentation was warranted. Chelsea was never asked to describe the Raeanna incident in detail or to describe the alleged statement to her mom that I had been molesting them and their mom didn't believe them in specific detail. Chelsea never said she told her mom, let alone that Martha, herself, and Raeanna had been molested. Ms. Hankel had statements from Kerri and the CPS which supported a vigorous cross-examination of Chelsea in this area. Ms. Hankel declined to ask Chelsea why she was sending me threatening emails that she would report me as a child molester if I didn't leave her friends alone when she had testified that she was scared to disclose because of my supposed threats.

Ms. Hankel failed to question Chelsea about her statement that she felt a lot safer telling her friends. Also, her statement that she was afraid that she was going to have to go back to Kerri's house. A timeline of disclosures, emails, statements from other witnesses, and the CPS documentation shows Ms. Hankel's negligence in this cross-examination. Ms. Hankel had specific evidence that Chelsea told Det. Rutowski in the May 2008 supplemental interview that she had called me a child molester in front of a large group of people, including Tyler and Leif, on August 3rd, 2007.

When Chelsea denied this during cross-examination, Ms. Hankel failed to use the interview to refresh Chelsea's memory and also neglected to introduce the very evidence which impeached Chelsea's testimony. This May 2008 supplemental interview with Det. Rutowski, in which Chelsea said she called me a child molester, revealed that Tyler Clarke and Leif Medrud were with her. Chelsea stated to Det. Rutowski that "Oh those boys don't know anything" when he asked her what Tyler and Leif said after Chelsea supposedly yelled at me in front of them. The fact is that Ms. Hankel had a statement written by Tyler Clarke on that same day, August 3rd, 2007, in which Tyler makes no mention of any child molester accusation being yelled out, nor any mention of his own knowledge of any type of abuse by me. Ms. Hankel never utilized this document at any time during trial.

On the topic of rape, Chelsea yelled out in the courtroom in response to questioning by Ms. Hankel that she never said "rape." Then, on Wednesday in the morning of day 3, Chelsea admitted that she told Tyler after telling Alex Ellis. Chelsea never mentioned Jordan Moriarty at all. Ms. Hankel missed here as well when she didn't cross-examine Chelsea on this vital topic to my "escalation" theory. Ms. Hankel's own interviews with Jordan Moriarty revealed that he was going to testify that Chelsea disclosed rapes and showed him bruising on her inner thighs in February or March of 2007. I had told Ms. Hankel this was a crock of shit for a couple reasons. First, I had no contact with Chelsea in February or March of 2007. I was busy with other stuff and Kerri didn't want me coming over, she was having trouble with the girls and their efforts at school. Secondly, Chelsea never wore skirts or shorts because she thought her knees looked fat and did not want the kids at school to see them. Besides, it was 15 degrees out when Chelsea went to school during that time of the year, and to suggest that Chelsea somehow want to catch the bus dressed like that was ridiculous.

I thought it was absurd that Ms. Hankel was going to call Jordan as a defense witness in support of her "plan" defense, knowing full well that Chelsea had never mentioned him. Ms. Hankel did not want to ruin her "plan" defense, even though it was based on speculative theory, not adduced facts. Det. Rutowski clearly knew about "those boys" (Leif, Jordan, and Tyler) and never investigated them as witnesses. Then, at the last possible minute, Ms. Hankel decides she wants to use them to bolster her misguided theory at my expense. She never questioned Chelsea about this obvious and major inconsistency that had nothing to do with memory and everything to do with changing her story and false testimony by her friends hoping to help Chelsea after the fact.

Ms. Hankel forgot to ask Chelsea about her alleged suicide attempt at the home of Chandra Burnett, even though Ms. Hankel had intervied Ms. Burnett and was going to call her as a defense witness specifically to discuss the alleged suicide attempt. Ms. Burnett felt that Chelsea was manipulating Alex Ellis. This issue was a cornerstone to Ms. Hankel's assertion that the girls and Chelsea in particular were manipulating the system, that they were "system savvy." Ms. Burnett had already told Ms. Hankel that Chelsea had faked the suicide attempt. Ms. Burnett said there was no way Chelsea could have gotten the pills that she told Alex she had taken in order to commit suicide. Ms. Burnett told Ms. Hankel that Chelsea faked her suicide attempt in order to move back to Bishop to be with her sister and live in the Lindsay's lax foster home.

Ms. Hankel had detailed evidence of Chelsea having visited Martha in Bishop a few weeks prior to the fake suicide attempt and Chelsea wound up smoking pot and getting "falling down drunk." This evidence was from a report from Ellen Thompson to Alex Ellis and also involved a series of letters between Ms. Burnett and Ms. Ellis. Ms. Burnett was a major development in my case that I knew nothing about, until then. Ms.

Hankel forgot to ask Chelsea about all of this and Ms. Hankel said she would get it in through Ms. Burnett.

Ms. Hankel refused to ask Chelsea about the big fight with her mom, which preceded her running away from home. It seemed Chelsea was arguing with Kerri and Kerri finally got fed up and told Chelsea she was going to box up her stuff and sell it on eBay. Also, Chelsea was to switch bedrooms with Martha so Martha got the bigger bedroom. This argument was pivotal because it was central to my assertions about motive which led to an escalation of accusations.

If Chelsea had a plan to make allegations against me in order to be removed from her home, then the big showdown in Kerri's front yard would have been a good time. A review of all the court records in Kerri's WIC §300 case, including Kerri's statements, would reveal an escalation of accusations that actually began against Kerri with no mention of me. Only later, when the girls were going to be returned home was I implicated in sexual abuse and even then it was that Kerri and I made the girls watch us having sex and escalated from there. Ms. Hankel neglected to ask Chelsea if I was even at the Guthrie home in early 2007 when Jordan says he saw bruises on Chelsea's inner thighs after hearing her tales of rape. Ms. Hankel also ignored asking Chelsea about whether she had seen Martha's "Why did you leave" note and she never asked Chelsea if there was a plan, why didn't Martha know about it? Ms. Hankel did not want to push the issue of whether Chelsea had called the CPS from her boyfriend's house. This inquiry showing Chelsea did not call the CPS at any time would obviously have disrupted the "plan" defense and bolstered my premise that there was an escalation of allegations. Ms. Hankel needed to show the record and motive component of Chelsea's actions.

There were no Sheriff reports, no mandated SCARs, no CPS reports, not even personal notes by Alex Ellis that show Chelsea called any authority at any time while a runaway. Ms. Ellis had notes that showed she was needed to respond to pick up Chelsea after Kerri had located her at Tyler's. Chelsea did not want to return home. Ms. Hankel had all the notes, the Sheriff phone records, everything, and still she did not force the issue, nor did the defense investigator, Mr. Morganstein, investigate Shaylynn Ellis. Ms. Hankel did not ask Chelsea anything about Shaylynn Ellis.

Ms. Hankel was going down with the "plan" defense ship, but it was me heading down to Davey Jones locker as a result of these critical omissions. Ms. Hankel should have pursued the rational line of questioning and thinking which showed the rewards of the allegations of sexual abuse. Then she should have shown the relationship between those rewards and the allegations in a timeline, then compared it to the inconsistencies and contradictions in a cogent manner.

Ms. Hankel never asked Chelsea why there was no corroboration of Martha's claim that Chelsea had been a witness to many purported molestations of Martha. There was zero corroboration of sexual abuse ever and I mean ever and Ms. Hankel failed to bring this fact to the fore. And thus ended the morning session of day three, November 4th, 2009. Next up was Cathy Boyle, the SART nurse who performed sexual assault physical examinations some six months after my arrest.

TWENTY-THREE

After my lunch, it was back to court for Cathy Boyle, a pediatric nurse practitioner at UC Davis Medical Center. Mr. Graham got things going with some general questions.

Q. by Mr. Graham: Basically, how does your CAARE [Child and Adolescent Abuse Resource and Evaluation] center operate?

A. by Cathy Boyle: It is an outpatient clinic. But most of our kids that I see for sexual abuse or suspected sexual abuse come to us being referred by law enforcement or Child Protective Services.

Q. And at the Center, are these where the physical examinations are performed?

A. Yes. Unless they are acute and they are after hours, then they are done in the emergency room.

Q. What does "acute" mean?

A. It means that the actual incident has happened within a time frame where we have the possibility of being able to collect potential biological evidence.

Q. Is there a number you give to that time frame?

A. Usually it is 72 hours … our adolescents exams will actually go up to a week after the alleged incident.

Q. Are exams conducted by nurse practitioners?

A. Yes. At UC Davis they are all nurse practitioners or physician assistants.

Q. How many number of children would you say you have conducted sexual abuse examinations on?

A. Over 6,800.

Judge DeVore then gave Ms. Hankel a chance to voir dire Norse Boyle and then following that Ms. Hankel objected to her as an expert on the grounds of foundation and Judge DeVore agreed to reserve his ruling until Dr. Gabaeff testified for my defense. Then the judge gave a lengthy instruction regarding expert witnesses, opinions, and weight of opposing opinions and opinions in general. He also gave a general witness instruction and off we went.

A. by Mr. Graham: Can you give us the title of the presentations you've listed in your C.V.?

A. In 2007 we published a paper on the healing on non-hymenal genital injuries on pre-pubertal kids, before they've gone through puberty and adolescent girls.

Q. Going to the next page.

A. The second article was Healing of Hymenal Injuries in Pre-Pubertal and Adolescent Girls.

Q. What is a cleft?

A. A cleft is an irregularity in the hymen. The hymen is the tissue that goes around the vaginal opening and a laceration. So a tear to the hymen where the edges are torn and they create sort of a V-shaped cleft, and that is called a cleft.

Q. And are you familiar with the alleged victims in this case, Martha and Chelsea Guthrie?

A. Yes.

Q. Did you see and examine them?

A. Yes.

Q. When did you examine the two girls?

A. I saw Chelsea on February 13th, 2008, and I saw Martha on February 14th, 2008.

Q. How old were the girls when you examined them?

A. They were 13 years and 11 months.

Q. Would it refresh your memory to look at the individual records of both girls when we are referring to details about the exam?

A. Yes.

Q. Go ahead.

A. On the medical history, we ask a question if they've ever had any falls or surgeries to their private parts that would have left any marks or scars that we see. And Martha said yes, she had fallen on her bike. She had been horseback riding. So there were two different incidents but never any blood or bruising.

Q. With regards to Martha, what was the history? What was the history relayed to you by Martha or anyone else before you started the exam?

A. It was by Martha and her medical history included abdominal pain, genital pain or discomfort with the incidents, genital discharge.

Q. What incidents did she refer to?

A. The things that happened to her in regard to her sexual abuse. Genital bleeding with one incident and that was it.

Q. Did she identify the person who had done these things to her?

A. Yes.

Q. Who was that?

A. And I need to back up. That history I did not get. That history was given to me by the social worker.

Q. All right. During your examination of Martha did you note any injury to the genitalia?

A. Yes, I did.

Q. I just wanted to ask – from the social worker, what did you understand?

A. There was penis to the vagina and finger to the vagina. She described both pain and bleeding.

Q. Following your examination of Martha, did you reach an opinion that she suffered from any internal or had suffered from any internal injury to her genitalia?

A. Yes.

Q. And what was that opinion?

A. That she had a cleft at 7 o'clock and that it was this cleft or narrowing in that area that could represent healed trauma. Because it is uncommon to be seen in children who have no abuse history.

Q. Did you examine Chelsea in much the same manner?

A. Yes.

Q. And with regard to Chelsea's history, what did you understand the history was of sexual abuse before you did the exam?

A. She described penis to vagina with pain, oral copulation, genital fondling by the assailant of the patient, and also fondling and kissing of her and force and threats.

Q. During your examination of Chelsea, did you notice any internal injury to her genitalia?

A. Yes, I did.

Q. Going on to the knee/chest position of the exam.

A. The knee/chest position, we see a very similar finding that she also has a cleft at the 7 o'clock position. Seen best in the knee/chest where the fold actually becomes a cleft.

Q. Now in your list of things that you – studies you have been involved with and have your name associated with, do you remember going over that list?

A. Yes.

Q. Did one of the publications involve the healing of hymenal injury?

A. Yes.

Q. You studied hymens that had been injured, is that correct?

A. Yes.

Q. Have you also studied the subject of normal exams in girls who had allegedly been penetrated?

A. Yes.

Q. Tell us about that.

A. The bulk of kids who have a history of sexual abuse have normal exams. Right now, the literature stated that about 95 percent of kids who give a history of sexual abuse have normal exams.

Wait just a minute, she can't have it both ways. She was saying that if they are molested or raped the injuries heal up and leave a hymen with a micro tear, but if there is no sign of a healed tear, no injury at all, they are the victim of sexual abuse if they report it. Wasn't that what she was saying? I hope Ms. Hankel gets it. Why am I even in jail???

Q. by Mr. Graham: In your report, tell me what it says in the section entitled Additional Comments?

A. "Area of narrowing likely indicates healed trauma and is rarely found in studies of non-abused children."

Q. Regarding Martha, were your findings consistent or inconsistent with the history that she gave of sexual abuse with Mr. Harris?

A. They were consistent.

Q. Regarding Chelsea, same question?

A. They were consistent.

Q. In your studies of or in your research or involvement in the study of hymenal tears, can you describe for the jury how a hymen might heal after it has been torn?

A. Hymenal tissue is like the same tissue that is inside your cheek. And so if you think about that, when you bite your check and if you really bite it hard to where it actually bleeds, it really hurts. But in 24 hours, because it is mucosal tissue, it is already healed, and it doesn't hurt anymore; it is already healed. Hymenal tissue is exactly the same kind of tissue. So when a hymen is torn, it doesn't heal back together to form a scar. So we don't see scars down in that area. What it does is the tear occurs, and each edge of the tear actually heals. So you can actually have a configuration like a cleft or a concavity.

Q. Did Martha's hymen look normal to you.
A. No.
Q. Did Chelsea's hymen look normal to you?
A. No.
Mr. Graham: Nothing further, Judge.
The Court: All right, Ms. Hankel.
Ms. Hankel: Your Honor, may I examine the witness from my chair?
The Court: Yes, you may, I understand you are having some problems.
Ms. Hankel: Thank you. Very much.
Q. by Ms. Hankel: I am just going to hand you what has been admitted subject to my objection on foundation as People's Exhibit 68, which is the report of the exam on Martha. Did you prepare that report?
A. Yes.
Q. You have testified that the findings on the exam were consistent with the history?
A. Yes.
Q. I note on page 3 of this [report] that you have under Martha Guthrie here are some words saying "not interviewed today."
A. Correct.
Q. And I noted that you have testified the history for this exam came from Martha's social worker, Alex Ellis?
A. Yes.
Q. So the entire basis for your – that supports your findings in this case come from a history given to you by a social worker in this case?
A. Yes.
Q. not from the patient?
A. That's correct.
Q. And when you say that these findings are consistent with a history as given to you by the social worker, would that history be page 2 of the [report]?
A. That's correct.
Q. And so the history would be "Martha stated she was fondled by perp on repeated occasions from the age of ten years to 14 years. One occasion at age 14 years he completed a rape and she bled."
A. Yes.
Q. Is it your belief that genital tissues after multiple acts of intercourse are not more likely to show more physical findings than on this examination?
A. Not necessarily. I have seen kids that have absolutely normal exams even with that history.

Q. When you say "that history" has that history also been provided to you by a social worker?

A. No, from kids.

Q. What do you do to verify the history?

A. It's not my job to verify it.

Q. Is it true that you just take whatever the statement is as the truth coming from the patient? So if they said they only had one physical act of intercourse, you would just believe that?

A. Yes.

Q. And if they said they had multiple acts of intercourse, would you believe that?

A. Yes.

Q. And if they had no acts of intercourse, would you believe that?

A. Yes.

Q. And if all those statements show a normal exam, how do you make the determination that the exam is consistent with the findings?

A. That it takes – it takes history. It takes other people other than me. I am just a piece of the puzzle. So I only have a small snippet of time with that patient. The only time where it will be different, if I see findings that don't correlate to the history I am talking about, and mostly I am talking about injuries that I see that don't go along with the history that I take, then we have to look further into that. But a normal exam, we know from the literature that the bulk of the kids have normal exams. Even in an acute setting, we don't always see findings.

Q. When you say "acute", you mean a matter of hours later?

A. Yes.

Q. And it could be that a matter of hours later, it could be that patient who is coming in to see you – it could be that that is a case of a false accusation?

A. It could be, or it could be that they don't have injuries.

Q. Going to Exhibit 69 which is the examination of Chelsea Guthrie.

A. Yes.

Q. And as in the report for Martha Guthrie, Chelsea Guthrie was also not interviewed?

A. Not about the incident, no.

Q. And all the information on her report would have also come from Alex Ellis; is that correct?

A. Yes.

Q. And that history is Chelsea stated – but this would be Alex Ellis stated that Chelsea stated –

A. Yes.

Q. So Chelsea stated as given to you by Alex Ellis, "She was fondled and kissed on her genitals and breasts from the age of 10 years to 14 years and stated that the perp reportedly attempted intercourse. And she does not know how far his penis was inside of her, but estimates three to four inches.

A. Yes.

Q. If you had additional incident history of repeated acts or penetration would that change your conclusion or your opinion as to whether the findings are consistent with the incident history of Chelsea Guthrie's case?

A. It wouldn't change my opinion, no.

Q. Do you disagree with the conclusion or the opinion rather that Martha Guthrie's exam is a normal exam.

A. Yes.

Q. Do you disagree with the opinion that Chelsea Guthrie's exam is a normal exam?

A. Yes.

So definitely a controversy existed. Ms. Hankel was done and Mr. Graham had a few redirect questions.

Q. by Mr. Graham: Ms. Boyle, there was mention of bike riding and horseback riding. In the history, I am not going to refer to the girl. Let's take that as a general proposition, if somebody bike rides and horseback rides, would you expect to see a deep cleft in the hymen of a 15-year-old girl who had previously, let's say months before, engaged in horseback riding?

A. No.

Q. Same question in regard to bike riding?

A. No.

That was that and I was utterly confused. Nurse Boyle said that Martha and Chelsea had exams consistent with their history, yet their allegations weren't consistent with their histories. And all that normal exam talk was just subterfuge for the fact they were liars. Nurse Boyle was quite simply a loose cannon. Her opinions didn't reflect an understanding of the voluminous claims the twins had made.

A History as revealed by Alex Ellis of one attempted intercourse belied the actual allegations. I have voiced concerns to both Mr. Gephart and Ms. Hankel that if the exams showed both girls still had intact hymens, then why was I still in jail? The discussions always centered on the term "cleft", which in this case, Nurse Boyle claimed showed healed hymenal tissue. I argued that if that were even true, it was likely a birth defect, since both twins had supposed clefts in exactly the same spot. I mean, what are the odds that, after I had supposedly raped each girl multiple times, that there would only be one cleft in each girl in the exact same spot?

Ms. Hankel retained an expert, Dr. Steven Gabaeff, to counter Nurse Boyle's activist opinions. No §402 hearings were held on this subject. I felt that Nurse Boyle's testimony should never have been allowed since it was highly prejudicial and lacked any probativity. I tried to get Ms. Hankel to understand WIC §324.5(a), which required a medical exam within 72 hours of the reported abuse. Even considering Ms. Hankel had the authority to make all strategy decisions, she still must make those decisions on the basis of proper investigation of the facts and research of the law applicable to those facts.

I asked Ms. Hankel to explain how an examination conducted six months after I had been incarcerated had any relevance and Ms. Hankel never explained. Especially concerning to me was her failure to elicit detailed testimony about the girls' activities once in foster care. Chelsea was found shacked up with her boyfriend while a runaway and her notes to Tyler showed a physical relationship. Martha's notes to Leif were much the same and other notes showed Martha had multiple relationships. Ms. Hankel also failed to bring out the CPS and psychologist's report to show Nurse Boyle Chelsea's and Martha's true history as they claimed prior to the February 2008 examinations.

Clearly the prosecutor put the girls' sexual activity into play when he asked them if they had sex with anyone besides me. Ms. Hankel did not object when Nurse Boyle used profile evidence to bolster an accuser's testimony in violation of Judge DeVore's pretrial ruling related to profile evidence. Nurse Boyle claimed that 95 percent of victims who claim sexual abuse and present themselves for an examination have a normal exam. How this statistic was relevant wasn't clear to me. Nurse Boyle clearly said the girls didn't have normal exams so she must have been arguing against my defense witness Dr. Gabaeff before he even testified. Nurse Boyle was an activist clear as day.

I really wanted Ms. Hankel to raise a ruckus over the issue that the underlying accusations were of repeated rape and digital penetration by an adult male of a young girl aged 10-11 years old, which was a Tanner Scale 3 by Nurse Boyle's own definition. That was incomprehensible how an adult penis wouldn't have caused substantial damage as expected. The hymen would be gone if the allegations were true. It doesn't take a biased nurse to explain that. I wanted Ms. Hankel to ask Nurse Boyle about

Martha's exam report in which she identified a white discharge after the LA rape and at trial she described a bloody discharge. The minutia was being swept asunder by either Ms. Hankel's ineffectiveness or Judge DeVore's desire to move this trial along quickly.

With a little time left on day three, Mr. Graham called a witness out of order. Mr. Brian Dressler was the chief investigator for the Inyo County District Attorney's Office and he was called for a very limited purpose.

Q. by Mr. Graham: Basically, tell us what minimal involvement you had in the case?

A. by Brian Dressler: I drove from my office to Bridgeport. I found a laptop and two hard drives. I returned to my office with them. I placed them in my safe. A few days later I gave them to Sgt. Wall from the Computer Crimes Task Force.

Q. And were they in your safe for the entire period of time before you removed them and gave them to Mr. Wall?

A. Yes.

Q. Did they ever leave your safe to your knowledge?

A. No.

And that was it. Just a chain of custody thing. The evidence has to be documented at every step from crime scene to courtroom. I had a feeling this was going to get more interesting as we got closer to Mr. Wall and the computer evidence. Ms. Hankel had a few questions on cross.

Q. by Ms. Hankel: Detective Dressler on [the bag containing the hard drives] under description and/or location it says two hard drives and the H.T. Is this SO-7?

A. I have no idea, I didn't write that.

Q. Where it says looks like Maxtor with a serial number, this serial okay, (indicating on ELMO) Did you check when you received this bag whether this 91080D5 was in fact the serial number of the hard drives that were in this bag?

A. No I did not.

For the record Ms. Hankel added:

Ms. Hankel: This bag would be Exhibit 28.

And that wrapped up a long day five. On the long drive to Independence, I couldn't help but wonder what it was about that Exhibit 28 item No. 1, the hard drive with the kiddie porn on it. I knew I didn't have or view kiddie porn on my computers and since the drive had failed I suspected foul play. I was waiting for Mr. Wall, but before that I still had to get through Raeanna Davenport.

TWENTY-FOUR

Raeanna Davenport was an oddity. She appeared to me to be the catalyst to the twins' claims. Out of nowhere she made an allegation against me and all I could figure was that she had heard about Michael Jackson's case and thought she could get something out of me. She was dirt poor and Kerri and I had the appearance that we had stuff. Raeanna was a reluctant, if not unwilling, witness. After a lengthy drive for the both of us, Raeanna took the stand and Mr. Graham started right in:

Q. by Mr. Graham: Good morning, Ms. Davenport. Do you want to be here today?

A. by Raeanna Davenport: No.

Q. Do you remember the first time you were called to testify in court a couple of years ago?

A. Yes.

Q. Did you eagerly want to come to court and testify in court a couple of years ago?

A. No.

Q. Since that time have you gotten and received numerous notices to come to court again to testify?

A. Yes, yeah.

Q. On any of those times, even though you didn't come to testify, were you excited about coming here to say anything?

A. No.

Q. Do you remember an incident in October 2003 where something happened to you that you didn't like?
A. Yes.
Q. And where did this thing happen?
A. In Chalfant.
Q. And was there a location in Chalfant?
A. A house.
Q. Do you remember whose house it was?
A. Michael's.
Q. Who else was living in that residence?
A. Martha and Chelsea.
Q. And was anybody else that you know?
A. Their mom.
Q. And was there a room that this incident happened in the residence?
A. The bedroom.
Q. And just before this incident happened, what were you doing?
A. Watching TV with the girls.
Q. And who was in the room when you were watching TV?
A. Both of the girls.
Q. And where were you in the room when you were watching TV?
A. On the bed with one of the girls.
Q. And which girl was that?
A. I don't remember.
Q. As you were watching TV and you were on the bed, tell us the very next thing that happened.
A. Then Mike came in.
Q. And what happened?
A. And he got on the bed.
Q. And what happened next?
A. And he started rubbing my legs.
Q. Were you wearing pants or shorts?
A. Shorts.
Q. And what did he do next?
A. He went under my shorts.
Q. And what did he do next?
A. Touched my private area.
Q. Before he took his hand away, did you say anything to him about what he was doing?

A. I said, "Stop."

Q. And at that point when you said "stop", did he stop?

A. Yeah.

Q. What did he do with his hand?

A. Took it away.

Q. What is the very next thing that happened that night that you remember?

A. We ate dinner.

Q. Do you recall, prior to coming to court today – about a month ago, you had spoken with my investigator about, well, we say generally not wanting to come to court at least? Do you remember that?

A. Yeah.

Q. And did you make any kind of statements about not remembering what happened?

A. Yes.

Q. As you sit here today, do you remember what happened?

A. A little bit.

Q. Prior to today's hearing, did you review your preliminary hearing testimony?

A. Yes.

Q. Through a transcript?

A. Yes.

Q. And you did that yesterday; is that correct?

A. Yes.

Q. As you testify today, do you have any doubt in your mind about what happened back in October 2003 when Mike Harris put his hand on your privates?

A. Yes.

No folks, that's not a typo. She simply stated the truth namely she had her own doubts whether it happened, she can't remember what never happened.

Q. by Mr. Graham: After the meal, what happened next?

A. I went home.

Q. And what happened next?

A. I told my grandmother what happened.

Q. Did you tell either Martha or Chelsea, let's say in the four or five days after this?

A. Yes.

Q. Did Martha or Chelsea, either one of them ever tell you that anything was happening to them from Mike Harris as far as sexual abuse?

A. No.

With that, Mr. Graham was done. Raeanna was an accuser who didn't want to be there even though Martha had apparently vindicated Raeanna by saying she saw the whole thing, albeit not the way Raeanna described it. The main problem was that Martha said she saw me rub Raeanna's back and then reach down the back of her pants, not shorts as Raeanna described. Then it was Ms. Hankel's turn and she made no headway. She got Raeanna to affirm her direct testimony, including the fact that she was wearing shorts, but when asked to remember specific things that happened during the incident, Raeanna simply couldn't remember anything. She couldn't remember if she told her grandmother right away, if she talked to a Sheriff's deputy, what the bedroom looked like, or even what the house looked like. Nothing, nada.

Q. by Ms. Hankel: Okay. Before you came here to testify today, you reviewed your preliminary hearing transcript?

A. Yes.

Q. The testimony you had in there.

A. Yes.

Q. And that helped you refresh your recollection?

A. Yes.

Q. You remember Mr. McCammond came out to your house?

A. Yes.

Q. And you talked to him about not wanting to testify in this case?

A. Yes.

Q. And you told him you didn't remember anything about what happened?

A. I told him I didn't remember that much.

Q. Okay. Your testimony today is that he, Mr. Harris, never rubbed your back, but he rubbed your legs, correct?

A. Yes.

And that was all Ms. Hankel could get out of Raeanna. A whole bunch of I don't remembers. Raeanna really was a reluctant witness and it was because nothing ever happened. Ms. Hankel should have asked the most relevant question of all: why are you reluctant to testify if recent events have vindicated your claims of molestation, that Martha and Chelsea had previously denied and which the Sheriff's Dept. and the CPS had said were unfounded or basically false allegations. At no time did Raeanna ever say she was threatened if she told. Neither her nor her family ever sought a restraining order or a civil judgment. Next up was Raeanna's grandmother, Anna Brennan.

Q. by Mr. Graham: Have you had any dealings with a Mr. Michael Harris before October 2003?

A. No, I haven't.

Q. Do you recall being alerted to some information at that time involving Mr. Harris by Raeanna?

A. Yes.

Q. What did you first learn?

A. She came home from their house.

Q. And what was her demeanor?

A. Just very different. When she came in the house she had a funny look on her face. And I knew something was wrong with her. And I asked her "What's wrong?" And she said "Nothing." And I said "did you and the twins get in an argument or something?" And she said "No, I want to take a bath, nan." And so we went in and she let water in and everything. And then in a few minutes, she called me in the bathroom and told me something happened.

Q. When she called you into the bathroom, did you question her further about what had happened, or did she just come out and say it?

A. She said, "I want to tell you something. Something did happen." And I said "Okay, what? What is wrong?" And then she told me.

Q. Do you know the name of the officer that you spoke to after this event?

A. I am pretty sure it was deputy Jeff Gordon.

Q. Did you tell Jeff Gordon that you asked your granddaughter if Mike had done something to her?

A. I might have after she was – I don't really recall if I told him that exactly or not.

And that was all from Ms. Brennan. Jeff Gordon was to be a witness in the days ahead, but Mr. Graham shifted gears into the computer evidence. I was eager to show them as liars just like all the other people. My mantra was "It's not paranoia if they really are out to get you." They might not have all started out to get me, but it sure wound up being the perfect storm.

TWENTY-FIVE

Finally, it was time for the computer evidence. Before their star witness Mr. Wall could testify, the People had to lay a proper foundation through the chain of custody in which each person who handled the evidence from Search to Seizure to trial had to testify. Next up then was Det. Paul Robles of the Mammoth Lakes Police Dept.

Q. by Mr. Graham: On August 20 of 2007 did you help execute a search warrant at a trailer?

A. Yes.

Q. Do you know whose trailer that was?

A. Yes.

Q. Who's was it?

A. Mr. Harris.

Q. Who did you go there with?

A. I was with Frank Smith, John Madrid who was a deputy sheriff, and Det. Rutowski showed up later on – and Brian Dressler from the Inyo County DA's office.

Q. What specifically did you find?

A. I found a SONY laptop that was on top of the – like the dining table.

Q. Did you give it to anybody at that time? Was there a person collecting all the evidence?

A. Det. Rutowski was taking possession of all the evidence,

Q. I am going to show you what has been marked as Exhibit 30. It is an evidence bag with what appears to be a laptop in it. Do you recognize that laptop as the laptop you seized or not?

A. It has been a long time. It is a SONY. I know the one I recovered was a SONY.

Mr. Graham: Nothing further.

The Court: Ms. Hankel?

Q. by Ms. Hankel: You just testified about People's Exhibit 30, this laptop?

A. Yes.

Q. And sitting there today, you have no way of knowing whether the laptop that is in this bag is the same laptop you saw in the trailer; is that correct?

A. Yes.

Q. Okay. Did you also have anything to do with the collection of these two hard drives?

A. I was there when they were found. Deputy Madrid is actually the one who found those.

Next was Detective Rutowski, a 32-year veteran of the Mono County Sheriff's Department. All these witnesses were still trying to authenticate the computer items as those actually seized during the search.

Q. by Mr. Graham: On August 20, 2007, did you execute a search warrant on one of [Harris'] residence?

A. Yes. Sir.

Q. All right. And were you there for the entire search or part of the search?

A. No sir. I was there for just the second half of the search.

Q. And during the search did you yourself seize in this residence or in this trailer any computer-related items?

A. Yes sir. I seized all of the items, once I arrived, that had been located previous to my arrival and compiled on the defendant's table. I took all the evidence from the trailer.

Q. I am going to show you what is Exhibit 30 – Do you recognize any of the writing on Exhibit 30 on the bag?

A. Yes sir.

Q. And is any of that writing yours?

A. Yes sir. It is.

Q. Okay. Can you take the computer out of the bag and compare the serial number on it to the serial number on the bag?

A. Okay. They appear to be the same.

Q. Specifically relevant to the laptop. Did you record in your report the laptop serial number that we have been discussing?

A. Yes sir.

Q. Let me show you Exhibit 28 – Again I want you to look at that bag first and see if you recognize any of the outside writing on the bag?

A. Yes sir. I do.

Q. And do you see any of your writing on that bag?

A. There is some of my writing on this bag, yes sir.

Q. Now there is some writing here below [your] description and location? Is that your writing or not?

A. No sir. That is not my writing.

Q. It looks like serial numbers, is that your writing?

A. No sir. It is not.

Detective Rutowski then explained how he took the evidence and placed it in his car and then drove up to the Crowley Lake substation where he put the evidence inside the substation in a file cabinet. The next morning, he bagged the evidence into similar bags with his case numbers and item numbers written on the outside. He then placed the evidence in the evidence locker. Why he didn't put the evidence there the night before baffles me. He left the evidence in the evidence locker until Deputy Delaney, the Mono County Sheriff's Department evidence officer picked them up some time later. Detective Rutowski didn't remember the date, but said it was approximately two weeks later. He verified that Deputy Delaney did in fact pick up the evidence for transport to Bridgeport.

Q. by Mr. Graham: Did you ever record the serial numbers during your involvement in the collection of the evidence?

A. Just the laptop serial number.

Q. Between the time that you seized and obtained this evidence to the time that you put the evidence in the evidence locker and had it at the Crowley sub[station] and eventually all the evidence including this went to Deputy Delaney, did you in any way alter the evidence or manipulate the evidence or do anything to change this computer?

A. No sir.

Ms. Hankel then began cross-examination of Det. Rutowski by asking him if he wrote down the serial number for the laptop.

Q. by. Ms. Hankel: And what was the purpose of writing down the serial number when you collected this evidence?

A. Well, for several reasons. Lots of times on traceable expensive items, we log the serial numbers as far as to verify what it is or whose it is.

Q. Okay. And is that to later on tell that the computer that you actually seized is the exact same computer that is in evidence later on in a case?
A. It could be, but not necessarily.
Q. In your POST [Peace Officer Standard and Training] training manual, do they tell you it is best to record a serial number when you collect evidence?
A. I don't recall that specific statement in the manual. But I would agree with that.
Q. Would you agree with me that it is a pretty important thing that the evidence you actually seized is the evidence adduced at trial later?
A. I would agree with that, yes.
Q. Okay. You had some involvement with Exhibit 28, the collection of hard drives; correct?
A. That's correct.
Q. And this evidence bag which is being projected onto the screen has evidence properly at the top, and you testified that this is your handwriting at the top? The first three lines with MCSO [Mono County Sheriff's Office], the subject's name, and then there is a description in lower case and looks like – this is your handwriting with the two hard drives, correct, just the words?
A. Yes, ma'am.
Q. So you yourself did not ever make any kind of determination as to the serial number on either one of the hard drives in this bag, is that correct?
A. Yes, ma'am.
Q. And is it important, when evidence can be altered, for you to note this serial number of evidence that can readily be altered when you collect it?
A. I don't know what you mean by altered. You can alter something with or without a serial number. I don't think the serial number would matter as far as altering something.
Q. Is it your understanding that you can actually change information on a hard drive?
A. I don't have a clue ma'am. I am not computer literate.
Q. You have not been taught in all the search warrant seminars and things that you have gone to that it is important, particularly for computer evidence to identify a hard drive by a serial number?
A. No ma'am. I have never been taught that.
Q. Okay. And is it your testimony that there is no serial number on your inventory list that is the same serial numbers on the two hard drives that are in evidence bag 28?
A. No. It shows the description as two hard drives.
Q. So the answer is there is no serial number on the inventory list; correct?
A. That's correct.

Q. Did you have anything in your office, or do you have anything sitting there today which shows that you made a report where you actually wrote down the serial numbers of the hard drives that are in evidence bag 28?

A. I did not write down the serial numbers of the hard drives.

Still unauthenticated the hard drive No. 1 is becoming an anomaly. We were moving along quickly through the chain of custody for what it's worth on the hard drive. The laptop was well documented but this loose hard drive was causing the police fits. The next person to testify was retired Sheriff's deputy Tim Delaney.

Q. by Mr. Graham: Good morning Deputy Delaney. What was your previous occupation?

A. Deputy Sheriff with the Mono County Sheriffs.

Q. Tell us what your involvement with evidence was at the Sheriff's Department?

A. I was the custodian of the property room.

Q. Tell us basically what you would do with the evidence.

A. The deputies would typically enter the evidence into a locker and lock the door. I would go to the substation and unlock those particular lockers.

Q. Where is the substation?

A. Crowley Lake and June Lake.

Q. Do you know Investigator McCammond?

A. Yes.

Q. Have you ever brought evidence from an evidence locker to him directly?

A. Numerous times.

Q. I am going to show you Exhibit 28. And this is the bag containing the two hard drives. Do you see any writing on that bag that is your?

A. Yes, I do.

Q. I will put this up on the projector and why don't you stand up and point to where your writing is for the jury.

A. The second line where it says CL evidence locker 2D1 and the date is my writing. And then D1 DA Investigator McCammond and the date 8/30/07 is my writing.

Q. Now do you have in your mind, as you sit there today that you did this, or would you say this refreshes your recollection?

A. I can tell you on many occasions I have on the same day taken it from a locker straight to the DA's office for Mr. McCammond.

Then it was time for Ms. Hankel to cross-examine Deputy Delaney and I thought that was going to go well for me. It was becoming apparent nobody wanted to admit not writing down the serial numbers. Ms. Hankel started off by going over the bag, Exhibit 28, with Deputy Delaney and he affirmed his handwriting. Ms. Hankel then asked him if it's his handwriting for the two serial numbers written on the outside of the bag.

Q. by Ms. Hankel: That is not your handwriting?

A. No, it is not.

Q. Was there anything you did, when you received this evidence, to ascertain what the serial numbers were on the hard drives in the bag?

A. No.

Q. And do you have any recollection, or is it your custom and practice, when you go on the computer and you put the evidence in the property room, that you write down the serial number of the hard drives that went into the property room.

A. No. Typically, I think that would be done by the investigating officer that put the property into evidence.

Q. Okay. So typically, the investigating officer who seizes the evidence would be the one to write the serial numbers on the bag?

A. Yes.

Q. After you put Exhibit 28 and Exhibit 30 into the evidence locker, you then delivered Exhibit 30 to Wade McCammond?

A. After I took them out of the evidence locker, assigned them their bin in the property room, I walked it over to Investigator McCammond.

Q. For both Exhibit 28 and Exhibit 30.

A. Yes.

And that wrapped up Deputy Delaney's testimony and so it was time to follow this odd chain of custody and see what Wade McCammond had to say. Mr. McCammond was actually Investigator McCammond of the Mono County District Attorney's Office. He handled many major cases in Mono County. On August 30th, 2007, he received some evidence from Deputy Delaney.

Q. by Mr. Graham: Is your memory consistent with [Deputy Delaney's] memory about him bringing computer evidence to you?

A. Yes, it is.

Q. Did you receive these two bags we've been talking about, Exhibit 30 and Exhibit 28 containing a laptop and one containing two hard drives?

A. Yes, I received that.

Q. From Mr. Delaney?

A. From Mr. Delaney.

Investigator McCammond then went on to detail his receipt of the evidence, the manner in which he stored it and the reasons why he needed to expedite the transfer of the computer evidence to Lydell Wall for forensic analysis. Brian Dressler was given the two bags of evidence, Exhibit 28 and Exhibit 30, in order to transfer them to the Sacramento Valley High Tech Task Force and Mr. Wall.

Q. by Mr. Graham: So you made contact with Mr. Dressler. What did he do?

A. He came to my office and I turned over specifically those two bags of evidence to him.

Q. And did you review those two items?

A. I have reviewed them, and I've seen them presented here in court.

Q. Is your writing on either of the two items, Exhibit 30 or Exhibit 28?

A. My writing is not within the description of the chain of custody.

With regards to Exhibit 30 and Exhibit 28, Investigator McCammond was asked about the chain of custody and the fact his name was not found between Deputy Delaney's and Brian Dressler's where it should have been. Instead, it was found at the bottom of the chain where he wrote his name picking up the evidence after the examination by Mr. Wall.

Q. by Mr. Graham: They came back to you in August of this year [2009]. What did you do with them?

A. Periodically manipulated them and I believe there is even – they have been opened since their return to me.

Q. You say "manipulated them." Are you doing anything to the hard drives themselves? In other words, hooking up to a computer or anything?

A. No. They have been removed and the labels photocopied.

Mr. Graham then produced the photocopied labels as Exhibit 31 and Exhibit 32 and he moved to admit the evidence.

Ms. Hankel: I am going to object. I am going to ask the witness to lay a foundation.

The Court: Go ahead. Are you done with the examination? Can she proceed with cross-examination?

Mr. Graham: Yes.

Q. by Ms. Hankel: Did you make the photocopies?

A. by Wade McCammond: Yes. I did.

Q. When did you made those photocopies?

A. I believe the same day I brought them back from Turlock, that I brought these two hard drives back.

Q. So you didn't make the photocopies before the evidence went to Turlock?

A. No, I did not.

Q. Okay. You also did not sign off in between – on Exhibit 28 – in between Brian Dressler and Tim Delaney's handling of the evidence?

A. Correct.

Q. Did you ever fill out anything that showed that you had received those two hard drives?

A. No.

Q. Did you ever fill out anything that clearly identified the serial numbers on these two hard drives when you received them?

A. No, I did not.

During the lunch break, Ms. Hankel filed a motion to exclude the evidence from the hard drives based on chain of custody issues relying on People v. Diaz, (1992) 3 Cal.4th 495, 559. The judge read and considered the motion over the lunch break. After lunch, Judge DeVore came back to the bench and without the jury being present he questioned counsel about the nuances of the foundation to admit Exhibit 28. The next witness, Mr. Wall, was to be the final link in the chain of custody and so the judge was satisfied and he denied the motion to exclude.

The Court: At your request, there has been drafted a limiting instruction relating to this computer evidence that we are going to give to the jury peremptorily.

TWENTY-SIX

Judge DeVore read the instruction and Mr. Graham and Ms. Hankel were both satisfied so the jury was brought in and the instruction was given to them. It basically told the jury that if you decide the defendant is responsible for any such images and/or text you may but are not required to consider that evidence for the limited purpose of deciding whether or not the defendant was the person who committed the offense as alleged in this case.

With that completed, Mr. Lydell Wall was called to the stand and he and Mr. Graham went over his career in law enforcement and his forming of a computer consulting firm in 1999. As part of his law enforcement career, he helped develop an extensive undercover operation program that sought out child sexual predators preying on children and distributing child pornography. In 2001, he was assigned to the Chandra Levy case and in 2006 he was assigned chief computer analyst for the Laci Peterson case. He officially retired from the Sacramento High Tech Crime Task Force in February 2009. In 2007, while he still worked in law enforcement, he was first contacted by Inyo County DA investigator Brian Dressler who had a computer to analyze and who told Mr. Wall he had some evidence from Mono County as well.

Q. by Mr. Graham: In September of 2007 did you gain some information that you were to pick up some computer evidence that had been collected in this case for your examination?

A. by Lydell Wall: Yes, we did.

Q. I'll show you what is marked as People's 28. And I want you to look at the bag and tell me if you see anything on there indicating your involvement from the beginning?

A. Yes, there's a case number indicating the two hard drives that are listed in the description or list that are of my partner at the time when I worked at that crime task force. I recognize his handwriting, his name, the Ryan West. That is his handwriting and down below my initials and my handwriting appear on five, line six, line seven, eighth line.

Q. Just so we're clear on the date of 9/26, is Exhibit 28, is your writing above – well the box, is it in the box next to that?

A. Yes. My writing is initialed as L. Wall as received it, and everything below up until the bottom line is not mine.

Mr. Wall then went on to describe meeting with Brian Dressler and actually reviewing the evidence physically, both Exhibit 30 and Exhibit 28, before flying back to Stanislaus County.

Q. by Mr. Graham: Regarding the two hard drives in Exhibit 28 as you look through the back description do you see any marks on the drives?

A. Yes, I do.

Q. There were two drives. And let's refer to them by their identification numbers as you would deem appropriate. But go ahead and tell us what you recognize on the back of the drive as any kind of writing?

A. I have used a Sharpie marker and wrote the same case number HIS-111 and labeled it as item No. 1 and the other drive I labeled with the same case number item No. 2.

Q. So we are clear when we talk about the two different drives, is there a number associated with the item No. 1 that you have just referred to?

A. Yes. This would be the primary drive of the computer, the bootable drive of the computer.

Now how could he have known when he picked up the evidence that item No. 1 was bootable? Both drives were out of the computer sitting on a bench and both were jumpered as slave drives. Mr. Wall would have had to had tried to access the drive to know that, or at least somebody did, you can't tell it is bootable without trying to boot it.

Q. by Mr. Graham: Is there a number on the label that I am referring to that you have used in your documentation?
A. Yes, I have to refer to my report.
Q. Would it refresh your recollection by looking at it?
A. Yes, it will. I documented two serial numbers, one for item No. 1 910S0D5. And for item No. 2 the serial number of 9DN0SC-326. However, there were additional numbers because hard drives have so many numbers on them, other numbers might appear – might also be present on the drives as well.
Q. When you look at the drive labeled item No. 1 in your handwriting what are the different numbers? You said one, what are the other numbers on there that relate to identification numbers?
A. Well, on he label there is going to be a model number listed, which is sometimes listed as the serial number because it's visible. And the model number on drive No. 1 is 91080D5.
Q. Is that the one you just read us off your report?
A. Yes.
Q. And what is the number used on the No. 2 drive, the one you've labeled No. 2?
A. The part number was listed as 9DN03C-326.

Mr. Wall then described things much as he had during the Evid. Code §402 hearings during the previous summer. He went ever the EnCase program, the creation of an exact copy called the "image file" and he produced his initial report and his supplemental report where he miraculously came up with the key.dat file, the keylogger printout Exhibit 60. Mr. Wall then described how a computer works and how users get information and how it's saved et cetera.

Q. by Mr. Graham: Throughout your examination of item No. 1, have I impressed upon you the importance of differentiating between items that would take user action to create versus items that you might find on the drive that were the result of something coming in unwanted, in an unwanted fashion?
A. Yes, you have.

So then, Mr. Wall was led through a parade of documents created by me, such as business cards, business correspondence, email addresses using my name, Mike Harris, and other indicia of my having used that drive item No. 1. Mr. Wall then went through the registry values for different programs showing me as the registered user of the programs on item No. 1.

Next, Mr. Graham asked about a variety of emails in the Outlook Express user created folder Saved Stuff. This folder resided in a file called saved_stuff.dbx and this was a file I had kept trying to get Mr. Albee to locate in order to identify users in the directory structure of the drive pivotal to my assertion that I did log on to a hard drive and created a user cache for ski which was used by the programs they just went through in the registry values. Mr. Wall then described me as an advanced user of a computer and discussed my business as a computer consultant. After this a break was taken and after the recess, before the jury was brought in, Judge DeVore ruled that all the documents presented thus far by the People were foundationally sufficient and admissible.

Ms. Hankel: I would like to add one thing for the record. That is that my foundational issue is expressly related to it as the court has noted that the foundation is laid because of the analysis of item No. 1 being the hard drive that was seized from the residence. And my continuing objection is that there has been no foundation laid to establish that the hard drive that is being referred to as item No. 1 is the actual hard drive that was seized at the residence.

The Court: Yes. I understood. We have dealt with that in the chain of custody witnesses and so forth.

Ms. Hankel: That is correct.

The Court: That is your objection. That is what I understood it to be. On that basis, respectfully, that is overruled as well.

After the jury was brought in, Mr. Graham started in on the Key Logger printout Exhibit 60.

Q. by Mr. Graham: All right. Is this a document you prepared?

A. Yes, it is.

Q. Tell us first. You labeled Actual Key Logger?

A. Actual Key Logger is a program that was installed on item No. 1 to log actual key strokes. It was installed in the program files as AK Program and the key log file was found in the logs folder in a file called key.dat which is this document.

Q. Now the key logger program, based upon your experience and training, what are the main purposes behind having a key logger program?

A. Well, a key logger program simply captures key strokes. It is used for a variety of reasons as an audit trail to indicate what actions had been taken, or it could be used by a person to keep track of what a child was doing on the computer.

Q. If you were someone with above average computer experience, say a person designated as a webmaster, is this something you would ordinarily find on a computer there?

A. It's hard to say whether it would be common or not. A lot of times people with extraordinarily high computer skills will test various programs to see what actions they take and determine their viability and functionality.

Q. This document you have here, Exhibit 60, in general, what does it depict without going into content?

A. Basically, it is key strokes on a computer item No. 1 that began on March the 12th and I believe ended on April 19th of 2006.

Q. All right. Now you have received this document prior to coming to court today; is that correct?

A. Yes, I have.

Q. As a general idea, what was your impression after you viewed this document and the recordation of key stroke activity and that relation to the user who is entering these key strokes interest of any kind?

A. Yes, there was a direct correlation to the user of the computer that was previously identified as Mike Harris and that there was an above average amount of websites and keyword searches that were done for young girls and preteen models.

They then proceeded to go through all 92 pages of Exhibit 60. It was exhausting, and I thought a bit of overkill, but that was how Judge DeVore ran things. What they failed to explain was that the keystroke logger logged a URL whenever a page popped up a new browser window and registered that address in the file. Many of the URLs were popups or pages spawned by one page opening another. Many pages didn't even load as shown by the lack of content recorded by the windows cache directory. This was obvious because there was no data found on item No. 1 corresponding to the recorded URL. Just to be fair, there were searches for preteen models, preteen bikini, preteen Lolita and the like. But there were no sex related searches, and as I said, there was no data form the URLs on item No. 1. The amount of material presented by Mr. Wall was extraordinary. Judge DeVore should have limited the amount that was admissible just to be fair because I wasn't even charged with illegal use of a computer.

Mr. Wall then went into newsgroups saying I had subscribed to nasty newsgroups looking for child porn. But that was belied by the reality that I only looked at lists of message titles and did not look at any messages. Mr. Wall tried to say I read a child incest story but never in fact showed any access to that message. Some of the newsgroups included: alt.binary.pictures.child.female or alt.binaries.pictures.erotica.child.female for example.

Q. by Mr. Graham: Give us the overview of your familiarity with newsgroups like these.

A. Of course, during my training and the investigations that we have done, distribution of child pornography and child erotica is prevalent on the internet. And there are those who would openly trade those types of images through various means. And newsgroups are one of the most popular means, especially during the Windows98 period of distributing child erotica and child pornography. Back in these days, it required a trust relationship to be developed between users, a handshake so to speak. So someone would not make available child pornography readily to someone he wouldn't know because of the ramifications that it may be a law enforcement officer looking for an investigation to prosecute. So there had to be some type of relational development that occurred between parties. And these typically did not contain child pornography in a rampant manner. The distribution of child pornography was usually done through specific file sharing or through CD-ROMs being delivered. You could purchase it. But there was not an overwhelming amount during this period of time where child pornography was distributed through newsgroups.

So that was all well and good but where was the evidence that I created relationships or sought out pornography of any type? An example of how prejudicial this evidence was is contained on page 59 of Exhibit 60. It shows the letters in all caps "PTHC LINKS ARCHIVE!" Mr. Wall was asked what that meant and he replied that PTHC is another acronym for pre-teen hardcore. The problem was it was an unrequested file. It was in the keylogger but it wasn't keyed in, it just popped open in a new window. No images or text was ever found, yet Mr. Wall swore that this showed the user accessed child pornography. This went on for hours.

Mr. Graham: This is Exhibit 81.

Q. by Mr. Graham: Do you recognize this document?

A. Yes, I do.

Q. And did you create that document recently?

A. Yes, I did.

Q. And tell us what was the process by which you created the images in this document?

A. This series of images was as a result of my analysis in a virtual environment. What I am able to do was … I can mount these image files I talk about from the EnCase program and I can actually see what the computer looked like when it was booted up. So it gives me the ability to access the program for computer in a virtual environment on my computer, go through the entire login and be able to access everything on the computer, including programs, be able to see the desktop and a host of other issues that are present on a computer system, a live environment virtual, a live controlled environment with no date being written to the data file.

Q. The last statement you made, you are now going to show the jury the screen shots that was what the screen would look like when you go to different parts of the computer; that's correct?

A. That's correct.

Ms. Hankel was a little confused so she asked to voir dire Mr. Wall on this issue.

Q. by Ms. Hankel: Mr. Wall, you said you used a program called VMWare to create these pages?

A. Yes.

Mr. Wall then went on a lengthy narrative of EnCase image files, the creation of the image file, and the emulation of it hence the name VMWare (Virtual Machine Ware).

Q. by Ms. Hankel: Then is it accurate to say that your exhibit shows images from data on the computer [item No. 1] itself?

A. This is a series of screen shots of what I saw while manipulating item 1 as it would appear if someone had turned the computer on and booted it up. It is a set of screen captures of that process and different functions of different programs.

Q. And what did you have to manipulate to get this data in this exhibit?

A. I would go to the start bar, just like I would see the computer as it would be booted up, if I had the real computer and booted it. I would see the start bar, and I would click the start bar and activate the programs. And when that program popped up, I would take a screen capture of it or the settings pertaining to that particular package that it was running in that mode.

After that answer, Ms. Hankel finished and renewed her objections on relevancy and foundation grounds. Mr. Wall began showing the screen captures. After this it was time to go home. After another long trip to Independence and back I was in the saddle again, ready for another day in court. Ready for the computer evidence to end I should say. It seemed endless and I so wanted to testify right then and there to put Mr. Wall in his place. First thing that morning Mr. Graham dove right in to more balderdash that had Mr. Wall stating I went into newsgroups and actually viewed content even though Mr. Albee had said the newsgroup messages weren't even accessed, just the subject title lists had been. I never went into any newsgroups as described by Mr. Wall and I wanted Mr. Albee to prove it.

A quirk of the whole trial process is that upcoming witnesses are not allowed to be in the courtroom except to testify. This meant Ms. Hankel had to relay what was being said by Mr. Wall on to Mr. Albee at the end of the day. Me, I was 90 miles away in basic radio silence. Teenage girls, preteen girls, preteen girls in tights, Lolita, those were all links Mr. Wall said I viewed. Even one called Real CP for "child pornography," but it was obviously a popup, not a link, since there was no page with that as a link on the computer. Mr. Graham then brought up the issue of users of item 1 which Mr. Albee had testified at the §402 hearing had used the computer, such as Christina Jump for example.

Q. by Mr. Graham: What did you determine about that name in relationship to the hard drive?

A. In conducting the analysis, I reviewed the data pertaining to the names submitted to me. And this specific name was identified as a potential user of the computer. The only place I identified this in an active content was an allocated space in the drive I named a spam folder. And I do know a spam filter was in place and it contained over 5,000 emails.

Q. Was one of the emails associated with Christina Jump?

A. It was in that spam folder.

Mr. Graham then went through the list of names Mr. Albee had testified were potential users of item 1 and showed what I already knew. Mr. Albee had made a big mistake at the §402 hearing when he said he had identified other users of the drive, item 1. Of special importance was the fact that of thousands of emails there was not one porn email, child, teen, or adult.

Mr. Graham then moved on to the Exhibit 81 VMWare screen captures. Mr. Wall walked the jury through the 21 pages explaining that the first thing he saw was the welcome to windows login screen which allows a user to input a user name and password to customize the computer setup for different individual users. I know Mr. Wall testified that this feature wasn't available in Win98 first edition back at the §402 hearing. I wanted Ms. Hankel to jump him on that point because the cache file system relied on a user login profile to create directory structure. Mr. Wall testified the computer did have a boot error which caused it to "crash" stating that "when a computer crashes, it does not shut down properly. A thing called the checkdisk will enable itself."

I didn't see the checkdisk program run when Mr. Wall virtually booted up the system and instead of logging in as ski which was my login, he bypassed the login screen by hitting cancel and began viewing content with default as the user and I don't think Mr. Wall understood the difference. Mr. Wall then described the crash and an unwanted shutdown which would activate the next time the computer was booted up. He then went into some mumbo jumbo about Word and how that program would make a temp file so that the file being worked on can be recovered to some degree after a crash. First, that feature wasn't available in Win98 first edition. Second, Internet Explorer and Outlook Express use a cache file system. A temp based system wasn't available or installed on my hard drive in early-to-mid-2006. Photoshop and some other programs do work on a temp file basis however the programs at issue here do not.

Mr. Graham continued to go through the screen captures, all 21 of them and he reviewed the mail settings. Wrapping up the screen shots, Mr. Graham launched into the "exemplary evidence" which was a collection of web pages purportedly viewed by me but were in reality pages recreated by Mr. Wall surfing the web in 2009 and hypothesizing that these pages were examples of what I supposedly looked at in 2006. Confused yet? I was. This was all based on a file Mr. Wall said he found on the pst1002.tmp file which showed pages viewed by some user at some time.

There were images on those pages that offended everyone in the courtroom and they didn't even come from my computer hard drive, if you could call it that. On top of that, Mr. Wall actually visited the sites twice several months apart and wound up producing 116 pages with up to 21 images each that he opined showed something like what I had viewed 3 years earlier. The jury was excused and after they left the court asked:

The Court: Do I understand correctly that the People offer these as representative of material that the visited — that the URL sites found on the hard drive we were talking about now produced and do not purport to be what has been there at any previous time precisely?

Mr. Graham: Correct.

The Court: And in the previous hearing, did I understand correctly that these sites change with regard to specific content, but Mr. Wall's testimony has been and again will be the content is generically the same; is that correct?

Mr. Graham: It is — Ms. Hankel, you wanted to express objections to this?

Ms. Hankel: Yes. I am objecting as to relevance, as to foundation. I'm objecting under §352, more prejudicial than probative because the witness cannot testify that any, I think, not a single image from any single one of the URL sites located on the computer were actually found on the computer, nor can the witness state that any of these images were found on the computer, the computer case, or any other place on the computer. So the witness cannot even state that the URL sites were ever visited. So that is my objection. They are called visited sites without any indication on the computer, any image was seen from the visited URL sites.

The Court: I understand that to be your position.

Ms. Hankel: Yes.

The Court: The People's offer is that Mr. Wall will testify that these were sites that were visited, but because of the change in content, virtual change in content, you can only produce representatives to show that the content remains essentially the same over time, one from April and one from November; am I correct?

Mr. Graham: Correct.

Ms. Hankel: I want to make clear my objection is that there are no visited website with any image whatsoever on the computer. So that you cannot tell whether any of these URL sites were ever visited, that is my objection.

The Court: If that is your objection. I do understand. On each ground the objection is respectfully overruled on the §352 grounds. I specifically concluded the relevance in connection with the probative value and the potential for undue prejudice. I have also considered the other factors of §352, including that this is not cumulative. It is not unduly consumptive of time, nor does it have any potential to confuse the jury in any respect. So on each grounds, including §352 evidence, respectfully your objections are overruled, and 55A and 55B will be admitted. And you are free to do what you will in terms of attacking it with regard to weight and so forth. But that is the ruling.

Geez. It felt like hate on Harris day. Things were going terribly what with all the bogus computer evidence and the evidence wasn't even over yet. I felt like I was being attacked from all sides with nothing but bull-shit. I couldn't wait to take the stand. So the jury was called back in and the judge read a limiting instruction that Exhibits 55A and 55B do not represent actual images that were taken off the hard drive. Mr. Graham then started asking Mr. Wall about that pesky pst1002.tmp file found in unallocated clusters on item No. 1 one more time.

Q. by Mr. Graham: And what again is a temp folder?

A. This is a file that was created as a result of the crash we are talking about. The crash can happen in a variety of ways.

Q. Okay. We go down to these different URL names; is this correct?

A. That's correct.

Q. You see the list. And did you enter those URL names into your computer to see what came up?

A. Yes, I did.

Q. Did you on Monday go through this list and enter these visited URL sites and printout what you first observed when the site was linked and images were up on the screen?

A. Yes.

Q. Can you just give us three pages of examples and show us what we are looking at? Can you first show us the visited URL that is on that list and where that visited URL name is on this exemplary page?

A. Yes. This comes from line 8 of the spreadsheet, where the name Lolita was entered with safe search off. It shows here that the exact link was copied in by Internet Explorer with the resulting Google images search for the name Lolita.

Q. Did you type in that word Lolita?

A. No, I did not.

Q. Is that word Lolita, produced when that screen comes up by the sheer fact that you have the URL name in the upper bar?

A. Yes, copied from the URL spreadsheet.

Q. When you look at these two stacks, 55-A, the first one we just showed the jury, and 55-B, what is your opinion as to the similarities showing similar types of images as a result of the URL's that were entered?

A. There is obvious distinct similarities showing similar types of images as a result of the URLs that were entered.

Now that the jury had been completely offended with graphic porn images which were not even child porn, Mr. Graham wanted to fall back to Exhibit 58, the pst1002.tmp file. This file was clearly not a part of item No. 1 as presented. Nowhere in this file were there any html files, cookies, text, video, or other type files. My analogy was that at no time would there be a history file which is a text file and then no others. It just wouldn't happen that way.

Q. by Mr. Graham: Showing you Exhibit 58, what is this exhibit?

A. These are the images that were recovered from the pst files. These were all the temporary files that were in the Windows subdirectory of temp on item 1.

Q. You have a document here containing 80 pages; is that correct?

A. That's correct.

Q. And what basically does this document contain?

A. During my analysis, I recovered all of the images files that were contained in the Windows subdirectory of temp.

Q. Do you believe these were affirmatively accessed images?

A. Yes.

Q. Why?

A. These are images that were recovered from websites that were visited commonly referred to as thumbnails for images that were actually clicked on to create the image viewed in a web browser environment.

Q. And do these images here have any similarity to the previous two exhibits of 55-A and 55-B?

A. Yes. They are images that were recovered from pst1002.tmp and they are images that were from the viewed websites from the viewed URLs, that of young girls posing in sexually suggestive poses.

Q. Now, we're clear these images were found on the hard drive No. 1; is that correct?

A. That's correct. In the Windows temp folder.

Q. Now were there other nonchild involved images in this temp file?

A. Yes.

Q. As you go through these images, page by page, are there going to be clusters of child related images and clusters of random stuff images?

A. Yes, normal web surfing activity from the browser.

If there is web surfing going on, then where are all the graphics like buttons and bars and divider lines and ads, not to mention scripting and html web pages? Mr. Wall is trying to say he found a URL history file in a graphic file but not the web pages or newsgroup messages. It simply was not making sense to me. He just a moment ago seemed to say the images were clicked on because he had the thumbnails, but he never showed a thumbnail and a full-sized image with its container file albeit it html or message. And why were all the bad images in one suspect location? A location not used by Internet Explorer or Outlook Express.

Mr. Graham then produced a CD-ROM created by Mr. Wall that had all the bad images collected together for easy display. They went through those (as though they jury didn't get it already), and Ms. Hankel objected as cumulative, §352, relevance and foundation with Judge DeVore overruling her every step of the way. It was all the same stuff already presented and it really was cumulative. Judge DeVore was going to let the prosecution have their day. Finally, it was over and I took a much needed break in my holding cell with the single bench along the wall.

TWENTY-SEVEN

After a short recess, it was Ms. Hankel's turn. She started in on Mr. Wall's background first.

Q. by Ms. Hankel: And so you are a very experienced law enforcement officer?

A. Yes, ma'am.

Q. And a very experienced law enforcement officer also in computer forensics?

A. Yes, ma'am.

Q. Do you teach seminars to show other law enforcement how to handle evidence and how to do forensics?

A. How to do forensics. Evidence is done at the academy level.

Q. So is that kind of elementary?

A. It is basic stuff.

Q. And what about your partner?

A. Brian Wentzel, yes, he was a partner of mine at the Stanislaus County Sheriff's Dept. He worked in our unit.

Q. And he was working there when you received the evidence in this case?

A. Yes, he was.

Q. I see here Exhibit 28, which contained those two hard drives we were talking about, one of which is item No. 1 that you testified about all morning. There is the bag you signed for the chain of custody?

A. That's correct.

Q. And on that one, two, three, four, five, six, seventh line, are those your initials there?
A. Yes, it is my writing.
Q. And then the date you received the evidence bag was —
A. It is listed there as January 3rd of 2007.
Q. Is that the date you received the evidence down in Inyo County?
A. No.
Q. What does that date reflect?
A I think it was in September of '07.
Q. Then is there a notation on that bag for September of '07?
A. Yes, there is.
Q. And then it went on the 26th of September you were with Mr. Wentzel when you got this evidence?
A. Yes.
Q. And then the next line that says - tell me what it says. Is that your handwriting?
A. Yes, it is. It says Sac. High Tech., L. Wall evidence room 9/26/07.
Q. So on the same day you received it, you put it in an evidence room?
A. Yes.
Q. Okay. The next line I saw would be the line where I saw just the L. Wall and that is 1/3/08?
A. It says L. Wall office imaging.
Q. And then there is another line under that with your initial and your last name. And it says evidence room with — I am not seeing a date there.
A. Yeah, the date is blank. It is not written in.
Q. Is there a reason why it's not written in there?
A. I have no idea, it was probably inadvertently left off.
Q. Did you ever, when you had received this evidence in September, you were working for high crimes task force?
A. High Tech Crimes Task Force, yes, ma'am.
Q. And the entire time you were doing the computer analysis, were you also working for that high tech task force?
A. Up until I retired. I retired in February of 2009.
Q. Okay.
A. But I didn't work on it the entire time, no.
Q. And I see this date of 9/26/07, when you got the evidence and put it in the evidence room and then I see the one January 3, 2007, where you've indicated that you are taking it to your office for imaging?
A. Yes.

Q. So in between receiving it and imaging it there is a - how many months is that?
A. Four months.
Q. Were you with Brian Wentzel when he wrote on that bag the model number for a hard drive and the serial number for a hard drive?
A. Yes, I was. I was in the same room at Inyo County at their county facility.

Now the question looms, why did they wait four months to image the hard drive when there was such urgency that they had to fly into Inyo County to get the drive? And why didn't they fly into Mammoth or Bridgeport? Why did the drive need to go to Inyo County?

Q. by Ms. Hankel: So by the phraseology, I would imagine you are telling me you weren't present when he did that?
A. I was present, but I didn't look over his shoulder necessarily. I don't recall watching him write it on there. But I do recognize that as being his writing.
Q. Have you ever, before this case, had to write down the actual serial number of the hard drive that you are going to be analyzing before?
A. Yes, ma'am.
Q. Do you know the difference between a serial number and a model number?
A. Yes, ma'am.
Q. Can you tell me the difference?
A. Usually one says model number and one says serial number.
Q. Did you train Brian Wentzel?
A. Yes, I did train him.
Q. Did you train him to write down the model number of a hard drive that you guys are going to be analyzing?
A. Part of our training includes model numbers and serial numbers.
Q. Did you train him to put down the serial numbers of those hard drives rather than a model number?
A. Yes. We are trained to do serial numbers.
Q. And do you always record the serial number of hard drives when you do it?
A. Yes. I try to do it but I make mistakes sometimes.
Q. You wrote a report in this case; correct?
A. Yes, I did.
Q. And the date of your report is a little bit after that January 3rd 2007 date? Do you have the date of that report as April 25, 2008? Do you have that report in front of you?
A. Yes.
Q. At the top of your report, you itemize evidence that you have analyzed in your report; correct?

A. Yes.

Q. And you have identified item 1 here as the Maxtor hard drive which purports to be in the bag in front of you; correct?

A. Yes.

Q. And you have here the S/N which would stand for serial number; correct?

A. That's correct.

Q. And do you not have a model number there after the serial number indication?

A. That is correct. That is the model number for that drive.

Q. And so it is not a specific identifier for the hard drive that you analyzed; correct?

A. Yes, that is correct.

Ms. Hankel then went on to show that they wrote down the serial number for item 2, the other hard drive; and item 3a, the laptop hard drive. Yet, they neglected to do so on the one piece of evidence with one suspect file that had what the prosecution was calling bad stuff. None of the other drives, discs, tapes, images, negatives, videos, or correspondence seized upon my arrest had bad stuff on it. Just pst1002.tmp. It was a railroad job gone crazy.

Q. by Ms. Hankel: It is only item 1, the only piece that you had, that no one thought to put a serial number on, including yourself, that had any bad stuff on it; correct?

A. I actually did record the actual serial number on my forensic worksheet when the drive was examined.

Q. And it is not anywhere in the report; correct?

A. Correct.

Q. Okay. And you received this hard drive in January of '07? Or you began working on it in January of '07; is that correct?

A. Actually, I believe that is a common mistake, it would have been January 3rd, '08.

Q. Can you tell me how much you billed from February of 2007 until today on this case?

A. It's probably in the area of $20,000.

Q. And so it is a pretty serious case, is it not?

A. I consider the case serious.

Q. So it is important, is it not, to make sure that you are not making mistakes when you draft your report, when you fill out evidence bags, when you complete identifying marks on evidence. These are pretty serious mistakes, are they not?

A. I would say they are mistakes. I don't — I mean we are human, we do make mistakes. How serious they are could be left to interpretation.

Q. Is it important in your analysis that you found only three, what you've identified as child porn images on a nine-year-old hard drive?

A. I considered it a very low amount of images, yes.

Q. And do you agree with me that in the newsgroup listing that you found very little evidence of any messages that were viewed on this computer from the newsgroup listings?

A. I believe there were only two that were introduced.

Q. So all those lists and lists and lists of newsgroups, what they had as titles or subheadings; you found two messages that you thought that were actually viewed?

A. Yes.

Q. Then aside from the three child porn images, and the two newsgroup messages you had a list of what you called visited URL sites?

A. That's correct.

Q. So this list of what we call visited URLs — these are the URLs which you found on the computer; correct?

A. That's correct.

Q. And then all the other stuff here is a document you created and generated from a different computer where you went in and looked for what these URLs might contain last Monday?

A. That's correct.

Q. And then I think there is another exhibit here, where you did the same thing back in April of 2009; is that correct?

A. That's correct.

Q. And also, none of these images were actually found on item 1?

A. No, that is incorrect.

Q. Are you stating that these images were found on item 1?

A. Not those images, but images similar to that when the URLs were activated on the computer were found or are in the exhibit that is entitled PST images. The similar images of child models, child erotica are contained in that exhibit.

Q. Okay.

A. So they were on the computer.

Q. All right. The images you found in PST were on the computer. So then why did you recreate a whole new list if the actual images were already on the computer?

A. Because not all the images are going to remain on the computer. The ones that are in PST, those in pst1002.tmp. There is going to be a lot of those images that are still there that are associated with the web pages visited. But I don't have the capability of rejoining the images on the actual webpage that was visited. So what I was able to do, at the request of Mr. Graham was to take the URLs and show images similar and how they would appear.

Q. Now you gave us a lot of what you called snap shots, screen shots.

A. Screen captures.

Q. Screen captures. And you put those in evidence to show what the screen looked like at various times when a user looks at that screen; correct?

A. That's correct.

Q. You didn't have any screen captures of child porn, did you?

A. No, I did not.

Q. You didn't have any screen captures of child erotica, did you?

A. No, I did not.

Q. You didn't have any screen captures of any newsgroup messages?

A. No, I did not. Just the parent directories and the individual files I think showed up in some of those screen captures.

Q. If you are the sole, exclusive user of a computer, is there any reason to install a key stroke logger?

A. There are many reasons to install a key stroke logger.

Q. What are those reasons?

A. To be able to create an audit trail, to test software, to monitor other people's activity on your computer, to capture passwords.

Q. What is an audit log?

A. To audit your own keystrokes, to find out — go back and see what you were doing to test software and see what the output of the program is.

Ms. Hankel then tried to ask a question regarding Mr. Wall's extensive forensic computer career analyzing close to 500 computers.

Q. by Ms. Hankel: So between the 360 and 480 [computers analyzed] did you find in the analysis of this computer [item 1] a vast amount of child erotica, comparatively?.

Mr. Graham: Objection. Can we approach on this issue?

A discussion was held out of earshot of everyone in the courtroom. Once concluded, Ms. Hankel launched right back in.

Q. by Ms. Hankel: In your experience in analyzing — forensically analyzing computers, would you say this is a great deal of child erotica that was found on this computer?

Well, that did it. Mr. Graham objected again, another sidebar discussion occurred and then Mr. Graham asked for a full-blown hearing of his objection. The jury was excused and the hearing began. Mr. Graham was concerned that the questioning was going to write reversible error into the record.

Mr. Graham: We are getting into evidence, a spectrum — well if you have this amount of bad-stuff on your computer, would you expect to see more child porn, more child erotica?

The Court: Are you concerned for Mr. Harris' due process rights?

Mr. Graham: I am.

The Court: That isn't your role specifically, but I understand. This is a considered judgment that has been made as a tactical decision to inquire on this topic?

Ms. Hankel: You bet.

The Court: Is it not?

Ms. Hankel: Yes.

Mr. Graham: We are getting into profile evidence of what a child molester would have on his computer.

The Court: Are you arguing now that you should be allowed to go into those areas if it comes out?

Ms. Hankel: He has already done it.

Mr. Graham: I have not done it Judge.

Ms. Hankel: You asked him to render an opinion that merely because this was shown on his computer, he has shown a sexual interest in little girls. If that is the state of the record, then I get to say really? Shouldn't you find more of this to show a sexual interest in little girls. The prosecutor is saying he gets to say it is there and it shows a sexual interest in little girls, but I can't say there's not enough of it to show?

Mr. Graham: I didn't show — I didn't ask for a quantity.

The Court: You're cutting it too fine. I respect your concerns for integrity of the process including the due process rights. With all respect, I am not going to interfere with counsel's considered handling of the case and consultation with her client on this topic in this way.

Before moving on, I just want to comment that Ms. Hankel never consulted with me on tactics she was developing ad hoc at the lectern. Ms. Hankel occasionally listened to me but she made her own calls without my input. So the jury was brought back in and Ms. Hankel was allowed to ask her question over Mr. Graham's objection.

Q. by Ms. Hankel: Mr. Wall, in your experience forensically analyzing computers, would you say this is a great deal of child erotica that you found on item 1?

A. No.

Ans that was that. Mr. Graham then had a few questions of redirect.

Q. by Mr. Graham: With regard to information management, whether it is allocated or unallocated, the expansion of those two concepts on the drive — do you see what I am saying?

A. Yes, it is clearly user intervention. It takes a user to be able to create files and delete files. So allocated would be the creation of it; deletion or deletion of data would be the unallocated, and that requires user intervention.

Mr. Wall said that a user had to do something to create or delete yet failed to mention that a popup webpage would create a cache file as it is loaded and create a history entry even if it isn't viewed. Also, the program settings flush out the cache periodically thus files are created and deleted without user intervention.

Q. by Mr. Graham: What happens to those URL's as I operate a computer over time?

A. The default setting for an internet browser is typically 20 days. That is the default. So it will cache things up to the 20-day period. The first amount of data captured on day one will automatically roll off or get flushed out or deleted by the browser and sent to unallocated space. And it just — every day that data falls off — first in first out theory.

Q. Was there shredding software on that drive?

A. Yes, there was.

Q. Explain what shredding software is.

Ms. Hankel: I am going to object as beyond the scope.

The Court: Sustained.

That was a peculiar thing, that last colloquy where the subject of shredding software came up. Shredding software simply overwrites all data in unallocated space; temp files and the like. My concern with Ms. Hankel was that she didn't get the nuances of Mr. Wall's "techy talk". She shouldn't have objected then raised the specter on her own that if I had shredding software and had shredded data then why was there stuff on the hard drive that didn't get shredded? That being said, Mr. Graham was done and it was Ms. Hankel's turn to close things down.

Q. by Ms. Hankel: Most of the dates of creation and the dates of access to the newsgroups were exactly the same, were they not?

A. Yes, there are some similarities between them.

Q. And would you say that most of the dates of creation, the very first date that the user subscribed to those newsgroups was the very last date of access? It was done the exact same time and date; correct?

A. Yes.

And then Ms. Hankel was done. The computer evidence was in and it was bad. I felt terrible. Even I would vote guilty at that point except I knew the truth. I just had to get Ms. Hankel and Mr. Albee to understand my counter "techy talk" . This was way over most people's heads, even mine, because it was all bullshit. Mr. Wall was wrong and they had messed with that drive to add misery to my lot.

I was upset with Ms. Hankel for not informing me of Mr. Wall's treachery the night before he testified. Mr. Wall had a telephonic conference call with all the parties except for me and he outlined even more new evidence he was going to present from the hard drive. I was frustrated with Ms. Hankel for not informing me of important developments in my case. All of them. Especially in regards to this last-minute change in evidence to be offered at trial. I wanted Ms. Hankel to inform me of all the changes occurring during this fluid and dynamic period. I wanted to be in the loop as to all strategic decisions being made.

Judge DeVore, in overruling Mr. Graham's objection related to due process at the end of Ms. Hankel's cross of Mr. Wall, said he wasn't "going to interfere with counsel's considered handling of the case and consultation with her client on this topic." This is contradicted by Ms. Hankel's steadfast reluctance to consult with me on strategy and tactics. Even if I was the most knowledgeable of all the experts in the room. Computer-wise anyway. Mr. Wall and Mr. Graham were being bullies toward Ms. Hankel and Mr. Albee with abstruse descriptions of evidence and leaving it to the defense to figure it out, and leaving me unable to assist because I was still in the Inyo County Jail. Mr. Graham contended that the hard drive was the evidence and whatever they chose to put forth at trial was properly disclosed through discovery of the drive. Basically, we gave you the drive copy so you better be ready for anything we decide to introduce based on it or from it.

Mr. Albee said that he was only required to respond to items that were to be presented to the jury, he couldn't be responsible for over 100 gigs of data on an ad hoc basis. I told Ms. Hankel that I was an expert in that evidence, the drive was a fraud and I could prove it. I told her she should declare me an Evid. Code §702 witness for the purpose of responding to the People's subterfuge. These new pieces of evidence were those introduced at trial. Exhibit 55-A was one of those and it was prejudicially unfair. Mr. Wall spent much of his time engaged in "techy talk" meant to confuse others understanding of the technology and thus enhance his own authority over the matter at hand.

I explained to Ms. Hankel that she needed an additional Windows expert to counter the "techy talk" but she said the court would not go for it. Subtleties I was trying to get her to understand with notes passed during trial included for example: Mr. Wall testified that he knew item No. 1 was bootable in September 2007, that's why he listed it as item No, 1 on the evidence bag. When he picked up the drive in the bag, he knew it was bootable but he said nobody tried to access it. The dichotomy is obvious. Either you knew or you were lying. My drive seized from a shelf in my trailer was jumpered as a slave and could not boot.

Another example pointed out to Ms. Hankel in a detailed written hypothetical addressing Mr. Wall's misrepresentation in testimony was when he said that if somebody has surreptitiously copied a file such as pst1002.tmp to item 1 then the access date would have changed to the date it was copied and the HASH value of the hard drive would also have changed. That was a false statement or at least a misleading one by him. Ms. Hankel could not have responded even with Mr. Albee sitting right there next to her since this "techy talk" was far beyond either of their ken.

I tried to explain in my notes that if a person copied a file to the drive before Mr. Wall ran an EnCase scan, then the new HASH value would be the only one he had. He wouldn't know of any previous values for previous dates. And remember, they had the drive from 8/20/07 to 1/3/08 before they supposedly scanned or imaged the drive. By the way, a HASH value is a numerical quantification of the files as they sit on the drive and any change to a file, no matter how miniscule, changes the HASH value.

Going further, Ms. Hankel did not understand the crux issue in Mr. Wall's misrepresentation, that being if a person copies a file from one drive to another, it automatically changes the access date. This was also a false or misleading statement. On a fundamental level, if one drive running Windows copies a file to another drive also running Windows then the file would get a new date reflecting the date it was placed in its new location. It would keep its creation and last accessed date from the source disk.

However, if a person copies a file from a drive to another drive and Windows is not running, then no dates associated or embedded in the file would change. One example is copying installation files from a disk onto a hard drive before it is booted with an operating system. Another example is if you are copying Windows onto a new drive and Window's is not running off the CD. The files are simply copied over to the empty drive and then the Windows files are activated to expand and install thus creating new dates. In a nutshell, the file moves but there are no new dates.

Mr. Wall also presented printouts from a program called VMWare. I tried to get Ms. Hankel to confront him about this evidence. None of the printouts made any sense such as the newsgroup messages not being formatted correctly as Win98 first edition and Outlook Express were configured on my system. An example, the VMWare program is a virtual emulation program, or in laymen's terms, a program that pretends to run item 1 by running a copy of it.

Specifically, Mr. Wall showed purported screen captures related to the newsgroups and the server news.verizon.net. Ms. Hankel never objected to the manufactured items of evidence that had not even been presented at the §402 hearing, outside the presence of the jury. Also important was the fact Ms. Hankel did not understand the complexities of what I was asserting. Namely, the evidence was fraudulent and one example would be contained in images 4-8 of Court Exhibit 56 which shows a graphical representation of newsgroup access by the Outlook Express program, but how could the newsgroup be accessed without being online?? The printed output from VMWare showing Outlook Express accessing news messages depicts the message pane showing the mail and news folders; the message list pane which displays available messages; and the preview pane which is the area where a message would display if it is selected from the list. I wanted Ms. Hankel to point out the error in the screen captures which showed that the top bar of the program, the title bar, shows news.verizon.net and the directory pane shows some nefarious group being selected and a list of messages in the message list pane. This message list is a forensic impossibility.

To put it bluntly, a list of messages in the message list pane can only be displayed while connected to a news server such as news.verizon.net. It doesn't matter whether an actual computer is running or VMWare is pretending to run it. Only if connected to a news server will messages be displayed and a newsgroup be selected from a list as shown in the exhibit described. Newsgroup messages never stay saved on a computer unless the user saves them and then they would be saved in a user created and named folder such as saved news and then the computer would create the file called saved news.dbx and place it in the news folder under the

Outlook Express folder under the users name similar to the management of mail messages which would be in inbox.dbx in the mail subdirectory of Outlook Express in the users directory of Windows. There is no temp involved in the tree.

Mr. Wall had shown the court a user created mail folder named saved stuff.dbx in the directory tree of Outlook Express just like inbox.dbx does. During Mr. Wall's testimony, Ms. Hankel notified me that my ex-girlfriend was going to take the stand and sling some more mud at me. The day couldn't have ended quick enough for me. Thank God it was Friday. Mr. Graham was loving it. It was time for Kathy Shultz (Barrickman).

Q. by Mr. Graham: Ms. Barrickman, do you know Mike Harris?
A. by Kathy Barrickman: Yes.
Q. Back in approximately 2001 were you dating Mike Harris?
A. Yes.
Q. Did Mr. Harris ever make any statements to you, conditional statements about if you do something, he's going to do something to you?
A. Yes.
Q. Can you tell the jury the statement you remember like that that he told you?
A. In reference to a restraining order, "If you do that and I go to jail, then I will get out and what do you think I'll do then? If you won't be with me, I'll kill you and your kids."
Q. Okay.
A. Stuff like that. I don't know exact statements — he said he would burn down my trailer and kill my kids.
Q. Did Mr. Harris ever make any statements on what he would do to you if you called the police regarding his behavior?
A. He would say often "If you do that you fucking bitch, I will kill you."
Q. Did he ever make any statements about if he was to go to jail what he would do to you?
A. He said, "If I go to jail, one day I'll get out, and then -
Q. What did you take that as?
A. A threat that he would come and kill me.

Finally, it was over. Just like that. Ms. Hankel refused to cross-examine Kathy and I was upset but I figured I would cover that in my testimony. The day was over. The hate on Harris day. The hate on Harris week. It was all pretty much hateful thus far. But my day was coming. Judge De-Vore read an instruction to the jury about Kathy's testimony and that it was only to be considered if the juror believed it to be more likely than not, the preponderance standard. I was whisked off to Independence for a boring weekend. No visitors, no phone calls. I did have a good book though. A thriller by Perri O'Shaugnesy and I had junk food I had bought from the commissary. I was praying that the Mono County Jail would reopen soon. I missed my luxury cell.

TWENTY-EIGHT

The first witness Monday morning November 9th, 2009, was Cathy McLennan, the CSAAS expert. She started out going over the five stages or elements of CSAAS. The first is secrecy, the second is helplessness, the third is called entrapment and accommodation, the fourth is delay in reporting, and the fifth element is recantation. Ms. McLennan had said at the §402 hearing that CSAAS was outdated but at trial she was offering detailed explanations for each element. The court declared her an expert in Child Sexual Abuse Accommodation Syndrome testimony. Ms. Hankel objected and we were on our way.

Q. by Mr. Graham: Ms. McLennan, prior to today's hearing, you were provided a couple of video interviews of the alleged victims in the case; correct?

A. Correct.

Q. Did you view the videos?

A. Yes, I did.

Q. Other than the videos, have I told you any of the background facts relating to the history, the detailed history leading up to these interviews?

A. No.

Q. I want you to assume the following facts: Twin girls before the age of ten. They lived on and off with their verbally abusive and unreliable mother. Both girls had contact with CPS regarding their mother's inability to care for them. CPS repeatedly returned the girls to their mother's care.

Before he died, the girls clearly preferred their dad and staying with their dad. The mother would leave the girls alone for days at a time when they were very young, unattended. Mother had a boyfriend that was both physically abusive and verbally abusive to them. When they were ten years old the girls moved in with their mom and her new boyfriend. The new boyfriend lived with the girls or was commonly around the girls for the next five years.

You got those facts in mind?

A. Yes.

Q. The background there is early on the boyfriend was very controlling, extremely verbally abusive as well as physically abusive towards the girls. Mom was unable to protect the girls from this abuse. Both girls have expressed extreme resentment that the mother did not adequately protect them from the new boyfriend. From age 10 to approximately their 15th birthday this boyfriend repeatedly molested and had forcible intercourse with both twins in different locations. The boyfriend tells the girls early on not to tell anyone and shortly thereafter says multiple times he will kill them if they disclose. The question I have is would the twins continue to do things recreationally with this boyfriend even though he was verbally, physically, and sexually abused them? Is that something you would see?

The Court: Wait a second. Can I see you please?

(Whereupon a discussion was held but not reported)

Q. by Mr. Graham: If the twins were to do things recreationally, continue to kind of do social things with the boyfriend, would that be consistent with Child Sexual Abuse Accommodation Syndrome factors?

A. Yes, absolutely.

Q. Why?

A. Because of the dependency issues, the fact that the powerlessness issues that children are inherently helpless. And because of the accommodation issues. The fact that they had this sort of negative aspect to their relationship and no one would deny the threats were negative. Children are not going to sort of define or -- again, it is about that whole issue of thinking that children are going to tell somebody or put a stop to the behavior themselves. If there are certain positive aspects of the relationship, this person spends time with them, this person might be a fun individual, that is not at all inconsistent with what we see.

In fact, I would say the reverse would be terribly inconsistent to see a child that would draw limits and say that well, because he does this bad thing, I am not going to go anywhere. I am certainly not going to allow him to take me to the movies anymore or go motorbiking with me or do anything positive with them.

Absolutely, that adds to people's incredulity about this. Because I see this even when children aren't terribly bonded, when the guy down the street has a garage filled with nifty kids toys that he attracts everyone to. The kids have got to tolerate the weird behavior on the side, but the kids continue to go there. That is the norm.

Q. Ms. McLennan. Let's just go back a little bit to the basic nature of CSAAS. It assumes that a molest or a molestation has occurred; isn't that correct?

A. Yes.

Q. And in any case, you have no idea whatsoever whether or not there has been any true allegations of molestation in this case at all; is that correct?

A. Correct.

Q. So we are talking about a hypothetical, hypothetical victims and facts, do you understand that?

A. Yes.

It may have been advertised as a hypothetical, but the facts were identical to the allegations in this case. Ms. McLennan continued on for quite some time opining that inconsistencies are common in disclosures and they can be attributable to multiple interviews from different people. That children don't write down in a calendar the time the sexual abuse started or what the exact frequency was. She went on to say that there is some line of thinking that trauma can actually enhance memory by making it sharper if you are really upset by something. And finally, Ms. McLennan noted that kids accommodate the sexual abuse by disassociating or thinking about something else while the abuse is going on. She closed by saying that if you do it often enough, and you get really good at it, it can interfere with your memory.

So that finished Ms. McLennan's direct testimony and now it was time for Ms. Hankel to point out the inconsistencies of Ms. McLennan's testimony.

Q. by Ms. Hankel: Would you agree with me that one way to tell if a child has been sexually abused is that the child immediately discloses sexual abuse?

A. I guess — well I guess the part I am struggling with is to tell if the child has been abused, my job in receiving disclosures is not to pronounce that is has or has not happened; it is to obtain information from the child. An immediate disclosure is one way in which that a child would come to someone's attention. That wouldn't necessarily prove that it had or hadn't based on an immediate disclosure, I guess that is where I am struggling with a yes or no on this.

Q. Okay, you would agree then, that if that child immediately discloses sexual abuse, that doesn't necessarily mean the child has been sexually abused?

A. Correct.

Q. And then if a child waits for a time before they disclose sexual abuse, that also doesn't mean they have been sexually abused?

A. Correct.

Q. If a child waits a week before saying I was abused a week ago, that doesn't mean the child was sexually abused?

A. Correct.

Q. If the child says I was abused five years ago, that doesn't mean the child was sexually abused?

A. Correct.

Q. Was it your testimony that if a child delayed disclosing sexual abuse, that is consistent with CSAAS?

A. Yes.

Q. And is it your testimony also that if a child discloses partially, that is also consistent with CSAAS?

A. It can be.

Q. Is it your testimony that a partial disclosure may or may not be consistent with CSAAS?

A. It could go either way. I mean that is something he [Dr. Summit] observed in it.

Q. So the answer to my question was yes?

A. I guess it is the yes/no part of it that I am struggling with a little bit. It is not inconsistent with it to do either.

Q. Okay. So the answer to my question is yes?

A. Yes, I guess, yeah.

Q. Is it also your testimony that not a partial but an inconsistent disclosure saying one thing this day and one thing that day is also consistent with CSAAS?

A. That is outside the whole Child Sexual Abuse Accommodation Syndrome. It has nothing to do with that.

Q. You talked about five stages of CSAAS?

A. Correct.

Q. And you explained how, by the nature of sexual abuse itself, that it was something that is done behind closed doors. So it would likely be a secret between the perpetrator and the victim?

A. Yes. That is common for most sexual abuse situations is that other people don't — aren't privy to it or know about it; certainly other adults.

Q. But if this was a false allegation, there wouldn't be any secret that the kid is not talking about. It would be something that never occurred; correct?

A. Well, sure.

Q. Because the very nature of CSAAS is one assumes that a molest occurred; correct?

A. Correct, uh-huh.

Q. And if, in fact, a molestation has not occurred, then there is no secret except for the secret of telling a lie?

A. Sure, yeah.

Ms. Hankel, then questioned Ms. McLennan about the levels of difficulty a child faces relative to reporting physical, verbal, or emotional abuse versus sexual abuse. Ms. McLennan said that a sexual abuse claim is a much more difficult thing to talk about, that societally it is taboo. Continuing, Ms. McLennan said kids are very free and will tell about getting spanked or how their parents act unless they are system savvy. Ms. McLennan added that kids don't think through a plan to relocate themselves. That is a sophisticated thing to do.

Q. by Ms. Hankel: Well, you talked about -- just a second ago -- you used the phrase "system savvy". Can you define what you meant by that; a child who is system savvy?

A. Well, kids who have been exposed to CPS or law enforcement, I think, that can contribute to their reluctance to reengage. It is not a pleasant system. Kids don't look forward to this -- And if kids have been interviewed by CPS, have been removed by CPS, have been placed somewhere else, I think that would contribute to their reluctance, again, to tell anybody about it because it is not necessarily a good thing for kids.

Even kids who are being abused would generally prefer to stay with the abuser rather than face something that they don't necessarily know or can't anticipate.

Q. Is it consistent with a true disclosure of sexual abuse to lie to law enforcement about disclosures?

Mr. Graham: Objection.

The Court: Sustained.

Q. by Ms. Hankel: Let me see. Maybe I have misunderstood this witness' testimony. Because you are testifying about something that Roland Summit called a syndrome, but then said it wasn't a syndrome, the CSAAS, Child Sexual Abuse Accommodation Syndrome, and that assumes that a molest has occurred; correct?

A. Well, sure. When he is describing what he observed in his patients who have disclosed molest, he is assuming there is a molest, sure, yeah.

The Court: Ma'am. Where I have difficulty is every time the word Child Sexual Abuse Accommodation is used, whether it is a reference to an acronym or something else, you seem to go back to Roland Summit's paper from 30 years age.

The Witness: Because that is what the term harkens to. That is what it is.

The Court: Does that term have to any relevance 30 years later, today?

The Witness: In the sense that the theoretical framework that he developed, the sort of stages, are still accepted for the most part based on subsequent research or literature that was never an empirical paper ... it was never like a diagnostic. Nobody ever took it to mean that if these things happen, then that person has been molested.

Q. by Ms. Hankel: Prior to today's hearing you said a couple of months ago you saw a couple of videos of the disclosure of some of the children in this case?

A. I did.

Q. You are not today vouching as to the credibility as to anything said in those videos; correct?

A. No, I am not.

Q. Because you have no information as to whether or not these children are or have disclosed true allegations of sexual abuse?

A. That's correct.

That finished up Ms. McLennan. I was unsure whether she said anything unequivocally. Ms. Hankel had failed to object to the whole CSAAS line of questioning since during the previous §402 hearing on 7/14/09 Ms. McLennan had repudiated CSAAS in favor of her own findings or those of more current researchers. Ms. Hankel's preparation in this area was detrimental to my defense because she neglected to focus on the incoherence of her plan defense. In essence, Ms. Hankel and our expert, Dr. Coleman, were keyed in on the suggestibility line of questioning which contradicted the plan defense and coalesced with my escalation and reward defense strategy. I really felt Ms. Hankel was playing to both sides of the coin. Her plan defense simply did not meld with Ms. McLennan's testimony that "kids don't think through a plan to relocate" and her rhetorical reply to Ms. Hankel "What are you going to do, move out of the house?"

Ms. Hankel should have focused on Ms. McLennan's statement, "Often you will get a partial disclosure and then upon subsequent questioning of them and "cueing" you will get a full disclosure." I was contending to Ms. Hankel that the twins were responding to "cueing" and that they did not have a plan. The typical disclosure often seen by Ms. McLennan involved the disclosure of physical abuse with the sexual abuse disclosures coming much later I reminded Ms. Hankel. She was ignoring the credible facts I pointed out to her which the evidence and testimony were validating, the fact that the girls' allegations about sexual abuse escalated in response to questioning; physical abuse and threats weren't even disclosed until much later, counter to the expert testimony.

The next witness was Detective Rutkowski who was appearing for the second time in order to review his videotaped interview with Martha. A transcript of the video was presented to the jury as a reference aid and then the video was played. After the video, Mr. Graham had no questions and nothing to add so Ms. Hankel started in on her cross-examination.

Q. by Ms. Hankel: The video tape we just saw was a video tape of August 2007?

A. by Det. Rutkowski: Yes, ma'am.

Q. It was August 3rd of 2007 when you interviewed Martha Guthrie; correct?

A. Yes, ma'am.

Q. What was the date of the second videotaped interview with Martha Guthrie?

A. May 27, 2008.

Q. Were there any other interviews or any interviews you conducted with Chelsea Guthrie?

A. Yes, ma'am.

Q. What were the dates of the interviews you conducted with Chelsea Guthrie?

A. Chelsea Guthrie was brought in for an initial interview on August 8th, 2007. While I monitored the interview, I did not conduct that interview. But I did record it. And then the second interview with Chelsea was on May 16th, 2008.

Q. Given Martha's age of 15, was there a particular interviewing style that you thought you should use with Martha Guthrie when you interviewed her on August 3rd, 2007, dependent on her age?

A. Most definitely.

Q. And what interviewing style was that?

A. Well, I was aware that both Martha and Chelsea had predisclosed.

The Court: You need to tell us what style you utilized. That was the question.

The Witness: I utilized the same style with her as I would have used on an older teenaged child or adult.

Q. by Ms. Hankel: Is it your understanding that Martha Guthrie had made several different disclosures prior to your interview of her?

A. Correct.

Q. How is the circumstance of Martha Guthrie's making prior disclosures going to change your interview style?

A. Because I was aware of the sexual acts she was claiming had been made against her; therefore, with that knowledge, I can tone my interview as to listening to what happened during those acts and not so much on the act itself.

Q. And was it important at all in your interview of Martha Guthrie to go over the various prior allegations she had made?
A. No, ma'am.
Q. Had you had discussions with those folks to whom she had made the prior disclosures about the content of her disclosures?
A. No, ma'am.
Q. Then how is it you came to know that she had previously disclosed?
A. I had minor discussions with DDA Graham and with the social worker about the type of allegations, but not the specifics.
Q. Did you have at the time of your interview with Ms. Guthrie in your hand the nature and content of each of the prior disclosures she had made before you interviewed her?
A. No, ma'am.
Q. Did you ever, after this interview, compare the content of the disclosures she made to you with the content of any previous disclosure or subsequent disclosure?
A. No, ma'am.
Q. Did you ever compare the content of Martha Guthrie's interview with Chelsea's interview with Karen Smart?
Q No, ma'am.
Qs Did you ever compare the disclosures made to Child Protective: Services with the disclosures made to you during this; videotaped interview?
A. No, ma'am.
Q. Did you ever compare the disclosures made to CPS with the disclosures made to you during the supplemental interview in May of 2008?
A. No, ma'am.
Q. Did you ever compare the content of Martha Guthrie's interview on August 3rd, 2007, with her testimony that she gave at the preliminary hearing in this case?
A. No, ma'am.
Q. Did you ever compare the content of Chelsea Guthrie's interview with Chelsea Guthrie's preliminary hearing testimony in this case?
A. No, ma'am.
Q. Did you believe at the time that you were interviewing Martha Guthrie on August 3rd, 2007, that it was appropriate for you to use leading questions during that interview?
A. Yes, ma'am.
Q. Did you ever interview any of the girls' counselors at the schools they attended?
A. No, ma'am.
Q. Did you ever interview any of the psychologists at the girls' schools they attended?

A. No, ma'am.

Q. Did you ever interview any neighbors of the girls?

A. No, ma'am.

Q. Did you ever interview any of the girls' friends?

A. No, ma'am,

Q. Did you interview Chelsea Guthrie about the content of Martha Guthrie's interview with you?

A. No, ma'am.

Q. Did you ever interview Martha Guthrie about the content of Chelsea Guthrie's interview with Karen Smart?

A. No, ma'am.

Q. Were you ever told by Deputy DA Todd Graham that Martha Guthrie's statements that she made at the interview were inconsistent with the statements that she made at the preliminary hearing?

A. No, ma'am.

Q. Did anybody ever discuss with you the inconsistencies in Martha Guthrie's statements to you at the interview with her statements at the preliminary hearing?

A. No, ma'am.

Q. You never heard that from the social workers?

A. Not that I recall.

Q. In any of the seminars you attended, did you learn that it was important to look at all the evidence in the case when you investigated the credibility of allegations of sexual abuse?

A. In some cases, yes, ma'am, but not this one.

Q. Is it your understanding that in certain cases you look at all the evidence and other cases you only look at part of the evidence?

A. That is not what I said ma'am. But in this case I had specific tasks that I was asked to complete, and I completed all of those tasks. A lot of what you asked me were not tasks I was asked to complete.

Q. So is it your testimony that nobody ever asked you to look at all the evidence in this case?

A. No. Nobody ever did say that.

Q. Is it your understanding that your investigation of the sexual abuse allegations in the case were limited to one certain aspect?

A. Yes, ma'am.

Q. Is it your testimony, then, that you reviewed all of the relevant evidence surrounding Martha Guthrie's disclosure of sexual abuse in this case?

A. No, ma'am. I did not.

Q. Did you have an understanding that there was another investigator who was investigating these sexual abuse allegations made by Martha Guthrie?
A. Yes, ma'am.
Q. Who are the other investigators investigating these allegations?
A. The DA's office itself ma'am.
Q. And aside from the DA's office, was there another law enforcement officer with the Mono County Sheriff's Office who was investigating Martha Guthrie's allegations of sexual abuse in the case?
A. No, ma'am.
Q. Did you ever learn that Martha Guthrie, instead of testifying or disclosing that she had maybe a dozen acts total of sexual conduct in the Chalfant trailer, later testified at the preliminary hearing that Mike Harris put his hands on her vagina almost every day?
A. No, ma'am.
Q. What did you do about the contradiction in the case?
A. That was being handled by the District Attorney's office, ma'am, not me.
Q. Was there a reason why you didn't interview Mike Harris' father about the allegation that Martha had been raped in his house?
A. There are several reasons.
Q. Give me the first one.
A. I wasn't asked to. It wasn't part of the task I was assigned in the case.
Q. What is the second reason?
Q. I assumed that somebody else may be interviewing. That is why I wasn't asked.
Q. What is the third reason?
A. I don't know.
Q. Are those the only two reasons?
A. That I recall, ma'am.

After that exchange Ms. Hankel was finished and then Mr. Graham asked some general questions about how investigations work and adduced that quite often different people are assigned different tasks. My question was: Who's calling the shots? I previously had problems with Mr. Graham prosecuting me overzealously in the Kathy Barrickman case and I had voiced my concerns of that in the Raeanna Davenport case. I felt like there was no investigation. Just a railroad going straight to prison. There were no investigation reports whatsoever until just days before trial. All there was against me lay on contradictory transcripts and a couple of bungled video interviews that couldn't even be heard in court.

I wished Ms. Hankel would have gone into this detail with Mr. McCammond regarding the investigation of all three girls' false claims. Mr. McCammond was the chief investigating officer for the Mono County DA's office. Ms. Hankel followed Mr. Graham with a couple recross questions.

Q. by Ms. Hankel: My question is, after your supplemental interview of Martha Guthrie, what additional investigation or interviews did you conduct after Martha Guthrie gave the supplemental information in May of 2008?

A. None.

Q. Detective Rutkowski, can you tell me everything you did to assert whether Martha Guthrie was making false allegations of sexual abuse?

A. Nothing other than interview her on tape so her comments could be viewed and read and submit them to Mr. Graham.

Q. And the same question with respect to Chelsea Guthrie?

A. Well, I would say the same thing but add obviously an interview with Mr. Harris and Mrs. Guthrie.

So, there you have it. Detective Rutkowski had one thing to do: interview and record the interviews of Martha and Chelsea. The finished product is of low quality with poor audio. I guess it's a good thing he wasn't more involved.

After court, I was told that I was going to the Bridgeport jail. They were reopening it just to house me. I guess they were sick of driving the 135 miles to Independence every morning to pick me up. I was going to miss the eastern escarpment of the High Sierra at sunrise every day. I got back to Bridgeport and was welcomed with a BBQ'd double cheeseburger. It seemed that the kitchen was still closed. I had a TV and all was well except for the fact I was facing a life in prison for crimes that never happened.

The next day I got to sleep in a little bit. Then I got dressed in my sport coat, slacks and tie. Following this I was transported to court in Mammoth by my trusty companion Officer Scott Bush who was my bailiff and transport officer.

TWENTY-NINE

To travel hopefully is a much better thing than to arrive. I was hopeful that Mr. Graham was done with his case so I could finally go on the offensive. The first witness on Tuesday November 10th, 2009, was Mr. Stanford from Yahoo! Mr. Graham asked some perfunctory questions related to how mail is stored and saved. Mr. Stanford verified that the disk of emails received by the DA's office was the same as the disc sent by Yahoo in response to a subpoena from Mr. Graham. Mr. Stanford verified my email as skibumgonegood@yahoo.com.

Q. by Mr. Graham: Was there anything to your knowledge relating to the computer operation, the server operations, that would give you reason to believe the server where this information was obtained from that was not operating properly?

A. No. Nothing.

Mr. Graham then said he was finished and Ms. Hankel then asked a question I had posed to her:

Q. by Ms. Hankel: Did you ever -- in reviewing this account, did you notice whether or not there were any reports of abuse or inappropriate activity associated with the use of this subscriber?

A. I did not.

Following Mr. Stanford, the Yahoo! representative, Mr. Graham recalled Mr. McCammond back to the stand. Mr. McCammond testified regarding the search warrant that led to the Yahoo! evidence being produced in court. He was then asked:

Q. by Mr. Graham: Mr. McCammond, in assisting in the investigation in the case, did you attempt to interview what you believe to be Mr. Harris' father, Thomas Charles Harris?

A. Yes, I did.

Q. And how did you try to contact him?

A. I first developed information as to where he possibly lives and then found a phone number and then placed several phone calls to that number.

Q. Did you state any messages during that time?

A. Yes, I left messages on a telephone answering machine.

Q. And was there any response back to you in any way?

A. I never received a response.

Mr. Graham: Nothing further.

Q. by Ms. Hankel: Mr. McCammond, did you bring anything with you today to show when you placed those phone calls to Mr. Harris?

A. No, I did not bring anything with me today, no.

Q. Sitting here today, can you recall when that may have been?

A. My estimation is that all those attempts most likely occurred in the last 12 months.

Q. Did you ask for assistance from any law enforcement agency in the area in which Mr. Harris lived?

A. No, I didn't.

Q. Did you ever draft a declaration for a search warrant to obtain evidence from Mr. Harris' home?

A. I don't believe so, no.

Q. You had received information that Martha Guthrie alleged to have been raped on a couch in Mr. Harris' home; correct?

A. Yes.

Q. Did you ever attempt to obtain DNA evidence off that couch?

A. No, I did not.

Ms. Hankel: Nothing further.

The Court: Mr. Graham, do you have any further witnesses at this time?

Mr. Graham: No, Judge. Thank you.

It was day 7 of my trial and I was finally stoked. Hallelujah. It was our turn. I was a little miffed that Ms. Hankel hadn't gone after Mr. McCammond about his lack of investigation like she had done with Det. Rutkowski. There was a break in the action so the county counsel could try to quash the subpoenas for the social workers and psychotherapists.

Their objection action to quash stated that it seems logical and the law, more importantly, that oral testimony concerning privileged information or confidential information is likewise confidential. The county counsel also believed that the oral testimony of the social workers and psychotherapists would be privileged under Evid. Code §1040.

They were also objecting via Welfare and Institutions Code §827 to the release of the confidential records and CPS case files, notes, reports, and the like. Mr. Magit and Mr. Berrey were the litigators in this hearing. Mr. Graham stayed out of it, he didn't have a dog in the fight. Any evidence released to us would also be released to him. The crux was that we had the evidence but; did not know what would be admissible at trial, nor what information the social workers and psychotherapists might be asked to divulge while on the stand.

I wanted the social workers and psychotherapists grilled on the inconsistent CPS file, the contradictory dates of the alleged allegations, and SCAR's never sent or received as required by state law. Ms. Hankel wanted to question Ms. Douglas and Ms. Ellis concerning the contents of those records so I was happy, but I wasn't sure she was buying into my conspiracy theory. Ultimately, Judge DeVore ruled:

The Court: I want to permit the examination in certain areas and the use of whatever records by their content relating to these areas. And I think that satisfies the obligation.

The judge then went through the topics he was allowing to be explored, such as the complaints the girls had made about me or Kerri, including inconsistent statements related to physical, emotional, and sexual abuse; and general neglect. Also, incomplete and inconsistent reporting to the county workers including the foster home evidence. The Judge had one caveat however,

The Court: If the CPS records say we are taking Chelsea out of the Smith's home because the Smith's say she is defecating and stealing, and sneaking out, and smoking dope; whatever it is, that is a hearsay statement in there.

Ms. Hankel: Yes.

The Court: You are not going to get it in through Alex Ellis, but I am not going to prevent you from getting into that with the foster parents if that is appropriate with the circumstances, even though your information about that comes from an examination of the foster parents may necessarily include a report to social services; okay?

Ms. Hankel: Got it.

Judge DeVore was then asked about the Suspected Child Abuse Reports (SCAR) and all mandated reports and he replied:

The Court: I think the mandatory reporting by those reporters is admissible. Certainly to the extent that it may indicate the inconsistent statements, inconsistent reporting, and that sort of thing. So the mandatory reporting by those people -- again, if you intend to use those documents or do you intend to examine the witnesses or the subject matter?

Ms. Hankel: Yes, the latter.

It was complicated, but in a nutshell, if it shows inconsistent, incomplete, or contradictory statements it was fair game. Ms. Hankel was going to start off the defense of me by calling one of the three boys I called "those boys" because of Chelsea's statement on 5/16/08 which was "Oh, those boys don't know anything." Ms. Hankel was going against my wishes right out of the gate, because these boys were lying to help Chelsea and they were not exculpatory for me, they were inculpatory as far as I could tell. Ms. Hankel wanted to use them to show the girls were planning on leaving home and had reported sexual abuse to their friends prior to the disclosures to Ms. Ellis. The girls consistently said they told nobody except each other and their mom, yet Ms. Hankel wanted to stake my life on those boys telling the truth. I was upset. This who said what first issue was pivotal to my assertion that the girls made it up as they went along in an escalating manner based on questioning by authorities and the dynamics of the WIC §300 case. First up was Chelsea's boyfriend Tyler Clarke.

Q. by Ms. Hankel: When did you meet Chelsea?

A. May of '07.

Q. And did you subsequently begin a dating relationship?

A. A few days later, yes, we did.

Q. And when you started dating was it in the early part of May, or the end of May?

A. Toward the end.

Q. Did you go over to Chelsea's house?

A. No, no.

Q. Did you ever take her to the movies, like dropping off and picking her up at the house?

A. No.

Q. Did Chelsea come to meet you at night?

A. Sometimes, yes.

Q. Was she sneaking out of her mom's house to do that?

A. Yes.

Q. At some point did Chelsea tell you she was going to run away?

A. She did.

Q. And did she make statements to you about her mother?

A. She did.

Q. Tell us what she told you about her mother.

A. She told me that her mom was; physically and mentally abusive, not just toward her, but towards her sister. She told me her mother would hit her sometimes, throw her up against the wall, made her do way more, did everything her and her sister made her do everything. Chelsea told me they would wake up at 5:00 o'clock in the morning and not be in the house until nine o'clock at night.

Q. Do you know what kind of chores?

A. Mostly woodcutting, weed moving, the stables, doing the horses, doing yardwork.

Q. You and Leif had a tent at the park; correct?

A. Yes

Q. And Martha and Chelsea would come and join you while you were camped at the park?

A. Yes, but they would not stay overnight. They would hang out until eleven o'clock or midnight and they would go back and sneak in the house.

Q. How long of a time did this occur?

A. Until she was put in to the foster home.

Q. And during this time, when you were getting to know her and you had been dating her for about a month, did Chelsea tell you that Mike Harris had sexually abused her?

A. She did.

Q. Did she tell you that Martha had been raped by Mike Harris?

A. She did.

Q. Did she tell you she had been raped by Mike Harris?

A. She did.

Q. Did she ask you if you would help her, to provide a place for heir to go and live?

A. She did ask for help.

Q. And did she subsequently run away?

A. Yes.

Q. Did she run away to your house?

A. Yes.

Q. And did your father and your father's girlfriend know that she was staying with you?

A. They did, yes.

Q. And how long did she stay at your house?
A. Not even a full day. We got back to my house at around the afternoon of that day, and then we told her to call the — to call the social services, whatever it is, for her to come let them know that she ran away. And she did that. And then the next day around noon is when the Mono County Sheriffs were at our door.
Q. Do you remember that she was surprised in fact when the police came?
A. Yes. She was pretty surprised.
Q. And she didn't want to go with the police, did she?
A. No. She kind of felt like - not pushing them away, but she ran back to me and was telling me "Don't let them take me."
Q. Because she thought she was in trouble?
A. Yeah, she thought she was going to jail.
Q. And after that Chelsea was placed in foster care; correct?
A. Yes, ma'am.
Q. And you continued to date her through the summer; correct?
A. Yes, ma'am.
Q. Hew was it you were able to see Chelsea throughout that summer?
A. Well, her social worker gave her some boundaries. Her social worker would bring her from the foster home, and she was able to stay two or three hours.
Q. Do you know the name of the social worker who was transporting Chelsea to see you?
A. Alex Ellis.
Q. And do you recall hew often Alex Ellis would chauffeur Chelsea to your house that summer?
A. It was pretty much every day.
Q. Did Martha ever tell you that she was being sexually molested by Mike Harris?
A. She did not.

And Ms. Hankel was finished. I was still upset that Ms. Hankel had Tyler testify to the fact that Chelsea said she was raped since Chelsea had said she never said she was raped and she never told Tyler anything before Alex. She might have said all that after she was in a foster home, but not before because Mr. Clarke gave a statement to the police after the "theater incident" on August 3rd, 2007, and he made no mention of Chelsea's claimed abuse. I was pleased though with Ms. Hankel's effort regarding the whole runaway phone call to CPS that never actually happened. Tyler was lying and I wished Ms. Hankel would jump all over him, but it looked like she was buying into Tyler's bullshit. Next it was Mr.

Graham's turn and he started off right away by pointing Mr. Clarke to the day and time Chelsea made her disclosure to him.

Q. by Mr. Graham: How did that conversation begin to where that topic came up?

A. Well, one day we were hanging out and I asked her, because she constantly wore sweaters during the summertime. And I asked her "Why are you wearing a sweater? It is 90° outside." And she told me she was covering her bruises that her mom and Mike had given her.

Q. Did you ask to observe any of the bruises?

A. No, I did not.

Q. What was the next thing that was said between the two of you?

A. Like I said, I was like, okay. And then she -- a couple seconds and then she came out and said "Well, I've got something else to tell you." And then she said like "Mike raped me."

It is worth considering that if it is 90° out when she supposedly disclosed to Tyler so it wasn't at night, it was after that period of time … just sayin'.

Q. by Mr. Graham: And can you recall the words that she used when she made the disclosure?

A. She said that "Well, my mom's boyfriend raped me and my sister."

Q. Did she make any statements after her disclosure about the sexual abuse whether or not she wanted you to tell anybody?

A. No, she told me not to tell anybody, and I told her there's no way I will.

Q. How many times, if any, after that initial disclosure, did she make any further statements discussing sexual abuse by Mike Harris?

A. None. Because after I told her that, you know, we don't need to talk about this anymore, that was it. Because I didn't want to hear any more about it. I can honestly tell you she didn't want to talk about it herself, so I told then let's just not talk about it.

Q. At any time did she make any statements to you about whether she had told her mother and her mother's reaction?

A. She did tell me she told her mother and she told me that her mother was like, you know, you are lying. I know Mike wouldn't do that.

Q. Mr. Clarke, did Chelsea and/or Martha ever approach you in any way to try to get you into a plan or scheme or some kind of setup to make up sexual abuse allegations against Mike Harris so they could get out of the house?

A. No, they did not.

It was almost over. Ms. Hankel had one final question:

Q. by Ms. Hankel: How long of a time elapsed between the time Chelsea told you that she had been raped by Mike Harris and you let her run away to your house?

A. About two weeks after

That ended Tyler Clarke's testimony and it was quite an end. He said he knew for two weeks before Chelsea ran away that she had been raped, yet when he testified on direct he said he started dating Chelsea toward the end of May and then a month later she told him she was raped. This was critical and Ms. Hankel failed to capitalize on this issue. Chelsea ran away in late June, a month after starting to date Tyler. Ms. Hankel was bordering on malpractice for asking the last question and letting it go so she could support her plan defense strategy. I wasn't believing a thing Tyler said, but Ms. Hankel bought into him hook, line, and sinker. These boys all came forward at the very last minute in an apparent attempt to bolster Martha and Chelsea's claims of abuse.

Despite having had numerous opportunities to help the girls previously, they waited until the last minute, on the eve of trial, to reveal their information. The information lacked credibility for a variety of reasons, yet Ms. Hankel wanted to use them in order to enhance her newly formulated plan defense. Mr. Clarke was present at the August 3rd, 2007, theater incident I just described and in which Chelsea told Det. Rutkowski that she had yelled out at me in front of a bunch of people that I was a child molester. This supposedly occurred while the movie theater was letting out. Tyler Clarke and Leif Medrud were with Chelsea. After the incident Tyler gave a handwritten statement to police at the scene and made no mention of the child molester outburst nor his own knowledge of sexual abuse. This was August 3rd. Police reports that night make no mention of any child molester or any threatening statements being yelled at anybody. Even Chelsea's foster parent, Ian Lindsay, who filed a declaration regarding Chelsea's statements to him, made no mention of any child molestation or sexual abuse statements by Chelsea.

During the theater incident, Ms. Ellis showed up at the theater parking lot and served me with a restraining order protecting Martha and Chelsea. The order made no mention of sexual abuse nor did Alex Ellis' notes that were in the CPS file reflect any child molester claim made by Chelsea. Mr. Clarke testified that Chelsea was surprised when the sheriff's dept showed up at his house to pick her up. Tyler never told the deputies, nor did his parents, that Chelsea was at the Clarke's home because she was being physically, emotionally, and sexually abused at her home in Chalfant. Tyler was never investigated or interviewed by law enforcement or CPS related to Chelsea's claims of abuse at any time prior to trial. Ms.

Hankel never asked Tyler if Chelsea told him she had told other people besides her mom like her sister or her other friends and family. Ms. Hankel should have asked if he was the only one she told. Tyler Clarke was never asked if I was living in Chalfant while the girls were sneaking out. (I wasn't.)

Mr. Clarke was not asked about the notes including the red letter which in detail describes Chelsea and Tyler's nocturnal activities such as shooting things, burning things down, and paintballing people and things, among other activities not permitted by Kerri. Ms. Hankel never asked Tyler why he kept his secret for years instead of talking to authorities, especially after I was in jail. Ms. Hankel never asked him if he discussed his knowledge with his stepmom, Kathleen Traynor, since she had told my investigator that Chelsea had disclosed to her my sexual abuse activities.

This was important since it was clear evidence of lying after the fact. Ms. Hankel never asked if and when "those boys" all decided to come forward at once or if it was a coincidence. Also, when exactly did they all know each other knew? I pushed Ms. Hankel to pursue these logical lines of questioning which would tend to disprove her "plan" defense theory and show the allegations were not as they or anything else appeared.

After all that, it was time for Jordan Moriarty who was supposedly Chelsea's good friend even though Kerri and I had never heard him mentioned before. I still didn't understand why Ms. Hankel was calling these boys as witnesses who were helpful to the prosecution, but there was nothing I could do.

Q. by Ms. Hankel: Do you know Tyler Clarke?
A. by Jordan Moriarty: Yes.
Q. Sometime in May of '07 did Tyler start dating Chelsea Guthrie?
A. Yes.
Q. And did you know Chelsea?
A. Yes.
Q. And did you know her sister, Martha?
A. I did.
Q. Did you hang out with Tyler and Chelsea?
A. Tyler yes. Chelsea, not so much. Just on occasion I would be hanging out with them.
Q. Did you learn at some point that Chelsea had run away from home?
A. Yes.
Q. Did you know where she ran away to?
A. I did not at first, and then I went over to Tyler's house, and she answered the door.

Q. So were you surprised that she was answering his door?

A. Yes.

Q. And did you come to learn that she was staying there?

A. I came to learn a couple days later that she was there for a couple of days.

Q. Before Chelsea ran away to stay at Tyler's house, did she make a disclosure to you that she was being sexually abused by my client?

A. Yes, she did.

Q. And did she say anything about her sister Martha being sexually abused?

A. No, just beaten I guess would be the word.

Q. And a couple weeks after Chelsea made that statement to you that she was being sexually abused by my client, did you have a discussion with Tyler Clarke about that?

A. I did, yes.

Q. Did Tyler Clarke talk to you about what should happen to Mike Harris in general?

A. He did say he belongs in jail for the rest of his life for doing such a terrible thing.

Q. Did you have an understanding that he wanted to help her?

A. Yes.

No sooner had she started than she was done. I was perplexed how these kids are talking about putting me in jail for life, yet they somehow kept their secret for years. I didn't get it. It was then time for Mr. Graham to cross-examine Jordan.

Q. by Mr. Graham: Well, if you think to when you had the discussion with Chelsea - please make sure Chelsea is the one that made the statement to you regarding sexual abuse; is that correct?

A. Yes.

Q. Can you give us an approximate time based upon the time of year or month when she made that statement to you?

A. I'm going to guess February or March of '07.

Q. And you know that Chelsea ran away towards the end of June. Do you know that? Does that ring a bell?

A. Of that year?

Q. Yeah.

A. That's when I found out, in the summer.

Q. Now where were you when you had this discussion in February or March of '07?

A. The school bus.

Q. Could you recall what she was wearing that day?

A. No.

Q. On that day, how would you describe your relationship with her generally?

A. Decent friends, good friends.

Q. And during these months - I am just going to go three or four months -- of the disclosure of sexual abuse, did she confide anything to you about what was going on in her house?

A. No.

Q. Let's go to this time in February of March '07, and you are on the bus with her. And tell me how this discussion starts.

A. Well, I noticed a very large bruise on her leg and I asked her what it was from.

Q. What did she say?

A. At first she said she didn't want to talk about it. And then I am like "It is okay, I am here if you need to talk to me." and then she told me, "it's from my mom's boyfriend."

Q. And where on her body was the bruise?

A. On her inner thigh.

Q. What is the next thing that was said?

A. She said, "And that isn't even the worst of it."

Q. And what did she say next?

A. At first she said once again she didn't want to talk about it. And then I once again told her that I was here for her if she needed me. And then she said that he had raped her.

Q. Did she make any further statements about any abuse at that time?

A. No -- she said "Don't tell anybody, and when I say anybody, I mean anybody."

Q. Did at any time Martha or Chelsea ask you or try to get you in any way to join in a scheme or plan where they would falsify allegations of sexual abuse against Mr. Harris so that they could be out of the house?

A. No.

So, the question looms, why is Chelsea wearing sweaters in the summer to hide her bruises and now in winter she is wearing something to where Jordan can see her inner thigh. This was all a bunch of hooey because when Mr. Graham asked Jordan when exactly this incident occurred, he conceded it was in the summer.

So, the whole bus story in winter was bogus. Jordan was actually one of Martha's many suitors and one of the notes shows that Martha wants Jordan to either feel her up or fill her up depending on how you read the handwriting. This fact was never brought up by Ms. Hankel who instead focused on a purported bus ride in which Chelsea supposedly said to Mr. Moriarty that I had raped her and showed him the bruises on her inner thigh to prove it. First off, I already showed that Jordan said this disclosure happened in summertime. Secondly, I wasn't anywhere near the Guthrie house in early 2007, especially when the girls were sneaking out. Finally, Chelsea rode horses all the time and cantering a horse will cause bruises.

It was time for lunch in my little room with the bench along the wall. Mr. Morganstein brought me lunch that day, a Big Carl®, fries and a coke. I felt better after that. After lunch Leif Medrud, the last of "those boys" was called as a witness by Mr. Graham, who was being allowed to reopen his direct-examination. Leif took the stand.

Q. by Mr. Graham: Do you know Martha and Chelsea Guthrie?
A. Yes, I do.
Q. Approximately what grade were you in when you first met them?
A. Sixth grade.
Q. Where were you living at that time?
A. Chalfant Valley.
Q. What school did you go to with the girls?
A. Edna Beamon Elementary.
Q. Did you become close with either one of them?
A. Yes.
Q. Which one?
A. Martha.
Q. And at some point during your relationship with Martha, did she discuss anything of a personal nature with you?
A. Yes, she did.
Q. Do you recall what grade you were in when this first talk about her home life came up?
A. Seventh grade.
Q. And do you recall the location where you were specifically when the discussion took place?
A. The school bus on the way home from school.
Q. And how did this conversation begin?
A. She was telling me she didn't want to go home. She didn't like going home, and I asked her why.
Q. And what did she say when you asked her why?
A. Because of her mother and her mother's boyfriend, Mike.
Q. What else did she talk about?
A. Certain things Mike had done to her. She said that Mike had raped her, physically abused her, and she didn't tell how long it had been going on.

Q. At some point in time in 2007, do you recall that her sister Chelsea ran away?
A. Yes.
Q. And at that point in time, what was your relationship with either of the girls?
A. I was dating Martha and Chelsea was a friend.
Q. After the disclosure that occurred two to three weeks after the first disclosure, did you have any further conversations with Martha where she disclosed anything else about sexual abuse by Mr. Harris?
A. We had conversations about it. She didn't tell me anything. She mostly tried to avoid the conversation because I knew it would upset her.
Q. How many times would you say it came up after that second time? During your knowing her from 7th grade [2004] to the summer of '07?
A. Three to four times.
Q. Did Martha make any statements about whether she wanted you to tell anybody or not?
A. Yes, she did. She told me not to tell anybody.
Q. Was there any request by Martha to you in any way, shape, or form, any kind of communication where she was trying to get you to go along with a plan or a scheme to make up false allegations against Mr. Harris about sexual abuse so she didn't have to go home and live under the strict rules of her mom?
A. No.

Okay. So then it was time for Ms. Hankel to cross-examine and I wanted her to hammer Leif on the whole 7th grade he knew and said nothing until after he has graduated high school. Besides, Martha and Chelsea were in the Bishop school until 2005 and Leif was a grade ahead so, bottom line, Martha couldn't have been on a bus with him until much later. Martha reports to him that this is happening almost every day supposedly yet I am living in LA and even so, Martha and Leif tell no one. Somehow though it was okay for Leif and Tyler to talk all about it instead of keeping their secret? And what about Jordan, yeah, right. Ms. Hankel handed Leif a stack of notes to review and then asked him if he recognized any of them.

Q. by Ms. Hankel: Mr. Medrud, were you dating Martha in the summer of 2007?
A. Yes.
Q. Fair to say that you really cared for her?
A. Yeah.
Q. You were handed a stack of documents, and were those notes, notes that you wrote Martha while you were dating her?
A. Some of them yes, some of them no.

Q. At the time Chelsea ran away from home, were you dating Martha?
A. I think I was.
Q. And do you remember that you and Tyler had been camping out at the park in Chalfant?
A. Yes.
Q. And do you remember the girls were sneaking out of the house at night to come and see you and Tyler?
A. Yes.
Q. And do you remember telling my investigator that it was your recollection that the girls would sneak out around midnight and come hang with you guys until 3:00 or 4:00 in the morning?
A. Yes.
Q. Do you remember talking with my investigator about Martha's disclosure to you that Mike was sexually abusing her?
A. Yes.
Q. Do you remember that my investigator asked you if she could have made that disclosure to you in June of 2007?
A. Yes.
Q. Do you remember telling him that she could have made that disclosure at that time?
A. Yes.

Well, well. Seventh grade, tenth grade, how do you get that confused? Ms. Hankel didn't want to impeach Leif but I sure did. Mr. Graham had seme redirect and tried to get to the bottom of the issue.

Q. by Mr. Graham: You said Martha told you in seventh grade that Mike Harris had been sexually abusing her.
A. Yes.
Q. Is it your recollection that that is accurate? In other words, seventh grade disclosure?
A. Yes.
Q. And there were subsequent disclosures after that; correct?
A. That is correct.
Q. What in your mind makes you think that this occurred in seventh grade?
A. Well, I had first met her in sixth grade. We got to know each other. We became friends through that entire school year. And the next grade, which would be seventh, she started telling me private and personal information because I think she knew she could trust me.

Mr. Graham had nothing further so Ms. Hankel took another crack at Leif.

Q. by Ms. Hankel: In June of 2007, what grade were you in?
A. I was in tenth, grade I believe.

Q. What school did you go to in tenth grade?
A. Bishop High School.
Q. Where did you live?
A. Chalfant Valley.
Q. Were you riding the bus from Chalfant Valley to Bishop High School?
A. I don't recall because they did end up canceling the bus sometime.
Q. And during that time you were camping at the park with Tyler in June of 2007 were you riding the school bus?
A. No.
Q. I'm handing you that stack of documents I handed you before and ask you to look at the first page of the note you wrote to Martha.
A. Okay.
Q. And do you now remember that during the time you were camping at the park with Tyler at the Chalfant Park, you were also riding the bus back find forth to Bishop Union High School with Martha?
A. Yes.

Ms. Hankel wrapped things up with "those boys." I was stunned that she didn't push harder on the whole seventh grade disclosure issue. I got that last bit about riding the bus when also camping but it was a bit abstruse. The reason I was perplexed is because Martha was in the Home Street Middle School until the middle of seventh grade when she transferred to Edna Beamon. Mr. Medrud was a grade ahead of Martha so he would have been in eighth grade. The whole story was whacked out. Tyler had been a new friend in 2007, not 2004, according to the notes Kerri found.

This fact was unknown to me or Kerri when on July 9th, 2007, Martha snuck out of the house after Kerri went to bed. This was after Chelsea had been removed from the home and placed in foster care. Kerri happened to wake up and she discovered Martha missing. After looking for her she called me. I drove the 13 miles out to Kerri's house to help her look for Martha. After talking with Kerri about a car that had been circling her block, I went outside and lo and behold there was a car circling her block. I followed it to 221 Hunter St. in Chalfant. I discovered it was the home of Leif Medrud. After an all-night search and subsequent confrontation at the Medrud residence, Martha suddenly appeared at home.

Kerri and I found Martha and Leif's webpages on MySpace and they listed each other as fiancés. Kerri was upset with Martha for sneaking out and having a secret profile on MySpace against Kerri's rules. The web page was a sore spot because Martha and Chelsea had been caught before with secret webpages.

Ms. Hankel knew all about this story and I wanted Kerri to testify about this and a bunch of other stuff. Ms. Hankel knew about Kerri's concerns which she had expressed to the sheriff's dept and the CPS regarding Leif Medrud, the sneaking out, the threats against herself for reporting the kids' unwholesome activities discovered in the notes as well as other issues. Also, the contentious and confrontational situations between me and Kerri against "those boys" and their families was an enormous and important dynamic not presented to the judge or jury.

Why weren't Tyler's parents in trouble for keeping Chelsea for three days and forcing Shaylynn Ellis to find out where she was in order to tell Kerri where she was? Ms. Hankel should have questioned Leif as to why in the midst of all the enmity and confrontations, he didn't report his knowledge of Martha's alleged abuse?

THIRTY

Things were moving quickly, but not in the direction I had hoped for. Thus far my defense had consisted of three witnesses who talked about how I had molested Martha and Chelsea. I wanted more testimony that showed I didn't. Go figure, right? That's what you do on defense. Anyway, the next witness was Melissa Chamberlain who was a horse-riding instructor from Newnan, CA. She was friends with Chelsea's short term foster mom, Chandra Burnett, who was also going to testify. Ms. Chamberlain was asked:

Q. by Ms. Hankel: Do you know Chelsea Guthrie?

A. Yes, I do.

Q. How do you know her?

A. She was Chandra's foster daughter, and she came to take riding lessons.

Q. When did she take riding lessons from you?

A. It would be 2008. She was there for about three months, so it would be October, November, and December.

Q. Did you get to know Chelsea very well?

A. Yes, very well. She was - not only did she take lessons from me, she helped. The deal with her was she paid for a lesson and then she worked off a lesson. So she was there an extra day a week helping with the animals, cleaning stalls, and she became friends with my daughter.

Q. So she was there three to six hours a day?

A. Yes.

Q. Three to four times a week?

A. Yes.

Q. Some folks you would say move with grace, and other folks are kind of "klutzy", what was Chelsea? Was she graceful or was she klutzy?

A. Chelsea was clumsy. She was a good rider. But on the ground, she was always running into things, tripping around. She bruised so easy. She was so white you could see the bruises. So we were always teasing her about falling down and getting bruised.

Q. And while she was taking lessons from you, did she ever tell you that she wanted to go and live back in Bishop with her sister?

A. Yes, she did.

Q. When did she tell you that?

A. It was close to Christmas. She was going to spend a week with Martha. She was very excited about it. She talked about — she loved being with Martha. And she went up to stay with her. And when she came back is when she was all excited about how she wanted to go live with Martha.

Q. Did Chelsea make a statement to you that she had tried to commit suicide?

A. Yes.

Q. When did she make that statement to you?

A. After she had been to Bishop, she was over riding.

Q. Did she tell you what she had done?

A. Yes.

Q. What did she tell you?

A. She said she had taken a bunch of pills the night before.

Q. Did she look to be in any great distress after having taken a bunch of pills?

A. No.

Q. Did you ask her if she had been to the hospital?

A. Yes.

Q. What did she tell you?

A. No.

Q. Did you question whether or not that really occurred?

A. Yes, I. did. And I asked her if she had told her foster mother and her foster mother knew nothing about it.

Q. Did she tell you that she had told Alex Ellis?

A. Yes, she did.

Q. Did she tell you she had asked Alex Ellis to remove her from Chandra Burnett's foster care because of it?

A. Yes.

Obviously, Chelsea was manipulating the situation to her advantage. That was the end of Ms. Hankel's direct examination and I expected that Mr. Graham would spin this into a poor ol' Chelsea story.

Q. by Mr. Graham: You don't know for a fact Chelsea tried to commit suicide or not; do you?

A. I only know what she told me from her mouth. I never saw any pills.

Q. Prior to that, had Chelsea shown mood issues, mood swings where she would be depressed, upset one day, and happy some other moment?

A. Yes.

Q. So when she's talking about trying to commit suicide, isn't that consistent with at least her moods that you saw?

A. No.

Q. Why not?

A. Because I think that at that point she was bent on coming back to Bishop and she knew that was a way to get there.

Okay, I think we landed a punch. Chelsea was a great manipulator and a complete stranger saw that. I still didn't understand how the plan defense fit in with Ms. Hankel's use of suggestibility evidence. I wasn't entirely sold on the suggestibility theory either but it more closely resembled my escalating allegation theory which I was pushing. In any event, the suggestibility evidence was going to contradict the plan defense which so far only had evidence produced by "those boys" which actually supported the prosecution IMHO.

Ms. Hankel's calling of a witness who says Chelsea bruised easily seemingly bolstered Mr. Moriarty's testimony regarding a bruise seen on Chelsea's inner thigh. Once again, points for the prosecution. The use of these defense witnesses to bolster the prosecution's case is and was completely incompetent. The next witness I prayed would offer some attacks on the girls. Ms. Chamberlain did have her moments so I was still trying to be upbeat. Next was Chandra Burnett, Chelsea's foster mom in Newman, CA.

Q. by Ms. Hankel: And so when you have foster kids -- and you had Chelsea Guthrie as a foster child; correct?

A. Correct.

Q. And how do you handle the medications at your home?

A. By law, we are required to lock them up in a locked closet so that the kids don't have access to any of the medications. And then the medications are dispensed by myself.

Q. And while Chelsea was a foster child in your home, were you dispensing medication to her?

A. Yes.

Q. When Chelsea came to live with you in October or 2008, when did she leave your home?

A. It was right after Christmas.

Q. And did Chelsea express to you a desire to leave your home?

A. No.

A. Did she go for a visit with her sister?

A. Yes.

Q. And was there anything that when Chelsea returned home from that visit to your home? Was there anything about her behavior that had changed?

A. She was a completely different child.

Q. In what way?

A. I have never seen. She was verbally abusive. She was very agitated, very distraught, very restless. We were just like wow. We haven't seen this side of her.

Q. Who was supervising Chelsea while she was visiting her sister in Bishop?

A. That is a very good question. I asked that same question to Alex Ellis, because we discovered Chelsea finally copped to she had been smoking marijuana. And I'm like "Where were you?" That you know she's a high-risk kid and high-risk kids are not supposed to be left unattended. I was like "Where did this opportunity come from? Who was taking care of you?" And to my surprise it was another foster parent somewhere, I believe in Bishop.

Q. Did you express your displeasure to Alex Ellis?

A. Yes.

Q. At some point did you address Chelsea's behavior with her?

A. Yes.

The Court: Did you check to see if all the meds were where they were supposed to be?

The Witness: Yes. Yes.

The Court: Were they?

The Witness: Absolutely.

The Court: Okay.

Q. by Ms. Hankel: And was it explained to you that Chelsea tried to commit suicide in your home?

A. That is what Melissa told me… Melissa told me that supposedly Chelsea claimed that she took about 40 or something, 30 or 40 pills. And I am like, there is no way.

Q. And you saw her the next morning?

A. Yes.

Q. And was she vomiting the next morning?

A. No.

Q. Did you have to take her to the hospital?

A. No.

Q. Is it your belief that she concocted this story to get out of your home?

A. Yes. As the day went on and I started getting more bits and pieces of how this all transpired, the fact that she called Alex over at Melissa's to say "I tried to kill myself," instead of doing that at my home, kind of let me know, you know, okay. Ever since she's gone to see Martha, she has not been the same, so it is clear to me she wants to go back to Martha.

Q. Did you then contact Alex Ellis?

A. Yes, I did.

Q. Why did you contact Alex Ellis?

A. Because Chelsea told me they're coming to get me tomorrow.

Q. So she was immediately removed from your home after her call to Alex Ellis?

A. Yes.

Q. Did you object to Alex Ellis?

A. Absolutely.

Q. Did you think that was a good thing for Chelsea to be able to be removed like that from your home?

A. No.

Q. Did you think it was in her best interest to be removed from a facility such as yours with a high level of supervision?

A. Nope. Absolutely not.

Q. Did you advise Mono County Social Services that you thought Alex Ellis was unprofessional?

A. Yes, I did. Yes, I did.

After some objections regarding phone calls the examination continued:

The Court: To the question "Did Alex Ellis ever tell you Chelsea told her she had tried to commit suicide in your house?"

The Witness: Yes.

Q. by Ms. Hankel: Did she ask you if Chelsea was exhibiting any symptoms of an overdose?

A. Nope.
Q. Did she follow-up at all on whether you had to rush Chelsea to the hospital?
A. Nope.

To this, Mr. Graham had nothing. He did not cross-examine Ms. Burnett. I thought overall Ms. Hankel and Mr. Morganstein did a fine job getting these two women from Newman to drive over the mountains to testify. I was convinced Alex Ellis was the root of my evil.

THIRTY-ONE

Finally, we were getting down to brass tacks. The next witness was Rose Douglas. She was a social worker for CPS who had multiple contacts with the girls.

Q. by Ms. Hankel: Do you recall, in November of 2003, being called out to talk to Martha and Chelsea Guthrie in Chalfant?

A. Well, I remember being called out to talk to them.

Q. Do you remember the incident where Raeanna Davenport claimed that my client touched her sexually?

A. Yes. I remember that was the allegation we went on.

Q. Do you remember going out and actually talking to Martha and Chelsea about that incident?

A. Yes, I do.

Q. Do you recall whether Martha told you that Mike Harris had done anything sexually inappropriate with Raeanna Davenport?

A. Yes. I recall she didn't disclose anything.

Q. Do you remember that Chelsea Guthrie did not disclose that Mike Harris had inappropriately touched Raeanna Davenport?

A. Yes, she did not disclose anything.

Q. How is it you were having these discussions with Martha and Chelsea Guthrie?

A. There was concern that Mike Harris was fondling — Raeanna was her name — I forget which one was reported about — that he could also be sexually inappropriate with them.

Q. And when you went out to talk to Martha and Chelsea, did you also ask them if Mike Harris had been sexually inappropriate with them?

A. No. We're not allowed to ask a direct question like that unless they disclose something.

Q. Do you recall going to speak to both of the girls at their home?

A. No.

Q. Would any document refresh your memory as to whether or not you had gone to their home to speak to them?

A. Yes, yes.

Q. Would your [delivered] service log from that time frame assist you in refreshing your recollection?

A. Yes.

Ms, Hankel then gave her the DSL for late 2003 and asked her if it refreshed her recollection and Ms. Douglas said it did.

Q. by Ms. Hankel: Do you recall going to speak to both of the girls at their home in early December 2003?

A. No, I do not.

Q. Do you recall speaking with the mother of the girls in early 2003?

A. Yes, I do.

Q. Do you recall going to the girls' school to speak to the girls in early December 2003?

A. Yes, I do.

Q. Do you recall that the girls were friendly?

A. Yes.

Q. Do you recall they did not disclose any kind of abuse occurring within their home?

A. Yes, I do.

Q. Do you remember there was a concern that Martha and Chelsea may have been sexually abused in their home?

A. Yes, I do.

Q. Do you remember that the concern was that Mike Harris was sexually abusing them?

A. Yes, I do.

Q. Did you find that allegation to be substantiated?

A. No.

Q. Did you find that allegation to be unfounded?

A. Yes.
Q. Can you tell me what it means when you determine that an allegation is unfounded?
A. It is we have found no evidence; nobody has disclosed any abuse to us.

Ms. Hankel then pointed out the girls' many reports of abuse to CPS against their mom and their mom's former boyfriend, Marty Teichmann. Ms. Douglas acknowledged that after the fact she learned of these reports from her supervising social worker Alex Ellis.

Q. by Ms. Hankel: As a social worker, when you receive repeated allegations of abuse, you can do an investigation; correct?
A. Yes.
Q. And you investigate that allegation of abuse?
A. Yes.
Q. And what kinds of things do you do to investigate the allegations?
A. We look into past history, previous reports. Obviously we go out and speak to the victim first. Then we go out and speak to the parents. And usually one of them is the perpetrator. But if we feel it could be founded, we also speak to the perpetrator to get their story also.
Q. Do you speak to anyone other than the alleged victim and the perpetrator?
A. And the parent who may or may not be the perpetrator. Sometimes we can speak to other county social services, sometimes law enforcement.
Q. Do you speak to neighbors?
A. No.
Q. When you conduct your investigation, do you write a report about the people you spoke to and the investigation itself?
A. Yes.
Q. And then do you have a conclusion about the truth or falsity of that report or allegation?
A. Yes.
Q. And you can either substantiate an allegation or you can find that an allegation is inconclusive?
A. Correct.
Q. Or you can find that an allegation is unfounded?
A. Correct.
Q. When you substantiate an allegation, what does that mean?
A. That means the abuse has been disclosed and there is some kind of evidence, believable evidence, that abuse has occurred.
Q. So it is believable, credible evidence that abuse has occurred?
A. Correct.

Q. And when you have an inconclusive determination about an allegation, what does that mean?
A. It means there is a kind of he said she said kind of — usually there is some on each side and we just don't know. We just don't know.
Q. Okay. And when the allegation is unfounded, what does that mean?
A. That means we didn't get evidence from anybody that abuse occurred.
Q. Can you tell me what a [delivered] service log is?
A. It is basically reporting a summary of the contact that we had on the investigation. Or it could be actually any contact in an open case file.
Q. So when you say contact, could it be a report of a phone call?
A. Yes.
Q. Could it be a report of a visit you made?
A. Yes.
Q. Do you recall in early November of 2006 delivering service to Chelsea Guthrie and Martha Guthrie?
A. Yes.
Q. Do you recall they made allegations of abuse against Mike Harris?
A. Yes.
Q. Do you recall that you told them that they did not have — that you didn't have enough evidence that they were in danger to keep them out of the home against their mother's will?
A I don't recall if those were my exact words.
Q Do you recall telling them the gist of that?
A. Yes.
Q. Do you remember, sitting here today, what the nature of the complaint was?
A. Yes, I do.
Q. What was it?
A. They said Mike had been angry because one of the twins — I don't recall which one at this time — was talking to a boy on the way to the bus stop, and he had said, "You just wait until you get home." And I forget if he said "You'll pay." But when I asked what "You'll pay" means, it was, like it wasn't physical abuse. So —
Q. Do you remember asking them if they were mad because they — because Mike didn't let them go trick or treating?
A. Yes.
Q. And do you remember that they told you that — one of them told you that they were mad because they couldn't be on the ski team?
A. Yes, I do.

A. Do you remember they told you their mom wasn't violent with them?
A. Yes.
Q. Do you recall whether the allegation the girls made in November of 2006 was substantiated?
A. In November? I recall — I know it was not substantiated.
Q. Because you, in fact, told them that they had not told you enough to warrant any concern?
A. Well, I basically told them that wasn't abuse.
Q. You said a while back in your testimony that you weren't permitted to ask if someone in the home was sexually abusing them?
A. Correct.
Q. And can you tell me why you are not permitted to ask a child the direct question, is so and so abusing you?
A. Because it would be a leading question leading them to give that answer.
Q. Is there a belief that, if you lead a child, that they may just agree with you?
A Yes.
Q. You wouldn't want to put that suggestion into a child's head?
A. Correct.
Q. And you wouldn't want someone to be falsely accused because you are suggesting something just happened to them?
A. Correct.
Q. Did you assist in an investigation of any allegations made by Martha Guthrie in the summer of 2007?
A. Yes.
Q. What allegations did Martha make in the summer of 2007?
A. She alleged that Mike Harris was sexually inappropriate with her.
Q. And did she make the allegation to you?
A. Actually, that allegation was reported to me, and then it was reported to me by someone else.
Q. Who reported that to you?
A. I don't recall the exact counselor. It was somebody from mental health, a counselor from mental health.
Q. In the summer of 2007, did Alex Ellis ever advise you that she had directly asked both Martha and Chelsea Guthrie whether Mike Harris was sexually abusing them?
A. No, she did not.
Q. As a social worker for CPS are you what we call a mandated reporter?
A. Yes.

Q. Can you tell me what that means?
A. It means under the law you are obligated to report abuse, suspected child abuse. If you believe, have a reasonable suspicion that a child is being abused, you are mandated to report that.
Q. How do you define the reasonable suspicion?
A. A reasonable suspicion, just whatever. If you believe there's abuse, make the report.
Q. So when in doubt, make the report?
A. Yes.
Q. And you said Martha had made an allegation that Mike Harris was inappropriately touching her but you did not report that. Can you tell me why you didn't?
A. I was the social worker — I don't know if you recall it, making a suspected child abuse report when you are a social worker with the county.
Q. Did you just say you don't make a suspected child abuse report when you are a social worker?
A. I report that — the way I would say that is I report it to the social worker handling the case. But you wouldn't —
Q. To whom did you report that?
A. To Alex Ellis and my supervisor.
Q. Do you remember Chelsea Guthrie telling you that Mike Harris had molested Martha and "tried to molest both of us"?
A. I don't recall her saying that. Not to me.
Q. What events have been refreshed for you after having looked at this document [DSL 7/9/07]?
A. I recall Mike Harris bringing Martha in my office to try to get Chelsea's phone number, saying she wanted contact with her, and I would not provide that.

After handing Ms. Douglas another document, Ms. Hankel asked:

Q. by Ms. Hankel: Is this document in your handwriting?
A. Yes, it is.
Q. And did you write this document on the 9th of July, 2007?
A. Yes, I did.
Q. But you note at that time that Chelsea Guthrie had told you that Mike Harris had molested Martha and then tried to molest both of them?
A. Yes.
Q. And that was the 9th of July, 2007?
A. Correct.
Q. Did you file a report of suspected child abuse when Chelsea made this statement?
A. I am sure I reported it to the social worker handling the case.

Q. And who was the social worker handling the case?

A. Alex Ellis.

Ms. Hankel gave Ms. Douglas another document and asked if it refreshed her memory and Ms. Douglas said it had.

Q. by Ms. Hankel: Did you write this document?

A. Yes, I did.

Q. And is this a part of that delivered service log that we talked about earlier?

A. Yes.

Q. Where you delivered service to a client?

A. Correct.

Q. And on July 12th of 2007, after Chelsea made the statement to you about Mike Harris molesting Martha and trying to molest both of them, do you remember going out to visit Martha Guthrie at her mom's home?

A. Yes, I do.

Q. Do you remember that nobody was there when you went to see them?

A. Yes, I do.

Q. Okay. So Chelsea discloses on the 9th. You go out to see Martha on the 12th. And then it is your recollection that it was the date that Martha disclosed to you that she was being molested by Mike Harris.

A Yes.

Q. How long after?

A. I do not recall exactly.

So, with that answer, Ms. Hankel concluded her examination of Ms. Douglas. Why she didn't confront her regarding the fact that she just testified that Martha didn't disclose to her, and said the mental health counselor and someone else told her.

Before Mr. Graham could start his cross-examination, Judge DeVore ended the proceedings for the day. The next day was November 11th, Veteran's Day. Therefore, there would be no court until Thursday. Before he left, Judge DeVore outlined the revised schedule that would require a two week break in the trial due to court conflicts and juror unavailability during the holiday week of Thanksgiving.

So, the 12th and 13th of November, Thursday and Friday, were going to have to be productive since the judge wanted to be finished and give the case to the jury the week of the 30th. That was the week we were coming back after a two-week break. Judge DeVore was putting enormous pressure on the lawyers to wrap up their cases and I thought it was unfair.

THIRTY-TWO

After a luxurious day off in my private suite I quickly found myself back in court. Right off the bat Judge DeVore had some questions for Martha and Chelsea's grandmother who had been sitting in the audience throughout the trial.

The Court: Ma'am, I understand you have been here throughout the trial, and I understand you are the grandmother of Martha and Chelsea.

Ms. Cole: That's correct.

The Court: What is your name?

Ms. Cole: Sharon Cole.

The Court: Ms. Cole, it has been reported to me that Alex Ellis has engaged you in some conversations and may have been making notes after conversations with you. Have you been talking to Alex Ellis at all during trial?

Ms. Cole: Yes, I have spoken to her.

The Court: Has the conversation in any sense concerned what has gone on in this trial? What people have testified about?

Ms. Cole: No, sir.

The Court: Nothing of that nature?

Ms. Cole: No, sir.

Judge DeVore then asked Ms. Hankel and Mr. Graham if they were okay with that and they were, so the day's testimony began with Ms. Douglas resuming her direct examination. Ms. Hankel started off by handing her another document dated 7/9/07 on the computer with a revised date of 7/11/07.

Q. by Ms. Hankel: Ms. Douglas, we were talking about a discussion you had with Martha Guthrie in July of 2007 — when she came to talk to you about foster care?

A. Correct.

Q. Do you remember that Martha talked to you about Chelsea having a lot of problems?

A. I remember some mention of some problems, vaguely.

And thus Ms. Douglas was given another note taken contemporaneously by her to help refresh her recollection as to what Martha said.

Q. by Ms. Hankel: Does that refresh your recollection as to the date you would have written that note?

A. Yes.

Q. Would it have been July 9 of 2007?

A. Yes.

The Court: Did you accurately record what you were told by Martha Guthrie?

The Witness: Yes, I did.

The Court: Did Martha Guthrie tell you "I love my mom to death," and did you record that contemporaneously with the statement made by Martha Guthrie?

The Witness: Yes, I did.

Ms. Hankel asked nothing further and I felt like she left a lot on the table that she could have asked. But I had to abide her strategy since she was captain of the ship. Mr. Graham stepped up to the lectern and jumped in right away to the summer of 2007.

Q. by Mr. Graham: In the summer of 2007, just so we are clear, did you hear from both of the girls, Martha and Chelsea, that Mike Harris had sexually abused them?

A. Yes.

Q. You specifically remember Martha making a statement to you?

A. Yes, I remember the basic message that Martha told me.

Q. Where were you and Martha when that statement was made?

A. I was in my office.

Q. Were you on the phone with her? Were you in person?

A. I was in person with Martha. We were both in my office.

Q. And can you tell us how the conversation began that led to this disclosure?

A. I had just received a suspected child abuse report alleging that Martha had expressed that Mike Harris had been sexually inappropriate with her in some way.

Q. Do you know where that report came from?

A. It came from a counselor at mental health.

Q. Going to the November of 2006 contact with Martha and Chelsea, do you remember the defense asking you about that?

A. Yes, I do.

Q. When you were in this contact, were both girls talking to you at the same time, or were you talking to them separately?

A. Both girls were talking to me at the same time.

Q. And did they relate to you an incident that you have given a brief statement on regarding something at a bus stop with Mr. Harris?

A. Yes, they did.

Q. Where were they?

A. The bus stop.

Q. And did they say anything about why Mr. Harris reacted in a certain way?

A. Because they were talking to a boy.

Q. And what happened?

A. And he asked them why they — "Why the fuck are you talking to that boy? What is he your boyfriend or something?" Or "You want him for a boyfriend?" I think is what he said.

Q. And then what did they say Mr. Harris did?

A. That he said — he said that they had better not tell their friend about the incident or there would be hell to pay if they told their friend about the incident, and he spun off.

Q. Did they make any statement regarding whether or not they wanted to go home and their feelings about that?

A. Yes. They said they didn't want to go home. They were afraid of Mike.

Q. Did they indicate why they were afraid of Mike?

A. They spoke of an incident in the past of him throwing — I forget which one — into the wall, pushing her into a wall and something about a bucket, which were incidents that I was aware of that were previously investigated.

Next, Ms. Hankel had some redirect questions and she started off by giving Ms. Douglas Exhibit 91, a document she wrote and the suspected child abuse report for Martha Exhibit VV. Referring to Exhibit VV, the Martha SCAR, Ms. Hankel asked:

Q. by Ms. Hankel: Is this the document you were referring to?

A. Yes, it is.

Q. Is the date of the report 7/19/07?

A. Yes, it is.

That was it. Ms. Hankel may have been buying into my conspiracy theory on some level because Ms. Douglas testified that she talked with Martha on the 9th or the 11th of July about sexual abuse yet the SCAR from Mr. Hultz was dated the 19th of July. Martha was removed from the home on July 16th. Ms. Douglas stopped working for the CPS on July 13th, 2007.

Next up was Patricia "Trish" Jackson, Martha's first foster mom and a friend of the family.

Q. by Ms. Hankel: Do you know Martha and Chelsea Guthrie?
A. by Patricia Jackson: Yes, I do.
Q. How do you know them?
A. They were friends with my daughter. Michelle Jackson.
Q. When did your daughter come to know Martha and Chelsea Guthrie?
A. She met Martha in 5th grade or maybe 4th grade and Chelsea in 5th grade.
Q. And did Martha and Chelsea visit with your daughter over at your house?
A. Yes.
Q. Did they spend the night with your daughter?
A. Yes.
Q. How much would they spend the night with your daughter?
A. I would say once a month, once every two months.
Q. And did your daughter think of them as good friends?
A. Yes.
Q. In the summer of 2007, did you become aware that Chelsea Guthrie had run away from home?
A. Yes.
Q. Did you become aware that Martha Guthrie was going to be placed in foster care?
A. Yes.
Q. Did you have a licensed foster care facility?
A. No.
Q. Did Alex Ellis contact you to see if you would take Martha Guthrie into foster care?
A. Yes.
Q. And when Martha was first placed in your home, how did — how did Martha and your daughter get along?
A. Fine.
Q. Subsequently did you become aware that Martha had to go in to interview with law enforcement?
A. Yes, I went with her.

Q. Were you the support person for that interview?
A. I was.
Q. And were you in the room with her while she gave her statement?
A. Yes, I was.
Q. Where was your daughter Michelle at that time?
A. She was in another room watching on a video.
Q. And who was in that room with your daughter while she was doing that?
A. Alex Ellis.
Q. Was there anything about [Martha's] behavior in your home that caused concern?
A. Yes.
Q. What was that?
A. She lied. She cut herself. Do you want specifics?
Q. Yes.
A. Okay, well when Martha first came to my house I talked to her about why she didn't tell her mother that this abuse was happening to her. And she told me she tried to tell her mom, and her mom didn't believe her. After we went to the police station for her to make her statement, she said that her mother was involved in the abuse. So I kind of started thinking that she wasn't quite telling the whole truth. She lied about going to a friend's house and spending the night. I talked to the grandmother where she was going to spend the night. The grandmother said she would be there. Alex Ellis told me that when she found out that the girl — that Martha had spent the night at her friend's house it was three girls and three boys. The grandmother left after Martha had gotten there. Martha lied about cutting herself. She lied about saying my daughter beat her up, and that my daughter was being mean to her.
Q. What did you do about all that turmoil in your home?
A. I wanted Martha out of the house and I called Alex Ellis to have her removed.
Q. And how long did — how many phone calls did you make to Alex Ellis to have Martha removed from your home?
A. At least 10.
Q. Do you remember if that was over a period like a week or a month?
A. It was over a period of a week and a half. Alex Ellis was looking for somewhere for her to go. On the weekend before Halloween 2007 the girls were supposed to go out, Martha, Chelsea, and Michelle. And Martha and Michelle were getting ready to go out. They were going to Leif and Tyler's just to hang out. Chelsea called me and said that she was going to kick Michelle's ass because Michelle was being rude to Martha.

Well, the girls were getting ready to go out. I wouldn't let Martha go out that night, so I let Michelle go out. Michelle came home that night and told me there was a phone call made to Chelsea from her friend Leif pretending to be Mike. So Michelle told me what happened, that Leif called, left a — I don't know if he talked to her or left a message saying "This is Mike. I am out of jail. Your mom bailed me out."

So that Halloween 2007 I was at work and a police officer called me at work and said he was at school arresting my daughter for felony terrorist charges for making this phone call. I went down to the school. I got in a fight with the officer. I ended up getting arrested and finally figured out that Michelle didn't make the call. It was Leif.

So I am not sure if it was Martha or Chelsea who told the school it was Michelle who made the call, but after that, I didn't want any part of them, none whatsoever. And I told Alex Ellis, "You need to come and get her today."

Q. As a result of the allegations made against your daughter with respect to the phone call and the terrorist threats, did you remove your daughter from school?

A. I did.

Ms. Hankel. I have nothing further for this witness.

The Court: Mr. Graham?

Q. by Mr. Graham: What is the nature of the disputes between the two [Martha and Michelle] in the summer, as we roll through the summer?

A. They were nit-picking about everything. Martha kept calling Chelsea, telling her Michelle was picking on her. Michelle spent most of her time in her room after they were not getting along.

Q. Do you think your daughter, Michelle, had any blame in the deterioration of the relationship?

A. Yes, I do.

Q. Isn't it fair to characterize their deterioration in the relationship as just teenage girl conflicts between the two of them?

A. Yes.

Q. Did you hear a statement from Chelsea regarding Chelsea's denying sexual abuse by Mike Harris?

A. Yes.

Q. When did you hear that?

A. Michelle told me. I don't remember. I don't remember when she first said it. I just blew it off. She told me again when Therese [Ms. Hankel] came to our residence to talk to us.

Q. Did you tell any law enforcement after you heard that statement?

A. No, I didn't.

Q. Why not?

A. I just wasn't sure what I believed anymore.

Q. You know at that point both girls had made allegations against Mike Harris; correct?

A. Correct.

Q. And now you are hearing that there is a possible recantation or at least a change in that story; correct? By Chelsea; correct?

A. Correct.

Q. And you did nothing about it?

A. I did nothing about it.

Q. Did you do anything about it after, let's say within the next two years?

A. No.

Q. At all?

A. Nothing.

Now Ms. Hankel had a couple follow-up questions on redirect.

Q. by Ms. Hankel: Ms. Jackson, did Detective Rutkowski ever call you to ask about statements made to you by Martha or Chelsea Guthrie?

A. No.

Q. Did Wade McCammond ever call you to ask about any statements made by Martha or Chelsea Guthrie?

A. No.

Q. Anybody else from any other law enforcement agency, Karen Smart ever call you?

A. No.

Q. What was the statement that Michelle had told you that Chelsea had made?

A. That Mike never raped her.

That was a heckuva story Trish related and it was all true. She didn't have to testify and she owed me nothing. Ms. Hankel missed a golden opportunity when she failed to ask Trish about her relationship with me and Kerri, her experiences with us over the years, and especially the period of time surrounding Chelsea's running away incident. Ms. Hankel did not ask Trish about her contacts with Chelsea while Chelsea was at the Clarke's house.

Trish was also not asked about the supposed phone call listed in Alex's notes and also in the 7/16/07 DSL. Martha was removed from her home on 7/16/07. Prior to that on 7/6/07, I took Martha over to the Jackson's and dropped her off for a few hours while I went golfing. The is no DSL entry for Martha having called CPS on either the 6th or the 16th.

Ms. Hankel never asked Trish about leaving Michelle for me to babysit with no complaints. Later on, Kerri and I would babysit Michelle with no complaints then either. Ms. Hankel should have asked Trish some general questions about her opinion of me and my character which should have been helpful to my defense. Following Trish was her daughter Michelle Jackson.

Q. by Ms. Hankel: Michelle Jackson, you are a friend of Martha and Chelsea Guthrie; correct?
A. I used to be.
Q. A former friend?
A. Yes.
Q. Did Martha Guthrie ever tell you that Mike Harris had been inappropriately touching her?
A. Not until she pressed charges.
Q. And that would be?
A. That was in the summer of 2007.
Q. What was the first statement she made to you about my client, Mike Harris?
A. That he molested her.
Q. Do you remember when she said that to you?
A. I would say in June of 2007.
Q. Did she use the statement "molested her" or did she use any other statement?
A. She said "raped".
Q. At the time she made the statement to you was she living in your home as a foster child?
A. It was about two weeks before she moved in with us.
Q. Do you know whether or not it was before or after Chelsea's run away incident?
A. It was about a week after she ran away.
Q. Did Chelsea Guthrie ever make any statements to you that she was being molested or inappropriately touched by Mike Harris?
A. No.
Q. Did your family go on a vacation?
A. Yes.
Q. With Martha?
A. Yes.
Q. While you were on vacation, did anything occur that made you angry?
A. Yes.
Q. What was that?

A. On the last day that we were there, we decided not to go to bed right away because it was going to be a long drive and we could sleep. So we stayed out by the river, right next to our cabin. And there were couple of guys with us and one of them was 12 years old and Martha started making out with him.

Q. When you got back from your trip did you ever advise Leif Medrud what Martha had done?

A. Yes.

Q. What did he do?

A. He called Chelsea pretending to be Mike Harris and he said "Your mom bailed me out." And he hung up the phone.

Q. Were you in the room when he did that?

A. We were actually outside, but, yes, I was there.

Q. Subsequently, were you accused of making that call?

A. Yes, I was.

Q. Who were you accused by?

A. Martha, Chelsea, and Leif.

Q. Did police officers come to your school?

A. Yes.

Q. And did they advise you that they were going to file terrorist felony charges against you?

A. Yes.

Q. Subsequently did they learn that Leif Medrud had made that call?

A. Yes.

Q. Did Chelsea ever tell you she was not molested by Mike Harris?

A. She told me she was never raped.

Q. When did she tell you that?

A. After she made her testimony at the police station in Crowley Lake.

Q. Did you have a conversation with. Chelsea after she gave her statement?

A. Yes.

Q. Did you ask her what. Mike Harris had done to her?

A. Yes.

Q. What did she say?

A. She said he didn't rape her.

Q. Did Martha and Chelsea ask you to come with them to the sheriff's substation?

A. Yes.

Q. Do you know why they asked you to come?

A. Because we were still close friends and they wanted my support.

Q. Was it your understanding that something else was going to occur at the substation besides the interview?
A. Yes.
Q. What was that?
A. To make that phone call where you try and incriminate him.
Q. And what was Martha's feeling about whether they should make that call?
A. She didn't want to do it.
Q. What was Chelsea's feeling about whether they should make that phone call?
A. She really wanted to do it.
Q. My client received some emails from people accusing him of being a child molester. Did you write those emails?
A. No, I did not.
Q. Did you ever sit down with Chelsea Guthrie and help her draft an email to my client that he was a child molester?
A. No, I did not.
Q. Michelle, while Martha was living in your home, did you ever choke her?
A. No.
Q. Did you ever hit her in her arm?
A. Yeah, once.

Ms. Hankel closed with a series of questions that related to whether anybody from CPS or law enforcement ever contacted Michelle about the purported choking of Martha by her. She said nobody contacted her. Mr. Graham then began cross-examining Michelle minimally asking to confirm what she had already said during her direct testimony. Mr. Graham did elicit some testimony about Chelsea's denial that she had been raped.

Q. by Mr. Graham: Before you heard the statement from Chelsea "I have not been raped by Mike Harris," did you understand that Chelsea had given a statement to the police officer about being raped by Mike Harris?
A. No.
Q. Did you understand why Chelsea was there at the substation?
A. Yeah, because of the allegations against Mike.
Q. So you knew Chelsea was there to give an interview about allegations against Mike; correct?
A. Yes.
Q. And it was right after that that Chelsea says to you "Mike never raped me?"
A. Yes.
Q. Did you tell anyone?

A. No.
Q. Why not?
A. Because I didn't know what she was accusing Mike of.
Q. Had Chelsea told you prior to that anything about her allegations?
A. No.

So, hold on a minute. Michelle didn't know at Chelsea's August 8th interview that Chelsea was claiming sexual abuse? And she supposedly knew from Martha a week after Chelsea ran away. They were all best friends. I put forth that Michelle was not accurate in her memory of the sequence of events. "Those boys" were also all over the place. I believed Michelle when she said Chelsea denied being raped mostly because Chelsea had yelled it out in court during her testimony. Remember it had been over two years since the events had transpired.

Q. by Mr. Graham: After you heard Chelsea say "Mike had not raped me," did you tell anyone that Chelsea said that?
A. No, not until now.
Q. Do you recall telling your mother in October of 2007 that statement?
A. No, I didn't — the first time I told her was when Nathan and Ms. Hankel contacted us.
Q. You waited that long to tell anybody that Chelsea had stated that Mike had not raped her, why?
A. Because I was trying to forget everything.

Michelle began to cry but after a few moments she pulled it together. Mr. Graham wrapped things up with a couple quick questions and then the attorneys were done with the Jacksons. Ms. Hankel never asked about "Bob" from the email I received that she had asked Chelsea about. Ms. Hankel went into the emails a little bit but not enough for my liking. Ms. Hankel and Nathan Morganstein did a fine job getting these witnesses to come all the way from Eureka, CA. However, Ms. Hankel neglected to ask Michelle about hanging out at the park in Chalfant with Martha, Chelsea, Jessikah, and "those boys" during the early summer of 2007 when the girls were supposedly telling their friends about the abuse. If there really was a plan, why didn't Ms. Hankel capitalize on Michelle's inside knowledge?

Michelle always had good things to say about me and Ms. Hankel failed to bring that to the fore. Sure, she might have opened the door to evidence of my bad character, but I felt that ship had already sailed, while Ms. Hankel is captain of the ship, she may elect to avoid character evidence in order to avoid opening the pandora's box of testimonial debate about whether I am a bad person or not. Ms. Hankel should have asked Michelle if I was ever inappropriate with her at any time or did she ever feel threatened by me. I felt that for all the trouble getting the Jackson's over to Mammoth to testify on my behalf, Ms. Hankel shirked her duty to prepare adequately and failed to ask the most important question left hanging: Why are you testifying for the defense?

THIRTY-THREE

Following the Jackson's, the next witness for my defense was Dr. Lee Coleman, a medical doctor specializing in adult and child psychiatry and had been for forty years.

Q. by Ms. Hankel: Have you ever treated a child who has claimed that he or she has suffered child abuse?

A. by Dr. Coleman: Yes. It was never a big part of my practice, but I have done that.

Q. What about teenagers? Have you ever treated a teenager that has claimed they were a victim of sexual abuse?

A. Yes.

Q. And adults, have you ever treated on adult who has claimed he or she has suffered sexual abuse?

A. Yes.

Q. Have you ever examined a teenager by conducting testing on a person who had claimed to have been sexually abused to determine whether they have been sexually abused?

A. There isn't such testing. So I wouldn't try to do it, because it doesn't exist.

Dr. Coleman then went through a discussion about forensic psychiatry and CSAAS as well as his lectures on investigation techniques, his experience testifying in court, and his published articles.

Q. by Ms. Hankel: And do these articles focus on investigation techniques?

A. That was always the very heart of the matter, yes. Everything I was talking about you could think of them as spokes of a wheel, that is, the different parts of the articles might be different spokes. But the central thing that would connect it all was these problems that I was discussing were part of legal investigations. That is, I was not talking about therapy as a clinician with children who were molested. The subject was the process by which we try to decide if a child has been sexually molested. In one part it might be interview techniques. Another view might be medical examinations. Another part might be failure to adequately question different people. Another one might be different kinds of alleged syndromes. But all of it came in the center to how is the system doing at trying to decide whether a particular child has been a victim of child abuse.

Dr. Coleman then went on to discuss the same things related to CSAAS and suggestibility that he testified to at the §402 hearing back in July. Once the basics were out of the way, Mr. Graham sought to destroy Dr. Coleman's credibility through voir dire.

Mr. Graham brought out that Dr. Coleman was not a member of the American Psychiatric Association, the American Psychology Association, the American Medical Association, or the American Academy of Child Psychiatry. In fact, Dr. Coleman was not board certified in psychiatry or any medical field. Dr. Coleman fought back, pointing out he was board certified in medicine by the National Board of Medical Examiners, noting that it wasn't a specialty board but was a required general board he had to practice medicine.

Further on, Mr. Graham raised the specter of Dr. Coleman being critical of the DSM-III and psychiatry in general when he asked:

Q. by Mr. Graham: You have often taken positions that are contrary to the dominant view of psychiatry; isn't that true?

A. Yes. That is true. Sometimes I have, sometimes I haven't. But that has happened in many examples.

Q. In 34 years of your private practice, how many children have you seen who are the victim of child abuse?

A. About 10.

Mr. Graham then went on to show that Dr. Coleman had never interviewed an accuser to determine if they were telling the truth, repeating that there was no credibility test to determine the veracity of an accuser. Following this, Mr. Graham rattled off several prominent medical magazines and journals and asked Dr. Coleman if he had ever published an article about child sexual abuse and Dr. Coleman said "No." He did however admit he had been published in Hustler Magazine, Chick Magazine, and Gallery Magazine, but explained they were articles about psychiatry and were not pornographic. And after that barrage, Mr. Graham concluded his voir dire. Judge DeVore then accepted Dr. Coleman as an expert in a variety of fields. The Court then instructed in part:

The Court: Dr. Coleman, and all experts, are allowed to testify and give opinions, but you must consider the opinions — while you must consider the opinions, you are not required to accept them as true or correct. Consider the experts' knowledge, training, and education, the reasons the expert gives for any opinion, and the facts or information on which this expert relies in reaching that opinion. You must decide whether that information on which the expert relied was true and accurate. And you may disregard any opinion that you find unbelievable, and unreasonable and unsupported by the evidence.

At the close of Judge DeVore's instruction to the jury, Ms. Hankel began her direct examination.

Q. by Ms. Hankel: Dr. Coleman, were you asked to review certain materials?

A. Yes.

Q. what did you review?

A. The social service records of the two girls which went back to 2002, I believe, the police investigation reports that started in 2007, taped interviews and transcripts. I think about three or four of those. There were preliminary hearing transcripts, some medical records, some therapy records, psychotherapy records.

Q. Did your review of records and materials in this case also consist of supplemental interviews of Martha and Chelsea Guthrie in 2008?

A. Yes.

Ms. Hankel then entered into a stipulation that the DVD she was about to play did not have to be transcribed and consisted of Chelsea's supplemental interview dated 5/16/08 and Martha's on 5/27/08. Ms. Hankel then played the videos from the DVD. After the jury had viewed the material Ms. Hankel asked Dr. Coleman:

Q. by Ms. Hankel: Dr. Coleman, do you have any opinion as to whether there were potential issues of suggestibility in the interview of Chelsea Guthrie by Detective Rutkowski which was the first interview we looked at?

A. Yes, I do.

Q. What are those opinions?

A. That the failure to pick up on potentially important leads in that interview, would — the failure to do that would encourage and enhance suggestibility that had already existed from earlier interviews. And I guess I would need to explain what I mean.

Q. Please.

A. The interview, the entire interview seemed to be done, in my opinion, in a rather flippant, lighthearted manner which I think is very, very inappropriate. Second of all, when Chelsea said "Oh, I had a diary in which I wrote some things about what Mike was doing," that would seem to be extremely important in the process of getting to the truth.

Because if you find material which would have appeared to have been done contemporaneously with abuse, that might go to support the credibility, depending on what was said, what other information he had. And I was struck by the fact the interviewer never asked her, "Well what happened to them? Where are they? We'd like to see them." It was as if they don't exist and nobody really cared. At least that is my understanding of it.

And so my impression was it's because the interviewer already said we are here just to clean up a few questions that the defense wants us to ask, but we know it happened and you are the victim, words to that effect. The other thing was that they were asking about, who have you talked to about this? Who did you tell? And that is a very good question, because of what it leads to next.

You go out and you talk to those people, and you see whether the story you've heard from one person both content wise and timing. There was no indication. In fact I now know they never went out and talked to Jessikah Luffman and her mother until the last 24/48 hours.

So to me, all this indicates a flippant, unprofessional attitude because they had already made up their mind. You're a victim. End of story. And likewise -- well I guess you haven't asked about the second interview.

Q. Do you have an opinion as to the potential suggestibility of the cheerleading in the background of that interview?

I must point out here that during Chelsea's supplemental interview Alex Ellis was seen and heard in the background leading a cheer P-R-I-S-O-N prison, prison, go to prison right in front of Chelsea and Detective Rutkowski. Now for Dr. Coleman's answer.

A. It is not just the impact at the moment which, of course, basically broadcast loud and clear that not only is she convinced she knows what the truth is, even though there has been no trial, and how she would be so sure, it is hard for me to know. But the fact she would feel free and comfortable to come out with such a thing, that cheer for prison, to me, indicates that she apparently sees the entire context;

her relationship with Chelsea, her relationship with Rutkowski, the entire investigation.

Q. And what about with respect to the second interview, the interview between Martha Guthrie and Det. Rutkowski? Did you see any areas of potential suggestibility in that area?

A. Basically the same. She mentioned she had written at least one thing in a poem. And again, that would be very important. But there was no discussion about, well, if she says it's gone -- I don't know what you would say -- but if it wasn't available, why not? This is the way you test somebody's credibility.

And I felt the entire tone with Martha was the same, inappropriately cozy, and failing to follow up on the poem, and failing to follow up on the statement that said "You told Jessikah," which turns out to be the very girl, along with her mother, that was along at that interview and that was done only within the last day or so. So it is like my God, there is a chance to get to the bottom of things and it is being ignored.

Q. Did you review the interview between Detective Rutkowski and Martha that was conducted in August of 2007?

A. Yes, I did.

Q. Do you have any opinions about the potential suggestibility of that interview?

A. Well, I think there was more suggestiveness in that interview. I still think the biggest problem is what they didn't do, rather than directly suggesting things. I think there is some of that. But, I would say the biggest problem is the entire tone of the interview, in my opinion, was one in which it was taken as a given that the child was a sexual abuse victim. And the point of the interview seemed to be let's get a list.

Let's get a compilation of all the things that he did, with plenty of encouragement, okay, what else? What else? Without doing anything to test the statements to find out who she's been in contact with. What the circumstances were. Basically just a blanket and uncritical acceptance of the allegations and nothing more.

Q. And what about the interview by Karen Smart of Chelsea? Did you see any issues of potential suggestibility in that interview?

A. Well, I think the fact that Alex Ellis is in the interview is, I think, a big mistake. I think that there's great dangers when you allow anybody else to be present. And given the information that I -- and the fact that she was one of the first persons to be told the allegations, I think you should not allow the person to be there. Because that is the way you test out different people's version of what was said and what the context was.

After a short recess Ms. Hankel continued:

Q. by Ms. Hankel: Dr. Coleman, in your review of the materials in this case, did you review an interview between the District Attorney's office and Jessikah Luffman and Gina Luffman?

A. Yes, I did listen to it.

Q. And in that interview, did Gina Luffman discuss a conversation that she had with Martha and Chelsea Guthrie in approximately June of 2007?

A. Yes.

Q. Was that conversation that she had prior to the time Chelsea ran away from home?

A. That is my understanding.

Q. In listening to that interview, were you concerned about any potential suggestibility out of the conversation that Gina Luffman had with Martha and Chelsea Guthrie in June of 2007?

A. Yes.

Q. What was that concern?

A. Well, again, the background in which there was a dispute between Gina Luffman, mother, and Kerri Guthrie, the mother of the girls, and Michael Harris, there was a dispute about whether the girls were going to be brought back to their house or whether or not they should have been allowed out of the house. It was quite a hostile interaction according to Gina Luffman's description. And she did not want the girls to be forced to go back.

She suggested to them that she had been sexually abused herself and that she wondered if that was going on with them. So the suggestion came from her, and only then, from everything I studied, did a statement; yes, that is what happened. So that's in my opinion highly relevant to the process of deciding the meaning of the allegations.

Q. Given the background of Martha and Chelsea Guthrie related to prior allegations made by Raeanna Davenport, do you have an opinion as to whether a prior questioning by law enforcement of Martha and Chelsea Guthrie could have led to potential suggestibility in the making of allegations against my client?

A. I have an opinion.

Q. What is that opinion?

A. That it is very relevant.

Q. And, why so?

A. Because I think every time you have a person being informed by either people that they have a concern or a belief or a worry or a fear that any, or all of those, that a certain person is doing certain things, you can basically be clueing this individual into certain possibilities.

Dr. Coleman then continued to describe the five stages of CSAAS. Secrecy, helplessness, entrapment, delayed and conflicted disclosure, and recantation. Dr. Coleman opined that CSAAS is not a syndrome at all. He explained that because every one of the stages singularly or any combination of the stages is just as strong a characteristic if the allegation is false as if it is true. The cause could be sexual abuse in one scenario and a false allegation in the next, and you would have exactly the same behavior by the child.

Dr. Coleman then went through each of the five stages in detail supporting his thesis that CSAAS does not help you determine if an allegation is true or false. He continued to criticize CSAAS and assert that it wasn't a syndrome: it was one man's observation 30 years ago.

Q. by Ms. Hankel: Does repeated questioning abort whether something is wrong have a potential for suggestibility?

A. It could depending on what other information I might have.

Q. And you've already testified that an adult suggesting to a child that he or she has been molested that has the potential for an unreliable disclosure of sexual abuse?

A. Yes.

Q. Doctor, do you have an opinion about whether multiple interviews of young adults can lead to potential suggestibility of about a subsequent disclosure of sexual abuse?

A. I think it has that potential to do that. It depends on how they are presented, not just multiple, but the content of how it is being done. But it could if other things are present.

Q. Do you have any opinions as to whether there could be potential suggestibility by the vilification of the alleged suspect?

A. Yes, I do.

Q. What is that opinion?

A. I think that is inherently suggestive and may complicate the problem of assessing the liability if an interviewer is doing that.

Q. And did you see in the interviews of Martha and Chelsea Guthrie any vilification of any of the suspects?

A. Yes, I did.

That finished up Dr. Coleman's direct testimony and I thought Ms. Hankel did okay with him but I felt she could have delved deeper into the specifics related to a timeline which would show both deficiencies in the witnesses testimony against me as well as show a definite escalation of allegations.

Following this, Mr. Graham launched his attack directly at Dr. Coleman's failure to know that the notebook/journal was found at Kerri's house as a result of a search warrant executed 9/13/07. Then Judge DeVore and Mr. Graham agreed to read CALCRIM 1193, the jury instruction which states you can use CSAAS testimony in deciding whether the conduct of any victim testifying in this case was not inconsistent with the conduct of someone who has been molested and in evaluating the believability of that testimony. Mr. Graham then went over articles about CSAAS with Dr. Coleman.

Q. by Mr. Graham: Do you have any evidence CSAAS was used in this trial that the victims were molested, any evidence at all?

A. To my knowledge, no.

Q. Do you have any evidence at all that CSAAS was misused in this trial?

A. I would have to hear the testimony of Ms. McLennan.

Q. At this point you don't have any evidence; correct?

A. No.

Q. Isn't it correct that with regard to suggestibility, 15-year-olds are no more suggestible than adults?

A. No, I wouldn't agree with that — I think that in some ways in terms of their intellectual capacity and the development of their memory, they are no more suggestible or less suggestible. They are about like adults. They are like adults. There are other ways where they can be more suggestible, because they are not yet adults in other ways besides their memory and intellect. They are still children. They may still be more susceptible to pressures and to pressures from their own community, from the adult community. So in some ways they would not be any more suggestible. But in other ways they very well could be.

Judge DeVore got a bit impatient and asked Dr. Coleman to describe the difference between psychology and psychiatry. Mr. Graham followed this with questions regarding implanted memories. I was confused by the way they were using suggestibility in the context that the girls somehow were having their memories altered like in some science fiction movie. The girls were lying and making it up as they went along. What happened one time didn't happen the next. Remember, the only thing they got right all day long was the bucket incident. Mr. Graham continued for quite some time with the false memory line of questioning and then scored some points when he asked:

Q. by Mr. Graham: I asked you if you testified that it was possible for a child to remember more in subsequent interviews?

A. Possible, yes.

Q. You've also testified that you would expect inconsistencies from a long term molest victim in recounting their abuse; correct?

A. A genuine long-term victim, I would expect inconsistencies.

Q. You've testified that you would not be concerned if a child could not remember the number or sequence of acts involved in an ongoing molest. You testified to that; correct?

A. Yes.

Q. Did you ever talk to either or any of the victims in the case, the alleged victims?

A No.

Q. You never talked to their mother or any relatives; correct?

A. No.

Q. You never talked to the nurse who examined the girls; correct?

A. No.

That completed Dr. Coleman's testimony. Mr. Graham slandered Dr. Coleman at every step, yet failed to mention that Dr. Coleman testified for the prosecution in the landmark case of People v Ledesma (1987) Cal 3d 171. But then again, I didn't see Ms. Hankel pointing it out either. Ms. Hankel should have used a hypothetical with Dr. Coleman to counter Ms. McLennan's detailed hypothetical thesis. The whole plan defense was shown to be in direct conflict with suggestibility. Especially in the context of suggestibility as being the creation of false memories. The plan, if there was one, sure wasn't very good.

If there was a plan, then Gina Luffman would have been the ringleader. It should be pointed out here that the incident Gina was referring to is a blurring of two incidents. I called for Martha at Gina's house and I was told that Martha was out running around town and so I called Kerri and told her. Kerri called Gina and told her Martha wasn't allowed to roam the streets of Bishop without supervision. Gina thought that was hogwash. A fight ensued on the phone, but in the end, Martha stayed the night in Bishop with the Luffmans. Chelsea was not there an all. She was in Chalfant with Kerri. The other half of the story is the girls going over to Gina's house after Chelsea ran away. Gina lived in Bishop, not Chalfant at that time. Both girls were in foster care in Bishop. Careful scrutiny by Ms. Hankel would have led her to use a timeline and detailed questioning to illuminate the facts in the case which showed there was an escalation of allegations, not a plan to deceive. These deficiencies should have been pointed out by Dr. Coleman, but he did explain a lot and I hoped the jury understood.

THIRTY-FOUR

Coming up next was Ms. Lindsay, the foster mom favored by most foster kids in the Bishop area because of her lax discipline. Ms. Hankel started her off with some basic questions about where she lived, how long she had lived there and whether she provided foster care. Ms. Lindsay replied that she had lived in Bishop for about ten years and did in fact run a foster home there.

Q. by Ms. Hankel: And in the performance of those services, did you come to know Chelsea and Martha Guthrie?

A. Yes.

Q. Were either of them placed in your home as foster care?

A. Yes, both of them.

Q. How long did you have just Chelsea in your home?

A. Chelsea was with me maybe four to six weeks before Martha came to live with us.

Q. How long did you have just Chelsea in your home as foster care?

A. Let me see. She stayed through her 16th birthday, February 23rd.

Q. And so it is your recollection that she stayed from about July 2007 through February?

A. Beyond February, I just don't remember when she left.

Q. Do you remember the circumstances where she left your home?

A. She chose to leave. She requested to move -- She requested Alex her social worker.

Q. Do you recall prior to requesting to leave your home she had been in an altercation at her school?
A. Yes.
Q. And was that altercation with another girl?
A. Right.
Q. And do you recall that the school was not going to permit her to attend a dance because of that altercation?
A. That's correct.
Q. And do you recall that you also told Chelsea that as a result of this altercation she would not be able to attend this dance?
A. Correct.
Q. Is it then your recollection that the school relented and told her she could attend the dance?
A. That's correct.
Q. Did Chelsea that same day have an altercation with her sister, Martha?
A. Correct.
Q. After the altercation with Martha what happened?
A. I decided that neither one of them could go to the school dance. That's because of their behavior, that I was restricting them from the school dance also.
Q. And what did Chelsea do as a result of that restriction?
A. Chelsea became angry and the girls argued and then Chelsea left.
Q. You say she left, do you know where she went?
A. Probably, no. I don't know exactly where she went. She probably went over to one of her girlfriends.
Q. Did she return that day?
A. No, she didn't. Her social worker called me.
Q. Was her social worker Alex Ellis?
A. That's correct.
Q. Was she removed from your home that day?
A. Actually, she did not come home that night. And then a couple of days later she came by, and we packed up her clothes, and she went to a new home.
Q. And then how long after that did Martha remain in your home?
A. Probably for maybe four or five weeks.
Q. Do you recall around Halloween you and your husband being gone for about three days?
A. Yes.
Q. And do you recall that Martha was going to spend time not in your house but in somebody else's home while you were gone?

A. Right.

Q. Do you remember as a result of leaving to go on this vacation you gave Martha some rules to abide by?

A. Yes.

Q. And when you arrived at home from that vacation did you find that she had abided those rules?

A. No.

Q. As a result of that was Martha placed in another home?

A. That's correct.

It is worth noting hare that Judge DeVore, in a contentious sidebar conversation, 86'd Ms. Hankel's venture into Martha's bad behaviors. The sneaking out, the drinking, the smoking, the smoking pot, the who knows what. Quite a wonderful way to live instead of at her mom's house. I was the victim, not the accusers. That wrapped up Ms. Lindsay and I was disappointed for not getting Martha's vices in there. Next on the stand was Deputy Gordon, the responding officer the night Raeanna's grandmother made her allegation. Deputy Gordon had worked for the Mono County Sheriff's Department for many years and I liked him, but for now it was all business.

Q. by Ms. Hankel: Deputy Gordon, were you involved in the investigation of allegations of inappropriate touching made by Raeanna Davenport in 2003?

A. Yes, I was.

Q. Did you investigate that allegation?

A. I did.

Q. Did you speak to Raeanna Davenport about the incident?

A. Yes.

Q. Did you make a report of that investigation?

A. Yes. I did.

Q. And do you have that report with you?

A. I do.

Q. Do you recall today the facts around that investigation?

A. Yes.

Q. Do you remember learning through the course of your investigation that Raeanna's grandmother was asking her leading questions?

A. Yes.

Q. Do you remember that you learned during the course of the investigation that she suggested to Raeanna Davenport that Mike Harris had done something to her?

A. Yes.

Q. Do you remember learning through the course of your investigation that Anna Brennan [Raeanna's grandmother] was repeatedly questioning her granddaughter about what was wrong with her?

A. I recall in my report that she'd asked her several times what was wrong, if something had happened.

Ms. Hankel: I have nothing further.

Mr. Graham then asked some questions on cross.

Q. by Mr. Graham: Is the sequence of the leading questions, in other words, when the leading questions occurred by Ms. Brennan to Raeanna Davenport, is that accurately reflected in your report to the best of your recollection?

A. Yes.

Then Ms. Hankel. asked a couple of redirect questions and then a bench discussion ensued whereby it was decided that there was to be a stipulation between counsel that Deputy Gordon's narrative report consisting of the first paragraph on page 2 of 4 and the first three paragraphs of page 3 of 4 may be introduced into evidence as his past recollection recorded.

That wrapped up day 8, the 12th of November, 2009. I kept waiting for a Perry Mason moment and was also hoping that Mr. Albee was doing his homework and could blow away the computer evidence. But in the meantime, it was a scenic trip back to my cell in Bridgeport. A fitful night's sleep led me to a trip back to Mammoth slightly dozing in the car. It was Friday the 13th. I figured nothing bad could happen to me that hadn't already happened. In fact, maybe I might get lucky, you never know.

First up that morning were the psychotherapists who took Martha and Chelsea's supposed first disclosures. It should be obvious from the girls' sworn testimony that they told Alex Ellis first before anyone else. No friends, no psychotherapists, no cops. Just Alex Ellis. So off we went with Michael Hultz who was a psychiatric technician with the Mono County Mental Health Dept.

Q. by Ms. Hankel: During your tenure with Mono County Mental Health did you come to know Martha Guthrie?

A. I did.

Q. How did you know her?

A. She was assigned to me as a case in July of '07.

Q. And was Martha Guthrie in foster care at the time she was assigned to you?

A. Yes, she was.

Q. Do you recall Martha Guthrie reporting child abuse allegations to you?
A. Yes, I do.
Q. Do you recall if that was the very first time you met with her?
A. Yes, it was.
Q. Do you recall Martha Guthrie telling you that she didn't want to discuss it at that time?
A. Yes, I do.
Q. Do you recall she was also complaining about treatment by her mother?
A. Yes, I do.
Q. Do you recall if she was talking about verbal abuse by her mother?
A. Yes, I do.
Q. Do you remember specifically what the allegation Martha Guthrie made to you that first day was?
A. Yes, I do.
Q. What was that?
A. That she was sexually abused, molested by the defendant.
Q. Was that as specific as she got or was she more specific than that?
A. She gave a time frame, she said it began in the fourth grade and continued until she was removed from the home.
Q. Did you as a result of that first conversation you had with Martha Guthrie prepare a Suspected Child Abuse Report?
A. I did.
Q. And are you what is called a "mandated reporter?"
A. Yes, I am.
Q. Do you recall who you reported that allegation to?
A. Alex Ellis.
Q. Did Alex Ellis ever tell you that she had a prior discussion with Martha Guthrie wherein she'd asked Martha Guthrie if she was being sexually abused by my client?
A. No. Not from Alex. I was aware that the allegations had been made and I believe that was from the director of mental health. When the case was assigned to me, I understood that there was sexual abuse, when I received the case.
Q. So, if you made your first report, you understood at that time you actually were filing a suspected child abuse report there had already been an allegation of sexual abuse made by Martha Guthrie?
A. That's correct.
Q. Did you come to file another suspected child abuse report?
A. I did.

Q. How much time passed, rather, between the first filing and the second filing, do you recall?
A. I don't recall exactly. I believe it was the next time I saw Martha, but I can't be sure of that.
Q. Mr. Hultz, I'm handing you a document. Do you recognize that document?
A. Yes. I do.
Q. What is it?
A. It's a Child Abuse Report.
Q. Is that reported July 19th, 2007?
A. Yes.
Q. In the narrative description of this report of abuse, you've written "Martha reported being raped by her mother's boyfriend, Mike, while in Los Angeles." Do you recall that?
A. Yes.
Q. Mr. Hultz, I'm handing you [another] one-page document entitled "Suspected Child Abuse Report." You see the date there?
A. I do.
Q. What is the data of this report?
A. The 30th of July, 2007.
Q. And you reported that Martha had reported being molested sexually by Mike Harris beginning in fourth grade through the removal of her from the home in July 2007; correct?
A. Correct.
Q. To whom did you make this report?
A. Alex Ellis.
Q. Other than these specific allegations of abuse related to Michael Harris, is it fair to say Martha Guthrie never made any other allegations of abuse against Mike Harris?
A. No.
Ms. Hankel had nothing further and so Mr. Graham took to the lectern and asked Mr. Hultz about the fact his sessions with Martha were supposed to be confidential. Mr. Graham continued on by asking about the process by which the disclosures were made and whether Martha volunteered the information.
Q. by Mr. Graham: Before she mentioned anything about sexual abuse by Mike Harris, did you prime her in any way with any kind of words or statements related to sexual abuse?
A. Absolutely not.

Q. And so if you could tell us the words or the statements that were being used by either of you prior to the disclosure, can you recall those words or the general gist of them?

A. I don't really recall anything more specific than what I just stated. I simply, in a sense to provide comfort and security and a sense of empowerment to her, I simply let her know that I was aware of her allegations but that she didn't have to tell me anything she didn't want to.

Q. As she made the disclosure of being raped by Mike Harris did it appear when she began -- you said she was crying and upset?

A. Uh-huh.

Q. Did it appear based upon your common experience, that she was feigning or faking that reaction?

A. Absolutely not.

Q. What other forms of abuse did she report in that meeting?

A. She reported physical abuse and what we call emotional or verbal abuse.

Mr. Graham then went into Martha's demeanor in detail and the claims that I had hit her leaving marks repeatedly. Mr. Hultz said Martha was upset, crying, shaking, and had difficulty speaking. Then Mr. Graham asked a final question:

Q. by Mr. Graham: Again, was there anything about her physical reaction or emotional reaction that caused you to believe that she was faking that reaction to gain any kind of sympathy or advantage over you?

A. No, there was not.

The next therapist to testify was Ellen Thompson, a psychiatric technician at Mono County Mental Health, who offered psychotherapy services.

Q. by Ms. Hankel: In the performance of those duties, did you come to know Chelsea Guthrie?

A. I did.

Q. Okay. Do you remember -- you were giving her psychotherapy; correct?

A. No. Initially my work with her, I was asked to do a psychological evaluation and when that was finished, we began a course of psychotherapy.

Q. And how was it you were asked to do a psychological evaluation of Miss Guthrie?

A. There was a request. It didn't come to me directly; it came to the person who -- through our intake process but I was given the information, a psychological assessment or evaluation was requested by a number of people actually including the court, Chelsea's mother, and CPS.

Q. Do you recall if the, during the first session, when you first met her, if Chelsea Guthrie made an allegation of sexual abuse?

A. At some point during my -- the process of psychological assessment -- I don't remember if it was in that very first session or the second session; we met several times -- in the process of doing that psychological evaluation, she did make an allegation of abuse.

Q. And did you complete a Suspected Child Abuse Report?

A. I did not at that time. I did so probably a month or so later.

Q. And when are you supposed to report an allegation of sexual abuse?

A. I have to report what seems like new information as soon as I get it.

Q. Do you recall completing a Suspected Child Abuse Report arising out of an allegation made by Chelsea Guthrie?

A. Yes.

Q. Do you recall what the nature of that allegation was?

A. It was about sexual abuse.

Q. Do you recall any of the details?

A. I recall that she told me that she had first been sexually abused by her mother's boyfriend, Mike Harris, when she was young. I'm thinking but, again, I would need to look at my records to tell you for sure — maybe around ten years old. And she described -- she gave me detailed information about three events that took place. She remembered something that happened -- what she told me was the first time where Mike Harris sexually assaulted her and was interrupted by someone at the door. She told me another time where Mike Harris had put her hand on his penis while he was having intercourse with her mother. She also told me there was another time when she was older in her mother's home where he came to her bedroom and attempted to have sex with her and she indicated to me that those things happened numerous times, his attempting to have intercourse with her.

Q. And I'm talking about the first time you filled out a Suspected Child Abuse Report. Are you testifying that she told you all of those things the first time?

A. No. She — those were the things she told me that prompted me to fill out a Suspected Child Abuse Report. And that was not in the course of our psychological evaluation procedures.

Q. Did you ever come to learn that her sister, Martha Guthrie, had made allegations of sexual abuse against Mike Harris?

A. Yes.

Q. When did you come to learn, that?

A. I really couldn't tell you exactly when I came to learn that. It was weeks if not months later.

Ms. Hankel handed the witness a one page exhibit.
Q. by Ms. Hankel: Is that a Suspected Child Abuse Report completed in your hand?
A. Yes. Yes, it is. I forgot about this one.
Q. Is it dated July 20 of 2007?
A. It is.
Q. And did you write that Chelsea had been sexually abused by Mike Harris, "sexual abuse began shortly after her 13th birthday"?
A. Yes.
Q. Handing you a document. Do you recognize that document?
A. Yes.
Q. Is that another Suspected Child Abuse Report that you filled out?
A. Yes.
Q. Dated October 19, 2007?
A. Yes.
Q. Is this the report you referred to earlier?
A. Yes, this is the one I was remembering.
Q. Where you have put down the date and time of the incident as "unknown".
A. Yes.
Q. And the narrative is "Chelsea reported that on one occasion Mike Harris made Chelsea put her hand on his penis while he had intercourse with Chelsea's mom, Kerri.
A. Correct.
Q. When [Chelsea] made these allegations to you on the first day or in your first report when she didn't want to give you details, you didn't press her for any details; correct?
A. No.
Q. And who did you report the July 20, 2007 report to?
A. I don't remember. It says CPS here. I don't remember which worker I spoke to, if that was Alex Ellis or Rose or someone else. I'm sorry. I don't remember.
Q. And what about the October 19th, 2007, report, who did you report that to?
A. Alex Ellis.
Q. And is there something in this -- on this report, that will show me that you directly reported to Alex Ellis?
A. Yes, there is. In the top third of the page there it says "Official Contacted" and the title and I wrote Alex Ellis, social worker.
Ms. Hankel: Okay, I have nothing further.
Cross examination began after a sidebar.

Q. by Mr. Graham: Miss Thompson. I need you to go to the first meeting in your mind with Chelsea, okay?

A. All right.

Q. Regarding the first time she ever mentioned anything regarding sexual abuse -- can you just go to that point in time?

A. Alright. The very first moment that I heard anything about sexual abuse from her came about in the form of a sentence where she was explaining to me her experiences at home and she said she had been abused in every way possible by Mike Harris. And when I asked her -- just reflected back to her "every way possible"? indicating I wanted a little more information from her and she indicated physical, psychological, and sexual abuse. That was the very first, what I recall her telling me initially.

Q. Did it appear to you when she first mentioned sexual abuse, given your common experience just dealing with people and everyday life, that what she was -- how she was reacting to you, was she feigning it, that she was faking it?

A. No, there was nothing in her presentation to suggest that she was faking.

Q. And did she express any -- make any statements about fearing Mike Harris during that first meeting?

A. She told me many times how fearful she was, that if she said things or told what Mike Harris had done to her, that he would find her and that he would hurt her, that he would kill her.

Mr. Graham then finished up with a discussion about Chelsea being scared for her life around August 3rd, 2007, which is ironic because that was the exact time Chelsea and her friends were harassing me with threatening phone calls and emails. They were also trying to scare Kerri then too. Ms. Hankel had a few more questions on redirect.

Q. by Ms. Hankel: On July 20th, 2007, is it fair to say that you noted that Chelsea was disappointed because Martha had said things that gave Chelsea the impression that Martha was siding with her mother and being critical of Chelsea?

A. Yes.

Q. And then, at the next session, August 3rd, 2007, the same note Mr. Graham showed you, do you also note that "Chelsea was concerned about her relationship with her sister, she said that Martha seems to be siding with her mother and judging and blaming Chelsea, this hurt Chelsea's feelings and she has decided to limit her contact with Martha until Martha can be more supportive?"

A. Yes.

And that ended it. Ms. Hankel did not go for the jugular with the therapists. I was astonished that Mr. Graham was allowed to ask whether they thought Chelsea and Martha were faking it. I thought Ms. Hankel should have objected to that kind of testimony. I'm not sure if Judge DeVore was hindering Ms. Hankel or what, but there was a lot more to cover, like Chelsea's suicide/move back to Bishop episode where she got falling down drunk and smoked pot according to Miss. Thompson's documentation. I sure hoped Ms. Hankel would go for it with the next witness, Mary Traynor, who was the girlfriend of Tyler's dad and she played an integral part in Chelsea's run away episode. Kerri couldn't figure out how the Clarke's and Mary Traynor could harbor a runaway for four days without calling anybody and not be in trouble. Ms. Hankel started right in on Ms. Traynor.

Q. by Ms. Hankel: Do you know Chelsea Guthrie?
A. by Mary Traynor: Yes.
Q. And do you know Martha Guthrie?
A. Yes.
Q. And how did you come to know them?
A. Through Tyler.
Q. Was there a period of time when Chelsea and Tyler were sneaking out or Chelsea was sneaking out of the house to meet with Tyler?
A. That I'm not aware of.
Q. Was there a period of time when Chelsea ran away and stayed at your home?
A. I wouldn't say ran away. She wanted to come to Bishop and get some help.
Q. Do you remember that she ran away in the end of June 2007?
A. Not running away, no. I wasn't aware of that.
Q. You never learned that Chelsea ran away to your house at the end of June 2007?
A. She was reported as a runaway but that wasn't my understanding of it in the beginning of it.
Q. Okay. Did you have a conversation with Chelsea Guthrie at the end of June or sometime in June of 2007 that she was being sexually abused?
A. Yes.
Q. Can you tell us what she told you?
A. She didn't get into details. She said that there was trouble at home and that she was being -- her and her sister were being sexually abused.
Q. And were you trying to help her when she made those statements to you?
A. Yes.
Q. Do you remember the first time Chelsea told you she was being sexually abused?
A. I'd have to say that was sometime in June when she had run -- when she had come to the house to get some help.

I have to point out here that her comment isn't a typo, she actually started to say run away but caught herself. It's well documented that Chelsea ran away and stayed at the Clarke's home but it is an example of how deceptive Ms. Traynor was being. I wasn't sure why Ms. Hankel had called her.

Q. by Ms. Hankel: Okay. And then subsequently did you have other conversations with her about that?

A. Never anything in detail, no.

Q. Did you have conversations with Martha Guthrie about being sexually abused by Mike Harris?

A. Just that she had been sexually abused. Nothing in detail.

Q. Did Martha Guthrie ever tell you that Mike would take her to his trailer in J-Diamond and have sex with her?

A. Yes.

Q. Do you remember -- Chelsea ran away first?

A. Correct.

Score one for Ms. Hankel with that last question. Ms. Traynon specifically said that Chelsea did not run away and now she said she ran away first. Gotcha.

Next was Mr. Graham, and his cross-examination. He started by clarifying that Tyler began dating Chelsea in late May 2007 and that Ms. Traynor met Chelsea in June of 2007.

Q. by Mr. Graham: Okay. And how would you describe your relationship with Chelsea leading up toward the end of June, as far as just generally speaking?

A. I met Chelsea when she left home so it wasn't a whole lot of getting to know her until later in the summer.

Q. And when she came into your home, you indicated there was trouble at home; correct?

A. Uh-huh. Yes.

Q. And when she said there was trouble, did she describe what that meant in its entirety?

A. Her mother being strict and not believing the girls about Mike, and how Mike was inappropriately touching and saying and wanting things and favors from them.

Q. Let's go to the first time there is any mention of sexual abuse by Chelsea to you.

A. That would be June 28th, when she wanted a ride into town and I directed her to social services.

Q. Where were you and her when she made that disclosure to you about sexual abuse by Mike Harris?

A. In my vehicle driving to Bishop.
Q. How did that conversation come up?
A. Because I asked what was going on. Tyler had said it was an emergency, we needed to get her into Bishop.
Q. Now you drive with her in the car. And to your knowledge had any authorities been called prior to that?
A. No.
Q. At some point were authorities called?
A. At some, point, yes.
Q. How long after she first came to the home, your house, she makes this disclosure in the car. How long after that did the authorities got called?
A. You know, I don't know if it was the following evening or it was the next day -- but it was very shortly afterward. She was reported a runaway, so…
Q. And did authorities eventually come to your house?
A. Yes.
Q; Was [Chelsea] happy to have all the authorities there?
A. No, she was very scared. She was crying.
Q. How much further contact did you have with Chelsea after the authorities took her?
A. When she was placed in foster care, she would come over quite often.
Q. At any point in time, from the time that she had first come to your house and had left her home to when you stopped having regular contact with her, at any point in time did you ever sense that she was involved in some kind, of scheme or plan to make up false allegation against Mike Harris regarding sexual abuse?
A. It never entered my mind. The child was telling me this was going on. I believed her.
Q. All right. At any point in time, did you get the sense, either through anything she said or did or reactions, that she was trying to manipulate her sister into making up false allegations against Mike Harris to support her efforts to get out of the house?
A. No, I only saw her frightened when Mike was around, both of them -- both of the girls, they would panic.

And nothing further was said by either side. No official records exist of any report by the Clarke's or Chelsea related to abuse. Ms. Hankel failed to press this point. She was dropping the ball. At every turn Ms. Hankel was calling witnesses who supported the girls' claims and she was never trying to impeach those claims. Chelsea ran away on June 26th, 2007. That is a fact, yet Ms. Traynor said she got involved because of Tyler on June 28th. This was the same day Chelsea was discovered at the

Clarke's home based on Kerri's call to the Mono County Sheriff's Department and there is a record of that.

Ms. Hankel never questioned Ms. Traynor regarding her confrontation with me after I had informed her that Kerri Guthrie was mad at her because of the whole runaway thing and the fact that Tyler was sneaking Chelsea out late at night and driving around in violation of the curfew and restricted driver laws as well as other nefarious activities discovered in the notes Kerri had found. Ms. Traynor wanted to see the notes and I had told her that Mr. Hammond, Kerri's lawyer, had them and she should contact him which she never did. Kerri should have sued them but that is none of my business. Basically, Ms. Hankel had important areas to impeach and failed to do so. And it was her witness.

THIRTY-FIVE

Next it was time for the heavy hitters. Dr. Gabaeff who was an emergency room physician, board certified, and who has a clinical forensic medical practice where he does the work he was now going to discuss. He was a 25-year member of the American Professional Society on the Abuse of Children and was also a reviewer for published reports. He went through his lengthy history including, 20+ years in forensic medicine. Dr. Gabaeff said that 60% of his work was in forensic medicine and the balance in practice as an emergency room physician. He rarely worked for the prosecution, maybe 10% of his forensic work was for them.

Ms. Hankel then moved to have Dr. Gabaeff qualified as an expert witness and Mr. Graham asked to voir dire the doctor. Judge DeVore allowed him to voir dire Dr. Gabaeff but kept cutting off Mr. Graham because he kept asking questions that were not qualification examination questions. Mr. Graham did point out the same thing I noticed which was that Dr. Gabaeff had worked at 17 different hospitals in 30 years. Dr. Gabaeff described his different situations and added that he had done 50 to 60 sexual assault exams and had reviewed 600 to 700 in his career. Mr. Graham then dove into the fact that Pioneer Hospital where Dr. Gabaeff works in Jackson, CA, sends its sexual assault cases to UC Davis if time allows. To Nurse Boyle's team no less. But after hours, the hospital does the sexual assault exams as an ad hoc response. Ultimately Judge DeVore put an end to Mr. Graham's contentious questioning and told Ms. Hankel to resume her direct examination. Mr. Graham nonetheless objected to Dr. Gabaeff and onward we went.

The Court: Let me tell you something. You're arguing your objections to this man's testimony. You can do that to the jury at the appropriate time. I'm not going to hear it now. Have a seat. Let's move on.

Mr. Graham: Thank you, Judge.

Q. by Ms. Hankel: Dr. Gabaeff, did you review certain materials in this case?

A. by Dr. Gabaeff: Yes, I did.

Q. What did you review?

A. I reviewed the police reports, some emails between the District Attorney and the twins; the child abuse report of Chelsea and Martha; the screener narrative for the Child Protective Services; more emails between the DA and Martha from around the date of August 29, 2007; I reviewed the OCJP forms, which are those state-mandated forms that we've seen that we fill out for sexual assault exams for both Martha and Chelsea; I reviewed the video of the entire exam of both girls on DVD; taped interviews of the girls; the preliminary hearing transcripts, both volumes; there were some additional emails between Chelsea and one of the friends of hers, a girl named Michelle Jackson; and a -- police reports from 2003.

Q. Do you have any opinions in this case about whether these girls had been victims of sexual assault?

A. Yes, I do.

Q. Let's take Martha Guthrie. Do you have any opinions as to whether Martha Guthrie was sexually assaulted prior to --

A. My general impression was that she was not. My statement is based on the physical findings and the lack of any damage to the hymen. I disagreed with Nurse Boyle's interpretation of the examinations. I did not see any damage to the hymen or clefts, I saw abundant hymen in the area that she thought was injured and in the area that's most likely to be injured if there has in fact been sexual assault with rape and penetration of a penis into a small girl, so, for Martha.

And that same situation applied to Chelsea. I found the exam to be completely normal, abundant hymen in the area Nurse Boyle considered to be abnormal, I felt was normal. And I'd like to at some point show some photographs of those areas.

As far as the medical history was concerned, I found -- I was concerned about some of the irregular -- inconsistencies that further impacted my impression that this -- that sexual abuse had not taken place in this case.

Q. Doctor, I'm handing you a document.
A. Yes.
Q. That's the OCJP for the -- form for the sexual abuse?
A. Yes.
Q. And that's for Martha Guthrie; correct?
A. Correct.
Q. As you reviewed this form, did you notice anything that stood out as peculiar to you?
A. Let's see. Well, there were a number of things that I made notes about concerning you know, what she told the nurse and so forth.
Q. Is it important when you are taking medical history to get a complete and accurate medical history for this type of examination?
A. It's extremely important. If you're going to end up expressing an opinion about the case, I think -- doctors generally accept and completely endorse the notion that the history is in many cases as important and in some cases more important.
So getting an accurate history looking the, you know, asking the person who's making the allegations what happened and looking them in the eye while they're telling you what happened, making some determination about how credible they may be, or if there's any credibility issues, it would be a big part of doing an exam like this. The physical findings can be demonstrative of sexual abuse in a very clear-cut way, in some cases negating the history.
But in cases where the physical findings are equivocal, inconclusive or normal, the history is really, virtually, the only thing you have to go on. So the importance of taking a good history on your, not relying on someone else, is absolutely essential, in my opinion.
Q. And as you reviewed this form did you note who gave Nurse Boyle the medical history for this examination?
A. Yes, the social worker did.
After an admonition by Judge DeVore to move on from the form issue, Ms. HankeI asked Dr. Gabaeff:
Q. by Ms. Hankel: You viewed the -- an actual examination, a video examination of Martha Guthrie; correct?
A. Yes.
Q. And that video examination was taken with a colposcope?
A. That's correct. The camera is hooked up to the colposcope and the operator and the camera see the same thing. You just turn the camera on and there's an optical system to allow you to take a picture with the camera of exactly what you're looking at.

Q. And do you agree with the findings on the last page, page six of that examination, as to what you saw and the colposcopic examination that you reviewed?

A. No.

Q. Why not?

A. Well, I have pictures of the exam. I can use the exhibits that the — Nurse Boyle used and I can demonstrate. So I can use the exhibits to show that the posterior, the bottom part of the hymen is intact and that there's no cleft at all, that there's an abundant amount of hymeneal tissue in the area most likely to be injured, and that there's no evidence of any injury whatsoever. And what she interpreted as a cleft was really a -- kind of oddity of the way she conducted the exam, which was quite unusual. She had the girls laying on their side while she was trying to examine them instead of laying on their back, which is -- it's really unheard of. I really hadn't seen that technique used before, and, you know, led to a lot of difficulties in showing and seeing things clearly. But these were definitely images we could use and pictures she brought demonstrate the abundance of hymen in the posterior rim, which is the area we'd be most interested in, and the lack of any clefts in the area that she describes.

And I'm just using the term "cleft" to describe a tear from the rim of the hymen all the way down to the vaginal wall. That's what a cleft is.

The doctor and Ms. Hankel then proceeded to go through all the pictures that Nurse Boyle had shown which to me looked like the girls were total virgins. But I am not the doctor, right? Dr. Gabaeff continued to assert that Nurse Boyle had examined the girls on their side and that there was abundant hymen throughout. He opined also that if there was full penetration one would expect to see the hymen virtually destroyed. Dr. Gabaeff noted that the little notch in the hymen was insignificant compared to the full thickness of the hymen. He continued that Martha's hymen was normal and in abundant condition. There were absolutely no tears of the hymen that extend down to the vaginal wall. Dr. Gabaeff went on and commented further that typically once a person, an adolescent, begins having sex, they'll end up having two or three breaks in the hymen in different places. He summarized that the average adolescent who is sexually active has two or three major clefts that would go right down to the vaginal wall. And he didn't see any clefts at all.

Q. by Ms. Hankel: And doctor, did you review the medical exam for Chelsea Guthrie?

A. Yes.

Q. And did you have, in reviewing the conclusions on the medical exam as written by Nurse Boyle, do you agree with those conclusions?
A. No, I do not.
Q. Why not?
A. Well, as you'll see in the pictures that we're going to look at, we're going to see essentially the same type of situation with abundant hymen in the area that's alleged to have been damaged. So we don't have any clefts and absent clefts, which one would expect after intercourse of a prepubertal child, one that intercourse would take place immediately before or after puberty, one would expect to see the beginning of the first clefts forming on the way to getting the two or three clefts that a sexually active adolescent female is known to have because the hymen, as the infant, and even as a young adult, is small, too small to accommodate the penis, the shaft of a penis. Once the hymen is stretched around the shaft of the penis it will stretch out and then rupture and break like a rubber band; it goes all the way. Once it starts to rip, it goes right to the vaginal wall. There's no way it tears halfway. It's just like if you are pulling a rubber band tight. When it goes, it goes all the way. As it's going, it's getting weaker and weaker because more and more of it is gone so it just keeps going until it hits the vaginal wall. And in the worst cases the vaginal wall can be torn apart.

Dr. Gabaeff then went through Chelsea's pictures and he had the same observations and opinions as with Martha's. He noted that once puberty occurs, the hymen takes on a scalloped-edge appearance. Ms. Hankel asked if there was any difference if a subject was on her side or her back and Dr. Gabaeff said that gravity comes into play and he didn't think it made a lot of difference, it was just an unusual thing to do.

Q. by Ms. Hankel: Doctor, in your exam -- in your review rather, of this -- the colposcopic examinations and the photographs that Nurse Boyle put together, do you have any opinions as to whether these examinations are normal or abnormal for Martha and/or Chelsea? And let's take Martha first.
A. Normal.
Q. For Martha Guthrie?
A. Normal.
Q. And for -- what about Chelsea Guthrie?
A. Normal.
Q. Was there anything at all about the examination of Martha Guthrie that was problematic in the least?
A. No.

Q. And what about for Chelsea Guthrie, anything that showed any evidence of sexual assault?

A. No.

Q. Or any evidence of sexual activity?

A. Well, "sexual activity" is vague. And fondling and things of that nature are not going to leave physical findings. Regarding the issue of penetration, there's no evidence of penetration or damage to the hymen from penetration.

Q. And is that the same for Martha Guthrie, that there's no evidence of any penetration?

A. Correct.

Dr. Gabaeff was then permitted to show a PowerPoint presentation that he had collected from various articles. The pictures were hard to take and I'm not sure how the jury felt about them either. The pictures showed victims of rape and the associated injuries. One picture was from Dr. McCann's 2007 study that says women revert back to normal after they've been sexually assaulted. Dr. Gabaeff said that was not really true in his opinion and that the purpose of that article was not to show that people revert back to normal, but instead to show the rate of healing of injuries of this type which is substantial. Another picture demonstrated that there is healing in that the bloodiness goes away but the actual tearing of the hymen persists.

He went through numerous images all showing the same thing, raped girls aged 11 to 14 and the associated damage. And that was Dr. Gabaeff's point for showing such disturbing images, that the acute nature of the injury heals up but the configuration is consistent. So that was how he explained clefts going down to the vaginal wall and that an injury prepubertally persists into adolescence.

Q. by Ms. Hankel: Doctor, you reviewed materials from the preliminary hearings and the interviews of both girls?

A. Yes.

Q. And you read about the amount of penetration that each girl was claiming?

A. Yes.

Q. Is that consistent with the exams that were taken of Martha and Chelsea Guthrie?

A. It is not consistent. I want to say about penetration, once the hymen is stretched out and is around the shaft of the penis, whether it is one inch in or four inches in, it doesn't matter anymore. The injuries that occur are not related to in-and-out movements, they're related to the stretching of this tissue beyond its capacity.

Once it reaches its capacity it tears and that capacity is reached when the hymen is completely around the shaft.

Q. Why do you believe your findings of the examinations are not consistent with the penetration as expressed by the girls?

A. There's no evidence of damage to the hymen.

Q. Doctor, if these girls had consensual intercourse, would you expect to find some kind of findings of penetration?

A. Yes, it's about the same.

Q. If there had been the kind of penetration as expressed by Martha Guthrie in her interview and preliminary hearing, would you expect to find consistent findings, physical findings in her examination?

A. Yes.

Q. If there had been penetration consistent with that expressed by Chelsea Guthrie at her interview, preliminary hearing, and testimony at this trial, would you expect to find findings of that penetration in her medical exams?

A. Yes.

Q. Is it true that injuries caused by penetration can heal up and result in a normal exam?

A. No.

Q. Why not?

A. There's no tissues in the body that do that. And these tissues -- I mean I could show you literally hundreds of pictures demonstrating the scarring and the deformity of the genital tissues that takes place after intercourse. I also know that among everyone who participates in consensual intercourse, that they're going to disrupt the hymen to the extent they'll end up with two or three clefts until that hymeneal opening has to approach the size of the vagina so that on every subsequent act of intercourse there's not bleeding every time somebody has intercourse.

Q. Doctor, do you hold your opinion that Martha Guthrie had a normal sexual abuse exam to a reasonable degree of medical certainty?

A. Yes.

Q. Do you hold your opinion that Chelsea Guthrie had a normal exam to a reasonable degree of medical certainty?

A. Yes.

Ms. Hankel ended it right there, nuff said. I thought that went pretty well except for the rape pictures. Once again, I found myself wondering why I was still in jail. I knew Mr. Graham was about to explode in anticipation of his cross-examination.

Q. by Mr. Graham: What's a SART Nurse?

A. A SART Nurse is what Nurse Boyle represents herself to be, which is a Sexual Assault Response Team is what SART stands for.

Q. And you send sexual assault cases from your county to Nurse Boyle's facility, UC Davis; correct?

A. That's right.

Q. And you know UC Davis is one of the primary training centers for sexual assault nurses; correct?

A. That's correct. Dr. McCann was there for a long time, did some of his best work at UC Davis, and then moved on.

Q. You think Dr. McCann is a reputable man in the field?

A. Yes.

Q. And you know that 2003 study that you mentioned in your direct, Cathy Boyle was one of the co-authors; correct?

A. Yes, I know that.

Mr. Graham kept on the attack having Dr. Gabaeff try to recite the Penal Code section for Minimum Standards for Examination and Treatment of Victims of Sexual Assault or Attempted Sexual Assault, Penal Code §13823.11. Finally Judge DeVore intervened.

The Court: Time out, time out, time out. You need to be a little less hostile and settle down.

Mr. Graham: Okay.

The Court: And I would ask you to let him finish because he trails off and then he starts up again.

Mr. Graham: I will.

The Court: This man's not a police officer. He's not involved in the collection of evidence, he's a physician making exams. Limit your examination.

Mr. Graham: All right.

The Court: The Penal Code isn't his responsibility. Limit your examination. Settle down.

Mr. Graham: I'm asking about the minimum standards for examination and treatment of sexual assault --

The Court: There may be standards that are inclusive of an investigative process. That's not his job. Let's deal with the physician's role and the opinions he's expressed in this, his training, his education, his experience, his knowledge. Relevant factors.

Mr. Graham: All right. I'll be moving on.

Q. by Mr. Graham: Regarding the McCann study in 1992 that you mentioned, you know that study; correct?

A. Yes.

Q. That study involved three children; correct?

A. Correct.

Q. And is it your opinion that that study is – the conclusions in it are wrong, that's your opinion?

A. No.

Q. What is your understanding of the basic conclusions of that study?

A. You know, over time things – the acute injury will heal up but the physical damage to the tissue persists.

Q. So the injuries can heal, correct, according to this study, and become difficult to detect, correct, the hymeneal injuries?

A. No. we saw examples of acute injury that healed and we saw the end result of the reconfiguration of the tissues. So healing to me means no more bloody, no more black and blue, no more bruising, everything in a stable and permanent state of tissue structure.

Q. Okay, In the 2007 study co-authored by Boyle involving 239 prepubescent and pubescent girls, have you read that study?

A. Yes.

Q. Let me read you a quote. Do you agree with the statement "The hymeneal injuries healed rapidly and, except for the more extensive lacerations, left no evidence of previous injury." Do you agree with that conclusion in the realm of healing of hymeneal injuries?

A. Well, to the extent that they identified seven patients in that study that had hymeneal clefts that did not go away and not really having a clear idea of what the other 232 patients exactly had done. I think it is a reasonable statement in the context of evaluating what actually happened in those cases because fondling could have occurred, non-penetration could have occurred, and fabrication could have occurred.

Mr. Graham then went back into attack mode challenging Dr. Gabaeff's knowledge of the proper SART forms and what he did at all the hospitals he worked for. Dr. Gabaeff pointed out that although he filled out a few reports himself by 1990 the role of the ER physician became supervisor of SART programs, supervisor of the nursing examination.

The Court: Come here.

(A discussion was held off the record)

The court: Ladies and Gentlemen, it's my job to monitor a certain part of the integrity of this process. Lawyers have certain responsibilities as well. That's what's going on right now. And I might have to become more active in this process if it continues.

Mr. Graham. I understand.

Q. by Mr. Graham: In your practice, have you ever followed any acute injury cases from injury all the way through to looking at how they heal yourself?

A. In my clinical forensic practice, yes. In my emergency medicine practice, no.

Q. Have you ever done any studies involving non-acute injuries in sexual assault cases, you yourself involved in this study?

A. I've never done any studies in the way UC Davis would do them. It's not something that's done at Sutter-Amador Hospital or the types of emergency departments that I work in.

Q. Is it your opinion that a hymen cannot heal, from a hymeneal wall, in? In other words, from the hymeneal wall in towards the center of the vaginal opening?

A. You mean the vaginal wall?

Q. Yes, from the vaginal wall in.

A. A little tiny bit at the base, a little tiny bit. It's scar tissue. If the tear itself is a perfect "V" and not bigger than that – like we saw some pictures where there was actually a little gap, an eight or a quarter of an inch – those are populated with scar tissue and scar tissue can populate the pointy part of the "V" creating the impression that there's some gluing back together of the parts but really it is typically a scar tissue reaction that's very minimal.

So to answer that, it's going to basically kind of heal back up this way, no, this does not happen.

Q. Is it your testimony that all hymeneal injuries when you have penetration from a penis are going to rip all the way to the vaginal wall; is that your testimony?

A. Correct, like a rubber band.

And Mr. Graham had nothing further. I was still concerned as to what the relevance was of an exam conducted six months after I had been put in jail. Another concern was that I felt Ms. Hankel should have had a DVD player in court so Dr. Gabaeff could specifically support his contention that the girls were laying on their sides, since it was imperative to his opinion. I repeatedly asked Ms. Hankel to elicit testimony that it is highly unlikely that both girls would have a sexual injury in the exact same spot and I argued that they were abnormalities probably born that way. Ms. Hankel countered that there was no cleft, the examination was normal and that's what Dr. Gabaeff is saying. It was all semantics though. Dr. Gabaeff said clefts had to go all the way down to the vaginal wall while Nurse Boyle said there are different levels of clefts. I remonstrated that regardless of the cleft/partial cleft debate, the underlying face should have been more emphasized, that the anomalous area at seven o'clock in the twins' hymens was not the result of repeated, forced, unlubricated, penetration of 10–11-year-old girls by an adult male. There would have been some serious damage as discussed by Dr. Gabaeff.

Now there was going to be a two-week hiatus so Judge Devore could handle some matters calendared before my trial began. I felt the judge had misinformed the jury hoping he could get 12 to serve when he told them that the trial would only last 10 days. We were just completing day 9 and we had a ways to go. And that didn't count the five days of jury selection. I was going to testify and so was Mr. Albee, not to mention Alex Ellis and other miscellaneous witnesses. Then there would be redirect and surrebuttal examinations, final arguments, jury instructions, and deliberations.

It was a time for reflection during that two-week break. I was nervous and anxious but I tempered that with thoughts of Dr. Gabaeff's strong statements that the girls' stories didn't match the evidence.

THIRTY-SIX

After a decent Thanksgiving and a reflective respite from the daily grind of court, I was eagerly back in court. I had a good turkey dinner and got to watch football, but jail was still jail. It was Monday, November 30th 2009, day 10 of my outrageous trial. Much to my dismay the first thing Judge DeVore did was apologize for his treatment of Mr. Graham when Mr. Graham was getting pretty aggressive with Dr. Gabaeff. Mr. Graham accepted his apology and I felt nauseous. I was positive the jury felt sorry for Mr. Graham, but I didn't.

First up was Mr. Albee with my side of the computer story, minus the multiple user fiasco of the §402 hearing. That could still come back to bite us, but I was hopeful things would all work out.

Mr. Albee was the owner of DataChasers Inc. He had been doing that for ten years. Before that he was a Lieutenant for the Riverside Police Department in Southern California, the IE or Inland Empire to be exact. He had 29 years on the force doing a variety of jobs. During his service he was awarded the first Medal of Valor ever awarded from the Riverside Police Dept. and the State Attorney General's Certificate of Valor.

During his experience in law enforcement, he handled pedophile cases and oversaw computer forensics. He had a Masters degree from USC. The guy was solid and I was glad to have him on my side. But then, he was on the side of truth, I was just the interested party. He was certified in EnCase and Windows just like Mr. Wall. Mr. Albee was accepted as an expert after a short amount of questioning.

Q. by Ms. Hankel: Mr. Albee, what did you look at in preparing to testify here today?

A. by Mr. Albee: Over the course of the last several months, there has been the discovery that we've been provided that was primarily the image of the hard drives. And I believe the one we are specifically talking about is hard drive No. 1 or item No. 1.

Q. And have you also gone through the exhibits that were prepared by Mr. Wall in the case?

A. His first testimony report. Not the one that we just got last week. I haven't finished going through it yet. I ran out of steam last night.

Q. But when you were going through the reports and through the trial testimony, did you see any discussions about the chain of custody in the case with the computer evidence and the hard drives.

A. Yes, I did.

Q. Is there anything that you noticed about the chain of custody in the case that may have been of concern?

A. I believe there were six or seven individuals who handled the evidence that went through the chain of custody. And at least on a couple of occasions, the evidence was handed off. There was no recording of the serial numbers on the hard drives.

Ms. Hankel then produced Exhibit 28 and went over the bag holding the two hard drives with Mr. Albee. He recalled that the officer who seized the evidence, made notations or the bag so that the bag had been filled out when Detective Rutkowski took possession of the bag of evidence containing the hard evidence.

Q. by Ms. Hankel; In your experience, is it unusual for an officer who has not collected or seized the evidence and put it into an evidence bag to have written on the evidence bag what the evidence bag contains?

A. Not specifically, but there is another step in there. The officer who seizes the evidence is responsible for what is in the bag. So that officer would fill out the evidence tags or the bags, or the chain of custody form.

Ms. Hankel next went through the chain of custody on the bag and then produced a simple form from Mr. Albee and went though that with him. Ms. Hankel then proceeded to highlight the use of the model number to identify No.1. Ms. Hankel was real thorough at this point. I was getting bleary eyed and so was the jury. Mr. Albee used an analogy that a car's PIN is a serial number and a model number would specify it is a

Toyota Camry. The bottom line was that Mr. Albee would always check the serial number before examining a piece of evidence like a hard drive.

Moving along after the judge put a halt to the whole line of questioning the court took a quick break and then following the recess, Ms. Hankel established that the number was not a serial number on item No. 1 for the record. Handing Mr. Albee Exhibit 42, Mr. Wall's report, Ms. Hankel asked about the report.

Q. by Ms. Hankel: Is it your habit and custom when you write a report of a computer forensics analysis of a hard drive to identify the hard drive by a PIN number or a serial number.

A. By a serial number.

Mr. Albee then went over the computer hard drives seized, three of them, and pointed out that only item No. 1 had any bad material on it. He next discussed the user on that item No 1 as being Kerri, Martha, Chelsea, and myself. He also noted that item No. 1 was running Windows 98 which had a splash screen allowing a user to log on and customize the user settings. This splash screen could be bypassed by hitting the cancel button.

Mr. Albee went on and described why he thought I was a sophisticated user of the computer as a webmaster and described how a key logger might be a useful tool. This was all the same as Mr. Wall's testimony and I wanted to get to the good part.

Q. by Ms. Hankel: Are you familiar with a popup, the term "pop up"?

A. Yes, I am.

Q. Tell me what that is.

A. Popup is a display of an image or advertisement or an item that you have not requested for a website. When you go to a website, and it is very common, when you go to a website or you are on the internet to have popups come up. You can be researching anti-virus software and popups advertising its functionality will pop up on the screen.

Q. Have you ever heard the term "bait and switch" in relation to web sites?

A. Yes, I have.

Q. Tell me how the term "bait and switch" is used in relation to a web site.

A. An example would be something that happened to my wife. If I may use an example.

Q. Sure.

A. We were getting ready to go on a trip, and she wanted to see what the weather was from that area where we were going to. So in our browser she put in weather.

And when she clicked on that she got bombarded with porn web sites. And she was just looking for weather. Bait and switch is also used in a redirect. For example, on my website, I have an old website DataChasers.com. If someone goes to DataChasers.com and you look at what pops up it is going to be DataChasersComputerForensics.com

Q. A redirect can be used for legitimate reason or as a way to take someone from point A and completely redirect them to something they are not anticipating, right?

A. Absolutely. Could be used for good or nefarious reasons.

Q. On this item No. 1, Mr. Wall found three images of what he described as child pornography. Do you agree that there were three images of child pornography on this computer?

A. I do. I agree with that.

Q. He also found some of what he described as child erotica. Do you agree that there was child erotica found on item No. 1?

A. I do agree.

Q. He said there were newsgroups that had been found that were subscribed to on item No. 1; do you agree with that?

A. Yes, I do.

Q. Lets take the three child porn images. Can you tell me where those child porn images were found on item No. 1?

A. There is a file that was identified on the computer by Mr. Wall. And it is a temporary file. The title of the file is pst1002.tmp. It is a temporary file. It is used by many, many programs to dump data into. It is referred to as a dump file. It is not accessible to the user. That file contained two child pornography images that were not accessible by the user. All three of them, the two in this file – and I'll talk about the other one in a minute – was never accessed.

The creation date and the access date and times are identical. That is not possible for a human being to do. You cannot create and access something within the same time frame. The computer is going to record it too quick. So, we know that the two pictures in that temporary file were never seen by the user of the computer. however they got there. And when I say however they got there, this is a nine-year-old computer. It has two images in a temporary file not accessible that nobody can identify the source of. Nobody can tell how these pictures got there, how long they have been there, and that they were not accessed again. That is the two.

Q. And there is one other.

A. There is one other and it was found in one of the newsgroups and the subtitles within the newsgroups of what the content would be. The content of this picture in the newsgroups was the child pornography that carried the exact same creation date and access date. Although it would have been accessible to the user of the computer, it was never accessed.

Q. You also said there was child erotica found on item No 1?

A. The child erotica on item 1 was all found in what is called unallocated space on the hard drive. When a file goes into unallocated space -- all it means is that at one time the pictures or documents or whatever it is, at one time, it was somewhere on the hard drive. It is generally not accessible by the user except using computer forensics tools which Mr. Wall and myself both used.

Q. So when you say it was located at some time on the hard drive, it could have been on a page on the internet that wasn't actually being viewed by the user of the computer?

A. Absolutely. Because the internet, when you go to a page on the internet – and, for example, my website – if you go to my website, you are going to click on the homepage of my website. Temporary files on the computer is going to download the images, a lot of the images, not all of the images from the subpages of my website. So they are all going to go into temporary internet files – all these images go to an unallocated space and are just sitting there and you have never seen them. You are unaware of their content on the computer.

Q. So is it true that you could have seen the first page but then have ten pages you never looked at?

A. That's correct.

Q. What about you said where were 12 to 14 newsgroups and there were many titles of newsgroups; correct.

A. Correct.

Q. So some three-thousand titles of newsgroups?

A. 3,300 and change.

Q. Of those 3,300 and change newsgroup titles, how many had been accessed?

A. None. Should I define how I know that?

Q. Yes, please.

A. Detective Wall supplied us with a CD of the evidence he had extracted on discovery, very common. And on that there were several spreadsheets, and the spreadsheets identified the main newsgroups. And within the main newsgroups they had all the subcategories that one would have been able to access on all the pictures and everything in the subcategories.

With that spreadsheet, he gave the create date of the subpages and the last access date. And on all 3,368 approximately and change, they were all identical. So we know – and dozens of them within a hundredth of a second. So we know that it is not possible for a computer user to go in and click on one of those, look at it in any amount of time and click out of it. The access date would have changed after the creation date.

Q. Are there also lists of what Mr. Wall identified as visited URLs? Did you see these?

A. Yes.

Q. And there was an exhibit, I think 55-A and 55-B. And 55-A shows a stack of documents, and they show little thumbnails or little pictures or images that purported to be a representation from April of 2009 of what the visited websites might look like or did look like in April of 2009, did you see that

A. Yes, I did.

Q. Did you see the actual item No. 1 that it contained any images that were on the actual item No. 1 that were from the visited URLs?

A. There were no images on item No. 1 that I found or I believe Mr. Wall found, actual images from any of the purported visited URLs or visited websites.

Q. Did you see any intentional saving of child porn images on item No. 1?

A. There is no intentional saving of child porn images on item No. 1.

Q. Did you see any bookmarking of child pornographic websites on item No. 1?

A. No, I did not.

Q. What about an adult pornographic website?

A. No, I did not.

Q. You have analyzed many computers?

A. That is correct.

Q. And you supervised the analysis of many, many, more computer?

A. That is correct.

The Court: Is there a substantial amount of child pornography on this computer?

The Witness. No.

Q. by Ms. Hankel: Is there a substantial amount of child erotica on item No. 1?

A. No there is not.

Q. Can you tell me when you looked at the hard drive in question, do you have in your mind the length of time that hard drive was in use, the age of the hard drive?

A. Approximately nine years. I'm sorry, it was a nine-year-old hard drive. I think it may have only been in use about seven years. I have to check.

Q. If a computer user showed a sexual interest in young girls, would you expect to find such an insignificant amount of computer porn on the hard drive?

A. I would expect to find a lot more.

Q. Would you expect to find actual viewing of newsgroups?

A. Absolutely.

Q. What else do you expect to find?

A. I would expect to find the categorized places on the hard drive. I would expect to find folders that were labeled with the – identifying -Saying the type of pictures within them. I would expect to find collections on the hard drive of various types of child pornography or child erotica.

I would expect it to be labeled. I would expect to find not only pictures, but movies. And I would expect to find a lot of them. Because people with this proclivity, value their collections. They keep them. I would expect to find the ability of the person obviously sharing and trading in this type of material. Live Ware or Bare Ware or peer to peer networking where people share files back and forth because they want to be able to collect more.

I would expect to find email and email accounts that with a bunch of different people where they talk about their collections and compare their collections. In general, I would expect to find a whole lot more. And this comes from not only my experiences, but from a number of sources.

Q. Did you find significant organized files of item No. 1 of any data?

A. Yes, I did.

Q. Did you find thousands of pictures within such organized categorized files.

A. Yes, I did.

Q. What were those files of?

A. Almost the vast majority of them were of mountains or skiing or outdoor scenes. And they were categorized by location and type of photograph, thousands of them.

Q. When you say "thousands" you mean one thousand or how many thousands?

A. Well, there were, I believe, there are 21,000, approximately 21,000 JPEG-type images on the computer.

Q. In your opinion, does item No 1 demonstrate that a computer user of item No. 1 had a sexual interest in little girls?

A. No, it does not.

Now it was time for Mr. Graham to go after Mr. Albee. Mr. Albee had not covered many of the areas I wanted him to cover so I guessed it was going to have to be me to point out Mr. Wall's two-sided testimony. Mr. Graham started off by attacking Mr. Albee's experience, then got him to admit I was a user of item No. 1. What was getting lost in the shuffle was the fact that indicia of me or that hard drive didn't mean that was the hard drive seized from my trailer. Mr. Albee also conceded that he hadn't had time to go over the evidence that had just been provided the week prior. Mr. Graham that went through the letters and business cards which tended to show me as the primary user of item No. 1. Judge DeVore then finally told Mr. Graham that he had gone over this enough already. Mr. Graham next went through Mr. Albee's mistaken identification of users on my computer from the spam email headers he had found.

Q. by Mr. Graham: Isn't it true that the overwhelming email communication was sent from ski@365.com; correct?

A. I believe so, yes.

Q. Newsgroups, what is your simple understanding of what a newsgroup is?

A. Pretty much what it sounds. Newsgroups are areas you can go on the internet, and it will give you information on just about any subject. I like fishing and get just about any kind of information I like.

Q. Now regarding the newsgroups that were found on item No. 1 that have been subscribed to, you testified somebody went and downloaded the title pages or subject pages; correct?

A. Well, somebody had to access – had to look at the main heading newsgroup, yeah.

Q. The newsgroups that relate to "child sex." The ones that have been found on the hard drive. These are the ones that had to have been subscribed to by the user, correct?

A. No sir, you can access newsgroups without actually subscribing to them.

After having shown Mr. Albee Exhibit 56, the VMWare screenshots, Mr. Graham asked:

Q. by Mr. Graham: Mr. Wall testified that this was a screen shot, it was actually a compiled set of screen shots of the newsgroup subscriptions relating to child sex. If you start with that foundation, and if you were to see this on your computer, what can you conclude when you look at this exhibit?

A. That is pretty obvious that it looks like child erotica or child-sex newsgroups.

Q. What about them is relation to this document?

A. Right now, sir, I don't even know what this document is. I wasn't supplied with the VMWare pictures.

Q. Let me show you Exhibit 56 up closer. Does it appear to be a screen shot containing a list of the subscribed to newsgroups relating to child-sex?

A. They have the same titles that we saw in the spreadsheets Mr. Wall produced.

Q. Now these newsgroups relating to this child-sex, were subscribed to, isn't that correct?

A. I don't know sir.

Q. Regarding the newsgroups, is it your opinion that for them to show up on the hard drive as they were currently when you examined the drive that the user had to engage an affirmative action to click and select those newsgroups for them to show up?

A. That's correct sir.

Q. Regarding the visited URLs, isn't it true that like the newsgroups, the user had to affirmatively click on those visited URLs for them to be on a hard drive as they currently are today relating to child-sex?

A. Yes, for the most part. But many URLs show up on a hard drive without clicking on them. So you will go to URLs. You go to websites and you will get a multitude of other websites appear in your temporary internet files that you did not click on.

Q. The user of that drive, item No. 1, typed in keywords in Google searches; correct?

A. Yes.

Q. Are those keywords included the word name nymphet; correct?

A. I believe so. Yes sir.

Q. What does nymphet mean?

A. Young child. Young girl.

Q. Lolita was a keyword typed in; correct?

A. I believe so.

Q. What does Lolita mean?

A. That is a common term for a young girl also.

Q. The search for leotard nymphet was typed in correct?

A. I believe so.

Q. The search term "3D porn" was typed in; correct?

A. I remember that one, yes sir.

Q. The search term "preteen tights" was typed in by the user; correct?

A. I remember the preteen. I am not certain about the tights.

Mr. Graham then proceeded to go through the keystroke logger yet again, line by line, with Mr. Albee, using a condensed version of Exhibit 61 called Exhibit 95. This condensed version took out all the good stuff and left all the bad stuff. Mr. Albee didn't have enough information to work from. The keystroke logger showed any URL that popped up in the browser, even if it wasn't typed in. Thus a link to a website opened in a new window logged in as though it was typed in. It was a small point but the only one who knew this was me apparently.

Mr. Graham continued on through incest, erotica, child-sex, and the like but it was getting old and even the judge and jury had heard enough. Moving back into the PST images Mr. Graham asked about a Lolita image found in the pst1002.tmp file.

Q. by Mr. Graham: I should clarify Google image searches using the term – and there were recovered images with the term "Lolita." Do you think it is a coincidence?

A. On that recovered image with the term "Lolita" in it, it is my opinion that it has no evidentiary value at all. You cannot tell where that came from or – nobody can – or when it hit the hard drive. That is very important, sir.

Q. There were Google searches for using the term "model"; correct?

A. Yes, sir.

Q. If there were recovered images that had the word or that showed apparently teen girls or model poses, do you think that is a coincidence?

A. I think I would want to know where they came from. It is very important not to make a generality like that. And the reason it is so important is that because when people have items that are recovered off a hard drive with no dates or times or source or anything that is available, there is no telling how that stuff hit the hard drive. That hard drive is nine-years-old. I am very suspect of anything unless we can see where the data came from.

Keeping in mind that none of these have been viewed. None of them have been accessed by the computer used out of all those images. None of them. And that is using Mr. Wall's evidence. He gave us the dates and times. So whatever the purpose was for the search, whatever the search accomplished, and whatever is or the hard drive was never accessed using your term from the last time, "the bad stuff." It was never accessed. It was never seen by the user that we can tell.

Mr. Graham: Nothing further, Judge.

The Court: Ms. Hankel?

Q. by Ms. Hankel: Did you find any picture of a Lolita that was accessed as a result of these searches?

A. Well, actually to broaden that a bit, there were no images from any visited websites on the hard drive. So whatever was produced by the searches in the keystroke logger never hit the hard drive that I could tell as an image on as an item or the hard drive.

Q. Did the searches seem to go to more searches?

A. Well, they do, yes.

Q. Does that suggest that the computer user wasn't looking for an image but was, for an example, analyzing the DNA of a webpage?

A. Specifically with Mr. Harris' background and that would be a very good explanation for that, yes.

Q. As a webmaster, he would need to be analyzing different codes on the internet; correct?

A. Yes.

Q. And he would need to be designing webpages to do things like redirect sites and make popups for his clients; correct?

A. Correct.

Q. What did you do when you went home for lunch today?

A. Well, I came in in the morning and had an opportunity to look at the hard drive for the first time.

Q. What did you do with that hard drive?

A. Well, even though I had seen a photocopy of that hard drive previously, I noticed on the hard drive it has a manufacturing date on the hard drive. And from my experience with Maxtor drives, they frequently carry a manufacturer date, depending on the model number. When I saw the manufacturing date on the hard drive it occurred to me that I had an opportunity yesterday when I was speaking to Mr. Harris to go through all the date codes on the computer, which I may have done previously, because I have done date analysis on the computer, on the hard drive.

But I didn't notice that the date of manufacture on the hard drive appeared to be later than the date codes on the evidence on the hard drive.

Q. What does that suggest to you?

A. It is very difficult for me. It suggests to me that that is not the proper hard drive that was put into evidence.

Q. And did you make some notes when you took a look at the dates on the actual computer and the manufacturer date and compared them? What was the beginning date that you found on the image of the hard drive?

A. The hard drive has a manufactured date of May 12, 1999. That is stamped on the label. I went back to my room, and I carry with me a forensic laptop. I took out the laptop and I booted up the image file of the hard drive that was supplied to me by Mr. Wall. And I checked the dates on the hard drive.

Now it is not uncommon to have early dates come up on the hard drive for created items or what have you. Because when they manufacture a hard drive, they will put on some system files, and the last written date is what we call technically last written, means the last time it was modified. And those become unique when the files are put on a hard drive. I found a number or a bunch of files, and I didn't have – quite frankly I had an hour. I didn't have time to write down all those numbers. But the date I noticed that had 316 folders that were either created or last accessed on the hard drive was January 7th, 1999. And that is approximately five months before that hard drive was manufactured, an impossibility.

Q. How can it be that that image copy you had had some material that which related to my client if it is not the actual hard drive that was seized at his residence?

A. Somebody altered that hard drive. I don't know – I – I am very hesitant. I feel terrified about this. But there are – in my time, there are indications on that hard drive especially the creation of, like, the desktop.ini that is created when the hard drive is put up. The mouse drivers that were installed. Somebody installed Dr. Solomon's anti-virus. The day after – a plethora of dates were January 7th 1999. That is when a lot was done what look to me like creating a hard drive. That is when the set up was accessed. Quicken was put on the hard drive on January 7th, 1999. These programs don't come from the factory installed on a hard drive. Those programs don't come from the factory installed on a hard drive. Hard drives don't come with these programs on them. The System32 was last written to – System32 is the primary Windows system folder – was written on January 7th, 1999.

Dr. Solomon's, I don't know if I said the date of Dr. Solomon's anti-virus. All of those were January 7th. That was installed on January 8th as someone would do who got a new hard drive. They would then install the anti-virus the next day.

But there were 450 files and folders either created, last accessed, or last written to on January 8th, 1999. The day after the first significant activity that I saw.

And I don't know what else to say. That shows the hard drive was in use. A hard drive, not this hard drive, a hard drive which date on it was in use for the date from that original hard drive five months too late. I don't know how else to explain it.

Q. Is there any way to tell what date would have been originally on the original hard drive versus the hard drive that is manufactured five months too late?

A. No. Not to my knowledge. There is – it depends on what platters are in it, what was done with the hard drive. I am at a loss to explain it. No, you cannot. There can be – there is no telling what the data is that is on this hard drive. And that is my opinion right now.

The Court: There's no telling what the data is on that hard drive? That is a lot of impersonal articles there.

The Witness: There is no telling how accurate the data is that is represented on this hard drive.

Q. by Ms. Hankel: Have you ever received in your business a hard drive that you could not access?

A. Only if the hard drive has a physical failure. By that I mean a physical failure, not a software failure. Where a spring broke, the head is contacting the disk. Something is physically causing the hard drive not to function.

Q. In that kind of situation, what do you do with that hard drive? How do you analyze it?

A. We have a service that is a clean room. They are located in Texas. We have had a very good amount of luck with them. We send the hard drive out to have the data – see if they can recover the data from the hard drive.

Q. And when that entity tries to recover data, do they use a similar model hard drive? Because they have to put the data on another hard drive, do they not, to reassemble the hard drive as it were?

A. When they can, they use the exact same model, because the platters and everything fit the same. So we have had cases that have been held up for months while they are looking for the exact same drive.

Q. The serial numbers of the hard drive can be different; correct?

A. Yes.

Q. But the model number would be the same?

A. Correct.

Q. And the manufacturing date might be different?

A. That's correct.

Q. Once you get back the new hard drive that you could actually operate, could someone then access the new drive from the clean room?

A. Almost certainly. As long as everything was repaired correctly, yes. We have done it many times.

Q. And could the original data from the first drive have been altered at that point?

A. Well there would be no way to tell what data was altered or not.

Q. Is there any other way to explain how this Maxtor hard drive has a manufacturing date five months after computer programs were installed?

A. From user created files, these programs that are installed, not to my knowledge.

And that ended Mr. Albee's try at explaining the unexplainable. Ms. Hankel was finished. Mr. Graham didn't ask any questions and I assumed he would bring back Mr. Wall to try to explain the unexplainable yet again.

Mr. Albee and Ms. Hankel worked hard to get the facts to the jury despite the everchanging evidence put forth by the prosecution. Mr. Albee had made some valid points regarding the chain of custody issue. Ms. Hankel failed to elicit testimony related to Windows however and also internet technologies which were crucial to my assertations.

Chief among these deficient areas of examinations was the failure to explain the user directory structure, the cache file system, and the fraudulent nature of the manufactured evidence including the "exemplary images" and the VMWare captures which were printed out screen captured images. Why not show the computer in court? Why the need for bogus screen captured images. Ms. Hankel and Mr. Albee failed to rebut Mr. Wall's claim regarding the BIOS time and the copying of files surreptitiously in light of the chain of custody issues and lack of authenticity concerns.

They also should have reviewed all the seized media such as pictures, tapes, DVDs and the like, not just the hard drives to show the lack of any pornography except in that pesky pst1002.tmp file. This review would have bolstered Mr. Albee's opinion that as a forensic investigator he would have expected to find porn and especially child porn collections saved somewhere in a typical child molester or pedophile investigation. Ms. Hankel should have prepared Mr. Albee and presented evidence related to my assertions. The topics I intended to testify about should have been showcased by Mr. Albee. Items I requested including the rew HTML files on my computer which show how information is hidden in webpages. Also, the .htaccess files I created which were used for filtering on a webserver to enhance search engine findability. In addition, I wanted Mr. Albee to show the actual directory tree structure which would show the user directory in a easy to see format. I wanted to show the user directory and the cache file structure in order to rebuke Mr. Wall's testimony that a crash caused the pst1002.tmp file to be created.

The PST temp files such as pst1002.tmp files which contained one file that contained numerous images but no HTML or TXT files, yet somehow had an internet history file. That was one magic file. The pst1002.tmp file did not contain any other web content associated with the images in question. Mr. Wall's claim that the crash caused the temp file simply does not hold water. Internet Explorer and Outlook Express do not write to PST temp files, period. The problem I kept pointing out to anyone who would listen was that Mr. Wall's contention that if Internet Explorer crashed then the program or Windows itself wrote out a temp file. This was so wrong on so many levels that I requested Ms. Hankel to get a Windows expert or allow me to testify as an Evidence Code §702 witness. That is an expert in the specific evidence by familiarity with the evidence and my professional occupation as a Windows and internet technologies consultant.

These specific facts that Ms. Hankel failed to bring forth were directly related to the term "crashing," the Windows98 cache file system, and the process by which Windows98 saved the cached files for later use by Internet Explorer or Outlook Express unbeknownst to a typical computer user. Also integral to this discussion is the writing of temp files by programs residing in the Windows 98 operating system environment. Some background facts are needed here.

If a computer hard drive mechanically fails it is commonly called a computer crash since all programs reside on the hard drive. When this happens, everything stops and nothing is written or saved, all activity ceases immediately and the hard drive never starts again. This is what happened to my hard drive. I saved the drive so that I could pay to have the data mined off the drive by a company that extracts lost data.

If the Windows98 operating system, which is a bunch of programs running together crashes which is often called the blue screen of death due to the error message screen, which displays with this type of crash, then the entire group of programs that is running stops. No files are written or saved but the hard drive may be restarted to begin working again.

If the version of Internet Explorer used on Windows98 systems crashes it simply freezes up but all the other programs are still running as is the Windows 98 operating system, and the hard drive is still functioning as well. When this type of crash occurs, a user can simply use the task manager to close the crashed program and then the program can be restarted normally.

Important to this discussion is the fact that Internet Explorer uses a cache file system in this Windows98 first edition operating system environment. It doesn't use the newer temp based format. The two file systems are distinguishable. Whenever you view a website in Windows98 first edition running Internet Explorer, all the files viewed are cached onto your hard drive in the particular users cache directory.

All files means HTML, scripts, cookies, images, videos, ads, anything on the websites, not just images. This action occurs so that upon any future visits to the same website the browser checks to see if it already has downloaded the content into the cache and if it is found, it doesn't need to be reloaded again which speeds up the page load time and increases the overall speed of the internet by eliminating redundant traffic. (Whew, what a mouthful□).

Individual users can control and vary their cache settings and each separate user of Windows98 can log on and have different cache settings as well as bookmarks, email address and such individual settings. Once the files are cached, they remain there until flushed out by user action or automatically by the user defined cache settings.

If Internet Explorer crashes in the Windows98 environment, it does not delete or alter any cache files, it does not create cache files, it does not create temp files. Internet Explorer simply stops doing anything when it crashes and Windows98 does not write or delete any files upon an Internet Explorer crash either. It doesn't need to. That is the purpose of the cached file system, the files are always there ready to be reused. Another important fact to consider in this discussion has to do with the fact that PST files are Photoshop temp files, not used by Internet Explorer.

I instructed Ms. Hankel and Mr. Albee to prepare for my testimony in these areas repeatedly. I told them to copy the drive data provided by Mr. Wall to a blank drive and put it in a dual boot environment to compare the data provided with the post boot data for the purpose of showing that the hard drive had not shut down correctly, or it had been altered. They should have looked at the bootlog.txt file and the scandisk.log file. Specifically, the bootlog.txt file recreates itself each time the computer boots. Mr. Albee was stating off the record that the bootlog.txt file was dated two months prior to the last boot of item No. 1 which either showed Mr. Albee was deficient or the hard drive data set had been altered.

These are highly technical issues that go to the heart of the authenticity of the hard drive which formed the foundation upon which numerous pieces of prejudicial information ware introduced.

Mr. Hankel did not elicit testimony from Mr. Wall or Mr. Albee explaining the lack of HTML or newsgroup messages in the PST files nor the lack of URLs in the visited sites to correspond to tilesaw of shower images. I specifically asked Ms. Hankel to go into cookies. Cookies are webpage tracking tools used by websites to track usage and enhance the visitor experience on a particular site by remembering your preferences like on Amazon when they know what books you have bought.

I wanted to show that there were no cookies to show visits to porn sites since these types of sites make extensive use of cookies. There were no porn site cookies on item No. 1.

Mr. Wall was permitted to introduce hundreds of pages of "representative" web pages printed out and not found on item No. 1. I expressly asked Ms. Hankel and Mr. Albee to point out there was no HTML or PHP web files either in allocated or unallocated space on item No. 1. They never went over it and I am not sure that they understood what I wanted. A user cannot delete files from unallocated space, it is inaccessible to the operating system user for retrieval. During the §402 hearing and at trial Mr. Graham tried to imply there was "shredding software" on item No. 1 that would overwrite the bad stuff or the unallocated space. Mr. Graham's contention falls short since it would have shredded the pst1002.tmp file if it was used, or perhaps it is proof that the pst1002.tmp file came from an outside source. I believe it did regardless of the software I had installed.

If there were so many images in unallocated space then why didn't Mr. Wall show the container pages that held the image. He said he didn't have the capability to match up pages with images but a simple search for file names would pull up the page containing the image file. The title is embedded in the image. Containers and images go hand in hand. Outlook Express doesn't show images, it hands them over to Internet Explorer to do it. An image must appear "inline" in a message to be seen in Outlook Express. Specifically, I wanted Ms. Hankel to pin Mr. Wall down with his error in his opinion that the one child porn image from the newsgroup file was somehow in the dbx file and not in the cache. Just like website viewing, news viewing uses the same cache file system and any images viewed in a newsgroup message would have a text or html message with them. Ms. Hankel failed to highlight Mr. Wall's patently misleading statements and failed to impeach him to the extent allowed by the facts and she weakened my defense as a result.

THIRTY-SEVEN

A short break was taken after Mr. Albee and then Sgt. Karen Smart from the Mammoth Lakes Police Dept. took the stand. She was the person who interviewed Chelsea way back on August 8th, 2007. Sgt. Smart had several 40-hour courses of study in child abuse investigation, sexual assault investigation, and criminal investigation. She had extensive experience as a police officer but very little actual experience interviewing sexual assault victims.

Q. by Ms. Hankel: Did you interview Chelsea Guthrie when she made allegations of sexual abuse in August 2007?

A. by Sgt. Smart: I did a partial interview, yes.

Q. When you say a "partial interview" was there a reason you didn't complete a full interview of Chelsea Guthrie?

A. I did not do a forensic interview. She had already disclosed allegations and an investigation was underway by Investigator John Rutkowski of the Mono County Sherriff's Department. I was asked to speak with Chelsea about specific sex acts mentioned in her allegations, because she was uncomfortable about discussing intercourse, oral copulation, and other topics with a male investigator.

Q. Is it important that an interviewer have a neutral interviewing style when interviewing a teenager making allegations of sexual abuse?

A. Yes.

Q. Can you tell us why that would be important?

A. It is important in any interview. You are gathering information at that point, not necessarily drawing an inference from it.

Q. So there could be a problem if you were overly critical of the teenager making the allegations?

A. That could cause a problem, yes.

Q. If you were hostile that may make a person not divulge information to you?

A. That could be a possibility, yes.

Q. And similarly, if you were very, very familiar with that person, that could encourage a false allegation; could it not?

A. It potentially could, I suppose, depending on the person.

Q. In all of the trainings that you went to, all the seminars and courses that you took, did you learn that you should not have an overly familiar or supportive attitude when interviewing a teenager making allegations of sexual abuse?

A. No. I would say the training went more to younger children, that teenagers were largely considered to be adults in terms of interviewing.

Q. Is it your understanding from the training and the seminars you took and the years and years of them that when you are interviewing an adult making allegations of sexual abuse, if the atmosphere of the interview is overly friendly, that could lead to tainted information coming out?

A. If the adult was inclined to lie, the adult would lie, I believe, regardless of the interviewer's demeanor.

Q. But would you agree with me that the adult would have an easier time of lying if you were very, very friendly to that adult?

A. That adult may perceive that he or she had an opportunity to fool someone, yes.

Q. And if you were asked many questions about specific details, it would be more difficult for that adult to lie to you?

A. Yes.

Q. At what age would you start using leading questions as an appropriate interview method when interviewing a teenager making allegations of sexual abuse?

A. I wouldn't say there was a specific age, but generally teenagers are cognitive and socially old enough to provide information in – they are either going to lie or they are going to tell the truth. But it is not going to be unduly influenced by how questions are asked of them. They will already have made the decision to lie or tell the truth.

Q. In all the training and seminars that you took, did you learn that a law enforcement officer should never assume that an allegation of sexual abuse is true?

A. You never assume that in any case.

Q. Because you want to keep an open mind; wouldn't you?

A. Yes.

Q. And is it important to consider multiple hypothesis when addressing an allegation of sexual abuse?

A. If I was the investigator, yes.

Q. When you were interviewing Chelsea Guthrie were you aware she had a motive to make a false allegation?

A. No.

Q. Did you know anything about her relationship with her sister?

A. No.

Q. Did you have a confirmatory bias when you interviewed Chelsea Guthrie?

A. No.

Then Ms. Hankel played the videotaped interview for the jury. In it were Chelsea, Sgt. Smart and Alex Ellis. The jury was provided with a transcript of the entire interview but there were a lot of missing parts which were inaudible. About two-thirds of the way through, the judge called it quits for the day. The next day was the day scheduled for Alex Ellis. I couldn't wait.

The next morning, the audio on the tape was terrible and the court staff tried to provide better equipment so the jury could hear the interview. None of the interview was transcribed during the court's session. After the video was played Ms. Hankel resumed.

Q. by Ms. Hankel: Sgt. Smart, would you agree with me that the style of your partial interview with Chelsea Guthrie was such that you discussed certain things she should tell you with respect to the allegations of sexual abuse?

A. No.

Q. You've heard that portion of the tape where Chelsea stated that Mike Harris tried to kiss her, and you asked her "Where?" And she said "All over." And you asked her "Okay. Did he kiss you on your breasts?" And Chelsea replied "Uh-huh." And you asked her, "How about in your genital area after he got your pants off?" After Chelsea responded to you "Uh-huh." Wouldn't you agree with me that you were offering to her that exact location of where you believed Mike Harris had kissed her?

A. No. She told me he had kissed her all over, and I was trying to get specifics.

Q. Did the seminars that you attended teach you that this style of interview to suggest that there were rumors about the alleged perpetrator was an appropriate interviewing method?

A. Yes, it is a standard interview technique.

Q. Is that a standard interviewing technique even if the information is false?

A. Yes. I am allowed to lie.

Ms. Hankel: Nothing Further.

The Court:

Mr. Graham?

Q. by Mr. Graham: Ms. Smart, when you say you are allowed to lie in an interview of someone, give us some more information as to what you mean by that please.

A. I can offer a ruse in an attempt to get information.

Q. When you asked that question regarding rumors without going into the background, did you have any factual basis in your mind?

A. Yes.

Q. And regarding the style of questioning that you conducted with her, did her age affect your style of questioning?

A. Yes.

Q. How so?

A. I felt that she was old enough to understand right from wrong, understand truth from lie, understand that she was responsible for the consequences for her own actions. And again, I went into the interview knowing that she had already disclosed to at least one other person some allegations of a sexual nature, and so I was just trying to get the facts.

That was it for Mr. Graham's cross. He was relying on the shock value of his manufactured computer evidence, and was not that interested in cross-examining our witnesses. Ms. Hankel next called Nathan Morganstein to discuss his interview with Kathleen Traynor. Ms. Hankel wanted to impeach her with an audio recording of the interview but couldn't get it cued up and ready quick enough for Judge DeVore, so she just had Ms. Morganstein testify briefly.

Q. by Ms. Hankel: You are a private investigator; are you not?

A. I am.

Q. And did I retain you to conduct various investigations for this case?

A. Yes.

Q. Did you in this course of investigating for me did you interview a woman by the name of Kathleen Traynor?

A. Yes, Ma'am.

Q. Did you ask her whether or not she was aware of whether Martha and Chelsea Guthrie were fighting about the allegations they were making against my client, Michael Harris.

A. Yes, I asked her about that.

Q. Did she acknowledge to you that they had a physical fight?

A. Yes, she did ell me that.

Q. can you tell me specifically what she said in that regard?
A. She said that – I believe she said Martha had gotten angry, and they had gotten into a big fight I believe were her words.
Q. Did she elaborate on that?
A. I believe she was – it was in the context of her saying that Martha didn't wan to partake in – coming forward and saying, you know, accusing Mr. Harris.
Q. Kathleen Traynor advised you that Martha did not want to make the allegations against Mike Harris; correct?
A. Correct.
Q. And did Kathleen Traynor advise you that Martha had said they had gone too far and that they would never be able to go back?
A. She did. She said once they got too far, they could not go back.

Now it is important to note that Ms. Hankel had all this recorded. But she couldn't present it to the jury for whatever reason. I believed this to be a tremendous loss but Ms. Hankel said she got it in with Nathan. In any even t it was done and it was time to move onto Frank Smith, an investigator with the Mono County DA's Office. He used to work for the Mammoth Lakes Police Dept. When he worked for the MLPD he conducted the interview I gave following Raeanna's allegation.

Q. by Ms. Hankel: Did you investigate the case of sexual allegations against my client made by Raeanna Davenport?
A. Yes, I did.
Q. The date of that occurrence was October 19th, 2003; correct?
A. Correct.
Q. At any point were you asked to reopen your investigation after you ceased investigating on October 22nd, 2003?
A. I don't recall if I was or was not.

Yeah, right. This guy went out of his way to have me charged and he was that girls had steadfastly denied that anything untoward had occurred. Anyway, it was time for Marlo Preis to take the stand accompanied by Allen Berrey, the county counsel representing the CPS workers who were testifying under subpoena. Before she could testify, Judge DeVore reminded the jurors that questions were not evidence at any time, only the witnesses answers were evidence.

Q. by Ms. Hankel: Have you ever completed a Suspected Child Abuse Report with respect to Martha Guthrie?
A. Yes.
Q. Did you have a chance to review the one-page document that I handed you?
A. Yes.

Q. Is that the suspected Child Abuse Report that you completed?
A. Yes.
Q. And you completed that on the 14th of November, 2007?
A. Yes.
Q. You completed that with respect to an allegation of physical abuse made by Martha Guthrie?
A. Yes.
Q. She made that allegation against her foster sister, Michelle Jackson; correct?
Q. She claimed that Michelle had choked her?
A. Yes.
Q. Can you tell me if you investigated this allegation against Michelle Jackson?
A. No, I did not.
Q. Did anyone from Child Protective Services investigate this allegation against Michelle Jackson?
A. That I don't know. It occurred in Bishop, which is Inyo County.
Q. So your answer is?
A. I don't know if they investigated it or not. I cross-reported it to Inyo County.
Q. Is it your practice and procedure to complete a Suspected Child Abuse Report and then do nothing to investigate it?
A. The procedure that we use when there is an allegation on a child that lives in a different county is to refer it or cross-report it to the county that the child lives in. Then it becomes their referral.

So ended Ms. Hankel's direct examination. Mr. Graham had no cross and that was that. I had provided Ms. Hankel with a detailed analysis of all the CPS documentation and referral number 5 was included. Ms. Hankel did not confront Ms. Preis with the documentation because she was unable to find it amongst her many papers. This referral was important since Martha had falsely accused her best friend of physical abuse. The referral would show that the reports and testimony were being manipulated to help the girls. Ms. Preis testified it wasn't her job to investigate Martha's allegation of abuse. The referral actually stated that Inyo County referred it back to Mono County since Martha was in Mono County foster care. And what about the lack of sheriff involvement or the DA? They both are supposed to get copies of all SCARs. Ms. Preis knew all of this and denied any knowledge in an evasive manner. Ms. Hankel should have produced referral number 5 and the paper trail then asked why the Mono County CPS was covering for the two girls. By impeaching Ms. Preis, Ms. Hankel would have supported the Jackson's as relevant witnesses.

THIRTY-EIGHT

Finally, it was showtime. Or showdown time as it were. Alex Ellis was hopefully going to face some pointed questions. I had given my questions to Ms. Hankel but she was going to do her own thing regardless. It was her prerogative not mine, but it was my ass on the line.

Q. by Ms. Hankel: Ms. Ellis, are you a social worker?
A. Yes.
Q. Are you a licensed clinical social worker?
A. No.
Q. You are the caseworker for Martha Guthrie and Chelsea Guthrie?
A. Yes.
Q. Do you remember your first contact with them?
A. Yes.
Q. When was that?
A. I think it was January '05.
Q. What was the nature of the contact?
A. I was investigating a report of suspected child abuse.
Q. Who made the report?
A. The Sheriff's Department.
Q. Did you go out and speak to Martha and Chelsea Guthrie?
A. Yes.
Q. Did Chelsea Guthrie disclose that she had been beaten up a couple of times?

A. I don't remember her saying that.
Q. Did she tell you she was mad because she had lost her dad.
A. No, I don't think so.
Q. Did she tell you that her mom was yelling at her?
A. I think so.
Q. Ms. Ellis, I'm handing you a document. Could you read though that document, please, and see if it refreshes your recollection.
A. Okay
Q. Do you remember speaking to Chelsea and Martha on January 5th, 2005, about the situation at home?
A. Yes.
Q. And do you remember that Chelsea was telling you that she had gotten beat up two times in the last year?
A. Well, I believe that she did say that since I wrote it down and now, I have this in front of me.
Q. Did this document refresh your recollection that the girls were telling you that they missed their dad?
A. I think the girls did tell me they were sad about their dad having died, yes.
Q. In January of 2005 did they tell you they were being sexually molested by Mike Harris?
A. No.
Q. In June of 2007 Chelsea Guthrie ran away from home; correct?
A. Yes.
Q. She ran away from her mom's house?
A. As far as I know, yes.
Q. Is it a true statement that before Chelsea Guthrie made any disclosure of sexual abuse allegations you suggested to her that she was being sexually molested by my client?
A. No.
Q. Is it a true statement that you advised Martha Guthrie, before she had made any disclosure of sexual abuse, that her sister had accused my client of sexual abusing her?
A. Would you restate it for me?
Q. Certainly. Did you tell Martha Guthrie before she had made any allegations of sexual abuse, that her sister had accused my client of sexually abusing her and asking Martha if she was also being sexually abused by my client?
A. I'm not sure what order those things happened in.
Q. Did you investigate the sexual abuse allegations against my client?

A. No.

Q. Why not?

A. When we get the reports of suspected child abuse, both Martha and Chelsea were already out of their mother's home, which made the allegations against the perpetrator – it was an out-of-home perpetrator is what we call that – and that means that it is not the CPS's job to investigate, that falls into the lap of law enforcement.

Q. So who was assigned to investigate these child abuse allegations against my client, do you know?

A. It was John Rutkowski.

Q. Did you have discussions with John Rutkowski about his investigation?

A. I am sure I did.

Q. Did you watch Martha give her interview from another room?

A. Yes.

Q. Were you present when Chelsea Guthrie gave her interview to Karen Smart?

A. Yes.

Q. Were you present at the preliminary hearing?

A. Yes.

Q. When each of the girls testified?

A. Yes.

Q. Did you ever discuss with John Rutkowski that the girls statements between interviews and their testimony at the preliminary hearing were not consistent?

A. I am not sure if I did.

Q. Did you ever talk to Ellen Thompson prior to Chelsea Guthrie making her disclosure of sexual abuse allegations to Ellen Thompson of July 19th, 2007?

A. I don't remember a conversation on that date you just said.

Q. What about July 20th, 2007? Do you remember having a conversation with Ellen Thompson about child sexual abuse allegations made by Chelsea Guthrie?

A. I could have, I don't remember the specific date.

Q. Is it your recollection that that was the first time that Chelsea had made an allegation of sexual abuse against Michael Harris?

A. Yes, I think that is what I recall.

And on and on it went. Ms. Ellis was vague and evasive. She had always taken notes of everything that went on around her and for her to say she can't recall was ridiculous. Her response above was typical hogwash where she replied "I could have. I don't remember the specific date." Ms. Hankel should have been working her over but Ms. Hankel was just going along with Judge DeVore's program which was in essence that we were not going to be using all the CPS reports as a defense strategy.

Ms. Hankel did bring out some testimony that the girls had repeatedly called the CPS in five different counties. She also brought out the facts surrounding the suspected child abuse reports by Ellen Thompson and Mike Hultz. Ms. Hankel failed to score any points asking Ms. Ellis to explain why she didn't file a SCAR even though both girls testified that they told her first and both clinicians testified there had both disclosure prior to their first meetings.

Q. by Ms. Hankel: The allegations made by Raeanna Davenport were not investigated by you; correct?

A. Correct.

Q. And there was some concern expressed and a report was made that the Guthrie girls could be at risk because they were sharing a household with Mike Harris; correct?

A. I think that is in some CPS documents, yes.

Q. And the disposition of that concern and those allegations were that they were unfounded; correct?

A. Whoever had this report did dispo that it was unfounded.

Q. So those reports were unfounded. Can you describe or define for me what it means when a disposition is unfounded.

A. It could mean more than one thing. But we only have four choices. When we have a report of suspected child abuse unfounded is one of them. If we really think that what was reported didn't happen, then we would call it unfounded. If what was reported was not a legal child abuse issue, we would call it unfounded on maybe not investigate at all because not investigating then it is one of the choices. Sometimes we feel like there is something in a report or in a family but we don't really have enough to call it unsubstantiated. So, we don't. We call it unfounded, even though we have some concerns.

Q. In your discussion with Chelsea Guthrie in January of '05 did she tell you that she didn't get along well with her sister?

A. Yes.

Q. Did she have a discussion with you about her mom's boyfriend with you at that time?

A. She said some things about her mom's boyfriend, yes.

Q. Who was her mom's boyfriend at that time?

A. The defendant, as far as I know.

Q. Reviewing your report, do you see whether or not you noted that they had made any allegations, either Martha or Chelsea, of physical abuse against my client?
A. I put under Martha "he hits and he throws things." I didn't put – or her statement – at least this one statement didn't say who he was hitting. But that is what I wrote in here. "He hits and he throws things and drags mom by the hair."
Q. And do you see whether or not you wrote down where he made any – there were any allegations of verbal abuse?
A. Um, I don't see that. I put "Martha states she is kind of scared of Mike and her mom."
Q. Did Rose Douglas advise you that she had advised Martha and Chelsea Guthrie in November of 2006 that they had not expressed enough danger in their mom's house in November, 2006?
A. I think Rose talked to me about something very similar to that, yes.
Q. Were you aware at that time that Rose Douglas suggested counseling for the girls?
A. Yes.
Q. On June 28th, 2007 after Chelsea Guthrie ran away, when did you become involved in this case?
A. When the Sheriff's Department called me that afternoon.
Q. What was your involvement?
A. They asked me to come to Chalfant and help deal with the situation they had.
Q. And what did you do as a result of that request.
A. I went to Chalfant. We had – I don't know if you could call it a meeting. There were a lot of sheriffs there, and Chelsea was in the Sheriff's car, and she was refusing to go home.
Q. What did you do as a result of that refusal?
A. I talked to her about it, and the sheriffs and I decided to place her in protective custody.
Q. And then what?
A. Then I took her to a foster home to stay the night.
Q. Do you know ho many foster homes Chelsea has been in since that first night.
A. I know the number is in my records because I keep a record of that.
Q. Is it more than 10?
A. I think so.
Q. Is it more than 15?
A. I don't know.
Q. Is it more than 20?
A. It could be.

Q. Have you been involved in placing Chelsea in each and every foster care placement she has been in since June 28th, 2007?

A. Yes.

Q. Have you ever removed her for not following the rules?

A. That is not the reason in my mind why she is being moved as simplistic as because she is not following the rules.

Q. Did you ever remove her from Frieda Lindsay's foster care?

A. Yes.

Q. And did Frieda Lindsay tell you that she had forbidden Chelsea to go to a dance?

A. She told me she didn't want her to go to a dance that day.

Q. Did you remove Chelsea Guthrie from Frieda Linday's home that day?

A. Not as a result of that, no

Q. Why did you remove her from Frieda Lindsay's home?

A. She left, and she refused to go back. And the foster father had made a comment to her that she wasn't willing to get past, that was very hurtful to her.

Q. What was the comment?

A. I think it was him saying to his wife "Oh, just get rid of them. Just get rid of both of them." Something like that that was dismissive of her.

Q. Did you remove Martha Guthrie from the Lindsay's home?

A. Yes.

Q. Did you remove her after she broke Frieda Lindsay's rules?

A. I am sure that Martha on one occasion broke one of Frieda Linday's rules. But no, that is not why I removed her from that home.

Q. Did you remove Chelsea Guthrie from Chandra Burnett's foster care?

A. I wasn't there but in essence, yes.

Q. Why did you remove Chelsea Guthrie from Chandra Burnett's foster care?

A. Chelsea reported having the foster father saying something to her that she was not able to get past, that really hurt her feelings, and that she wanted to leave the house.

Q. Isn't it true that Chelsea told you that she tried to commit suicide at Chandra Burnett's foster care?

A. She told me that after it occurred, while she was still in the home.

Q. So the answer is, yes?

A. I don't know that she said that she tried to commit suicide, but she did take an overdose. She said that she had taken an overdose.

Q. Did you speak to Chandra Burnett about that?

A. No, not that day when I heard about it. After Chelsea was removed from the home, Chandra and I spoke about it.

Q. Did Chandra Burnett tell you that Chelsea had been smoking pot with her sister during a visit about a week before her removal from Chandra's home?
A. It may have been Chandra. I had heard that. I had heard that.
Q. Did you verify that information?
A. No.
Q. Did you talk to Martha or Chelsea about whether they had been smoking pot during that visit?
A. I didn't.
Q. Did Ellen Thompson discuss with you her concerns about Martha and Chelsea sneaking out of their foster care and drinking alcohol?
A. She did.
Q. Do you remember arranging for Martha Guthrie to be in a residential care facility for drug and alcohol treatment?
A. Yes.
Q. And Martha was scheduled to go?
A. Yes.
Q. And then Martha told you that she changed her mind and she didn't want to go anymore, right?
A. Yes.
Q. And so you cancelled the treatment?
A. Yes.
Q. And you let Martha stay in a home that was not a home geared to address her substance abuse issues?
A. She stayed in that same home.
Q. Did Martha tell you she didn't want to go to the placement facilities because she felt pressured by Chelsea to request that treatment initially?
A. I remember her telling me that. I don't think that she said that to me before I cancelled the placement.
Q. Do you think Martha was manipulating you when she told you that she didn't want to go to that treatment facility?
A. Not in my way of thinking she wasn't manipulating me.
Q. Did you ever talk to Cheryl Scott about why Martha no longer wished to go to the residential treatment facility?
A. Probably since that is where she stayed.
Q. Isn't it a fact that Cheryl told you Martha had actually met a boy and that is why she no longer wanted to go to the treatment facility?
A. She might have. I don't remember that specific right now.
Q. I'm handing you an exhibit and ask if you recognize it please.

A. Yes.
Q. Is that your handwriting?
A. Yes.
Q. Is that a note about a conversation that you had with Chandra Burnett on the 8th of January 2009?
A. Yes.
Q. Where she was describing to you that Chelsea Guthrie was hell on wheels?
A. Yes, she did.
Q. Was she telling you she was cursing like a sailor?
A. Yes.
Q. That she stopped taking her meds?
A. Yes.
Q. That she had hit Tyler's girlfriend?
A. That is what it says.
Q. Was Chandra's complaint to you that every time Chelsea visited Martha, she has problems?
A. I believe she did say that, yes.
Q. On the second page did you write "Every time Chelsea goes to Bishop, she appears traumatized after a visit."
A. Yep, I did.
Q. Did Chandra express to you that she felt that girls were manipulating you?
A. I think she did, yes.
Q. Aside from Chelsea Guthrie running away from the Lindsay's house and declining to return, did Martha Guthrie also ran away from the Lindsay's placement and refuse to return?
A. I wouldn't call it running away. They both let the house and refused to go back.
Q. Did you come to learn that Chelsea Guthrie had run away from home at the end of June, 2007, and was staying with her boyfriend?
A. Yes.
Q. And did you learn that she had planned to run away for quite some time to her boyfriend's house?
A. I don't know.
Q. Did you learn she had stayed for several days with her boyfriend without calling authorities or without calling CPS?
A. That is what I think happened, yes.
Q. Did you then take Chelsea Guthrie every single day to Tyler Clarke's house that summer so that she could visit her boyfriend?
A. I don't remember how many times.

Q. You don't have any recollection that it was everyday of the summer?
A. No. Since my office is in Mammoth and that is in a different county, that would have certainly been a challenge for me to do that every day.
Q. Did the county pay you to do that?
A. When I transport Chelsea to friends, including her boyfriends house, that would be on paid time.
Q. Did you talk to Chelsea Guthrie after she ran away in June of 2007 about her relationship with her mom?
A. Yes.
Q. Did you talk to her for some length of time about that?
A. Yes. And more than once.
Q. And did she tell you that she wasn't getting along with her mom?
A. Yes.
Q. Did she tell you that she wasn't getting along with her sister?
A. Yeah, she probably did.
Q. Did Chelsea tell you she hated her mother?
A. Yeah, I think she did.
Q. And did she tell you her mother was blaming her because her mother's boyfriend had broken up with her?
A. That's possible. I am not positive.
Q. Did she tell you that the main reason she wanted to be in foster care was because of her mother?
A. Yes.
Q. Did you ever have a conversation with Rose Douglas on or around July 12th, 2007 where Rose told you that Chelsea Guthrie had claimed that Mike Harris had molested Martha and tried to molest both of them?
A. I believe so, yes.
Q.. Did you ever talk about Chelsea about that conversation she had with Rose?
A. I am not sure.
Q . Do you remember removing Martha from her home on or about July 16th, 2007?
A. Yes.
Q. And at that time Chelsea was already in foster care; correct?
A. Yes.
Q. Do you remember arranging a sister visit on that date?
A. Yes.
Q. It had been the first time in two and a half weeks they had actually seen each other?
A. I think so.

Q. Three days later they both made allegations of sexual abuse; didn't they?
A. I think it was three for Martha and four for Chelsea.
Q. Did you file a suspected child abuse report for either Martha or Chelsea in July of 2007
A. I don't think so. I could look at my records, but I don't think I did.
Q. In August, specifically August 25th, 2007 do you specifically recall receiving an email from Chelsea Guthrie that she did not want to discuss her abuse in front of Martha with Todd Graham?
A. I remember that happening, uh-huh.
Q. Did you discuss with Martha Guthrie that she did not want to make the allegations of sexual abuse against my client, Mike Harris.
A. I am not sure. Martha certainly discussed with me her fears and her feelings with me about the allegations.
Q. Did you discuss with Chelsea Guthrie that she did not want to make the allegations against my client in this case?
A. I am not sure the way you asking it. Again, I had talked to Chelsea about the allegations and her fear.
Q. Have you ever heard or do you know whether it is ethical for a social worker to have a dual relationship with a client?
A. I am not sure where that would be written, if it is written.
Ms. Hankel: I have nothing further.
The Court: Mr. Graham?
Mr. Graham: Thank you, Judge.
Q. by Mr. Graham: In June of '07 you refer to this time Chelsea ran away; correct?
A. Yes.
Q. And you were involved in that initial response down to that scene where the sheriff's dept. had Chelsea, correct?
A. Yes.
Q. Can you tell us why Chelsea was refusing to go home?
A. She said that – this is from my memory without looking at anything I have written from my notes – that her mom was belittling to her, was what – she probably didn't say emotional abuse – but name calling, things I would characterize as emotional abuse – on a daily basis for weeks, and months, and years; that she suffered those things from her mom and she was done.
Q. After Chelsea ran away at the end of June 2007, what was the approximate date when you or – set in time here in the month of July when you first heard that there was nay mention of sexual abuse by Mike Harris on either of the twins?

A. If my memory served correctly it was the statement from Rose that – Rose Douglas – that Chelsea had said that Harris had tried to molest Martha, I believe was the first I had heard.

Q. And were there any statements made to you about either of the twins before either of them saw their counselors toward the end of July about sexual assault by Mr. Harris?

A. I don't believe so.

Q. At any point in time in your involvement with the twins after Chelsea ran away, did you ever receive information that caused you to believe that they were manufacturing the sexual assault allegations against Mr. Harris in order to stay out of the home and be away from their mother?

A. No.

Q. Did you ever hear either of them make statements along the lines of "We don't want to go forward with these charges because they didn't, in fact, happen?

A. Definitely not.

Q. Did you ever hear either of them that they were arguing about the fact that Chelsea was upset that Martha wouldn't go along with her in making allegations against Mike Harris?

A. No, I don't remember that.

Q. Did you ever observe from Martha an attitude that how we are making up these sex allegations up against Mr. Harris and now I don't have to go back in the home, and it is all relieved and everything is happy?

A. No.

Q. Did you ever get the sense from Chelsea that making these allegations was going to be a huge benefit to her and make her life better?

A. No.

And it was over. No Perry Mason moment here either. I was bummed. Ms. Hankel has let me down. All the CPS and mental health witnesses had major inconsistencies. Psychiatric Technician Mike Hultz testified that he had been made aware of Martha's allegations prior to his initial meeting with her. Mr. Hultz stated he was made aware of the prior allegations by perhaps the Director of the Mono County Mental Health Dept. Ellen Thompson, also a Psychiatric Technician with the mental health dept. testified she did a psychological evaluation of Chelsea based on a request by the court and others, not because she had been sexually molested.

Chelsea testified that Martha told first. Martha testified that she first met with Mr. Hultz about a month after she was removed from her mother's home on 7/16/07 not three days later as Mr. Hultz testified. Ms. Hankel failed to create or present a timeline either verbally or visually to cogently place all the inconsistencies in proper context.

The 16th is the day Martha supposedly told Alex Ellis in the car about the sexual abuse. July 19th Martha reportedly told Mr. Hultz about the abuse and he said he already knew of Martha's allegations. On July 20th, Chelsea told Ms. Thompson. So how did it figure that Chelsea testified she told Michelle after she told Alex and Alex says Chelsea told Ms. Thompson first then Alex says she learned of the abuse from Rose Douglas who says she learned of the abuse from a worker from the Mono County Mental Health Dept. See the problem yet?

My discussions with Ms. Hankel during this time period centered on my "escalation of accusation" theory of defense which was enhanced by my assertions that if the girls made it up as they went along, then the people involved in supporting the girls had to have been trying to make a paper trail that supported the girls. This paper trail was at the heart of my claims and Ms. Hankel did not want to highlight this paranoid thinking. Ms. Hankel wanted to stick to the "plan" theory of defense and ignore the inconsistencies. She said they were irrelevant. She was firm in her belief that the girls had a plan to get away from their mom, which somehow included claiming I had sexually abused them for years, yet they failed to mention it until asked about sexual abuse.

Ms. Hankel's flawed from the start "plan" defense did not comport well with a vigorous attack on the CPS caseworkers Ms. Douglas and Ms. Ellis. I had already claimed at my first Marsden hearing on June 4th, 2008 that the collegiality of the Mono County Justice System all housed on the same floor of the same building led to Ms. Hankel's desire not to attack and interrogate aggressively the Mono County Mental Health and CPS workers. Ms. Hankel had to work with the live with in the same small quaint town of Mammoth Lakes, pop. 4,000.

Ms. Hankel also failed to investigate the inconsistent facts of her defense strategy. She failed to research the law correctly as well when she confronted the CPS and psychotherapist witnesses regarding the Child Abuse and Neglect Reporting Act, §11164 et seq. In The CPS documentation of Raeanna's allegation Ms. Douglas filed a report in the CPS file that stated Raeanna's allegations were "unfounded." Ms. Hankel neglected to question Ms. Douglas about her own definition of unfounded and inconclusive. This after Ms. Douglas offered her own definitions that were inconsistent with §11165.12.

According to Ms. Douglas' own report, she had found Raeanna's claim to be unfounded which by law means she found proof that Raeanna's claim was false. Otherwise, she would have had to make a finding of inconclusive. This is the typical he said/she said finding in the absence of evidence of abuse.

The legal distinction was relevant and I had faxed Ms. Hankel from the jail a detailed analysis of this relevant part of the California Penal Code. I also provided a detailed analysis of Ms. Douglas' reports. I told Ms. Hankel during Ms. Douglas' testimony to raise the issue of her findings but Ms. Hankel stood pat. Clearly the record in this action reflects the obviousness that there was a passing of the buck and flat-out contradictions. Who know what, when, and who was investigating what were and are legitimate questions in my mind. Ms. Hankel should have pressed on these issues more assertedly if not aggressively.

Whether it was Det. Rutkowski saying he wasn't the investigator or Alex Ellis saying he was. It was and is a huge contradiction. Why didn't Ms. Hankel therefore press Mr. McCammond about the lack of investigation since he was Mr. Graham's investigator. What about Rose Douglas stating she was handling Martha's case but then saying she didn't file a mandated SCAR because she referred it to the person handling Martha's case, Alex Ellis. All roads lead to Alex Ellis and Todd Graham. Whether Ms. Douglas received a report of abuse is a hotly contested issue in my mind, but not in Ms. Hankel's mind.

No SCARs in the record were either submitted or received by Rose Douglas as required by law. There was no SCAR in the Raeanna Davenport case either. These facts were all well known at the time of trial. Prime evidence related to these facts included all the released CPS records, the referral No. 10 issue involving the Big note/Little note claim and the purported SCARs never sent the Sheriff or the DA's office.

Nowhere in Ms. Douglas' notes or DSL entries is there any mention of a SCAR, a referral to Ms. Ellis or Mr. Hultz, a report of Mr. Hultz, or any entry by Rose Douglas after 7/13/07, Ms. Douglas' last day of work with the CPS office.

I had consistently argued that the girls reports started when they thought they were going to be placed back in their mother's home. At this same time, Chelsea, who claims she was scared senseless, began sending me threatening emails and her friends began sending me threatening emails as well as placing harassing phone calls to me.

How Ms. Douglas received a SCAR after her last day of work is every bit as perplexing as Ms. Hankel's failure to point this out. The dates of the SCARs were never authenticated. Ms. Hankel may be "Captain of the Ship" by statue and case law but that doesn't give her the right to protect her standing in the community and professionally by protecting her associates on the Third Floor at my expense.

Ms. Hankel repeatedly told me she was going to call a bombshell witness, another client named Ted Carlton. He had also been falsely accused of child molestation by his wife concerning their daughter. Ms. Ellis handled that case as well and she had Nurse Boyle do a SART exam. Ms. Boyle did not find any signs of abuse. Despite this lack of physical evidence, Ms. Ellis went ahead with charges of sexual abuse against Mr. Carlton. Ms. Hankel then met with the director of Mono County CPS and vociferously attacked Ms. Ellis' ethics or pursuing a claim with no basis of fact.

This highlighted two important issues. First, Ms. Ellis and the CPS will make claims conform to their caprice even in the absence of credible evidence, or in the presence of evidence that shows claims have no basis in fact. Second, the collegiality of the Mono County Justice System, the meetings and the sharing of information on the "Q.T." violates a defendant's rights to proper confrontation as well as confidentially to a certain extent. Whether it is Ms. Hankel talking to me about Mr. Carlton's case or Mr. Gephart telling Mr. Graham and Mr. Wall about my computer evidence statements or what Mr. Graham tells the girls about my relationship with Mr. Gephart, there seems to be a dysfunctionality to the adversarial process in Mono County.

Ms. Hankel failed to point out important issues with Ms. Ellis which I asked her to look into and challenge Ms. Ellis with. These issues were related to facts associated with the inconsistent and contradictory documentation. My key contention was that the allegations were part of a series of events that began with Chelsea's making allegations of physical and emotional abuse against her mother and escalated from there.

THIRTY-NINE

And then it really was showtime. Next up was me. I wasn't going down without a fight despite the fact Ms. Hankel advised me not to testify. Yeah right. Before we started, the judge asked me a couple of questions.

The Court: Ms. Hankel, you have advised me the Mr. Harris desires to testify?

Ms. Hankel: Yes, he does.

The Court: Mr Harris, is that your intention?

The Defendant: My intention is to exercise my First Amendment right to free speech.

The Court: You also have a Fifth Amendment right.

The Defendant: It doesn't apply in this case.

The Court: Well you have a privilege not to testify. The corollary request is that you have a right to testify. You understand clearly –

The Defendant: I clearly choose –

The Court: Both sides of the coin?

The Defendant: Yes, sir.

The Court: We'll be glad to honor that.

So, after a bit of housekeeping about how I wasn't going to miss this chance for anything, the jury was brought in and all eyes were on me.

Q. by Ms. Hankel: Are you a little nervous?

A. Yes. It's a high pressure situation, but I'll ease into it.

Q. Tell me when you met Kerri Guthrie.

A. Well, I met Kerri online in the fall of 2001 and physically met her in person for the first time December 31st, 2001.

And so Ms. Hankel led me through the basics of living in Nevada City, CA., moving to Bishop and moving the horses, Dale Guthrie being in jail and then getting released etc.

Q. by Ms. Hankel: Did Chelsea come live with Dale after he was out of jail?

A. Yes, she did.

Q. What was the incident that preceded that?

A. I was going to the Westminester Kennel Club Dog Show. I go every year. And I had Kerri come over and look at the Millpond Equestrian Center for her horses. Because where she lived it was 4,200 feet of elevation, right at the snow/ rain line over there which is pretty harsh on horses. So she came over and liked the facility. She took my dogs back to care for them while I was gone.

While she was taking care of my dogs, she was going to bring over her horses to Millpond. I made arrangements with the owner Hilke Ungersma to board the two horses and kind of wean the colt, the yearling of the mom.

She brought her horses over, and there was an incident with CPS that transpired that caused the girls to be removed from the home for a day. Chelsea made some allegations against her mom, and therefore Kerri wound up saying 'Dale, can you help me with Chelsea. She's a bit more than I can handle right now."

Q. And had Kerri been having some problems around that time with Chelsea stealing things?

A. I came to be aware of the fact that Chelsea had some situations at school in regards to stealing stuff from classmates.

Ms. Hankel then led me through the basic story of how we came to live in Bishop and then Chalfant. Also how Chelsea came to leave her dad and came to live with us in Bishop, and how I was running my internet business. We then discussed Raeanna Davenport.

Q. by Ms. Hankel: Do you remember when Raeanna Davenport came to spend the day in October 2003?

A. Very much so.

Q. Tell me what happened that day.

A. The girls came and asked me that Raeanna's grandmother had basically wanted me to watch Raeanna for her and I didn't really know what to say. And so I said fine. It sounded like for an hour, something like the grandma had to run to town. And so Raeanna came over and played outside basically with the girls. And then it got pretty late and no grandmother was there.

So I started to cook dinner, and I cooked dinner and Raeanna wound up going home.

Q. Did you sexually touch Reanna Davenport?
A. I absolutely did not touch Raeanna in any way.
Q. Do you remember if you rubbed Raeanna's back?
A. In retrospect, because we discussed this at length over many years, I believe the situation was that Raeanna was singing the blues about always having to go to Uncle Greg's house in Benton. And she was glad she didn't have to go there this day. And I got up from sitting on the bed and said well, that's ok, or good, or something very innocuous to me.
Q. And did Raeanna have dinner with you guys?
A. She sure did, yeah.
Q. When did you learn that you had been accused of sexually touching Raeanna Davenport?
A. When they arrested me the next night.
Q. So they brought you up to jail?
A. Yes.
Q. And how long did you stay in jail?
A. I believe I was in there just shy of 48 hours, which was a kind of legal threshold that they had to fish or cut bait.
Q. And after you were released, where did you return?
A. I returned to the Guthrie's – my house.
Q. Did you resume living with Kerri and the girls?
A. Yeah, absolutely.
Q. Was there any hostility between you and the girls at that time?
A. We were all just confused, what the heck was going on.
Q. You resumed living with the girls, and then you resided with them until what time.
A. I lived there until July of 2004.
Q. Did you move out in July of 2004?
A. I did.
Q. Why did you move out?
A. Well, the prior fall I had to put down one of my dogs, and it was a big issue with the burden it created in the house. So now I had another 13-year-old dog that was in a bad way and Kerri didn't want to go through what we went through the prior fall. She forced me to put the dog out in the yard, and the dog pretty much couldn't get up. It would dig a hole and lay in the hole and flies would get at its ears and all this stuff. And I was like "I want to put this dog inside the house."
So it escalated into a battle. I wound up going down south and buying a brand new travel trailer to basically protect my dog from a living situation that was not good.
Q. Was your living situation with Kerri volatile?

A. Not at that point. It became more volatile as we battled over, you know, that I didn't have a room in the house, you know, that kind of stuff. For me, I have never lived in somebody else's house like that. That was unique, a new situation for a relationship for me.

Q. Where did you move your travel trailer?

A. Initially, I moved it to Big Pine.

Q. How long did you live in Big Pine then?

A. Until about October of 2004.

Q. And throughout that time did you continue to see Kerri?

A. Yes, I did.

Q. Was there anything at all that changed in your relationship between October 2004 and January 2005?

A. There were a lot of things that came to a head at that point in time, with my business, with my relationship with her, with pressures from my dad, a variety of issues came to manifest themselves in that period of time.

Q. Do you remember you had a falling out at the fairgrounds when Chelsea first came over to live in Bishop?

A. Yeah, we had a big blowout at the fair.

Q. Tell me what happened.

A. I was working at the fair in the office. And I came out and there was liquid under my car. And I was like "What's going on?" And they were like "I don't know, I don't know." And I finally got it out of them that Martha had peed inside my dogs water dish inside my van. And I was upset about it, and they started talking back. It became a tag team between those two against me. And I wasn't going to win because they were going to stand up for each other.

And so we got to the house and it kept this battle going on. I wound up throwing the bucket at the trash can in the corner. I can't use this bucket for my dog. And they were telling me oh, yeah, it's no big deal. You don't have to get so overreactive about it.

The bucket bounced off the wall and hit Martha and Chelsea was standing over there yelling at me, you know, "leave her alone," and it was just this big fiasco.

Q. Aside from that incident, was there ever an incident where you held Chelsea up against the wall?

A. When she first came over – yes, there was.

Q. Tell me when that occurred.

A. The first week that Chelsea came back I paid extra for her to go to a horse camp at Freedom in Motion. There wasn't even space for her. She got to go to a birthday party. I did all this stuff for her, and then to pay me back, she stole some cake and lied about it. And that was exactly what her mom had warned me about she would do. And this was all within the first week or two that she was there. I gave her grief about it and she blew up at me. I grabbed her and said "We're not going that route."

Q. Did her mom have a concern about Chelsea eating sugar? A. She said it was a tell-tale sign of BiPolar.

Q. Going up to January of 2005, do you remember an incident in January of 2005 with the girls where they ran away to the neighbors?

A. Very much so.

Q. Do you know whose house they ran away to?

A. They ran away next door to the Worley's.

Q. Were you living with the family, with Kerri and Martha and Chelsea at that time?

A. No, I was not.

Q. Did you have any involvement when they ran away to the neighbor's house?

A. Yes. I was called to come down and mediate the situation.

Q. Who called you?

A. I believe Kerri called me.

Q. And did you go over to the Worley's?

A. I did. I tried to talk to them but Ms. Worley was definitely running cover for them at that point.

Q. So she wouldn't let you talk to the girls?

A. No. Well, she did – can I continue?

The Court: Sure.

The Witness: She did, and then there became some animus, and I would try and go back over and talk to them. And this went on for several hours.

Q. by Ms. Hankel: When you say you went, you were going back and forth between Kerri's house and the Worley's house?

A. Yes.

Q. And were you brining messages from the girls to their mom?

A. Exactly.

Q. And from Kerri to the girls?

A. I was trying to, Ms. Worley was running cover.

Q. Was CPS called out?

A. They weren't called out. In Chalfant you don't get emergency services like CPS or sheriff to show up in a timely fashion. So what was going on is that a sheriff's deputy was dispatched but it would be two hours before he showed up. And CPS was on the phone. Alex Ellis was on the phone with Ms. Worley.

Q. At some point did the girls return home to the mom's house?

A. Yeah. About 2:30 in the morning, I believe it was.

Q. In November of 2006 there's been some testimony about a van incident. Are you familiar with that incident?

A. I am extremely familiar with that incident.

Q. Can you tell me what happened?

A. I was going over to the house, prior to the girls going to school. They had to walk to the bus which is about – I don't know, about a half mile – to give them some lunch money and pick up something at the house or whatever. They were already on their way, trying to go to the bus stop. And they were actually trying to get into a van and I was like, what's up with that? And so they got out of the van, they came over to the side of the truck. And there were a couple other kids in the street because they all go at the same time.

Chelsea started lighting up into me "Don't tell me what to do. You're not my dad." And Martha was standing there not saying anything and it kept escalating until the point I told Chelsea she couldn't be on the ski team. And that was a big blowout. And then I turned around to leave and Chelsea was running after this kid who was somewhat of a problem child in the neighborhood, and Kerri didn't like the parents. I was driving by and I told Chelsea "Don't go running after that boy. If he wants to wait for you, he can have some manners. But, don't you go flogging after him."

Q. In November of 2006 that is just about six months before Chelsea ran away; correct?

A. It was her first year of high school, yes.

Q. Were the girls getting along with their mom at that point?

A. They had a dichotomous relationship that fluctuated pretty regularly.

Q. So sometimes they would get along with her?

A. Yes, sometimes they would get along with her.

Q. And sometimes they wouldn't.

A. Sometimes they wouldn't.

Q. What kind of things did the mother ask them to do?

A. The regular stuff. Clean out the cat box, pick up the horse poop, throw out the feed. Mom would weigh the feed. Finally, she trusted the girls to weigh the feed but at the beginning she didn't trust them. So mom would have it already sitting there. Basically, throw some scratch out there for the chickens in the morning and throw out the flakes to the house on your way out to school in the morning. In the afternoon they would pick up some horse poop and the standard issue of chores on the weekend, clean your bedroom, clean the bathroom. And then every night they were responsible for cleaning up the kitchen.

Q. Did they resent doing these chores?

A. It seemed like they did.

Q. How would you define Kerri's disciplinary style?

A. Like I always do. She is a rancher woman; she runs a ranch.

Q. And so describe for me how someone disciplines who runs a ranch.

A. You don't talk back to your mom.

Q. Was Kerri strict?

A. Not as strict as some parents I have seen.

Q. Did she let her kids drink alcohol?

A. No.

Q. Did she let them date?

A. If their behavior was good, she let them go to dances. So, I guess. Did she let them date at 14? I don't think 14 is an age that any of their friends were dating. That term "date" is kind of like an older kids term.

Ms. Hankel continued going through my living situation. After Big Pine I had moved to Mammoth and then after a blizzard, had moved down to my dad's house in Seal Beach, CA. I then moved to nearby Huntington Beach until September of 2005. I was commuting back and forth to Chalfant staying with Kerri on the weekends. Next, I discussed my ongoing relationship with Kerri and her mare. I had leased it from her to breed an Appaloosa/Thoroughbred colt. In September of 2005 I moved into Kerri's house again and parked my trailer in her yard for my dog. I only had one dog left. The colt was born April 26th, 2006 so on July 26, 2006 it was time to wean him off his mom I told the jury.

There was a bit of a battle over control of the colt but I had a lease and so I took the colt, my dog, and my trailer and moved up to Mammoth for the summer. I told the jury that I was done with doing winter in Mammoth other than for skiing. At the end of summer I moved down to Bishop at the J-Diamond trailer park.

Throughout this period of time I was continuing to see Kerri a couple of times a week and even more often after I moved down to Bishop. I lived there until my arrest on August 20, 2007. Ms. Hankel wrapped up this section of the interrogatory and segued into a party the girls had attended at the Bartlett Ranch.

Q. by Ms. Hankel: Can you tell me about the day of the party at the Bartlett Ranch?

A. It was late February or early March of 2006.

Q. Did Martha and Chelsea attend the party at the Bartlett Ranch?

A. Yes.

Q. Did something unusual occur at that party?

A. Many things.

Q. Tell me what they were.

Q. It started out that they were having a party for their fifth-grade friend. Whatever. So, the older sister of the fifth grader was going to come out and pick them up, which we thought was okay, that's fine. Then it turned out that a 16-year-old girl and an 18-year-old boyfriend showed up to pick them up in a mini-truck. There wasn't even seat belts for it. So, it started out weird. We wound up taking them out there to the party. And the next day, we went to pick them up, none of the other fifth graders were there that were also supposed to spend the night. It was a bunch of 18-year-old boys running around and no mom either.

Q. How did Kerri react when she found out there were 18-year-old boys at the slumber party.

A. I don't think that bothered her as much as the mom not being there.

Q. When you say "the mom" you mean the mother of the child having the slumber party?

A. The fifth-grader, yeah.

Q. Did anything else happen at the Bartlett Ranch party that was disturbing to you or Kerri?

A. It looked like they had been up all-night partying, and Martha came back with her belly button pierced.

Q. Was the Bartlett Ranch party a turning point vis-à-vis a relationship between the girls and their mother?

A. It was a turning point in their whole life.

Q. Why is that?

A. Well, prior to that day were active in school sports, and they were leaders in the Edna Beamon athletic teams. And then after that, they began hanging out with the wrong crowd. I hate to say that but it was obvious that they were hanging with the wrong crowd.

Q. At some point did you and Kerri come to learn that the girls had established Yahoo! profiles?

A. We went online to find the kids who were at the party that had MySpace pages. And so we created an account in order to look at kids who are under 18 years of age. In order to look at their site or page you have to register as being under 18 or you can't view it.

So Kerri and I logged on, viewed – found some unbelievable stuff about their friends but didn't find anything about Martha or Chelsea and no links from their friends, not any of that. So Kerri really grilled the girls on it and came to find out that they had those Yahoo! accounts.

Q. Did the girls know – did their mother permit the girls to have any kind of online profiles?

A. No. She was – the girls were not allowed to create online profiles or have online accounts other than the ones their mom knew about.
Q. Were there accounts their mother knew about?
A. Yes. There was the Marthawitch and Chelseawitch.
Q. Where were those accounts?
A. Those were at Yahoo!
Q. Can you tell me where you were living when Chelsea ran away?
A. I was living in the J-Diamond trailer park.
Q. You were still dating Kerri?
A. Yeah.
Q. How did you come to learn Chelsea ran away?
A. I heard it on the scanner.
Q. Is that a police band scanner?
A. Yes.
Q. What did you do when you heard that?
A. I called Kerri up.
Q. Did you go out to see Kerri?
A. No, I didn't.
Q. Why not?
A. Well she was pretty stressed out. She didn't have any call waiting or anything on the phone. She didn't want me calling her.
Q. Were you worried about the whereabouts of Chelsea?
A. I figured – personally, I figured, she was at Jessikah's house.
Q. Jessikah was her friend, Jessikah Luffman?
A. It was her best friend that lived like two blocks over; yeah.
Q. What did you do – did Kerri ever ask you to assist her in finding Chelsea?
A. While she was a runaway?
Q. Yes.
A. No.
Q. What about afterwards?
A. Afterwards she wanted to know what the hell was going on, if you'll excuse my French.
Q. Did you assist in finding Chelsea afterward?
A. After she had run away or after she had been taken? I assisted Kerri after Chelsea had been removed from the home, after what had transpired.
Q. And then did you use that MySpace account to send her friend a message?
A. Much later. A lot of stuff happened in between. There is quite a lot that went on.

Here is where I wanted Ms. Hankel to permit me to expand on this topic to discuss all the confrontations that led up to the girls making their allegations but Ms. Hankel simply moved on.

Q. by Ms. Hankel: Was Martha upset that Chelsea had run away? A. Martha was torn on that subject.

Q. Did you have a discussion with Martha about it?

A. I not only had a discussion with Martha, I took her up to the CPS office to meet with them over the whole issue so Martha could contact her sister.

Q. You brought her to the Mono County CPS offices?

A. Right here.

Q. And what was the purpose of bringing Martha to meet with CPS?

A. So she could see her sister and see if she wanted to be in foster care with her. Martha was extremely torn that now her sister had run away and she was stuck with all the chores. But the other aspect was that Martha felt Chelsea was starting a lot of the problems around the house, that if Chelsea wasn't there, Martha loved her mom and Martha got along with her mom great. She loved her mom. She loved her sister. She was torn.

Q. When you brought Martha up to talk to CPS, did Martha express a desire to be in foster care?

A. No. She asked about it, but she chose not to – want to be.

Q. And you brought Martha back to her mom's house?

A. Yeah.

Q. And Chelsea was already in foster care; correct?

A. Yes.

Q. Were you getting along with the girls at the time?

A. More so with Martha than with Chelsea.

Q. Is it fair to say you were having disagreements with Chelsea?

A. Chelsea never got over the fact that I had told her she couldn't be on the ski team. I tried to take it back. And her mom said "You can do it next year, but not this year." It was reaching a point because Martha wound up being the real hero of the ski team that year, and Chelsea was jealous. She never lost her animus for me after that event.

Q. She was resentful of you?

A. I felt so. I heard a lot of "You're not my dad" stuff. So I just kept my distance.

Q. How much time elapsed between the time you took Martha to talk to CPS and Chelsea accusing you of being a child molester?

A. Yeah, the first email I received, I believe was the TeaBag emails. And then I received an email direct from Chelsea on the 30th, but prior to that on the 28th, the 27th and 28th, I received phone messages implying I was a child molester. So I took Martha on the 9th of July to CPS office. And the first contact that I received was the phone call on the 27th. The 28th email, the 29th, and also emails from Chelsea on the 30th and the 31st.

Q. And these emails just came out of the blue?

A. The TeaBag email came from out of the blue, and the phone call messages came from out of the blue. The emails from Chelsea were a result that I had found Martha and Chelsea's pages, and I clicked on the add a friend from the account that I had, that Kerri and I both setup. And I received an email from Chelsea, no response from Martha.

Q. And the email that you received from Chelsea, was she pretty hostile with you?

A. At first she wondered who the heck I was and then there is three possibly four emails that were sent. I never responded so they kept escalating.

Q. What did you do if anything with these emails?

A. Well the phone calls and the emails – I took them to the Bishop Police Department and showed them, you know, what's going on. These kids are out of control. I had a battle going on with quite a few people at that point because of the situation with the people who had harbored Chelsea as a runaway for several days.

I took it upon myself to get to the bottom of the situation which led me into a cornucopia of people and situations and feelings I didn't know were there.

Q. Was it fair to say this was a pretty tumultuous time?

A. Very much so.

Q. And were you spending a lot of time with Kerri during this time?

A. And so when Martha was removed on the 16th I started staying nights at Kerri's house to give her comfort. Prior to that, I wasn't staying. So there was a change in my dynamic with Kerri the moment Martha was removed from the home.

Q. What was changed in the dynamic with Kerri?

A. Intense emotional support. Kerri was very distraught at losing Martha.

Q. Did you ever take the emails to Detective Rutkowski?

A. Yes, I did.

Q. When did you do that?

A. August 16th, 2007.

Q. When you gave him the emails did he tell you he had already seen them?

A. That's my recollection, yes.

Q. You have heard Mr. Wall state that you, or somebody who was accessing a hard drive, that you had a sexual interest in little girls, Do you have a sexual interest in little girls?

A. I do not have a sexual interest in little girls.

Q. Can you tell me what you know about hard drive item No. 1?

A. The hard drive item No. 1 that is in the bag identified as piece of evidence no. 28, if I am not mistaken, is not my hard drive.

Q. How do you know that?

A. Because the label that she Maxtor is in blue and mine was in black

Q. How do you know how the label of the hard drive was in black.

A. Because it was sitting in my trailer.

Q. Why was it sitting in your trailer?

A. Because the hard drive had failed, mechanically failed. It wasn't even accessible by a floppy drisk drive boot in slave mode, which means you are not even using the operating system. You are just trying to spin the disk, read it with a floppy. It wasn't readable. There were very important digital elevation model data from the State of California which is how you redertopo maps in 3D on the hard drive that I wanted to retrieve. I could not purchase it. It was proprietary from a particular client I got.

So I bought the second drive to have it copied over.

Q. How long had this hard hard drive you just testified about sitting in an inoperable state in your trailer?

A. The hard drive that was sitting in my trailer – mechanically failed in June of 2006 and remained in my trailer until my arrest, at which time I returned to my trailer and it was no longer there.

Q. Mr. Harris, did you install a key stroke logger on a computer that you owned?

A. Yes, I did.

Q. Why did you do that?

A. Because the girls were using the computer and they weren't supposed to. Martha had been chatting with people online and wasn't copping to it. So I was going to bust her.

Q. Did you ever perform any searches for preteen models or prepubescent young girls?

A. Yes, I did.

Q. Can you tell us why you were performing searches for prepubescent young girls?

A. From the inception of my business, when Alta Vista was the primary search tool for Yahoo!, I have always analyzed search results for real estate agents, business owners, whoever, to optimize their webpages for search results.

Probably 90 percent of the internet was powered by porn in the beginning and porn sites are what – were the initiators of exploitation of search engine results. They battle it out over search engine results where the normal person puts their page on-line and calls it good. Over a period of time, I have analyzed search results since 1995 through to this day. And at that point in time that we're talking about, on the keystroke logger, the preteen prepubescent stuff – there was a certain exploitation going on with Google that had to do with preteen models. But if you did a search for prepubescent or preteen breasts or any of that you wouldn't get any of that, you wouldn't get any of these sites. You would only get like a doctor site about something or another. It wasn't a porn site at all.

So I tried to figure out that exploit, what else was going on with it, why was that exploit there and what was it all about.

Q. Why were you interested in it?

A. Well, the genesis – I mean anybody that uses the internet knows that one thing leads to another, leads to 12, then pretty soon you have 50 different things going on. So I think the genesis of it all was the fact the girls were online, the predator series. There was an issue with Yahoo! User created chat rooms, which were kind of tied together with Perverted Justice who was attempting to lure people on the internet and throw spam.

You just look at it, it is not prosecutable. There was a compilation of all different things going on. Ultimately it came down to the fact Google sells advertising based on keywords. I am a charter member of AdSense with Google, which is a way you make income by advertising Google ads on your site. Leveraging these words to me was very important, and I tried to understand every facet of how these words were leveraged.

Q. Do you recognize Exhibit 60 as a program that you installed on your computer?

A. It is a log file from a program that was installed on my computer.

Q. Can you explain to the jury what you are doing on page 7?

A. Well, first, this line next to the date line that is one entry. So this entry is an example, shows a 3/14/06 6:51 in the evening, I guess, a title bar of Google News. The program being used is Internet Explorer. The machine name, the computers name basically is ski, and then a search on Google News was commeneed for preteen models and the enter key was struck.

Q. And what happened next at 3.14.06 6:52:41?

A. The next entry shows that Internet Explorer didn't return a title bar on that which could have been I went to Google News, and Google News didn't have an Index Title Bar to put with the index result, or it could be a plethora of what came up. Internet Explorer came up without a title bar, shows Internet Explorer as the application and a machine name, a delete, and an enter.

Thus Ms. Hankel led me through the key stroke logger log file line by line page by page and I explained the sophisticated nature of search engine results and the esoteric nature of the study of them. We then moved on to the newsgroup access of the title headers but I pointed out

I didn't view any of the messages. By this time the jury had heard enough computer geek speak to last them quite a while. I'm sure they wanted to hear why I didn't molest these three girls who had made false allegations.

Q. by Ms. Hankel: Can you characterize what exactly you were doing with these searches?

A. With the internet, one thing always leads to another. You make discoveries, you try to analyze them, you look for other ways to exploit it, see what is being exploited. There is really no rhyme or reason to web programming analyzation. You just kind of follow where the programming takes you.

Q. Were you ever doing these searches because you had a sexual interest in little girls?

A. No. Once again, I do not have a sexual interest in little girls, or young girls.

Q. Did you ever look at these images?

A. I may have looked at some images at some point in time. But generally what would happen if I went to one of those sites, I would generally stop the download at this point in time of this particular logger because of the fact I was using dial up in Chalfant which is extremely slow.

These websites are generally image intensive, which takes forever to load. I am interested in the source code, the actual programming behind the scenes, the actual HTML, the hypertext markup language.

Q. Aside from these searches, there were some newsgroups that were found on the hard drive. Have you ever subscribed to newsgroups?

A. Well the term subscribed is a bit of a misnomer. It is not the same as subscribing by email, in essence, where you repetitively receive the same account all the time. The way that the tab displays in the windows dialog box is that there is all subscribe or select subscribe as the two different options. And it lists subscribed to any you have selected to look at. It doesn't mean anything other than you looked at the list of headers that were in that group.

Q. Were you in the habit of reading messages about preteen sex?

A. I looked at the list of messages, the headers of a couple groups, I think but I didn't look at all of the – I forgot the evidence item that showed, the 50 or whatnot. Those were not – even though the term was used as subscribing, those lists weren't even looked at. If I did look at a list on messages, I was looking at the titles to see what was going on just in general in relationships to things I read on the news and the fact that this is Verizon and Verizon isn't filtering it. Because that is what it comes down to are these being filtered? What is left? There is a variety of things to look at. You don't need to look at a message to look at what the subjects are.

Q. There were three images of what has been described as child porn on the compuer. Have you ever seen any of these images?

A. I never saw these images on the hard drive that was produced in court. They were not on the hard drive that was in my trailer prior to my arrest.

Q. Were you in the habit of looking at child porn.

A. There was no way to see that kind of content on a Google search. Even with Safe Search off, you are not going to get that kind of content available.

Q. Why not.

A. Because it is ultimately filtered out. It is generally only available from people who are trading personal type photos on that level. Normally what you are going to find is a site that says I've got preteen girls and then it's some 18-year-old in pony tails that is trying to look like she is a preteen.

Q. Have you ever subscribed to a child porn site?

A. Never.

Q. Have you ever traded child porn?

A. I have never traded, received, or sent any emails regarding child porn whatsoever.

FORTY

Ms. Hankel was finished and an eager Mr. Graham sat licking his chops. He pounced to the lectern.

Q. by Mr. Graham: You testified that this hard drive is not your drive. And yet you've heard evidence from our computer expert describing your indicia as well as other indicia on that drive item No. 1? How do you reconcile those two facts?

A. Well, I reconcile it in that my hard drive had a mechanical failure that resided in my trailer for approximately a year. It was retrieved by persons unknown and handled through the chain of custody at which point it was sent away to be rebuilt in order to retrieve the data from the hard drive. And then it was imaged from that rebuilt hard drive to the hard drive that was presented here in court.

Q. So are you saying that the image of item No. 1 that has been referred to by Mr. Wall and Mr. Albee is a doctored image purposefully doctored by someone to make it look like you had all this nasty material on that drive along with your personal indicia; is that what you are saying?

A. I have no way of knowing that.

Q. Isn't that consistent with what you just expressed previously to that question?

A. It could be.

Q. At this point you have heard no evidence that what you just referred to has occurred; correct?

A. I know those images weren't on that hard drive when it was retrieved from my trailer.

Q. So they appeared somehow – correct? – according to you, you don't know how. Is that basically your argument?

A. Exactly.

Q. The newsgroups – I refer to Exhibit 56 – I will put it up on the screen. Just so I understand, do you recall this exhibit Mr. Harris?

A. I do, yes I do.

Q. And this is a compilation screenshot of the newsgroups at issue; correct? Or at least were named as being subscribed; correct?

A. That is what Mr. Wall testified to, yes.

Q. Now correct me if I'm wrong. It is your prerogative to do, but let me make sure I understand you. Are you saying that you clicked on the subscribe button in order to have all these newsgroups on your hard drive?

A. Well, the newsgroups weren't on the hard drive. That is just simply a list of titles of groups. And the way it works on the newsgroup, where it says all, would have shown 33,000 different groups. All that it shows is that I went through a list and selected those particular groups by using the control key to go through and add than into what is called subscribe, but they are not technically subscribed to yet.

Q. Describe the a master list that you say you got these from – describe that.

A. That is going to have a couple hundred other alt binary pictures and the erotica and alt sex and then there are other groups that are non-sex related.

Q. Why did you pick these out Mr. Harris?

A. Because I wanted to see if there was any trolling going on within these groups, but mostly I selected them just to see what was in the list subjects.

Q. Why did you focus on so many of these titles, sexual titles, that deal with sex with teens or young kids?

A. Well, because after the whole Raeanna incident, I felt there was a certain element of society that would try to entrap people in the predator series on Dateline as far as child predators. It was somewhat of an entrapment period show, and there was a lot of information on the internet about not only that, there was entrapment from groups like Perverted Justice, but also agencies such as officer Smart saying you could lie to get whatever you want. And what they will do is actually put material over there and try to entrap you into contacting them or try to set sophisticated software like spyware back onto you computer.

So there was a lot going on at this particular time, and I think until this day that this is the primary focus on the internet for all law enforcement agencies right now.

Q. So you felt you had to have a long list of subscribed newsgroups dealing with sex with young girls and teens in order to do what?

A. I was looking to see if anybody was there trolling to entrap and what kind of software they were setting because ultimately, there are police agencies and vigilante groups that are out there setting some pretty sophisticated software, and I wanted to get that.

Q. So you wanted to be able to have regular access to these teen and girl sex newsgroups to do your research; is that what you are saying?

A. No. That is not what I am saying at all. This is a one time one deal, and those aren't subscribed to yet. This is a dialog box to get you to subscribe or unsubscribe from the other. You can reset the list. I haven't even gone to view them in the Outlook Express screen.

Q. Now you testified with Ms. Hankel that you were looking at the newsgroups and the titles to see if Verizon was filtering them out. Isn't that different than what you just testified to?

A. Obviously, they are there. I selected them from a list. When I see erotica, early teens, hardcore, just because it is listed in this, just didn't mean I had access to this server. The way it works with news servers, each one of those has its own named computer somewhere. Verizon is mirroring – they are basically taking a copy of a news server and they are reproducing it here. But they might not have any content in that particular machine name.

Mr. Graham continued on a bit more repetitively covering the same ground trying to trip me up and then he moved on to the web searches.

Q. by Mr. Graham: And you have indicated that for a particular purpose you were doing these searches. Lets start with Google, using words like preteen space model et cetera. Explain for us in clear terms as possible why you were doing all these searches, doing these terms, or using these terms?

A. Preteen models is a topic that was heavily in the news at that point in time, that they couldn't remove these sites. These sites are legal, and they are allowable just like a parent wants their kid to become the next Brooke Shields. They can put a website up there and nobody can stop them.

So these preteen model sites, which may have started out legitimately were exploited by people possibly wanting to trade, in child vigilante groups wanting to bust perverts. So it is a battle over preteen models as a keyword. But if you search for something like prepubescent or naked little girls, you do not get any of these sites. So it was very interesting that there was so much energy, it was actually in the news in Google and on MSNBC. These are topics covered by mainstream media.

And that wrapped up day 11. I had a lot left to say and couldn't wait to say it. I had told Ms. Hankel in our brief meeting before I testified that I wanted to be questioned on a variety of topics such as "those boys", the Luffmans, things having to do with Kerri, and Shaylynn Ellis. I had asserted my First Amendment right to speak freely and give a full exposition of my defense.

Ms. Hankel did not allow me to do so. I wasn't allowed to talk about the series of events which preceded the allegations being made. Ms. Hankel declined to ask me about the whole Kathy Barrickman saga nor offer me an opportunity to explain to the jury the facts involved or the chance to deny her allegations. Ms. Hankel never let me explain the interview with Det. Ruthkowski which Kerri and I volunteered to give on 8/16/07, and she wouldn't play the recording of the interview in which Kerri and I denied having sex in front of the girls, in which I deny raping the girls, and in which Kerri stated the girls never reporting any molestations, rapes, or abuse to her. I was not allowed to testify about "the cabin" implicated in the girls notes as with their friends which was discussed in detail with Det. Rutkowski and had already been discussed with Det. Estridge. He had visited Kerri's house after she had discovered "the cabin" party spot and called the sheriff's department wanting something done about the state of affairs in Chalfant.

I was not allowed to testify about the reasons for the trips to Disneyland which were precipitated by a couple of factors. Chief among them was the fact that the girls had visited their grandfather's house in Cerritos, CA. a couple times where they stayed a few days. He couldn't or wouldn't take them to any of the amusement parks during their visits. I would have also explained that the girls had been in band at school since fifth grade and at the conclusion of seventh grade they would have been able to go with the band for the girls first ever trip to Disneyland. The fact was however that Kerri took them out of the Bishop school halfway through the year and sent them to the school in Benton which was their regular district school, not the Bishop school.

Therefore, the girls missed out on another chance to go to Disneyland. I would have further described had I been invited to testify that the girls were told by their mother that if they did well in school, did their chores, got along with each other and were respectful of her they would be able to go to Disneyland during the coming summer. They did well as a result and so we went. I would have explained why Kerri chose not to go with me and the girls which had to do with Kerri's schedule, horses, avoiding the heat, sun, crowds and other issues.

If given the chance I would have explained the events which took place after Kerri called me up asking for help on the night of 7/8/07. It seemed that Martha had snuck out after Kerri had gone to bed, and Kerri wanted me to help find her. I eventually found her by pressuring Leif Medrud about where Martha was. Ms. Hankel did not allow me to discuss all my interactions with all the players in this drama and Kerri in the first half of 2007, leading up to the escalating allegations.

I was denied the opportunity to testify about my relationship with the girls best friends and their families. I also wasn't allowed to detail the series of events involving Alex Ellis, Rose Douglas, and Mary Stanley ant the CPS office in Mammoth. This included the meeting Martha and I had with Rose Douglas on 7/9/07, the delivery of Chelsea's property to Alex Ellis by me, and my request to Mary Stanley and Rose Douglas that they remove Martha from her mother's home temporarily. This request was so that Martha, Chelsea, and Kerri would be forced into a group counseling situation and relieve me from the burden of mediating their familial discord.

Ms. Hankel did not let me explain "the notes" that Kerry had shown Det. Rutkowski and which reflected poorly on the girls behavior and made no mention of molestation or abuse by me, through they complained about Kerri quite a bit. I was not allowed to describe the numerous trips Kerri and I and the girls took which showcased the normal dynamic of our relationship. I was also denied the chance to explain in detail a timeline of events during this time I was in a relationship with Kerri. Furthermore, I was not afforded the chance to offer an alibi to each and every crime charged even though I specifically asked Ms. Hankel to allow me to do so. I wasn't allowed to discuss the 8/3/07 "theater incident," the restraining order preceding my arrest that made no mention of sexual abuse, nor the note to mom dated 7/16/07 either. This note was written to Kerri and given to her before Martha was removed from the home, not after as Todd implied.

Ms. Hankel effectively blocked me from testifying about details that could have been independently corroborated by Kerri. For example, I was not permitted to explain the impossibility that the two girls slept on the same couch in the Bishop trailer as Martha described. The fact was that Chelsea never corroborated that testimony, and Ms. Hankel never raised the issue at trial. I pointed this oddity out to her in detail. Martha only slept on the couch at night or two by herself because Kerri immediately after moving the horses to Bishop, she brought the bunk bed for the girls.

The next day, December 2nd 2009, I was advised that Ms. Hankel had suffered some type of seizure in the Judge's chambers and there would be no court that day. I was not in the courtroom when the Judge discussed with the jury and the newspaper reporter the reason for the delay even though I had requested to be present to avoid the appearance that I was faking some illness to avoid cross-examination or other inference that may have been speculated on by the jurors. I the end I took a long drive home stewing on what would happen next.

FORTY-ONE

The following day, December 3rd, 2009, all was well. Ms. Hankel was alert and ready and I was back on the stand being cross-examined by Mr. Graham.

Q. by Mr. Graham: Just so I understand, what you were saying about your searches on the key logger. You say you were basically doing research using child sex related newsgroups, URLs and Google searches; correct? You were doing research?

A. which URL are you referring to?

Q. The ones relating to preteen, sex, child sex. That information, basically doing research. I am trying to qualify that; is that correct?

A. I think what I testified to and I believe is that I actually did different things for differing reasons at different times.

Q. But you are saying that you did none of this activity as it relates to preteen sex, teen sex, preteen models, any of this quote bad stuff? You didn't do any of that because you were interested in having sex with preteens or teens; correct?

A. Correct.

Q. So it is fair to characterize what you were doing as research for non-nefarious purposes; is that correct?

A. Absolutely.

Q. When did you stop doing this kind of research into child-sex related material?

A. I believe I stopped when I had my hard drive mechanically fail, which I believe was the result of something nefarious installed from those sites.

Then Mr. Graham wanted to go through the key stroke logger again, this time with a condensed list that unfairly showed all the "bad stuff" searches all together. I called him on it and the Judge agreed so Mr. Graham went back to using the full log so I could put things into context.

Q. by Mr. Graham: All I'm asking you is why you were interested in the word incest as part of your research.

A. As a comparative search result, what is being produced. I explained that quite at length. All right?

I was getting testy. All he was asking me about was the computer evidence and nothing about the crime itself. I was not happy about that. It was apparent that Mr. Graham just wanted to put the offensive material on the screen over and over helping the influence the passions and the prejudices of the jurors.

Q. by Mr. Graham: So you are using the word "web surfing" surfing through all these different sites involving child sex-related terms; isn't that correct?

A. I don't know if I would categorize it as surfing these sites. I'm investigating the URLs and their results.

When I am looking at my Reg Editor, see, right below there, to see what they might have popped in. Because in your Registry they will place different things. Very sophisticated sites don't just place a cookie or spyware in your temp folder or inside your cache as the Internet Explorer uses. They will install things into your registry, and that is where you would look to see what they have done. Before you close down and then boot up, to where you might have nefarious stuff then installed, you can actually investigate before shutting down.

Q. Mr. Wall testified that for this to be on that – in his evidence that he found you had to click on Oh daddy, I like it so much when you slide down my little pink and it continues on that title to get the text that is listed down below which begins with I have always been a naughty little girl. Did you click on that title?

A. No, I did not.

Q. You turned your Google Sace Search filtering function off to allow explicit images onto you computer; isn't that correct?

A. That is incorrect.

Q. Mr. Harris, Mr. Wall described and I'll use the phrase "a universe of information" that he analyzed and discussed here in court, is that fair to say?

A. Sure.

Q. And you – correct me if I'm wrong – you have acknowledged some of the information that relates to the "bad stuff" you're responsible for; correct?

A. Not to – you said I could say if I thought you were wrong. But I think you were referring to the "bad stuff" in such a general overarching way that is a little misleading. Are we talking about pictures, are we talking about a URL as an actual –

Q. Okay, what information, referring to the bad stuff where there are URLs, news-groups, any of that, are you saying it is not yours, you are not responsible for it?

A. I believe there are several pieces of evidence that you showed me that you have put on the record that are inaccurate representations of what was contained on my hard drive as it sat in my trailer.

Q. What were those pieces of evidence?

A. I believe they would be the representations contained within the screen captures. It would be the erotica images. It would be the pornographic images, and it would be the PST files. I believe that was how that exhibit was labeled. I believe the newsgroup messages as well.

Q. Are you claiming that Mr. Wall deliberately tampered with evidence in this case to frame you?

A. based on my extensive experience with computers, I believe there is some suspect areas that somebody did something that wasn't me.

Q. Mr. Wall is the only People's witness that has been described as doing any kind of analysis of the computer information obtained from any kind of hard drive from your residence; correct?

A. There was also his assistant, who was described as a participant in the process. So I am not sure about how you factored that in.

Q. Are you saying that Raeanna's detailed description under oath about sliding your hands up her shorts, lifting the elastic of her underwear, and touching her vagina was a lie?

The Court: Excuse me. That for of questioning is inappropriate. Don't answer that question.

Q. by Mr. Graham: Did – as Raeanna described it, did that happen.

A. No, it did not.

Q. As Martha and Chelsea have described in several years of sexual abuse by you, did that happen?

A. There was no sexual abuse of any of the three girls in the case.

And so ended Mr. Graham's crusade to railroad me into oblivion so he could boost his career. I then hoped Ms. Hankel would take my lead and get into the technical reason why Mr. Wall was incorrect or even corrupt.

Q. by Ms. Hankel: Mr. Harris, I am showing your Exhibit 50 which contains the so-called child porn images which you have just testified is part of the bad stuff that was not – that you were not responsible for; correct?

A. That's correct.

Q. Can you tell me why you believe you were not responsible for those images?

A. Well, there's three images, two of which have a file name of pst1002.tmp and the third has the name of UA1.jpg. Then it has the full path listed. The full path of the first two were also listed, and all three of those paths are not logical paths as they would sit on a Windows 98 first edition system in the way Internet Explorer and Outlook Express operate within that operating system environment.

Q. When you say they are not a logical path, what do you mean by that?

A. In simple terms, Internet Explorer and Outlook Express reside in a certain location on your computer. And these images don't correlate to a location where they would have been placed by any Internet Explorer or Outlook Express usage.

Q. What does that suggest to you?

A. It could suggest a wide variety of things, but ultimately, the PST files as contained in the other exhibit, which this is a derivative of, the Exhibit 50 is a derivative of the other exhibit that contains all the PST images, and that isn't a file created by Outlook Express or Internet Explorer, and further, PST is a photoshop temp file that creates a temporary file for every image that you ever open up in Photoshop individually.

And knowing that each one would be created individually, the fact that there are numerous images all within the same pst1002.tmp for example, shows that it is what we call a dump file where many objects have been placed into this temp file which is absolutely not what Outlook Express or Internet Explorer would do on its own or even in the event of a program or system error. It just wouldn't happen.

Q. Is it your testimony that you have never seen these images prior to the evidence being produced by Mr. Wall; correct?

A. Not only have I never seen the images, they would never have been on the hard drive for the reasons I have stated.

Q. Mr. Harris I am showing you what has been admitted as Exhibit 51, which is certain images of so-called child erotica. Why do you believe you were not responsible for the child erotica that Mr. Wall alleges to have been on item 1?

A.. Except for the first image, all the other images are from unallocated clusters, which could mean anything. The first image in the list of – I guess there's five – there's seven total images labeled in this Exhibit 51, the first of which shows a path – and I'm going to disregard the first couple of items because they are items listed by Mr. Wall in the creation of this document. But it shows windows\application *data\microsoft\outlook express\saved stuff.dbx\DBX volume\unallocated clusters.*

This particular path caused me tremendous grief in that saved stuff.dbx folder named is a representation of a file that resided on my hard drive called saved stuff.dbx which is a compressed mail file. Basically if you have a folder within your Outlook Express program it creates a file that is called the same name as the folder name.dbx. But what is important to know is that particular folder is associated with a particular user on the computer and so therefore, it would be placed in a location specific to the user, not in the general location of windows application data, especially because Windows98 first edition uses the path windows\program files in order to place Internet Explorer and other programs into it.

It does not use the application data path under windows either. So there are numerous errors within that path that I can't even logically deduce other than somebody took a name from my hard drive and replicated it into a path on a document to suit their needs.

Q. And sitting here today, can you tell me you've had an opportunity to look at the images in that exhibit. Do you recall ever seeing any of these images?

A. I have never seen any of the images contained in Exhibit 51.

Next Ms. Hankel, who was doing a fine job, went into the PST files, the Exhibit 58 which was like 80 pages of images, two of which were child porn. There was no HTML, text, or email/newsgroup messages, etc.

Q. by Ms. Hankel; Are there images that are child erotica that are contained in that PST document?

A. I have a general problem with this entire document that revolves around the path of all the images within this document.

Q. Could you please explain the problem that you have with respect to the path that is seen in exhibit 58 for the PST images?

A. Irrespective of whether I did or didn't view any images in the document, whether they are porn, erotica, or a picture of a horse, they all contain a path which is very simply windows\temp\pst. And then there is about six variations of a four number– whether it is 1002, 1121 or 1083 and continues with the file extension .tmp.

Nowhere as I explained before, while viewing anything on the internet whether it's with Outlook Express, an email message, a newsgroup message, or web page with Internet Explorer would a windows\temp file with a pst prefix everbe created. It would not happen in the Windows98 first edition program.

Next Ms. Hankel broke out Exhibit 61, which was the newsgroup message I supposedly viewed.

Q by Ms. Hankel: Can you take a look at page 8?

A. Yes. I have looked at that page.

Q. And is this an other example of material that Mr. Wall described was contained on item No. 1 that you are not responsible for?

A. Yes. For a variety for reasons, I disagree with Mr. Wall's testimony.

Q. Can you tell me why you disagree with it please?

A. The first reason would be at the very second line under the title. The first line is alt.sex.young.dbx. The second line contains a line that appears to be generated by Mr. Wall that simply says item 1\alt.sex.young.dbx implying it is a path on a computer. Yet when I look further down at the path, I see that some problematic path that we described previously of windows\application data\microsoft\outlook express\ et cetera, which is in conflict with the normal path which would be windows\program files. Or more importantly would be windows\users\user name\program files on down the line, which signifies that a particular use had used Outlook Express and had retained the settings.

Everybody knows that you log on to your computer and it retains your settings, whether it is your bookmarks, mail access settings, whatever it is and the message you saved in your mail folders. This is a generic path that makes no sense. Because if you bypass the login screen as we saw in the screen capture logging in with ski and you can bypass that screen, then you will go into the users directory as .default. But there would always be a separate user path in order to identify separate user settings for programs. So this path is extremely suspect.

And finally, in this document it shows a sent and created date as the same, but it does not show an access date. And every file has an access date or it wasn't accessed.

Ms. Hankel then continued to go through the other pages in Exhibit 61.

Q. by Ms. Hankel: And that exhibit which is Exhibit 61, are there any other paths that are suspicious to you aside from page 8?

A. I will quickly verify that every one of those separate messages which don't correlate exactly with the pages – there are some that are one page and some that are several pages – but every one of these pages has the same path, and more importantly, it has a header at the top of the document and every document has a header.

That isn't a normal Windows Microsoft generated header or a news server generated header. This is a header that has been generated by somebody in order to produce this document for here, for court.

Q. Mr. Harris, I am handing you an exhibit, Exhibit 62, the heading of which is alt.binaries.pictures.erotica.peachfuzz.dbx.

Is it your belief that you are not responsible for the images contained in that document?

A. I am not responsible for that document.

Q. Can you tell me why you believe that to be true?

A. The same issue that we just discussed with the previous exhibit, but also, this has an added bonus topic of attachments.

Without going into technical details, the attachment path is shown as item 1\alt. binaries.pictures.erotica.bdx\little sister et cetera. And those – that type of path is common with every image attachment within messages in this Exhibit 62. That is not an actual path used on my hard drive as it sat in my trailer.

Q. Mr. Harris, I am handing you Exhibit 63 which reflects certain screen captures.

A. Yes.

Q. Mr. Harris, do you recognize the screen captures as being screen captures that would have existed on your hard drive?

A. These are screen captures that don't represent the state of my computer at the time that hard drive was seized.

Q. Mr. Harris, I am handing you Exhibit 56. Can you tell me if you were responsible for the data contained in Exhibit 56?

A. No, I am not.

Q. Why not?

A. There are several reasons.

Q. What is the first reason?

A. The first reason is that this shows someone is accessing the sever news.verizon.net and are sorting through the lists of newsgroups contained on that news server. But in the very top it shows inbox Outlook Express and specifically it shows that the newsgroup function has not been entered yet.

Q. When you say the inbox has not been entered yet, what is your conclusion?

A. What I said was that it shows inbox in the taskbar. Everyone will understand the taskbar shows the running program on your screen at the top or bottom. And when it shows the inbox here, that means you are in the inbox of your Outlook Express at the present time. This dialog box shows that somebody has attempted to access a newsgroup and sort through the lists. But in a logical sense, it would have shown the news server up there.

Because the way it works in Outlook Express, for those of you that have Outlook Express, on the left side of the screen it will list your mail server account and then it will list your inbox, your sent, your trash, and any folders you have created. And then further down it will list a news server that may be accessed.

Now if somebody was actually accessing a news server, the news server would show up, not inbox. It is pretty much impossible to be in your inbox and accessing the news server to retrieve the list at the same time.

Q. Is it your testimony that that is not an accurate screen shot of what you would actually see on the screen on the computer at any time?

A. It is impossible to generate that screen shot.

Q. You said there were other reasons why you were not responsible. Can you tell me any other reason why you are not responsible for that material?

A. Assuming that someone did access a news server they would be generating a new list. And any time you access a newsgroup or generate any lists, it still resides on the server at news.verizon.net. It never resides on your computer. So, any time you access the list server and it repopulates the list on your computer. Those lists do not reside on your computer to be reused at any time.

Q. is there another reason why you claim you are not responsible for that data?

A. It has no date on there whatsoever, and the screen captures conveniently crop out where the date would be at the top. It shows the time, but it conveniently doesn't show the date. So the whole document is suspect to me, and I don't believe it is an accurate screen capture on any computer. I believe it is a manufactured document.

Q. Mr. Harris, I am handing you Exhibits 55-A and 55-B. Can you explain to me why you are not responsible for the data in Exhibit 55-A?

A. The first four pages of Exhibit 55-A contain a list of visited URLs that also come from the suspected path we just discussed which we do not need to go into but concluded with pst1002.tmp. So this is an extension of those files put in a different wrapper. They don't necessarily represent pages that were successfully loaded or retrieved, especially in the context of the content he's provided subsequent to the list.

Q. can a URL exist on a computer if the actual page has not loaded in?

A. The URL can exist without the page, yes?

Q. The page will be partially loaded and the URL will be there?

A. Yes.

Q. You also said that the exhibit didn't necessarily represent pages that were successfully loaded. Can you explain that please?

A. I can explain that in the context that those two particular documents show pages that don't match. One page may appear one way in 55-A, and appear a different way in 55-B, and may exist in one and not the other. And it's a vivid example of the way search engines and web sites talk to each other, and the term "bait and switch" becomes very evident in these documents.

Q. And would the differences between 55-A and 55-B be explained merely by one of those exhibits was created in November, and one of them created in April?

A. Sure.

Q. Are there other reasons that those difference may exist?

A. Definitely, because of the way websites manipulate and use what is called bait and switch or redirecting or error document not found handling. But a page exists one way a one time, exists another way at another time, and this evidence has been produced over the last two years ten different ways we are seeing right now.

Q. Is there any other material that you testified to earlier that you are not taking responsibility for that I have not gone over with you?

A. I saw Mr. Graham and Mr. Wall go over numerous screen captures of which you only showed me two. So all the other screen captures were suspect as well.

Q. Why do you think those screen shots are suspect?

A. Among other reasons, the main reason I would suggest is that Mr. Wall testified that he used the program as outlined at the top VMWare Workstation 8th Edition to emulate my computer as that hard drive was retrieved, and he just simply attempted to log onto it as it sat or as it was given to him. And this does not represent that as being a truthful statement.

Q. Why not?

A. On page 4 it shows the inbox for Outlook Express and shows subfolders that did not exist on the hard drive as it sat in my trailer and was seized at the time of my arrest.

Q. Are there any other screen captures which are suspect?

A. Page 5, page 6, and page 7 in a variety of ways show what appears to be news-group lists or messages in a list. But that, once again, shows that the computer or the hard drive as it were, needed to be connected to the server news.verizon.net, which is shown on page 6.

In order for this list to be populated, it had to connect. And so to show that it is connected by also show the message of unavailable while offline is a highly suspect document because the list wouldn't exist if you were offline.

You need to be connected to the server to have any messages or lists of newsgroups contained within the program. That is just the way it works. So as I discussed previously, it regards to the inbox and the taskbar, this one has the taskbar hidden, but does show the alt.sex.young group name in the titlebar for Outlook Express. But it's not showing that group being in the list or even highlighted as though you are in that group.

But most importantly, the group lists as represented here are not the state of the hard drive when it was seized as testified by Mr. Wall.

Q. How do you know that?

A. Well, I personally know that it – I know when the hard drive mechanically failed, and I know what was going on with it at that time. And no news groups were in access or connected to. So this is a manufactured capture of some point in the time on a computer I can't even make sense out of.

Q. During that time frame, March through mid-April or so of 2006, was that when the Predator series was highly in the news?

A. That is my recollection, yes.

Q. And is it your recollection that some of the searches were performed as a result of those news headlines?

A. Among other reasons, yes.

Ms. Hankel: I have nothing further.

All right now. I got in my two cents worth but unbelievably, I left a lot unsaid. Now Mr. Graham would try to beat me down but my opinions on the paths and screen captures were indisputable.

Q. by Mr. Graham: Are you responsible for any images as reflected in that document [Exhibit 58, the recovered PST files]?

A. I recall seeing some of these images, yes.

Q. When?

A. I couldn't tell you. I just – some of them look familiar.

Q. In what context did you see them? What were you doing when you saw them, the ones that you say you saw?

A. I knew I was doing a remodel of a shower in June, and so when I see tile saws or information in regards to like the shower repair, I don't know what date it was. But I do recall looking up information about tile and showers like right here.

Q. And you flipped open to page 48?

A. Uh-huh.

Mr. Graham then brought up a picture of cartoon incest sex and kept after me even though I never saw the entire image. All he had was what is called an image slice where an image is chopped up into little pieces for faster page loading. Finally Judge DeVore had had enough and told Mr. Graham not to use compound questions.

Q. By Mr. Graham: Did you – are you responsible for those cartoon-- I am going to use the term "sex images" that are in this document Exhibit 58?

A. My computer is not responsible for the generation of any PST temp file as displayed in the exhibit.

Q. Going back to page 39, image 151 isn't that a temp file that involves a shower?

A. It is, yes.

Mr. Graham: Nothing further, Judge.

I really wanted to address the fact that Mr. Graham and Mr. Wall were fixated on an image of a tile saw that I might have seen yet they never showed a webpage, a URL, or any search query associated with the image or when, if at all, it was viewed.

My main concern though was that I was not allowed to discuss Kerri nor was I permitted to deny that there was any sexual activity in front of the girls. I wasn't allowed to deny that I forced Chelsea to participate in a sex act with her mother, count 24. This deficiency was compounded when Ms. Hankel refused to call Kerri to testify as a defense witness. Kerri had denied that any forced watching of sex or forced participation had occurred. Kerri would have changed the whole dynamic of the trial. I had explained to Ms. Hankel that based on my legal research; the Judge could have granted Kerri judicial immunity if she was a defense witness with extremely exculpatory information.

Kerri was worried that Mr. Graham was going to charge her with some crime for vindictive purposes. Kerri believed that I was being railroaded in a witch hunt after the WIC §300 Juvenile Dependency Hearing held 7/30/07. I contended that if Ms. Hankel showed how important Kerry's testimony was through my testimony, then either Mr. Graham would have to call her and grant her immunity, or the Judge would have been obligated to hold a Mincey hearing and determine the need for any immunity based on anticipated testimony or invocation of Fifth Amendment privilege and act accordingly.

Ms. Hankel ignored all my carefully reasoned requests regarding Kerri's testimony. Ms. Hankel had no credible reason not to call Kerri to testify, the only witness to know the whole story.

I also wasn't asked to explain the 2007 time period, especially important in light of the fact that I had virtually no contact with Chelsea during this time except for the fact we went skiing a couple of times, the four of us. This was critical since Jordan Moriarty testified about Chelsea's claim of rape during this same period of time. Chelsea failed to mention this rape and never said a word about Jordan Moriarty.

I was not permitted to explain my dad's relationship with the girls and our visits to his home. Also, my dad's availability to be reached by cell phone at any time. The DA and Mr. McCammond had my dad's cell number since all my calls to him were recorded in the jail phone system. I wanted to tell the jury about a conversation that me, my dad, and Chelsea had about Chelsea's anger at her mom for getting Dale Guthrie's SSI death benefit checks.

I also wanted to tell the jury about my phone call to the Sheriff's dept. asking them to return to Kerri's house after a domestic disturbance between Kerri and myself. I wanted them to take Martha aside and ask her if she wanted to be removed from the house. Martha had been complaining that her mom was going "mental" but Martha told the deputy she wanted to stay in the home.

I was never asked about my involvement with Kerri in her WIC §300 proceedings and the escalations of accusations within the CPS reports prior to any sexual abuse allegations. Kerri would have corroborated me if she would have been called to testify. These areas of deficient performance by Ms. Hankel had no rational or reasonable explanation.

FORTY-TWO

As soon as it began, it ended. Ms. Hankel rested her case without calling Kerri. I was upset. Mr. Graham began his rebuttal. His first witness was the girls' neighborhood friend Jessikah Luffman.

Q. by Mr. Graham: Do you know Martha and Chelsea Guthrie?

A. Yes, sir.

Q. When did you first meet them?

A. They came to my school in the seventh grade, like in the middle of the year.

Q. At any point in time after you first met them, up until, say, July of 2007, did either of them tell you in any kind of conversation abut anything regarding abuse that was occurring to them at home?

A. Yeah.

Q. And when – if you can think back, when was the first time you heard about any of the abuse from either one f them?

A. Probably around eight grade or maybe ninth grade.

Q. Who made the mention of abuse to you?

A. The one – well, they both told me.

Q. Were they together when they told you?

A. I think they did it separately.

Q. And what do you remember Martha telling you?

A. She just said that he – he was – sorry. He touched them and she said that he raped them.

Q. Before Martha told you about being touched and raped by Mike Harris or by him – did you ask her a question about that that led to that answer?

A. Well, because she said that he, like, pushed her mom before, and I asked her if he did anything to her, and she said Mike raped her.

Q. And what did Chelsea specifically tell you about the abuse?

A. She said that he raped her. She didn't give specifics, though, because she was really upset. She couldn't really talk about it. And I didn't want to press her for questions because she was really upset.

Q. Did either of the two girls indicate whether or not they wanted you to tell anybody else about what they told you?

A. I think they wanted me not to tell anybody because they didn't want to get in trouble.

Q. When you first heard this information from the girls, did you tell your mother when you first heard about it?

A. No, I didn't tell anybody.

Q. Did you eventually tell your mother about it?

A. They told her, and I kind of told her too after they did, because they did it in front of me. So, I figured it was okay to, like, talk to her about it.

Ms. Hankel then cross-examined Jessikah Luffman about her interview with Frank Smith of the Mono County DA's office.

Q. by Ms. Hankel: And do you remember that he asked you many, many, many times about what you remember Martha or Chelsea telling you about abuse?

A. Yes.

Q. Do you remember what you told him several times that you didn't remember really when the girls talked to you about being abused?

A. Yes, ma'am.

Q. Could it be that it had been that the girls talked to you about being abused by Mike Harris in July of 2007?

A. Yeah, maybe, yeah.

Mr. Graham then had a couple more questions.

Q. by Mr. Graham: How much time passed between when the girls told you something about the abuse that occurred and they told your mother in your presence?

A. Maybe six months to a year.

With that last question Mr. Graham was finished with Jessikah and her mom, Gina Luffman was supposed to go next but he said he wasn't going to call her. I was frustrated because the girls had told her mom that they were mad at me for leaving them to fend for themselves with their mom. Martha had testified that she didn't tell Jessikah until after she told the CPS. I pointed out to Ms. Hankel that Jessikah was just another example in the inherent flaw of the plan defense. Neither Martha nor Chelsea said they told Jessikah of the sexual abuse or involved her and her mom Gina in their plan to get out of their mother's home by disclosing sexual abuse allegations.

Ms. Hankel should have asked if there was a discussion among all of them regarding the purported abuse or plan for that matter. Ms. Hankel should have tried in this instance, as she should have with the other witnesses for the girls, to make an attempt to box them in in order to expose all the contradictions among all the witnesses for the girls. This would have tested the witnesses and shown their likely bias.

Ms. Hankel's persistence in focusing on the "plan" defense led her to rationalize that all the girls' friends and others who testified for Martha and Chelsea and gave conflicting testimony and information and dates were simply confused. For Ms. Hankel not to confront Jessikah about her part in the who knew what/when dilemma was detrimental to my defense. In essence, by supporting a theory of a plan with supporting witnesses, Ms. Hankel was blindly supporting the accusers.

As I pointed out prior to trial, Gina and Jessikah Luffman were showing up at the last minute in an effort to bolster the girls' credibility. Expecting to be believed that they kept the girls secret before and after their disclosures is unreasonable especially since Alex Ellis would have known that Jessikah was a good friend. Ms. Hankel's refusal to discredit the Luffman's also thwarted a reasonable doubt defense by allowing the claims of Jessikah, which weren't even consistent with Martha and Chelsea's testimony to stand unassailed was a deficient performance that worked to deny me a potentially meritorious defense.

Following Jessikah's testimony was Mr. Wall's redirect testimony. Mr. Graham was trying to show the hard drive was manufactured in line with the operating system file dates. Mr. Wall analogized that if you have a file cabinet that was manufactured on May 12th, 1999, that is going to store a host of files inside this filing cabinet, because a hard drive is nothing more than a filing cabinet and a way to organize files.

Q. by Mr. Graham: Referring to the date, when was drive No. 1 in Exhibit 28 first fired up?

A. On October 9th, 1999 at 9:46:36pm.

Q. How did you determine that?

A. By a file called MSDET.EXE.

Q. What is significant about that file and that date?

A. When you push a button on a computer and you start it, there Is a very specific set of instructions that are activated to begin the instillation process and start the computer to initialize the computer so it can be used by the user.

Q. When you received item No. 1 from Mr. Dressler and created the initial forensic image of the drive via EnCase, after that, did you insert any additional information into that image that wasn't already there?

A. No.

Q. If you wanted to do that after the forensic image was created for you analysis, could you have done that?

A. No. The forensic software prevents us from doing that.

The Court: How about prior to the time you created the forensic image, is there a method by which the data on which you have referred to as item No. 1 could have ben altered?

The Witness: Yes.

Mr. Graham then asked a series of questions aimed to put the rest the switched hard drive assertion I was swearing by. My hard drive did not work mechanically and they had to have done something to get my date off of it.

Q. by Mr. Gram: You received the drive from Brian Dressler, that particular drive. At any point in time, did you replace out that drive with another drive, mark it No. 1 and put it back in evidence so that drive we have here today marked No. 1 is a different drive than the one you received from Brian Dressler?

A. Absolutely not.

Q. When you first received the two drives from Mr. Dressler, did you record in your case file the serial number of the drive that you labeled No. 1?

A. Yes.

Q. Do you have that record with you?

A. Yes, I do.

At that point Ms. Hankel stepped out of the room and passed out. The judge took a break and following the break Judge DeVore told the jury what had happened. I sat at the defense table with my investigator, Mr. Morganstein. Judge DeVore then gave the bad news that the trial would continue into the following week. He asked the jurors if anyone had a problem with that and none responded.

Ms. Hankel had some medical issues. The EMTs were called. Ms. Hankel regained her composure and was taken to the judge's chambers where I was able to meet with her briefly before they took her to the hospital. She told me she was feeling better. Ms. Hankel also said that the judge had offered a mistrial if Ms. Hankel wanted to request one. I told her to take him up on his offer so we could go to the Court of Appeal regarding our evidentiary issue. Ms. Hankel said she would think about it but she never moved for one.

No court was in session the rest of the day. We wouldn't be back in session until Tuesday December 8th, 2009. I spent an anxious four days not knowing what was going to happen next with Ms. Hankel and my verdict. I heard from no one during these trying days of despair mixed with a little hope.

Starting out on Tuesday morning Judge DeVore ruled on my §1118.1 motion for acquittal and he shot it right down.

Mr. Wall was supposed to take the stand and resume his testimony but he was benched so Nurse Boyle could testify again.

She began by stating that colposcopes are instruments that have a pair of binoculars. But focal distance and how you actually focus – the instruments is on a rolling stand. As you move it closer to the patient or further away, and remember that you have a moving patient as well. So, a child and even a teenager doesn't exactly hold still. And trying to focus the colposcope in such a way that you can get closer clear pictures in a way that aren't blurry is difficult.

Q. by Mr. Graham: There has been testimony based upon the photographic evidence that the girls, the twins, Martha and Chelsea Guthrie were examined and photographed by you on their sides. Is that an accurate statement?

A. No.

Q. Was a Dr. Gabaeff in the room with you when you did the exam of Martha and Chelsea?

A. No.

Q. Regarding examining on their sides, is there something odd about that opinion – in relation to the photographs that are in evidence showing the girls genitalia?

A. Yes.

Q. Explain why.

A. A side lying position is called lateral recumbent. We sometimes use that position when we are looking specifically at the anal area or use in a person that needs to have specimens collected from the anal area. Other than that, that position is not used because you have no assistance of gravity to help tissue fold out. It is very difficult for kids to relax in that position. Very different from the knee/chest position which is superior in actually getting a complete exam.

Q. If there is full penetration as I have defined it, based upon your training and experience, would you expect to see the hymen completely destroyed?
A. No.
Q. Can you explain why?
A. They hymen will tear to accommodate an object. But it doesn't completely go away. It can somethings tear in more than one area, but sometimes there is just one tear with that kind of history.
Q. Based upon your training and experience, is the statement, in adolescents who are sexually active would have two to three major clefts that would go right down to the vaginal wall; is that an accurate statement?
A. No.
Q. Based upon your training and experience as you have previously testified to, what is your opinion of that statement?
A. That you can have tears to the hymen. There can be multiple tears. But they don't have to go completely to the vaginal wall. They can be superficial small little tears which are just past the edge of the hymen. They can be intermediate tears that are greater than 50 percent but not to the vaginal wall.

Nurse Boyle continued on at length about hymens and clefts but she never explained repeated penetrations of a 10- or 11-year-old girl like Martha and Chelsea had alleged I did to them for years, every day or almost every day. What history was Nurse Boyle comparing to I wondered.

Nurse Boyle challenged Dr. Gabaeff's assertion that the hymen doesn't tear partway it always goes to the vaginal wall tearing like a rubber band, stretching until it finally ruptures. Then Nurse Boyle continued on about how a torn hymen can heal, regardless of the type of tear. She then showed photographs of healed hymens and I was pretty maxed out on the imagery and I suspected the jury was too. The images kept showing the same thing and after a bit Mr. Graham was finished and Ms. Hankel jumped right in.

Q. by Ms. Hankel: You testified that with full penetration you wouldn't necessarily expect to see the hymen completely destroyed; correct?
A. Yes.
Q. Would you expect to see a certain portion of the hymen injured?
A. You could, but in a third of teenagers, you don't have a tear with first intercourse?

And with that Nurse Boyle was done again. I was hopeful that Dr. Gabaeff was going to come back and help me out with this whole teenager first intercourse thing. The girls had claimed forced intercourse for years starting when they were ten years old. They were teenagers when they made their allegations. Ms. Hankel said she wasn't going to recall Dr. Gabaeff and I was bummed.

Then it was back to Mr. Wall who had produced another document after the fact. The People proposed to recall Mr. Wall to the stand and then an issue arose with regards to the new document that had been marked as Exhibit 100. In essence the issue was why the work product hadn't been produced previously as the court had ordered. Ms. Hankel objected.

The Court: May I see Exhibit 100? You have something that is illegible. And for that reason you believe there is a violation of People's discovery obligations to you and/or a due process concern for the use of Exhibit 100 and/or its contents by way of testimony by Mr. Wall. Have I accurately postured or characterized at this point Ms. Hankel?

Ms. Hankel: Yes.

After much discussion about the document versus the document on the CD that Mr. Wall provided that was blurred out on the front but appeared the same from handwriting on the back. Ms. Hankel made some strong arguments but the judge was having no part in that and he denied Ms. Hankel's motion to strike Mr. Wall's testimony and block further testimony about Mr. Wall's recordation of the serial number of item No. 1 contemporaneously.

Mr. Wall then took the stand and though his testimony admitted the Exhibit 100 case report as Exhibit 100a. This report seemed to show he wrote down the correct serial number at his office at the High Tech unit. When he actually wrote it down is pure speculation since Mr. Wall liked to manufacture documents to suit his needs.

Next Mr. Wall went back to discussing the files he was presenting when Ms. Hankel had her unfortunate incident. He described 27 out of 12,006 files that were not installation files.

The Court: Excuse me, can I just ask a clarifying question? Did you just tell us someone bought a new computer and transferred something from an older computer to create those 27 files?

The Witness: Very easily done, Your Honor.

The Court: And to follow up on that, that is why the created date appears on a given computer prior to the hard drive – prior to the time that specific hard drive may have been built?

The Witness: Correct. Because the files were created before the hard drive was built.

Q. by Mr. Graham: How could those – hypothetically, how could those files gotten onto that hard drive? What media or process could have been used?

A. There is a number of ways. CD-ROM during this time was the most common form of transferring files. Files could be simply created on a CD-ROM and then placed onto a new computer and transferred. And they would typically have the same exact date of last accessed of the files being transferred over to the new computer.

Q. The Judge asked you a question previously relating to before you created your forensic image of item No. 1, if someone took that drive, they could input files on that drive; correct?

A. Yes, it could conceivably occur.

Q. Between the time that you received the item No. 1 and the time that you created the forensic image, did you hook that drive up and insert any files onto that drive?

A. No, I did not.

Q. If someone was to take the drive that you received from Dressler, item No. 1, and before imaging it loaded a bunch of other files on that drive, what would happen regarding the file dates on that drive?

A. In order to do that, you would have to hook up the hard drive, the original media, it is going to change potentially thousands of files based on the date and time of your computer system you are hooking up to. There would be – and then files would have to be placed onto that computer in a specific place that is consistent with the investigation of the case.

Q. Regarding newsgroups, if you have – I'm going to use the term "saved," a newsgroup title to your computer does a computer have to be online in order to see those newsgroup titles on the screen in the newsgroup windows?

A. The titles themselves, you do not need to be online. They are clearly visible.

Following this exchange Mr. Graham asked Mr. Wall if he found additional material on the drive in recent days and Mr. Wall said yes, he found affirmatively accessed material from two different newsgroups, the peach.fuzz group and the alt.sex.young. Mr. Graham then moved to admit the screen shots Mr. Wall had provided. Ms. Hankel objected and asked to voir dire Mr. Wall.

Q. by Ms. Hankel: Mr. Wall, did you create those screen shots using VMWare?

A. No, I did not.

Q. Can you explain the process of how you created the screen shots?

A. I used a program called Snag It that captures what is on the screen at the time it is on the screen.

Q. And when you say "on the screen" who's computer screen are you talking about? Your computer screen that you hooked the software up to or the computer screen as it existed on the hard drive on its last day of use.

A. No, this is the forensic software view. So it would be on my screen, on my – what I am viewing while I am doing the forensic analysis.

Ms. Hankel: My objection remains the same. Lack of foundation.

The Court: What does affirmatively accessed mean in the context of the question she was just asking?

The Witness: Affirmatively accessed means a person would have to click on a file to be able to view. That file is present on the computer.

The court: And does clicking on a file necessarily mean one viewed the file?

The Witness: Yes, it does, Your Honor.

The Court: You can't click on a file and before it loads up or some slow program decide I am not looking at this. I am going off to something else?

The Witness: Yes, Your Honor. That could happen, or you could turn your head away.

Ms. Hankel: I have one further question.

Q. by Ms. Hankel: Showing you what has been marked for identification 103. I don't see a date of access. Can you point?

A It is not shown. The date of access is the date created.

Q. There is not date of access on this exhibit?

A. Well, date of access is a subjective term. It depends on the type of file, what type of date and time stamps are associated with it. There is clearly a date that is created. And there is also a column where it says date sent.

Q. You can't tell us sitting here today when the date of last access was?

A. I can tell you the date it was created on the computer, that date, and the date the that the file was sent under the sent column it has a date and time.

Q. You have testified that you created this document [Exhibit 100-100a] when you received the evidence; correct?

A. Yes.

Q. Isn't it true that you did not prepare Exhibit 100-100a contemporaneously with the receipt of evidence in Exhibit 28?

A. It was created when we returned to our office with the evidence.

Q. Isn't it true that you put the evidence in Exhibit 23 into the evidence locker at the Sacramento Valley Hi-Tech Crime Task Force evidence room on September 26, 2007?

a. I don't recall that date. I know what date I created the intake report for the evidence.

Q. I am putting on the ELMO Exhibit 28.

The Court: Do you see the entry for 9/26/07?

The Witness: Yes, I do.

The Court: Does that reflect that date you deposited that in the Hi-Tech evidence room?

The Witness: That was the date it was returned or picked up from Dressler. And the one below it was probably placed in the evidence room because of the late hour. And the very next day, this report was generated.

Q. by Ms. Hankel: Can you show me where on Exhibit 28 you show that you removed this bag from the evidence locker on 9/27/07 so you could generate Exhibit 100a?

A. No, I cannot.

Q. Mr. Wall, I am handing you a document which has the title Item 1 Computer Data at the top. Do you recognize this document?

A. Yes.

Is this a document that you produced to me that you prepared from item No. 1?

A. Yes.

Q. And earlier you testified that there would have been a report prepared by you with respect to the date that the operating system had been installed; correct?

A. That's correct.

Q. And is this that report?

A. Yes, it is.

Q. What is the date you prepared this document?

A. Well, it would have been January 3rd, 2008.

Q. This report that you prepared indicates that the first install date of the operating system was January 7th, 1999; correct?

A. Correct.

Q. And you have listed here not that serial number that you put on a worksheet which you purport was prepared September 27, 2007, but instead that model number of the Maxtor hard drive; correct?

A. That's correct.

The Court: And is that noted as the product, the ID? What is that? Where is that noted?

The Witness: Righ there.

Ms Hankel: Under notes.

The Court: Notes. Thank you.

Q. By Ms. Hankel: Mr. Wall, if a pst1002.tmp file had been copied onto a hard drive and then copied onto another hard drive and in the second copy the computer wasn't even booted up, Windows wasn't even open, the pst.tmp file would have kept or retained its creation date, its modified date, its first access date, its last accessed date would it not?

A. Not necessarily.

Q. Why not?

A. Well, accessed in order to put a file onto another computer, it would have another last access date from another hard drive onto another hard drive.

Q. How does that differ from the DEM file [digital elevation model] that we saw had the creation date in 1997?

A. It had a different last accessed date of 2004.

Q. And if Windows wasn't even booted up, it would have a new access date?

A. I don't understand. Windows wasn't booted up?

Q. In the computer – if you are just simply taking one file from one hard drive to another?

A. Right.

Q. Would there be a new last accessed date?

A. Yes. It has nothing to do with a computer being booted up. A computer has to be booted up to place data onto it.

Q. Even if Windows was not running?

A. Windows would have to be running.

Mr. Graham and Ms. Hankel continued on trading redirect and surrebuttal examinations and it was getting old. Ms. Hankel did not grasp the nuances of Mr. Wall's subterfuge. He was playing semantics with her. She wasn't asking for or taking my advice at that point.

Q. by Ms. Hankel: Mr. Wall, are you suggesting that Windows computer was built and put together and that operating system was installed and that January 7th, 1999 date couldn't be a real date of January 7th, 1999?

A. Okay, you asked a kind of confusing question. I'll try to answer it the best I can. When the files were put on by the manufacturer, it has nothing to do with the January 7th date. The January 7th date was when the user pushed the on button and started the process of those files being expanded and being added to the computer and will also add some new creation dates, because new files are being created on that computer.

So it has nothing to do with the manufacturer for that date; it has everything to do with the user for that January 7th date.

The Court: That is what you determined to be the first date an end user used the computer?

The Witness: No. It is somewhat confusing. That is the first date that was recorded by the BIOS. But the BIOS isn't necessarily going to be accurate, because it was not on until that button was pushed, and until the BIOS clock is updated.

So it could have any date on it. But the first date that the operating system captures is from the Bios before it is ever set by the user.

The Court: Okay. Did you ever make a determination of the first date that the end user did something with this computer?

The Witness: Yes, Your Honor.

The Court: When was that?

The Witness: October 9, 1999, is when I observed two specific files being created that are consistent with an operating system being loaded, those files being the MSDET file, is a command to start loading the processes for Microsoft. And the second file was a password file that was created titled ski.pwl and they were merely second apart.

The Court: Okay.

Ms. Hankel: I have nothing further.

I thought Ms. Hankel left it hanging with that last colloquy between Mr. Wall and Judge DeVore. Ms. Hankel was not prepared to re-examine Mr. Wall based on the same complex and sophisticated topics already discussed. She gave it a good try but missed the mark in a couple of areas. For whatever reason, Ms. Hankel was not ready to confront and cross-examine Mr. Wall about the install package, the contradiction in Mr. Wall's testimony about copying files, and the effect that action may or may not have on associated file dates. Ms. Hankel left it on the table regarding the BIOS clock being a random entity. Anybody who has built a computer knows you can set the BIOS clock with a floppy and you can copy files back and forth all day long with no change in dates. Just look at the driver install disks for example. Anyway…

Ms. Hankel did not challenge Mr. Wall's contradictory assertion that files copied from one drive to another would have a new access date. Mr. Wall had testified that it was not possible to copy a file from one drive to another without changing the date when discussing the pst.tmp files. Then Mr. Wall on redirect said it was possible to transfer files from one drive to another with no effect on the access dates and that some file dates changed in October 1999 which he said showed the computer never can until that date. Who ya gonna believe, the BIOS clock or Mr. Wall's mysterious MSDET file? Mr. Wall was so wrong I almost laughed out loud when he said Windows had to be running for the computer to run.

All you have to do is boot it from a disk, load your drivers and there you go, computer sans operating system. Without Windows anyway. Move files back and forth, burn CDs et cetera.

I told Ms. Hankel to confront Mr. Wall on the dichotomy of his testimony and use his contentions that files can be copied without changing the date to explain the pst.tmp files which were not even a part of the Internet Explorer file system to begin with. Mr. Wall never challenged my testimony about the cache file system, the user directory, or the VMWare representations, in fact, Mr. Wall steered clear of all my contentious remarks I made under oath. Mr. Wall's analogy that you could put old files in a new filing cabinet was a good one but Ms. Hankel failed to use it to her advantage by showing it to be a two-edge sword. That was because you could put files in without knowing what date the files were placed in the filing cabinet, right?

Now it was my turn again, this time on surrebuttal and I could hardly contain myself.

Q. by Ms. Hankel: Mr. Harris, when did you purchase the computer that the black labeled hard drive came out of?

A. Sometime in March of 1999.

Q. After you received you computer, did you install a Browser on the computer?

A. I definitely installed Netscape Navigator. It was a much more advanced browser in the early 1999 time period.

Q. Did your computer come with a different browser when you received it?

A. It came with Windows98 preinstalled and Windows 98 was the introduction of Internet Explorer being integrated within the operating system of Windows 98.

Ms. Hankel: I have nothing further.

The Court: Mr. Graham?

Q. by Mr. Graham: How do you reconcile the fire up date in 1999, October, with your receiving it in March. What happened in that time frame?

A. As I recall, I moved the computer from the house to my office, and with my employees at my office, I installed a password on that computer.

Mr. Graham then quit and so did Ms. Hankel

FORTY-THREE

The show was almost over. All that was left were the closing arguments and the jury would have the case. I was frustrated that Ms. Hankel had not allowed me to testify about all the misrepresentations Mr. Wall had made in his redirect testimony as well as the ease with which someone can spoof a date on a file or the associated dates on a computer. Ms. Hankel denied me my last chance to set the record straight. Mr. Graham couldn't wait to get started. He had a Power Point presentation and so the lights wer turned down low as he started in on me.

Mr. Graham: Well, we made it to the end of this process. I want to thank you for sitting and listening so intently. The first thing I waned to say is I would just pose a question to you after weeks of listening to the evidence, that is, these girls are making it up? They're making these allegations up? That is what this case comes down to is whether or not Raeanna Davenport, Martha and Chelsea decided to essentially frame the defendant with horrible allegations of sexual abuse…

You really have two versions in this case. You have the People's version of events, and you have the Defense version of events. One is a reasonable version for you to believe and convict on. One is an unreasonable version that is full of holes and problems and unreasonableness.

How do you decide? Once you go back in the jury room, how do you determine which version to believe?

Let's do a People's case overview. We have the 2003 molestation of Raeanna Davenport. We have the 2002 to approximately 2007 sex abuse of Martha. We have the 2001 to approximately 2007 sexual abuse of Chelsea. We have the defendant's threat to kill his prior girlfriend if she went to the police regarding his actions. We have the twins emotional disclosures to friends before the runaway by Chelsea. We have the twins consistent yet gradual emotional disclosures to CPS and Mental Health. We have the medical evidence, torn hymens consistent with penetration as testified to by Cathy Boyle. And we have the defendant's clear sexual interest in having incest with young girls via the computer evidence. We'll call that motive and intent evidence…

The question has to be asked, when you think back and look at how Raeanna Davenport testified, did she fabricate her emotions, her tentativeness on the stand? Did she fabricate all the detail in all of her disclosures? The shy, demure, little girl, did she do that?...

No. You saw a reluctant witness. You saw someone who was doing the best she could under difficult circumstances. But after swearing to tell the truth, she told you what happened.

The twins. They gave you detailed descriptions of the year of sexual abuse in the Bishop trailer. They remember the touchings, the place, the general time frame, approximate ages 10 to 11. They can't remember the exact number of times or dates. And really, what should we expect?...

The girls gave details, descriptions of two to three years of sexual abuse in the Chalfant trailer. Again, they remember the touchings, the place, again, the time frame, and they remember it happened – some of them they remember it happened more than one time. Some of them it was a single event. Again they can't remember the exact number of times or the specifics. If you think about it, that is a reasonable way for someone to recall events that occurred multiple times over a long period of time…

Let's talk about the prior threats to Kathy Shultz [Barrickman]. You watched her come in here and take the stand, take the oath. And it is fair to say her demeanor was less than thrilled about being here. She was asked if she knew Mr. Harris and her answer was kind of a contained "yeah." Something like that. But it wasn't pleasant and she saw Mr. Harris sitting over there.

Let's talk about what she testified to. She testified she had a volatile relationship with Harris prior to Harris entering the twins' life. She clearly feared him. She testified that Harris threatened to kill her if she called the police about his actions. Her testimony was never challenged. She got off the stand and walked out.

Why is this important? This testimony shows how Harris is controlling those he is close to in his life when he fears they may disclose what he is doing to them. Remember, the girls spoke about his threats to kill them in a similar way to what Ms. Shultz testified about what he does. If you get in his way. If you are going to go to the authorities, he is going to use threats to keep you in line. And Mr. Harris kept these girls quiet for years through threats.

Years.

Look at the prior disclosures to friends. Now, with regard to Leif, possibly Jessikah, we have disclosures essentially about being raped and molested by Mike for a year, maybe more, prior to Chelsea running away. The girls were consistent that they – or the witnesses were consistent that the girls said they were told not to tell anybody. Before I get to the next point, if this is all a scam, all a plan by Martha and Chelsea to frame Mr. Harris, if that is what this is all about, how come it started all the way back with Leif? How do we explain? Leif talked about seventh grade. A year and a half, maybe two years prior to the bus. Okay…

The importance of these prior disclosures is it destroys the idea that there was a deceptive plan by the twins to frame the defendant. Both girls have deep clefts to their hymen, their hymens. You got to listen to Cathy Boyle come in here and present you with some more evidence on that yesterday. Look at Cathy Boyle, a highly qualified woman. When you listened to her talk about her research and involvement in this area, I think there is no other way she can come across other than extremely, highly qualified…

Her conclusion was both girls' hymens showed cleft hymens consistent with penetration…

And she did not waiver. Those two girls had clefts in their hymens consistent with penetration.

Finally, we go to the ad nauseam computer evidence that went on and on and on. I am not going to apologize for it. But I know it was tedious. I know it was hard to listen to, and there was lots of microscopic issues we delved into. There was a purpose. The purpose was to give you an idea of the motivations and intent of the defendant. Let's look at the chain of custody. Mr. Rutkowski seizes two hard drives and a laptop from the defendant's residence via search warrants, places the two drives into the evidence bag, places the laptop into an evidence bag. Writes the case number info on these two bags. He testified he gave those two bags to Delaney from the Sheriff's Department. Delaney testifies he gave these three bags containing the three items to DA Investigator McCammond. McCammond gives the two bags to Dressler. Dressler gives the two bags to Wall on 9/26/07. On 9/27/07 Wall documents the serial numbers for both drives referring to the drives in Exhibit 28. He writes No. 1 and No. 2 on those two hard drives. The two drives in evidence have Wall's No. 1 and No. 2 on them and the same serial numbers are recorded on 9/27/07 in his report. Most importantly Wall found mountains of evidence relating to the defendant…

Let's look at the content of drive No. 1 that Wall examined. It is overwhelming evidence that that was defendant's drive. It lists a number of indicia here. There is a small amount of usage by the twins and Kerri on the drive.

There is overwhelming evidence against the defendant in multiple ways, the newsgroup image searches and websites sought out information showing clear sexual and incestuous interest in prepubescent and teen girls.

The key logger and newsgroup lists say it all. He admitted both were his. He admitted the activity. The key logger was his, and he admitted that news group list was his. That is his creation. Key Logger – the window into the mind of Mr. Harris. Some overall key logger observations, you look at that document there were 23 days of searches. Only 6 were not child related searches, he searched using the word child 11 times. Preteen 20 times. Lolita 4 times. And model or models 21 times.

We see a little bit of redundancy in his work. You will look at that document, key logger, there is not a search using the word Dateline. There is not one search using the term predator. There is not one search using the term perverted, and there is not one search using the term justice which should have been terms floated out here by Mr. Harris as justification for what he was doing.

Let's look at the Key Logger sites he researched. These are the sites that were indicated or the key logger that he went to. You haven't seen all these yet. Little Top Model sites, Little Princesses.com, Sweet Tyler Super Fashon Teen Mode, Diapers World, Preteen Models Google image search, Lolita Preteen Google image search. These images searching, looking for photos, images, preteen bikini, google search for preteen, mini model site for current photo galleries.

Sweet Strawberry, non-nude child, pre teen and teen models, Little Cuties Preteen Models, Little preteens, Elite names Pics, Preteen Breasts, Preteen incest, child bikini. Remember, these are the sites. These are part of the Key Logger which he admitted was his activity. Child Beach Google image search, Voyeur Beach young, nine year old Google image search, younggirl google image search. So many – so much of an indication of a desire to look at young kids.

All the way up to the lunch break Mr. Graham kept reading off websites after website. Lolita, incest, nude girls, you name it, he was going to feature it, but where were all the images he said I was looking at? It was all overkill and besides most of those were popups. You could tell because it was the name alone, no keyed in characters, no space bar, no enter pressed. The tricky thing about the key logger is that it shows keys being struck but not mouse clicks. It shows windows that open up anew by showing the titlebar text but not those you click through to unless the new page pops a new window. This cuts both ways I know, but in all fairness, it has to be considered. In court I have found that you take your gravy with a bit of grease anyway. After lunch Mr. Graham started right back in hammering me on the computer evidence some more.

Mr. Graham: What was he doing looking up all this information? It is highly reasonable that he was doing this search to sexually gratify himself. He was accessing these sites because it excited him. It got him hot. He liked it. That is why he went back time and time and time again.

He likes to look at girl gymnasts. And you'll see that a number of photos in the PST temp file document are all spreading their legs. Do you think this is a coincidence that all these temp file images of a gymnast spreading her legs is random chance? There is probably two dozen of them.

Key Logger focused on the word Lolita. In the newsgroup there is a newsgroup with the name Lolita in it. In this PST temp file there is an image you'll see that has the word Lolita toys. If you'll recall, Mr. Harris tried to distance himself from those PST temp files.

And then I believe he testified that he was responsible, he recognized some of them he had been into. And then I think he made a statement "Oh those temp files could never have been on the hard drive I had in my residence." The record has what he testified to, and that is what you must refer to. But that is what the recollection at this point that I have…

In the key logger, he went to an incest site, in the newsgroup we have an incest story. Is that just a coincidence? Is it just a coincidence he testified these links were into just the newsgroups maybe for a split second?...

He used the term "incest" in a search in the key logger. So are you to believe that newsgroup incest story that Mr. Wall identified the title had been clicked on and its content on Mr. Harris' drive.

Is it just a coincidence?

The defendant's computer shows the defendant has a clear, intense drive to have sex with preteen and teen girls. He likes little girls in bikinis. He likes them in tights. He likes their legs spread. And he likes incest. That is what the computer shows..

Mr. Graham then went through the weaknesses of Dr. Coleman, Dr. Gabaeff, and Mr. Albee, then went after me and my testimony and the PST temp file.

Mr. Graham: There are no implanting's of that file on that drive before Wall got it or after Wall got it. Bottom line, Wall analyzed the file taken from the researcher in child sex sites. That is basically what he is saying. Incredible. But he doesn't have it. It is not for a bad reason. You know. Doesn't keep notes. It is all in his head. 15 years here. It is important work. I want to figure it out. But I don't keep any notes. What?

He in essence said "I was accused in '03 of molestation. From January '06 to the end of June, '06" – coincidentally the period of time containing the bad stuff – "I decided that because I was so concerned about being accused of (sic) here and I better start intensely researching child porn, erotica, and incest websites to see if Google or Verizon or a host of others to see if they let that stuff through."

Does that ring true to anybody? That is ridiculous. The ridiculous unreasonable nature of his testimony – He lied to you. He lied to you. The idea that this is not my hard drive. Never seen that. That is a lie. We have a chain of proof that it is not a lie. Wall's document on September 27th, we checked with a serial number. Shows it is a lie. He lied to you big time. Finally get to use that word.

Been waiting. Big time. He got up on the stand and he talked more mumbo, jumbo, and you go over his testimony. There are so many contradictions. Never seen any of those PST files. Wait. I saw some. I recognize some. Okay.

He lied to you ladies and gentlemen. And what can you do with it? You can reject it. All of it. The law allows you to reject all of it. He significantly lied to you. He did.

Recapping. The defendant was just a logger researcher whose important work focused on child and preteen websites and newsgroups. Okay.

And with his attack complete Mr. Graham went into the charges and some jury instructions.

Mr. Graham: When the twins were pressed for a specific number of times or dates, "I don't remember, I wasn't keeping count." You are not going to get out of the girls how many times did his hand touch your breasts? "I don't know, it just happened." That is why I was asked one time or more than one time, more than one time. What does that get you? Well, it is completely unreasonable to expect them to know the specific dates and times and exact number of touchings. So for most of the charges we charged each touching at a specific location as a first time and a last time. You will see them. They are paired. Counts 1 and 2 for example lists Martha Count 1 defendants hand touched Martha Guthrie's breasts the first time at defendant's trailer in Bishop, okay.

I went through these questions and answers with Martha and Chelsea on these specific descriptions in the charges. All that is required is you must be unanimous that the defendant's hand touched Martha's breast at least two times, and that there was a first time, and there was a last time in the Bishop trailer. Okay? With the requisite intent for each touching while she was under 14 years of age. You are not required to determine the exact number between the first and the last.

The Court: I need to interrupt you. Counsel to the bench please. (A discussion was held but not reported)

The Court: There is a slight misstatement of the law here that we want to disabuse you of.

Mr. Graham: Let me clarify. You could find a first time, in other words, only one time and not a last. Okay. So if I have a first time charge you could find the first time meaning one time, but there was not a last time, and find the defendant not guilting on count 2. This is an option that you have. But you are not being asked to determine the exact number of touchings within a period of time if we have more than one time.

Whereupon Mr. Graham proceeded to go through each of the 25 remaining counts (one having been dismissed), 23 of which were §288(a) lewd and lascivious acts on a child under 14 and two or which were §269(a)(1) Aggravated Sexual Assault or Rape of a child under 14 years of age. Then the jury was to be asked if there were multiple victims in the case with guilty verdicts rendered. This was so the One-Strike law would apply mandating a 15 years- to-life sentence.

Clearly I was facing some serious time in prison and after hearing Mr. Graham's closing argument I would have voted me guilty right then and there but I still had Ms. Hankel to get me back in the game.

FORTY-FOUR

I was a bit disappointed in Ms. Hankel for not objecting when Mr. Graham called my defense ridiculous and when he repeatedly argued his own bald-faced opinion that "Harris lied to you." Neither statement was in the record or inferable thus was not arguable. Regardless, it was now in her hands to provide my closing argument.

Ms. Hankel: In the United States we hold dear the principle that an individual cannot be deprived of life, liberty, or property without due process of law. That is, that in our system of government, safeguards are taken to protect those charged with crimes. People who are arrested are considered innocent unless proven guilty in a court of law. Is Mono County a different standard? It is the same standard as in all the rest of the United States an just because we live in a small town, doesn't mean that we do anything differently. And when I know about due process is – one of the things I know about due process is that " P-P-P-R-I *(clap, clap, clap clap)* S-S-S-O-N *(clap, clap, clap, clap, clap)* R-I-S-O-N, *prison, prison, we are going to send him to prison "in the middle of a law enforcement interview when you are trying to ascertain the truth, that is not due process. That is not due process.*

Instead, this case is about manipulation. It is about two girls who didn't want to be at home anymore. I don't know the reason why. I don't know if it was valid reason. I don't know. We have never heard from mom. I don't know. What I do know is the girls never, ever, ever, had a problem speaking their minds.

You saw these girls on the stand. Those girls never had a problem saying what is what. In a court of law, you saw the deference they gave this Court. From 2001 to 2006 Martha and Chelsea made repeated allegations to CPS. In Nevada County, El Dorado County, Placer County, Mono County, Inyo County.

What's odd about that? I didn't see any CPS worker telling you which of those allegations were substantiated and which were unfounded. No one has told you "Oh that allegation that Chelsea made back when she was nine, that was substantiated." Nobody told you that…

Did you hear that was substantiated? Nope. She stated that Marty Teichmann got mad and picked her up and threw her across the room. Did you hear that substantiated? Nope.

Ms. Hankel then went through all the numerous CPS contacts none of which were substantiated. Then she went through the litany of things Martha did and did not remember regarding those CPS contacts.

Ms. Hankel: The surprising lack of detail in this case is just shocking to me. You never heard anything at all about detail about any kind of allegations of sexual abuse. Not one. You never heard, you know, "When I was 12 and it was my birthday and I was sitting in my room with all my stuff, and all of a sudden I heard the door open and I knew it was him. And I was wearing a blue and green flowered shirt that my dad gave me. My dad who I just loved. And he gave it to me right before he died. Then Mike came in and pushed me and it ripped."

You never heard anything like that. Why is that? Why is it the only detail you heard was more than one time? "Yeah, he touched my breasts more than one time. And he touched my vagina more than one time."

"One time, or more than one time."

"More than one time."

What do we say about liars? It's not that they say the same thing over and over and over. It is the lack of specificity; it is the lack of detail. And it is the inconsistencies between one story and the next. And you know what, I think that everyone has heard this one; Oh what a tangled web we weave when first we practice to deceive. Because that is exactly what this case shows.

Let's talk about Raeanna Davenport. She went to the twin's house. And she went there for dinner. She went there for maybe a couple hours. She couldn't remember how long she was there. Remember, that was a long list of questions I asked her. She didn't really remember anything that they did that day, except that she did remember, before she came in and testified, she read that preliminary hearing transcript to kind of refresh her recollection about what she testified at the preliminary hearing…

Let's take a look at Officer Gordon's report. Officer Gordon went out to the house that day on 10/19/03 at approximately 21:35. He contacted Anna Brennan, the grandmother, who told him that her granddaughter came home from some friends' house and was acting strange. Anna said her granddaughter is usually active. However, she was quiet and subdued. Anna told him she asked her granddaughter what was wrong and her granddaughter said nothing.

Anna said her granddaughter went into the bathroom and took a bath which was normal at that time. Anna went into the bathroom and asked her granddaughter what was wrong again. The granddaughter again told her nothing was wrong. Anna said she picked up her granddaughter's panties and found what appeared to be blood in them. Remember when we asked Raeanna Davenport about that? She didn't remember anything about that. Anna asked her granddaughter her the blood got in her panties and Raeanna Davenport told her "Maybe I am starting my period." Anna told him that her granddaughter hadn't had any periods yet. She said she asked her granddaughter if Mike had done something to her. Anna told him that her granddaughter hesitated and then told her Mike had touched her private parts. Anna asked her what had happened and her granddaughter said she and Martha were lying on the bed, watching TV.

Mike came in and laid on the bed and started rubbing Martha's back. She said Mike reached over and touched her private parts and she said stop and he did. When we talked to Raeanna Davenport I said "Raeanna, was there any type of investigation?" And Raeanna said "Yeah, I thinka couple of days later they videotaped my statement." Where is that videotaped statement? How come you have never seen it? You saw Martha's videotaped statement. You saw Chelsea's videotaped statement. And then you saw two more supplemental videotaped statements. Where is Raeanna's videotaped statement?

Remember Frank Smith? Got on the stand and said "I started my investigation October 21st. I ended my investigation October 22nd."

So that is a couple days after October 19th. Maybe he's the one who took that videotaped statement. I don't know. All I knew is he stopped the investigation and never – he told you he never reinitiated it.

We don't have any report of any investigation saying what Raeanna Davenport – what really happened to her there. We don't have a medical report. We don't have a video. We don't have anything. All we know is the investigation was curtailed October 22nd, 2003, and then years later, when Martha and Chelsea make allegations against Mike Harris, the state thinks it's a pretty good time to revive Raeanna's allegations.

Why do you think they did that? Because Martha and Chelsea aren't credible, and they tried to find somebody they thought was a little more credible.

Do you remember when Mr. Graham was examining Raeanna Davenport and he said "As you testify today, do you have any doubt in your mind about what happened in October 2003 when Mr. Harris put his hand in your privates?" And Raeanna Davenport said "Yes." He had that read back to you.

Remember when Mr. Graham asked Raeanna Davenport if she had ever heard that Martha and Chelsea had made allegations against Mike Harris and she said yes? And he got a little excited there, and he said "When did that happen? When did you hear it? Was it within the next year? He said – he said

Question: Let's go with the year after Mike touched you, did you hear it from them during that time?

Answer: Yes.

Question: Who told you of the two girls, or both of them, that Mike was doing something like that?

Answer: I don't remember.

Question: I want to make this very clear. Are you positive that one of the twins, within a year after Mike touched you, that Mike was doing something sexual to the girls? Answer: I don't know who told me, but I found out somehow.

Question: Was it the first time you found out about any allegations of touching by Mike Harris on either of the two twins when this case started?

Answer: Yes, yes. It was when this case started.

Raeanna Davenport was a little kid back when she claimed that Mike Harris touched her. I don't think Raeanna Davenport was part of any plan or scheme to get Mike Harris in trouble. That is not the Defense's theory of this case. We don't think that Raeanna Davenport intentionally did anything whatsoever. We think she was simply mistaken or maybe her grandmother suggested it just like Todd Graham suggested to her, "Did you hear about it within a year?" And she just agreed "Yes." Because sometimes kids do that. And they don't really know how to articulate any differently…

It is true the State doesn't have to put on every single witness, but they should at least give you enough evidence so that they actually meet their burden of proof, which they haven't done in this case. As for Martha and Chelsea, they were clearly upset about their mom and about their dad's death. It was a recurring theme for them, as it should be. They were very sad about their dad's death. And they were already talking to their friends in 2007 about "How do I get out of my mom's house?" Amanda was writing Martha notes saying "I wish I knew somewhere you could go and stay to get away from your mom."

I didn't see any notes whatsoever, and there has never been any evidence whatsoever of a note about Mike Harris. Not one..

Both the girls told their friends they just wanted to be emancipated, just wanted to get out of their mom's house so bad.

Martha testified she told all kinds of her friends about the planned emancipation. She said she told Sara. She told Amanda. She told Jessikah. She told Annie Crane. Chelsea wrote it in a journal. Chelsea wrote a lot of things in her journal.

I didn't see a single journal entry from Chelsea Guthrie that is in evidence today where she talks about Mike Harris molesting her. I think that she claimed there were some pages that were missing from her journal, the journal that she gave to Martha for safekeeping. So I don't know why Martha would have removed any entries from Chelsea's journal. That just doesn't make sense.

Do you remember this journal entry from August 13, 2005? When she is talking about going to Ridgecrest, getting three shirts and Martha – "She's gets to go to LA for a week. It sucks that I can't go." This would have been after the Disneyland rape.

Why would she have written a journal entry saying that she doesn't get to go on the second trip to LA if she had been raped on the first trip to LA?

Ms. Hankel proceeded to remind the jurors of all of Chelsea's angry journal entries and none of them mentions me. Writing about her mom she wrote, "she just loves to try to control my research paper, and she is trying to tell me what has to be in it." Continuing on:

Ms. Hankel: Nothing in there about Mike Harris touching her breasts and her vagina…

Martha and Chelsea both talked to you about how they were sneaking out of the house. A little different testimony. One of the guys said, "Oh, they were sneaking out around 11:00 or 12:00 and staying out until 3:00 or 4:00 in the morning.

The other one didn't think it was that long. But they were both sneaking out of their mom's house because their mom said they couldn't date, but they were going to date anyway. And things had become different in their home.

It is clear that Chelsea was having a really hard time. It is clear she didn't want to be there anymore. It is clear that Chelsea had a plan. She talked about it with Martha. And I think in all fairness to Chelsea and Martha, I don't think they meant for it to go the way that it did. I think initially all they were trying to do was to get out of their mother's home. I think that's where they meant to take it.

You know why I think that? Because neither Martha nor Chelsea called CPS. Neither Martha nor Chelsea called the cops.

Now this is where I disagree with Ms. Hankel's plan defense and I am confused because she seems to say their intentions "escalated."

Ms. Hankel: Instead. what they did was they told their boyfriends Mike Harris is sexually abusing us. And you know what? Remember in November, November 3rd of 2006 remember Rose Douglas testified that she had two occasions to meet Martha and Chelsea Guthrie.

The first one was way back when Raeanna Davenport made her allegations against Mike Harris. Rose Douglas is the person who went out there and talked to Martha and Chelsea Guthrie about Raeanna Davenport. She said hey, she talked to them, wanted to find out what was going on in their lives, and they did not disclose a single thing to her. They didn't tell her Mike had done anything with Raeanna Davenport. They didn't tell her that Mike Harris had done anything with them either. And, in fact -- they kind of – they all went out there to make sure that Martha and Chelsea were okay. Because they had a concern for them. Completely an appropriate thing to do. Make sure they are all right, because the neighbor girl made an allegation against the guy they are living with. What was the result of that report? Rose Douglas said unfounded.

The second time she had occasion to meet Martha and Chelsea was in November. November 3rd of 2006. Just about six months or so before Chelsea ran away. That was the van incident when the kids said "Mike was yelling at us because he saw us talking to some boy."

And Mr. Harris testified "I came out to give them some lunch money. I saw them getting into a van. Their mother doesn't even let them date."

They called CPS and what did Rose Douglas say? I said "Didn't you tell them they just hadn't told you it was dangerous enough to keep them out of the house?" She said "No, I said they hadn't told me it was abuse."

So, the next time they made sure to use the right language. They made sure it was serious enough so they never had to go back to their mom's house…

Both Martha and Chelsea denied ever telling Leif and Tyler or Jordan. If these are true allegations then why wouldn't they say I told Tyler, I told Leif, I told Jordan? What is the big secret? Why wouldn't they admit that? Why, when law enforcement asked them who did you tell, why did they say "We didn't tell anyone, I only told my mom" … And remember Detective Rutkowski asked specifically, he said to Chelsea "Who did you tell?" And Chelsea said "I only told my sister and my mom. But Martha told all kids of people." Detective Rutkowski said "She did?" And Chelsea said "Yeah." And she looked over at Alex Ellis, who was sitting behind her and said – well she started laughing a little bit, and then she said "Well. But you can't contact any of them." Which I thought was kind of strange. Why would she be telling Detective Rutkowski that he couldn't contact the people they told or people Martha told? And she said, "We told all these people at the party." At the party.

Martha told people at the party, all kinds of people at the party about being molested by Mike Harris for five years? Use your common sense. Does that sound like someone who would have any kind of difficulty talking about anything that was happening to her? Does that sounds like a real allegation? Does that make sense to you? Does it make sense for either one of these girls?

They would have no problem saying everything they could possibly think of to say about their mom and even about their mom's former boyfriend. Think about him hitting them, hitting their mom. But they could never open up to their mom to say one thing about my client? Do you think the girl who screamed "This is fucking bullshit," in a court of law would have any problem whatsoever telling CPS any little thing that happened to her?

Do you think Martha, who was mouthing off to the DA, who threw the Exhibit back at him, do you think she had a problem?

Tyler said he knew good and well that Chelsea was going to run away to his house because they planned it. He said "Yeah, I told my dad. I told his girlfriend." They were waiting for Chelsea to run away to his house. Once she got there, he says "She was only here for like a half a day and then she called CPS." We know that isn't true. We know she was there for several days.

They were putting up missing children posters, Martha and her mom, looking for her. I think Tyler just didn't want to get in trouble. Neither did Kathleen Traynor. However, we know she was there for more than a day. If she had called CPS we would have all heard about it by now. Chelsea would have testified, "I called CPS." It didn't happen.

Martha and Chelsea were trying to manipulate law enforcement. They were trying to manipulate the DA. And I think they were very successful in doing that. They started out making their allegations of sexual abuse not because they picked up the phone and called CPS, but Martha and Chelsea testified you know how this first started? It started when Alex Ellis asked Chelsea "Is Mike Harris molesting you?" She suggested to Chelsea after Chelsea had run away and when she was worried about having to go back and live with her mom. And she said, "Yeah, yeah he is."

Then when Martha is taking Martha to her foster home, after Martha gets removed July 16, 2007, just a couple weeks after Chelsea she said, "Martha, Chelsea says that Mike has been molesting you and Chelsea. Is that true?"

She didn't say "Oh my God yes, he has been molesting us for five years." And she didn't burst into tears. She didn't do any of that... Let's talk about that Nevada County in Nevada City charge. Chelsea says that she was sitting in a chair with Martha. I don't know if they were each sitting in a different chair or sitting in the same chair. She says she was about nine. And she was trying to show you how little she was before, so maybe she was about this little. And she says that Mike called her over and had her place her hand on his penis while it went in and out of her mom.

Let's think about this for a minute. If she is about this little and she's next to a bed and she's supposed to be placing her hand on Mr. Harris' penis, remember how she said they were laying like, on their sides? Okay.

So, we know she wasn't putting her hand underneath Mr. Harris. She has to be reaching over Mr. Harris and she is about this little. She has to reach over his form. How is this physically possible? How does that really happen? I think it can happen in your imagination, but not in real life.

Remember what Martha said about the incident? Martha's story was completely different. In this incident she said, "My mom was giving Mike a blow job, and he made Chelsea put her hand on his penis while my mom gave him a blow job."

What a tangled web.

Let's talk about the rapes, the so-called rapes of Chelsea where Chelsea says she's in a motel at Disneyland, and there are two beds right next to each other. She says "Martha and I wanted to be in that bed together, but Mike wouldn't let us sleep together. Mike made me sleep with him. He came and pulled me out and put me into my bed. He held me down."

That is what she told Karen Smart. "He held me down and I fell asleep. Then I woke up again because he was taking off my clothes. And he was going to rape me."

And she described this horrifying scene, and it would have been a horrifying scene where she was being forcibly raped by Mike Harris while her twin sister was in the bed next to her. And she said Martha woke up and Martha started getting up and Mike said, "Martha, go back to sleep."

So Martha does. And remember when Martha goes to talk to Investigator Rutkowski in her interview, the videotaped interview, and he said to her "Have you ever had intercourse with Mike Harris?" And she says "Yes." And he says, "How about Chelsea? Has Chelsea ever had intercourse with Mike Harris?" And Martha says "I don't know about that." They hadn't gotten their stories straight enough yet.

Martha testified on the stand she had never seen Chelsea being raped by Mike Harris. She has never even seen that. And yet Chelsea described not one but two incidents of rape.

Chelsea described being raped in the Chalfant residence. She said while she was being raped by Mike Harris, Martha walked right in on them and looked at her and looked at Mike. They didn't say anything, and she walked out.

How is that possible if Martha says it never happened? Martha said, I have never seen anything like that." Why would their stories be so different? And how in the world can one twin be so forcibly raped at the age of 14 in the bed next to her sister and have the other twin wake up, see all that was happening. We didn't hear any testimony about this happening in concert, ever, just this one time. And Martha couldn't recall that? How is that possible?...

There were all kinds of contradictions between the girls' stories of where they were raped, how they were raped, how they were touched, all kinds of contradictions. At the prelim Martha said she had never given Martha a blow job. Her in court she said, "I remember it now." She never told Detective Rutkowski about that blow job, and you know, it was really not making sense whatsoever, was gibberish, when Chelsea described how Mike tried to force her to give him a blow job. And the way she described it, he had to pry her jaw open, and then try to place his penis in her mouth. He just pried it open.

I don't think any guy was going to try to put his penis in someone's mouth that he had to pry open.

Martha testified at the preliminary hearing that she was only touched on the couch in the living room. She said it always happened at night. And she said something interesting, that she and Chelsea slept on the long couch and Chelsea would be at the other end of the couch.

She testified differently. She said no, no, now it happened in his bedroom and on the couch. She doesn't remember Chelsea being there at all…

In the interview Martha tells Rutkowski not that she tried to tell her mom one time, but that she tried to tell her mom more than one time. She tried to tell her mom after she was raped in Los Angeles. But she only said that one time. She only said that in the interview with Rutkowski. Every other time she has said she has only told her mother one time because it is really hard to keep your story straight.

She also testified that beginning at age 10 all the way up until she is removed from the home in 2007, she was being molested by my client. If that is true, then why in the world would they not have conducted an immediate medical exam of the girls? Why would they wait until February of 2008?

Dr. Gabaeff testified that neither Martha nor Chelsea were sexually molested. And he said, "You know how I can tell that? I can tell because of the hymen. The copious amounts of hymen…"

We know one thing. We know that these allegations in a 25 count information, also called a complaint sometimes, they were never, ever, ever investigated by anyone with the exception of Raeanna Davenport. They investigated hers, and they stopped after a few days.

With Martha and Chelsea, what did we find out? Investigator Rutkowski was the lead investigator, and he never investigated at all. When I asked him, when you are trying to get to the truth of this, did you ask their friends? Did you go out and talk to their teacher? What about their neighbors? What about their history? He didn't do any of that. He said this was just an interview. It was just an interview? If it was just an interview then who was the investigator? You know what Karen Smart said. "Not my job. I just did a partial interview. I didn't investigate. It was investigator Rutkowski's case."

What did Alex Ellis tell you? Other than the fact we know she is very biased and wants the best for the girls, I can't say I blame her for that, but who wants the best for my client? Where is the checks and balance? How come nobody is there protecting the rights of my client? Why is it just, you know, these girls have said it, and therefore, it is true and we won't investigate any of it?... Karen Smart did tell you she gets to lie. She didn't investigate anything. She put it all on Rutkowski's plate. Alex Ellis told you we don't investigate it because it is out of the home; so, we just give it to the Mono County Sheriffs. Marlo Preis, she was in charge of that other Suspected Child Abuse Report, the one that she made after Martha Guthrie accused Michelle Jackson of choking her. Was that investigated? No. Why not? Is it because it was yet another false allegation? She gave it to Rutkowski…

Next, Ms. Hankel moved into the initial foster care situation for Martha with the Jackson family. Referring to Trish Jackson's testimony that they didn't have any kind of license, but they wanted to do the right thing, and took Martha into foster care.

Ms. Hankel: Do you remember that she said that, you know, she felt sorry for her, and she wanted to believe in her. But she said, "I had problems with her lying." And she said, you know, she was at that interview to Detective Rutkowski. And she said, "There was something about that that didn't hit me right." And I said, "Well what was it?" She said, "It was when she said that she told her mom," and she said "But then she was talking about her mom being involved in the whole thing and how Mike and her mom would force them to watch sex. So why would she have to tell her mom about it? She was a perpetrator. That didn't make any sense to me."...

How did the girls manipulate? Because it was so easy. All they had to do was say "He put his wee-wee in me," and the DA just bought it. Never any detail. Nothing. Inconsistent stories left and right. They never told their friends.

And why is it that the DA had to make liars out of his own witnesses? He tried to call people to say I told this friend and that friend. The girls said themselves, they never told anyone.

This is the true Martha and Chelsea Guthrie, and these are the same girls you saw on the stand having hissy fits as soon as someone dared to challenge them or ask about their statements.

Ms. Hankel then went into the twins foster placements, something like 20 for Chelsea. Ms. Hankel then delved into the whole manipulation of Alex Ellis by Martha and Chelsea. Chelsea faking an overdose to get placed back with Martha. Martha breaking a rule and poof! She's out of the Lindsay's home. Alex Ellis was the girls Mr. Wizard who could be summoned at a moments notice to save the day. The girls were sneaking out; spending the night with boys unchaperoned, getting drunk, and smoking pot. These are things their mom wouldn't let them do. Mom made them work and expected certain behavior in order for them to curry favor with her.

Ms. Hankel: There is absolutely no case here. Certainly not beyond reasonable doubt. You must have an abiding conviction, proof that leaves you with an abiding conviction that the changes are true.

How reasonable is the testimony? Does the evidence prove or disprove any fact about which the witness testified? Did the witness admit to being untruthful?

The DA had no case, but he thought he could convince you all that he had a case if he could just show you in the computer evidence, the stuff on my client's computer...

The computer evidence was – was this the worst chain of custody in the western world? The DA asked you several times not to hold it against him if the actions of the police were not like CSI.

Remember he kept saying that over and over and over during voir dire. But just because we live in Mono County doesn't mean we should expect a lesser standard in our law enforcement...

We haven't heard any testimony from the first person who found those hard drives. You didn't hear from him at all. I'm assuming that one of those officers is the one who seized the hard drives. All we know is that Rutkowski comes and collects the evidence, and Rutkowski says he has been an investigator for about 7 years and in the department for over 32 years, briefly on the S.W.A.T. team, executed several dozen search warrants as an investigator, even going to specific search warrant schools…

He says he was only there for the second half of the search. Remember, he comes in and says, "I seized all the items once I arrived that had been located prior to my arrival, and I compiled them all on the defendant's table. I took all the evidence from the trailer." And then he said he compiled two evidence lists. The he says he took it all to the Crowley Lake substation.

He said someone had recorded a serial number for the laptop before he got there. He wrote the serial number on the evidence bag when he packaged the computer. He agreed that it was a pretty important thing that the evidence actually seized during an investigation be the evidence that is later adduced at trial.

Rutkowski never wrote down the serial numbers for the evidence in the evidence bag. We don't know why. But he never did. He wrote down the number for the SONY laptop on the bag. And if you listen to his testimony he specifically told you he was the officer who inventoried that evidence. But then, later on, he talked about an inventory sheet by someone else, someone who had never been on the inventory sheet who said they wrote an inventory sheet. It was only Detective Rutkowski.

Exhibit 23 notes that he seized a bag of photo negatives, a SONY laptop computer, video tapes, eleven SONY Mini DV tapes and 8 VHS tapes in addition to those two hard drives. Not one single piece of evidence that he seized, anything, no child porn, no child erotica, nothing at all. None of the video tapes, none of the other computers, none of the other hard drives, nothing…

Who's the guy who wrote the hard drive numbers on the evidence bag? Brian Wentzel. You never saw him. He's the guy who wrote the numbers on the bag.

How come he didn't come in and testify?...

Why is it never did they record a serial number, oh, until we had that Exhibit 100A where Mr. Wall told you "I took the evidence. We went right to my office. I looked at the hard drives. I wrote it all down on the sheet, and then we booked it into evidence." And he didn't do that. The date on that report is 9/27/07. The date he wrote on the bag that he put into evidence is 9/26/07. It was generated at a later date.

How do we know that? Because none of the EnCase stuff, none of the reports had an accurate serial number. Why would his worksheet be the only place that mentions a serial number? You know why? Because the manufacture date of that hard drive is May 12, 1999. It is after that computer was first turned on.

And remember before we know that, we didn't find out until in the midst of trial. Where is it? There it is. When he first testified, know what he told you? He said – I asked him "How can you age that hard drive?"

He said "There should be a report right there – I made an exhibit right in my report, the operating system report." It says right on it when Windows would have been installed, and Windows was installed on the computer January 7th and January 8th of 1999. January 7. January 8.

He wanted to say that's probably just because the BIOS clock wasn't there yet. My client testified "I got the computer in March. I installed Netscape March 6, 1999. Couldn't possibly be the same drive."

He said "You know, it had a black label." You know what really makes you know my client is telling the truth? He knows that is not the same hard drive. We know it is manufactured way after he even actually got the computer. And he never, ever, ever told you, "I'm not responsible for most of the stuff on the hard drive." He looked you in the eye and said "A lot of that stuff is mine."

He could have disavowed everything, because you know what? It is not the same hard drive. Did he? Absolutely not. He said "You know what I was doing? I was doing bits and pieces of research."

Mr. Graham says there's nothing about the Predator on that. That is not what my client said. My client said the Predator was in the news. And Mr. Wall, who is the computer expert, he never got on the stand and is "No, it wasn't."

We all know it was in the news. We all know people were talking about entrapment issues. Wouldn't that have caught your eye if you had been falsely accused of child molestations? You bet it would. He never got on the stand and said "I was worried it might happen again." What he said was "You know what I thought was interesting is if you put the word preteen into a search, it would bring up all these different sites. Put if you put in prepubescent, it really wouldn't. You can see the difference, subtle differences with a dash over here, a comma over there.

Remember what Mr. Albee said "If he had a sexual interest in little girls then why isn't he looking at any of it." Why would he have hundreds and hundreds of newsgroups without even looking through them or accessing them or reading them?

Even Mr. Wall said "I only saw a couple messages that had been accessed." I didn't make any sense. And he said "I know that the people from Perverted Justice were trying to entrap people. That was fascinating to me too. And one thing led to another. And sometimes I got on a bit of a tangent."

If he wanted to lie to you, he would have said "You know what, it's not my hard drive." That is not what he said to you.

With that Judge DeVore called a halt to the days activities. I was pensive. The jury looked tired and the thought of one more day in jail was upsetting to me. I was innocent, clearly. But why was it so hard to prove. Why did I have to prove my innocence at all, I was clearly framed. Ms. Hankel was missing the point in some areas and doing a fine job in others. I thought about a lot of things on the way back to jail.

FORTY-FIVE

The next day was December 10th, 2009, day 16 of my trial. It was the day I could be set free and I was excited. I awoke fresh and eager to hit the road for what could hopefully be the last time. I just knew the jury was going to find me not guilty right away. I was certain they would see through all the lies and contradictions. Ms. Hankel began to finish up her closing argument by talking about reasonable doubt as a burden of proof in a criminal trail. It is a tougher standard then that in a civil trial which is the preponderance of the evidence standard.

Ms. Hankel: Proof beyond a reasonable doubt is a significantly higher burden, an abiding conviction based upon proof beyond a reasonable doubt. It is the highest left of certainty recognized in the law.

So what evidence can you rely upon to form such an abiding conviction? Can you rely upon the testimony of Raeanna Davenport who said she was wearing short shorts and that Michael Harris put his hand in the front of her shorts up the leg? When Martha Guthrie said, no, no, no. She was wearing long jean pants and Mike Harris put his hand down her pants.

Can you rely on Raeanna Davenport when Martha and Chelsea said nothing happened back in 2003? Remember when she was asked by Mr. Graham,

When you spoke with my investigator and you said you didn't remember, were you saying that because you actually don't remember or were you saying that because of another reason?

And Raeanna Davenport said "I was saying that because I actually didn't remember."

Question: Now as you sit there today, has there been anything that has helped you remember?

Answer: No.

In fact, when the DA asked her did you feel the skin of his finger touch the skin of your vagina? She answered "I don't remember." Can you rely on the testimony of Nurse Boyle, the person who conducted the exams of Martha and Chelsea, who said the exams were abnormal and whose supervisor, a medical doctor, wasn't here to confirm her findings, who yesterday said she was going to correct Dr. Gabaeff. She was going to school him on anatomy.

How come she only had that one picture that was missing the hymen on the right side and Dr. Gabaeff showed you all those picture? Why didn't she go through the pictures and quarrel with him about what it looks like when someone has been sexually molested? Why didn't she do that?...

Can you rely on the statements of Martha and Chelsea given to law enforcement? Well, do you remember what Dr. Coleman said about what kind of an interview elicits truthful information, a lack – you have to watch to see if there is a lack of investigatory independence. Is there a pursuit by the investigator of a preconceived notice?...

Can you rely on the statements of Martha and Chelsea in this courtroom who said they were abused from 2002 to 2007? According to the DA, they are tough, independent girls – nobody is going to put words in their mouths – who testified they fought back every single time they were molested. They kicked. They screamed. They hit. Chelsea talked about kicking Mike Harris in the stomach. If they are fighting so much day after day after day after day, then why when they are talking to the counselor, Aaron Storey, aren't they telling him about it? How come when they are talking to their counselor Vicka Stout, they aren't telling her about it? Does that make any sense whatsoever?...

And what about the emails? Those emails that Chelsea and her friends got together and they were writing to Mike Harris accusing him of being a child molester. The emails that they turned over to Detective Rutkowski? Did you rely on the testimony of a witness who was asked why she and her friends wrote emails to go to Mike and to responding. And the answer was "Because I wanted to get him in trouble."... Why did the girls say that they had only been molested in the Bishop trailer, in the Chalfant trailer, their home, and in LA? Why in the world if Mike Harris had such a sexual interest in little girls, why wouldn't he be groping them in the car? Why wouldn't he take them over to Pleasant Valley Dam, find a place back there or anywhere else. He must know a million places he could take them where there is nobody around. How come he didn't take them there?

Is there a reasonable doubt in this case?

Ms. Hankel then went through 50 reasonable doubts and I will present a few of them here.

Ms. Hankel: Reasonable doubt #1: Would Martha and Chelsea make allegation after allegation against their mom and her former boyfriend Marth Teichmann in Nevada City when they were nine and not be able to make a sexual abuse allegation against Mike Harris?

Reasonable doubt #3: Wouldn't Martha and Chelsea have told CPS about Mike abusing Raeanna Davenport in 2003?

Reasonable doubt #4: Why didn't Martha and Chelsea tell Alex Ellis they were being abused in January 2005 after the first trip to Disneyland when Chelsea claimed she was abused?

Reasonable doubt #5: Why didn't Martha and Chelsea tell Rose Douglas they were being sexually abused in November 2006 when they were 14 years old?

Reasonable doubt #8: Why does Martha change her story about giving Mike a blow job?

Reasonable doubt #9: How come Martha doesn't know that Chelsea was forcibly raped in front of her at the motel in Disneyland?

Reasonable doubt #10: How come Martha doesn't know that Chelsea was raped in front of her in the Chalfant trailer?

Reasonable doubt #11: How come Chelsea says that Mike Harris put her hand on his penis when he was having intercourse with her mom, but Martha says "No, he did it while her mom was giving him a blow job?"

Reasonable doubt #15: How could the girls have abundant hymens when Mike Harris had repeatedly tried to forcibly force his penis in them every day?

Reasonable doubt #16: How come the twins testified that Alex Ellis suggested to them each before they had ever discussed that Mike Harris had sexually abused them?

Reasonable doubt #21: How come Chelsea wrote in her journal that it sucked she couldn't go back to LA on that second trip, the one after she had been raped at Disneyland?

Reasonable doubt #22: How come the only specificity in this case came from a 17 ½ year old who can tell you in vivid detail about the bucket incident can't come up with any details about years and years of sexual abuse, not even one time, much less that more than one time.

Reasonable doubt #23: How come Martha and Chelsa didn't disclose in 2003 that Raeanna Davenport had been molested right in front of them? Didn't they care about their friend?

Reasonable doubt #30: How come we didn't get to see the video of Raeanna Davenport's statement?

Reasonable doubt #33: How can you be sure of the integrity of the hard drive manufactured 5 months after the operating system was installed?

Reasonable doubt #36: How come Mr. Wall had to make his exhibits on his own computer for the visited URLs? Why couldn't he just find them in the computer cache?

Reasonable doubt #40: How come the twins said they never told anybody else about the abuse?

Reasonable doubt #45: Why did Leif Medrud agree with my investigator that they told him in the summer of 2007? Remember how he said that Martha's disclosures to him were a couple weeks apart?

Reasonable doubt #48: When isn't there any DNA evidence from that couch at Mike's dad's house

So are we ridiculous when we say that the girls made these claims to get out of the house, maybe to get revenge against their mom? In some other case maybe, that would be a ridiculous argument. Not in this case.

The girls said "Why would I put myself through all this pain and all this stuff I have to go through just to get him in jail and get back at my mom"

Why indeed…

Reasonable doubt is hard to define. I can tell you what it isn't. If you think Mike Harris was proven not guilty, that is an easy one. He is not guilty. If you think it is highly unlikely that he is guilty, that is not guilty. If you think it is less than likely he is guilty, that is not guilty. If you think it is possible that he is not guilty, that is he is not guilty. If you think he may not be guilty, that is not guilty. If you think he may not be guilty, that is not guilty. If you think "I don't really know if he is guilty or not, that is not guilty.

If you think "Perhaps he's guilty," that is not guilty. If you think, "I suspect that he might be guilty," that is not guilty. If you think, "I think he is possibly guilty," that's not guilty. If you think, "He's probably guilty," that's not guilty. Guilt is likely, that is not beyond a reasonable doubt. Guilt is highly likely. We are still not there. It has to be guilt beyond a reasonable doubt, an abiding conviction. Thank you.

After this a break was taken and the jury was offered donuts and pasteries and coffee. Their work was about to commence. First though would be Mr. Graham's final argument, or closing argument. Then would be the jury instructions. I was on edge. After the quick break, we were all back in position.

The Court: Mr. Graham, you can take your final closing.

Mr. Graham: Thank you, Judge. Given that the People have the burden of proof in the case, I get to make a final summation to you. And I know maybe we all smell a dead horse in the room. Maybe it has been beaten down a little more than it neeed to. We just need to go over a couple points, and I am not going to be long.

Ms. Hankel mentioned that Dr. Gabaeff was a director with nurses working under him. If you recall, Mr. Albee was a supervising detective, yet he had done no analysis of the hard drive at all as a cop. Just because you are a supervisor of somebody doesn't mean you are in there doing the work that you are actually supervising. Ms. Hankel has stated certain quotes to you about certain witnesses in this case. The record is the evidence. If you have a question regarding what a witness says, you can ask to read back what that witness testified to…

Ms. Hankel mentioned is it believable that Mike would kill them if they told? Well, the defendant threatened to kill Kathy Shultz, a prior girlfriend numerous times. Again, that evidence was not challenged as far as the type of thing he would do; threaten to kill you if you call the police…

And just because Ms. Hankel calls something reasonable doubt doubt doesn't make it actually reasonable doubt…

You can look at a fact or a piece of evidence in the full context of the case. Okay. I can look at it and determine if it is reasonable doubt or not or is it an unreasonable interpretation of the evidence by the defense. You can look at things in context. You can use your common sense when you evaluate the evidence.

Let's talk about reasonable doubt. Beyond a reasonable doubt is a great standard, a great standard…

Definition is: Proof beyond a reasonable doubt is a proof that leaves you with an abiding conviction that the charge is true. The evidence need not eliminate all possible doubt, because everything in life is open to some possible or imaginary doubt…

There are inconsistencies in the twins' statements. Yes. Expectedly, there are, but that is understandable. You'll be instructed that you shouldn't automatically reject inconsistent testimony. The automatic rejection rule. There is a rule that counters that. You can look at the entire testimony, all of the evidence and consider whether there is something important you should consider important or not. Okay.

And in sexual assault cases, as we've learned, okay, it is reasonable to see inconsistencies in versions of long time sexual assault victims. It is reasonable to see that. Coleman agreed with that.

The twins are lying because there was little detail in the disclosures. That is wrong. That is a wrong statement of the evidence…

There is a question: If they are lying, wouldn't it have been easier to say he raped them once? Wouldn't that be an easier way to keep it all together? Think about that…

Why develop this year long plan or this years long history of sexual abuse. That doesn't sound like a plan at all. That sounds like two girls who now realize "Hey, we are out of the house. I think we can disclose."

Chelsea wanted to go to LA even after the abuse. Well, we learned from Ms. McLennan it is not unusual for sexual assault victims to behave like that…

The girls are from a rural area. They don't have a lot of access. That was a big deal for them… Going to LA. Can you blame them? Now…

[regarding the July 16, 2007 letter from Martha to Kerri]

It was a letter right before the counseling session, first counseling. It was a letter written after the Ellis disclosure, but just before the meeting with the counselor. Question: If Martha is caught up in this scheme in foster care, why is she writing this letter? "Mom, I'm sorry." Is it a beg me to come back letter? Why is she writing this letter? She wants to be back with mom.

Conclusion, Martha was deeply conflicted about running away. Making the sexual assault allegations would close off her ability to be with her mom. Do you see the conflict there in the language of that letter, okay, versus disclosing sexual assault allegations against her mom's boyfriend?

It's a conflict of interest.

The letter strongly conflicts with the defense's theory of the case about a plan to be removed from the home. It cuts right to the heart of that idea.

It is imperative to mention here that the letter was written on 7/16/07 and given to Kerri that same day by Martha before Ms. Ellis came and removed her from the home. The letter was a later given to Detective Rutkowski on 9/13/07 by Kerri. The interesting part of this is that Mr. Graham's insinuations to the jury without mentioning that Kerri could not have received a letter from Martha while in foster care without a court order.

Mr. Graham: Here is a question regarding the medical evidence. It was determined in early 2008 by Boyle that the twins had deep clefts in their hymens by deep penetration of the penis. Do you think the girls knew the information when they were telling everyone in July and August of '07, and they hadn't seen the results of the medical exam. They hadn't heard Cathy Boyle's opinion yet. Did the twins manipulate the medical evidence?

As far as the computer evidence, Mr. Harris said he bought the computer in March of 1999 from a client. Wouldn't you expect documentation about that or the client testifying about the transaction? The defense has the same ability to call witnesses as the People. Wouldn't you expect to see the witness here?

The defendant said that "Drive No. 1" is not my hard drive. Let's think this through.

To switch – there has to be some kind of drive switch here that occurred with Wall? That makes no sense. Did Wall take an image from the drive from the residence, insert porn in some temp file image and discard the original drive and then replace it? He would have to mark No. 1 on the new drive and write its serial number on his report on 9/27/07 and then let his fraud stand for years and even under oath. That is a lot – that is a big story. Maybe it is a fun piece of fiction. But that's not reasonable to believe.

Okay. And let's look at Mr. Albee. I would expect to see a lot more. This is not a direct quote. It is the essence of what he testified to. "I would expect to see a lot more bad stuff on this drive if he had a sexual interest in young girls." Well, it is clear from the key logger that you don't need to save the bad stuff. You can go to it immediately, view it, and get whatever kicks you need and move on.

Remember regarding the hard drive No. 1 the defendant corroborates Mr. Wall. The defendant's drive was a crashed hard drive. Per Wall, this meant that the items that were "saved in the temp files given the crash." The material seen in essentially a snapshot in time of the defendant's use of that drive during the spring and early summer of 2006. The hard drive had not crashed. Thee material would have been written over.

Now I am going to finally say something and you are probably happy as hell to hear me say "finally." I am too. Think how unreasonable the defense case is. Martha lied to everyone and you. Chelsea lied to everyone and you. Raeanna Davenport lied to everyone and you. Martha, Chelsea and Raeanna Davenport faked all of their emotions during all their disclosures to all the different people. Came up tears and hesitancy and the fear and the shame. That was all a big manufacture.

Boyle doesn't know what she is talking about. And all those website searches and newsgroups were really research by the defendant. Think how unreasonable the defense's position is. The defense case is not reasonable and you can reject it. Adopt the reasonable and find the defendant guilty of all 25 counts.

And that was it. After two years of waiting, the case was in. I was way on edge. I was way mad that Ms. Hankel had not addressed a couple of issues such as Kathy Shultz' testimony about me threatening her. It was never clear to me what I was doing that she shouldn't tell the police about in the first place. Also missing what Ms. Hankel's argument about the statement by Mr. Graham that the hard drive was crashed and the files being created because it crashed. There was no mention that Mr. Wall had any trouble booting up the EnCase image with VMWare.

I had many doubts about my case but I was determined to prove my innocence. It was out of my hands though and that lack of control over one's destiny was frustrating. Mr. Graham had relied on a spiffy Power Point presentation with a bulleted item discussion of reasonable and reasonableness. Ms. Hankel in her final argument failed to offer a cogent tit-for-tat response to Mr. Graham's arguments and she failed to utilize display technology to emphasize her arguments and show a timeline in an organized way.

Ms. Hankel had offers to help her create a Power Point presentation but she declined due to lack of time. She was in essence a one woman show. She did not have a strategic or tactical reason not to use technology to emphasize her thesis. I asked Ms. Hankel throughout the case to consider the facts I outlined and to argue them with logic and verve. Ultimately Ms. Hankel made all the tactical and strategic decisions regardless of my desires.

Ms. Hankel did not provide a coherent and cohesive strategy from the start as I have already mentioned at length. Perhaps too much length, but alas I specifically asked her to outline her thesis in detail, provide numerous examples of the thesis in support, and to argue it using those examples in a comprehensive and through way. Ms. Hankel failed to do so.

Important in my mind was Ms. Hankel's refusal to utilize a timeline to show the many contradictions and outright lies told in court and elsewhere. A timeline is almost always used in court unless there are no dates of importance to reference, I thought the timeline of disclosures was paramount to a detailed presentation. The use of a timeline in my case would have been standard practice for an attorney adhering to prevailing professional norms.

In a credibility battle the who said what to whom, when test is an imperative to credibility evaluation. Ms. Hankel's lack of cohesiveness at trial was brought to the fore in argument. Ms. Hankel wanted to argue reasonable doubt but failed to respond to Mr. Graham's reasonableness challenge, "What is reasonable?" I wanted Ms. Hankel to argue that it was unreasonable to believe that all the girls friends kept their sexual abuse secret for years until their friends were forced to reveal their knowledge in court. I wanted Ms. Hankel to argue that it was unreasonable to believe that Martha and Chelsea told their mother that they were being molested after the Raeanna allegation and yet Kerri did nothing. Then Martha comes back from LA and supposedly tells her mom she was raped in LA and Kerri does nothing. Then later still, Kerri forces the girls to go on another trip to Disneyland according to the interviews and testimonies. Once at Disneyland, Chelsea says she was raped right in front of Martha yet Martha never mentions it to anyone at any time, including to Kerri.

Ms. Hankel also let me down by relying on the "plan" defense to avoid confronting witnesses who were lying to help the girls and then trying to use a strategy that suggestibility and leading questions caused in escalation in the girls' allegations. Ms. Hankel failed to highlight the actual leading questions which in sequence led to the escalation of disclosures.

Mr. Graham had argued "For what purpose would the girls make this up?" Ms. Hankel had no response even though the evidence of rewards was abundant. Ms. Hankel was so enamored of the "plan" defense she failed to argue the "Oh those boys don't know anything" statement by Chelsea. Also, Martha's statement that she "didn't plan any of this" and that she never told any of her friends until after.

This omission by Ms. Hankel combined with her unwillingness to show after the contradictions in a timeline as well as her failure to argue any alibi defense effectively denied me a potentially meritorious defense.

For example, at no time in the first half of 2007 did I stay at the Chelfant trailer. I had extremely limited contact with Martha and Chelsea. In fact, the only time I saw them was when Kerri and I took the girls skiing. Nevertheless, during Mr. Graham's final closing, the summation, Mr. Hankel failed to object to his act of prosecutorial misconduct when he stated facts not on the record. Specifically, Mr. Graham stated that I had "saved newsgroups" which was a fact not in the record. Ms. Wall had, in fact, testified that I saved no newsgroups or images. Mr. Graham went one step further when he argued that I could not delete the bad stuff from item No. 1 or I would have done so because the hard drive had crashed. Even if I had deleted it, it would still be in unallocated space. But beside that point, Mr. Graham's argument was contradicted by his own expert who said he hooked up the hard drive and accessed it normally. I am not sure how this was possible but the testimony is there.

Much more disturbing than Mr. Graham's misconduct was the fact that Kerri wasn't called to the stand by either side even though she waited in the lobby each and every day of the trial waiting to be called to testify. Why was Ms. Hankel blaming the State when she could have called Kerri herself?

I called the whole process a witch hunt and so did Kerri. I was being railroaded because people didn't like me, not because I was a child molester. Ms. Hankel ultimately failed to argue the very positions she advocated in all the pretrial proceedings for discovery of the juvenile records. Ms. Hankel let me down.

FORTY-SIX

The only thing left were the jury instructions. The attorneys and Judge DeVore had crafted acceptable instructions for the most part and Judge DeVore got right to it.

The Court: Ladies and Gentlemen of the jury, this is the point in time that I am going too instruct you on all of the law that applies to this case…

It is your job and your job alone to decide what the facts are. It is up you up to all of you, those of you who are deliberating as a jury, and you alone, to decide what happened based only on the evidence that has been presented to you in this trial

Judge Devore continued on discussing bias and evidence and the like much to lengthy for my purposes here. I will however include a couple of the basic instructions he gave for clarity's sake.

The Court: The fact that the criminal charge or charges have been filed against the defendant is not evidence that the charge or any of them are true. You must not be biased against the defendant because he has been arrested, charged with the crime, crimes, or brought to trial.

A defendant in a criminal trial is presumed to be innocent. This presumption requires that the People prove the defendant guilty beyond a reasonable doubt…

Nothing that the attorneys say is evidence. In their opening statements and closing arguments the attorneys discuss their cases, but their remarks are not evidence. Their questions are not evidence. Only the witness' answers are evidence. The attorney's questions are significant only if they helped you to understand the witness' answers. Do not assume that something is true just because one of the attorneys asked the question that suggested it was true.

Facts may be proved by direct or circumstantial evidence or by a combination of both. Direct evidence can be proven a fact by itself. For example, if a witness testifies, he saw it raining outside before he came into the courthouse, that testimony is direct evidence that it is raining outside. Circumstantial evidence may also be called indirect evidence. Circumstantial evidence does not directly prove the fact to be decided but it is evidence of another fact or group of facts from which you may logically and reasonably conclude the truth of the fact in question. For example, if a witness testifies that he saw someone come inside wearing a raincoat covered with drops of water, that testimony is circumstantial evidence because it may support his conclusion that it was raining outside.

While I liked this analogy, I was left wondering what if the guy with the raincoat walked through some sprinklers. You never can tell when making assumptions.

The Court: Both direct and circumstantial evidence are acceptable types of evidence to prove or disprove the elements of a charge include intent and mental state and acts necessary to a conviction, and neither is necessarily more reliable than the other. Neither is entitled to any greater weight than the other. You must decide whether a fact in issue has been proved based on all the evidence…

The testimony of only one witness can prove any fact. Conviction of a sexual assault crime may be based on the testimony of a complaining witness alone. Before you conclude that the testimony of one witness proves a fact, you should carefully review all the evidence…

You've heard testimony from Ms. Cathy McLennan and Dr. Lee Coleman regarding Child Sexual Abuse Accommodation Syndrome. Their testimony about Child Sexual Abuse Accommodation Syndrome is not evidence that the defendant committed any of the acts charged against him. You may consider this evidence only in deciding whether or not Martha Guthrie and Chelse Guthrie's conduct was not inconsistent with the conduct on someone who has been molested, and in evaluating the believability of their testimony…

The defendant is charged in count 1 through count 21, 24, and 25 with committing lewd or lascivious acts on a child under 14…

To prove the defendant is guilty of such crime, the People must prove that: The defendant willfully touched any part of a child's body, either on the bare shin or through the clothing, or the defendant committed the act with the intent of arousing, appealing to, or gratifying the lust, passions, or sexual desires of himself or the child and the child was under the age of 14 years at the time of the act.

The touching need not be done in a lewd or sexual manner…

The defendant is charged in count 22 and 23 with forcible rape of a female who is under 14 years of age and who is at least 7 years younger than the perpetrator. To prove the defendant guilty of the crime, the People must prove that the defendant committed the forcible rape of a female, and when the defendant acted, the female was under 14 years of age and at least 7 years younger than the defendant…

Evidence was presented that defendant, after Martha and Chelsea's 14th birthday, engaged in the crimes of forcible rape of a female on Chelsea Guthrie and engaged in the crime of lewd and lascivious act on a child 14 o 15 years old who was at least 10 years younger than the perpetrator on Martha Guthrie.

None of these crimes were charged in this case. You may consider this evidence on the above named uncharged offense/crimes that occurred after Martha and Chelsea Guthrie turned 14 years old, only if the People have proved by a preponderance of evidence that the defendant in fact engaged in such uncharged crimes…

Proof by a preponderance of evidence is a different standard or burden of proof beyond a reasonable doubt. A fact is proved by a preponderance of the evidence if you conclude that it is more likely than not that the fact is true. If the People have not met this burden, you must disregard this evidence entirely.

If you decide the defendant engaged in such above named crimes that occurred after Martha and Chelsea Guthrie turned 14 years old, you may but are not required to conclude from that evidence that the defendant was disposed or inclined to commit sexual offenses, and based on the decision, also conclude that the defendant was likely to commit and did commit the offense charged in this case on counts 1 though and including count 25.

If you conclude that the defendant engaged in such above named uncharged crimes, that conclusion is only one factor to consider along with all the other evidence. It is not sufficient by itself to prove that the defendant is guilty of the charged offenses.

The People must still prove each charge and allegation of the Complaint beyond a reasonable doubt…

You are not to take anything I said or did during the trial as an indication of what I think about the evidence on about what the verdict should be. You are the sole judges of the evidence and the believability of witnesses. And it is up to you to decide the issues in this case…

You must reach your verdict without consideration of the punishment.

And with that finished, Judge DeVore explained the verdict forms, the protocol for asking for further information such as readbacks, than be excused the alternate jurors and swore in the bailiff to take charge of the jury. The jury then went in to deliberate.

I won't kid around. I was scared. Ms. Hankel had made an effort, but I wasn't sure it was a winning effort. I was placed in my little room to wait it out. The judge was nice enough to permit me a chair, a heater, and his own copy of that day's LA Times. I took that as a positive sign that maybe things were going my way.

During the afternoon of that cold December 10th,the jury sent a question to the judge. The question was: Would like that portion of testimony on morning of November 2nd by Martha Guthrie where she said 'for the most part' in response to a question from Mr. Graham 'Are you telling the truth' or 'Do you clearly remember?'" The record was located and read. The jury then left the courtroom and continued their deliberations. The jury met for a couple more hours sent another questions as to whether they could have a transcript of Martha and Chelsea's testimony. The judge said no because daily transcripts had not been prepared. The jury then called it a day with no further questions and no verdicts. I was kind of hopeful that the jury was on the right track seeing how they had asked about Martha saying she couldn't remember. How do you remember a lie? I took another long ride home to my cell and slept fitfully with the TV on all night as my companion in turmoil.

The next day, Friday December 11, 2009 started out dreary and cold with fresh snow on the ground. I was hoping we would go faster than the 35-mph speed limit during chain controls so I could get to court early and talk to Ms. Hankel. She was not there as I arrived but at least I had a chair and a heater.

First thing that morning the jury sent another question in which they asked for clarification on the courts referred to as the "last time" counts. Can an implied "more than one time' without any specifics be accepted as proof beyond a reasonable doubt. The court's response was you must decide what happened, based only on the evidence that has been presented to you in this trial. Counsel concurred that that was an appropriate response and so the message was sent to the jury.

One hour later two requests were sent to Judge DeVore by the jury foreperson, the court clerk juror #12. The first of two delt with the jury wanting to use a DVD player to watch the physical exams. The judge said the only way they were going to be able to do that would be to bring them into the courtroom and run it on the screen as it was during the evidentiary phase. The problem as I saw it was that the exam video has never been played in court.

The other inquiry read "Read back of testimony by Martha…" and they asked for a bunch of testimony related to the specific touchings.

The Court: First, the jury inquiry No. 4 asks for a laptop/DVD player for 20 minutes. We've subsequently been advised – handed the specific exhibit that apparently is desired to be played. The other inquiry regarding readback of testimony by Martha or various things we believe we have identified the places in the record where the examination relevant to these questions occurs. We have on the phone the reporter who was with us then Juile Federico and were going to have her read the questions and answers that in consultation with counsel we believe is responsive.

Ms. Fedrico then proceeded to read back the relevant testimony. It was much of the "more than one time" mantra put several different ways.

The Court: All right ladies and gentlemen, apparently, we're still not set up with the video, although we've been trying hard for the last two hours.

The DA was in charge of the video and he couldn't set it up. Mr. Gonzalez, the court manager tried to the best of his ability, but he couldn't get the video to play. It was simply not able to be viewed.

The Court: How long is it going to take you now to set this up? I thought you had it done.

Mr. Graham: Well, Hector [Mr. Gonzalez] was expressing some issues on this computer, so we're going to try another computer.

The jury went back to their deliberations without seeing the exam video. As I looked outside it was beginning to snow. Two riders were approaching and the wind began to howl.

FORTY-SEVEN

After a couple of hours alone with my thoughts back in my cubicle there was suddenly a flurry of activity and I was summoned into court.

The Court: We'll return to the record in the matter of People v. Harris. All members of the jury are present.

Juror No. 12, you're our foreman and I understand the jury has reached a verdict or verdicts.

Jury foreperson: We have, Your Honor.

The Court: All right. They're in the envelope that you have.

Would you give it to the bailiff, please, who will deliver it to me

Thank you.

For those of you in the audience, I want you to understand something clearly. I want there to be no outbursts whatsoever. None. You're to receive this information without visible, audible, or other show of emotion.

And the judge read the verdicts.

The Court:

Count 1 Guilty,
County 2 Not Guilty,
Count 3 Guilty,
Count 4 Guilty,
Count 5 Guilty,
Count 6 Not Guilty,

Count 7 Guilty,
Count 8 Guilty,
Count 9 Guilty,
Count 10 Guilty,
County 11 Guilty,
Count 12 Guilty,
Count 13 Not Guilty,
Count 14 Guilty,
Count 15 Guilty,
Count 16 Guilty,
Count 17 Not Guilty,
Count 18 Guilty,
Count 19 Guilty,
Count 20 Guilty,
Count 21 Not Guilty,
Count 22 Guilty,
Count 23 Not Guilty,
Count 24 Guilty,
Count 25 Guilty.

My brain exploded. I was angry but I bit my tongue. How could I be guilty of some but not all charges or vice-versa. Why wasn't I just found guilty of all the counts. I was frustrated and upset to say the least.

The Court: We, the jury have found the defendant guilty of two or more counts of a lewd and lascivious act upon a child under the age of 14 that is charged in counts 1 though and including counts 21 and counts 24 and 25 hereby further find the following: The defendant committed the crime of lewd or lascivious act upon a child under the age of 14 against more than one victim, specifically Martha Guthrie, Chelsea Guthrie, and Raeanna Davenport…

Ladies and gentlemen, the jury, this concludes your service, and for those of you that are here as our alternates, yours as well. I can't begin to tell you how much I admire the dedication you brought to this matter. It went well beyond what you were told to expect in terms of time and disruption of your lives. I've been incredibly impressed at the attention that you gave this matter throughout, and your service is greatly appreciated.

Now I understand the jury wanted to make a statement of some sort following the entry of verdicts.

Jury Foreperson: Yes.

The Court: If you will please.

Jury Foreperson: Thank you.

We the jury would like to thank and commend the court staff, the bailiffs, the court reporters, the clerk's office for their fine work in this trial. We would also like to thank the Sheriff's Department for all their work also.

We the jury would like to thank and commend both sides of this case – the attorneys, investigators, and support staff. Your diligence, professionalism and legal skills were quite impressive. The jury asks that neither side feels deficient in any way by the decisions we have reached. We thank each side for their humility and grace and their self-deprecating sense of humor which helped break the tension we all felt in this case.

The jury would also like to note that the defendant assisted in his own defense quite ably and maintained a respectful demeanor in court throughout the trial.

Finally, we would like to thank the judge, who established in the firm basic principles in court, decorum, justice, and we feel made everyone in the courtroom feel welcome and important to the process of a public trial.

We, the jury, would like to thank and commend Ms. Worley – she's here today – the support person for Martha and Chelsea Guthrie. Ms. Worley would be stoic and invisible during the proceedings but was just a but away from Martha and Chelsea.

We, the jury, representing the People of California, extending a hug to Ms. Worley.

We, the jury, would like to address Martha Guthrie. Martha are you here?

Ms. Martha Guthrie: Yeah.

Jury Foreperson: Martha, you said that you did not want to talk about the abuse because it was your personal and private business and you did not want people involved in your private life. We would like to correct you. When a child is violated, it's not the child's private business. It's the business of the People of the State of California to protect our children.

We, the jury, representing the People of California extend our apology to Martha. We failed to protect you.

And we the jury, would like to address Chelsea Guthrie, Chelsea you're here, okay.

Even before law enforcement decided to get involved in this case you told the defendant that he started a war and you told him something like "bring it." But Chlesea, this was not your war to fight. It was the People of California's duty to investigate the allegations and prosecute the case, to wage the war.

We, the jury representing the People of California, have this message for you. Chelsea, you won the war.

And to Martha and Chelsea, we, the jury, would like to say that your strength is intact, your innocence, though violated is intact. We saw that about both of you. Your beauty is intact. You can continue to heal, to grow.

The nightmare is over.

Your future begins now.

The Court: Alright. Thank you.

And then all Judge DeVore had left to do was et my sentencing for January 22nd, 2010 and remand me into custody with no bail.

I went back to my holding cell and the chair, my heater, and the newspaper were all gone. It was just the bench and me. Welcome to hell. Ms. Hankel showed up and we talked a little bit about why the DVD was never played for the jury and other stuff that had happened over the past couple of days. In the end I told her I was going to ask for a Marsden hearing in order to substitute counsel or the purpose of making a new trial motion. This was to be based on Ms. Hankel's ineffective assistance at trial. I felt bad for her. I mean, she was in poor health because of all the work that she did but this was business, and I had to do what I had to do. And besides, I was extremely disappointed with her refusal to call Kerri Guthrie to the stand in my support. I asked Ms. Hankel about the jury's statement, I mean how biased can you be even though you found me innocent of 6 counts including one rape charge. Apparently, the jury didn't believe Chelsea that it happened more than one time. That or the jury compromised. I was confused. It was snowing hard outside and we had a long drive to Bridgeport. My life was in ruin and Ms. Hankel said she'd be in touch.

FORTY-EIGHT

Back in my cell in Bridgeport, I still had my TV and books. I quickly delved into my notes so I could make my Marsden motion as soon as possible. I wanted a new trial while the witnesses were still fresh and available.

As the weeks passed and Christmas quickly turned into the new year 2010, I waited to hear from Ms. Hankel. Nothing. Nada. Zip. Finally on January 6th, 2010. I filed my motion to substitute counsel commonly referred to as a Marsden motion. I also sent Ms. Hankel a Subpoena Duces Tecum asking for my case files and I asked the court for the transcripts.

Time was dragging by. I reflected on the offer that Mr. Graham made right before trial for a term of 6 years served half-time with the remainder in county jail. I said no way because I wanted to prove my innocence. That's a hard thing to do as it turns out. During deliberations Mr. Graham wanted to make me another offer and I said "No way." I really thought I was going to be found not guilty. I was, in fact, found not guilty, but not enough times to make a difference. I was now facing a 285 year to life sentence. Words can't describe the depths of despair that I was living under. I focused on my Marsden hearing coming up and did legal research with the few law books available in what was called the Mono County Jail Law Library which was really a joke.

I finally heard from Ms. Hankel in mid-January and she came to see me on January 24th, 2010. Just a few days prior, Judge DeVore had calendared my hearing for January 29th. He asked for my assignments in error declaration to be submitted forthwith. I wrote out an 82 page declaration with numerous claims of error within.

When Ms. Hankel came to meet with me, I gave her my declaration and she responded that she had some news on her front, namely, jury misconduct. It seemed that Juror No. 12, Larry Petrisky, who was the jury foreperson also worked at the Mono County Superior Court as a deputy clerk. Ms. Hankel said that she had interviewed him.

Mr. Pertrisky told her that the jurors were confused by the manner in which the case was charged and by the "first time/last time" instructions. He stated that he and his fellow jurors did not believe that the medical evidence related to the Guthrie twins supported repeated penetrations of them. According to Mr. Petrisky, the jury did not believe that Chelsea was raped by me. The jury further did not understand whether the "last time" could also refer to the "first time' if indeed it was also the last time I had touched an accuser. Mr. Petrisky further stated that the jury "wasn't going to give the DA the rapes, since they had already given the DA other felony charges" against me.

Mr. Petrisky noted that while the jury had asked to view certain medical evidence on a DVD during deliberations, they did not in fact review the evidence as the means by which to do so were not immediately available to them. Mr. Petrisky also related to Ms. Hankel that he was under pressure by his employers, "To get back and do his job." He noted that just prior to going into deliberations, he intended to write a memo to the Clerk of the Court, Hector Gonzalez, regarding the pressure being brought to bear on him, but he did not have the time to do so.

Mr. Petrisky was the same jury foreperson who gave the ridiculous biased speech after the verdicts had been read. Now I was beginning to understand his bias. Mr. Hankel wanted me to give her a chance to work on her new trial motion and she wanted me to basically take back my motion to substitute counsel. I still wanted to claim ineffective assistance of counsel but by the end of our meeting I agreed to take my motion off calendar in order to see what developed. I could always ask to place it back on calendar.

Based on my meeting with Ms. Hankel, she had the court withdraw my Marsden motion and she asked for a hearing to present a motion for a new trial. February 25th, 2010, was set for the hearing with final sentencing set for March 26th.

In early February I had met with the Mono County Probation Department who were tasked with writing a probation report. It was a futile gesture since I was not going to get probation even though technically I was eligible, sort of. The probation report is something that does need to be accurate because it follows a prisoner to prison and stays in his or her Central File.

I next began working on an even lengthier document. My §1200 Allocution. I outlined the legal causes which existed which should have prevented the court from passing sentence. It wound up being 148 pages long. I was on a mission to be heard. So it came to be February 25th before I knew it and it was the day for the new trial hearing but I had heard nothing from Ms. Hankel so I placed my Marsden motion back on calendar and submitted my Allocution. Judge DeVore was upset.

He had driven for many hours from his home court in Markleeville, CA. down to Mammoth and now he had to reschedule a Marsden hearing as well as digest my allocution.

The Court: I want you to understand me clearly. I have been and continue to be respectful of your rights and your concerns and the gravity of this matter is not lost on me and never has been. And I want to give at each and every stage what I believe is the same attention I have given to those, stage in the future what I believe I have given to every stage in the past and that is careful attention to issues that are raised.

However, there has to be an end to your submissions on any given issue such that it can come to the floor, I can digest it, analyze it, do what research it necessary to make appropriate findings and decisions to move incrementally through the various stages of the proceedings. I have to deal with issues. If you continue biting at the apple or shaking the tree or whatever metaphor one may choose, we will never end this process. That is not going to happen.

The Defendant: That's why I produced this early.

The Court: Stop. Listen to me. I want to know and I want to set it at a time appropriate, without undue prolonging this matter, I want to know at this point if you can tell me when you can have every assignment of error on every issue that you think needs to get addressed by the court prepared and submitted such that I can set a hearing and we can deal with every single issue and all of the evidence you may produce in support of those issues. I want to give you the opportunity but I don't want to disabuse you, I don't want to disabuse you of the idea that we are going to do this again and again and again and again. Tell me, what's the end?

The Defendant: The end is I need to inquire of the documentary evidence from Ms. Hankel that I have outlined in my declaration.

The Court: Okay. If you are asking for, you asked for material already in the materials I had before today. So are you asking for further information in this submission?

The Defendant: The documentary evidence that I requested in my subpoena duces tecum.

The court: I don't know what subpoena you are talking about.

The Defendant: It was contained with my initial motion, Marsden motion, it was contained with that. I issued a civil SDT to Ms. Hankel in regards to the materials in her position relevant to evidence not on the record.

Additionally, I felt it's appropriate I have given her a list of reported transcripts from the trial that bear directly on allegations contained within my declaration. So once I have those, if you would prefer written assignment rather than having oral argument at some hearing, it would take me a period of time subsequent to receive the materials in order to formulate a digestible final document for you to review.

The Court: All right. It's pretty apparent that I can't do anything until I read this document, until I see what this newest submission is. It's your intention to file this, lodge it with the court as a public document, not under seal?

The Defendant: Yes, Your Honor.

The Court: All right…I have proposed a hearing on Mr. Harris' Marsden motion as requested for substitution of counsel Wednesday March 10th. I will review the recently submitted material and consider each and every requested for documents that you need. I will advise the Clerk by minute order of my ruling on those requests. And at such time as you receive notice that there will need to work with those documents if the setting of this for March 10th is too problematic.

Do you understand what I mean?

The Defendant: Yes.

The Court: I am going to give you enough time to work with what you need to work with if you are going to be getting things to work with. Fair enough?

The Defendant: Thank you.

FORTY-NINE

The next two weeks went by really fast since I was immersed in legal books related to my crime and punishment. No documents from Ms. Hankel or the court came my way and this deflated my spirits. How was I going to prove Ms. Hankel's errors if she was withholding all my proof. Ms. Hankel was making a motion for new trial (§1181) based on errors she believed occurred at trial such as jury misconduct. She was also alleging ineffective assistance of counsel based on her own ineffectiveness; go figure. She claimed the proof was in my assignments of errors declaration. In that 82 page declaration I raised 77 claims of error some of which are as follows:

No. 3: I am only able to provide a cursory list comprising my assignment of error at this time due to a lack of possession of a full reporter's transcript and certain pieces of documentary evidence.

No. 5: Documentary evidence I am unable to produce not in my possession is possessed by Ms. Hankel and is listed in the subpoena duces tecum I issued to her on 1/6/10.

No. 6: I believe I am entitled to representation by counsel at this stage of the proceedings and yet during this and prior Marsden hearings none had been appointed to me and so I object to being forced into a propria persona situation.

No. 18: Ms. Hankel failed to object during Mr. Graham's closing arguments and she allowed him to assert falsely that the 7/16/07 note from Martha to her mom was written after Martha's purported disclosure to Ms. Ellis. Ms. Hankel did not challenge Mr. Graham with the assertion that the fact was that the note had been seized from Kerri Guthrie's home on 9/13/07as a result of a search warrant seeking to find the journals. If Martha did in fact write the note after removal from her mom's home, it would not have been in Kerri's possession because contact between Kerri and the girls was prohibited by court order.

No 23: Ms. Hankel did not call Kerri Guthrie to the witness stand even though when interviewed 8/27/09 Kerri supported my claims. Kerri expressed concern though about the threats she had been received since my arrest. These threats were coming from Martha, Chelsea, and their friends. I provided Ms. Hankel with letters Kerri wrote to me in jail which showed she had profound fears.

Mr. Graham may have caused the defense problems we had in calling Kerri by failing to call her himself and/or giving her immunity. Mr. Graham had an obligation to call her that is more a point of contention in a motion for new trial but Ms. Hankel nonetheless should have raised issues I presented to her regardless.

Ms. Hankel should have called Kerri since I asked her to, and otherwise I was denied a potentially meritorious defense based on statements Kerri had made in court on 8/28/07 at my bail review hearing and when interviewed on 8/27/09 by Ms. Hankel and Mr. McCammond.

No. 24: Ms. Hankel failed to call Steve Cupp, Shaylynnn Ellis, or Dee Berner even though I asked her to. Steve Cupp was also accused by Martha of being a child molester and he is not one and would have so testified. Shaylynn Ellis was the person who disclosed Chelsea's whereabouts to Kerri when Chelsea ran away to the Clarke's home and that was how Chelsea was located contradicting Tyler Clarke, Kathleen Traynor, and Chelsea Guthrie. Ms. Hankel did not call Don Clarke regarding the runaway incident either. Also, Ms. Hankel failed to question Trish or Michelle Jackson about this important event.

Basically, Ms. Hankel chose to hypothesize that the girls had a plan and then tried to fit the evidence to the hypothesis rather than following the facts as I have laid them out and as the evidence would have shown if all of it would have been presented at trial. Ms. Hankel did not have the time, resources, or manpower to pursue all aspects of my case. The gist of it was that Ms. Hankel did not want to burden the jury with minutia, did not feel the court would give her enough time, and did not think the jury would get it. This highlights the basic dichotomy of my attorney–client relationship.

Ms. Hankel's statement such as "I don't want to confuse the jury," or, "That's too much minutia for them to get," contradicted with statements such as "you never can tell what a jury is thinking or is going to do," or, "they're tough to read." This impacts my case in that I wanted to ferret out the truth while Ms. Hankel saw it as a contest of strategy and tactics. Who is the trier of fact? Is it the jury or the attorney? If Ms. Hankel can't opine what a jury will decide as a matter of fact then she must zealously advocate my position unless they violate the rules of professional conduct. I asked her to call many witnesses and she didn't call them.

No 28: Ms. Hankel did not use the physical exam DVD to validate Dr. Gabaeff's assertion that the girls were examined on their sides, nor did Dr. Gabaeff provide digital captures from the DVD in print form to contradict Cathy Boyle's contrasting claims that they were not on their sides. Ms. Hankel failed to address the issue of the physical exam being six months after I was arrested and held in jail awaiting trial. The girls were out partying and staying weekends alone with boys according to Trish Jackson's testimony, and the general concept that the girls were more sexually active than their testimony implied.

Ms. Hankel did not address with Dr. Gabaeff the whole notion of Cathy Boyle's that 95% of sexual assault forensic exams result in normal exams. This in the context that there are fondling versus forcible rape trauma injury discrepancies as well as the claim that Ms. Boyle made regarding typical clefts and their appearance and likelihood after the first instance of sex by a "Turner Scale - 5" teenage female when in fact the allegations during trial were forcible rape of 10-11 year old females more like a "Tanner Scale - 2 or 3" according to definitions provided by Ms. Boyle. Ms. Hankel refused to question Dr. Gabaeff regarding the reasonable doubt that two twins would have identical clefts in identical locations. Ms. Hankel wanted to stick to the script that the twins did not have clefts. Okay. Fine. Identical irregularities. Either way, no argument was made regarding the physical exam and Dr. Gabaeff's testimony.

No. 32: Ms. Hankel did not question or argue regarding the issue that during Chelsea's direct testimony on 11/3/09 she said she first told Alex Ellis and second told Det. Rutkowski then Mr. Graham led her into changing her story to Ellen Thompson second. This is all relevant to the Big Note/Little Note issue as well as Ms. Hankel's failure to adequately cross-examine Rose Douglas, Alex Ellis, Ellen Thompson, and Det. Rutkowski regarding my potentially meritorious defense that there was some serious lying going on.

No. 42: Ms. Hankel did not play the tape of Kathleen Traynor and failed to prepare other tapes for review by the jury in a timely manner, although it may be that the court did not permit her time to prepare and play the tapes. This might have been due to constant pressure the court placed on Ms. Hankel to hurry up or "We're going to lose this jury." This may have exacerbated her medical condition in addition to her inability to get the tapes cued up in a timely manner.

No. 52: Ms. Hankel absolutely missed the whole situation leading to Chelsea's running away incident, and the fight with her mom, having her stuff taken away, and other issues not involving me in any way. I was not living in the home with them at the time described.

No. 54: Ms. Hankel did not want to use "Chelsea's trippin' Poem" dated 2/9/09 and I tried to insist she use it based on the way the poem showed further evidence that Chelsea was fabricating her story and could never get it right two times in a row to save her life. Chelsea should have been confronted aggressively with the fact she couldn't have it both ways; remember events, then don't, then remember again. This deceptive testimony should have been highlighted by Ms. Hankel and that it wasn't, denied me a factor of a potentially meritorious defense.

No. 57: Ms. Hankel should have shown and argued to the jury graphical Power Point outlines of all the contradictions such as the 11/3/09 testimony by Chelsea the she told nobody, not her mom, not her sister, not Tyler, not Kathleen Traynor. Nobody. Then on 11/4/09 Ms. Hankel asked Chelsea if she told anybody referring obliquely to Tyler, and Chelsea responded nobody but Alex. No mention of Ms. Douglas, or Ms. Thompson. The whole 7/9/07-7/12/07 Big Note/Little Note issue I wanted raised and zealously argued was not even brought up and this was very disconcerting to me.

No. 60: Another simplistic example of argument not made that was worthy of the jury's consideration in light of Mr. Graham's arguments would be that not only is it hard to believe that all these people lied to get me, but it is also harder to believe that all these people conspired to keep a secret and not try to help the girls. Why would Gina Luffman, who told investigators she was a sexual abuse victim, keep Martha's secret for as long as she claimed to have kept it even though she hated Kerri and myself. Why would Leif have kept the secret even after my initial arrest when he wrote a multi-page letter to the court supporting Martha and attempting to help the DA have me put in jail after bailing out?

Why would Raeanna Davenport fail to tell anybody when after years of no prosecution in her own case, when she now had validation of her own claims that were never believed according to the whole "unfounded" issue. What about Kathleen Traynor or Tyler Clarke? Why wasn't this argument made?

No. 64: Ms. Hankel refused to call Gina Luffman who had evidence to bear benefitting me, including the statement she was told by the girls that "They were mad at [me] for abandoning them at their mom's and not helping them deal with her." This among other statements that would have shed light on the truth in this matter.

No. 70: Wade McCammond was not questioned about his interview with Kerri and the exculpatory statements she made that contradicted Martha and Chelsea's statements and testimony.

No. 71: Ms. Hankel never argued that if scar tissue can form in a hymen in only 10 days and lead to a normal exam then isn't this a contradiction by Cathy Boyle; either they had a normal exam or they had scar tissue. She said they had a abnormal exam. I was entitled to the contradictions argument but also to the argument that if it only takes ten days for scar tissue to form, then the physical exam evidence should have been excluded as lacking proactivity since I was in jail for 180+ days prior to the exams.

No 73: going back to Ms. Hankel's refusal to call Kerri as a witness, her refusal to question Wade McCammond regarding his interview with Kerri, and Ms. Hankel's refusal to likewise question Det. Rutkowski, she did not argue these points and denied me a logical and potentially meritorious defense.

For example, are we supposed to believe that Martha and Chelsea told their mom that they had been abused and raped by me but did not tell her that Raeanna had been molested? Then after supposedly being raped in LA, Martha tells her mom that she was raped and Kerri still doesn't believe her, and then Martha wants to go to LA again with me and Kerri lets her go. The denial of these arguments to my defense by Ms. Hankel was unreasonable and it is likely that the jury would have rendered a different verdict if they had this and the other evidence withheld to them by Ms. Hankel.

No. 74: Ms. Hankel did not effectively handle the testimony by Martha and Chelsea and did not reserve the right to recall them thus denying me my right to confrontation and cross-examination. I have previously mentioned some of my issues regarding Chelsea. As to Martha, some glaring omissions would involve Martha flat out stating that Chelsea told first; or the whole forced blow job issue never before disclosed, and explained away in a bogus manner. Then there was the whole never saw my penis issue even though they both described being forced to give me a blow job.

I felt like I had some valid claims which should entitle me to substitute counsel for the purpose of making a new trial motion in part based of Ms. Hankel's ineffectiveness. Time was flying by quickly and before I knew it, March 10th was upon me. I awoke early that day for my long-anticipated Marsden hearing and I was excited. I truly believed I was going to get a new attorney. About a half-hour before my hearing, I got a FAX from Ms. Hankel that was her 27 page response to my declaration. I was surprised to say the least. A few examples of her responses include:

*In response to No. 18(a) Mr. Harris claims that Mr. Graham asserted in his closing argument that "Mr. Harris lied to you." I do not specifically recall this statement, but I do not believe highlighting this comment with an objection to it in closing argument would have been helpful to Mr. Harris. Moreover, such is not misconduct.

*In response to 18(b) and the allegations that "Mr. Harris saved newsgroups," made by Mr. Graham, I do not recall if Mr. Graham made this statement in closing. The defense computer expert, Mr. Richard Albee, testified that no newsgroups were saved, and Mr. Harris testified to that effect.

*In response to No 18(c) and the hard drives being "crashed," I believe Mr. Wall testified to a crash but stated he was able to obtain data from the drive regardless. Mr. Albee also testified about the hard drive and program crashes. I agree with Mr. Harris that the computer evidence was highly prejudicial and should have been excluded.

* In response to No. 18(e) I did not object to Mr. Graham's closing argument, but I attempted to express the many, many reasonable doubts in this case in a proactive fashion. I did advise Mr. Harris that the jury, collectively, consisted of 12 people who would work together to sort

out inconsistencies and that the lawyers could not possibly address every single piece of paper in a case such as this involving hundreds of documents as potential exhibits in a manner the jury would find helpful.

* In response to No. 23 (Not calling Kerri Guthrie) I considered calling Kerri Guthrie all during the trial. However, I was not confident that the jury would believe anything that Ms. Guthrie told them, as in her interview on 8/27/09, she told the District Attorney's investigator that Mr. Harris was violent with her. She completely contradicted prior testimony (at Mr. Harris' Bail Review hearing) in which she averred that Mr. Harris had never been violent with her or her children. Moreover, instead of characterizing her twins as "liars" as she had at the bail hearing, as of August '09 she was taking the position that she didn't see any sexual abuse. If she had testified in accordance with her statements in my interview and the DA's interview, she would have stated that her daughters never told her that Mr. Harris abused them, yet she also wanted to assert in the interview with the DA's investigator that she now thought that Mr. Harris "did something." Moreover, she was just beginning to have visitation with Martha Guthrie, perhaps not for reunification but in an attempt to repair her relationship with her. She did not want to testify against her daughters. I do not know whether Ms. Guthrie would have claimed a privilege not to testify pursuant to the Fifth Amendment. The Court advised counsel that it would not permit Ms. Guthrie to assert the Fifth Amendment privilege as to her entire testimony, but only on a question-by-question basis. I did not want the jury to see Ms. Guthrie assert the Fifth Amendment privilege not to incriminate herself.

I did discuss with Mr. Harris requesting that the court grant Kerri Guthrie "judicial use immunity." I believe I raised that issue, rather than the reverse. I researched this issue early in my representation of Mr. Harris, but found it to be unresolved in California.

The Court asked Mr. Graham several times in chambers whether he was going to grant Kerri Guthrie immunity. Mr. Graham declined to do so.

In addition, I found it troubling that Ms. Guthrie had changed her story about the lack of domestic violence in her relationship with Mr. Harris. She also made comments in her interview with the District Attorney's investigator that she now "believed Martha." While I am not opining that Kerri Guthrie's vouching for Martha would be admissible, I viewed Kerri Guthrie as a loose cannon. Ms. Guthrie was present in the hallway, sitting in a chair behind the elevator for much of the DA's case and I caught her eye now and again on my way through the halls. She was not particularly friendly to me and never called me over to ask me if I was going to call her to testify. She did, however, speak to me briefly and advised me that the DA's office had subpoenaed her. I expected that I might be called upon to cross-examine her.

I knew Ms. Guthrie's position on having state agencies interfere with her parenting of her daughters. She had declined reunification with one of her daughters (Chelsea) and was attempting at least a partial reunification with the other (Martha). I feared that the jury would dislike her and that this would bolster the twins allegations that their mom loved Mr. Harris more than them and would let him do as he liked just to keep him as her boyfriend.

*In response to No. 24: I declined to call Steve Cupp, Shaylynn Ellis, or Dee Berner because I did not find them necessary witnesses to Mr. Harris' defense. Martha Guthrie admitted that she did not have personal knowledge that Mr. Cupp was a child molester. The jury did not need to hear Mr. Cupp's personal denial of the same. I did not find the fact that Shaylynn Ellis allegedly disclosed Chelsea Guthrie's whereabouts to Kerri Guthrie after Chelsea ran away, to be relevant to the issues in the case.

Don Clarke, the boyfriend of Kathleen Traynor, had cumulative information that Chelsea stayed with their family, after she ran away. I found this information to be merely cumulative.

*In response to No. 28: I did not show the physical exam DVD to the jury to corroborate Dr. Gabaeff's assertion that the twins were examined on their side, because it was cumulative and I did not see the need to do so. I did not see the need to request that Dr. Gabaeff provide digital captures from the DVD to contradict Cathy Boyle's assertions. I did address the length of time between the physical exams and the allegations made by the twins in cross-examinations and argument. I did not suggest that the medical evidence was caused by people other than Mr. Harris, because this was not consistent with the testimony of the defense expert, Dr. Gabaeff, who opined that the girls' medical exams were "normal" and inconsistent with repeated penetration. I disagree with Mr. Harris' statement that "Ms. Hankel did not address with Dr. Gabaeff the whole notion of Cathy Boyle's that 95 percent of exams result in normal exams," in the context that there are fondling vs. forcible rape, trauma, injury, discrepancies, etc. Dr. Gabaeff did refute Nurse Boyle's testimony in this regard, and in particular, testified "to a reasonable degree of medical certainty" that each twin had a normal SART exam. Regarding the allegations that I was sticking to a "script" that the twins did not have clefts, Dr. Gabaeff testified that the twins did not have clefts.

* In response to No. 32: I cross-examined Chelsea on her various versions of her allegations. The defense theory in large part, was based on the inconsistencies in the twins' various stories.

* In response to No. 42: I called investigator Nathan Morganstein to impeach certain testimony by Kathleen Traynor. I did not believe that I also needed to play a tape of Mr. Taynor corroborating Mr. Morganstein's testimony.

* In response to No. 52: I did not share in Mr. Harris' belief that the jury would buy into the theory that Chelsea Guthrie ran away from her mother's home and accused Mr. Harris of molesting her because her mom made her change her room and take the smaller bedroom.

* In response to No. 57: It is true that I did not have a graphical Power Point outline of the twins contradictions.

* In response to No. 71: The defense elicited testimony from its expert, Dr. Gabaeff, which refuted Nurse Boyle's assertions that repeated sexual penetration can result in a normal exam.

* In response to No. 77: I would have elicited this testimony from Mr. Albee had I been permitted to recall him.

* In response to No. 80: Mr. Harris and Mr. Albee addressed many of the issues of which Mr. Harris complains in this paragraph. I maintain that the computer evidence should have been excluded pursuant to Evidence Code §352 and for the State's failure to show a proper chain of custody. And its inability to authenticate the same.

So there it was. My word against hers. A real he said, she said, redux. What I found real perplexing was the fact that Ms. Hankel had put forth a motion for a new trial based on her own ineffectiveness. She was arguing against me now on one hand with her responsive declaration, and on the other hand she was arguing for me, advocating my assignments in error declaration as the very evidence of her ineffectiveness.

FIFTY

The Marsden hearing is supposed to be strictly for the purpose of determining whether to substitute counsel or not. My Assignment of Error declaration was to be my reasons why I should be given new counsel. They were not however, my only claims of error to be raised in a new trial motion. Ms. Hankel filed her opposing declaration and in effect opposed my claims of error. Then she argued that my Assignment of Error declaration was the basis for the new trial motion based in part on Ms. Hankel's ineffectiveness. She had an obvious conflict of interest, mine and hers. Otherwise, why did she respond to my declaration? She could have said nothing.

From the Motion for a New Trial:

The duty of a trial court to afford every defendant in a criminal case a fair and impartial trial is constitutional dimension. Where the procedure has fallen short of that standard, an accused has been denied due process, and the inherent power of the court to correct matters by granting a new trial transcends statutory limitations. Defendant has filed a declaration under seal requesting that the court appoint counsel to review his asserted points of error supporting a motion for new trial based upon ineffective assistance of counsel. He requests that the court grant him a new trial based on the grounds stated therein.

I made no such request, Ms. Hankel did. With the battle lines clearly drawn, I went across the street to the stately Bridgeport Courthouse.

There I met briefly with Ms. Hankel who hadn't spoken to me since our January 24th meeting. She told me the judge was going to rule against me. We took our places at the defendant's table. Judge DeVore then advised me that he had read all my documents and he wanted me to expand a little bit on several issues that came to mind during his review of the material. He proposed to go through my assignment of error one by one and when he reached a questionable area, he would give me the opportunity to more fully express myself.

The Court: All right. First, I want to deal with these matters, well, I will go through the beginning with paragraph eight, which I think is the beginning paragraph of the 82 page document for assignments of error. I will simply characterize it by summary.

Paragraph eight, the assertion that counsel did not create a comprehensive argument with a clear thesis, supporting points of specific examples through courtroom evidence or testimony, didn't follow through with coherent arguments. I find that to be a courtroom event complaint. I observed that matter, and without substitution of counsel, I feel that I am capable of dealing with that issue. When I indicate courtroom even complaint, I mean that entire statement I just made, that it's something that I feel I can deal with, which does not in and of itself, or unless I indicate to the contrary, cumulative warrants the appointment of separate counsel to deal with.

Also, I should say at the outset that while we are at the Marsden portion of this, at such time as we get to the motion for a new trial phase, either with new counsel or with existing counsel, I recognize that, notwithstanding it's not a statutory basis, the IAC claim, ineffective assistance of counsel claim is appropriately raised in a motion for new trial. It's recognizable by the trial court motion for new trial, so if we move on to a motion for new trial, much of the comments may have some applicability there as well.

And so Judge DeVore went one by one though my assignments of error and declared each one a courtroom event. He was basically saying that the record illustrates the event and from his observations he can rule from the bench. The flip side of the coin is evidence not a part of the record. Extrinsic evidence. When he got to paragraph 23 and paragraph 24 he ruled them not to be courtroom events. This was important since those complaints went to the heart of the plan defense and the failure to call witness such as Kerri Guthrie. I felt I was entitled to the documents from Ms. Hankel which would prove my contention and I also felt I was entitled to an evidentiary hearing with unbiased counsel. I got neither.

The Court: 23. The failure to call Kerri Guthrie, I believe has aspects of both outside the courtroom as well as courtroom efforts. Do you have something specific you can tell me about the significance of the failure to call Kerri Guthrie that you would like considered?

The Defendant: The significance of Kerri Guthrie as being a party to one of the courts, I am not sure which count that was, but that would be the hand on the penis during intercourse count where she was an alleged active participant. Statements she made in an interview with both Therese Hankel and Mr. McCammond in the District Attorney's office that were opposite of Ms. Hankel's claims in her response, which basically are that Kerri said the same thing and denied any culpability, let's call it, in the girls' making claims to her that she ignored or participating in sexual events that the girls were forced to watch. And I believe if you look at the sum totality of the record, she is probably the most important witness who could have been called for either side.

The Court: But in terms of you having, from advancing a defense, full defense, Ms. Guthrie's testimony would have done what, contradicted the girls?

The Defendant: It would have supported my position.

The Court: Which would be?

The Defendant: That the girls were not molested. They did not tell their mom. They did not suffer any abuse. They like me. Everything she said in the interviews and in her testimony was important to the ascertainment of the truth…

Th Court: With Regard to number 24, you complaint here is with the failure to call certain witnesses, Mr. Cupp, Ms. Ellis, Ms. Berner, Mr. Clarke. You also seem to indicate that Ms. Hankel did not have the time or the resources to pursue all aspects of you case. What is it that leads you to believe that those witnesses individually would have had testimony of significance that prejudiced you from the absence?

The Defendant: Steve Cupp, friend of the girls and the mom before I ever even got involved with them, has an overarching knowledge of the family dynamic, far beyond mine.

The whole incident with Alicia King is kind of important because of the contemporaneous synchronized nature of the girls and this girl, Alicia King's claims. Dee Berner lived across the street with her and used her for work from time to time. Steve Cupp, Alicia King, and Dee Berner, and this whole dynamic was important to understanding where the girls came up with their plan because I disagreed with Ms. Hankel's assertion that the girls had a plan before they ran away. I have evidence that shows they didn't.

And Shaylynn kind of ties it all together because Shaylynn Ellis was the one who ratted out Chelsea for being there at the Clarke's house, called up Martha and Kerri and told them where Chelsea was. Kerri Guthrie then called the Sheriff's Department who went and got her, Chelsea, and took her back to the home. So there was this whole incident that contradicted everything Kathleen Traynor, is that the name she used? Kathleen Traynor, Chelsea and Tyler Clarke's testimony is impugned by facts as recorded by the sheriff's department and third-party witnesses such as Shaylynn Ellis…

A little further along I asked Judge DeVore for a clarification.

The Defendant: Your Honor?

The Court: Sir?

The Defendant: Item number 23 and 24, did you find those to be courtroom events?

The Court: No.

Thus, Judge DeVore left a slight opening for further litigation of the issues involving Kerri, the other witnesses, and the logic of Ms. Hankel's "plan" defense. I was hoping to get a new attorney but it wasn't looking too good. I needed the attorney-client file and the transcripts to show that my claims were valid. Ms. Hankel and I went back and forth. She was aggressively opposing my declaration of errors which formed the basis of my IATC claim in the new trial motion. I had no attorney representing me in this Marsden hearing which was in essence also the new trial motion hearing based on ineffective assistance of trial counsel. Following some comments by Ms. Hankel, Judge DeVore replied:

The Court: This might lead us into a broader discussion than is appropriate now, but it's going to have to be had at one time or another. I understood that the principal conceptual defense that you presented, was that the Guthrie girls… were lying, that they had an ulterior motive to accuse Mr. Harris, which you referred to as a plan, that motive being to extricate themselves from their mother's care, custody, and control, and to demonstrate that they have made many complaints against their mother over the period of time, that subsequently they alleged that they were suffering mistreatment by Mr. Harris, had multiple opportunities, multiple individuals and public agencies, entities, school folks, and so forth, to make these allegations contemporaneously and that their failure to do so made the later allegations, later made allegations, all suspect, and that that in a nutshell was the attack on the veracity of the victims and the establishment of ulterior motives of the victims to make all allegations against Mr. Harris.

Is that a fair characterization?

Mr. Hankel: That's a fair characterization. Substantially that is true. And I would supplement that by noting that there were several other allegations made by Chelsea Guthrie with respect to allegations of abuse made.

The Court: By others?

Ms. Hankel: Made by others or perpetually by her mother that were contained in numerous diary entries. There were no such allegations made by Chelsea against Mr. Harris of any kind of abuse that were found in her journal or diary entries.

The Judge continued through my assignments of error and noted that if there was something of a confidential nature being brought up by Ms. Hankel then by all rights I could interrupt.

The Court: I tried to tell you not to interrupt a minute ago, but that's the exception.

The Defendant: And I don't want to interrupt. I have way too much respect for you.

The Court: Okay.

The Defendant: In regards to some of the things that have been raised that I haven't had the opportunity to rebut, is this a first pass through and its over, or am I going to have a chance to address any of these topics, because I am completely at odds with statements that she is making that aren't factually correct? And so I want to state clearly that I state opposite things to what she is saying.

The Court: I understand that there is a disagreement, that you disagree with things.

The Defendant: The record disagrees with her as well.

The Court: The issue presently is whether or not Ms. Hankel's representation of you constituted ineffective assistance of counsel such that in order to present a motion for a new trial you should be given a new attorney. I mean, that's the context here right now.

The Defendant: The context isn't whether there is a conflict of interest in her representing a position against me as well as for me?

The Court: That's part of it.... Let me tell you, you seem to be, you seem to want to talk about things that have happened, some of it in the distant past, preliminary hearing, pre-preliminary hearing with Mr. Gephart. We are here to find out whether Ms. Hankel can effectively present a motion for new trial.

The Defendant: Part of my motion for new trial is based on ineffective assistance of counsel to include Mr. Gephart's actions in regards to this in regards to this DNA evidence which was possibly the most exculpatory evidence possible. Because what Ms. Hankel just said about blood and semen being found is not actually correct. According to a document lodged with your own court on July 17, 2008, the issue exactly was the court would require detailed showing to justify the $25,000 expense for the testing. So can Ms. Hankel effectively argue the point *that she isn't making now? And furthermore, the evidence showed a protein that may or may not and did not ever actually show blood or semen.*

So the specificity of what Ms. Hankel just told you with what was on that couch as told by her by Mr. Gephart to me. So I believe it goes to the whole gist of what I am saying, can Ms. Hankel effectively argue a position of mine for a new trial when we are at odds what the position even is.

The Court: I understand your position. Number 72 is a failure to use some records of a sheriff's office. And I wonder if you can tell me, that's sort of a courtroom event, sort of not, relates to something that wasn't there, can you tell me what relevance or significance you think that exists with regards to the sheriff's office records, please.

The Defendant: On the incident July 11, 2007 I spoke with officer Scott Bush, and there was an incident at the home in regards to me and Kerri having a fight. Martha basically saying her mom has gone mental and wanting me to help et cetera. And so I called the sheriff attempting to – actually, Kerri and I got into a wrestling match over a pair of skis I was taking back. Martha called the cops and said we were having a fight and the cops responded. During that response I told them what Martha had told me, that she wanted to be removed from the home. Chelsea had already been removed from the home. It was really a problematic situation, and I left the scene. I called back and asked them, because I had just talked to Martha and she still wants to be removed out of the home. So the sheriff went back over there and took Martha away from the home because previously she had been talking in front of her mom. They separated her away from her mom and asked her, and this is Martha stating in the sheriff's document, "She wanted to leave earlier, but now she is okay, she wants to stay."

The fact that I am calling up the sheriff to remove Martha from the home and trying to help Martha shows that I am not trying to intimidate Martha or threatened to kill her if she talks to the cops. I had the cops go over there and talk to her away from her mom, away from everybody, and that's in this document, because this is three different documents.

Furthermore, I requested, because Leif Medrud had been stalking the house according to Kerri, and I had a whole incident with him, finding out he was the stalker, and he had lied to me and in my statement of facts, I had the cops go over and confront Leif Medrud. Leif Medrud did not say oh he's been molesting her or you need to watch him or anything of that sort.

On the 17th, the day after Martha had been removed from the house, there was a whole incident where the night that Martha was taken from the home, Kerri was taking a bunch of pills and booze and effectively wanted to kill herself she was so mad. I went to get help. There wasn't much they could do, so I went to my mental health counselor that I had in Inyo County and reported through that, because then they had to go. They are mandated reporters. They had to go over and so there was this whole incident of them trying to confront Kerri and her trying to blockade herself in her room.

The Court: Your argument is this sheriff's office record would have supported the litany of events you just related and they were not admitted, they were not used?

The Defendant: All of the events of the summer of 2007 which led up to the reporting and subsequent to the reporting and finally my arrest were all relevant and were not used at trial.

The Court: Ms. Hankel, your written response indicated that this was too vague to allow you to respond. Is this giving you any further information that permits you to respond at this time?

Ms. Hankel: Yes, Your Honor. With respect to the first record where Mr. Harris spoke with Officer Scott Bush regarding incidents in the home, I did not find those records to be helpful to Mr. Harris as they highlighted the domestic violence in the home and the fight that occurred in the presence of Martha Guthrie. Martha Guthrie was quite upset, Kerri Guthrie was quite upset, Mr. Harris was quite upset, everyone was crying, and it was an extremely tumultuous situation. I did not think that the records show that he wasn't trying to manipulate Martha or Kerri Guthrie, I thought they showed the reverse.

With respect to the issue with the confrontation with Leif Medrud and the suggestion that he was stalking Martha. We actually investigated the scenario, had several discussions with Leif Medrud, and I did not find that the testimony or the factual scenario that Leif Medrud would have testified to again be helpful to Mr. Harris but instead suggested that perhaps Mr. Harris who was stalking Leif Medrud.

The documents that show that Kerri Guthrie had taken a bunch of pills and perhaps tried to commit suicide I did not think would be helpful to Mr. Harris defense. I thought that it actually may have shown a guilty conscience and that Ms. Guthrie was committing suicide because of the events that had occurred in her family with respect to Mr. Harris.

The Defendant: Your Honor, this is an important issue, if I might respond just briefly?

The Court: Briefly.

The Defendant: Kerrie Guthrie could have testified specifically to her telling me who was stalking the house. It wasn't me. It was Kerri Guthrie. And in regards to –

The Court: You mean it was Leif Medrud.

The Defendant: Leif Medrud.

The Court: You said it was Kerri Guthrie stalking.

The Defendant: Kerri Guthrie said he was stalking and had me go and find who was circling the block. They had been doing this for days on end, and this is going into all the sneaking out or whatever. But there is also email that, there are emails from Kerri that were contained in that CPS release where she specifically outlined her position with CPS and the facts she is suicidal, because CPS was going to charge her so much, and render her homeless. It had nothing to do with her culpability in any crimes. It had to do with the financial situation as to the State taking her daughters away. Those are in the emails.

Now, it is worth noting here that not only did I have a problem with Ms. Hankel during the trial, but then in my motion for substitution of counsel Marsden hearing, which was to form the basis of a new trial motion on IAC ground, I had a big problem in that she was arguing against me with privileged information and all I could do was make allegations. I couldn't argue against her much, if at all. I was not allowed to present evidence. I was not allowed to confront and cross-examine Ms. Hankel as she argued against my position. Basically, I was screwed.

The Court: But No. 82 is a kind of a catchall, "I've got more complaints," I want to give you the opportunity to air them without arguing the law to me.

The Defendant: Right. It is a little difficult without the documents that I requested to be complete.

The Court: I'll deal with that at this time. I am going to deny your request for documents that basically go back to the start of this case. I don't deem that to be necessary or appropriate to the issues before the court at this time.

What the … how is the new trial motion not a critical stage of the proceedings warranting the production of documents necessary to the proof of ineffectiveness? This discussion went on for some time; I made an allegation of inadequacy of my representation and Ms. Hankel and the court shot me down. Finally, it came to a head and I had my final say for what it was worth. I started off talking about the trips me and the girls took and I pleaded with the court to understand that Ms. Hankel did not let me testify fully and completely.

The Defendant: They liked it. Their mom testified at my bail hearing that they liked it. They wanted to go with me. They never came back and complained about a thing.

The Court: Okay. What else?

The Defendant: I guess the list isn't actually showing the Leif Medrud or Jordan and the Tyler Clarke incident such as the incident at the theater, what I will call the theater incident, I will call the Chalfant Market incident they are in the Statement of Facts.

The Court: And these were events, at least the theater events that you mentioned earlier that you thought was susceptible and some damaging conclusions to the effect that Mr. Harris might be seen as stalking the girls?

Ms. Hankel: That's correct.

The Court: Or whatever girl it was, whatever it was.

The Defendant; I was with Kerri at that time. So I mean, for her to opine a position isn't necessarily factually correct. The incident that had to do with Michelle Jackson and taking Martha over to Michelle Jackson's, I didn't testify to it. There was a whole bunch of me taking Martha over there. Michelle Jackson, excuse me, Trish Jackson, the mom, is a good friend of the family, like I testified, we have known her since fourth grade. Since this is like the biggest family friend. Shaylynn Ellis was the biggest family friend since fourth grade. Michelle Jackson and Shaylynn Ellis were the girls' best friends for the longest period of time. They knew everything. The situation that had to do with the notes as far as what was contained in the notes for Martha, we were going to go down to Disneyland again the summer of 2007 and there was a note where Martha states as much, that she wants to go down there and go shopping at a store called "Hot Topic" because that's what we did every year and it was something she looked forward to.

The theory that they had this plan that somehow fit into some kind of container, it didn't address the issues that had to do with other people's testimony whether it was my meetings with Alex Ellis, my meetings with Rose Douglas in their office and the specificity of those meetings. It was just brushed upon in a generalized way. And if somehow I am seen as a person who commits domestic violence, previous counsel's strategy was: Okay, but does that make you a child molester? So I mean to simply avoid all evidence that may paint me as a not perfect person isn't fair in rebutting allegations of such a serious nature as being a child molester.

So hey, if I grabbed a girl or something, I testified to that, I spoke truthfully. So, for me to testify about all the events in 2002 all the way through 2007 was important because those were the sum total of the charges. And anything that was eliminated because it was too burdensome for the jury and not likely to elicit a response from the jury puts the lawyer in the position of trier of fact, and the trier of fact should have all the facts to decide from. Thank you.

The Court: All right. Are there any other issues on the questions of substitution of counsel for the motion of counsel for the motion for a new trial that you need to address?

The Defendant: Yes, Your Honor.

The Court: Go ahead.

The Defendant: Ms. Hankel's motion for new trial I believe you have; correct?

The Court: I do. We aren't dealing with the motion for a new trial.

The Defendant: I understand that but it's important.

The Court: Okay.

The Defendant: Page eight of her motion, like 30, 31, where I request the court to grant me a new trial on the grounds therein of an 82-page document is not what I am seeking to do. The grounds for a new trial based on ineffective assistance of counsel are not contained within that, or I shouldn't be obligated to argue the positions. I am simply seeking to have independent counsel argue my positions, which are obviously at odds with Ms. Hankel's. Why should I be forced to argue in propria persona in a case so serious?

The Court: you aren't being asked to argue your position, what you are being asked to do is provide the court with your assignment of counsel's errors…

The Defendant: All documents in the possession of the attorney I would like to be placed in the record.

The Court: I am going to respectfully deny that request.

The defendant: The CPS notes are in the same format, all the CPS records are highlighted.

The Court: Mr. Harris, I am not going to require Ms. Hankel to produce every document that she has received in the course of discovery –

The Defendant: They are my documents.

The Court: Excuse me – and make it a part of this hearing…

The Defendant: My documents that Ms. Hankel has included the complete petition you are familiar with Mr. Gephart filed in regards to his civil relievement motion are in her possession, not a part of this case. She has those, those are mine. They have no bearing on this case as far as her, unless they are part of some argument that she is going to make for a motion for a new trial that should include Mr. Gephart's ineffectiveness, not just her own.

The Court: We are arguing now. I think we are going to move on.

The Defendant: I don't have any rights to my own documents?

The Court: At this point I am denying all your requests for a transcript of this proceedings, as well as the documents that you have asked for.

The Defendant: And the subpoena to her?

The Court: Exactly, including the subpoena to her. What I am going to do in terms of preserving the record here is direct Ms. Hankel to preserve her file in regards to this matter until and unless there is an application to this court to do something with it, so that if there ever is an interest by anyone to secure those, review those and do anything further with them, that they are available. And I think it would be prudent to anticipate that there is going to be a need for that, that is, for somebody else to look at this. That gets to part of my rulings here.

In terms of the Marsden motion for appointment of substitute counsel for the presentation of a new trial motion, as to the identified in trial occurrences, things that were observed by me and I am able to assess the significance of without the appointment of new counsel, I think I have listed most of them that appear to me to be of that nature. To the extent that there may have been identified things as outside of the record occurring other than before me in the courtroom, on the presentation here and taking them individually, as well as taking the entire assignment of errors collectively, I don't find that there has been a colorable claim of inadequacy of counsel on the strictly held standard that governs these matters. And to the extent that there may have been a colorable claim, I find that given the length of the trial, the obvious need for many, many, many documents and probably considerable investigation to further explore and develop the issues and the intended delay that obviously occurred given Mr. Harris' large, large litany of assignments of error that a motion for new trial would not be the proper venue for it anyway, and it appears it would be better for it to appeal under habeas…

I have already stated my thoughts about in court issues and the colorable claim or the essence of the colorable claim being established. What I am impressed by in terms of the complaints of counsel and the performance of counsel since she became involved in this is that she made and argued very complex pretrial motion very appropriately and, in my judgment, very effectively. She participated effectively and vigorously in the jury selection process. She made a coherent, cogent opening statement. She found and utilized appropriate experts on the Child Sexual Abuse Accommodation Syndrome, medical, and computer evidence issues. She had consistent defense throughout that the victims had ulterior motives, gave a myriad version of events, made complaints about their mother and other persons, and had many, many opportunities to make these reports concerning Mr. Harris and didn't do so, apparent manipulation of their friends and manipulation of the CPS social workers and those folks, the poor CPS law enforcement work, poor at best, and worst, the suggestion of contamination and all part of a plan, this ulterior motive to extricate themselves from their mother's home I thought was consistent throughout, and the evidence was presented in a way that put the best face forward on it. I think Ms. Hankel investigated and produced witnesses to support the defense theme. And it is counsel's determination to determine what available defense is presented and what evidence to adduce and when to object and when not to object. Counsel runs the trial. She conducted both cross and direct ex-

amination of trial witnesses effectively, and she made an organized and relevant closing argument…

We are told that by having professional representation the accused surrenders all but a handful of fundamental rights to counsel's complete control, defense strategies, and tactics. That came from the Supreme Court In re Horton 54 Cal. 3d 32. And the defendant does not have the right to present a defense of his own choosing, rather he has the right to an adequate and competent defense. Supreme Court told us that in People v Hamilton 48 Ca. 3d 1142. And the tactical disagreements between the defendant and his attorney do not in themselves constitute irreconcilable conflict. The Captain of the Ship doctrine and the concept just referred to come from the Supreme Court in People v Carpenter 15 Cal 4th 312 and, People v Welch 20 Cal. 4th 701.

So as to those performance complaints, I don't find that any of them, either collectively or individually reflect that Mr. Harris was deprived of effective assistance of counsel, nor that his due process rights were impaired. I don't find any basis to conclude that it is reasonably probable that a more favorable outcome would have been attained, notwithstanding each and every and all of those complaints that he has raised.

So, for those reasons, the motion to substitute counsel at this juncture for further proceedings here at the trial court, specifically the motion for new trial is denied… So that's the court's ruiling.

I have felt like I had been rode hard and put up wet. I was simply unable to get any traction with Judge DeVore and that didn't bode well for sentencing, which was set for April 9, 2010, in Mammoth. I still had the public motion for a new trial based on juror misconduct, the admission of prejudicial evidence, the failure to allow Mr. Albee to be recalled after Mr. Wall had offered rebuttal testimony, and that the verdicts were contrary to law and evidence.

Judge DeVore shot down all the claims of error at the hearing of the new trial motion as articulated by Ms. Hankel who was still my attorney. A plain conflict of interest. The judge did however leave a door open when he allowed Ms. Hankel to get the contract information for all 12 jurors and gave Ms. Hankel permission to make contact and appropriate inquiry. Judge DeVore stated "The Motion for New Trial on the other grounds is denied, and I am reserving on this issue."

The discussion continued as to the process and the reporting of the search queries. Then the court discussed the documents required in the Marsden hearing.

The Court: Ms. Hankel, with regard to documents, we talked earlier about your filing of the matter.

Ms. Hankel: Yes.

The Court: I think it would be prudent for you to have a duplicate copy made in anticipation that you are going to be required to turn over your original file at some point in time, and I'll authorize funds to have that done. I would tell you not to have it done through any outside copy service because of the sensitivity of the information. Do you have the ability to do it in house through persons that you higher to assist you and so forth?

Ms. Hankel: Yes, I believe so, Your Honor.

The Court: Why don't you go ahead and do that.

FIFTY-ONE

In the days that followed, Ms. Hankel and Mr. Morganstein attempted to contact the jurors and they were soundly rebuffed. I had met with the Mono County Probation Dept. for a perfunctory interview so they could create a report for sentencing. I received that report and they were denying me probation and recommending only 200 years-to-life. This led me to investigate the sentencing statute §667.61. (All further statutory references are to the California Penal Code unless otherwise notes). This statute, the so-called "One-Strike" law provides for a life sentence for child molestation for multiple victims.

However, only one life sentence may be imposed for multiple counts committed on a "single occasion." At the time of my alleged crimes a previous version of §667.61 was in effect and there were some substantial differences with the current law. (All further references are to the former §667.61 statute unless otherwise noted). The former version of §667.61 requires that a defendant be unqualified for probation before §288(a) can be considered in §667.61's sentencing scheme. §667.61(e)(5) requires a defendant be convicted of an offense [(c)(7)] against more than one victim. In order to make that finding the special allegation verdict form and the amended complaint should have pled and listed that fact for the jury to find as listed in §1203.066(c) et seq. such as the fact that probation would not be in the best interest of the child, (c)(2), or a threat of harm exists if probation is granted, (c)(5), for example.

The jury does not need to find a defendant ineligible for probation, only that a fact exists which precludes the court for granting probation. The effect of this finding would permit §288(a) as listed in §667.61(c)(7). This in turn would permit the application of §667.61(b) and the jury would have found all the requisite facts for imposition of the enhanced sentence. I was trying to explain to Ms. Hankel that the court and Mr. Graham had been relying on the current version of §667.61 all along. The complaint stated that I was ineligible for probation when in fact I was. Moreso, the county probation office and the district attorney both read the law differently with both of them agreeing that indeterminate and determinate sentences may be appropriate. From the district attorney's sentencing brief:

Therefore each PC 288(a) count that relates to Martha and Chelsea Guthrie, that can be concluded to have bee committed on a separate occasion, the court should impose a 15 year to life sentence. For those PC 288(a) counts that relate to Martha and Chelsea Guthrie that the court does not deem to have been committed on separate occasions (but rather could have occurred on the same occasion as another PC 288(a) count), the court should assign a determinate sentence. (i.e. one principle term of 3, 6, or 8 years, with the rest being given a 'one third the middle term' consecutive sentence or a full term consecutive sentence).

I was adamant with Ms. Hankel that the fact the County and the State were proceeding against me based on the newer version of the "one-strike" law was denying me my right to fundamental fairness, or due process. The former §667.61(g) was not in the new version of §667.61 and it stated:

The term specified in subdivision (a) or (b) (15 years-to-life) shall be imposed on the defendant once for any offense or offenses committed against a single victim during a single occasion. If there are multiple victims during a single occasion the term specified in (a) or (b) shall be imposed on the defendant once for each victim.

The term "single occasion" in §667.61 former subdivision (g) meant the sex offenses were committed in close temporal or spatial proximity. Ms. Hankel began to understand my contentions and she did some research related to the "single occasion" requirement in §667.61(g). I believed that the state had failed to prove the separateness of the first time/last time language in the complaint and verdict forms. Ms. Hankel went into radio silence mode while she wrote out two motions for a new trial and a sentencing brief. I spoke to her from time to time. The probation report included statements from Martha and Chelsea. They seemed to be written by Alex Ellis. Raeanna Davenport refused to make a statement or even submit one for the record.

I began pushing Ms. Hankel to investigate a number of areas that I thought would be productive and she told me about a case, Blakely v Washington 542 US 296 (2004) in which the Supreme Court held that a jury must find all the facts necessary to a conviction, the judge cannot extrapolate from his own observations. Here, the jury did not find all he facts necessary to subject me to an indeterminate "life" term for a violation of §288(a). The jury did not find a multiple victim allegation for any particular count pursuant to §667.61(e)(5) nor did the jury find any fact from which the court could conclude that I was ineligible for probation pursuant to §667.61(c)(7).

Ms. Hankel wrote in her sentencing brief:

Section 667.61 was significantly amended, effective November 8, 2006, by voter approval of proposition 83, section 12. These amendments further changed the predicate offenses required for the penalties in the One-Strike law to apply. The United States Constitution and the California Constitution proscribe Ex Post Facto laws. Both Constitutions protect against the later adoption of a statute that inflicts a greater punishment than the law in effect at the time of the commission of the crime. Therefore the Ex Post Facto of the United States and California Constitutions preclude sentencing under the current §667.61 for offenses committed before November 8, 2006. Instead, Defendant is entitled to be sentenced under the formerly applicable versions of §667.61.

All that being said, I was still concerned that I was going to prison for a crime that never occurred. I wanted to find that perfect argument that would get me to the promised land; a new trial.

I contended under Blakely I was entitled to have the jury determine the "separate occasions" beyond a reasonable doubt before multiple life terms could be imposed. Because of the way the Third Amended Information referred to in court as simply "The information" was pled, it was impossible to ascertain which of the crimes occurred on separate dates or at separate times. The jury instructions and the verdict forms did not demonstrate that the jury made such determinations.

Section 667.61 specifically required the jury to find as true the fact that I had been convicted of committing an offense (such as §288(a)) against more than one victim. The statue does not state that the jury need only find, as true, that there were multiple victims against whom I had committed a lewd and lascivious act. The statue clearly requires multiple victims in one offense, not in one case.

So everything sped up as I raced toward my April 9, 2010 sentencing. I stayed up late pounding the books, writing out declarations and pleadings, and in the end I felt pretty good about my chances. Ms. Hankel had stepped it up despite our differences.

FIFTY-TWO

Suddenly it was April 9th and I took what may very well have been my last drive ever to Mammoth Lakes. I took in the scenery and tried to relax. Once in the courtroom Judge DeVore denied everything Ms. Hankel and I threw at him.

Mr. Graham: Your Honor, the victim is asking for her statement to be read.

The Court: Go ahead.

Ms. Martha Guthrie: This trial is by far the most painful emotional thing I have ever gone through. I personally think Mike Harris deserves about 55 to 65 years in prison with no parole. I think he deserves that because he ruined half of my life. So now half of his life will be ruined.

I lived a good life except for little problems through the years before I met Mike Harris. As soon as he came into my life, I learned that he wasn't that nice guy that he put himself out to be. He was only the nice guy when he got something that he actually wanted for something that made him feel tingly and great inside.

Half of my life was pretty much ruined because of what he did to me. The things he did to me were just plain stupid and very sick. I never did anything to him to make him do those things. I was only 10 years old. I was still a growing child. I was still learning about the world and the stuff involved in it.

Does he really think that I liked being touched in inappropriate places and that was what I wanted to learn about so early in life? I was a growing child. What is his problem. He put me through so much stuff in my life, I could not even have a life. All my friends were afraid of him and never wanted to come over. I was always afraid to come home, but I knew I had to because, if I didn't, he would take his anger out on my mom and I didn't want that to happen. I love my mom very much, but he being in her life changed her so much. She wasn't my mom anymore. He put her against my sister and me. He manipulated so many things in my mom.

I will most definitely never, ever, forgive him for what he did. He knew what he did to me, he knew what he did to my sister, and the fact that he wants to lie about it, that's pretty pathetic. He tried so hard to take me down during this whole trial. Yes, I started crying and freaking out, but that was because of my anger, but he actually made me a very much stronger person.

He took half my life away, and now he is going to get half his life taken away from him. I hope it hurts badly. I hope he feels the pain like my mom and my sister and I had to. You can only live once, and he decided to mess that up. He could be out there just living up life and having a grand old time, but now he is stuck in a cell.

He should have thought with the head that's on top of his body, not the one that hangs. Maybe he would have had a very nice life, but since he can't live life to the fullest now doesn't mean I'm not going to. So while he is in prison, I'm going to be living my life, like hiking and skiing and more skiing and eating great delicious homemade turkey dinners and whatnot. It will be great. I will make sure to keep him updated on how the slopes are on the mountain.

Well, that's the last thing I have to say to Mike Harris, is don't drop the soap.

The Court: Does anyone else want to be heard?

Mr. Graham: This is Ms. Chelsea Guthrie.

Ms. Chelsea Guthrie: I was only 10 years old when I was violated, taken advantage of. That lasted five years of my life. From ten years old to fifteen years old, my right to be a child was taken away from me. My family was torn apart. My dignity was stolen. I felt powerless to protect myself from the man my mom told me was caring. I do not call myself a victim. In fact, I was. The impact of his hurtful words, violent hits, violating touches, the impact of him forcing his body on top of mine, his fist hitting my face and throwing me against the wall. He forced me to do sexual activity that I never wanted to do. I was only a little kid.

Months and years I lived in fear of my life. I lost all self-respect. I blamed this all on myself. I always asked myself why would I let this man take control of my life? Why would I let him take away my self-image? For years I was unable to be who I wanted to be, to act like a kid.

The one and only thing I owned was taken away from me, my virginity. I tried telling my mom what was going on but she never believed me.

Now right there when Chelsea said "She never believed me," implied that she told her mom more than once, contradicting her testimony.

Living with a mom who didn't care and her sexually abusive boyfriend made me feel so helpless. I wanted to give up and just end it. I stared cutting myself at age 12, hoping that I would just end everything. I kept this going on even when I left my house at 15.

When I ran away from home, I thought everything was going to be better, but every night I had nightmares and woke up just trying to kill myself. My mom said she never wanted to talk to me ever again because of her boyfriend. All I wanted as a kid was a loving mother and father to take care of my life after my dad passed. But Mike Harris made me feel disgusted and not worth living. I am 17 now and still struggling with the sexual abuse. I just really want this creep off the streets. I think he should get life, but I knew that's not possible. Mike took one-third of my life and put it through pain and suffering. So I think he should have one-third of his life taken away.

The Court: Thank you.

After making sure Raeanna wasn't there to make a statement the court rendered its tentative sentence. Judge DeVore said that he intended to sentence me to 19, 15 years-to-life terms, fully consecutive, for a total of 285 years-to-life. I suddenly realized Judge DeVore was out to screw me over. I had kept an open mind throughout but in the end, the system was failing me. Judge DeVore made his own finding that I was not eligible for probation.

The Court: It is my intention to sentence him for the following reasons: I determined that as to each individual victim among them all no offense of which Defendant which convicted occurred on a single occasion. I have in mind the testimony of Chelsea Guthrie and Martha Guthrie that the molestation that they suffered at the hands of the Defendant occurred on an almost daily basis; that is, they were of a serial nature at whatever location they happened to be living or visiting at any point in time. The manner of charging, a somewhat convoluted presentation of evidence by the People notwithstanding, I find beyond a reasonable doubt, although I recognize the applicable standard is by a preponderance of the evidence, that none of the offenses found by the jury occurred on a single occasion or during a single episode or transaction.

For each offense on which the jury found the defendant guilty, he had significant opportunity to reflect on his actions and nonetheless continued for a period of many years his serial molestation of the young and vulnerable victims.

Defendant had separate, distinct, and independent objectives on each occasion of molest and rape, although his motives were the same, that being his sexual gratification. It is my belief that this implicates no Sixth Amendment issues pursuant to the recent case of Oregon v Ice 129 S.Ct. 711.

I have in mind the evidence as to the first time/last time counts, dealing specifically with the same parts of the body and perhaps the same locations, which is what I referred to as the somewhat convoluted charges and evidence presentation. Nonetheless, I also have reviewed my notes and memory of the trial, and the testimony by each of the victims that had multiple counts relating to them, that is, Chelsea and Martha, were that the conducts were occurring on a daily basis. And I believe as to each of them there may well have been testimony that they occurred on multiple times. Sometimes the testimony I think was focused on more than one time, and sometimes It was ten or more times. Sometimes there were numbers put on it. Sometimes there weren't. But it's clear to me – and the standard in People v Murphy is preponderance – nonetheless by even a greater standard of beyond a reasonable doubt those first time/last time offenses I believe and I find permit and the circumstances warrant and justify the imposition of full consecutive terms of 15 to life.

The Court: Ms. Hankel?

Ms. Hankel: I understand the Court's ruling Your Honor. I am going to rely on my submissions to the court with respect to my objections about the prior version of §667.61 and my objections pursuant to Blakely, Booker, Cunningham, and Apprendi.

I am not certain if the court has made a determination as to section (g) of the former version of §667.61 which states that the term specified in (a) or (b) shall be imposed on the defendant once for any offense committed against a single victim during a single occasion. If there are multiple victims during a single occasion, the term specified in subdivision (a) or (b) shall be imposed on the Defendant once for each separate victim.

The Court: I think that People v Murphy dealt with that concept, but even if it didn't, I did not find multiple victims on a single occasion as to any of the 19 counts of which Mr. Harris was found guilty.

Ms. Hankel: And if I understand the court's ruling correctly, the court's made a determination that each of the counts occurred at a separate occasion.

The Court: Yes, That's the People v Murphy determination that's left to the court, again the preponderance of the evidence standard, and it's well in excess of that amount of evidence in my judgment.

(Discussion between Ms. Hankel and myself.)

Ms. Hankel: for clarification, Your Honor, is your ruling with respect to the separate occasions based upon the Court's review of the Court's notes or based upon he verdict in the case on the facts the jury found?

The Court: Both. My memory of the trial, my notes of the trial, the findings of the jury…

The Court: I recognized the law does not require it and further that if it's not permitted by the court that he be required to be under oath. Nonetheless, Mr. Harris has conducted himself well during the course of these proceedings and if he wanted to address the court at this point –

Ms. Hankel: Yes, Your Honor.

The Court: -- not to argue the legal issues, but to argue against the tentative decision by the court – in any respect, that is, not to grant probation – I think he is ineligible for it, but I wouldn't grant it if t were a matter of discretion – or the nature of the sentences, I'd give him that opportunity.

The Defendant: Yes I do. Absolutely.

The Court: Alright. Go ahead.

The Defendant: Would you like to take a break first? This might take a minute.

The Court: No, I'm ready.

The Defendant: Okay.

The Court: But it's not going to take up the rest of the day, I'll tell you that. I'll give you the opportunity, but I am going to ask you to be concise and brief and not repeat yourself.

The Defendant: Absolutely, Your Honor. First off, Martha and Chelsea lied –

The Court: No, no.

The Defendant: Yes.

The Court: You are not going to address anybody else. You will only address me.

The Defendant: I will only address you Your Honor. Martha and Chelsea lied, absolutely lied to you, right to you.

The Court: Let me indicate that Mr. Harris turned around and attempted to address victims in the audience directly, and that's what I cautioned him against. He is not appropriately addressing the court.

The Defendant: Thank you Your Honor. They lied to you Your Honor, very clearly. They contradicted themselves or they were justified in their contradictions, but they lied. They said – specifically the record reflects in my papers I filed with you – I believe they might have been sealed papers, but nonetheless, identified specifically where Chelsea said she never told anybody, the boys, anything.

Then suddenly the boys materialized and testified, oh, they'd been told everything. And Chelsea specifically – now it could have been Martha – in the interviews they made in 2008, told Detective Rutkowski who is an honorable and smart –

The Court: Mr. Harris, let me interrupt you. You seem to want to impeach the jury verdict and that's not the point of the –

The Defendant: No.

The Court: -- statement at this point in time.

The Defendant: No. I am furthering the truthfulness of myself and my character as an honest and decent person who's lived here for 30 years, over 30 years. So I'd like to continue in that vein that I am boosting myself and my credibility.

Maybe I should rephrase in how I present it, but nonetheless, if Detective Rutkowski receives information that those boys don't know anything, then all of a sudden in order to impeach me at he last minute, the People bring those boys in who fabricate stories right before you. You should be offended because I was truthful every step of the way. I went to a voluntary interview with Detective Rutkowski at the genesis of this case, and so my veracity was unimpeachable. Nobody impeached my veracity, and nobody can.

And more importantly, why didn't Kerri Guthrie appear? If, as the victims just stated that mom was such a victim and she is so handicapped, why didn't she appear and slander the hell out of me. She would have been here. You know she is a strong woman. For you to characterize her the way you just did, I don't think you, Your Honor, could get on a 17-hand thoroughbred from the race track, hopped up on grain the way she can break it flak jacketed and helmeted up. I'd have preferred that she'd been called, and she would have testified the same as she did in her interviews or as she did at the bail hearing.

Then Martha, who stated to Detective Ruthkowski in the interview that she came back from LA when she was raped and she told her mom that she was raped and her mom said "Oh, Mike wouldn't do that," and yet you never heard a word in this court about how she told her mom. And if mom would have known her daughter was raped, I would have a caved in a skull because she's a great woman.

And so for them and for you to impugn Kerri Guthrie in this courtroom based on innuendo and hearsay is about as offensive as I can ever imagine, and I don't mean that personally Your Honor. It's a position that perhaps Ms. Hankel, perhaps Mr. Graham by not calling her, by not offering her immunity – because specific testimony was that Chelsea said I made her put her hand on my penis while her mom was giving me a blow job.

Now if that doesn't cause you a bit of concern – clearly case law all the way around the books support the position that children are more credible than they've been given credit for. So for them to come in and make that kind of false statement before the court and for the mom to have been interviewed by Wade McCammond, who's in the courthouse today, was interviewed by him and denied it to him and they know it and she denied it at the bailhearing, it's absolutely offensive to me that this evidence wasn't produced. So Kerri Guthrie is a great person. I didn't take advantage of anybody. I could not take advantage of her. She is too strong a woman, but she had trouble handling her two twins. And the evidence wasn't produced in this court, and I gave you a lengthly diatribe or two about the facts that weren't presented to this court that should have been presented and would have boosted my veracity and impugned theirs.

So the fairness of the trial and the presentations that were made weren't accurate reflections of any facts that were ongoing in the four-year period that the crimes were charged. More specifically, Martha testified at the preliminary hearing --

The Court: We don't need to review evidence in detail of the trial. I am inviting you to tell me why you think probation should be grated or why you think the intended decision that was announced at the outset is not appropriate, not to rehash evidence of the trial

The Defendant: I believe I am doing that Your Honor.

The Court: I am not going to listen to your concerns about preliminary hearing evidence, this matter went to trial. The jury –

The Defendant: Let me –

The Court: Excuse me. The jury made credible determinations. The jury heard from you. The jury heard from the victims. They heard from a variety of witnesses. The findings were made, and were here at the time of judgment and sentencing. We're not here to revisit the motions for a new trial or holding orders at the preliminary hearing or anything else. Confine your comments to the relevant points at this point please.

The Defendant: Then perhaps I should couch it in the general terms that my character in the community doesn't match the allegations that were made in court, and the fact that the two primary complaining witnesses could have corroborated with each other and didn't is a profound statement as to their credibility and their character versus mine.

The Court: Again, the motion for a new trial has been ruled on. The jury –

The Defendant: I understand that. I'm speaking to character.

The Court: The jury made credibility determinations. Confine your comments to the relevant matters, please.

The Defendant: I have worked in the community for 30-plus years. I lived with the Guthrie family in a beneficial way to them. They spoke highly of me to all of their friends. Any statements that were made that were otherwise were untrue. I attempted to have additional friends show up, but the fact that their best friend Michelle Jackson, showed up, testified on my behalf and not theirs, shows that my credibility and my character was sound, and my character in the community was never impugned…

As far as why I shouldn't be sentenced to the maximum, I won't go into legal commentary, but as a person, you have to have your own reasonable doubts, you have to know that I didn't commit the crimes that were alleged, and therefore, why you chose not to exercise any discretion and create such a monumental sentence when it is obviously not required. So somehow I am finding it hard to understand why I'm not allowed to offer in evidence of mitigation, letters from people or items of that nature. I don't understand why they're not in the probation report, and I don't want to argue points that you've already ruled on, but I brought up the issue, and so the probation report as an objective report should have pursued the items I requested them to pursue, but they didn't.

And so I wonder how much I'm being railroaded through the system in order to just get it to the appellate court so they can foot the bill and Mono County's off the book and let somebody else take the blame for any charges that are made in the small little collegial atmosphere of the third floor.

So I mean, these are issues of – there is my character, which is unimpeached. Nobody came in here and said I was a liar. I took the stand and defended myself. I didn't shy from one question. I'm accountable for my actions. But for Chelsea to say I held her up and stuck her to the ceiling and Martha never said that happened should cause you some concern because my character isn't one to grab a girl and hang her up against the ceiling. Nor was their any evidence of anybody being beaten or hit.

So the fact that my character wasn't considered in this sentencing causes me some concerns, and that's why I requested the presentence hearing in order to resolve the probation report that was flawed on every page, on every level. There was nothing accurate in it, and I itemized the list to you in my presentation.

So I would argue that I deserve and am entitled to complete and fair evidence being produced in mitigation of my character and how I am in this community and what I did because I didn't go molesting anybody at any time.

But nonetheless, my character and my veracity and truthfulness in this matter should warrant a reasonable sentence and fair consideration of all the issues that have been raised, including my request for a stay so I can stay the execution of the judgment order so I can pursue the fertile grounds for appeal. Thank you.

The Court: Thank you Mr. Harris. It is the judgment of the court that the defendant Michael Jay Harris be sentenced to state prison under the custody and control of the Department of Corrections and Rehabilitation for a term of 285 years-to-life, allocated as indicated previously in my tentative decision, that is, a term of 15 years-to-life, fully consecutive, on each of the 19 counts.

The judge went on to state each and every count and sentence. I then received 1103 days credit for time served and got a $10,000 fine to be paid out of my prison salary if I earned one. Parole was to be for five years if I lived to be paroled. I immediately filed my notice of appeal. Ms. Hankel was told her appointment would continue for a period of ten days. It was over and I was whisked to a waiting patrol car for my last ride home. But not if I could help it.

FIFTY-THREE

Having been sentenced to 285 years to Life for a crime which never occurred I was back in my cell ruminating over my twisted fate. I wanted to scream but I didn't. I was going to stand tall and fight this out. All the way to the United Supreme Court if need be. The first thing I did was write to the California Appellate Project for California's Third Appellate District. I had filed a notice of appeal and in so doing I had applied for indigent counsel. The Appellate Project is the organization that handles and dispenses assignments for the indigent attorneys. When I contacted them I was told I wouldn't have an attorney assigned to me until my record on appeal was complete and that would likely take months.

I was frustrated. I wanted a new trial while the witnesses were still fresh. I decided right away to file my own habeas petition in the Third District Court of Appeal

3rd DCA). I didn't have much information to go on from a legal perspective. I had some old Witkin law books, and some old Deering's annotated codes. The jail staff gave me some forms and I quickly sent in two petitions under the misguided assumption that was how you made separate claims. Boy, was I wrong.

In the first petition I raised the issue of illegal conviction and sentence. In the second petition I alleged ineffective assistance of counsel. I thought for sure I would get a hearing because Judge DeVore had told me in no uncertain terms that my claims were better suited for appeal under habeas corpus. This then was my indoctrination into the world of law, where there always were two sides to an issue.

Of those two habeas petitions, the second was my best shot. The first one, the illegal conviction and sentence was weak. I wrote that the basis for asserting the illegal conviction and sentence relied on the prerequisite determination by the court in its fact-finding mission to identify specific occasions in order to compensate for the People's failure to elicit specific facts in the jury's verdict which were required for legal sentencing to occur. It was inappropriate and beyond the court's authority to hypothesize which acts the jury may have based its verdicts on, or what dates might have been attached to certain acts such as "more than one time" or "first time/last time" and other generic testimony elicited during the trial. The ambiguous evidence adduced at trial and the trial court's factfinding actions amounted to judicial impingement upon the traditional role of the jury. (See Blakely v Washington 542 US 296, 309 (2004)).

If the jury had convicted on all charged counts unanimously, the separateness of occasion issue would still be unclear, confounded by the lack of any specific occasion descriptor with which the court could make a verdict based determination. The factor of same occasion or separate occasion is the gateway to any sentence derived from a multiple count, multiple victim criminal action.

The absence of facts determined by the jury through its verdicts did not allow the court to sentence in an indeterminate way pursuant to the former §667.61 (g) or in any discretionary way involving a determinate sentence and §1170. Also see California Rules of Court, rules 4.420, 4.425 and 4.437.

Clearly, the People's use of generic testimony based on "first time/last time" descriptor lowered the burden of roof making it easier to bear. However, their ability to plead and prove separate and distinct occasions through the judge's fact-finding mission rendered the entire case reversible error. (See United States v Booker 543 US 220 (2005); People v Black (2005) 35 Cal. 4th 1238, 1262-1262-1263; Cunningham v California ____ US ____ (2007)). Even the leading case on generic testimony in a §288 (a) action, People v Jones (1990) 5 Cal. 3d 294, holds that the minimum quantum of proof would require the victim to describe a general time period in which an act occurred. (Id. at p. 316).

Noteworthy in my habeas petition was the People's error in pleading and proving the requisite separateness of occasion necessary for proper sentencing as well as the trial court's willingness to perpetuate the People's failings by imposing consecutive "One Strike" sentences even in the absence of any tangible factual finding by a jury required to support the sentence. This is plainly error with prejudice in my opinion, beyond a reasonable doubt and as such required a reversal of the conviction. (See Chapman v California 386 US 18, 24 (1967)).

During sentencing, Judge DeVore justified his sentence by citing People v Murphy (1998) 65 Cal.App. 4th 35 as allowing multiple consecutive terms, but that was error. While Murphy does describe two consecutive terms, the holding notes the separate occasion and the same occasion multiple act criteria outlined in §667.61 (g). In Murphy, the allegation was six §667.61 (c) offenses against Carma L. and one §667.61 (c) offense against Kristi R. Absent the former §667.61 (g) directive, Murphy would have been sentenced to seven life terms pursuant to §667.61 (b) but because six of the subdivision (c) offenses were committed against a single victim (Carma L.) on a single occasion, §667.61 (g) limits the punishment to one life term instead of six. Murphy was also convicted of a single subdivision (c) offense against Kristi R. on a separate occasion under one of the circumstances specified in subdivision (e) therefore Murphy was sentenced to another life term on that conviction. (Id. at p. 40).

Addressing the former §667.61 and the subdivision (c)(7) proviso regarding probation, it was interesting that should the court grant probation to the defendant found guilty of §288 (a) against more than one victim then the life terms would not apply and the penalty provision of §667.61 would be withdrawn from the option of the People without a determination by a jury. I'm just sayin'. This issue becomes more intriguing if you consider that one victim may want treatment and reconciliation while another victim opposes probation for the defendant. Though I had not standing to argue the People's positions, it was my contention that the weakness in their pleadings led to the sentencing errors.

A proper pleading could have and should have simply alleged separate occasions for each act charged, alleged that probation would not be in the best interest of the child, of allege that a substantial threat of harm exists. The jury could have then decided and found all the facts necessary for a legal sentencing phase. A proper multiple victim special allegation verdict form should have had specific, count by count, victim by victim checkboxes so the jury could have articulated the specific facts they found. These facts were necessary for Judge DeVore to legally pass sentence instead of being forced to extrapolate his own facts in order to sentence me as he had. Statutory and decisional law requires all facts in a criminal action to be found by a trier of fact (a jury) unless the defendant requests a bench trial' (judge only) which I did not do.

When a judge inflicts punishment that the jury's verdict alone does not allow, the jury has not found all the facts which the law makes essential to the punishment and the judge exceeds his authority.

(Blakely v Washington, supra, at 304).

Now my second and arguably better petition alleged ineffective assistance of trial counsel (IATC) and I was counting on it to get me a new trial even if I failed on my other petition. The right to the assistance of counsel is a fundamental right granted to and individual through Article I sections 15 and 24 of the California Constitution, and the Sixth and Fourteenth Amendments to the United States Constitution. The effective assistance of counsel is a function of due process. The Due Process Clause of both the State and Federal Constitutions require a prevention of unjust deprivation of an individual's right to life, liberty and property. Included rights retained by a defendant in a criminal action related to due process are access to an impartial jury, the right to confront those witnesses against and to compelled testimony for a defendant, the right to a speedy trial by an impartial jury, and the effective assistance of counsel, among other rights not relevant here.

The due process safeguards required for protection of an individual's statutory interests must be analyzed in the context of the principle that freedom from arbitrary adjudicative procedures is a substantial element of one's liberty.

(People v Ramirez (1979) 25 Cal. 3d 260).

Denial of the right to effective assistance of counsel is not only reversible error per se (in and of itself), but is reviewable on habeas corpus after the final judgment of conviction. The right to counsel is guaranteed as detailed above and if impaired by ineffectiveness then it is reversible error per se. (See People v Ibarra (1963) 60 Cal. 2d 460, 466). The farce or sham test of Ibarra is no longer controlling however. Replaced by the Pope test (People v Pope (1979) 23 Cal. 3d 412), Pope held that effectiveness of counsel must be determined by standards based in due process.

The burden of providing a claim of inadequate trial assistance is on the defendant and the defendant must show that trial counsel failed to act in a manner to be

> *expected of a reasonably competent attorney acting as a diligent advocate and that counsel's performance resulted in the withdrawal of a potentially meritorious defense.*

(Id. at p. 425)

The federal courts have similarly held that the appropriate standards for testing the adequacy of counsel is "reasonably effective assistance." (See Strickland v Washington 466 US 668 (1984); also McMann v Richardson 397 US 759 (1970)). Strickland has held that the benchmark or test for judging a claim or ineffectiveness is whether counsel's conduct so undermined the adversarial process that the trial court cannot be relied on as having produced a just result. Further holding that any claim by a defendant of ineffective assistance of counsel requires a showing of both deficient performance by an attorney as well as proof of resulting prejudice. The prove prejudice, the defendant must show that there is a reasonable probability that but for counsel's unprofessional errors, the result of the proceeding would have been different.

Another relevant and leading case is People v Marsden (1970) 2 Cal. 3d 118 and its holding that a defendant may have knowledge of conduct and events relative to the diligence and competence of his attorney not apparent to the trial judge from his observations in the courtroom. (Id. at pp. 123, 125-126). The California Supreme Court has consistently upheld the Pope and Marsden standard. Reasonably effective assistance must be provided to a defendant and the burden is on the defendant to demonstrate that absent counsel's failings it is reasonably probable that a more favorable determination would have resulted.

It is a slippery slope indeed when a defendant disagrees with the actions of appointed counsel. Longstanding case law supports counsel's exclusive authority to demine trial tactics and strategy despite differences of opinion or open objections by the defendant. (See People v Jackson (1969) 186 Cal.App. 2d 307, 315; People v Stewart (1967) 250 Cal.App. 2d 829, 832; People v Marsen, supra,) These cases illustrate the "captain of the ship" doctrine and California Code Civil Procedure §285 which enforces the state's denial of standing to a defendant receiving the assistance of appointed counsel. (See People v Monk (1961) 56 Cal. 2d 288, 299). A defendant is never provided counsel to challenge appointed counsel and therefore any challenge to an appointed counsel's actions or omissions is done Pro. Per. (by yourself) and alienates both attorney and judge alike. To make the required showing based on decisional law a defendant must possess both skill and factual evidence to support any claims made.

The crux of my case was actually twofold. First, does appointed counsel have the right to impinge upon my constitutional rights by way of statutory or decisional law authority and; second, does the court have the authority to withhold factual documentary evidence from myself thereby restricting my ability to demonstrate the ineffectiveness of Ms. Hankel, who was withholding the evidence in the first place. I am entitled to every right which is embraced within the constitutional guarantee of procedural due process. Even if a statutory right I possess has not been held to be an element of due process, it may be considered such an important limitation on the powers of the trial judge that a violation is an act in excess of jurisdiction. (See People v Kiihoa (1960) 53 Cal. 2d 748).

The statutory authority of my attorney, Ms. Hankel, to be my sole voice at trial (Cal. Code Civ. Proc. §285) is a procedural directive. Ms. Hankel did not possess to authority to assert or waive my constitutional rights including my due process rights. (See Townsend v Superior Court (1975) 15 Cal. 3d 774, 780). Despite the broad authority of Ms. Hankel to act on my behalf, there are situations where the authority of Ms. Hankel to act on my behalf, there are situations where the authority is, in fact, limited. The decision regarding Ms. Hankel's power to decide which defense to present is one such situation. Another is the limit on Ms. Hankel to not allow me to testify or tell my story.

My right to decide whether to present a particular defense applies to on if credible evidence exists to support the defense. (See People v Jones (1991) 533 Cal. 3d 115, 1139-1140, upholding People v Frierson (1985) 39 Cal. 3d 803). Distinguishable is that while Frierson is "qualitatively different from the bulk of decisions which have a properly confirmed counsel's broad control over 'trial tactics' and is analogous to those cases which have recognized the defendant's personal choice on the most 'fundamental decisions' in a criminal case" (People v Frierson at p. 814).

The question then begs, how can I assert my right to a particular defense by making a showing that credible evidence exists to support that particular defense if I am denied access to the evidence and the opportunity to make the required showing of "demonstrable reality?" A "defendant's insistence on presenting a particular defense will impinge on counsel's handling of the case, but this is so whenever a defendant chooses to exercise a personal right over counsel's advice." (Id. at p. 816).

Another similar holding in the Court of Appeal says that Ms. Hankel cannot deny me the right to opportunity to take the stand and that the "accused has the right to give his story to the jury even though in the attorney's judgment it may be fatal to his chances of acquittal." (People v Blye (1965) 233 Cal.App. 2d 143, 149). If I am not allowed to testify or my testimony is curtailed by defense counsel's limited questioning, it is not a question of waiver, but instead a question of adequate representation by Ms. Hankel. If Ms. Hankel's error keeps my story from being presented to the jury and if the testimony is not perurious then "his real complaint is that he was denied effective representation by counsel, not that he was denied the opportunity to waive his right to testify in open court." (People v Mosqueda (1970) 5 Cal. App. 3d 540, 545; People v Shells (1971) 4 Cal. 3d 626, 631).

Ms. Hankel cannot deny me the right to confront or cross-examine a complaining witness by incompleteness or a lack of thoroughness either. The importance of the opportunity to cross-examine was stressed in Lee v Illinois 476 US 530 (1986):

"The confrontation guarantee serves not only symbolic goals. The right to confront and to cross-examine witnesses is primarily a functional right that promotes reliability in criminal trials...The mechanisms of confrontation and cross-examination advance the pursuit of the truth in criminal trials."

(Ibid.)

In order for me to make a successful claim of ineffective assistance of counsel, I had to clearly demonstrate both error and prejudice.

"Defendant must demonstrate that counsel's ineffectiveness deprived him of a potentially meritorious defense. Nowhere in the petition or even in the declarations in support of the writ of habeas corpus was there any hint of the nature of the exculpatory testimony [petitioner] might have testified."

(In re Noday (1981) 125 Cal.App. 3d 507, 521).

Going further, related to Ms. Hankel's failure to call Kerri Guthrie as a witness;

"To sustain a claim of inadequate representation by reason of a failure to call a witness, there must be a showing from which it can be determined whether the alleged additional defense witness was material, necessary, or admissible, or that defense counsel did not exercise proper judgment in failing to call [her]."

(Id. at p. 522; also People v Shaw (1984) 35 Cal. 3d 535, 542 [failure to investigate potential alibi defense to probation violation charged constituted ineffective assistance]; People v Bess (1984) 153 Cal.App. 3d 1053,

1060, 1062 [defense counsel's failure to interview potentially favorable eyewitness constituted ineffective assistance counsel])

My ability to produce evidence relevant to my claim of ineffective assistance of counsel is directly related to my ability to bear the burden of proof through clear demonstration of Ms. Hankel's errors. In my case, I believe prejudice had clearly been shown. Article I, section 28(f)(2) of the California Constitution provides that all relevant evidence is admissible unless ruled inadmissible by the court on Evidence Code §352 grounds. Judge DeVore's withholding of relevant evidence related to my claim of ineffective assistance of counsel was an abuse of discretion. It was arbitrary and capricious. There would have been no prejudicial impact upon me if the evidence had been let in. There could have been no confusion of the issues and there would have been no undue consumption of time since the withheld evidence was the material issue of my IATC claim.

This abuse of discretion in withholding the necessary evidence violated my right to due process and had the corollary effect of denying me the effective assistance of counsel by foreclosing the opportunity to clearly demonstrate the inadequacies of Ms. Hankel's representation of me in this action.

The law is well settled that I can make a motion for a new trial based on the grounds of IATC, even though that ground is not enumerated in §1181. The trial court has a constitutional duty to ensure that I am accorded due process of law and that duty may not be limited by statute. (See People v Fosselman (1983) 33 Cal. 3d 572, 582). It is also well settled that I can raise the issue of IATC by means of a motion before, during, and after trial, to discharge my attorney and have a new one appointed. (People v Marsden, supra, 2 Cal. 3d 118). Once a Marsden motion is made the court must allow me to have an opportunity to speak on behalf of my request and fully explain the reasons for my dissatisfaction with appointed counsel. I had unique knowledge of conduct and events relative to the diligence and competence of Ms. Hankel which were not likely to be apparent to Judge DeVore from his observations in the courtroom. A Marsden motion is equally available to a defendant before, during, and after trial. (See People v Smith (1993) 6 Cal. 4th 684, 694). In fact, I had a reduced burden to obtain appointment of substitute counsel posttrial. (Id. at p. 692; also People v Stewart (1985) 171 Cal.App. 3d 388; People v Garcia (1991) 277 Cal. App. 3d 1369).

A defendant seeking to attack his conviction in the trial court on the basis that his attorney's ineffectiveness led to his conviction is in a far different position than a defendant seeking appointment of new counsel before he has been convicted. If there was any deficiency in his attorney's performance, the defendant needs effective assistance in demonstrating that deficiency and its bearing on the conviction.

If the attorney was ineffective in the preconviction stage, counsel's ability to effectively pursue the postconviction motion for new trial is suspect. And one can hardly expect the attorney whose performance is being directly challenged to assist the defendant in making the challenge. This is exactly what happened in my case. In such a case, the attorney has an inherent conflict. (See People v Smith, supra, at p. 692; also, People v Stewart, supra, at p. 395).

Distinguishable in my case is that Marsden looks to the future and Fosselman looks to the past. Clearly, trial counsel set on the following professional norms would see the inherent conflict of defending one's own positions while advocating another's. There is an inherent conflict in defending one's own positions while advocating another's simultaneously. Regardless of whether Ms. Hankel provides effective assistance before or during trial, effective representation of myself in a new trial motion based in part of Ms. Hankel's ineffectiveness is virtually impossible. Reversal is the plain, speedy, and adequate remedy if my interests are paramount to Ms. Hankel's acting as a conscientious and diligent advocate. Her failure to recuse herself led me to believe and infer that her interests were the focus and self defense the priority in my posttrial proceedings before Judge DeVore. All of this went into my second petition and I hoped for the best. I felt that I must reverse my life, I cannot live in the past.

FIFTY-FOUR

I felt really optimistic about my argument sitting in my cozy little cell with the TV. I thought that the law was on my side. I slept well knowing this was all going to be behind me soon.

At 5:00 am on May 3rd, 2010, I was awakened by Officer Bush and I were told to pack my stuff. I was going to prison. The jail staff were only too eager to see me go. I had stayed in Mono County Jail longer than anyone had before. I was there 2 years and almost nine months. Nothing to brag about really, but I was going to miss my cozy little cell which I had all to myself.

I had been up late the night before sending the appellate projecting copies of my two habeas petitions. Across the Sierra Nevada mountains we went in the early morning dawn. It was beautiful and I was sad. We were heading west towards the Great Central Valley of California. To be precise, we were heading for Tracy, CA., where I would be processed into the California Department of Corrections and Rehabilitation (CDCR) at Duell Vocational Institute known by everyone as DVI. This was a nice name for a dirty old prison. "Kashmir" by Led Zeppelin played on the radio as we entered the prison gates. I commented to Officer Robles that maybe I could learn a vocation and he quipped "yeah, his name is Bubba." Haha.

I processed in with the perfunctory strip search but surprisingly no cavity search. I was able to keep my box of legal papers but there was a strict policy that mandated nothing could come into prison with you yet somehow I made it with my box of papers. I had a crossword puzzle book secreted in with my legal papers and they let me keep that but they took out the answer pages. Welcome to prison. I went into a holding cell and tried to eat my horrendously bad lunch without getting beat up or raped. My imagination was getting the best of me at that point. I waited.

After a while my name was called and off I went. I grabbed up a box of papers and my bedroll and began walking down the longest hallway I had ever seen. It was like half-mile long if a foot. I quickly tired and had to stop a couple of times. The guards were pissed but I wasn't sprayed with pepper spray or beat with clubs or anything like that. I took that as a good sign. Yes on legal papers. No on beat down. The guards kept cajoling me to keep moving. I finally got to my cell block and it was downright scary. It was three levels high on both sides and 50 cells deep. There were doors on the cells, no bars.

I had been placed in a Special Processing Unit (SPU) since I was getting protective custody due to my commitment charges. That all didn't matter though, this was prison and nobody likes sex offenders. My first roommate called a "celly" was Juan, a visually impaired illegal alien who did some bad things. I never found out exactly what though. In prison, especially protective custody in prison, you don't talk about your personal business because it will always be used against you. Especially if you have sex crimes on your jacket. Those are the worst crimes you can be convicted of in prison culture. In prison, people won't even talk to you unless you show your paperwork. Paperwork consists of your Legal Status Summary (LSS) which is given to each inmate upon arrival. You are thus forced to hang out with other sex offenders or those who are also afraid to show their paperwork.

I should mention at this point that there are also retired or 86'd gang banger "drop-outs" in the mix and many of them are still what is called "active" which means they deal with vice and violence. They will beat up or stab a "chomo" at will. "Chomo" means child molester – don't ask me why it's not "chimo" but I digress.

The next morning I went to breakfast and managed to avoid getting beat up while attempting to eat the biscuits and gravy that can only be described as meat soup. I already missed the Mono County Jail and it was my first full day in prison. I went and applied to go to the law library while coming back from chow. More marching down endless halls with the occasional "Klaxon" alarm bringing everything to a standstill. Face the wall. Get down. Then more sweating in the cell with broken windows and no air conditioning. More waiting for the mail. More waiting. No TV. No radio. It was going to require some personal adjustment but at least I had a couple books and some crossword puzzles with no way to cheat.

After a few days I received notification from the 3rd DCA that both of my petitions had been denied summarily and without prejudice. Drats. I thought I had it in the bag. I had requested an evidentiary hearing and that was denied as well. After another week I got to go to the law library and it was awesome. They had all the law books and computers with searchable case files. You couldn't copy and paste or print though. Everything had to be copied by hand. I think that's where my handwriting got to be so sloppy. I learned to write fast, I had only an hour or two per week. I immediately started drafting a new habeas petition for the Mono County Superior Court. It seemed that the two petitions I sent to the 3rd DCA should have been put together in one comprehensive petition to the Mono County Superior Court in the first place. Then if it is denied there, I could go to the 3rd DCA. Following a denial there, I could go to the California Supreme Court. If I failed there then I would have to go to the federal courts; the US District Court for the Eastern District of California, the Ninth Circuit Court of Appeals, and ultimately the US Supreme Court. I really hoped I didn't have to go that far.

I wanted relief and I wanted it then and there. I really tried to conform my third habeas petition to the insights I had gleaned from the law library. I had three grounds or claims of error in one bombproof petition. I was still claiming illegal conviction and sentence and ineffective assistance of counsel but to that I added the arguably illegal Marsen hearing to the mix. I sent it to the court on June 28th, 2010 and it took the court exactly two weeks to kick me to the curb. I was crestfallen. I mean, I had the legal argument that should have got me out and yet I failed. I had no legal training. I was winging it. My expectations were getting blistered.

While this was going on, my record on appeal was finally delivered to the appellate project and the 3rd DCA. The appellate project assigned my case to Ms. Diane Nicholas of Grass Valley, CA. She wrote me right away with some basic information and she told me to knock it off with the serial habeas petitions. It turned out there was case law that says it is an abuse of the writ to keep filling in new forms and filing new petitions, improved or not. Statutorily there is no bar to successive petitions but in reality I was abusing the writ.

I was frustrated with Ms. Nichols' slow pace what with all her augmenting and correcting of the record. I felt like this was all slipping out of my control. I wanted to tell my story, completely. So I wrote out a fourth petition even though Ms. Nichols said to stop it. I wanted Ms. Nichols to expand her appointment to include a habaes petition but she refused to do so. Based on my legal research it was clear I could keep pushing the habeas proceedings while the direct appeal was ongoing. I sure didn't want to wait a couple of years to file a new detailed petition so I got busy. I went through all of my notes since I didn't have the transcripts to work from, Ms. Nichols had the only copy.

I wrote 163 pages detailing every last error I could think of. I wrote all about the facts with only 25 pages of law argument because it was plainly evident that my legal arguments were being ignored. This time the facts were crystal clear. The minimal argument was solid. I couldn't lose.

I was contending in my limited argument that reasonably competent assistance by an appointed attorney acting as a diligent and conscientious advocate is measured by "prevailing professional norms" and that was regardless of whether counsel was appointed or retained. Without a doubt, Ms. Hankel's withdrawal of potentially meritorious defense (the escalation defense) irrespective of excuse or level of recompense; whether by choice of counsel or by ignorance of the facts, or by failure to adequately investigate the facts, or by failure to research the law applicable to those facts, is nevertheless a withdrawal of the potentially meritorious defense and as such meets the duality of the Strickland standard which is deficient performance and resulting prejudice.

I felt like I met the criteria outlined in all the case law I had read, but it really depended on the court whether they wanted to give a convicted child molester any love. The key was whether Ms. Hankel's actions or omissions affected the outcome or led to a probability that is sufficient to undermine confidence in the outcome.

A fair trial is one in which evidence is subjected to adversarial testing and is presented to an impartial tribunal for resolution of the issues defined in advance of the proceedings. Proper preparation by counsel should be based on informed strategic choices made by me, based on information provided by me. That is how it should work. The reasonableness of counsel's actions may be determined or substantially influenced by my own statements or actions. A proper investigation of all the facts supplied by me, and, Ms. Hankel's research of the law applicable to those facts in the crux of any reasonableness test that evaluates the assistance of counsel that Ms. Hankel has provided and the reliability of the adversarial testing process. Any act or omission by Ms. Hankel that undermines this adversarial process undermines confidence in the outcome. "Fundamental to counsel's role is a duty to make reasonable investigations or to make a reasonable decision that makes particular investigations unnecessary." (Strickland v Washington supra, at 691).

Reasonableness has been defined as not extreme. Not arbitrary or capricious. Reasonableness depends on a variety of considerations and circumstances. It is an elastic term which is of uncertain value in a definition. Finding a bright line of reasonable and unreasonable really is a fielder's choice proposition. "Strategic choices made after less than complete investigation are reasonable precisely to the extent that reasonable professional judgement support limitations on investigation." (Ibid.)

As I have previously noted, the Strickland court has defined reasonableness to mean measured under "prevailing professional norms." The American Bar Association Standards for Criminal Justice have consistently been relied on by the United States Supreme Court as relevant indica of the "prevailing professional norms."

(See Rompilla v Beard 545 Us 373, 380 (2005)).

The ABA standards articulate:

" is the duty of the lawyer to conduct a prompt investigation of the circumstances of the case and to explore all avenues leading to facts relevant to the merits of the case and the penalty in the event of conviction."

(ABA Standards Rules of Professional Conduct).

'Before counsel undertakes to act or not to act, counsel must make a rational and informed decision on strategy and tactics founded upon adequate investigation and preparation."

(In re Marquez (1992) 1 Cal. 4th 585, 602).

"Counsel's primary 'duty is to investigate the facts of his client's case and to research the law applicable to those facts'. (People v Ledesma (1987) 43 Cal. 3d 171, 222). Counsel's decision regarding strategy and tactics must be rational and 'founded upon adequate investigation and preparation.' (In re Thomas (2006) 37 Cal. 4th 1249, 1258)."

(People v Doolin (2009) 45 Cal. 4th 390, 417).

It is important to point out that Ms. Hankel didn't start her investigation until mere weeks before my trial, over two years after my arrest. This was the result of having Mr. Gephart, who did nothing, and then Ms. Hankel couldn't get an investigator to work on my case. This was extremely frustrating. When things finally did start developing, I was left out of the discussions such as the Jackson's involvement and "those boys" statements for example. I bear the burden of showing the act or omission which has undermined confidence in the outcome. Which the acts or omissions involve improper investigations or research of the law based on evidence not a part of the record, then the only means of making the proper showing is with an evidentiary hearing in which an inquiry can be made into my claims in order to answer the factual questions necessary to the determination of whether Ms. Hankel's acts and/or omissions were based on reasonable decision making or not.

I requested an evidentiary hearing before with no luck. Several times. I just wanted the attorney-client case file and an evidentiary hearing to show what I believed was inadequate representation. I truly believed that Ms. Hankel was operating under a conflict of interest, her own and mine. I wanted the attorney-client file and a hearing to prove my claims of error. Ms. Hankel wanted to keep the file to support her contention that her representation of me was constitutionally adequate.

"A criminal defendant is guaranteed the right to the assistance of counsel by the Sixth Amendment to the United States Constitution and Article I, §15 of the California Constitution. This constitutional right includes the correlative right to representation free from any conflict of interest that undermines counsel's loyalty to his or her client. (See Glasser v United States 315 US 60, 69-70 (1942); People v Douglas (1964) 61 Cal 2d 430, 436-439)."

(People v Doolin, supra, 45, 45 Cal. 4th 390).

I have steadfastly contended in my case that I am innocent and Ms. Hankel's and Mr. Gephart's actions and omissions have cause evidence to be missing from the record. I sought the due process remedy outlined in Fosselman by seeking a new trial based on the claimed deficiencies. Ms. Hankel, the actual trial attorney, labored under an actual conflict of interest for reasons described above. A conflict of interest can occur when,

"[a]n attorney's loyalty to or efforts on behalf of a client are threatened by his responsibilities to another client, or a third party, or his own interests. (People v

Cox (1991) 53, 3d 618, 653; quoting People v Bonin (1989) 47 Cal. 3d 808, 835)."

(People v Doolin, supra, 45, 45 Cal. 4th 390).

The Doolin court held that it was bringing California jurisprudence in line with federal law outlined in Mickens v Taylor 535 US 162 (2002) by adopting the Strickland standard for review of conflict of interest claims brought forth in post conviction proceedings. The Doolin court also explained that:

"An 'actual conflict' and an 'adverse effect' on a counsel's performance are not separate considerations. An actual conflict is 'demonstrated' precisely when it can be established that a conflict of interest 'adversely affected' counsel's performance."

(People v Doolin, supra, 45, 45 Cal. 4th 390; citing Mickens v Taylor, supra at 171).

The Mickens court specifically held that a defendant must show that counsel's conflict of interest adversely affected their performance and wrote about any confusion regarding presumed prejudice previously outlined by the High Court that the majority now thought:

"An actual conflict of interest meant precisely a conflict of interest that affected counsel's performance as opposed to a mere theoretical division of loyalties... 'A defendant who shows that a conflict of interest actually affected the adequacy of his representation need not demonstrate prejudice in order to obtain relief."

(Mickens v Taylor, supra, at 171; citing Cuyler v Sullivan 446 US 335, 349-350 (1980)).

I have alleged that Ms. Hankel clearly defended and protected her own interests at my expense by not providing me with my own documents necessary to making a demonstrable showing of error by the very person withholding the documents. Ms. Hankel argued against the very same evidence she put forth as grounds for a new trial which was an obvious action taken to protect her own interests.

Traditionally, appointed counsel such as Ms. Hankel, has retained ultimate control over trail strategy and tactics, is "captain of the ship" as it were. Counsel's statutory authority encompasses decision making over all but the most fundamental decisions involving fundamental constitutional rights. The "fundamental" decisions have been defined as pleading guilty, waving jury trial, waving counsel, and waving self-incrimination. (See In re Horton (1991) 54 Cal. 3d 82, 95).

The authority to control strategy and tactics as discussed above is a statutory authority, California Code of Civil Procedure §285, as such is a procedural directive distinguishable from a constitutional authority. While Cal. Code of Civ. Proc. §285 requires the court to exclusively recognize appointed counsel unless replacement pursuant to Cal. Code of Civ. Proc. §284, the trial court did have the discretion to allow a defendant like myself to participate in the presentation of my case thus there was no statutory or constitutional mandate that Ms. Hankel was in fact "captain of the ship." (See People v Hamilton (1998) 48 Cal. 3d at pp 1162-1165).

A motion for a new trial is a critical stage of the proceedings. "Trial courts have a constitutional duty to insure that defendants be accorded due process of the law and this duty may not be limited by statute. "(People v Fosselman, supra, at p. 582; also, People v Smith, supra, 6 Cal. 4th 684).

An attorney such as Ms. Hankel was not and is not authorized to assert or waive any of my constitutional rights involving fundamental fairness. (See Townsend v Superior Court (1975) 15 Cal. 3d 774, 780). The Faretta Court detailed the rights guaranteed to me by the Sixth Amendment, holding that the right to defend is a given directly to the accused, of it is he who suffers the consequences if the defense fails. (See Faretta v California at 819-820). Although Faretta deals with self-representation, the court outlined the assistance of counsel provision thusly:

"It speaks of the 'assistance' of counsel and the assistant, however expert, is still an assistant. The language and spirit of the Sixth Amendment contemplates that counsel, like other defense tools guaranteed by the Amendment, shall be an aid to a willing defendant, not an organ of the State interspersed between an unwilling defendant and his right to defend himself personally."

(Ibid.)

Even the dissenting Justices in Faretta made it abundantly clear that defense counsel does not enjoy an unlimited discretion to employ any trial strategy or tactic it chooses when the strategy or tactic overrides a defendant's wishes on matters of fundamental importance.

In the case of People v Bloom (1998) 48 Cal. 3d 1194, the California Supreme Court understood the basic teaching in Faretta to be:

"that the state may not constitutionally prevent a defendant charged with the commission of a criminal offense from controlling his own fate by forcing on him counsel who may present a case which is not consistent with the wishes of the defendant."

(Id. at p.1220; citing People v Windham, supra, 199 Cal. 3e at p 130).

The California Supreme Court has also repeatedly upheld the "captain of the ship" doctrine which allowed Ms. Hankel to present a case which was inconsistent with my wishes. For example, "A defendant does not have the right to present a defense of his choosing, but merely the right to an adequate and competent defense." (People v Cole (2004) 33 Cal. 4th 1198, cert. denied 125 S. Ct. 1931; upholding and citing People v Welch (1999) 20 Cal. 4th 701, 728-729, quoting Hamilton)

The core rationale of Faretta is that unwanted counsel represents the defendant only through a tenuous and unacceptable legal fiction. (See Faretta at 821). Of course the difference between self-representation and having the assistance of counsel are substantial. I have argued that the Sixth Amendment does in fact guarantee me the right to a defense of my choosing. The Sixth Amendment is quite clear. I am entitled to the assistance of counsel for my defense.

At no time when I was appointed Ms. Hankel or Mr. Gephart as my defense counsel was I informed about or asked to waive my constitutional rights in order to receive public, indigent, representation. The main issue I have raised is one of distinguishability; is the assistance of counsel really assistance, or a take it or leave it proposition? Certainly the California Supreme Court has been sensitive of the need to respect a defendant's "personal choices" on the most "fundamental' issues.

"The right to the assistance of counsel and the correlative right to dispense with a lawyers help are not legal formalisms. They rest on considerations that go to the substance of an accused's positions before the law. The public conscience must be satisfied that fairness dominates the administration of justice. An accused must have the means of presenting his best defense. He must have time and facilities for investigation, and for the production of evidence. But evidence and truth are of no avail unless they can be adequately presented. Essential fairness is lacking if an accused cannot put his case effectively in court.

(Adams v US ex rel McCann 317 US 269, 279 (1942); citing Johnson v Zerbst 304 US 458, 468-469 (1938)).

Presenting the best defense is paramount, but who gets to decide the best defense?

Ms. Hankel was asked to cross-examine and present witnesses, but she refused to comply. The main and essential right of confrontation is to secure for the opponent the opportunity for cross-examination. The public has no interest in convicting on the testimony of witnesses who have not been rigorously cross-examined and thoroughly impeached as the evidence permits. Cross-examination provides a jury the opportunity to fully assess the credibility of the witnesses and their testimony. The judiciary has an obligation to insure that the constitutional right of an accused to a fail trial is realized. If that right would be thwarted by the enforcement of a statue, the statue must yield. (See People v Memro (1985) 38 Cal. 3d 658, 677; People v Raiser (1956) 47 Cal. 2d 566, 586; Hammarley v Superior Court (1979) 89 Cal.App. 3d 388, 401).

I have also posited that credible evidence exists which precludes any waiver of fundamental rights held exclusively by myself. Ms. Hankel erred in not calling exculpatory witnesses, not presenting exculpatory evidence, for not cross-examining to the extent the evidence allowed in order to impeach the evidence against me, and also in opposing my demand for a speedy trial, albeit late in the game.

Even more to the point, the denial of due process through the ineffectiveness of counsel is a two-fold error; a denial of the assistance of counsel, and the denial of the effective assistance of counsel denied me my right to receive a fair trial by lowering the People's burden of proof. Ms. Hankel's actions and omissions, simply put, constituted a denial of due process of law and fundamental fairness.

The First Amendment to the United States Constitution provides quite succinctly that "Congress shall make no law abridging the freedom of speech, or of the press." (Ibid.) Despite its literal words, the First Amendment applies not just to Congress but equally to all branches of the federal and state governments. I submit to you that this means that Cal. Code of Civ. Proc. §285 is not constitutionally permitted to abridge the ability of myself to testify freely and fully in my own defense.

The right to testify is a fundamental decision over which the defendant rather than his counsel must have ultimate control. (See People v Robles (1979) 2 Cal. 3d 205). The Robles court rejected the argument that defense counsel has the authority over the calling of the witnesses including the defendant in making "tactical" decisions and explained:

"Although an attorney representing a criminal defendant has the power to control the court proceedings, that power may not be exercised to deprive a defendant of certain fundamental rights. We are satisfied that the right to testify in one's own behalf is of such fundamental importance that a defendant who timely demands to take the stand contrary to the advice given by his counsel has the right to give an exposition of his defense before a jury."

(Ibid.)

At trial, I asserted my First Amendment right to speak freely when I told the court I was going to testify on my own behalf despite Ms. Hankel's opposition. Her concerns were unfounded and with all that had transpired, what with the girls' testimony and the voluminous computer evidence, I felt obliged and eager as a citizen of my community to stand up for myself. Besides, I was downright angry. I put forth in my fourth petition for writ of habeas corpus that choosing to testify is an exercise of the right to free speech, and an exercise of the right to present a particular defense if credible evidence exists to support the exercise. (See People v Jones, supra, 53 Cal. 3d at pp. 1139-1140). At trial, Ms. Hankel failed to ask me about the numerous events which led up to the allegations being made against me. Ms. Hankel also failed to ask me about the numerous other topics I listed in my note I gave her before testifying.

FIFTY-FIVE

While I worked on my fourth habeas petition I was getting prepared to transfer to another prison. I was still at DVI in "reception" as it's called. While there I had refused to cell up with some questionable cellies and so I wound up housed in Administrative Segregation (Ad/Seg). In Ad/Seg I was alone in my cell all day long so I was able to really focus on my petition. And I mean FOCUS. It was 187 pages long and filled with facts and arguments. I also included over 300 pages of exhibits so in total I had over 500 pages I needed to copy and mail out. While in Ad/Seg I was still able to use the law library and that was where I needed to go and get my copies. There is a limit in the California State prison system that you can only copy a maximum of 100 pages. I went to the law library and filled out the form and made my best argument why I should be allowed to exceed the page limit set by the CDCR. To my utter disbelief the library approved my request and made over 1,000 pages of copies.

I received the copies and envelopes on the same day that correctional officers told me to pack up my stuff, I was transferring to High Desert State Prison the next day. I mailed out my petition that night and the next morning I was awakened at 3:00 am and taken by bus to my new home in Susanville, CA., 90 miles north of Reno, NV.

Upon arrival things got scary right away. I asked to be placed in Ad/Seg because of my safety concerns and unwillingness to "cell up." The guards laughed at me. They told me to get in a holding cell with a bunch of other prisoners and I refused. The officers proceeded to take me down and rough me up. I screamed bloody murder. Then they got me up and put me in a six foot tall and three foot square cage made of steel mesh. These cages are technically called "therapeutic modules" but I wasn't getting any therapy. Off came my clothes and out went my sack dinner. All I could do was stand there freezing cold They ordered me to face the wall.

I then claimed I was suicidal and that got me in to see the nurse. I told her the officers were beating me up and she said nothing. The officers told me to shut up and just answer the questions. The officers then took me barefoot and in only my boxer shorts out into the freezing cold early November night. They hustled me over to the hospital for a suicide check. Just before taking me inside they hit me in my stomach and said "we don't like your type here. We have kids." I said nothing. I was taken into the hospital and put in my holding tank to wait for the doctor to arrive.

After a couple of hours the doctor arrived and quickly determined that I wasn't suicidal. He said I was just manipulating the officers so I wouldn't have to go into a cell with another inmate. The doctor was right but I didn't want officers to know that, they might write me up a Rules Violation Report, a "115." Anyway, off to "B" yard I went, into the cold and frigid night, still with just my boxers on.

"B" yard was a Special Needs Yard (SNY) for protective custody inmates. Besides sex offenders and former cops there were a lot of "dropout" gangbangers. I mean tattooed on the head and face convicts. Hardened convicts at that. These guys didn't care about anything except drugs and violence. Many of them were Life Without Possibility of Parole (LWOP) prisoners and many others had long sentences. "B" yard was a level 4 yard and that is the worst of the worst. So there I was, marching in my boxer shorts in the freezing cold toward 3 block on B-yard. There I was told to go into a cell by Officer Weeks with my new celly, Carlos. Officer Weeks told me that "If he wants you to sleep under the bed, you do it." I was nervous and I smelled bad. Carlos told me to shut the door and take a "bird bath." A bird bath is a bath using the sink and a rag with a milk carton cup. I did so.

When I was done he asked me if I was a sex offender. I told him I would rather not say and he said "Look, I'm your celly, you gotta tell me." So I replied "Yeah, but I'm innocent and I'm still fighting my case." He said that was fine but I was going to have to find another cell. He said he couldn't have me in his cell. He added that the guards wanted him to take me out but he said he "wasn't going to do their dirty work." The rest of the night was uneventful, he even gave me a soup.

The next morning Carlos made me some coffee and soon thereafter I was moved to a new cell . My new celly was "Ron" who was a convicted sex offender who had pled guilty to molesting a young boy. I was disgusted and prison protocol mandated that I beat him up, yet I felt safe with him. The other inmates worried me however because they all knew Ron was a sex offender. I figured they thought I was too.

Well, several days passed by and suddenly my habeas petition was sent back to me with a letter from the court clerk stating I had sent it to the wrong court, the trial court, and the clerk were wrong. I returned it right back to the Mammoth court and they mailed it to the Lassen County Superior Court in Susanville. I sent a motion to the Lassen court explaining the Mono County error and Lassen County agreed, sending the petition back to Mammoth.

After several months of back and forth my petition was assigned to visiting judge John Ball out of Santa Clara County. He issued an order for an informal response from the Mono County District Attorney. The DA asked for several extensions and the court granted them all.

Meanwhile, me and my prison experience were not very pleasurable. I was moved and got a new celly after I was attacked on the way to chow. It was a total sucker punch to the back of my head. I wasn't hurt but I was moved to a new building. I was moved in with a hearing impaired guy and that was great. He had a TV. Ron also got a new celly after I left and Ron was promptly beat up badly.

I remember vividly an incident one day in the medical clinic. I was being examined by a doctor and the correctional officer (c/o) was standing by the door. The c/o asked what I was in for, meaning what was I convicted of. I told him I would rather not discuss it. The c/o left and went to his computer and looked me up on SOMS. He quickly came back and in front of the nurse and the doctor detailed my 19 consecutive 15 year to life sentences for §269 (a)(1) and §288 (a). He also discussed the twins' victims impact statement contained in my probation report in my Central File (C-File). This is the CDCR master record for all inmates.

The officers were all over me after that. I lasted three days without my hearing impaired celly before he had them move me out. I was afraid to go to chow so I wasn't eating and he thought that was a sign of guilt or weakness. I later found out that a month before an inmate had been stabbed to death in his sleep for being a chomo in the same bunk I had been sleeping in. That was spooky and I am glad I moved.

I changed buildings again and moved in with "Jose." He was very muscular from working out. This made me apprehensive at first but as it turned out, he was a decent guy. He wasn't violent but he did work out a lot and take a lot of bird baths. I figured he was a sex offender because he had no paperwork at all and hid his legal mail. Most inmates asked me legal questions but not Jose. I settled into a routine of sorts but there were lots of lockdowns and getting to the law library was a real challenge. Overall I did my best but then one day I let things get the better of me. I said 'Fuck You" to a c/o. He was banging on my window everyday and waking me up for the "close custody" count. That really didn't go over well. He made me and Jose go in the shower and then proceeded to toss our cell. The c/o threw away a bunch of my important stuff like addresses, pens, and papers. He tossed all my legal papers loosely onto my bunk. It looked like a tornado had gone through the cell.

After that it was all bad. Jose got approval to switch cells which meant that I was getting a new celly. I had arranged to move in with a safe black celly (the blacks are a lot more forgiving about paperwork) but the c/o, Officer Robinette, said no way. He told me in no uncertain terms that I was taking the celly assigned to me or else. Officer Robinette is the c/o I said fuck you to so it was getting real. I began to rebel by laying out prone on the floor and told Robinette I wanted to speak with the sergeant. Robinette laughed at me and so did the inmates. This went on for several minutes then finally Robinette came over and told me to get up and cuff up. I complied but after handcuffing my hands behind my back, Robinette started hitting me in my head and face. I dropped to the floor where Robinette and another c/o started kicking me all over my body all the while yelling "stop resisting." This is c/o code for beat his ass. Remember, I was handcuffed during all this.

Finally after a minute or three a bunch of other c/o's showed up because the alarm had sounded. Medical staff responded a little bit later. I was manhandled over to the sergeants office and placed in a therapeutic module, a cage. I was ordered to strip out so the nurse could inspect my body for injuries. My side ribcage was killing me, my head and face were sore, and I felt dizzy and nauseous. I told the nurse this and she then had me placed on a backboard with a neck brace placed on my neck. I was strapped down tight and transported to the Correctional Treatment Center or CTC. Once there, a sergeant came in to speak with me and he asked if I was going to file a complaint and I said "Hell yeah." He said "that's bullshit." He then stormed off in a huff. I was taken to the hospital in Susanville where they said I was fine without so much as an aspirin for my pain.

When I got back to prison I told the medical staff I was suicidal and did not want to live any longer. In a way I meant it. Everybody laughed at me and the c/o's took me to a safety cell. I was told to strip down naked and go in with nothing; no blanket, no pillow, nothing. Inside of the small eight-foot square room I saw a one foot metal sink in the middle of the room set in the floor with a grate cover and I was told that was my toilet. I was in serious pain, I had not had lunch or dinner, and I couldn't get an aspirin because they were in my property and not prescribed to be administered by the nursing staff. I was depressed and super stressed out.

The next day came ever so slowly, I hadn't slept a wink. My breakfast came with no utensils of course, so I groveled on the floor and ate as best I could sitting naked on a cold, hard cement floor. The whole time I was in the safety cell there had been a nurse sitting outside the cell watching to make sure I didn't kill myself. I wasn't even sure if that were possible what with me sitting naked in a naked room. I decided then and there I was going to leave High Desert State Prison one way or another. I had had enough of their sadistic ways. After a couple days naked, I was given a safety smock which is a heavy blanket you wear like a poncho. I was then removed from the safety cell and placed in a "crisis bed" which was a large empty room with a built-in bed in the middle with a toilet and sink off to one corner by the door so everyone can see you. There was also a camera on the ceiling. Luckly I was also a foam mattress with a heavy cover that couldn't be torn and made into a noose.

I had heard that if you could stick it out for ten days in the crisis bed you would be transferred to the Department of State Hospital (DSH) where you will get enhanced therapy. Thus I began a regimen of eating, sleeping, and daydreaming about food, my case in the courts, and the universe as a whole. On my seventh day I met with the Inter-disciplinary Treatment Team (IDTT) and they recommended I go back to the yard where I had been before. They also recommended that I be placed in a less restrictive cell with no camera and lights that turn off. I knew my time was short and I had to do something.

My first night I rolled up my blanket they had given me and folding it up I made a loop on one end. Next, I stuck the two ends in a metal handle on the bed and stuck my head in the loop. Then I twisted around and around on the floor until the blanket was tight around my neck. The blood flow was cut-off. I waited. My left arm was in pain and my head felt like it was going to pop. Before I died a nurse came in and saw me hanging with a blanket while lying on the floor.

She set off the alarm and the c/o came rushing in and yanked the blanket off of the handle. He then pulled me out from under the bed and cuffed me up. I was escorted back to the safety cell, ordered to strip out, and in I went. This time I only stayed a day naked before I was placed back in a crisis bed bt this time with no mattress and no blanket. I did get a safety smock though. I tried to get the duty doctor to at least give me a mattress pad but he just laughed at me and said I would have to wait until Monday when the regular clinic doctor would return. It was Thursday so things were bleak. It was bad. I tried sleeping on the concrete floor by curling up inside my smock and using my fist as a pillow; this was crazy. Or was I?

The duty doctor kept coming by, asking how I was doing, but he wasn't giving me any love. In the end I somehow bivvied (bivouacked) until Monday morning when the doctor returned and said I could have a mattress. I didn't get it until that afternoon however. No blanket was given. I positioned the pad under the heater vent and let the warm air alternate with the cold air blowing over me. This cycle of comfort and misery is how I passed the time. A couple of days later I was told I could shower. That was like being in heaven. They wouldn't let me shave though for obvious reasons.

The next morning the guards came for me at daybreak and I was whisked away to the California Medical Facility at Vacaville, CA. I was thrilled to be leaving the nightmare that was High Desert State Prison. I cherished the memory of the rising sun and the brilliant glare piercing the guard tower and barbed wire electric fence as I left. It took about six hours to cross the High Sierra to Vacaville.

When I got there I was placed in a crisis cell with a smock, a mattress pad, and two blankets. I was given a hot lunch. Corned beef and potatoes. It was outstanding. I was depressed, but I was definitely having a positive moment. That lasted about as long as it took to eat. I was alone in a cell with a plastic bed glued to the floor and a thin pad. I did some real soul searching.

After lunch I met with my treatment team and I was pleasantly surprised to learn that when I went back to prison I would be what they called an Enhanced Outpatient or EOP for short. That meant I couldn't go back to High Desert. They didn't have an EOP program there. That was great news. I settled into a routine at DSH getting three hot meals a day instead of the normal two and a sack lunch in prison. We also got cold milk with every meal and a snack at 8:00 pm. This was unheard of. It was simply awesome.

I passed the time by watching the drama unfold outside my cell as patients came and went, some trying to commit suicide, others just being disruptive. I was across from the five-point restraint room where they tied you down and injected you with heavy drugs if you were out of control. Eventually I got clothes instead of a smock and they let me go to the law library. There I had to sit in a cage without any computer access. Only hardbound law books were available to me as a DSH patient. That was no way to do contemporary legal research but I did my best.

One day I thought they were taking a few of us down to the law library so I kicked my door a couple times when I thought they had forgot me. I yelled too. I really needed to get in to do some mailings. Well, the escort officer came to my cell and told me I was too agitated to go to the law library that day. The moment that happened was like an epiphany to me, being belligerent and disruptive was acceptable among the inmates but with staff, they either ignored you or beat you up. Then and there I decided to be quiet and work exclusively on proving my innocence.

After 37 days in DSH at Vacaville, I was discharged and transferred to Mule Creek State Prison in Ione, CA. Once there I was put right into Ad/Seg because there was a lack of bed space in the EOP building on the "A" yard. I like Ad/Seg. I was EOP so I had groups and movies and there was a law library right in the building. There were no computers though.

Shortly thereafter I heard from the Mono County District Attorney's Office with their informal response to my petition. They didn't really respond to my legal claims or my IATC complaints. Instead, Mr. Graham, the deputy DA focused on the facts adduced at the trial which were in his favor. It became clear in my legal research that once I had been convicted, all the accusations and insinuations became irrefutable facts that could be used against me ad hoc, forever. This despite my assertions and proof to the contrary. I simply had to win my collateral appeal. I filed an informal reply in October, 2011, in which I wrote:

"The People's informal response incorrectly argues that petitioners claims are vague and conclusory. Petitioner replies that at this juncture of the proceedings the court should assume all claims are true whether or not they seem vague or conclusory to the People. Petitioner further replies that 'overwhelming evidence' does not exist to negate the prejudice to petitioner during the criminal action. Petitioner has shown deficiency of counsel and a likelihood of prejudice and argues that the record in this matter is incomplete and cannot be relied upon to have produced a fair and just result."

(Ibid.)

I went on to discuss the lack of overwhelming evidence, the fact that the twins and Raeanna never successfully corroborated one another, the issues surrounding the contradictory statements related to the initial disclosures, the who knew what, when dilemma, CSAAS evidence, the medical evidence, and the computer evidence. I summarized by stating:

"The People have quite simply failed to respond to any of the specific errors presented by petitioner, and are instead relying on their own version of events to carry the day.

It is plainly evident that there is no response other that the People's assertion that there was 'utterly overwhelming evidence of guilt.' The People did not respond to the assertion that witnesses such as Kerri Guthrie were not called, that cross-examinations were flawed, especially related to all the contradictions and even non-existent in the case of Kathy Shultz (Barrickman).

The facts as presented by defendant Harris to appointed counsel were not investigated promptly or adequately, nor was the law researched and applied to those facts correctly. The People have failed to respond to the core issue which is whether the 'captain of the ship' doctrine is constitutional and if it protects counsel from being held responsible for their acts or omissions. The people have failed to respond to petitioner's assertions the appointed counsel's diligence was lacking and diligence, along with skill and ability, are the benchmarks of competence and adequacy of representation… Through the People's use of smoke and mirrors to introduce circular reasoning they may have convinced themselves that the evidence was 'utterly overwhelming,' that fact is not borne out by the facts extrinsic to the record."

(Ibid.)

The main thrust of the People's argument against me in their informal response was that I could not show prejudice because there was so much evidence against me. The People, especially Mr. Graham, threw everything including the kitchen sink at me utilizing the evidence he thought stuck. In his informal response, Mr. Graham argued that I had failed to reveal any deficiency or reasonable likelihood of prejudice and instead he relied on the supposed overwhelming evidence of guilt.

On another front, the fourth habeas petition also requested an evidentiary hearing because the denial of the new trial motion based on the Marsden hearing was unlawful. Simply put, "A judicial decision made without giving a party an opportunity to present an argument or evidence in support of his contention is lacking in all the attributes of a judicial determination." (People v Dennis (1986) 177 Cal.App. 3d 863, 873; citing Marsden). Even more to the point, perhaps, is that

"A judge who denies a motion for substitution of counsel solely based on basis of his courtroom observations despite defendant's offer to relate specific instances of misconduct abuses the exercise of discretion to determine the competency of the attorney."

(People v Marsden, supra, 2 Cal. 3d 118).

I also contended in my fourth habeas petition that the trial court erred in its application of Cornwell in my case. Judge DeVore should have appointed counsel to represent my interests when he decided to blow me off without taking evidence or argument. If Mr. Graham argues that habeas is not the proper venue for my claims I would point out that in In re Dixon the California Supreme Court wrote "it is of course, an established rule that habeas corpus may not be used instead of an appeal to review determinations of fact made upon conflicting evidence after a fair trial. [citations]" (In re Dixon 41 Cal. 2d at pp 760-761).

As already discussed, the record in my case is incomplete and thus cannot be relied upon to have produced a fair result. I insisted to the Mono County Superior Court that they should "examine the record to ascertain whether the facts relating to petitioner's contentions were before [the trial court] and whether any error therewith could have been raised on appeal." (Ibid.)

The Dennis court held "granting a motion for a new trial simply on the basis of a Marsden motion was error." This was exactly what Ms. Hankel asked the court to do. That was an incorrect understanding of the law by Ms. Hankel. I was never permitted the assistance of counsel during the Marsden/New Trial hearing nor was I allowed to present evidence and argument which would have been the opportunity to create a full, fair and complete record for review.

I filed my informal reply October 5th, 2011, and fully expected an order to show cause to issue right away with the granting of an evidentiary hearing as well. On November 1st, 2011, Judge Ball told me to go kick rocks and in a seething rebuke he wrote:

"While the petition alleges detailed facts regarding the conduct of Harris' defense of counsel, commencing with the first bail hearing, and though posttrial proceedings, it fails to allege any facts which 'establish prejudice as a demonstrable reality,' simply not speculation as to the effect of the errors or omissions of counsel."

(See In re Clark (1993) 5 Cal. 4th 750, 766; from Judge Ball's 11/1/2011 ruling).

Judge Ball went on to write:

"In the petition Harris seeks relief on the grounds of the ineffective assistance of counsel, these are the same grounds asserted in the first petition which the 3rd DCA summarily denied on April 29, 2010. That denial was on the merits. See Rule 8.385 California Rules of Court. "

Further still Judge Ball opined:

(Ibid.)

"A close review of the allegations of the petition discloses no new grounds for relief which were not raised in at least one prior habeas petition. Similarly, Harris' explanation for delay given in response to paragraph 15 of the habeas form, does not suggest the existence of newly discovered evidence or grounds for relief. Nor do any allegations of the petition purport to explanation why any 'new claims' in the petition were not presented in a prior petition. The successive petition is thus barred unless it falls within the exception of there having been a fundamental miscarriage of justice... The court finds that the allegations of the petition fail to establish (i) demonstrable prejudice resulting from counsel's alleged ineffective assistance, (ii) that there was an error of such constitutional magnitude as to render the trial so fundamentally unfair as to undermine confidence in the outcome; or, (iii) Harris' actual innocence."

(Ibid.)

And that was that. No mention of specific acts alleged, just a summary denial that I was procedurally barred. But what about my claim that Mr. Gephart disclosed privileged and confidential information to Mr. Graham without any authorization by me. As a general rule, an attorney's client may refuse to disclose, and my prevent another from disclosing, a confidential communication between the client and the attorney. The attorney-client privilege is codified in California Evidence Code §954 which provides in part:

"The client, whether or not a part, has a privilege to refuse to disclose, and to prevent another from disclosing a confidential communication between client and lawyer."

(Ibid.)

I claimed in my June 26th, 2008 Marsen hearing that Mr. Gephart had disclosed confidential attorney-client communications to the prosecution. Mr. Gephart denied my claim. He flat out denied having any conversations with Mr. Graham where he disclosed anything confidential in nature. However, on June 3rd, 2008, Mr. Graham wrote:

"Defense counsel Gephart told this prosecutor that Mr. Harris would explain away the child porn images, etc., by saying that he was doing research related to the Dateline Predator Series that discussed 100 Child Supermodels. In other words, from this prosecutor's perspective, Harris admitted to his lawyer, and his lawyer then relayed this admission to this prosecutor that Harris knew he had damaging information on his hard drive, but there was an innocent explanation for its existence. At no time did Mr. Gephart tell this prosecutor that what he was telling me was 'privileged' or somehow to be kept in confidence. This prosecutor ultimately emailed Mr. Wall."

(Mr. Graham's June 3rd, 2008, email)

Mr. Graham's email to Mr. Wall on June 3rd, 2008 read in part:

"Lydell, Spoke with the defense just a minute ago and he said that Harris will explain the child porn images etc., by saying he was doing research related to the Dateline Predator Series that discussed 100 Child Supermodels and this research coincides with information on his Yahoo! User account. I am sorry if that didn't make sense, but that is my best summary of what I was told, you will likely be asked to assess whether you see anything on his hard drive that supports anything like this.

Just a heads up.

Todd"

(Ibid.)

Now I don't know about you, but I felt this email vindicates me and my claim that Mr. Gephart disclosed privileged confidential work product to the prosecution. There can be no reason to disclose my statements to Mr. Graham behind my back. This is important because they key.dat file had not been found by Mr. Wall yet. All they had was a couple unallocated space images and some allocated space URLs which could have been there for years if at all. There was no way to tell. There were no bookmarks, no saved images, no video artifacts, nothing.

FIFTY-SIX

In a criminal case, the client/defendant has the total control over certain decisions because they derive from constitutional guarantees for criminal defendants. Also, the attorney-client privilege serves to preserve a defendant's rights against self-incrimination. To make adequate representation possible therefore, the attorney-client privilege assures criminal defendants that confidential statements to their attorney will not be admissible in any proceedings. (See People v Ledesma (2006) 39 Cal. 4th 641. 694).

In my case, I clearly waved my Fifth Amendment right against self-incrimination. However, Mr. Gephart's disclosures regarding the computer evidence weakened my position by divulging trial tactics and strategy to the People, who then manufactured evidence to attack those very tactics and strategies. Ultimately, Mr. Gephart's unauthorized disclosures to the People effectively lowered their burden of proof.

Having told Judge Ball all of this, he was having none of it. According to him, I was completely out of line filing for a writ of habeas corpus on the same grounds as my previous petitions.

Things at Mule Creek State Prison were going along fine when they finally found me a bed. I was scared and I liked my little world in Ad/Seg so I refused to move to the level 4 "A" yard. When the c/o's heard this, they told me I had to cell up with someone in Ad/Seg. When it came time to cell up with another inmate in Ad/Seg, I refused. Twice. All that wound up costing me three 115s.

I received a punishment of a six-month term in a security housing unit or SHU. With that my day at Mule Creek were over. Off I went to California State Prison at Sacramento and its Psychiatric Services Unit, the PSU. This is where EOP inmates do their SHU terms. There I was placed in a single cell and I was happy as a clam.

I had sent in a habeas petition to the 3rd DCA which was exactly the same as the one Judge Ball had denied. They quickly denied it without comment. Next I sent in a petition for review in the California Supreme Court. I asked them several questions having to do with the effective assistance of counsel and an evidentiary hearing. Little did I know that at the exact time the United States Supreme Court was deciding Cullen v Pinholster 131 S.Ct 1388 (2011) in which the high court held that evidence adduced after trial is irrelevant and that a habeas court could only review the record that was available at the time the case was adjudicated.

Shortly thereafter I received notice that my petition for review was being denied without comment. Thus, I ventured forth into the world of relevant federal law since my next step was the federal courts. While this was going on, Ms. Nichols was supposedly working hard on my appeal. She was identifying errors in state law but she was not really focusing on federal laws. Regardless of those efforts she was not raising the issues I was concerned with such as the ineffective assistance of counsel and conflict of interest issues related to the Marsden/New Trial hearing.

The issues she raised were the unduly prejudicial child sex-related evidence admission, the CSAAS evidence (Child Sexual Abuse Accommodation Syndrome), the jury instruction which invited the jurors to use the CSAAS evidence to evaluate the believability of the girls, the uncharged sexual acts evidence being prejudicial, the illegal use of propensity evidence, and finally her take on the illegal sentencing under §667.61 in which she argued that the court made its own finding that all of the acts were separate from each other and no one crime occurred on a single occasion. The opening brief went 122 pages and Ms. Nichols had to get special permission to file such a large appeal. I felt good about that.

I waited on the direct appeal in the 3rd DCA while my petition for review had been soundly denied by the California Supreme court. I was flustered but I still had some hope left. I couldn't go to the federal courts until I was completely done with my state appeals. I was already planning another habeas petition in state court alleging ineffective assistance of appellate counsel (IAAC), but I would have to wait until Ms. Nichols finished the direct appeal to both the 3rd DCA and the California Supreme Court.

After being at the PSU at "New Folsom," as it's called, for about 3 months, I never got to go to the law library and I was getting upset. The PSU was just like Ad/Seg but with single bed, single prison cells. I kind of liked that. The programming was great. Lots of groups and movies, even some "R" rated movies. But alas, it wasn't meant to be. At a meeting of the Institutional Classification Committee, or ICC as it's called, the associate warden told me they were suspending my SHU term and sending me to Corcoran State Prison. The home of Charles Manson. I was scared. Corcoran was notorious for housing the most violent prisoners in the CDCR. And they were sending me there? Why? I was besides myself. On the bus to Corcoran we stopped for an overnight layover at DVI in Tracy, CA. Once there, sitting in a cage awaiting my housing assignment, I ruminated on the full circle I had traveled. I told the nurses interviewing me that I was suicidal. I was escorted upstairs where I was given a smock, a mattress pad, and a blanket. I was placed in a large, empty room with a toilet and a sink. There was nobody watching me so I must have been a low suicide risk to them. I stayed there for a day and a half and then was sent to Vacaville. I was placed in the new 64 bed CTC crisis bed for observation. This was okay since I wasn't at Corcoran State Prison.

I saw a nice doctor, a Doctor White, every day. I really enjoyed his insights. Eventually the treatment team decided to send me to DSH, an intermediate care facility at Salinas Valley State Prison for extended treatment. I said great! Anything but Corcoran. As I arrived at Salinas Valley the Olympics were just getting underway in London and they were on the TV. Ahh, TV. I programmed beautifully in DSH custody. It was also single bed, single cell housing. They even gave me an allowance for every week of good behavior. It wasn't much but it was four dollars a week and I could buy snacks every Saturday.

On September 13th, 2012, the 3rd DCA denied my appeal in a scathing denial opinion. In essence they said I did it and I was a verrry baaaad man. Ms. Nichols quickly followed up with a petition for review, writing:

> *"This case presents an Internet-era question about whether the introduction of explicitly sexual and deviant images into evidence is so inflammatory, distracting, and time consuming, that the jury cannot focus on the issues of guilt or innocence*

as to the offenses with which the defendant is actually charged. This is of particular concern in this case, as in others, where the sexual images of incest, child pornography, and other deviant images and words are introduced into evidence as 'representative evidence' and 'exemplary evidence' although there is no proof that the defendant actually viewed what the jury was told to view in order to judge him guilty.

This case also presents several intriguing issues that are frequently litigated pretrial an child molestation cases, about Child Sexual Abuse Accommodation Syndrome (CSAAS) – a diagnostic model equally consistent with a victim's lying about being molested. A related issues is whether CALCRIM No 1193, the CSAAS pattern instruction which tells the jury that may use 'in evaluating the believability of the victim's testimony,' a violation of the permissible use of syndrome evidence and a change in the wording of the old CALJIC instruction.

The remaining issues involve the admission of uncharged sex acts with the same victims under Cal. Ecid. Code §1108, the constitutionality of that provision, cumulative and collective prejudice, and whether the failure to sentence defendant on seven counts to determinate sentences violates due process of law or the Sixth Amendment, the jury must determine all factual findings."

(Ibid.)

I had a difference of opinion with Ms. Nichols on the sentencing error. Fundamentally different. My opinion was that all the verdicts were unlawful and she believed some of them were lawful. I went about my business at Salinas Valley while I waited for a decision on my petition for review. It didn't take long. My petition was filed on October 23, 2012 and by December 19th it was denied without comment. I was crushed. All my hopes and dreams squashed like a bug on the windshield. I still had one shred of hope left though, habeas corpus. I had gone through the state appeals process for all my claims except one. I wanted to claim that Ms. Nichols was ineffective and failed to raise my off-the-record complaints I had pointed out to her.

While at Salinas Valley I tried to access the law library repeatedly and I was always turned down. It was a good thing I didn't have a deadline. I wanted to file a new (fifth) habeas petition back to the Mono County Superior Court in order to follow protocol. I went through all the papers I had in my cell and got rid of all the extraneous ones and prepared to move back to Mule Creek. I hoped anyway.

FIFTY-SEVEN

I received a new transfer endorsement in early April of 2013 to either Mule Creek or the dreaded Corcoran State Prison. I wanted Mule Creek obviously. On April, 23, 2013, I was given a trash bag and told to pack up my things. I was going on the bus right away. I hurriedly filled the bag and went to the departure area called Receiving and Release or R&R for short. There I was told I was going to Corcoran but they didn't have space on the bus. I thought "wow, that was close." Maybe I would get to Mule Creek instead. Mule Creek is a very safe and pleasant prison when compared to others in the CDCR system I was kicking myself for not celling up at Mule Creek when I had the chance, all things considered.

The officers at R&R told me to get back in the tank which was short for holding tank. I waited, and I waited. For a couple hours. Then the Director of the DSH program came to R&R and said that I was discharged from DSH and could no longer return there that day. I was then told I would have to go to Ad/Seg and wait there for transfer. I was sick, both literally and figuratively, I was catching a cold. I wasn't feeling any love from the officers so I told them I was feeling suicidal. They said "what the fuck?" The end result was that they put me in a smaller "tank" with my prison clothes and I slept on the floor. I sneezed all night long and the c/o's wouldn't give me any toilet paper. I was miserable. The next morning I was taken by high speed cop car to Vacaville and the 64 bed crisis center where I once again saw Dr. White. They went easy on me and let me have my reading glasses and some books. I read Ken Follett's "Pillars of the Earth" and thoroughly enjoyed it. I was still depressed and extremely anxious. Dr. White couldn't give me any type of sedative because they aren't allowed by the CDCR.

I spent about a month there seeing Dr. White most every day. One day I met with another doctor who told me I needed to start programming because if I was going to kill myself I would have already. Touche. Eventually Dr. White convinced me to roll the dice and give Corcoran a try. I would be in SNY and EOP custody which is as safe as it gets. I deided to go for it and that night before I was transferred I shaved my head to try and fit in better. I had no tattoos however.

I went to Corcoran by van and I was the only prisoner onboard. They call that a special transport and it was. It was the Friday of Memorial Day weekend and it was after 2:00 in the afternoon. I was relaxing with my new haircut and I was figuring that I wouldn't be transferred until after the holiday weekend because of the late hour. But, lo and behold, there they were. My transport officers had arrived. They were ready to haul me off to Corcoran State Prison, five hours south. Probably gonna be more though since it was holiday traffic in California. The officer's were working a double shift as they often do. Partway there they stopped for a burger and fries and the smell mad me really suicidal. All I got was a peanut butter and jelly sandwich. Prison sucks on so many levels.

I got to Corcoran in my thin paper transport suit and went to "3B" yard and block number one. Inside I was told to face the tower gunner holding a Ruger mini-14. I got my assignment to cell 127. When I went to my cell, my new celly, Malachi, told me he didn't want a celly. He said he would give me $15 if I went on suicide watch. When I said show me the money, he said it would have to be paid later. I said "yeah, right" I then yelled out the door to c/o Hicks that I needed some clothes. There were none in my bedroll. Hicks laughed at me and said I wouldn't be needing them. The night went by uneventfully. Malachi gave me some clothes and I slept all night through.

The next morning, Malachi told me he couldn't handle having a celly and he wanted me to tell the cops he was flipping out and to move me to another cell. The c/o's were like "whatever" and told me to sit at one of the tables in the dayroom. I waited for a bit and then another c/o told me to go door to door and find a bed for myself.

So there I was, a convicted sex offender, a "chomo," going door to door my first day at the infamous Corcoran State Prison looking for a good "house," on a level 4 yard no less. I was definitely apprehensive and uncomfortable. Nobody wanted a celly, especially a new "fish" as I was called. Things were looking grim when the tower cop told me to try cell 112. I did and the occupant, "Raul" said, "sure, no problem." He was mellow, had long hair, no visible tattoos and most importantly, he had a TV! In I went. After a few days I got my "fish" issue of clothes and a week or so after that I was taken off orientation status. I could then start going to EOP groups and the law library. Yard too. But that was sketchy deal for me. I went out there in my flip flops (they were out of boots) and was out there with no safety net. The c/o's are on the other side of the fence most of the time.

Well, time was ticking on my federal habeas appeal. I had one year and 90 days to file in the federal court and I still had to complete my last claim through the state courts. It was a simple claim that remained, sure to be denied, that being my ineffective assistance of appellate counsel claim. It is well settled case law that says an indigent defendant has no constitutional right to compel appointed appellate counsel to press non-frivolous points if counsel, as a matter of professional judgement, decides not to press those points (See Jones v Barnes 463 US 745, 751 (1983)).

My conviction had been affirmed by the California Supreme Court on December 19th 2012, so that meant I had until March 19th 2014 to file a complete yet concise petition for writ of habeas corpus in the United States District Court, Eastern District of California (district court). I went to the law library for the first time in mid-June of 2013 and it was awesome. It had state of the art computers running Windows 7. The computers had complete and searchable databases for all state and federal case law. In addition there were litigation guides, law books, Court Rules, etc. It was completely updated every quarter. The only downside was that you couldn't copy and paste or type up and print any documents. You had to copy everything by hand, rough out a handwritten version then neatly rewrite it into a legible final petition or motion or what have you. If you were rich, you could buy a typewriter for about $200 plus supplies. All this took time and all you got was two hours per week in the law library unless you had a verified court deadline and if you didn't have an attorney, you could get priority library user status (PLU) and with that you got four hours per week, minimum, depending on the librarian and demand for services.

I submitted my habeas petition claiming IAAC in Mono County Superior Court and within days Judge Magit denied it on August 12t, 2013. He explained that "the petition fails to state the prima facie case for relief and is procedurally barred. (People v Duvall supra, 9 Cal. 4th 464 and California Rule 4.551 (a)(4)(B).)"

He went on to point out that I had already raised my claims of ineffective assistance during my Marsden hearing and then he recapped my appeals thus far. Judge Magit, who was the attorney for the County of Mono and the CPS/Mental Health Dept. during my trial continued on in his last paragraph:

"Petitioner fails to provide a factual basis for the claim of ineffective assistance of trial counsel on direct appeal, and fails to show any prejudice. Appellate counsel and the Court of Appeal were provided the entire record from the trial court and were specifically aware that the petitioner raised the claim of ineffective assistance of trial counsel. Given the circumstances presented in the record of these related matters, the issue of ineffective assistance of counsel would have and should have been properly addressed by direct appeal."

(Ibid.)

On direct appeal? Say what? The whole point of my fifth habeas petition was the failure of Ms. Nichols to present evidence not a part of the record on appeal. Pinholster had mandated that only evidence in the record at the time the case was adjudicated would be considered. Therefore, I was left with no recourse but death in prison, apparently.

I immediately filed the same habeas petition in the 3rd DCA claiming IAAC and on Augst 29th, 2013, they denied it without comment. I then threw together a 15-page petition for review and sent it in to the California Supreme Court. They denied it promptly with a citation comment citing People v Duvall, supra, at p. 474; and In re Swain (1949) 34 Cal. 2d 300, 304.

Then there I was. I needed a full-on federal habeas petition and I didn't really know what I was doing. I went to the law library every chance I got. I also went to my EOP group therapy sessions. But mostly I begged and pleaded to get a pen or even a pen filler (the inner part) to no avail.

The CDCR has a rule book referred to by its statutory Code "Title 15" of the California Code of Regulations. In section 3138 is a description of the rules related to indigent inmates and mail usage. In subsection

(i) "Each institution shall establish local procedures for the issuance of writing supplies to indigent inmates." The funny thing is this, at Corcoran they hand out postage paid indigent envelopes from time to time, but never a pen or paper. In subsection (a) the rule states that each inmate shall receive 5 envelopes, 5 sheets of paper, and one writing implement usually a golf pencil, per week. This pencil is not entirely sufficient since the courts and the CDCR appeals forms require ink pens, black preferred.

Somehow, I was able to get paper and pens by trading food and on December 16th, 2013, I filed my lengthy 500-page petition in the district court. Included was over 300 pages of exhibits. I raised 25 grounds for relief in my federal habeas petition. I have already told you; I really didn't know what I was doing, but that was about to change. Only July 18th, 2014, the State Attorney General's office, a Ms. Tami Krenzin schooled me with a contentious response that said, quite thoroughly, you have nothing to stand on, your appeal is without merit.

I was stunned. I took what she wrote to heart though and then did a bunch of research. I delved into federal case law; Harrington, Pinholster, 28 USC §2254, and a variety of other topics. In her response. Ms. Krenzin laid out five arguments:

1. *AEDPA bars relitigation of petitioner's admission of evidence claims because the Supreme Court has not clearly established that the admission of evidence violates due process;*
2. *Petitioner's instructional error claim does not warrant federal habeas relief because the State court determination is binding;*
3. *Petitioner's sentencing claim does not warrant federal habeas relief because it does not involve a federal constitutional right;*
4. *AEDPA bars relitigation of petition's assistance of counsel claims because the state court's denial of the claims was reasonable; and*
5. *AEDPA bars relitigation of petitioner's cumulative error claim because he has not shown that the State court's decision violated any clearly established Supreme Court precedent.*

Following this I filed a reply to Ms. Krenzin's response also knows as a traverse. With that I argued the issue of my actual innocence. I discussd Dr. Gabaeff's opinion that the SART exam showed the twins were virgins and more specifically that the exam didn't show the damage one would expect to see if years of forced and serial abuse had occurred as alleged. I also raised the issue that the girls never once corroborated each other about the supposed sexual abuse. The only time Martha and Chelsea corroborated each other was the "bucket incident" which they both remember identically. And of course, I complained about Ms. Hankel's failure to call Kerri Guthrie as a witness.

Next, I moved onto the standard of review which was 28 USC §2254(d). I was new at the federal case law so I basically had to argue with Ms. Krenzin's interpretation. I followed that up with detailed argument about the fact evidence was improperly admitted, there was cumulative error, there was ineffective assistance of counsel error, improperly admitted CSAAS evidence, sentencing error, the unreasonable finding of facts (28 USC §2254(d)(2)), the 3/10/10 Marsden hearing error and my contention that the "captain of the ship" doctrine was unconstitutional. I finalized my argument with a discussion of fundamental fairness and my First Amendment right to testify fully and freely.

I felt pretty good about my argument once again but I thought about them some more and kept going to the law library. There I learned much more about the Anti-Terrorism and Effective Death Penalty Act, AEDPA, codified at 28 USC §2254(d) which states:

"An application for a writ of habeas corpus on behalf of a person in custody pursuant to the judgment of a State court shall not be granted with respect to any claim that was adjudicated on the merits in state court proceedings unless the adjudication of the claim –

(1) resulted in the decision that was contrary to or involved an unreasonable application of clearly established federal law as determined by the Supreme Court of the United States; or, (2) resulted in a decision that was based on a unreasonable determination of the facts in light of the evidence presented in the State court proceeding."

(Ibid.)

FIFTY-EIGHT

And so I waited for my ruling in the district court, stewing on the weaknesses of my petition, vowing to get it together for my next appeal. Should I lose, which I felt was likely, my appeal was actually over. The next step as it turned out was to go to Ninth Circuit Court of Appeals. There I would need to get a certificate of appealability just to be able to further appeal at all. I could get one from the district court but I needed to figure out how to do that. I applied for an attorney. Denied. I applied for an evidentiary hearing, three times. Denied. Denied. Denied. I was bobbing in the flotsam and jetsam of the justice system.

By then I had a new celly, JB, and he was from Belize. He had a TV and liked to watch movies so we did a lot of that. I got a job as a porter (janitor) in the EOP clinic where all the therapy occurs. I got paid more than some of the other jobs. I got 13 cents an hour instead of the usual 8 cents an hour other inmates got working in the cell blocks. I worked five days a week making 91 cents a day. The number of work days in a given month fluctuated but I was capped at $20 a month. Max. I owed $10,000 in a restitution fine so the CDCR took out 55% of my income leaving me with $9 per month. Max.

I really liked my job. I cleaned the bathrooms, the group rooms, the one-on-one therapy rooms, the staff offices, the break room, and mostly I took care of the floor stripping and waxing the linoleum floors with a couple buffer machines they had. I worked around the free staff (non-police professionals) and it was almost like being in regular society. There weren't any bars or grill gates or anything like that, and the staff were friendly towards me. Even the c/o's like Officer Clegg and Officer Andrade were decent and polite. Not like the cops I had left behind at High Desert State Prison.

I settled into a routine which in prison means I "programmed." I went to work, I went to the law library, I went to groups, I watched TV. After awhile JB transferred and I moved in with a new celly named 'Dennis." He also had a TV. I didn't have to worry about showing him my paperwork since he couldn't read. I didn't have to worry about him going through my transcripts. Trust is a big deal in prison only behind respect in importance. Once your cover is blown, you're a target and off to another prison you go if you are still alive. I continued to work on a plan for my certificate of appealability (COA) petition in the district court and Ninth Circuit if I was denied in the district court. I even started to dabble in United Stated Supreme Court rules related to a writ of certiorari, the final step in an appeal. In plain english a petition for a writ of certiorari is a petition of last resort in a court of last resort.

After about a year, I finally received what is called a Magistrate's report. These findings and recommendations were filed to the district Court Judge on October 12th, 2015. Quite abruptly my hopes were dashed. The magistrate judge who issues recommendations to the sitting district court judge presented a brutal report which asserted that I had not provided adequate case law according to the standards imposed by 28 USC §2254. The magistrate further stated that I was limited to the record that was before the court at the time my case was adjudicated. As I have explained, my record was incomplete and as to case law, the United States Supreme Court regularly declines to rule on many important issues so there is no precedential case law to rely on to prove any given point of law such as due process or ineffective assistance of counsel. It is all arbitrary and capricious based on my experience. I wasn't surprised that the recommendation was to deny my petition.

Two weeks later I filed my objections to the report with further argument and then dug deep into the underworld of habeas corpus law. It seemed there were tantalizing loopholes or openings in the law but in reality, it was locked up tight. If you want to get an evidentiary hearing you first have to prove that you were probably innocent. I am innocent and to say otherwise is to use circular logic and reasoning to say I am guilty despite the obvious error because I am soooo guilty. Under 28 USC §2254 I was hemmed in. I could not show I was in fact innocent, i.e., I could not overcome the presumption of correctness that the guilty verdicts were factually correct until I first showed that the proceedings at my trial were unconstitutional, unreasonable, or unfair, yet I could not show that the proceedings at my trial were unconstitutional, unreasonable, or unfair until I first showed that I am innocent. I am not kidding. Quite the conundrum.

In my objections to the magistrate's report I countered the findings section by section. I was by then familiar with the arguments in the report since they were almost verbatim the arguments made in the State's response. I was relying on shaky precedent and argument in my objections because there were no others.

Reasonableness was central to 28 USC §2254(d)(1) and the burden was on me to show the unreasonableness of the State Court's application of Supreme Court precedent. "Where the State Court decision has no explanation that habeas petitioner must still show there was no reasonable basis for the State Court to deny relief." (Harrington v Richter 178 L.Ed. 2d 624, 631 (2011)).

As will be shown below, there is no reasonable basis to show that fair-minded jurists could disagree on the State Court's findings. The state court was silent on my federal claims. In my criminal actions to date the record was incomplete as shown herein. Accordingly:

"A habeas court must determine what arguments or theories supported or could have supported the State Court's decisions; and then it must ask whether it is possible fair-minded jurists could disagree that those arguments or theories are inconsistent with the holding in a prior decision of this Court."

(Ibid.)

Having discussed reasonableness, it is also important to consider the contrary to clause in 28 USC §2254(d)(1):

"A federal habeas court may issue the writ under the 'contrary to' clause if the State Court applies a rule differently than we have done on a set of materially indistinguishable facts."

(Bell v Cone 535 US 684, 694 (2009))

I asked the court to specifically apply Estelle v McGuire 402 US 62 (1991) and the trial court failed to do so or did so silently leaving it to the district court to determine de novo the reasonable or contrary to presumptions which I asked them to do. I found that in the magistrate's report it was stated that:

"Factual findings of the State Courts are presumed to be correct, subject only to a review of the record which demonstrates that the factual findings resulted in a decision that was based on an unreasonable determination of the facts in light of the evidence presented in the State Court proceeding."

(Ibid.)

In my case, as I have explained, the record was incomplete and evidence was not allowed to be presented. I objected to the statement in the magistrate's report that all 25 grounds for relief were without merit. The first eight claims of error were matters of law to be decided under 28 USC §2254(d)(1) while the final 17 claims of error were factual findings to be considered under 28 USC §2254(d)(2) and (e)(1). Having discussed 28 USC §2254(d)(1) and (d)2) now is the appropriate time to venture into subdivision (e)(1). The text of 28 USC §2254(e)(1) states:

"In a proceeding instituted by an application for a writ of habeas corpus by a person in custody, pursuant to a judgment of a State Court, a determination of a factual issue shall be presumed to be correct. The applicant shall have the burden of rebutting the presumption of correctness by clear and convicting evidence."

(Ibid.)

Basically, I was arguing law on my first eight grounds for relief but I was seeking an evidentiary hearing on the final 17 grounds for relief in order to fill in the gaps of the incomplete record. The federal courts wanted nothing to do with my new evidence. It was a state matter and I was already done with the state thing. Besides, the presumption of correctness that left me with the burden to prove the error seemed to naturally require an evidentiary hearing to show errors not a part of the record at the time my case was adjudicated. Seemed simple enough but not so fast, bucko.

AEDPA requires federal courts to presume the correctness of state court factual findings unless applicants rebut this presumption with clear and convicting evidence. Factual findings under 28 USC §2254(d)(2) and also considered under subdivision (e)(1). From the Ninth Circuit:

"We interpret these provisions [28 USC §2254(d)(2) and (e)(1)] sensibly, faithful to their text and consistent with the maxim that we must construe statutory language so as to avoid contradiction or redundancy. The first provision – applies most readily to situations where petitioner challenges the State Court's findings based entirely on the State record. Such a challenge may be based on the claim that the

finding is unsupported by sufficient evidence... That the process employed by the State court is defective... or that no finding was made by the State court at all...

Once the State court's fact-finding survives this intrinsic review or inthose cases where petitioner does not raise an intrinsic challenge to the facts as found by the State court – the State court's findings are dressed up in a presumption of correctness, which then helps steel them against any challenge based on extrinsic evidence i.e., evidence presented for the first time in Federal court. AEDPA spells out what this presumption means: State court fact-finding may be overturned based on new evidence presented for the first time in Federal court only if such new evidence amounts to clear and convincing proof that the State court finding is in error. See §2254(e)(1).

Significantly, the presumption of correctness and the clear and convincing standard of proof only come into play once the State court's fact-finding survive any intrinsic challenge."

(Taylor v Maddox 366 F. 3d 992, 999-1000 (9th Cir. 2004) cert denied 543 US 1038 (2004) cited by Wood v Allen 558 US at 299 fn. 1).

"In essence, therefore, 28 USC §2254(d)(2) can be viewed as dividing 'determinations of the facts' into two categories – State court fact-findings that are flawed because they are 'unreasonable' hence are a basis for habeas relief without more; and findings that are not flawed because they are reasonable hence are presumed to be correct unless the petitioner proves otherwise by clear and convincing evidence. The determinations of a factual issue made by the State court that 28 USC §2254(e)(1) tells courts to presume to be correct only those determinations that survive §2254(d)(2)'s winnowing out of unreasonable determinations when the evidence leads very clearly to the conclusion that a federal claim was clearly overlooked in the State court. §2254 entitles the petitioner to de novo review of the claim." (See Johnson v Williams 133 S.Ct. 1088, 1096-1097 (2013)).

One of the errors I claimed was that evidence was not considered despite my best efforts to present it. I claimed I wasn't given a fair hearing in my motion for a new trial on IATC grounds.

"The nature of an ineffective assistance claim means that the trial record is likely to be insufficient to support the claim. And a motion for a new trial to develop the record is usually inadequate. Thus a writ of habeas corpus Is normally needed to gather the facts for evaluating these claims."

(Trevino v Thaler 133 S.Ct. 1911 (2013)).

I was begging for the assistance of counsel and an evidentiary hearing in order to rebut the presumption of correctness attached to claims 9-25 of my petition. As I have stated, the record was incomplete and evidence was not allowed to be presented.

"Closely related to cases where the State courts make factual findings infected by substantial legal error are those where the fact-finding process itself is defective. If, for example, a State court makes evidentiary findings without holding a hearing and giving petitioner an opportunity to present evidence, such findings clearly result in an unreasonable determination of the facts. Obviously, where the State court's legal error infects the fact-finding process, the resulting factual determination will be unreasonable and no presumption of correctness can attach."

(Taylor v Maddox, supra, at 1001).

In my objections to the magistrate's report I listed grounds 1, 2, 4, 5, and 6 as my admission of evidence error. I followed Ms. Nichols' lead by citing Estelle v McGuire 502 US 62 (1991) and argued that the evidence admitted, including the computer and CSAAS evidence, rendered the trial completely unfair and had a substantial and injurious affect on the jury's verdict because it distracted them from the real issue of whether the accuser's claims were true or false. "Admission of relevant evidence offends due process when the evidence is so prejudicial it renders the defendants trial fundamentally unfair." (Id. at 70). "State law error permitting admission of propensity evidence rendering a trial fundamentally unfair violates due process and the right to a fair trial." (Ibid.)

"Propensity evidence is not permissible in any setting because it is unfairly prejudicial. "The term 'unfair prejudice' as to a criminal defendant speaks to the capacity of some concededly relevant evidence to lure the fact-finder into declaring guilt different from proof specific to the offense charged." (Old Chief v United States 519 US 172, 180). "Courts that follow the common tradition almost unanimously come to disallow resort by the prosecution to any kind of evidence of a defendant's evil character to establish a probability of his guilt." (Id. at 181; citing Michelson v United States 335 US 469, 475-476 (1948)).

I conceded that I was not entitled to a perfect trial but I asserted that I was entitled to a fair one by the State and Federal Constitutions. The Estelle case is not precedential to the concept that the admission of evidence that is prejudicial is somehow error. Instead, Estelle says that is left up to the states to regulate the admission of relevant evidence and only if the whole trial becomes unfair will constitutional error have occurred. In California all relevant evidence is admissible so basically, Estelle is irrelevant.

In my objections the magistrate's report I addressed grounds 9-25 as factual findings made by the trial court and rubber stamped in affirmance by the 3rd DCA and the California Supreme Court. I was up against a wall because the magistrate's report was clear that I had no leg to stand on. I was like, what is the point of an appeal if not to find errors and correct them. It's not that simple.

I'm not going to go over the numerous facts already presented thus far, instead I will point directly to the 3/10/10 Marsden hearing and my desire to be fully and fairly heard with my documentation presented. Ms. Hankel and Judge DeVore denied me my documentary evidence. I should have been allowed to show the errors I claimed then I could have shown the prejudice and made a clear and reviewable record. I claimed that Ms. Hankel was operating under a conflict of interest because she was protecting her own interests at my expense by arguing against the very evidence she put forth as grounds for my new trial motion. She then argued for her position that she was competent and diligent advocate. Judge DeVore knew of this conflict of interest and failed to rule on it despite my verbal protestations to the matter. "A defendant is required to establish that an actual conflict of interest adversely affect the performance of counsel in order to demonstrate a violation of the Sixth Amendment." (Cuyler v Sullivan 446 US 335).

I felt I clearly established error and resulting prejudice on at least the conflict of interest claim alone and I was counting on the district court to validate my claim[s] of error.

FIFTY-NINE

On February 19th, 2016, the district court denied my habeas petition. They also denied my COA request which I needed to appeal to the Ninth Circuit. I had no right to appeal the district court's ruling. Now it was crunch time. I only had one crack at the Ninth Circuit and one shot at the United States Supreme Court left. If I failed, it was only 272 years to go until my release. Writing a COA or a petition for a writ of certiorari is a daunting task. There is a limit to the number of pages allowed in each document. No more free-for-all submissions.

To describe it briefly, I would say it is all about the facts and how they relate to Supreme Court precedence. Most critical perhaps is the nexus of that relationship to issues of national importance. If the petition is worthy of attention you might have a slight chance, if not, then it is just fodder for the shredder. I got right to it and started on my COA petition to the Ninth Circuit. First thing I did was ask for an extension of the deadline since this was a one-shot deal. I had a 30 page limit. I grappled with the fact that I was going to have to cut some baggage much as I have done with this book to edit down to the marrow of the case. I started with an outline and focused in on the issues I was going to present. It was readily apparent that I couldn't raise 25 claims in only 30 pages so I compromised. My issues were consolidated into these four topics:

1. Whether the denial of a COA as to claims 1-7 were unreasonable because it is debatable that the claimed errors violated petitioner's right to due process;

2. Whether the denial of the COA as to claim 8 was unreasonable because it is debatable that the claimed error violated petitioner's right to trial by jury;

3. Whether the denial of the COA as to claims 9-25 was unreasonable because it is debatable that the claimed errors violated petitioner's right to the effective assistance of counsel and due process of law;

4. Whether petitioner has a right to an evidentiary hearing in light of Trevino v Thaler and Martinez v Ryan and how can a petitioner who was deprived of an evidentiary hearing and forced into pro se collateral review expand the record to include off-the-record complaints.

I felt comfortable with my issues presented. I really wanted to isolate my two most important claims, the sentencing error ground 8 and the 3/10/10 Marsden/New Trial issue which denied me the evidence and evidentiary hearing I needed o prove my claims as a demonstrable reality. If I could have just got one good and fair day in court I would have been able to cut this case off at the pass. The legal standard for the issuance of a COA was clarified by the United States Supreme Court in the case of Miller-El v Cockrell 537 US 322, 123 S.CT 1029 (2003):

"A prisoner seeking a COA need only demonstrate a 'substantial showing of the denial of a constitutional right.' A petitioner satisfies this standard by demonstrating that jurists of reason could disagree with the district court's opinion of his constitutional claims or that jurists could concluded the issues presented desrve encouragement to proceed further."

(Id. 123 S.Ct. at 1034; Citing Slack v McDaniel 529 US 473, 120 S. Ct. 1595 (2000)).

To recap, I was charged with 23 counts of lewd acts with a child under 14 years old. These consisted of 10 counts with Martha and 12 counts with Chelsea, the twin sister of Martha. Also, there was one count with the neighbor girl Raeanna. In addition to these charges there were two counts of aggravated rape of Chelsea. Raeanna's allegation had been investigated and dismissed in 2003 after an investigation deemed her claim unfounded. After Chelsea ran away from home in June of 2007 she and Martha were placed in foster care. After a time, they both alleged that I had touched them sexually and raped them repeatedly from 2002 through 2007. A small amount of child porn was found on a hard drive located at my residence when I was arrested. The People conceded that I never viewed or saved most, if not any of the content. I challenged the authenticity of the hard drive.

My defense was a concoction of Ms. Hankel's and I had no say in it. She held the position that Martha and Chelsea made false allegations against me in order to not live with their mother. Their mother, Kerri, was a strict mother who would not permit the 15-year-old girls to use alcohol or drugs and did not allow dating. Kerri made them do chores at their rural property, and according to the twins, Kerri verbally abused them, and ultimately cared more for me than them according to Ms. Hankel's hypothesis. Despite multiple opportunities to make allegations contemporaneously, including repeated contacts with CPS over the years such as when the girls were interviewed at school by the CPS about the Raeanna allegation. Also, when they made complaints about verbal and physical abuse by Kerri and myself, the girls did not disclose any sexual abuse. This failure made their first disclosures in 2007 suspect. There were inconsistencies in their disclosures during interviews, preliminary hearing testimony, and trial testimony.

I went on in my COA petition to outline my arguments to include the violation of my right to due process based on the use of improperly admitted evidence at trial, improper instruction to the jury related to the CSAAS evidence, my right to trial by jury related to the sentencing error, and cumulative error.

Of the factual findings I claimed ineffective assistance of both trial and appellate counsel based on numerous facts I believed were relevant. I demonstrated specifically that had the error of not calling Kerri to testify not taken place, the result of the proceeding would have been different, the epitome of prejudicial error. Here is a recap of what I wrote in my COA petition about Kerry's testimony at my 9/28/07 bail review hearing:

- She denied having sex in front of her twin daughters saying they lie a lot.
- She denied that Martha ever complained about any kind of abuse in the Chalfant trailer.
- She denied that Martha ever complained about any kind of abuse in the Bishop Trailer
- She denied that Chelsea ever complained about any kind of abuse in the Chalfant trailer.

- She denied that Chelsea ever complained about any kind of abuse in the Bishop trailer.
- She denied there was any kind of tension between me and the twins.
- She denied that Martha and Chelsea ever complained of physical or sexual abuse after traveling with me.
- She denied that either twin told her that I molested Raenna in the Chalfant trailer.

I made a play in the COA petition to be granted an evidentiary hearing. I wanted to get Kerri to testify regardless of what she had to say bad about me. I got technical in my arguments. I had a lot riding on getting my off-the-record complaints before the court. I still didn't have my attorney-client file and Ms. Hankel was extremely reluctant to part with it. The district court had denied my motion for an evidentiary hearing citing Cullen v Pinholster 131 S.Ct. 1388 (2011) which disallows evidence being presented for the first time in federal court. This denial was arguably unreasonable because the procedural bar or fact-finding by the State relied upon by the district court was flawed.

I requested an evidentiary hearing each and every time I filed a petition in any court. The trial court refused to order production of the attorney-client file held by Ms. Hankel. The Mono County DA's office refused to provide me with discovery without a court order since §1054.9 only allows post-trial discovery to condemned inmates or those serving life without the possibility of parole (LWOP). I researched this issue with the perspective that 285 years to Life is a LWOP sentence. The Legislature addressed this issue by creating a law for elderly parole (§3055) that gives me a chance for parole when I am at least 50 years old and have served 20 years continuously. I also looked at the equal protection issue by the court's had sewn that all up. It was not a lane to try, it was a dead end.

In my petition to the district court, I had been denied an evidentiary hearing three times and appointment of counsel twice. That was very frustrating. Pinholster at 1398 holds that review under §2254(d)(1) is limited to the record that was before the State court that adjudicated the claim on the merits. But what about the claim that was not decided on the merits? What if the record is incomplete? What about my case? My testimony had been abridged by Ms. Hankel. Important exculpatory witnesses were not called. The state's fact-finding was defective. Claims 9-25 were not decided on their merits in a reasonable manner. Even if they were, the record is silent as to why and there is no reasonable and obvious reason why that can be presumed. A court that does not state the grounds for its denial is presumed on the merits as held in Harrington but this presumption is subject to rebuttal. A court must state the grounds for its denial federally, or rebuttal is permissible by clear and convincing evidence. (28US§2254(d)(2) and (e)(1)).

Section note USC 2254(d) bars relitigation of any claim adjugated on the merits in state court subject only to the exceptions in §2254(d)(1) and (d)(2). However, "Federal habeas courts may take new evidence in an evidentiary hearing when §2254(d) does not bar relief." (Brumfield v Cain 135 S.Ct. 2269 (2015); referring to Pinholster at 1401). "§2254(e)(2) continues to have force where §2254(d)(1) does not bar federal habeas relief. For example, not all federal habeas claims by state prisoners fall within the scope of §2254(d) which applies only to claims adjudicated on the merits in state court proceedings." (Pinholster at 1401).

That means that an evidentiary hearing was permissible in my case contrary to the district court's denial. The district court's denial relied on a state court's decision that was not on the merits. Nor was it reasonable related to grounds 9-25. Besides, I was entitled to an opportunity to rebut the presumption of correctness adopted by the district court.

Regarding claims 10-25, the ineffective assistance of trial counsel (IATC) claims, the district court found that the denial by the 3rd DCA and the California Supreme Court were presumptively on the merits. Therefore, the findings were subject to rebuttal. Flowing form this is the assumption that rebuttal comes from a full and fair evidentiary hearing, especially when the issues are off-the-record complaints. Was this a witch hunt I wondered to myself.

As to claim 9, the IAAC claim against Ms. Nichols, the district court also ruled that the denial was on the merits. However, the California Supreme Court in its denial cited People v Duvall 8 Cal 4th 464, 474 (1995); and, In re Swain 34 Cal. 2nd 300, 304 (1949), which are a procedural bar, not a finding of fact. I did everything possible to put forth my claims of error and the state thwarted my every effort. 28 US §2254(b)(2) states in relevant part:

"An application for a writ of habeas corpus of behalf of a person in custody pursuant to the judgment of a State court shall not be granted unless it appears that...

(B)(i) There is an absence of State corrective process; or,

(ii) circumstances exist that render such a process ineffective to protect the rights of the applicant."

(Ibid.)

By review of the State Court's last reasoned opinion regarding claim 9 or 10-25 it is clear that I was not afforded a full and fair hearing, thus the State's process was ineffective or absent. I asserted in my COA petition that claims 9-25 were rebuttable with clear and convincing evidence. The proffered evidence included the testimonial evidence, the factual evidence, and all the evidence of off-the-record error I had, which I have discussed already. Testimony by Kerri was key to unlocking the pandora's box of the People's case.

SIXTY

Pursuant to the established California procedure, the claim of IATC was not raised during the direct appeal. I had asked Ms. Nichols to expand her appointment to include a habeas petition alleging IATC but she refused. I think that the attorneys stick together. Therefore, I was forced by the actions of the state and the state appointed attorney to put forth claims of error for the first time in the pro se collateral review. Trevino v Thaler 131 S.Ct. 1911 (2013) discussed this very issue referencing the holding in Martinez v Ryan 566 US 1 (2012) which concerns the initial collateral review of IATC claims. "A prisoner may obtain federal review of a defaulted claim by showing cause for the default and prejudice from a violation of federal law." (Travino v Thaler, supra, at 1917). I was similarly situated to Trevino. Both of us failed to obtain a hearing on the merits of our IATC claims because State appointed counsel neglected to properly present our claims in State Court.

"The nature of an ineffective assistance of counsel claim means that the trial record is likely to be insufficient to support the claim. And a motion for new trial to develop the record is usually inadequate. Thus, a writ of habeas corpus is normally needed to gather the facts for evaluating these claims."

(Id. at 1911).

I fairly presented my claims to the State. I was diligent in my efforts to plead and prove my claims of error. "A person is not at fault when his diligent efforts to perform an act are thwarted by the conduct of another or happenstance. (Williams v Taylor 529 US 420, 432 (2000) (Michael Williams)).

"Comity is not served by saying a prisoner 'has failed to develop the factual basis of a claim' where he was unable to develop his claim in State court despite diligent effort. In that circumstance an evidentiary hearing is not barred by §2254(e)(2). If there has been no lack of diligence at the relevant stages in the State proceedings, the prisoner has not 'failed to develop' the facts under §2254(e)(2)'s opening clause, and he will be excused from showing compliance with the balance of the subsection's requirements."

(Id. at 437).

Looking deeper, 28 USC §2254(e)(2) states:

"If the applicant has failed to develop the factual basis of a claim in the State court proceedings the court shall not hold an evidentiary hearing on the claim unless the applicant shows that:

(A) The claim relies on –

i. A new rule of constitutional law;

ii Factual predicate that could not have been previously discovered through the exercise of due diligence

(B) The facts underlying the claim would be sufficient to establish by clear and convincing evidence that but for constitutional errors no reasonable fact-finder would have found the applicant guilty of the underlying offense."

(Ibid.)

These facts detailed about proof of error or innocence as it were, most certainly needed to be found in an evidentiary hearing where evidence can be presented, and tested. The Trevino court addressed the structure of the appellate process thusly:

"Where, as here, state procedural framework by its design and operation makes its highly unlikely in a typical case that a defendant will have a meaningful opportunity to raise a claim of ineffective assistance of trial counsel on direct appeal, our holding in Martinez applies. A procedural default will not bar a federal habeas court from hearing a substantial claim of ineffective assistance at trial if in the initial review collateral proceeding there was no counsel, or counsel in that proceeding was ineffective. 566 US___; 132 S. CT. 1309; 182 L.Ed. 2d 272, 278, 288."

(Trevino v Thaler, supra, at 1921).

The question begs, was State appointed counsel's failure to pursue IATC claims a strategic decision or a negligent omission? A hearing was absolutely necessary to resolve this issue as well as all the others in grounds 9-25 of my habeas petition to the district court. The United States Supreme Court has ruled that:

"Where a habeas petitioner challenges State court fact-finding 'based entirely on the State record' the federal court reviews those findings for reasonableness under §2254(d)(2) but where a petitioner challenges such findings based on part on evidence that is extrinsic to the State court record then §2254(e)(1) applies."

(Wood v Allen 175 L.Ed. 2d 738 fn.1; citing Taylor v Maddox 366 F.3d 922, 999-1000 (9th cir. 2004); cert denied 543 US 1038, 125 S. Ct. 809, 160 L.Ed. 2d 605 (2004)).

I argued to the Ninth Circuit in my pro se petition for the COA that rather than review under §2254(d)(2)'s "unreasonable determination of the facts" standard, they should review under the arguably more deferential standard in §2254(e)(2). I asked the Ninth Circuit to grant me an evidentiary hearing and consider an expanded record before ruling on my petition for a COA.

I beat the odds and submitted my petition ahead of my April 25th, 2016 deadline and I prepared for an evidentiary hearing. I mean, I had all the facts and arguments on my side, right? What could possibly go wrong this time?

Spring turned to summer and it was a really hot summer at Corcoran State Prison, but then I heard they all were. Finally the heat broke and summer turned to fall and still no response from the Ninth Circuit I had spent my time sweating in my cell with Dennis when I wasn't able to enjoy the air-conditioning in the law library or the EOP clinic where I still worked every day. Thank God Dennis had a fan and a TV. I had a CD player with headphones that also had a radio which made things somewhat bearable. I listened to Chevelle, Tool, Five Finger Death Punch and other bands when I wasn't listening to The Blaze radio station. I liked the modern rock. I really couldn't take anymore classic rock, I don't know why but I never liked "oldies."

I went to the law library as often as I could. I prepared for a path forward if my COA was approved or denied. If denied, the path forward would be a petition for rehearing en banc which really is a motion for reconsideration, Ninth Circuit Rule 27-10. Following a denial of reconsideration I would need to file a petition for a writ of certiorari in the

United States Supreme Court. Beyond that my options were terminated with petition for rehearing in the High Court. Most all appeals to the Supreme Court are denied, like 98% of them. On December 9th, 2016, my COA was denied with a brief comment: "This request for a Certificate of Appealability is denied because appellant has not made a 'substantial showing of the denial of a constitution right.' See 28 USC §2254(c)(2); also Miller-El v Cockrell 537 US 322, 327 (2003),"

At the bottom of the page in bold caps was one word, DENIED. This left me heart-broken. I mean, I had it in the bag yet I was outgunned. Decisively.

I immediately got to work on my motion for reconsideration. First off, of course, was to file for an extension of time in order to grapple with all the issues that needed to be corralled into a 15 page petition. Condensing is an art form of writing I am obviously not good at. I struggle writing petitions and motions by hand, however I did have some ideas.

I started off by pointing out that Miller-El v Cockrell and Slack v McDaniel conflicted with the denial of my COA petition. I noted to the Ninth Circuit that the ruling in my case also directly conflicted with Lambright v Stewart 220 F. 3d 1022 (9th cir. 2000) (en banc); and, Jennings v Woodford 290 F. 3d 1006 (9th cir. 2002).

These cases illustrated that "Reduced to its essentials, the test is not where the petitioner makes a showing that the petition should have been resolved in a different manner, or, that the issues presented where adequate to deserve encouragement to proceed further." (Miller-El v Cockrell 537 US 322, 123 S. Ct 1029, 1039 (2003); citing Barefoot v Estelle 468 US 880 (1983)).

This all meant that in order to receive a COA from the Ninth Circuit, I didn't need to prove that the district court was necessarily wrong – just that the resolution of the constitutional claim was debatable.

I was out to show that several areas of my petition for the COA were debatable, were violations of my constitutional rights as determined by the United States Supreme Court. I truly believed that I had made a substantial showing of a constitutional violation notwithstanding my lengthy and complicated handwritten petition. This weakness was compounded by the lack of evidentiary support because Ms. Hankel wouldn't provide me with my attorney-client file.

In my motion for reconsideration, I went on to recite my previous claims of error in a succinct manner, choosing seven areas of contention:

1. The fact I should have received a COA because of a case law on COAs

2. The lack of an evidentiary hearing

3. Ineffective assistance of trial and appellate counsel

4. Conflict of interest and the 3/10/10 Marsden/New Trial hearing

5. The missing record/evidence issue

6. The sentencing error

7. The post-appeal record creation

The district court in its denial ruled on the COA application without acknowledging the "facial allegation" test. This test mandates that the court accept all the allegations in the habeas petition as true and look at the face of the petition to determine whther the petitioner has alleged the denial of a constitutional right. It was obvious that the district court failed to consider what my petition facially alleged, by failing to take my allegations as true in the habeas petition. Moreover, the district court focused instead on the contrary evidence that in their view, undermined the claim on the merits.

Becaue the COA ruling is not an adjudication of the merits of the appeal, it does not require a showing that the appeal will succeed.

The COA determination under 28 USC §2253© requires an overview of the claims in the habeas petition and a general assessment of the merits...When a court of appeals sidesteps this process by first deciding the merits of an appeal and then justifies its denial of a COA based on its adjudication of the actual merits it is in essence deciding an appeal without jurisdiction.

(Miller-El v Cockrell, supra, at 336-337).

I have covered the areas of contention thoroughly thus far and suffice to say, the arguments I have made are well thought out and decidedly written IMHO. The court was going to see things my way this time, I was sure of it.

Moving on to the evidentiary hearing issue, I was forced to acknowledge that there is no constitutional right to an evidentiary hearing. However, there is a due process right to one when the record is incomplete. Off-the-record complaints have a place in a habeas proceeding, especially when the evidence proves innocence by clear and convincing evidence.

In my case there was prejudice when the trial court did not permit me to present evidence of IATC and Ms. Hankel withheld the very evidence needed to prove my claims of deficient performance.

"An 'actual conflict' and an 'adverse effect' on counsel's performance are not separate considerations. An actual conflict is 'demonstrated' precisely when it can be established that a conflict of interest 'adversely affected' counsel's performance."

(Mickens v Taylor 535 US 162, 171 (2002)).

The Mickens court specifically held:

"A defendant must show that counsel's conflict of interest adversely affected counsel's performance and wrote about any confusion regarding presumed prejudice previously outlined by the High Court that the majority now thought an actual conflict of interest meant precisely a conflict of interest that affected counsel's performance as opposed to a more theoretical division of loyalties. A defendant who shows that a conflict of interest actually affected the adequacy of his representation need not demonstrate prejudice in order to obtain relief."

(Ibid.; citing Cuyler v Sullivan, supra, at 349,340).

Do you see where all of this is leading? I mean, is there any way I don't get relief? This all leads back to the circular reasoning whereby you have to prove error to prove innocence and you have to prove innocence in order to prove error. The justice system is rigged to say the least, it's a real lose/lose proposition. One final thought on this, a conflict of interest can occur when an attorney's loyalty to, or efforts on behalf of, a client are threatened by his or her responsibilities to another client, or a third part, or his own interests. (See Glasser v United States 315 US 60, 69,70 (1942)).

I really felt like I was getting focused and I was going to come in under 15 pages. I pointed out in my motion for reconsideration another constitutional right which was the right to trial by jury. The former §667.61(g) read:

"The term specified [15 years-to-life] shall be imposed on the defendant once for any offense or offenses committed against a single victim during a single occasion. If there were multiple victims during a single occasion the term specified [15 years-to-life] shall be imposed once for each separate victim. Terms for other offenses committed during a single occasion shall be imposed under any other law [determinate]."

(Ibid.)

The issue raised in my habeas petition in ground 8 was not ruled on correctly by the district court. My claim was that the crime was charged and tried generically and Judge DeVore was forced to make his own findings that all the charged offenses occurred on a separate occasion in order to sentence me to 15 years-to-life instead of a determinate sentence. Based on the verdict forms, there is no way to determine if an allegation happened on a separate or same occasion. Judge DeVore played semantics when he ruled that none of the charged acts happened on a single occasion. He opined that based on his notes and recollections the bad acts happened every day or ten times or a lot and thus none of the charged crimes occurred on a single occasion. Some of the alleged abuse could have occurred on any day between 2/23/02 and 2/23/06. There is no way to tell from the jury verdicts. Basically, the crimes were charged as a single event and somehow Judge DeVore extrapolated his own total and date of the abuse extraneous to the jury's verdicts.

"The essential Sixth Amendment inquiry is whether a fact is an element of the crime. When a finding of fact [separateness] alters that proscribed punishment so as to aggravate it, the fact necessarily forms a constituent part of the new offense and must be submitted to the jury."

(Alleyene v United States 133 S. Ct. 2157, 2162 (2013)).

The jury simply wasn't asked to find me guilty of serial molestation like §288.5, they were asked specifically if I touched this girl on some part of her body at some location, singular, with no date or time specified.

One last item; the question raised in my COA petition to the Ninth Circuit which was not addressed in the denial, and was of great importance in light of Pinholster, is whether a petitioner has a right to an evidentiary hearing to present off-the-record complaints. Also, how can a petitioner, who was deprived of an evidentiary hearing and forced into pro se collateral review expand the record to include the extrinsic complaints. I pointed out to the Ninth Circuit in closing that the issue of post appeal record creation was critical in light of Cullen v Pinholster, supra; Trevino v Thaler, supra; and, Martinez v Ryan, supra. The holdings and arguments I presented were in direct conflict which the decisions of the district court and the Ninth Circuit. I asked respectfully for reconsideration.

I ventured forth into the New Year, 2017, with high hopes and sent in my motion for reconsideration, en banc. The en banc meant I wanted the whole panel of the Ninth Circuit to rule on my case. This is reserved for cases of utmost importance. Mine was not such a case and on January 23rd, 2017, my motion for reconsideration was denied by two judges who wrote that based on General ordinance §6.11 a panel may reject a request for an en banc hearing on behalf of the court. That sucked. I was not ready for that, but in a way I was.

SIXTY-ONE

I had spent a lot of time in the law library up to that point. I mean hours and hours of tedious searching, reading, and copying by hand relevant law which led up to the final battle. A petition for a writ of certiorari is a beast unto itself. It is limited to 40 pages and review by the Supreme Court is not a matter of right, it is a matter of judicial discretion.

"A petition for a writ of certiorari will be granted only for compelling reasons. The following, although neither controlling nor fully measuring the Court's discretion, indicate the character of the reasons the court considers:

> A) a United States Court of Appeals has entered a decision in conflict with that decision of another United States Court of Appeals on the same important matter; has decided an important federal question in a way that conflicts with a decision by the State court of last resort; or is so far departed from the accepted and usual course of judicial proceedings, or sanctioned such a departure by a lower court, as to call for an exercise of this Court's supervisory power;
>
> B) A State court of last resort has decided an important federal question in a way that conflicts with the decision of another State court of last resort of a United State Court of Appeals;
>
> C) A State Court or a United State Court of Appeals has decided an important question of federal law that has not but should be, set-

tled by this Court, or has decided an important federal question in a way that conflicts with relevant decisions of this Court.

A petition for a writ of certiorari is rarely granted when the asserted error consists of erroneous factual findings or the misapplication of a properly stated rule of law."

(United States Supreme Court Rule 10)

As shown above, there is rarely an opening for the granting of a writ of certiorari. The place to start was obviously going to be the questions I was to present to the Supreme Court. Page 1 of any petition to the High Court. I had 90 days give or take and I figured I was going to need more time so as usual, the first thing I did was request more time. I then started formulating a plan to lay out relevant and important questions of federal law. My request for additional time sent under Rule 22 and Rule 30 of the Supreme Court Rules was promptly denied by the circuit justice, the Honorable Anthony Kennedy, Justice. No go, but still ok, I had 75 days and I had already done a ton of research. The issue for me was, could I get my statement of facts and all my argument into 40 pages. My research in the law library was empowered by the use of computers but no being able to copy, paste, and edit was a real hinderance. Everything had to be copied by hand, just like this book, and all that took time. And paper. And pens. All were in short supply.

I had a three-inch-high stack of handwritten notes that was at least 400 pages so that meant I could use less than 10% of my research. That didn't even let take into account my statement of facts which would run five pages or so.

I'll admit it. I was intimidated. I wrote to the Supreme Court, specifically to Justice Kennedy who is the Ninth Circuit overseer for certain requests, and I asked him for leave to file a petition in excess of 40 pages. Application for the granting of such leave is not favored. Rule 33-1(d) and Rule 22. I got another quick response telling me I had to send the proposed enlarged petition in with my application.

Cool. That was the ticket. I felt I could do it up real nice in 50 to 60 pages. I often wondered how the Supreme Court got back to me so quickly. They handle the entire nation's litigation at this level and they operate like a well-oiled machine. My kudos to the Clerks of this Honorable Court.

So, after that I set out to make the template. Supreme Court Rule 14 lists in detail the contents required in a petition; and the order in which they are to be presented. The rulebook and the application for a writ of certiorari can be had for free by writing to the US Supreme Court, 1 First Street NE, Washington DC 20543. In a nutshell, the petition should contain:

A cover
Questions Presented
List of Parties to the Action
Table of Contents
Table of Authorities
Opinions and Orders Below (first page of the 40-page limit
Grounds for Jurisdiction
Constitutional provisions
Statement of the Case (Shorter than that presented to the State)
Reasons for Granting the Writ (facts and Arguments)
Appendix (not included in the 40-page limit)

I eagerly got to work and bogged down right away. I had hundreds of pages of facts, arguments, and research. I needed to cull my thesis from this pile of fodder right away. I just decided to jump in and I came up with ten important and, I felt, relevant questions to present to the Court.

1. Did the trial court deny me the assistance of counsel during the Marsen/New Trial hearing and did defense counsel prejudice petitioner while operating under a conflict of interest.

2. What evidence would have been presented if an evidentiary hearing had been held?

3. How can a petitioner, who was deprived of an evidentiary hearing to present off-the-record evidence, and forced by the State into pro se collateral review, expand the record to include the off-the-record evidence in order to rebut presumed correctness and how do §2254(d)(2) and (e)(1) interact?

4. Did the trail court exceed its jurisdiction when it made findings that all the crimes occurred on separate occasions violating petitioner's right to have the jury make all the factual findings?

5. Did the trial court erroneously admit inordinately time consuming and unduly prejudicial evidence of child sex-related material from the portioner's alleged hard drive including hundreds and hundreds of graphic images it was conceded petitioner never viewed?'

6. Did the admission of expert testimony of Child Sexual Abuse Accommodation Syndrome (CSAAS) violate due process of law and the right to a fair trial?

7. Did CALCRIM No. 1193, the pattern instruction to the jury in CSAAS evidence, impermissibly permit the jury to determine the accuser's credibility and use CSAAS evidence to corroborate the claims of abuse in violation of due process of law and the right to a fair trial?

8. Whether admission of criminal propensity evidence under California Evidence Code §1108 violates due process of law and the right to a fair trial?

9. Did the admission of uncharged sexual acts with the same victims under California Evidence Code §1108 violate due process of law and the right to a fair trial?

10. Is petitioner entitled to raise ineffective assistance of counsel based upon the instant petition for writ of habeas corpus in an evidentiary hearing with the COA or back to the State?

I felt pretty good about 1, 3, 4, and 10. The others I kept in there because I didn't want to look back after a denial and wish I had played all my cards. I pleaded to the Supreme Court, much as I had to the lower courts, that the evidence not yet presented would unequivocally show that my claims for a writ of habeas corpus were valid. I should have received an evidentiary hearing somewhere along the line. I contended in my petition to the Supreme Court that an evidentiary hearing was appropriate. In a case where certiorari was denied sub nom Chappell v Gonzalez 133 S. Ct. 155 (2012), the Supreme Court silently affirmed the finding in Gonzalez v Wong 667 F. 3d 965 (2011) that said:

"Under Pinholster we may not consider those later discovered materials in reviewing Gonzalez's federal habeas claim. Because it appears to us that these materials strengthen Gonzalez's Brady claim to the point that his argument would be potentially meritorious -- that is, a reasonable State court might be persuaded to grant relief on that claim – it is not appropriate for us to ignore those materials, we remand that portion of the case to distract court with instructions to stay the proceedings in order to give Gonzalez the opportunity to return to State court." (Id. at 972).

Pinholster could actually be considered unconstitutional because a convicted prisoner who can show factual innocence cannot find relief in the federal courts, even if new, credible, and material evidence of innocence exists. In California, effective January 1st, 2017, the state habeas law was changed to lower the standard of proof required to present new evidence. (§1473(b)(3)(A)). Habeas relief is now to be granted when new evidence exists that is credible, material, presented without substantial delay, and of such decisive force and value that it would have more likely than not changed the outcome at trial. (See in re Miles (2017) 7 Cal.App. 5th 821 (depublished)).

Mr. Miles was convicted of robbing a check cashing store where someone got killed. Years later, two men came forward and said Mr. Miles had nothing to do with the crime. He was released from prison and sent back to Orange County Jail. While there, he was offered a deal for time served and so in order to be with his ailing mother he took a People v West plea. (People v West 3 Cal. 3d 595). He wound up released from prison after some 30 years and walked out of the Orange County Jail a free man at last. A great story perhaps but the system still screwed him in the end. He was innocent but still had to plead it out to be freed.

All this change does however put the State in charge of new evidence which then can be brought to the federal court satisfying Pinholster. The lower federal courts have been all over the place related to Pinholster and its implications regarding discovery, new evidence, and evidentiary hearings in general. For example, in Sample v Colson 958 F. Supp. 2d. 865, (2013) the district court determined "given the lack of district guidance from the Supreme Court or the Sixth Circuit of the breadth of Pinholster, the court will follow the plain language of Pinholster and limit its force to §2254 habeas review."

The petitioner has argued that Pinholster does not apply to discovery requests because the state withheld evidence during the state court proceedings. Petitioner also contended that any new evidence discovered would represent a new Brady claim. The district court agreed that first, Pinholster did not, strictly speaking, alter or even speak to the standards governing Rule 6 discovery. Second, Pinholster restrictions should not be invoked at the discovery phase where the petitioner is seeking discovery related to protentional Brady violations. (See Jones v Bagley 696 F. 3d 475, 486 fn. 4 (6th cir. 2012)). The district court decided that allowing a Pinholster bar on discovery would mean that the State could thwart any adjudication of facts underlying a federal claim simply by withholding the facts during the State court proceedings.

In juxtaposition with the Ninth Circuit which has mentioned Pinholster in connection with discovery but only in passing with little analysis.

The Court wrote that they were concerned with preventing "habeas by sandbagging." Jameson v Runnells 713 F. 3d 1218, 1226 (9th Cir 2013)). In the case of Runningeagle v Ryan 676 F. 3rd 758, 773-774 (9th cir. 20120) the Ninth Circuit opined that petitioner is not entitled to an evidentiary hearing or additional discovery in federal court because his claim is governed by §2254(d)(1) and in Peraza v Campbell 462 F.App'x. 700, 701 (9th cir. 2011) the court wrote in an unpublished opinion that Peraza seeks to expand the record through discovery or an evidentiary hearing, beyond what was presented to the state court, we conclude that such relief is precluded by Pinholster with regard to any of his claims under §2254(d)(1).

In the Fifth Circuit they were unpersuaded by petitioner that "Pinholster applies only when a fair and complete state court record is before the federal court." (Ross v Thaler 511 F. App'x. 293, 305 (5th cir. 2013)).

In the Sixth Circuit the court wrote that petitioner has not cited and the court is unaware of any language in Pinholster itself suggested that a petitioner who diligently attempts to convince the State Courts to consider new evidence but ultimately does not succeed can escape the reach of Pinholster to have a federal court consider his new evidence." (Lynch v Hudson 2016 US Dist. LEXIS 53430 (2016)).

All this illustrates the paradox I faced. Should I be granted an evidentiary hearing at the federal level to protect my constitutional rights; or, should I be granted a stay in order to return to the state court to present extrinsic and exculpatory evidence that was not considered in my state record on appeal. I had definitely been diligent in my efforts to gain access to the evidence as detailed herein. The Michael Williams court addressed this issue. Is the Sixth Circuit correct that the diligent pursuit of the truth by those unjustly incarcerated are not worthy of consideration or is it a matter of Sate's rights and the States should be the forum for taking in new evidence should as in California? "Failure to develop the factual basis of a claim is not established unless there is a lack of diligence, or some greater fault, attributed to the prisoner or the prisoner's counsel." (Williams v Taylor (Michael Williams), supra, at 432)).

SIXTY-TWO

Ms. Hankel did not respond to my continued request for my attorney-client file while I was appealing my case. I wanted to include exhibits with my petition to the Supreme Court but finally I didn't want to wait anymore so I mailed in my petition sans exhibits to the United States Supreme Court. This was April of 2017. My petition was 53 pages total so I included a motion to exceed the page limit. It didn't take long to get a reply. On May 4th, Justice Kennedy denied my request. I was then forced to whittle down my offerings to 40 pages. Luckily, the court gave me an additional 60 days to rewrite my petition. By the end of June I had knocked it out. I sent in the revised document and waited. I had been careful in my editing to not change the substance of the petition as directed by the Court. My petition was bounced right back to me this time. I was told I had two pages of what I thought were exempt statute included which caused me to fail to conform to the page limit. I fixed it up and sent it back in. Each time I sent in a new copy I had to send a copy to the Attorney Central of California. That cost me $20. I earned $9 per month so there went my monthly Ice Cream and Soda each time they returned my petition.

I had no idea how long I would have to wait for a decision. I knew from the news that the Supreme Court had made their last decision of the spring session and so I surmised that by early fall I would know something. Well, a month later my petition was returned to me. I had not entered anything in a couple of what I thought were irrelevant boxes in my In Forma Pauperis financial statement. I was quickly learning that the United States Supreme Court demands perfection in the documents it reviews.

I was able to make the changes by simply adding some zeros and spending another $20 for copies. I sent it back in right away and as I expected, it stuck. I was filed and placed on the docket October 4th, 2017. While all this was playing out, I filed a motion to compel Ms. Hankel to give me my attorney-client file.

I learned shortly thereafter than the Honorable Mark Magit would be hearing the case and I was not happy with that development. He had been the attorney for the CPS and Mono County Mental Health Department which had refused to give me the records I sought pretrial. He was now a judge in Mono County Superior Court. On June 22, 2017 I filed my verified challenge for cause against Judge Magit. (Cal. Civ. Code Civ. Proc. §170.1)

Shortly after that, Judge Magit filed his verified answer. The Honorable Judge Sarkisian of Fresno County heard the matter on August 16th 2017, and I was not a participant. Judge Sarkisaian denied my challenge for cause. I felt I had a clear, present, and substantial right to the performance of the duty to impartially adjudicate all maters before the court. When a motion to disqualify is made pursuant to Cal. Civ. Code of Civ. Proc. §170.1(a)(6)(A)(iii) the judge should recuse himself if a person aware of the record herein would reasonably entertain a doubt about Judge Magit's ability to be fair and impartial.

On August 25th, I filed a petition for a writ of mandate (mandamus) in the 3rd DCA. Just after that, Judge Magit issued an order to show cause to Ms. Hankel related to the motion to compel. I then filed a motion for a stay in the 3rd DCA to prevent Judge Magit from ruling in my case pending before the trial court.

On October 18th, 2017, the 3rd DCA issued an alternative writ of mandate and stayed the proceedings pending resolution of the issues. Rather than fight, the Mono County Superior Court. Hon. Judge Magit presiding, accepted the challenge for cause a week later. Judge Magit ordered the court clerk to seek an assigned judge for my matter. The Honorable Stan Eller had already recused himself from my case years before and in Mammoth and Mono County, that's all you have, two elected full-time judges.

On December 11, 2017, the Untied States Supreme Court denied my petition for a writ of certiorari, and you know what, I was expecting it. I had no evidentiary support for my claims. I was focused on getting my attorney-client file from Ms. Hankel so I could go back to the State court with a new habeas petition.

The first thing I did the day after my certiorari writ had been denied was file a renewed motion to compel in the Mono County Superior Court in a fresh attempt to get my attorney-client file. On December 21st the Honorable Dean Stout was assigned for the purpose of hearing this matter. He was a long-time judge in nearby Inyo County. He took the reins and quickly issued an order to show cause to Ms. Hankel which had to be responded to by January 22nd, 2018. My God, was it 2018 already? I was arrested on Augst 20th, 2007. This was really getting old, as was I.

Not to forget, I still had one more petition up my sleeve. I could file a petition for rehearing in the United States Supreme Court with, like, no chance of success. However, if I could convince a majority of the court that my issues warranted extraordinary attention, I could open the doors to a full blown hearing.

I had 25 days to file and I was only allowed 15 pages to work with. I was limited in subject matter to intervening issues of a substantial or controlling effect or to other substantial grounds not previously presented. I couldn't locate one template or other petition for rehearing to see what it should look like so I went with the Ninth Circuit's layout tweaked to look like US Supreme Court petition.

My intervening circumstances were that I had discovered additional information since I had written my original 53 page petition back in April, 2017. I reminded the Court that I was pro. per. with limited skills as an advocate. I mentioned the limited resources in the law library and stated that the questions I was raising were focused and important to prisoners throughout the country who were similarly situated. This time I was not going to hold back one iota and I presented 13 questions for review.

1. Were the district court's and Ninth Circuit's decisions unreasonable in their denial of an evidentiary hearing and a COA?

2. Was the trial court's new trial motion decision to not allow evidence, argument, and disinterested counsel unreasonable?

3. Should a defendant be provided independent counsel during a Marsden hearing when the content of the Marsden hearing decides the new trial motion?

4. During a Marsden hearing, which is the basis for a new trial motion on ineffective assistance of trial counsel grounds where a trial attorney rebuts defendant's assignments in error declaration, does the defendant have the right to confront and cross-examine and present evidence against the trial attorney's response on due process grounds?

5. How does 28 USC §2254(d)(1), (d)(2), (e)(1), and (e)(2) interact when a petitioner has extrinsic evidence not a part of the record on appeal and wants to prove innocence and proceed under 28 USC§2254(e)(2)(B) with an evidentiary hearing?

6. Does a trial attorney have a constitutional obligation to turn over all attorney-client property upon motion to sustitute counsel for the purpose of making a new trial motion based on IATC?

7. If a trial court declines to rule in IATC claims in a motion for new trial forcing the extrinsic issues into habeas proceedings, is the defendant entitled in counsel and an evidentiary hearing?

8. Is a district court reviewing a case de novo obligated by due process to hold an evidentiary hearing when petitioner alleges IATC and has been denied a full and fair hearing by the state?

9. Was the trial court unreasonable in its application of Strickland and its finding that trial counsel, Ms. Hankel, was adequate in this case?

10. Did Ms. Hankel operate under a conflict of interest when she opposed the defendant in the Marsden/New Trial hearing?

11. Does an indigent petitioner have a right to make an IATC claim in a court proceeding equal to that of a non-indigent petitioner?

12. Is petitioner entitled to an evidentiary hearing in order to prove a fundamental miscarriage of justice has occurred?

13. Is petitioner's 285 years-to-life sentence excessive and to be considered cruel and unusual?

14. In my petition for rehearing I decided not to argue questions point by point I felt I had made my arguments well known in all previous petitions. Instead I focused in on three areas. Right to counsel, 28 USC §2254, and cuel and unusual punishment.

My right to counsel was a hotly disputed area of contention. I had claimed my innocence throughout and I was still innocent as the numerous not guilty verdicts attest. It was unreasonable that the trial court forced me into habeas proceedings without at least appointing counsel to represent me. A habeas petitioner has no constitutional right to counsel. The error analysis regime becomes tougher in habeas proceedings i.e., the Brecht standard as opposed to the Chapman standard.

Unreasonable = not rational; arbitrary, capricious. This is what happened when Judge DeVore silenced me. For example, an indigent defendant receives appointed appellate counsel who then gets to speculate which areas in the record are most fruitful from which to raise an appeal. Here, my appellate counsel, Ms. Nichols, decided that habeas was not a good way to go. This decision was made without a proper investigation. "Indigent defendant had no constitutional right to compel appellate counsel to press non-frivolous points if counsel as a matter of professional judgement decides not to press those points." (Jones v Barnes 463 US 745, 751 (1983)).

I claimed in my petition for rehearing that Ms. Nichols made frivolous claims when she repeatedly cited Estelle v McGuire as a catch-all due process argument. This strategy was doomed form the start and was at the expense of pointing out the real errors I was claiming against Ms. Hankel and which showed my innocence. A defendant who can pay for appellate counsel, I argued, can compel the attorney to present the extrinsic claims of IATC.

I went on to argue that the United States Supreme Court had admitted on several occasions:

"The precise rationale for the Griffin (Griffin v Illinois 351 US 12 (1956)); and Douglas (Douglas v California 372 US 353, 357 (1963)) lines of cases has never been explicitly stated, some support being derived from the equal protection clause of the Fourteenth Amendment and some from the Due Process Clause of that same Amendment, Evitts v Lucey 469 US 387, 403 (1985). Due process requires States to offer each defendant a fair opportunity to obtain an adjudication on the merits of his appeal. Id. at 404."

(Smith v Robbins 528 US 1259, 1292-1293 (Justice Souter Dissent)).

I also raised the whole spectrum of law under the habeas statue 28 USC §2254. I started by conceding that the US Supreme Court was very familiar with

Cullen v Pinholster 131 S. Ct. 1388, (2011);
Harrington v Richter 131 S. Ct. 770 (2011);
Trevino v Thaler 131 S. Ct. 1991 (2013);

thus there was no need for a lengthy discussion of their features. At the core, I articulated that there is a right to the assistance of disinterested counsel to make a claim of IATC, or IAAC for that matter, in the first instance, when the court forces a defendant into habeas proceedings and where the federal court says it is only going to review the record on appeal at the time the State case was adjudicated.

This is a two-edged sword. First the record is incomplete when I am relegated to habeas to litigate extrinsic IATC or IAAC claims. Second the federal government requires me to overcome a presumption of correctness solely on the record on appeal. I also did not need to detail my 28 USC §2254 arguments to the Supreme Court, in fact, I did not want to cite cases because this was the court that wrote the case law. Suffice to say, in my case, the trial court and Judge DeVore in particular made a finding of fact that Ms. Hankel was competent, adequate, and diligent based on his own observations and personal knowledge of her without hearing argument or receiving evidence of off-the-record complaints.

Under 28 USC §2254(d) this is presumed to be a correct application of federal law, Strickland v Washington 466 US 668 (1984), and also presumed to be a reasonable determination of the facts in light of the evidence presented in the State court proceedings. Judge DeVore and Ms. Hankel withheld the evidence I needed to augment the record. It was up to me to rebut the presumptions of correctness with clear and convincing evidence, and I had no evidence.

Thus the real questions presents itself; was Judge DeVore's decision to send me to habeas proceedings without appointing disinterested counsel for the new trial motion an unreasonable application of case law?

I dabbled into reminding the Supreme Court in my petition for rehearing that I had numerous areas of contention to be presented in an evidentiary hearing as I have detailed above. Additionally, I emphasized further and more pointedly that the design and structure of the California justice system in actual operation makes it virtually impossible for an IATC claim to be raised in a new trial motion or on direct appeal with a state appointed attorney.

Finally, I raised the specter that the sentencing error complained of previously should also be considered cruel and unusual punishment prohibited by the Eighth Amendment to the United States Constitution. Recognized goals of the penal system include retribution, deterrence, incapacitation, and rehabilitation. Quite simply, the Eighth Amendment stands for proportionality review. Does the time fit the crime? In my case, I am innocent and the numerous not guilty verdicts prove that to a certain extent. A 285 years-to-life sentence is a death sentence, it's just a matter of time. Regarding excessive sentences, Chief Justice John Roberts wrote:

"Our cases indicate that courts conducting "narrow proportionality" review should begin with a threshold inquiry that compares "the gravity of the offense and the harshness of the penalty" Solem 463 US at 290-291...

This analysis can consider a particular offender's mental state and motive in committing the crimes, the actual hard done to the victims or to society by his conduct, and any prior criminal history. Id. at 292-293, 296-297, and fn. 22"

(Graham v Florida 130 S. Ct. 2011 (2010)).

I closed by reminding the Supreme Court that stare decisis counsels strict adherence to the narrow proportionality principle.

SIXTY-THREE

I sent my petition in and basically wrote it off. I had other fish to fry. I really wanted to get my attorney-client file and get going on my successive and delayed petition for writ of habeas corpus to the State. That was in and of itself an uphill battle. But I still had hope. It seemed to me that along the way there had been a communication breakdown so I was beginning to focus on tight, coherent arguments that also fully explained my concerns in detail. I knew that sounds oxymoronic but I swore I was going to pull it off. I'd better because on February 20th, 2018, I was denied rehearing in the United States Supreme Court which finalized my convictions and appeals. I was toast but I wasn't yet burnt.

I had some good news on the attorney-client file front. The trial court granted me an extension for my hearing until March 5th, 2018, and had granted me a fee waiver so I could appear in court by phone using CourtCall. The bad news was that the prison was passing the buck on how to facilitate the call. I asked for and received another extension until April 16th, 2018, and the Mono County Superior Court sent me and the prison the CourtCall verification receipt with calling instructions.

I had a brief hearing on April 16th and another hearing was scheduled for May 16th, 2018. Ms. Hankel was to have a report on the status of the attorney-client file at that time. On May 16th, I was escorted to the sergeant's office where we placed a call to court. On the line were myself, Ms. Hankel, Judge Stout, and the court clerk. Judge Stout began by asking me if I had anything to say and I replied "No, Your Honor." The judge then asked Ms. Hankel what the status of the file was. Ms. Hankel said she gave it to Ms. Nichols. Then Ms. Hankel corrected herself and said she gave part of it to Ms. Nichols. Finally Ms. Hankel said she hadn't thrown it away and that it was probably in storage. Judge Stout ordered her to comply with Rule 3-700(D) of the State Bar Rules of Professional Conduct. He also ordered that I was entitled to a full copy of the file in paper format. The judge further ordered that Ms. Hankel was to ascertain whether she had the entire attorney-client file and confer with Ms. Nichols regarding the location of the file if need be.

That was great news. While this had been going on, I had put another pot on the fire. I sued Ms. Hankel for $250,000 for withholding the attorney-client file. I received a default judgment when Ms. Hankel failed to respond and then I filed for a court judgment. I got a response for the court clerk which stated I was required to file some declarations and submit evidence and then a hearing would be scheduled. About that time I learned that Ms. Nichols did in fact have the digital file copy of my attorney-client file. I then amended my complaint to include Ms. Nichols as a defendant on June 4th, 2018.

This action nullified my default judgement and restarted the whole process. Ms. Hankel represented herself while Ms. Nichols was represented by Mr. Jacobus from Oakland, CA. Both defendants filed demurrers to my complaint. I was time barred and I needed to prove my innocence before I could file a claim against Ms. Hankel or Ms. Nichols for malpractice, which is what their responses called my claim.

On June 27th, Ms. Hankel was found by Judge Stout to have violated Rule 3-700(D) of the State Bar Rules of Professional Conduct and she was ordered to provide a full and complete paper copy of the original file. He ordered Ms. Hankel to have all audio evidence to be transcribed to include the video interviews. For some reason Ms. Hankel was appointed to represent me despite my vigorous objections and my pending lawsuit.

Back on the lawsuit front, I filed an opposition to the demurrers and several amended complaints which were lodged but eventually discarded. I ultimately settled on fraud as my cause of action. Fraud requires specific claims to be made in order to pass the demurrer stage:

1. False representation of a material fact;
2. Knowledge of the falsity;

3. Intent to induce another to rely on the representation;
4. Justifiable reliance;
5. Actual damages.

Now I had originally claimed negligence in my lawsuit against Ms. Hankel and Ms. Nichols. Their demurrers pointed out that I couldn't claim negligence because that was in fact a malpractice claim. When claiming malpractice against a former attorney from a criminal action, the claimant must prove that he has been cleared of the crime(s). (Cal. Code of Civ. Proc. §340.6).

Finding this to be basically true, I submitted a second amended complaint following a hearing on the demurrers. This was August 28th. I got beat up pretty bad at that hearing and on December 4th, Judge Pines politely told me to take a hike, I was shut down. He sustained the defendants demurrers without leave to amend. I was dead in the water.

I went back to work on getting my attorney-client file. I filed a motion to find out why I still hadn't received my file. It had been six months since Judge Stout had ordered it copied and given to me. The file had already been scanned and placed on a thumbdrive so what was the holdup? I also filed a motion to amend my abstract of judgement which Judge Magit had amended to take the §269(a)(1) count and place it in numerical order following the other counts instead of leaving it as it was, the first count listed. It was the first count judge DeVore sentenced me on which I assumed meant it was the primary offense. This was an important distinction since under prop. 57 a non-violent primary term is eligible for early parole consideration.

I argued that §269(a)(1) was not on the violent crimes list codified as §667.5(c) and therefore I should be eligible for early parole consideration after my primary term of 15 years-to-life is complete. My argument fell on deaf ears and on January 9th, 2018, Judge Pines denied my motion. He did however get Ms. Hankel to admit she would get sending me my attorney-client file within the week. Unfortunately, she wouldn't be sending all the CPS and therapist documents because they were considered confidential. Judge Pines said that I could file a motion at a later date and then I could explain the need for those other confidential files. I acquiesced and left that fight for another day. At least I was going to get part of the file.

By the end of January, 2019, I had the partial file and I was happy. In the months that this battle had unfolded my prison life took a dramatic turn. I was transferred to Salinas Valley State Prison in the scenic "Lettuce Bowl" aka the Salinas Valley near Monterey and Carmel, CA. The weather was perfect and it was a level 3 yard so it was much less violent. In fact, it was like being at a rehab facility. The law library was awesome and I got to use it more than two hours a week. I had left Corcoron with Dennis' old "bubble" TV; he had a new flat screen TV his mom had sent him. In leaving Corcoran I had gone to R&R to have my property packed up for transfer. The C/O at R&R was very upset with me because of the amount of paperwork I had. It was like six boxes worth. The C/O had to go through all my property and itemize it so he was not a happy camper. He looked at my old green Zenith "bubble" TV and then he looked at my CDCR number and he noted to me that I hadn't been in prison long enough to have a TV that old. I told him I got it fair and square. I had to gotten it engraved with my name and number by the property officer on B-yard but he did not put it on my property card. The C/O packing my stuff told me he was going to get my property card and see if it was on my "books."

Well, he called over to the yard property officer and got the card and to nobody's surprise, the TV was not on there. I was doomed. He sat the TV aside and packed the rest of my things. Following this I went back to my cell to await the bus and I told Dennis what had happened at R&R and he said "just relax" and he reassured me it would be put on the bus. If I could just believe him I thought to myself.

The next morning the bus came and as I walked through R&R to my waiting bus, I saw my TV on a shelf and I was crushed. I had been able to watch TV for the last five years straight with Dennis and now I was going to have nothing but my radio. Not everybody in prison has a TV, only the lucky ones do. I rode the bus for two days in total despair with a layover in Wasco State Prison near Bakersfield.

When I got to Salinas Valley State Prison that following morning, I was told to get off the bus and wait in a cell with the others. I complied. My, how far I had come. One by one the other prisoners all got their property inspected and given to them. My property did not make it on the bus with me. There was simply too much of it to get loaded onto the bus at Wasco. Now I was really bummed out. The C/O told me I would get it in the next week. I went to A-yard and went into a cell by myself with nothing but a bedroll. I fell into a fitful sleep.

About a week or so later, I received word that my property had arrived and so I waited in line… for two days and then it was finally my turn to get my property. I was sooo glad to see my six boxes of legal papers but alas, no TV. At least I could listen to my radio, right? As the C/O opened the second box to inspect my tuff for contraband, out popped my TV. I was over the moon. I went back to my cell and plugged it in and relaxed by watching some football. Outstanding.

About a week later I got a celly named Miguel who had food and he shared it with me much like Dennis had. Life was good as far as prison allowed.

SIXTY-FOUR

After I got the partial file from Ms. Hankel, I dug through it and found a transcript of Kerri's June 1st, 2010 interview with Wade McCammond, the investigator for the Mono County DA's office. I had tried to get ahold of this transcript since she gave the interview the week after I went to prison. I quickly read it and I was shocked, but more on that in a minute.

While that was going on I had also filed for a writ of mandate in the 3rd DCA asking the Court of Appeal to order the Mono County Superior Court to re-amend my abstract of judgement to reflect the count 22, 269(a)(1) charge as the primary term. Without fanfare, the 3rd DCA denied my petition. I then filed a petition for review in the California Supreme Court with little hope of success. None was offered with a quick denial sent my way. No explanation, just rejection. It was frustrating not to know why. I was left with my second or successive petition for writ of habeas corpus as the only thing between me and an eternity in prison.

Now back to Kerri's interview. She sat down with Mr. McCammond in Bridgeport, CA, and told quite the tale of abuse, rape, domestic violence…the works. As I said this all went down he week after I went to prison.

Kerri: I wanted to back up my kids and say that whatever they said then I want to back them up on that.

Mr. McCammond: Okay.

Kerri: With a few exceptions…
Kerri: Just – and some of those exceptions where I didn't force them into harm.
Mr. McCammond: Gotcha.

My initial takeaway from reading the interview was that Kerri seemed scattered and appeared to be using her lack of memory as an excuse for her not to be able to coherently blame me for specific events. Regarding her bail hearing testimony given August 28th, 2007, she said:

Kerri: When I said there wasn't any domestic violence, well of course there was domestic violence, and –
Mr. McCammond: Right.
Kerri: I went through a crap load of it. And some of it my children didn't see..
Kerri: I didn't mean to perjure myself on the stand in the bail hearing –
Mr. McCammond: Right.
Kerri: - and that's really weighed on my mind. And I – this isn't an excuse, but, like we talked about before, I – there's a lot of other circumstances that led up to that…
Kerri: I saw mike destroy one of his computers.
Mr. McCammond: Uh-huh.
Kerri: At the fairgrounds during Mule Days. And he threw it in the dumpster.
Mr. McCammond: How was this in time relation to the girls?
Kerri: When he got charged…

I got charged in August of 2007 and Mule Day is during Memorial Day weekend, the last weekend in May. Besides, all of my computers were seized when I was arrested and searched forensically.

Mr. McCammond: But it – you have an independent memory, recollection that the girls absolutely saw you and Mike in a sexual – is that true? Or is that something you're remembering form documents?
Kerri: I – I know – I don't know, you know?
Mr. McCammond: Okay.
Kerri: I'm trying to – cause my memory gets – if something trigger it, then I'll remember it and all be like, aha, that's when I remember…
Kerri: but if they said I did then we did…
Kerri: And I, - my whole thing is, I don't know he was doing the other sexual stuff…
Kerri: I didn't know he was – I didn't know that he wanted to have sex with them…
Mr. McCammond: But you don't remember your girls ever telling you: Hey mom –
Kerri: - that's where I can't pull that memory up…

Kerri was really trying to screw me over for some reason, perhaps she was trying to win back the love of her twin daughters, but she couldn't because the girls were never raped or molested. And they never told anybody that they were until Alex Ellis suggested to them that they should say they were.

Kerri: Just - I wanted to, like I said, defend my kids – but – while I still can. Since I have all this secret service, or whatnot, um – you know, on my ass across the entire country…

I kinda feel for Kerri in a way, she is losing it… but I have lost everything so the fight goes on.

Mr. McCammond: Did Martha or Chelsea tell you anything about Michael touching them in a sexual manner?

Kerri: And this was the one [question from the interrogatory] – I – I don't even know how to answer that one. 'Cause if I did say no and then they did, then I'm wrong.

Mr. McCammond: Do you recall?

Kerri: I – I – not – I don't know if I do.

Mr. McCammond: Okay.

Kerri: I – my answer to that is that if they said that I did, then I believe them.

Mr. McCammond: Okay.

Kerri: And that's what I came in to say…

Kerri: Whatever they said, so then I did.

Mr. McCammond: have you ever seen sexually explicit material in any computer used by Mike or yourself?

Kerri: Not on – I mean I've seen it pop-up by accident when you punch in Horse King or something –

Mr. McCammond: Right, right.

So Kerri said she saw pop-ups and she used my computer. Did anybody catch that? I sure did.

Kerri: -- weird crap, but I don't know he –

Mr. McCammond: You never saw him looking at porn or you saw porn on the screen?

Kerri: And I – not that I – no…

Mr. McCammond: So what's happened with your place there on Piute in –

Kerri: It sold to some – and that's the other one. I say the whole neighborhood is trying to kill me. I'm not just lying. It – sold.

Mr. McCammond: Okay.

Kerri really was losing her mind, especially when she said that I tried to rape her twice but didn't actually rape her. It was obvious to me that she was trying to gain favor with Martha, Chelsea, and the cops. But there were no rapes or molestations hence, no telling mom. Martha and Chelsea were adamant that they told her but Kerri said no. 'Nuff said.

I wasn't too concerned about Kerri's interview back in 2010 since it was now 2019 and I was focused on getting out of prison. I looked over the physical exam evidence that I did have and I found information about Dr. Gabaeff and Dr. Sinkhorn. I was familiar with Dr. Gabaeff but I was surprised to learn he had been disqualified from several trials and had a record of not that great a performance in court and some questionable extracurricular behavior.

I was interested in Dr. Sinkhorn and his opinion early on in my case that the girls simply couldn't have been the victims of rape. Unlike Dr. Gabaeff, who was an emergency room physician, Dr. Sinkhorn was a Board Certified gynecologist with many years of experience. I found Dr. Sinkhorn's address and wrote to him. He responded right away but told me he couldn't re-review my case unless I had an attorney to retain him. He added that he didn't work directly for inmates, only for attorneys. Well that lit a fire under my ass.

I filed a motion for discovery of the sexual abuse physical exam DVD(s) and all the relevant documents in the possession of the District Attorney and other agencies who were involved. Ms. Hankel had some of it but I wanted everything that they had in order to prove my point that no molestation or rape had occurred. I also filed a motion in the Mono County Superior Court asking for the appointment of counsel to help me in the presentation of this highly sensitive evidence. I couldn't even have the evidence in prison. During deliberations at my trial, the jury had asked to view the DVD exams but they were not allowed to do so. This was the main issue I was going to raise in a petition for a writ of habeas corpus. Judge Pines asked for briefing from the parties and set a hearing date of July 17th, 2019.

The day before the hearing Judge Pines faxed his tentative rulings to me at the prison and I was told at chow that I could pick up the fax later that evening. I was apprehensive. The tentative rulings had always gone against me. This time was a little different. Although the judge was going to deny my request for discovery, he ruled that the new §1054.9 post verdict discovery law was retroactive and applied to me. Yes, me. I was ecstatic. He also ruled that I had made both a good faith showing in my efforts to obtain materials from Ms. Hankel and said that I had shown good cause to review what he called "physical evidence." I disagreed with his opinion that a DVD is "physical evidence" and not "documentary evidence" but I digress.

On July 17th I appeared by phone from Salinas Valley State Prison and Judge Pines officially denied my motion without prejudice and he invited me to file a proper motion to raise my sworn and verified claims so that the People could properly respond. I was very happy. Finally something had gone my way. I had been denied but really I had won. But there was still work to do. I was stressed out about writing a full blown motion which includes a declaration and a memorandum of points and authorities. I reviewed my documents and felt more confident and less stressed. I realized I could pull it off.

The next day, out of nowhere, an acquaintance of mine in prison, "Huero" (we don't really have friends in prison), asked me if I could type something up for him and he would loan me his typewriter in return. Wow! I was stoked, it was an awesome development. Up until that point I had sloppily handwritten all my pleadings and I truly believed that that had hindered my success. I went to work that night on Huero's typing work and knocked it right out. I was worried that I didn't have enough ribbon and correction tape to complete my motion and my anxiety ratcheted back up. There is no way to go to the store and get supplies so I prayed and I was blessed with a plan. I would try to trade my brand new four-pack of rechargeable AA batteries for the ribbons I needed.

The next morning I approached my friend (I know, but I do have two friends in prison) Mr. Whitall and begged him to sell me all the ribbons so I could type my motion. He needed all his ribbons for his own pleadings but being the good friend he is, he went ahead and let me have them for the batteries. I had the supplies and the typewriter and I was off to the races. I rushed back to my cell and began typing. Now that was stressful. I was used to a word processor or computer where you can go back and fix errors later. With a typewriter, which I hadn't used in like 30 years, all you get is a correction key. On Friday the 19th of July I was able to get five perfect pages done. I finished up on Saturday with ten more pages and on Sunday, the Sabbath, I rested. I was done. I fired with full aim at Mr. Graham on Monday. I felt my motion was bombproof. Really, this time for sure. I copied it and mailed it off in the hopes of getting an attorney to help me present the DVD(s) evidence and put this story to rest.

Meanwhile, I decided that while I had the typewriter I would create another motion, a motion for reconsideration of my ability to pay restitution fines and fees. When I was sentenced, without any fanfare. I was fined $10,000, and it was a mandatory fine. In early 2019 the Seventh

Division of the Second District Court of Appeal (2d DCA) ruled that mandatory fines violated due process and that fines on indigent prisoners are only due and payable when the prisoner has a proven ability to pay. The People must prove this fact in order to collect the fine. This was great news to me because should I get a job and it were to pay me $20 per month as it stood at the time the State would take 55% or $11 and leave me with a paltry $9 for full-time work.

It was a big deal that any money a prisoner received who owed restitution was docked 55%. This meant that your friends and families were forced to pay the State in order to help you out. And you were forced by the State to work for like, four cents an hour. I went ahead and typed up this additional motion and after several wadded-up balls of paper I had an almost perfectly typed motion. I was so excited I typed up another one, leaving the name areas blank and the fine amounts empty as well so anybody could fill in the blanks and use the motion for themselves. I considered letting the law library hand it out for free but several inmates suggested I charge like five dollars to help inmates get their fine stayed until they had the proven ability to pay. The vast majority of inmates have restitution fines and needed help. This could be quite a windfall for me, broke as I was. I mulled my options and decided to keep it close to the vest and send my motion in on my case as a test-piece. I thought I should see what the courts do in my case before I tried to help anyone else. The court accepted my motion and a hearing was scheduled for August 21st, 2019.

SIXTY-FIVE

I was really excited as my court date neared. I liked having pots on the stove instead of the drudgery of prison life. To travel hopefully is a much better thing than to arrive. August 20th, 2019 came and I received a fax from Judge Pines outlining his tentative rulings. He was going to grant me access to the court exhibits, (the DVDs) but he made no mention of the supporting documentary evidence I was also seeking. I would have to raise that issue when I appeared in court via CourtCall.

As for the restitution fine issue, Judge Pines was going to rule that the court had no jurisdiction to grant the motion. "A court loses its jurisdiction over a criminal case once the defendant has been ordered committed to the custody of the Department of Corrections and Rehabilitation, thereby commencing execution of the sentence. (People v Karaman (1992) 4 Cal. 4th 335.)" (Court Opinion 8/20/19 p. 12). He went on to explain that the restitution fine imposed on me was not an unlawful sentence and was therefore beyond the court's jurisdiction to modify. (Court Opinion 8/20/19 p. 13).

My last hope for an attorney was quashed when Judge Pines tentatively ruled that the only way I was going to get an attorney was if he issued an order to show cause on my as yet unfiled habeas petition. Under California Rules of Court Rule 4.551 a court is required to appoint indigent counsel when an order to show cause is issued. An order to show cause is issued when a prima facie (on its face) showing is made whereby if a petitioner's claims are assumed to be true, would he be entitled to relief.

So, there it was, I had the DVDs but no attorney. I needed an attorney to hire Dr. Sinkhorn so I was effectively dead in the water. Somehow, I was going to have to produce a habeas petition which started a prima facie case for relief with only the evidence I had in hand. But at least I still had a chance.

On August 21st I made my CourtCall appearance after much confusion with the prison staff. Once connected I thanked the judge for his rulings as courtroom decorum dictates, then pressed him for the documentary evidence he was declining to rule on. He wasn't budging, commenting that he gave me the DVDs but the other stuff was not being considered at that time. So fine. I quickly analyzed my options and then decided to thank the judge and head back to my cell before I pissed him off.

Upon reflection I felt strongly that I needed to pull the trigger and submit a habeas petition to the judge. First though, I decided to file one last motion for the documentary evidence such as the missing SART exams, the missing peer review notes and reports, all the CPS files and other things I thought Dr. Sinkhorn would need to form his opinion. Dr. Sinkhorn was still not on board since I had no money to pay him with and no attorney to hire him on my behalf. I ventured forth anyway, undaunted by the task at hand. Also, I needed to file in the 3rd DCA right away to appeal the denial of my restitution fine reconsideration motion.

I was in over my head. It was obvious. But I still had the typewriter and I had managed to get more ribbons so I was optimistic that I could still be persuasive. First, I knocked out a petition for a writ of mandate to the 3rd DCA and sent it in September 3rd, 2019.

Next I drove into the new discovery motion. In it I asked for everything related to the SART exams, everything except the kitchen sink. At some point I was going to get all the evidence Dr. Sinkhorn needed, come hell or highwater. If I could just get a day in court to put all the evidence together, I knew I could at least get a new trial, if not be found completely innocent. I was waiting for the girls to crack. They couldn't lie forever. To get my day in court I needed to get an evidentiary hearing by submitting a petition for a writ of habeas corpus.

I started this task by going through the boxes and boxes of documents that Ms. Hankel had sent me. I whittled them down to several large stacks of relevant documents and then went through the stacks winnowing further; culling the wheat from the chaff. Ultimately, I was left with about 100 pages of transcripts and correspondence which really went to the heart of my claims. I outlined my petition and divided it into six grounds, or claims, for relief.

1. Ineffective Assistance of Appellate Counsel: Counsel did not investigate DVD evidence showing SART exam showed no sign of abuse consistent with alleged abuse;

2. Ineffective Assistance of Appellate Counsel: Counsel did not investigate peer review of SART exam not produced by the People per Brady;

3. Ineffective Assistance of Appellate Counsel: Founsel failed to investigate whether Alex Ellis lied while of the witness stand and under oath;

4. Ineffective Assistance of Appellate Counsel: Counsel failed to investigate whether Alex Ellis lied when she filled out the SART examination histories;

5. Ineffective Assistance of Appellate Counsel: Counsel failed to investigate the incompetence of trial counsel and defense expert related to the computer evidence;

6. Ineffective Assistance of Appellate Counsel: Counsel failed to investigate defense witness related to bias of Alex Ellis and Cathy Boyle.

In my petition, I started off reciting all my previous habeas petitions and explained why this latest one was being presented without substantial delay and with good cause for any unexcused delay. Substantial delay is measured from the time the petitioner or counsel should have known of the information offered in support of the claim and the legal basis of the claim. In assessing a petitioner's explanation and justification for delayed presentation of claims, the court should consider facts of which the claim is based, even though recently discovered, could have and should have been discovered earlier. Petitioner is expected to demonstrated due diligence in pursuing potential claims. If petitioner had reason to suspect that a basis for relief was available, but did nothing to promptly confirm those suspicions, that failure must be justified.

I basically laid out the arguments for delay and good cause then went right into the grounds for relief. In ground one I pointed out that Mr. Graham had not shown the video of the SART exam of the twins and instead used images reportedly captured from the video to show the supposed injuries to the twins' hymens to the jury. I felt this was complete hogwash. I mean, how do you identify a victim from an image of their vagina? It was all conjecture and nobody seemed to care. I wished Ms. Nichols had looked into this, but she and Ms. Hankel had me pegged as overly paranoid.

During the appeal, Ms. Nichols received the entire attorney-client file in digital format. I assumed at that time that she would investigate this issue since she had the DVDs containing the videos of the SART exams. I also figured that she would investigate it further because the jury did not deliberate after it was determined that they could not view the videos of the SART exams though they requested to do so. According to Ms. Hankel, she provided the entire attorney-client case file to Ms. Nichols, including the DVDs. This fact was belied by the information provided by Ms. Hankel in her May 29, 2019 letter to me in which she stated she didn't have the DVDs because she gave them to Dr. Gabaeff and he returned them to Mr. Graham.

I furthered raised in ground one that the jury foreperson, Larry Petrisky, had told Ms. Hankel that although the jury had specifically requested to look at the DVD video to see if the girls had been examined on their side, when no device was available to view the DVDs with, the jury rushed ahead and disregarded the evidence. Finally, I pointed out that Larry Petrisky was a clerk for the Mammoth Superior Court and he was pressured to get a verdict and get back to work. He was also reprimanded by the court for actions during my trial.

In ground two, I raised the issue of a peer review conducted of Nurse Boyle's Sexual Assault Response Team (SART) exam which was not presented to the defense. This evidence reportedly showed that the initial findings were inconclusive or indeterminate and no further details were provided. This was found to be a Brady violation by Judge DeVore. He asked Ms. Hankel during a closed session if she thought it was exculpatory and subject to a Brady requirement. Ms. Hankel responded that it was based on what Dr. Gabaeff told her. Mr. admitted that it came in late, the disclosure of a peer review. In the end the issue was dropped when Mr. Graham said he would avoid the subject in the future. Judge DeVore declined to make a ruling or give a corrective instruction. Ms. Hankel objected to the peer review because she had not received any documentation.

In ground three I turned my attention to Alex Ellis, the girls' CPS case worker. At trial it became apparent to me but not to Ms. Hankel that Alex

Ellis was at the heart of the who knew what, when dilemma. The girls testified that the told Ms. Ellis first, over and over again. Meanwhile, Ms. Hankel was calling witness after witness, friends of the girls, to testify that they were told weeks, months, even years before the girls made allegations to the authorities. I have went on and on about this issue already and will suffice by saying that Ms. Ellis lied while on the stand when she testified that the girls didn't tell her first or that she couldn't remember the exact order of the disclosures. This from a woman who takes notes voraciously of everything she does. In the end, I pointed out that when Ms. Ellis submitted a SCAR on August 21st, 2007, it was a day after I had been arrested and I believed it was evidence of a paper trail being created to hamper my defense.

In ground four, it was more of the same, lying by Ms. Ellis, but I shifted to her role in the portrayal of the girls' histories in the SART exams where Ms. Ellis, not the girls, gave their histories to Nurse Boyle. The girls personally gave a basic medical history but when it came time to relate their history of sexual abuse Ms. Ellis jumped in and gave that to Nurse Boyle. All the information in the final report which Nurse Boyle relied upon was from Ms. Ellis. Dr Gabaeff, the defense expert, testified that if the incident history was different then what is noted there, it could have an effect on the understanding of the findings of the examinations. Dr. Gabaeff concluded that the history is in many cases as important and in some cases more important than the physical findings.

With ground five, I revisited the whole computer evidence issue from a different perspective, that being the failure of Ms. Hankel and Mr. Albee to grasp the nuances of my arguments and the errors in doing so.

I concluded with ground six, which detailed a witness Ms. Hankel did not call, Ted Carlton, who had been falsely accused of child molestation by his wife. Ms. Ellis investigated with the help of Nurse Boyle to basically charge Mr. Carlton with child molestation even in the absence of any physical findings of abuse.

All told, the claims spoke for themselves and I submitted over 100 pages of exhibits to support my claims. I'd been down this road before however, and I didn't have much faith that I was going to get a fair shake. I was part worried, part excited. I was in the game and I had Judge Pines as the umpire, not Judge DeVore.

A writ of habeas corpus is a prisoner's last hope in a criminal proceeding. It is the final gatekeeper of justice as it were. But it could be looked at two ways. On one hand, it can free those unjustly incarcerated by the government. On the other hand, it could throw up seemingly endless roadblocks because of the requisite circular logic needed to gain freedom. In simple terms, a prisoner must prove he is innocent before he can prove constitutional error and he must prove constitutional error before he can prove his innocence. The rule is that constitutional error is defined by the United States Constitution as interpreted by the United States Supreme Court. The United States Supreme Court has repeatedly declined to rule on constitutional issues such as due process or the legality of evidence issues, in essence telling the states they have free rein to legislate as they see fit. This is a quandary for me. I am pro states rights. I believe that states should be free to regulate themselves, IMHO.

So I was back in the State Court with both barrels loaded. I really needed to get Dr. Sinkhorn onboard, and fast. He wanted money. I had none. He wanted to be hired by an attorney representing me. I had none. I was at my wits end. But onward I pressed, confident that the DVDs were going to show the girls were not molested or raped once and for all. The other issues were just so much fluff placed in the petition to add weight to the main argument that the girls were virgins.

While all this was going on, my celly Miguel went out to court and never came back. He was struggling with the San Bernadino County Superior Court. It seemed they wanted to add $200,000 in restitution fines to his sentence. I was outraged but I had my own fight. I decided to change buildings so I could stay "single celled," a luxury in prison. The building I moved into was not crowded and so the cops wouldn't need to put anyone in my cell, yet, knock on wood. The fall weather brought wind and fire to Northern California. Pacific Gas and Electric, (PG&E), the local utility company, started shutting off power grids to avoid liability for brush fires started by their equipment throwing sparks in the extremely dry brush of the fall season in California. These outages hit our prison for over two days. All we got were box lunches and we were locked in our cells 24 hours a day, the worst part was that the toilets didn't work without electricity. We all thought the CDCR would be better prepared for this type of shutdown which had been predicted well in advance, but then again, all of Northern California was in the same boat. No power mean no, nada, nothing was on. Being prepared was a pipe dream. The reality was lost business, lost food, lost homes, lost lives. The loss of lives and property due to the fires which invariably start was unavoidable. That is what happens when housing developments encroach on the urban/forest interface. It is frustrating all around, so what's a few thousand inmates crying about. Plenty. But that's another story. At least we got PBJ's.

SIXTY-SIX

On November 18th, 2019, I was concerned about my CourtCall hearing because I had not received my customary tentative rulings from Judge Pines. I was worried he was going to put the kibosh on my whole appeal. I had submitted my new and improved habeas petition and I had doubts I had made the right decision. I went to the visiting room for my CourtCall and right off the bat, things looked real good. Mr. Graham was conceding defeat in that §1054.9 was not prospective only as codified in §1054.9(i) and therefore I was entitled to the materials I had requested.

Ms. Hankel had many of the documents and after much discussion it was decided that Ms. Hankel would search the remaining attorney-client case file for the relevant documents I was seeking. During this discussion, I brought up my pending habeas petition, and Judge Pines abruptly said he was denying my petition on procedural grounds. I was bummed but I played through. I wasn't going to let a procedural error deny me any facts. I just needed to get a written ruling that I could work from.

In the end, Judge Pines ignored my habeas petition denial and instead focused on the discovery issues. He ordered an in camera review of the materials to be provided by Ms. Hankel for January 6th, 2020, and an open hearing for January 8th, 2020 scheduled for the release of all authorized documents. All in all, I was extremely optimistic.

About a week later, forest fire season was over and several inches of rain fell on California. Mammoth got several feet of snow and I was homesick. I got over that quick however since my cell had a leak in the room; I was flooded out. I was lucky none of my papers or the typewriter got wet. That same day I was fortunate to move to a dry, leakproof cell.

As I thought about things, I felt motivated to type this story up instead of continuing to handwrite it. I still roughed it out in cursive but now I was going to try typing it. I had enough paper, but I only had a couple of ribbons but I was optimistic nonetheless. I was motivated to throw the dice and figured I could take apart ribbons and reverse the tape to recycle them into double use.

In early December 2019, Miguel returned while we were on lockdown and he got a cell that didn't leak in 5 block. He told me on the yard that as it turned out, he had gone to court because the state had sued him for victim restitution saying he owed for the addition pension of the cop he shot. This added up to $285,000 and he was distraught to say the least. I consoled him as best I could and told him I would try to get him a stay in the payment of his restitution fine and also looked into his habeas and gun enhancement issues.

As the weeks had gone by and Christmas approached I eagerly awaited Judge Pines' written ruling regarding my habeas petition. It took forever but on Christmas Eve I was pleasantly surprised when it finally showed up. Judge Pines had ruled on November 18th but it hadn't been mailed until December 18th. i quickly tore open the envelope and read the contents. My heart was in my throat. Basically he ruled that I hadn't been entirely forthcoming in stating all the facts related to my previous nine habeas petitions in the state courts. In essence, I hadn't filled out the form correctly, the new HC-001 petition. Also, I had forgot to sign the verification at the end swearing that I had been truthful in my petition. I was still in the game!

I spent a glorious Christmas Day locked in my cell locating all my record from my previous appeals. I found all the denial orders and read them over. I then write a declaration describing my reasons for all the petitions and their denials.

I felt really good but I was not able to mail in my declaration because the prison was on a "lock-down." A lock-down occurs when there is a security threat or an institutional search, and also when there is a shortage of staff. This particular time there was a shortage of staff because of the holidays and the prison decided to do an institutional search during this holiday period to kill two birds with one stone.

Sometimes the guards really "toss" the cells when they search but this time I had everything organized and clean so the guards just did a once over and left me alone. Whew, that was close. I have way too many papers they could have tossed around but they didn't.

On January 8th, 2020, I was still on lock-down when I went to my CourtCall related to the protective order and the release of the remaining documents held by Ms. Hankel. Judge Pines told me that he had reviewed all the remaining documents held by Ms. Hankel and he had decided that several hundred pages were relevant and would be released. These included Ms. Ellis' notes, the CPS referrals, and other emails and the like. I was satisfied that at that point all the materials I needed would be forthcoming in short order. In closing my remarks on the CourtCall, I asked Judge Pines if he would entertain a declaration explain my procedural errors or would I need to submit a whole new petition for a writ of habeas corpus. He replied that I would have to file a completely new and verified petition which was to include all relevant documentary evidence. I was bummed but still hopeful. I mean, I ws about to get more ammunition, and I wasn't getting shot down so all in all, I felt pretty good about my chances.

Finally in mid-January, we were off lock-down and I could use the law library. I dug in and worked on my case. I made copies of my new declaration then decided to rewrite the whole thing and type it up all over again. At the same time I was helping some other inmates with their cases. I tried to help those I could but as I have always said, "You can't save all the dogs in the pound." As much as I felt for the other prisoners' plights, I was limited in my ability to help. I was pretty good on a computer so I looked up things for people as I had the time to do so occasionally.

In late January, 2020, I came across a story in the newspaper related to Pinholster and the Ninth Circuit court of Appeals. It seemed they had ruled that evidence obtained by the district court at a hearing on whether state postconviction counsel was ineffective could be used to grant habeas corpus relief, despite the ban on evidentiary hearings to develop facts that were not addressed in state court. This fit right in my wheelhouse since I was claiming error by Ms. Nichols, my postconviction counsel. I wasn't sure this ruling would hold up under United States Supreme Court scrutiny, but it was a nice turn of events and I felt I had a path towards freedom.

Shortly thereafter I finally received notice that my petition for a writ of mandate in the 3rd DCA had been denied. My stay in the payment of my $10,000 restitution fine was not to be. The petition had been denied back in October but I didn't get the ruling in the mail until January 2020. I quickly put together a petition for review in the state supreme court and I thought it was pretty good. I had really honed my argument on this issue. Typed up it looked like a professional petition. I really felt confident when I sent it in, but didn't I always say that?

Near to this time I worked on my habeas petition for the Mono County Superior Court and Judge Pines. I put my declaration regarding the delayed petition with the same petition that I had sent in before. I also attached a clarification of ground five based on a new piece of evidence I had found I my partial attorney-client file. This new piece of evidence was a document which showed Mr. Wall did not testify truthfully when he said he put the disk drive serial number on his worksheet (Court's exhibit 100a). He was adamant at the trial that he had documented the disk drive by its serial number when he examined it but this new document showed unequivocally that in January 2008 when he initially examined the drive he actually noted the model number as the serial number. This was consistent with every other document he produced except the mysterious court exhibit 100a. There was something hinky about that drive and this new document was just fuel on the fire.

I put the whole habeas package together, made copies, and sent it in to the court. I was on edge as I began another cycle of waiting. I had two pots on the fire: the petition for review in the state supreme court and now the petition for a writ of habeas corpus in the trial court.

While I waited, I turned my attention to my TV and the news (and all the hype) of a new virus in China killing a lot of people. This seemed to happen every year and I didn't think much of it. The new virus was called coronavirus. People were joking that they would rather have a modelovirus. Coronavirus had been traced back to the Hunan wildlife market in Wuhan, China. I heard that it was a disease found in bats, which they eat in China, and it had spread to humans. There were like seven types of coronavirus. Some are benign and are similar to a cold while other coronaviruses are deadly like SARS and MERS.

Well things got bad in China and they locked everything and everyone down tight. The Chinese were beating people up in the streets for going out without a mask. China is normally an oppressive country but this was extreme even by those standards. People could not leave their homes and the Hubei Province looked like a ghost town.

It was only a short time after the world knew of the rampant virus in China that it began to spread to other countries. President Trump ordered all flights from China grounded and began to evacuate Americans stuck in China using chartered flights. Those people lucky enough to get out China were greeted with a 14-day quarantine back in the US. Nobody wanted them in their neighborhood so the evacuees were quarantined on military bases throughout the country. Not too long after that, the first case was discovered in the US and it was in the state of Washington.

Within days, several people in a retirement home were ill and then one person died from coronavirus and that was completely unexpected. The date was March 1st, 2020. Heightened anxiety led to the blocking of a cruise ship from entering San Francisco Bay. It was forced to stay 100 miles off the California coast while it was decided what to do with the ship. Eventually the cruise liner was allowed into the Port of Oakland and the 2,500 passengers were allowed to disembark. But not before 24 people who had tested positive for the coronavirus had been evacuated and taken to quarantine. In the midst of all this live action TV news, I received notice from the Supreme Court that my petition for review and request for a stay in my $10,000 restitution fine was denied. I was crestfallen and I wasn't sure what my options were. I would have to look up the case law in the law library, if I could get in. The librarian had been having some personal issues that had been causing her to take a lot of time off. On top of that, the prison had a shortage of librarians, thus the library was only operating three days per week instead of five. Then adding in the librarian's personal issues, we were getting only one or two days per week. I would have complained except for the fact that according to CDCR rules, we were only guaranteed two hours per week of law library access. Any additional time was a luxury. I had been getting like four hours a week at least, so I knew that if I sent in a 602 grievance appeal, I would have been shot down because I was already getting extra time, even with all the closures.

Things on the outside of prison were descending into chaos by his time. School closures, people forced to stay at home with cancellations of major events the norm. For us in prison it was business as usual. Then Governor Newsom issued a statewide shelter in place order. Even with that in effect, we prisoners were still going out in the yard in large groups. We were being fed in our cells however. In discussions with other prisoners, it was apparent that there were two competing schools of thought. One was the idea that the coronavirus wasn't as dangerous as the flu and the media was blowing it all way out of proportion. The other line of thinking was that all the cops and staff were going to get sick and it was going to be anarchy in no time. I thought it was important to let the states do what they must to curtail the virus and any rights lost were temporary. I had learned in prison that you always covered your cough and washed your hands a lot because prison was basically a dirty and dangerous palace. I was practicing to avoid coronavirus before I ever heard of it.

SIXTY-SEVEN

By March 22nd, 2020 the prison system got its first confirmed case of coronavirus. The US had over 35,000 cases nationwide with a total of 471 deaths. This was all very sobering news. Once the virus was in the prison system I knew it was only a matter of time before we were on complete lockdown. We had already lost church, library, and group activities as well as our regular dayroom times. Things changed quickly after that. By the 24th there were 54,000 cases nationwide with 781 dead. It was common knowledge that it was going to get worse.

The CDCR put us on limited yard and dayroom with only one-third of a tier allowed out at a time (a tier is 50 cells). The news on the TV was grim and it seemed as though the world was coming to an end. I expected Christ to appear at any time. Two days later there were over 1,000 deaths nationwide. I was waiting for the first prisoner to die. I dreaded that day. I really didn't want that to happen but I felt it would have been a turning point for me. Personally, I thought the media was acting like Chicken Little while the reality was that I felt fine as did everyone else around me did. I wondered why the media didn't do a total death report to comparatively include car crashes, cancer, and the like. I wanted fair and balanced reporting. We didn't get FOX news at Salinas Valley State Prison.

Regarding "The Problem" as President Trump called it, all the prisoners were apprehensive because we were told very little by the prison staff.

The powers that be believed that safety and security are compromised when they give out any information related to the goings on in prison. However there exists a fundamental difference in those people who look for the government to do for us and then those who look to do for themselves. We got our info by calling people on the outside. An example of self-sufficiency. Another would be lost laundry. You could try to get your laundry replaced by staff bureaucracy but that was nearly impossible to do. Alternatively, you could barter with other prisoners to get it taken care of and it would get done. We were all in it together before that term started trending.

Reliance on the government is a slippery slope indeed. By depending on others who have no interest in your day to day problems can create a false sense of security. Only by being on a strong team can you count on a winning effort. By the end of March there were over 3,000 deaths nationwide from coronavirus and Dr. Fauci, the infectious disease specialist warned that 100,000 to 200,000 people could die if the virus was unchecked by "social distancing." People on the outside were taking a couple different approaches. One was shelter in place and the other was business as usual. I mean, the parks were packed and the beaches were crowded even though everyone was supposed to stay at home. As for me, I stayed put with my TV and room service meals. I had a cache of Top Ramen so I was doing OK. I was afraid of the shower though. I took "bird baths" in the sink instead of going out.

I was still waiting for a reply to my habeas petition and I was really hopeful that I would get relief this time. I wasn't sure what the world would look like by the time I got out but I wanted out nonetheless. I read Rip VanWinkle and ruminated on the possibilities. Watching the overnight news on ABC's World News Now I saw on the ticker that an employee of Salinas Valley State Prison had tested positive for coronavirus. I was stunned. It was just a matter of time before I got it, right? I was healthy and hydrated so I thought I could weather the storm but notwithstanding my good health, I worried that I may in fact be vulnerable.

I pondered throughout the day and night about the apocalyptic ramifications of this event ut tempered those thoughts with visions of home. I really wanted to be in the High Sierra where I had always felt safe and secure. I knew that if I could get there I would survive for sure.

Everybody knows the story about the coronavirus though. By April 1st 2020, there was no April Foolin'. There were over 200,000 cases of coronavirus nationwide with over 5,000 dead. This after only a month from an initial total of 30 cases and one dead on March 1st 2020. The news was ominous and so I tore up a t-shirt and made a mask. I was done messing around.

I still hadn't received my discovery documents from my attorney-client file which Ms. Hankel was supposed to have sent back in early February. I knew more or less what I was looking for, but I really wanted Judge Pines to see the whole story. I was worried that he had already denied my petition and I just didn't know it yet. This is what had happened back at Christmastime. If Judge Pines denied my petition I was kind of ready to go to the 3rd DCA but I would need the additional documents Ms. Hankel had. At the time, I wasn't even sure that the courts were open. It was on the news that the courts were in limited operation. The rules were all suspended though. For example, arrestees were unable to get arraigned for 30 days instead of the normal 10-day statutory requirement. Instead of the two-day mandate to be charged after arrest it was ten days. Jury trials were postponed. The whole justice system was dead in the water. Dead in the water, maybe, but Judge Pines was busy on my case and I felt hopeful.

Throughout April and May people kept getting sick and dying. The tally was spinning like an out of control speedometer. Some of the prisons had a few cases of coronavirus and one prisoner even died from it in Chino, CA, but overall, we were in quarantine of a sort and nobody got sick. We had no program, but we were safe.

Suddenly it was Memorial Day with no end in sight. Then a cop killed George Floyd in Minneapolis. You know how that went. In prison though, it was business as usual. Generally, there are not many riots in prison. The cops rule over us with an iron thumb, and a Ruger Mini 14. While all this was going on I waited, and waited. Finally in late May I received the CPS files and I was stoked. I had sent Judge Pines an Ex Parte request to crack the whip on Ms. Hankel and it worked. The CPS files contained all the caseworker notes, and the DSL files. Even the Big note/Little note were in there. Judge Pines also issued a request for an informal response and reply to my petition. Mr. Graham wrote a two paragraph response that made no sense. I was excited, maybe he was throwing in the towel. I wrote a two-page reply stating the obvious, that Strickland v Washington applied to appellate counsel and my appellate counsel, Ms. Nichols was woefully inadequate and I was prejudiced by her inadequacy.

In early June, with the response and reply in to the court, Judge Pines said he would rule on my petition by July 6th, 2020. I was mesmerized by the thought of freedom but well grounded with the fear of the unknown. By then there were 2,000,000 cases of coronavirus and 110,000 people had died nationwide. There was simply no end in sight.

States and counties began to loosen their grip on their citizenry. Businesses and sports opened back up to a new normal. It was status quo in prison though. We did nothing, day after day. But we were safe. I spent my time typing a re-edit of "The Ordeal" though not very well because I was reusing the ribbons two and sometimes three times. But it was all I had and I needed to kill a lot of time. It was cathartic to edit and type my story.

In the midst of typing I came across a statement by Mike Hultz, Martha's therapist, and he had testified on November 13th, 2009 that he was told by the Director of the Mono County Mental Health Dept. that Martha had predisclosed prior to his meeting with her or the first time. Bingo I had them now. Who told the director? It had to be Alex Ellis. Remember Rose Douglas said she was told by Mike Hultz so what gives? I suddenly felt a laser of hope bore into my soul.

It was the first day of summer, a few days before Judge Pines was expected to rule. I wrote to him immediately with my proof that Alex Ellis was the genesis of the sexual abuse allegations. At least I hope that's what I had. I told Judge Pines that all I needed was an evidentiary hearing and a subpoena for the Director of Mental Health back in 2007. I figured I was golden. I sent in my letter and prayed. That same day they started testing some prisoners for coronavirus in my building. Three prisoners tested positive in Salinas Valley State Prison. As usual they didn't tell us who or where, we got the information from the news on TV. I prayed that we would weather the storm.

Well, before I could get a response from Judge Pines, I got a denial. In a scathing 10-page opinion, Judge Pines said I had filed 16 previous appeals and had not justified my claims of actual innocence. Basically, he said I hadn't proved I was innocent.

I might have been shattered but for the fact that in my typing I had noticed that Mr. Graham, during his closing argument at my trial, had told the jury that the girls had disclosed to Alex Ellis prior to telling Ellen Thompson. This was huge. I quickly shook off the denial and worked on a new petition to the 3rd DCA. This took some time though. Millions of people tested positive for coronavirus and the deaths doubled to 220,000 before I was ready to file my newest petition.

I had no law library as the entire prison was on a modified program though. Luckily, I was able to mail my documents to the Senior Librarian who made copies of my petition and exhibits. I sent my petition to the 3rd DCA and I sent a copy to Mr. Graham in the hopes he would investigate my claims set forth in the petition. My main assertion was that the DVDs showed the girls to be virgins. My second claim was that Alex Ellis lied on the stand during my trial. This was proven by Mr. Graham's own words which showed he believed the girls had told Alex Ellis first. Ms. Ellis testified she had heard about the abuse from Ellen Thompson and Ellen Thompson said she had heard about the abuse from the CPS. There was treachery afoot and I was out to expose it.

It only took a couple of weeks for the 3rd DCA to shoot me down. In the quick and brief denial, the Court of Appeal cited In re Clark (1993) 5 Cal. 4th 750 which basically says if you can prove you are innocent, we will grant you relief even if you have been denied relief before. I was stunned. I mean, I had the proof. What was I missing.

I quickly put together a brief related to In re Clark for the California Supreme Court and attached it to another petition for writ of habeas corpus and sent it in. I thus began another waiting game. I knew it would be awhile because things go really slow in the California Supreme Court.

It was Christmas 2020 by then with over 330,000 coronavirus deaths and 20,000,000 cases nationwide. The Salinas Valley State Prison had an outbreak with hundreds of cases and many deaths but I was good to go. Go nowhere. We were on complete lockdown. The prison finally handed out N95 masks in early 2021 and I felt like I as going to make it. I wasn't sure why I was so optimistic but I just felt good about my chances. I had no celly and I never left my cell so I was in my own bubble. Besides, I had been healthy all my life which was a true blessing.

Nevertheless, I believed that this story could go on forever so I decided to publish what I had before I did die and then continue the saga on the internet. I really was at a point where I needed outside help. I needed an expert doctor and a lawyer to make headway against the criminal industrial complex. I found a publisher, got the domain name MichaelJayHarris.com, and set out to digitize my book for Kindle and the like as a free download with the epilogue on the website that I expected to update regularly. Email me at hairy@MichaelJayHarris.com if you want to donate to my cause or offer feedback. I will be very glad to hear from you. Thank you for your interest in my story and be sure to check out MichaelJayHarris.com/epilogue for the rest of the story…

CPSIA information can be obtained
at www.ICGtesting.com
Printed in the USA
BVHW041048060423
661869BV00013B/406